THE OFFICIAL DICTIONARY
OF MILITARY TERMS

THE OFFICIAL DICTIONARY OF MILITARY TERMS

Compiled by

The Joint Chiefs of Staff

Authorized for use by

U.S. Department of Defense (DOD)
North Atlantic Treaty Organization (NATO)
Inter-American Defense Board (IADB)

With a Directory of Departments, Agencies, and Facilities of the U.S. Department of Defense and U.S. Coast Guard

 **SCIENCE INFORMATION RESOURCE CENTER**

● **HEMISPHERE PUBLISHING CORPORATION**
Cambridge   Philadelphia   San Francisco   Washington
London   Mexico City   São Paulo   Singapore   Sydney

THE OFFICIAL DICTIONARY OF MILITARY TERMS

1 2 3 4 5 6 7 8 9 0   B R B R   8 9 8 7

Library of Congress Cataloging-in-Publication Data

Department of Defense dictionary of military and
   associated terms.
   The official dictionary of military terms.

   "Authorized for use by U.S. Department of Defense
(DOD), North Atlantic Treaty Organization (NATO),
Inter-American Defense Board (IADB); with a directory
of departments, agencies, and facilities of the U.S.
Department of Defense and U.S. Coast Guard."
   "Contains the complete text of the official
Department of Defense dictionary of military and
associated terms"—Pref.
   Bibliography: p.
   Includes index.
   1. Military art and science—Dictionaries.
I. United States. Joint Chiefs of Staff. II. Title.
U24.D47   1988   355'.003'21   87-23694
ISBN 0-89116-792-7   Hemisphere Publishing Corporation

CONTENTS

v

FOREWORD BY THE PUBLISHER

This hardbound edition contains the complete text of the official *Department of Defense Dictionary of Military and Associated Terms* and was compiled and prepared by The Joint Military Terminology Group under the direction and authority of The Joint Chiefs of Staff, in coordination with the Office of the Secretary of Defense, the Military Services, and Defense Agencies. Its use has been authorized and mandated throughout the Department of Defense to ensure uniformity in the application and use of terms and definitions. Appendix A, following the Dictionary, contains a complete directory of the U.S. Department of Defense and U.S. Coast Guard including their departments, agencies, and facilities. This section as well as the Dictionary itself should prove a useful tool for anyone dealing or communicating with the U.S. Department of Defense, the North Atlantic Treaty Organization, and the Inter-American Defense Board. It is especially recommended for contractors, suppliers, and consultants as well as editors and journalists.

The terms and definitions identified with *NATO* represent terms standardized and agreed upon for use within the NATO community. Entries identified with *IADB* represent terms standardized and agreed upon for use between member countries of the Inter-American Defense Board. The symbol *I* means that the entry has United States Government Interdepartment approval for national usage. The symbol *DOD* marks the entry as official for DOD components, all of whom have been directed to use these terms and definitions without alteration.

The criteria for creating and compiling the terms in this dictionary include their not being adequately defined in other standard dictionaries, that the terms have widespread military or associated significance, that weapons terms will be limited to important modern weapons, and that the terms and definitions in this Dictionary will not contain Classified information.

SYMBOLS EXPLAINED

(DOD) Established for use by all Department of Defense Components, which will use the terms and definitions so designated without alteration unless a distinctly different context or application is intended.

(I) United States Government interdepartmental approval has been achieved for national usage.

(IADB) Established for use by the member nations of the Inter-American Defense Board, consisting of:

Argentina	Costa Rica	Haiti	Paraguay
Bolivia	Dominican Republic	Honduras	Peru
Brazil	Ecuador	Mexico	United States
Chile	El Salvador	Nicaragua	Uruguay
Colombia	Guatemala	Panama	Venezuela

(NATO) Established for use by the member nations of the North Atlantic Treaty Organization, consisting of:

Belgium	Germany	Luxembourg	Spain
Canada	Greece	Netherlands	Turkey
Denmark	Iceland	Norway	United Kingdom
France	Italy	Portugal	United States

A

A-4—See **Skyhawk.**

A-6—See **Intruder.**

A-7—See **Corsair II.**

A-10—See **Thunderbolt II.**

ABAC scale—*(NATO)* A nomogram for obtaining the conversion angle to apply when plotting great circle bearings on a mercator projection.

abeam—*(DOD, NATO, IADB)* Bearing approximately 090° or 270° relative; at right angles to the longitudinal axis of a vehicle.

abeam replenishment—*(DOD, NATO)* The transfer at sea of personnel and/or supplies by rigs between two or more ships proceeding side by side.

abort—*(DOD, NATO)* 1. Failure to accomplish a mission for any reason other than enemy action. It may occur at any point from initiation of operation to destination. 2. Discontinue aircraft takeoff run or launch.

abrasion—*(DOD, NATO)* In photography, a scratch or mark produced mechanically on an emulsion surface or film base.

absolute altimeter—*(DOD, NATO)* Radio or similar apparatus that is designed to indicate the true vertical height of an aircraft above the terrain.

absolute altitude—*(DOD, NATO, IADB)* The height of an aircraft directly above the surface or terrain over which it is flying. See also **altitude.**

absolute dud—*(DOD)* A nuclear weapon which, when launched at or emplaced on a target, fails to explode.

absolute filter—*(DOD, NATO)* A filter capable of cutting off 100% by weight of solid particles greater than a stated micron size.

absorbed dose—*(DOD, NATO, IADB)* The amount of energy imparted by nuclear (or ionizing) radiation to unit mass of absorbing material. The unit is the rad.

AC-130—See **Hercules.**

acceleration error—*(NATO)* An error caused by the deflection of the vertical reference due to any change in acceleration of the aircraft.

acceptable product—*(NATO, IADB)* One which may be used in place of another for extended periods without technical advice. See also **emergency substitute; standardized product.**

acceptance trial—*(NATO, IADB)* Trial carried out by nominated representatives of the eventual military users of the weapon or equipment to determine if the specified performance and characteristics have been met.

access procedures—*(NATO)* See **explosive ordnance disposal procedures.**

access to classified information—*(DOD, IADB)* The ability and opportunity to obtain knowledge of classified information. Persons have access to classified information if they are permitted to gain knowledge of the information or if they are in a place where they would be expected to gain such knowledge. Persons do not have access to classified information by being in a place where classified information is kept if security measures prevent them from gaining knowledge of the information.

accidental attack—*(DOD, IADB)* An unintended attack which occurs without deliberate national design as a direct result of a random event, such as a mechanical failure, a simple human error, or an unauthorized action by a subordinate.

accidental war—*(DOD, IADB)* Not to be used. See **accidental attack**.

accountability—*(DOD, IADB)* The obligation imposed by law or lawful order or regulation on an officer or other person for keeping accurate record of property, documents, or funds. The person having this obligation may or may not have actual possession of the property, documents, or funds. Accountability is concerned primarily with records, while responsibility is concerned primarily with custody, care, and safekeeping. See also **responsibility**.

accuracy of fire—*(DOD, NATO)* The precision of fire expressed by the closeness of a grouping of shots at and around the center of the target.

accuracy of fire—*(IADB)* The measure of the deviation of fire from the point of aim, expressed in terms of the distance between the point of aim and the mean point of bursts.

accuracy of information—See **evaluation**.

acknowledgment—*(DOD, NATO, IADB)* A message from the addressee informing the originator that his communication has been received and is understood.

aclinic line—See **magnetic equator**.

acoustical intelligence—*(DOD)* The technical and intelligence information derived from foreign sources which generate acoustical waves.

acoustical surveillance—*(DOD)* Employment of electronic devices, including sound-recording, -receiving, or -transmitting equipment, for the collection of information.

acoustic circuit—*(DOD, NATO)* A mine circuit which responds to the acoustic field of a target. See also **mine**.

acoustic jamming—*(DOD, IADB)* The deliberate radiation or reradiation of mechanical or electro-acoustic signals with the objectives of obliterating or obscuring signals which the enemy is attempting to receive and of deterring enemy weapon systems. See also **barrage jamming; electronic warfare; jamming; spot jamming**.

acoustic mine—*(DOD, NATO)* A mine with an acoustic circuit which responds to the acoustic field of a ship or sweep.

acoustic minehunting—*(DOD, NATO)* The use of a sonar to detect mines or mine like objects which may be on or protruding from the seabed, or buried.

acoustic warfare—*(DOD, NATO)* Action involving the use of underwater acoustic energy to determine, exploit, reduce or prevent hostile use of the underwater acoustic spectrum and actions which retain friendly use of the underwater acoustic spectrum. There are three divisions within acoustic warfare:

1. **acoustic warfare support measures.** That aspect of acoustic warfare involving actions to search for, intercept, locate, record and analyze radiated acoustic energy in water for purpose of exploiting such radiations. The use of acoustic warfare support measures involves no intentional underwater acoustic emission and is generally not detectable by the enemy.
2. **acoustic warfare countermeasures.** That aspect of acoustic warfare involving actions taken to prevent or reduce an enemy's effective use of the underwater acoustic spectrum. Acoustic warfare countermeasures involve international underwater acoustic emissions for deception and jamming.
3. **acoustic warfare counter-countermeasures.** That aspect of acoustic warfare involving actions taken to ensure friendly effective use of the underwater acoustic spectrum despite the enemy's use of underwater acoustic warfare. Acoustic warfare counter-countermeasures involve anti-acoustic warfare support measures and

anti-acoustic warfare countermeasures, and may not involve underwater acoustic emissions.

acoustic warfare counter-countermeasures—See **acoustic warfare Part 3.**

acoustic warfare countermeasures—See **acoustic warfare Part 2.**

acoustic warfare support measures—See **acoustic warfare Part 1.**

acquire—(*DOD, IADB*) 1. When applied to acquisition radars, the process of detecting the presence and location of a target in sufficient detail to permit identification. 2. When applied to tracking radars, the process of positioning a radar beam so that a target is in that beam to permit the effective employment of weapons. See also **target acquisition.**

acquire (radar)—See **acquire.**

acquisition—See **collection (acquisition).**

action agent—(*DOD, IADB*) In intelligence usage, one who has access to, and performs actions against, the target.

action deferred—(*DOD, IADB*) Tactical action on a specific track is being withheld for better tactical advantage. Weapons are available and commitment is pending.

action information center—See **combat information center.**

activate—(*DOD, NATO, IADB*) 1. To put into existence by official order a unit, post, camp, station, base or shore activity which has previously been constituted and designated by name or number, or both, so that it can be organized to function in its assigned capacity. (*DOD, IADB*) 2. To prepare for active service a naval ship or craft which has been in an inactive or reserve status. See also **commission; constitute.**

activation detector—(*DOD, NATO*) A material used to determine neutron flux or density by virtue of the radioactivity induced in it as a result of neutron capture.

active—(*NATO*) In surveillance, an adjective applied to actions or equipments which emit energy capable of being detected.

active aircraft—(*DOD, IADB*) Aircraft currently and actively engaged in supporting the flying missions either through direct assignment to operational units or in the preparation for such assignment or reassignment through any of the logistic processes of supply, maintenance, and modification. See also **aircraft.**

active air defense—(*DOD, IADB*) Direct defensive action taken to destroy attacking enemy aircraft or missiles or to nullify or reduce the effectiveness of such attack. It includes such measures as the use of aircraft, interceptor missiles, air defense artillery, non-air defense weapons in an air defense role, and electronic countermeasures and counter-countermeasures. See also **air defense.**

active air defense—(*NATO*) Direct defensive action taken to destroy or reduce the effectiveness of an enemy air attack. It includes such measures as the use of aircraft, anti-aircraft guns, electronic countermeasures, and surface-to-air guided missiles. See also **air defense.**

active communications satellite—See **communications satellite.**

active defense—(*DOD, IADB*) The employment of limited offensive action and counter-attacks to deny a contested area or position to the enemy. See also **passive defense.**

active duty—*(DOD)* Full-time duty in the active military service of the United States. A general term applied to all active military service with the active force without regard to duration or purpose.

active duty for training—*(DOD)* A tour of active duty which is used for training members of the Reserve Components to provide trained units and qualified persons to fill the needs of the Armed Forces in time of war or national emergency and such other times as the national security requires. The tour of duty is under orders which provide for return to non-active status when the period of active duty for training is completed. It includes annual training, special tours of active duty for training, school tours, and the initial tour performed by non prior service enlistees.

active homing guidance—*(DOD, NATO, IADB)* A system of homing guidance wherein both the source for illuminating the target, and the receiver for detecting the energy reflected from the target as the result of illuminating the target, are carried within the missile. See also **guidance**.

active material—*(DOD, NATO, IADB)* Material, such as plutonium and certain isotopes of uranium, which is capable of supporting a fission chain reaction.

active mine—*(DOD, NATO)* A mine to be actuated by the reflection from a target of a signal emitted by the mine.

activity—*(DOD, IADB)* 1. A unit, organization, or installation performing a function or mission, e.g., reception center, redistribution center, naval station, naval shipyard. 2. A function or mission, e.g., recruiting, schooling. See also **establishment**.

actual ground zero—*(DOD, NATO, IADB)* The point on the surface of the earth at, or vertically below or above, the center of an actual nuclear detonation. See also **desired ground zero; ground zero**.

actuate—*(DOD, NATO)* To operate a mine-firing mechanism by an influence or a series of influences in such a way that all the requirements of the mechanism for firing, or for registering a target count, are met.

actuator—*(DOD, NATO)* A mechanism that furnishes the force required to displace a control surface or other control element.

acute radiation dose—*(DOD, NATO)* Total ionizing radiation dose received at one time and over a period so short that biological recovery cannot occur.

ACV—See **air cushion vehicle**.

add—*(NATO)* In artillery and naval gunfire support, a correction used by an observer/spotter to indicate that an increase in range along a spotting line is desired.

additional training assemblies—*(DOD)* Inactive duty training periods authorized for selected individuals to participate in specialized training or in support of training. These are in addition to the training assemblies an individual attends as a part of unit training.

adjust—*(DOD)* An order to the observer or spotter to initiate an adjustment on a designated target.

adjust fire—*(DOD, NATO, IADB)* In artillery and naval gunfire support: 1. An order or request to initiate an adjustment of fire. 2. A method of control transmitted in the call for fire by the observer or spotter to indicate that he will control the adjustment.

adjustment—See **adjustment of fire**.

adjustment of fire—*(DOD, NATO, IADB)* Process used in artillery and naval gunfire to obtain correct bearing, range, and height of burst (if time fuzes are used) when engaging a target by observed fire. See also **spot**.

ADM-20—See **Quail**.

administration—*(DOD)* 1. The management and execution of all military matters not included in strategy and tactics. 2. Internal management of units.

administration—*(NATO)* 1. The management and execution of all military matters not included in tactics and strategy; primarily in the fields of logistics and personnel management. 2. Internal management of units.

administrative airlift service—*(DOD, IADB)* The airlift service normally provided by specifically identifiable aircraft assigned to organizations or commands for internal administration.

administrative chain of command—*(DOD, NATO)* The normal chain of command for administration. See also **chain of command; operational chain of command.**

administrative control—*(DOD, NATO, IADB)* Direction or exercise of authority over subordinate or other organizations in respect to administrative matters such as personnel management, supply, services, and other matters not included in the operational missions of the subordinate or other organizations. See also **control; operational command; operational control.**

administrative escort—*(DOD, NATO)* A warship or merchant ship under naval control, carrying a convoy commodore and his staff, serving as a platform for simultaneous communication with an operational control authority and a coastal convoy.

administrative landing—*(DOD, IADB)* An unopposed landing involving debarkation from vehicles which have been administratively loaded. See also **administrative loading; administrative movement; logistics over-the-shore operations.**

administrative leadtime—*(DOD, IADB)* The time interval between initiation of procurement action and letting of contract or placing of order. See also **procurement leadtime.**

administrative loading—*(DOD, NATO, IADB)* A loading system which gives primary consideration to achieving maximum utilization of troop and cargo space without regard to tactical considerations. Equipment and supplies must be unloaded and sorted before they can be used. See also **loading.**

administrative map—*(DOD, IADB)* A map on which is graphically recorded information pertaining to administrative matters, such as supply and evacuation installations, personnel installations, medical facilities, collecting points for stragglers and prisoners of war, train bivouacs, service and maintenance areas, main supply roads, traffic circulation, boundaries, and other details necessary to show the administrative situation. See also **map.**

administrative march—See **administrative movement.**

administrative movement—*(DOD, NATO, IADB)* A movement in which troops and vehicles are arranged to expedite their movement and conserve time and energy when no enemy interference, except by air, is anticipated. *(DOD, IADB)* Also called **administrative march.**

administrative order—*(DOD, NATO, IADB)* An order covering traffic, supply, maintenance, evacuation, personnel and other administrative details.

administrative plan—*(NATO)* A plan, normally relating to and complementing the operation plan or order, which provides information and instructions covering the logistic and administrative support of the operation.

administrative shipping—*(DOD, IADB)* Support shipping that is capable of transporting troops and cargo from origin to destination, but which cannot be loaded or unloaded without non-organic personnel and/or equipment; e.g., stevedores, piers, barges, boats. See also **administrative loading; administrative movement.**

advance—*(DOD)* A request from a spotter to indicate the desire that the illuminating projectile burst earlier in relation to the subsequent bursts of high explosive projectiles.

advanced base—*(DOD, NATO, IADB)* A base located in or near a theater of operations whose primary mission is to support military operations.

advanced fleet anchorage—*(DOD, IADB)* A secure anchorage for a large number of naval ships, mobile support units and auxiliaries located in or near a theater of operations. See **emergency anchorage.**

advanced fleet anchorage—*(NATO)* A secure anchorage for a large number of naval vessels, mobile support units, and auxiliaries located in or near a theater of operations. See also **emergency anchorage.**

advanced guard—*(NATO)* The leading element of an advancing force. The primary mission is to insure the uninterrupted advance of the main body. It has the following functions: **a.** To find and exploit gaps in the enemy's defensive system; **b.** To prevent the main body of the advancing force running blindly into enemy opposition; **c.** To clear away minor opposition or, if major opposition is met, to cover the deployment of the main body.

advanced landing field—*(DOD, NATO, IADB)* An airfield, usually having minimum facilities, in or near an objective area. See also **airfield.**

advance force—*(DOD, NATO)* A temporary organization within the amphibious task force which precedes the main body to the objective area. Its function is to participate in preparing the objective for the main assault by conducting such operations as reconnaissance, seizure of supporting positions, minesweeping, preliminary bombardment, underwater demolitions, and air support.

advance force (amphibious)—*(IADB)* A temporary organization within the amphibious task force that precedes the main body to the objective area. Its function is to participate in preparing the objective for the main assault by conducting such operations as reconnaissance, seizure of supporting positions, minesweeping, preliminary bombardment, underwater demolitions, and air support.

advance guard—*(DOD, IADB)* Detachment sent ahead of the main force to insure its uninterrupted advance; to protect the main body against surprise; to facilitate the advance by removing obstacles, and repairing roads and bridges; and to cover the deployment of the main body if it's committed to action.

advance guard reserve—*(DOD, IADB)* Second of the two main parts of an advance guard, the other being the advance guard support. It protects the main force and is itself protected by the advance guard support. Small advance guards do not have reserves.

advance guard support—*(DOD, IADB)* First of the two main parts of an advance guard, the other being the advance guard reserve. It is made up of three smaller elements, in order from front to rear, the advance guard point, the advance party, and the support proper. The advance guard support protects the advance guard reserve.

advance to contact—*(DOD, NATO)* An offensive operation designed to gain or reestablish contact with the enemy. See also **approach march.**

adverse weather—*(DOD, IADB)* Weather in which military operations are generally restricted or impeded. See also **marginal weather.**

advisory area—*(DOD, NATO, IADB)* A designated area within a flight information region where air traffic advisory service is available.

advisory control—*(NATO)* A mode of control under which the aircraft commander selects his own speed, altitude and heading, and has freedom of action to accomplish the assigned task. The aircraft control unit will inform the aircraft of the current tactical picture and provide adequate warnings of hazards affecting aircraft safety.

Aegis—*(DOD)* A totally integrated shipboard weapon system that combines computers, radars, and missiles to provide a defense umbrella for surface shipping. The system is capable of automatically detecting, tracking, and destroying airborne, seaborne, and land-launched weapons.

aerial picket—See **air picket**.

aerial port—*(DOD, IADB)* An airfield that has been designated for the sustained air movement of personnel and materiel, and to serve as an authorized port for entrance into or departure from the country in which located.

aerial port squadron—*(DOD)* An Air Force organization which operates and provides the functions assigned to aerial ports, including processing personnel and cargo, rigging for airdrop, packing parachutes, loading equipment, preparing air cargo and load plans, loading and securing aircraft, ejecting cargo for inflight delivery, and supervising units engaged in aircraft loading and unloading operations.

aerial reconnaissance—See **air reconnaissance**.

aerodrome—See **airfield**.

aerodynamic missile—*(DOD, NATO, IADB)* A missile which uses aerodynamic forces to maintain its flight path, generally employing propulsion guidance. See also **ballistic missile; guided missile**.

aeromedical evacuation—*(DOD)* The movement of patients under medical supervision to and between medical treatment facilities by air transportation.

aeromedical evacuation—*(NATO)* The movement of patients to and between medical treatment facilities by air transportation.

aeromedical evacuation control center—*(DOD, NATO, IADB)* The control facility established by the commander of an air transport division, air force, or air command. It operates in conjunction with the command movement control center and coordinates overall medical requirements with airlift capability. It also assigns medical missions to the appropriate aeromedical evacuation elements in the system and monitors patient movement activities.

aeromedical evacuation control officer—*(DOD, IADB)* An officer of the air transport force or air command controlling the flow of patients by air.

aeromedical evacuation coordinating officer—*(NATO)* An officer of an originating, intransit, or destination medical facility/establishment who coordinates aeromedical evacuation activities of the facility/establishment.

aeromedical evacuation operations officer—*(NATO)* An officer of the airlift force or command who is responsible for activities relating to planning and directing aeromedical evacuation operations, maintaining liaison with medical airlift activities concerned, operating an Aeromedical Evacuation Control Center, and otherwise coordinating aircraft and patient movements.

aeromedical evacuation system—*(DOD, IADB)* A system which provides: **a.** control of patient movement by air transport; **b.** specialized medical attendants and equipment for inflight medical care; **c.** facilities on or in the vicinity of air strips and air bases, for the limited medical care of intransit patients entering, en route via, or leaving the system; and **d.** communication with originating, destination, and en route medical facilities concerning patient transportation.

aeromedical evacuation system—*(NATO)* A system which provides: **a.** Control of patient movement by air transport; **b.** Specialized medical attendants and equipment for inflight medical care; **c.** Facilities on, or in the vicinity of, air strips and air bases, for the limited

7

medical care of intransit patients entering, en route via, or leaving the system; **d.** Communication with destination and en route medical facilities concerning patient airlift movements.

aeromedical evacuation unit—*(DOD, IADB)* An operational medical organization concerned primarily with the management and control of patients being transported via an aeromedical evacuation system or system echelon. See also **forward aeromedical evacuation.**

aeromedical staging unit—*(NATO)* A medical unit operating transient patient beds located on or in the vicinity of an emplaning or deplaning air base or air strip that provides reception, administration, processing, ground transportation, feeding and limited medical care for patients entering or leaving an aeromedical evacuation system.

aeronautical chart—*(DOD, IADB)* A specialized representation of mapped features of the earth, or some part of it, produced to show selected terrain, cultural and hydrographic features, and supplemental information required for air navigation, pilotage, or for planning air operations.

aeronautical chart—*(NATO)* A representation of a portion of the earth, its culture and relief, specifically designed to meet the requirements of air navigation.

aeronautical information overprint—*(DOD, NATO, IADB)* Additional information which is printed or stamped on a map or chart for the specific purpose of air navigation.

aeronautical plotting chart—*(DOD, NATO)* A chart designed for the graphical processes of navigation.

aeronautical topographic chart—*(NATO)* A representation of features of the surface of the earth, designed primarily as an aid to visual or radar navigation, which shows selected terrain, cultural or hydrographic features, and supplementary aeronautical information.

aeropause—*(NATO, IADB)* Region in which functional effects of the atmosphere on man and aircraft cease to exist.

aerospace—*(DOD, IADB)* Of, or pertaining to, earth's envelope of atmosphere and the space above it; two separate entities considered as a single realm for activity in launching, guidance, and control of vehicles that will travel in both entities.

aerospace control operations—*(DOD)* The employment of air forces, supported by ground and naval forces, as appropriate, to achieve military objectives in vital aerospace areas. Such operations include destruction of enemy aerospace and surface-to-air forces, interdiction of enemy aerospace operations, protection of vital air lines of communication, and the establishment of local military superiority in areas of air operations.

aerospace defense—*(DOD, IADB)* 1. All defensive measures designed to destroy attacking enemy aircraft, missiles, and space vehicles after they leave the earth's surface, or to nullify or reduce the effectiveness of such attacks. 2. An inclusive term encompassing air defense and space defense.

aerospace projection operations—See **land, sea, or aerospace projection operations.**

affiliation with the Department of Defense—*(DOD)* Persons, groups of persons, or organizations are considered to be affiliated with the Department of Defense if they are: **a.** employed by, or contracting with, the Department of Defense or any activity under the jurisdiction of the Department of Defense, whether on a full-time, part-time, or consultative basis; **b.** members of the Armed Forces on active duty, National Guard members, or those in a reserve or retired status; **c.** residing on, authorized access to, or conducting or operating any business or other function at any DOD installation or facility; **d.** authorized access to defense information; **e.** participating in other authorized DOD programs; or

f. applying or being considered for any status described above.

afloat support—*(DOD, NATO)* A form of logistic support outside the confines of a harbor in which fuel, ammunition and supplies are provided for operating forces either underway or at anchor. See also **floating base support.**

afterburning—*(DOD, NATO, IADB)* 1. The characteristic of some rocket motors to burn irregularly for some time after the main burning and thrust has ceased. 2. The process of fuel injection and combustion in the exhaust jet of a turbojet engine (aft or to the rear of the turbine.)

after flight inspection—*(NATO)* General examination after flight for obvious defects, correction of defects reported by aircraft crews, replenishment of consumable or expendable stores, and securing aircraft. Also called **post flight inspection.**

afterwinds—*(DOD)* Wind currents set up in the vicinity of a nuclear explosion directed toward the burst center, resulting from the updraft accompanying the rise of the fireball.

agency—*(DOD, NATO)* In intelligence usage, an organization or individual engaged in collecting and/or processing information. See also **agent; intelligence cycle; source.**

agent—*(DOD, IADB)* In intelligence usage, one who is authorized or instructed to obtain or to assist in obtaining information for intelligence or counterintelligence purposes. See also **anticrop agent; antimateriel agent; biological agent; chemical agent; defoliating agent; nerve agent; riot control agent.**

agent—*(NATO)* In intelligence usage, one who is recruited, trained, controlled and employed to obtain and report information. See also **source.**

agent authentication—*(DOD, IADB)* The technical support task of providing an agent with personal documents, accoutrements, and equipment which have the appearance of authenticity as to claimed origin and which support and are consistent with the agent's cover story.

agent net—*(DOD, IADB)* An organization for clandestine purposes which operates under the direction of a principal agent.

age of moon—*(DOD, NATO)* The elapsed time, usually expressed in days, since the last new moon.

aggressor forces—*(DOD, IADB)* Forces engaged in aggressive military action. In the context of training exercises, the "enemy" created to add realism in training maneuvers and exercises. This method replaces the less realistic system of fictional "red" and "blue" armies.

AGM-28A—See **Hound Dog.**

AGM-45—See **Shrike.**

AGM-53—See **Condor.**

AGM-65—See **Maverick.**

AGM-69—See **short range attack missile.**

AGM-78—See **Standard Arm.**

AGM-84A—See **Harpoon.**

agonic line—*(DOD)* A line drawn on a map or chart joining points of zero magnetic declination for a specified epoch.

agonic line—*(NATO)* A line drawn on a map or chart joining points of zero magnetic declination for a specified year date. In nautical and aeronautical navigation, the term magnetic variation is used instead of magnetic declination.

agreed point—*(DOD, NATO)* A predetermined point on the ground, identifiable from the air, and used when aircraft assist in fire adjustment.

AH–1J—See **Sea Cobra.**

AIM–4, 26, 47—See **Falcon.**

AIM–7—See **Sparrow.**

AIM–9—See **Sidewinder.**

AIM–54A—See **Phoenix.**

AIR–2—See **Genie.**

air—*(DOD, NATO)* In artillery and naval gunfire support a spotting, or an observation, by a spotter or an observer to indicate that a burst or group of bursts occurred before impact.

air alert—See **air defense warning conditions; alert; ground alert.**

air and naval gunfire liaison company—*(DOD, IADB)* An organization composed of Marine and Navy personnel specially qualified for shore control of naval gunfire and close air support. Also known as ANGLICO.

air attack—*(DOD, IADB)* **1. coordinated**—A combination of two or more types of air attack (dive, glide, low-level) in one strike, using one or more types of aircraft. **2. deferred**—A procedure in which attack groups rendezvous as a single unit. It is used when attack groups are launched from more than one station with their departure on the mission being delayed pending further orders. **3. divided**—A method of delivering a coordinated air attack which consists of holding the units in close tactical concentration up to a point, then splitting them to attack an objective from different directions.

airborne—*(DOD, NATO, IADB)* **1.** Applied to personnel, equipment, etc., transported by air; e.g., airborne infantry. **2.** Applied to materials being or designed to be transported by aircraft, as distinguished from weapons and equipment installed in and remaining a part of the aircraft. **3.** The state of an aircraft, from the instant it becomes entirely sustained by air until it ceases to be so sustained. A lighter-than-air aircraft is not considered to be airborne when it is attached to the ground, except that moored balloons are airborne whenever sent aloft. See also **air transportable unit.**

airborne alert—*(DOD, NATO, IADB)* A state of aircraft readiness wherein combat-equipped aircraft are airborne and ready for immediate action. See also **fighter cover.** *(DOD, IADB)* It is designed to reduce reaction time and to increase the survivability factor. See also **combat air patrol; fighter cover.**

airborne assault—See **assault phase.**

airborne assault weapon—*(DOD, IADB)* An unarmored, mobile, full-tracked gun providing a mobile antitank capability for airborne troops. Can be airdropped.

airborne battlefield command and control center—*(DOD)* A United States Air Force aircraft equipped with communications, data link, and display equipment; it may be employed as an airborne command post or a communications and intelligence relay facility.

airborne command post—*(DOD, NATO)* A suitably equipped aircraft used by the commander for the control of his forces.

airborne early warning—*(DOD, IADB)* The detection of enemy air or surface units by radar or other equipment carried in an airborne vehicle and the transmitting of a warning to friendly units.

airborne early warning and control—*(DOD, NATO, IADB)* Air surveillance and control provided by airborne early warning vehicles which are equipped with search and height-finding radar and communications equipment for controlling weapons. See also **air picket.**

airborne force—*(DOD, NATO, IADB)* A force composed primarily of ground and air units organized, equipped and trained for airborne operations. See also **force(s)**.

airborne force liaison officer—*(NATO)* An officer who is the representative of the airborne units and who works with the air force on airfields being used for airborne operations.

airborne interception equipment—*(DOD, NATO, IADB)* A fire control system, including radar equipment, installed in interceptor aircraft used to effect air interception.

airborne lift—*(DOD, IADB)* The total capacities expressed in terms of personnel and cargo that are, or can be, carried by available aircraft in one trip.

airborne operation—*(DOD, IADB)* An operation involving the air movement into an objective area of combat forces and their logistic support for execution of a tactical or a strategic mission. The means employed may be any combination of airborne units, air transportable units, and types of transport aircraft, depending on the mission and the overall situation.

airborne operation—*(NATO)* An operation involving the movement of combat forces and their logistic support into an objective area by air.

airborne order—*(DOD, IADB)* A command and authorization for flight when a predetermined time greater than five minutes is established for aircraft to become airborne.

airborne radio relay—*(DOD)* Airborne equipment used to relay radio transmission from selected originating transmitters.

airborne radio relay—*(NATO)* A technique employing aircraft fitted with radio relay stations for the purpose of increasing the range, flexibility or physical security of communications systems.

airborne sensor operator—*(DOD)* An individual trained to operate sensor equipment aboard aircraft and to perform limited interpretations of collected information produced in flight.

airborne tactical data system—*(DOD)* An airborne early warning system capable of integration into the tactical data system environment. It provides an automated, operator-controlled capability for collecting, displaying, evaluating and disseminating tactical information via tactical digital information links. It is part of the Naval Tactical Data System (NTDS). Also called **ATDS**.

airborne troops—*(DOD, IADB)* Those ground units whose primary mission is to make assault landings from the air. See also **troops**.

air-breathing missile—*(DOD)* A missile with an engine requiring the intake of air for combustion of its fuel, as in a ramjet or turbojet. To be contrasted with the rocket missile, which carries its own oxidizer and can operate beyond the atmosphere.

airburst—*(DOD, NATO, IADB)* An explosion of a bomb or projectile above the surface as distinguished from an explosion on contact with the surface or after penetration. See also **types of burst**.

air cargo—See **cargo**.

air cartographic camera—*(NATO)* A camera having the accuracy and other characteristics essential for air survey or cartographic photography. Also called **mapping camera**.

air cartographic photography—*(NATO)* The taking and processing of air photographs for mapping and charting purposes.

Air Combat Fighter—*(DOD)* A single engine, supersonic, turbofan, all-weather multipurpose tactical fighter/bomber. It is capable of employing nuclear/nonnuclear weapons. Air superiority is its primary mission with air interdiction and close air support as secondary. An air refueling capability increases its flexibility. Designated as **F-16**.

air command—*(DOD, IADB)* A major subdivision of the Air Force; for operational purposes, it normally consists of two or more air forces. See also **command.**

air control—See also **air controller; air traffic control center; airway; area control center; combat zone(air); control and reporting center; control area; controlled airspace; control zone; tactical air control center; air traffic controller; air weapons controller; terminal control area.**

air controller—*(DOD, NATO, IADB)* An individual especially trained for and assigned the duty of the control (by use of radio, radar, or other means) of such aircraft as may be allotted to him for operation within his area. See also **air traffic controller; air weapons controller; tactical air controller.**

air corridor—*(DOD, NATO, IADB)* A restricted air route of travel specified for use by friendly aircraft and established for the purpose of preventing friendly aircraft from being fired on by friendly forces.

aircraft—See **active aircraft; inactive aircraft inventory; nonprogram aircraft; program aircraft; reserve aircraft; supporting aircraft; unit aircraft.**

aircraft arresting barrier—*(DOD, NATO, IADB)* A device, not dependent on an aircraft hook, used to engage and absorb the forward momentum of an emergency landing or an aborted take-off. See also **aircraft arresting system.**

aircraft arresting cable—*(DOD, NATO)* That part of an aircraft arresting gear which spans the runway surface or flight deck landing area and is engaged by the aircraft arresting system. Also called **aircraft arresting wire.**

aircraft arresting gear—*(DOD, NATO, IADB)* A device used to engage hook-equipped aircraft to absorb the forward momentum of a routine or emergency landing, or aborted take-off. See also **aircraft arresting system.**

aircraft arresting hook—*(DOD, NATO, IADB)* A device fitted to an aircraft to engage arresting gear. See also **aircraft arresting system.**

aircraft arresting system—*(DOD, NATO, IADB)* A series of components used to engage an aircraft and absorb the forward momentum of a routine or emergency landing (or an aborted take-off). See also **aircraft arresting barrier; aircraft arresting gear; aircraft arresting hook.**

aircraft arresting wire—See **aircraft arresting cable.** See also **aircraft arresting system.**

aircraft arrestment—*(DOD, NATO, IADB)* Controlled stopping of an aircraft by external means.

aircraft block speed—*(DOD)* True airspeed in knots under zero wind conditions adjusted in relation to length of sortie to compensate for takeoff, climbout, letdown, instrument approach, and landing.

aircraft captain—See **aircraft commander.**

aircraft climb corridor—*(NATO)* Positive controlled airspace of defined vertical and horizontal dimensions extending from an airfield.

aircraft commander—*(DOD, NATO)* The aircrew member designated by competent authority as being in command of an aircraft and responsible for its safe operation and accomplishment of the assigned mission.

aircraft control and warning system—*(DOD, IADB)* A system established to control and report the movement of aircraft. It consists of observation facilities (radar, passive electronic, visual, or other means), control center, and necessary communications.

aircraft control unit—*(NATO)* A unit with facilities and personnel, including controllers, for conducting aircraft control and which exercises tactical control of aircraft or a unit(s).

aircraft cross-servicing—*(DOD, NATO)* Services performed on an aircraft by an organization other than that to which the aircraft is assigned, according to an established operational aircraft cross-servicing requirement, and for which there may be a charge. Aircraft cross-servicing has been divided into two categories:

a. Stage A cross-servicing: The servicing of aircraft on airfields/ships which enables flights to be made to another airfield/ship. The servicing includes refueling, replenishment of fluids and gases, drag chutes (if applicable), starting facilities, and ground handling.

b. Stage B cross-servicing: The servicing of aircraft on airfields/ships which enables the aircraft to be flown on an operational mission. The servicing includes all Stage A services plus the loading of weapons and/or film, including the processing and interpretation of any exposed film from the previous mission. See also **aircraft transient servicing.**

aircraft dispersal area—*(NATO)* An area on a military installation designed primarily for the dispersal of parked aircraft, whereby such aircraft will be less vulnerable in the event of enemy air raid.

aircraft flat pallet—*(NATO)* A stressed pallet capable of supporting and restraining a specifically rated load. It is specifically designed for tie-down in an aircraft. See also **palletized unit load.**

aircraft guide—See **aircraft marshaller.**

aircraft handover—*(NATO)* The process of transferring control of aircraft from one controlling authority to another.

aircraft inspection—*(NATO)* The process of systematically examining, checking and testing aircraft structural members, components and systems, to detect actual or potential unserviceable conditions.

aircraft loading table—*(DOD, NATO, IADB)* A data sheet used by the force unit commander containing information as to the load that actually goes into each aircraft.

aircraft marshaller—*(NATO)* A person trained to direct by visual or other means the movement of aircraft on the ground, into and out of landing, parking or hovering points. Also called **aircraft guide.**

aircraft marshalling area—*(NATO)* An area in which aircraft may form up before take-off or assemble after landing.

aircraft mission equipment—*(DOD, NATO, IADB)* Equipment that must be fitted to an aircraft to enable it to fulfill a particular mission or task.

aircraft modification—*(DOD, NATO, IADB)* A change in the physical characteristics of aircraft, accomplished either by a change in production specifications or by alteration of items already produced.

aircraft monitoring and control—*(DOD)* That equipment installed in aircraft to permit monitoring and control of safing, arming, and fuzing functions of nuclear weapons or nuclear weapon systems.

aircraft picketing—*(NATO)* Securing aircraft when parked in the open to restrain movement due to weather or condition of the parking area.

aircraft repair—*(DOD)* The process of restoring aircraft or aircraft material to a serviceable condition.

aircraft replenishing—*(NATO)* The refilling of aircraft with consumables such as fuel, oil, and compressed gases to predetermined levels, pressures, quantities or weights. Rearming is excluded.

aircraft role equipment—See **aircraft mission equipment.**

aircraft scrambling—(DOD, NATO, IADB) Directing the immediate take-off of aircraft from a ground alert condition of readiness.

aircraft servicing connector—(NATO) A device fitted to aircraft and/or ground equipment which enables replenishment and/or servicing to be carried out.

aircraft store—(DOD, NATO) Any device intended for internal or external carriage and mounted on aircraft suspension and release equipment, whether or not the item is intended to be separated in flight from the aircraft. Aircraft stores are classified in two categories as follows:

   a. **Expendable store—**An aircraft store normally separated from the aircraft in flight such as a missile, rocket, bomb, nuclear weapon, mine, torpedo, pyrotechnic device, sonobuoy, signal underwater sound device, or other similar items.

   b. **Nonexpendable store—**An aircraft store which is not normally separated from the aircraft in flight such as a tank (fuel and spray), line-source disseminator, pod (refueling, thrust augmentation, gun, electronic-counter measures, data link, etc.), multiple rack, target, cargo drop container, drone or other similar items.

aircraft tiedown—(DOD, IADB) Securing aircraft when parked in the open to restrain movement due to the weather or condition of the parking area. (NATO) See **aircraft picketing.**

aircraft transient servicing—(DOD, NATO) Services performed on an aircraft by an organization other than that to which the aircraft is assigned, and for which there may be a charge. See also **aircraft cross-servicing.**

aircraft utilization—(DOD, IADB) Average numbers of hours during each 24-hour period that an aircraft is actually in flight.

aircraft vectoring—(DOD, NATO, IADB) The directional control of in-flight aircraft through transmission of azimuth headings.

air cushion vehicle—(DOD) A vehicle capable of being operated so that its weight, including its payload, is wholly or significantly supported on a continuously generated cushion or "bubble" of air at higher than ambient pressure. Also known as ACV. (Note: **NATO** uses the term "ground effect machine".)

air data computer—See **central air data computer.**

air defense—(DOD, IADB) All defensive measures designed to destroy attacking enemy aircraft or missiles in the earth's envelope of atmosphere, or to nullify or reduce the effectiveness of such attack. See also **active air defense; passive air defense.**

air defense—(NATO) All measures designed to nullify or reduce the effectiveness of hostile air action. See also **active air defense; passive air defense.**

air defense action area—(DOD, NATO, IADB) An area and the airspace above it within which friendly aircraft or surface-to-air weapons are normally given precedence in operations except under specified conditions. See also **air defense operations area.**

air defense area—(DOD, IADB) 1. overseas—A specifically defined airspace for which air defense must be planned and provided. 2. **United States—**Airspace of defined dimensions designated by the appropriate agency within which the ready control of airborne vehicles is required in the interest of national security during an air defense emergency.

air defense area—(NATO) A specifically defined airspace for which air defense must be planned and provided.

air defense artillery—(DOD, IADB) Weapons and equipment for actively combatting air targets from the ground.

air defense battle zone—(DOD, IADB) A volume of airspace surrounding an air defense fire unit or defended area, extending to a specified altitude and range, in which the fire unit commander will engage and destroy targets not identified as friendly under criteria established by higher headquarters.

air defense command—*(NATO)* The authority and responsibility for the air defense of a designated area.

air defense commander—*(NATO)* A duly appointed commander responsible for the air defense of a designated area.

air defense control center—*(DOD, NATO, IADB)* The principal information, communications and operations center from which all aircraft, antiaircraft operations, air defense artillery, guided missiles and air warning functions of a specific area of air defense responsibility are supervised and coordinated. See also **combat information center.**

air defense direction center—*(DOD, IADB)* An installation having the capability of performing air surveillance, interception control, and direction of allocated air defense weapons within an assigned sector of responsibility. It may also have an identification capability.

air defense division—*(DOD, IADB)* A geographic subdivision of an air defense region. See also **air defense sector.**

air defense early warning—See **early warning.**

air defense emergency—*(DOD, IADB)* An emergency condition, declared by either the Commander in Chief, North American Air Defense Command or Commander in Chief, Aerospace Defense Command, that exists when attack upon the continental United States, Alaska, Canada, or United States installations in Greenland by hostile aircraft or missiles is considered probable, is imminent, or is taking place.

air defense ground environment—*(DOD, NATO)* The network of ground radar sites and command and control centers within a specific theater of operations which are used for the tactical control of air defense operations.

air defense identification zone—*(DOD, IADB)* Airspace of defined dimensions within which the ready identification, location, and control of airborne vehicles are required. Commonly referred to as ADIZ. See also **air defense operations area.**

air defense identification zone—*(NATO)* Airspace of defined dimensions within which the ready identification, location, and control of aircraft is required. See also **air defense operations area.**

air defense operations area—*(DOD, IADB)* An area and the airspace above it within which procedures are established to minimize mutual interference between air defense and other operations; it may include designation of one or more of the following: air defense action area, air defense identification zone, and/or fire-power umbrella. See also **air defense action area; air defense identification zone; fire-power umbrella; positive identification and radar advisory zone.**

air defense operations area—*(NATO)* A geographical area defining the boundaries within which procedures are established to minimize interference between air defense and other operations and which may include designation of one or more of the following: **a.** Air defense action area; **b.** Air defense area; **c.** Air defense identification zone; **d.** Fire power umbrella.

air defense operations team—*(DOD)* A team of United States Air Force ground environment personnel assigned to certain allied air defense control and warning units/elements.

air defense readiness—*(DOD, IADB)* An operational status requiring air defense forces to maintain higher than ordinary preparedness for a short period of time.

air defense region—*(DOD, NATO, IADB)* A geographical subdivision of an air defense area.

air defense sector—*(DOD, NATO, IADB)* A geographical subdivision of an air defense region. See also **air defense division.**

air defense ship—*(NATO, IADB)* The ship detailed to assume responsibility for air defense.

air defense suppression—*(DOD)* In air operations, actions taken to degrade fixed and mobile surface-based components of enemy air defense systems so that offensive air forces may effectively attack a target.

air defense warning conditions—*(DOD, IADB)* A degree of air raid probability according to the following code. The term air defense division/sector referred to herein may include forces and units afloat and/or deployed to forward areas, as applicable. **Air defense warning yellow**—attack by hostile aircraft and/or missiles is probable. This means that hostile aircraft and/or missiles are en route toward an air defense division/sector, or unknown aircraft and/or missiles suspected to be hostile are en route toward or are within an air defense division/sector. **Air defense warning red**—attack by hostile aircraft and/or missiles is imminent or is in progress. This means that hostile aircraft and/or missiles are within an air defense division/sector or are in the immediate vicinity of an air defense division/sector with high probability of entering the division/sector. **Air defense warning white**—attack by hostile aircraft and/or missiles is improbable. May be called either before or after air defense warning yellow or red. The initial declaration of air defense emergency will automatically establish a condition of air defense warning other than white for purposes of security control of air traffic.

air delivery—See **airdrop; air landed; air movement; air supply.**

air delivery container—*(DOD, IADB)* A sling, bag, or roll, usually of canvas or webbing, designed to hold supplies and equipment for air delivery.

air delivery equipment—*(DOD, IADB)* Special items of equipment, such as parachutes, air delivery containers, platforms, tie downs, and related items used in air delivery of personnel, supplies and equipment.

air dispatcher (cargo)—*(IADB)* A person trained in the ejection of cargo from aircraft in flight.

air division—*(DOD)* A unit or its headquarters, on a level of command above wing level, composed of two or more combat wings, but sometimes adapted to other organizational structures.

airdrop—*(DOD, IADB)* The unloading of personnel or materiel from aircraft in flight. See also **air movement; free drop; free fall; high-velocity drop; low-velocity drop.**

airdrop—*(NATO)* Delivery of personnel or cargo from aircraft in flight. See also **air movement; free drop; high-velocity drop; low-velocity drop.**

airdrop platform—*(DOD, NATO, IADB)* A base on which vehicles, cargo, or equipment are loaded for airdrop or low-altitude extraction. See also **airdrop.**

air employment/allocation plan—*(DOD)* The means by which subordinate commanders advise the joint force commander of planned employment/allocation of organic or assigned assets of any expected excess sorties, or of any additional air support requirements.

air evacuation—*(NATO, IADB)* Evacuation by aircraft of personnel and cargo.

air facility—*(DOD, IADB)* An installation from which air operations may be or are being conducted. See also **facility.**

airfield—*(DOD, NATO, IADB)* An area prepared for the accommodation (including any buildings, installations, and equipment), landing and take-off of aircraft. See also **alternative airfield; departure airfield; landing area;**

landing point; landing site; landing zone; main airfield; redeployment airfield; regroup airfield.

airfield damage repair—*(NATO)* The range of activities required to restore the operational capability of an airfield after non-nuclear attack, including: **a.** Reconnaissance to assess the damage and essential recuperative work; **b.** Explosive ordnance disposal; **c.** Restoration of minimum operating surfaces, including aircraft maneuvering areas and access tracks; **d.** Restoration of services and facilities essential for the conduct of air operations. Also called **ADR.**

airfield traffic—*(DOD, NATO, IADB)* All traffic on the maneuvering area of an airfield and all aircraft flying in the vicinity of an airfield.

air fire plan—*(DOD, IADB)* A plan for integrating and coordinating tactical air support of ground forces with other fire support.

Air Force base—*(DOD)* An air base for support of Air Force units consisting of landing strips and all components or related facilities for which the Air Force has operating responsibility, together with interior lines of communications and the minimal surrounding area required for local security. (Normally, not greater than an area of 20 square miles.) See also **base complex.**

Air Force Component Headquarters—*(DOD)* The field headquarters facility of the Air Force commander charged with the overall conduct of Air Force operations. It is composed of the command section and appropriate staff elements.

airframe—*(DOD, IADB)* 1. The structural components of an airplane, including the framework and skin of such parts as the fuselage, empennage, wings, landing gear (minus tires), and engine mounts. 2. The framework, envelope, and cabin of an airship. 3. The assembled principal structural components, less propulsion system, control, electronic equipment, and payload, of a missile.

air freighting—*(NATO)* The nontactical movement of cargo by air.

air ground operations system—*(DOD, NATO, IADB)* An Army/Air Force system providing the ground commander with the means for receiving, processing and forwarding the requests of subordinate ground commanders for air support missions and for the rapid dissemination of information and intelligence.

airhead—*(DOD, NATO, IADB)* 1. A designated area in a hostile or threatened territory which, when seized and held, insures the continuous air landing of troops and materiel and provides the maneuver space necessary for projected operations. Normally it is the area seized in the assault phase of an airborne operation. 2. A designated location in an area of operations used as a base for supply and evacuation by air. See also **beachhead; bridgehead.**

air intercept control common—*(DOD)* A tactical air-to-ground radio frequency, monitored by all air intercept control facilities within an area, which is used as a backup for other discrete tactical control frequencies.

air interception—*(DOD, IADB)* To effect visual or electronic contact by a friendly aircraft with another aircraft. Normally, the air intercept is conducted in the following five phases: **a. climb phase**—Airborne to cruising altitude. **b. maneuver phase**—Receipt of initial vector to target until beginning transition to attack speed and altitude. **c. transition phase**—Increase or decrease of speed and altitude required for the attack. **d. attack phase**—Turn to attack heading, acquire target, complete attack, and turn to breakaway heading. **e. recovery phase**—Breakaway to landing. See also **broadcast controlled air interception; close controlled air interception.**

air interception—*(NATO)* An operation by which aircraft effect visual or electronic contact with other aircraft.

air intercept zone—*(DOD, IADB)* A subdivided part of the destruction area in which it is planned to destroy or defeat the enemy airborne threat with interceptor aircraft. See also **destruction area**.

air interdiction—*(DOD, NATO, IADB)* Air operations conducted to destroy, neutralize, or delay the enemy's military potential before it can be brought to bear effectively against friendly forces at such distance from friendly forces that detailed integration of each air mission with the fire and movement of friendly forces is not required. See also **interdict**.

air landed—*(DOD, NATO, IADB)* Moved by air and disembarked, or unloaded, after the aircraft has landed or while a helicopter is hovering. See also **air movement**.

air-launched ballistic missile—*(DOD, IADB)* A ballistic missile launched from an airborne vehicle.

air liaison officer—*(DOD, IADB)* An officer (aviator/pilot) attached to a ground unit who functions as the primary advisor to the ground commander on air operation matters.

air liaison officer—*(NATO)* A tactical air force or naval aviation officer attached to a ground or naval unit or formation as the advisor on tactical air operation matters. See also **ground liaison officer**.

airlift capability—*(DOD, NATO, IADB)* The total capacity expressed in terms of number of passengers and/or weight/cubic displacement of cargo that can be carried at any one time to a given destination by the available air transport service. See also **airlift requirement; allowable cabin load; allowable cargo load; payload**.

airlift control center—*(DOD)* An operations center where the detailed planning, coordinating, and tasking for tactical airlift operations are accomplished. This is the focal point for communications and the source of control and direction for the tactical airlift forces. Also called ALCC.

airlift requirement—*(DOD, NATO, IADB)* The total number of passengers and/or weight/cubic displacement of cargo required to be carried by air for a specific task. See also **airlift capability**.

airlift service—*(DOD, IADB)* The performance or procurement of air transportation and services incident thereto required for the movement of persons, cargo, mail, or other goods.

air logistic support—*(DOD, IADB)* Support by air landing or airdrop, including air supply, movement of personnel, evacuation of casualties and prisoners of war, and recovery of equipment and vehicles.

air logistic support operation—*(DOD, NATO)* An air operation, excluding an airborne operation, conducted within a theater to distribute and recover personnel, equipment and supplies.

airmiss—See **near miss**.

air mission—See **mission**.

air mission intelligence report—*(DOD, IADB)* A detailed report of the results of an air mission, including a complete intelligence account of the mission.

airmobile forces—*(DOD, NATO)* The ground combat, supporting and air vehicle units required to conduct an airmobile operation.

airmobile operation—*(NATO)* An operation in which combat forces and their equipment maneuver about the battlefield in helicopters under the control of a ground force commander to engage in ground combat.

airmobile operations—*(DOD, IADB)* Operations in which combat forces and their equipment move about the battlefield in air vehicles under the control of a ground force commander to engage in ground combat.

airmobility—*(DOD, NATO)* A capability of airmobile forces which permits them to move by air vehicles while retaining the ability to engage in ground combat.

air movement—*(DOD, NATO, IADB)* Air transport of units, personnel, supplies and equipment including airdrops and air landings. See also **airdrop; free drop; high velocity drop; low velocity drop.**

air movement column—*(DOD, IADB)* In airborne operations, the lead formation and the serials following, proceeding over the same flight path at the same altitude.

air movement officer—*(NATO)* An officer trained for duties in air movement/traffic sections.

air movement section—See air movement traffic section.

air movement table—*(DOD, NATO, IADB)* A table prepared by a ground force commander in coordination with an air force commander. This form, issued as an annex to the operation order: **a.** Indicates the allocation of aircraft space to elements of the ground units to be airlifted; **b.** Designates the number and type of aircraft in each serial; **c.** Specifies the departure area, time of loading and take-off.

air movement traffic section—*(NATO)* A section located on those airfields which serve transport aircraft. It is responsible for the loading and unloading of aircraft and for the handling of passengers, mail and material.

air observation—See air observer.

air observation post—See observation post.

air observer—*(DOD, NATO, IADB)* An individual whose primary mission is to observe or take photographs from an aircraft in order to adjust artillery fire or obtain military information.

air observer adjustment—*(DOD)* The correcting of gunfire from an aircraft. See also **spot.**

air offensive—*(DOD, IADB)* Sustained operations by strategic and/or tactical air weapon systems against hostile air forces or surface targets.

air operations center—See tactical air control center.

air photographic reconnaissance—*(DOD, NATO, IADB)* The obtaining of information by air photography, divided into three types: **a.** Strategic photographic reconnaissance; **b.** Tactical photographic reconnaissance; and **c.** Survey/cartographic photography—air photography taken for survey/cartographical purposes and to survey/cartographic standards of accuracy. It may be strategic or tactical.

air picket—*(DOD, NATO, IADB)* An airborne early warning aircraft positioned primarily to detect, report and track approaching enemy aircraft or missiles and to control intercepts. See also **airborne early warning and control.**

air plot—*(DOD, NATO, IADB)* 1. A continuous plot used in air navigation of a graphic representation of true headings steered and air distances flown. 2. A continuous plot of the position of an airborne object represented graphically to show true headings steered and air distances flown. 3. Within ships, a display that shows the positions and movements of an airborne object relative to the plotting ship.

air policing—*(NATO)* The use of interceptor aircraft, in peacetime, for the purpose of preserving the integrity of a specified airspace.

airport—See airfield.

air portable—*(DOD, NATO, IADB)* Denotes materiel which is suitable for transport by an aircraft loaded internally or externally, with no more than minor dismantling and reassembling within the capabilities of user units. This term must be qualified to show the extent of air portability.

airport surface detection equipment—*(DOD)* Short-range radar displaying the airport surface. Aircraft and vehicular traffic operating on runways, taxiways, and ramps, moving or stationary, may be observed with a high degree of resolution.

airport surveillance radar—*(DOD, IADB)* Radar displaying range and azimuth that is normally employed in a terminal area as an aid to approach- and departure-control.

airport traffic area—*(DOD)* Unless otherwise specifically designated, that airspace within a horizontal radius of five statute miles from the geographic center of any airport at which a control tower is operating, extending from the surface up to, but not including, an altitude of 3,000 feet above the elevation of the airport.

air position—*(DOD, NATO, IADB)* The calculated position of an aircraft assuming no wind effect.

air priorities committee—*(DOD, NATO, IADB)* A committee set up to determine the priorities of passengers and cargo. See also **air transport allocations board.**

air raid reporting control ship—*(DOD, NATO, IADB)* A ship to which the air defense ship has delegated the duties of controlling air warning radar and air raid reporting.

air reconnaissance—*(DOD, IADB)* The acquisition of intelligence information by employing visual observation and/or sensors in air vehicles.

air reconnaissance—*(NATO)* The collection of information of intelligence interest either by visual observation from the air or through the use of airborne sensors. See also **reconnaissance.**

air reconnaissance liaison officer—*(DOD)* An Army officer especially trained in air reconnaissance and imagery interpretation matters who is attached to a tactical air reconnaissance unit. This officer assists and advises the air commander and staff on matters concerning ground operations and informs the supported ground commander on the status of air reconnaissance requests.

air route—*(DOD, NATO, IADB)* The navigable airspace between two points, identified to the extent necessary for the application of flight rules.

air route traffic control center—*(DOD)* The principal facility exercising en route control of aircraft operating under instrument flight rules within its area of jurisdiction. Approximately 26 such centers cover the United States and its possessions. Each has a communication capability to adjacent centers.

airspace control—*(NATO)* A service provided in the combat zone to increase operational effectiveness by promoting the safe, efficient, and flexible use of airspace. Airspace control is provided in order to permit greater flexibility of operations, while authority to approve, disapprove, or deny combat operations is vested only in the operational commander.

airspace control area—*(DOD, NATO)* Airspace which is laterally defined by the boundaries of the area of operations. The airspace control area may be subdivided into airspace control sub-areas.

airspace control authority—*(DOD, NATO)* The commander designated to assume overall responsibility for the operation of the airspace control system in the airspace control area.

airspace control boundary—*(DOD, NATO)* The lateral limits of an airspace control area, airspace control sub-area, high density airspace control zone, or airspace restricted area.

airspace control system—*(DOD, NATO)* An arrangement of those organizations, personnel, policies, procedures and facilities required to perform airspace control functions.

airspace management—*(DOD)* The coordination, integration, and regulation of the use of airspace of defined dimensions.

airspace reservation—*(DOD, IADB)* The airspace located above an area on the surface of the land or water, designated and set apart by Executive Order of the President or by a state, commonwealth, or territory, over which the flight of aircraft is prohibited or restricted for the purpose of national defense or for other governmental purposes.

airspace restrictions—*(DOD, NATO)* Special restrictive measures applied to segments of airspace of defined dimensions.

air space warning area—See **danger area.**

airspeed—*(DOD, IADB)* The speed of an aircraft relative to its surrounding air mass. The unqualified term "airspeed" can mean any one of the following:
a. **calibrated airspeed**—Indicated airspeed corrected for instrument installation error.
b. **equivalent airspeed**—Calibrated airspeed corrected for compressibility error.
c. **indicated airspeed**—The airspeed shown by an airspeed indicator.
d. **true airspeed**—Equivalent airspeed corrected for error due to air density (altitude and temperature).

airspeed indicator—*(DOD, NATO)* An instrument which displays the indicated airspeed of the aircraft derived from inputs of pitot and static pressures.

air spot—*(DOD, IADB)* The correcting adjustment of gunfire based on air observation.

air staging unit—*(DOD, NATO, IADB)* A unit situated at an airfield and concerned with reception, handling, servicing and preparation for departure of aircraft and control of personnel and cargo.

air station (photogrammetry)—*(DOD, NATO, IADB)* The point in space occupied by the camera lens at the moment of exposure.

air strike—*(DOD, IADB)* An attack on specific objectives by fighter, bomber, or attack aircraft on an offensive mission. May consist of several air organizations under a single command in the air.

air strike coordinator—*(DOD, IADB)* The air representative of the force commander in a target area, who is responsible for directing all aircraft in the target area and coordinating their efforts to achieve the most effective use of air striking power.

air strip—*(DOD, NATO, IADB)* An unimproved surface which has been adapted for take-off or landing of aircraft, usually having minimum facilities. See also **airfield.**

air superiority—*(DOD, NATO, IADB)* That degree of dominance in the airbattle of one force over another which permits the conduct of operations by the former and its related land, sea and air forces at a given time and place without prohibitive interference by the opposing force.

air supply—*(DOD, NATO, IADB)* The delivery of cargo by airdrop or air landing.

air support—*(DOD, NATO, IADB)* All forms of support given by air forces on land or sea. See also **call mission; close air support; immediate air support; indirect air support; preplanned air support; tactical air support.**

air support operations center—*(NATO)* An element of a tactical air control system that is usually located at corps level.

air support radar team—*(DOD, IADB)* A subordinate operational component of a tactical air control system which provides ground-controlled precision flight path guidance and weapons release. See also **armstrong.**

air supremacy—*(DOD, NATO, IADB)* That degree of air superiority wherein the opposing air force is incapable of effective interference.

air surface zone—*(DOD, NATO, IADB)* A restricted area established for the purpose of preventing friendly surface vessels and aircraft from being fired upon by friendly forces and for permitting antisubmarine operations, unrestricted by the operation of friendly submarines. See also **restricted area.**

air surveillance—*(DOD, NATO, IADB)* The systematic observation of air space by electronic, visual or other means, primarily for the purpose of identifying and determining the movements of aircraft and missiles, friendly and enemy, in the air space under observation. See also **satellite and missile surveillance; surveillance.**

air surveillance officer—*(DOD, NATO)* An individual responsible for coordinating and maintaining an accurate, current picture of the air situation within an assigned airspace area.

air surveillance plotting board—*(NATO)* A gridded, small scale, air defense map of an appropriate area. It is maintained at the air control center. On it are posted current locations, number, and altitudes of all friendly or enemy aircraft within range of radar or ground observer facilities.

air survey camera—See **air cartographic camera.**

air survey photography—See **air cartographic photography.**

air target chart—*(DOD)* A display of pertinent air target intelligence on a specialized graphic base. It is designed primarily to support operations against designated air targets by various weapon systems.

air target materials program—*(DOD)* A DOD program established for the production of medium- and large-scale target materials and related items in support of long-range, world-wide requirements of the unified and specified commands, the military departments, and allied participants. It is under the management control of the Defense Intelligence Agency and encompasses the determination of production and coverage requirements, standardization of products, establishment of production priorities and schedules, and the production, distribution, storage, and release/exchange of the air target materials items and related products.

air target mosaic—*(DOD)* A large-scale mosaic providing photographic coverage of an area and permitting comprehensive portrayal of pertinent target detail. These mosaics are used for intelligence study and in planning and briefing for air operations.

air terminal—*(DOD, IADB)* A facility on an airfield that functions as an air transportation hub and accommodates the loading and unloading of airlift aircraft and the intransit processing of traffic. The airfield may or may not be designated an aerial port.

air terminal—*(NATO)* An installation on an airfield with facilities for loading and unloading aircraft and processing traffic (passengers, cargo, and mail).

air-to-air missile—*(DOD, IADB)* A missile launched from an airborne vehicle at a target above the surface.

air-to-surface missile—*(DOD, IADB)* A missile launched from an airborne vehicle at a surface target.

air traffic control center—*(DOD, NATO, IADB)* A unit combining the functions of an area control center and a flight information center. See also **area control center; flight information region.**

air traffic control clearance—*(DOD, NATO, IADB)* Authorization by an air traffic control authority for an aircraft to proceed under specified conditions.

air traffic controller—*(DOD)* An air controller especially trained for and assigned to the duty of airspace management and traffic control of airborne objects. See also **air controller.**

air traffic control service—*(DOD, NATO, IADB)* A service provided for the purpose of: **a.** preventing collisions: (1) between aircraft; and (2) on the maneuvering area between aircraft and obstructions; and **b.** expediting and maintaining an orderly flow of air traffic.

air traffic identification—*(DOD)* The use of electronic devices, operational procedures, visual observation, and/or flight plan correlation for the purpose of identifying and locating aircraft flying within the airspace control area.

air traffic section—*(DOD, IADB)* The link between the staging post and the local air priority committee. It is the key to the efficient handling of passengers and cargo at a staging post. It must include load control (including Customs and Immigrations facilities), freight, and mail sections.

air transportable unit—*(DOD, NATO, IADB)* A unit other than airborne, whose equipment is adapted for air movement. See also **airborne; airborne operation.**

air transport allocations board—*(DOD, NATO, IADB)* The joint agency responsible within the theater for the establishment of airlift priorities and for space allocation of available aircraft capabilities alloted to the theater. See also **air priorities committee.**

air transported force—*(NATO)* A force which is moved by air. See also **force(s).**

air transported operations—*(DOD, IADB)* The movement by aircraft of troops and their equipment for an operation.

air transport liaison officer—*(DOD, NATO)* An officer attached for air transport liaison duties to a headquarters or unit. See also **ground liaison officer.**

air transport liaison section (army)—*(NATO)* A subunit of the movement control organization deployed to airfields and responsible for the control of service movement at the airfield in connection with air movement operations and exercises.

air transport operations—See **strategic air transport operations; tactical air transport operations.**

air trooping—*(NATO)* The nontactical air movement of personnel. See also **air movement.**

airway—*(DOD, NATO, IADB)* A control area or portion thereof established in the form of a corridor marked with radio navigational aids.

airways station—*(DOD, IADB)* A ground communication installation established, manned, and equipped to communicate with aircraft in flight, as well as with other designated airways installations, for the purpose of expeditious and safe movements of aircraft. These stations may or may not be located on designated airways.

air weapons controller—*(DOD, IADB)* An individual especially trained for and assigned to the duty of employing and controlling air weapon systems against airborne and surface objects.

alert—*(DOD, NATO, IADB)* 1. Readiness for action, defense or protection. 2. A warning signal of a real or threatened danger, such as an air attack. 3. The period of time during which troops stand by in response to an alarm. 4. To forewarn; to prepare for action. See also **airborne alert.** *(DOD)* 5. A warning received by a unit or a headquarters which forewarns of an impending operational mission. See also **air defense warning conditions; ground alert; warning order.**

alert force—*(DOD, IADB)* Specified forces maintained in a special degree of readiness.

alerting service—*(DOD, NATO, IADB)* A service provided to notify appropriate organizations regarding aircraft in need of search and rescue aid, and assist such organizations as required.

alighting area—*(NATO)* A specified surface, reserved to vehicles that depend upon water surfaces for their landing.

alignment—*(NATO)* 1. The bearing of two or more conspicuous objects (such as lights, beacons, etc.) as seen by an observer. 2. Representation of a road, railway, etc., on a map or chart in relation to surrounding topographic detail.

all available—*(DOD)* A command or request to obtain the fire of all artillery able to deliver effective fire on a given target.

allied commander—See **NATO commander.**

allied headquarters—See **allied staff.**

allied staff—*(NATO)* A staff or headquarters composed of two or more allied nations working together.

allocation—*(DOD, NATO, IADB)* The translation of the apportionment into total numbers of sorties by aircraft type available for each operation/task.

allocation (nuclear)—*(DOD, IADB)* The apportionment of specific numbers and types of nuclear weapons to a commander for a stated time period as a planning factor for use in the development of war plans. (Additional authority is required for the actual deployment of allocated weapons to locations desired by the commander to support his war plans. Expenditures of these weapons are not authorized until released by proper authority.)

allocation (nuclear)—*(NATO)* The specific numbers and types of nuclear weapons allocated to a commander for a stated time period as a planning factor only.

allocation (transportation)—*(DOD, IADB)* Apportionment by designated authority of available transport capability to users.

allotment—*(DOD, NATO)* The temporary change of assignment of tactical air forces between subordinate commands. The authority to allot is vested in the commander having operational command.

all out war—*(DOD)* Not to be used. See **general war.**

allowable load—*(DOD, NATO)* The total load that an aircraft can transport over a given distance taking into account weight and volume. See also **load.**

all-purpose hand-held weapon—*(DOD, IADB)* A lightweight, hand-held, small arms weapon capable of projecting munitions required to engage both area and point-type targets.

allweather air defense fighter—*(DOD, NATO)* A fighter aircraft with equipment and weapons which enable it to engage airborne targets in all weather conditions, day and night.

allweather fighter—*(DOD, NATO, IADB)* A fighter aircraft with radar devices and other special equipment which enable it to intercept its target in dark or daylight weather conditions which do not permit visual interception.

alphabet code—See **phonetic alphabet.**

alternate airfield—*(DOD, NATO, IADB)* An airfield specified in the flight plan to which a flight may proceed when a landing at the intended destination becomes inadvisable. An alternate airfield may be the airfield of departure.

alternate command authority—*(DOD, IADB)* One or more predesignated officers empowered by the commander through predelegation of authority to act under stipulated emergency conditions in the accomplishment of previously defined functions.

alternate command post—*(DOD, IADB)* Any location designated by a commander to assume command post functions in the event the command post becomes inoperative. It may be partially or fully equipped and manned or it may be the command post of a subordinate unit.

alternate escort operating base—*(NATO)* A base providing the facilities and activities required for the support of escort units for short periods of time.

alternate headquarters—*(DOD)* An existing headquarters of a component or subordinate command which is predesignated to assume the responsibilities and functions of another headquarters under prescribed emergency conditions.

alternate water terminal—*(DOD, NATO, IADB)* A water terminal with facilities for berthing from two to five ships simultaneously at wharves and/or working anchorages, located within sheltered coastal waters, adjacent to reliable highway and/or rail transportation nets. It covers a relatively small area and is located away from population centers. The scope of operation is such that it is not designated a probable nuclear target. See also **water terminal.**

alternative airfield—*(DOD, NATO, IADB)* An airfield with minimal essential facilities for use as an emergency landing ground, or when main or redeployment airfields are out of action, or as required for tactical flexibility. See also **airfield.**

altimeter—*(DOD, NATO)*
1. **Barometric altimeter.** An instrument which displays the height of the aircraft above a specified pressure datum. The datum may be varied by setting the specified pressure on a sub scale on the instrument.

2. **Barometric altimeter reversionary.** An altimeter in which the indication is normally derived electrically from an external source (central air data computer or altitude, computer) but which, in case of failure or by manual selection, can revert to a pneumatic drive.
3. **Cabin pressure altimeter.** An instrument which measures the pressure within an aircraft cabin and gives an indication in terms of height according to the chosen standard atmosphere.
4. **Radar altimeter.** See **radio altimeter.**
5. **Radio altimeter.** An instrument which displays the distance between an aircraft datum and the surface vertically below as determined by a reflected radio/radar transmission.

altitude—*(DOD, NATO, IADB)* The vertical distance of a level, a point or an object considered as a point, measured from mean sea level. See also **absolute altitude; critical altitude; density altitude; drop altitude; elevation; height; high altitude; minimum safe altitude; pressure altitude; transition altitude; true altitude.**

altitude acclimatization—*(DOD, NATO, IADB)* A slow physiological adaptation resulting from prolonged exposure to significantly reduced atmospheric pressure.

altitude chamber—See **hypobaric chamber.**

altitude datum—*(DOD, NATO, IADB)* The arbitrary level from which vertical displacement is measured. The datum for height measurement is the terrain directly below the aircraft or some specified datum; for pressure altitude, the level at which the atmospheric pressure is 29.92 inches of mercury (1013.2 m.bs); and for true altitude, mean sea level.

altitude delay—*(DOD, NATO)* Synchronization delay introduced between the time of transmission of the radar pulse and the start of the trace on the indicator, for the purpose of eliminating the altitude hole on the plan position indicator-type display.

altitude height—See **altitude datum.**

altitude hold—*(DOD, NATO)* In a flight control system, a control mode in which the barometric altitude existing at time of engagement is maintained automatically.

altitude hole—*(DOD, NATO)* The blank area at the origin of a radial display, on a radar tube presentation, the center of the periphery of which represents the point on the ground immediately below the aircraft. In side looking airborne radar, this is known as the altitude slot.

altitude separation—See **vertical separation.**

altitude sickness—*(DOD, IADB)* The syndrome of depression, anorexia, nausea, vomiting, and collapse, due to decreased atmospheric pressure, occurring in an individual exposed to an altitude beyond that to which acclimatization has occurred.

altitude slot—See **altitude hole.**

altitude tint—See **hypsometric tinting.**

ambulatory patient—See **walking patient.**

ammo (plus, minus, zero)—*(DOD)* In air intercept, a code meaning I have amount of ammunition indicated left (type may be specified. For example:

ammo plus—I have more than half my ammunition left.

ammo minus—I have less than half my ammunition left.

ammo zero—I have no ammunition left.

ammunition—*(DOD, NATO, IADB)* A device charged with explosives, propellants, pyrotechnics, initiating composition, or nuclear, biological, or chemical material for use in connection with defense or offense, including demolitions. Certain ammunition can be used for training, ceremonial, or nonoperational purposes. See also **chemical ammunition; fixed ammunition; semi-fixed ammunition; separate loading ammunition.**

ammunition and toxic material open space—*(DOD, NATO, IADB)* An area especially prepared for storage of explosive ammunition and toxic material. For reporting purposes, it does not include the surrounding area restricted for storage because of safety distance factors. It includes barricades and improvised coverings. See also **Storage.**

ammunition controlled supply rate—*(DOD)* In Army usage, the amount of ammunition estimated to be available to sustain operations of a designated force for a specified time if expenditures are controlled at that rate. It is expressed in terms of rounds per weapon per day for ammunition items fired by weapons, and in terms of units of measure per organization per day for bulk allotment ammunition items. Tactical commanders use this rate to control expenditures of ammunition during tactical operations at planned intervals. It is issued through command channels at each level. It is determined based on consideration of the required supply rates submitted by subordinate commanders and ammunition assets available.

ammunition supply point—See **distribution point.**

amphibious assault—*(DOD, NATO)* The principal type of amphibious operation which involves establishing a force on a hostile shore.

amphibious assault area—See **landing area.**

amphibious assault landing—See **amphibious operation,** Part e.

amphibious assault ship (general purpose)—*(DOD)* A naval ship designed to embark, deploy, and land elements of a landing force in an assault by helicopters, landing craft, amphibious vehicles, and by combinations of these methods. Designated **LHA.**

amphibious chart—(DOD, NATO) A special naval chart designed to meet special requirements for landing operations and passive coastal defense, at a scale of 1:25,000 or larger, and showing foreshore and coastal information in greater detail than a combat chart.

amphibious command ship—(DOD, NATO, IADB) A naval ship from which a commander exercises control in amphibious operations. DOD designated as LCC.

amphibious control group—(DOD, NATO, IADB) Personnel, ships, and craft designated to control the waterborne ship-to-shore movement in an amphibious operation.

amphibious demonstration—(DOD, NATO, IADB) A type of amphibious operation conducted for the purpose of deceiving the enemy by a show of force with the expectation of deluding the enemy into a course of action unfavorable to him.

amphibious force—(DOD, NATO, IADB) 1. A naval force and landing force, together with supporting forces that are trained, organized and equipped for amphibious operations. 2. In naval usage, the administrative title of the amphibious type command of a fleet.

amphibious group—(DOD, NATO, IADB) A command within the amphibious force, consisting of the commander and his staff, designed to exercise operational command of assigned units in executing all phases of a division-size amphibious operation.

amphibious lift—(DOD, NATO, IADB) The total capacity of assault shipping utilized in an amphibious operation, expressed in terms of personnel, vehicles, and measurement or weight tons of supplies.

amphibious objective area—(DOD, NATO) A geographical area, delineated in the initiating directive, for purposes of command and control within which is located the objective(s) to be secured by the amphibious task force. This area must be of sufficient size to ensure accomplishment of the amphibious task force's mission and must provide sufficient area for conducting necessary sea, air and land operations.

amphibious objective study—(DOD) A study designed to provide basic intelligence data of a permanent or semipermanent nature required for planning amphibious operations. Each study deals with a specific area the selection of which is based on strategic location, susceptibility to seizure by amphibious means, and other considerations.

amphibious operation—(DOD, IADB) An attack launched from the sea by naval and landing forces, embarked in ships or craft involving a landing on a hostile shore. As an entity, the amphibious operation includes the following phases:
a. **planning—**The period extending from issuance of the initiating directive to embarkation.
b. **embarkation—**The period during which the forces, with their equipment and supplies, are embarked in the assigned shipping.
c. **rehearsal—**The period during which the prospective operation is rehearsed for the purpose of: (1) testing adequacy of plans, the timing of detailed operations, and the combat readiness of participating forces; (2) insuring that all echelons are familiar with plans; and (3) testing communications.
d. **movement—**The period during which various components of the amphibious task force move from points of embarkation to the objective area.
e. **assault—**The period between the arrival of the major assault forces of the amphibious task force in the objective area and the accomplishment of the amphibious task force mission.

amphibious operation—(NATO) An attack launched from the sea by naval and landing forces, embarked in ships or craft involving a landing on a hostile shore.

amphibious raid—*(DOD, NATO, IADB)* A limited type of amphibious operation; a landing from the sea on a hostile shore involving swift incursion into, or a temporary occupancy of, an objective, followed by a planned withdrawal.

amphibious reconnaissance—*(DOD, NATO, IADB)* An amphibious landing conducted by minor elements, normally involving stealth rather than force of arms, for the purpose of securing information, and usually followed by a planned withdrawal.

amphibious reconnaissance unit—*(DOD)* A unit organized, equipped, and trained to conduct and support amphibious reconnaissance missions. An amphibious reconnaissance unit is made up of a number of amphibious reconnaissance teams.

amphibious shipping—*(DOD, IADB)* Organic Navy ships specifically designed to transport, land, and support landing forces in amphibious assault operations and capable of being loaded or unloaded by naval personnel without external assistance in the amphibious objective area.

amphibious squadron—*(DOD, NATO, IADB)* A tactical and administrative organization composed of amphibious assault shipping to transport troops and their equipment for an amphibious assault operation.

amphibious striking forces—*(DOD, IADB)* Forces capable of projecting military power from the sea upon adjacent land areas for initiating and/or conducting operations there in the face of enemy opposition.

amphibious tractor—See **amphibious vehicle.**

amphibious transport dock—*(DOD, IADB)* A ship designed to transport and land troops, equipment, and supplies by means of embarked landing craft, amphibious vehicles, and helicopters. Designated as LPD.

amphibious transport group—*(DOD, NATO)* A subdivision of an amphibious task force, composed primarily of transport ships.

amphibious vehicle—*(DOD, NATO, IADB)* A wheeled or tracked vehicle capable of operating on both land and water. See also **landing craft; vehicle.**

amphibious vehicle availability table—*(DOD, IADB)* A tabulation of the type and number of amphibious vehicles available primarily for assault landings and for support of other elements of the operation.

amphibious vehicle employment plan—*(DOD, IADB)* A plan showing in tabular form the planned employment of amphibious vehicles in landing operations, including their employment after the initial movement to the beach.

amphibious vehicle launching area—*(DOD, NATO, IADB)* An area, in the vicinity of and to seaward of the line of departure, to which landing ships proceed and launch amphibious vehicles.

amphibious withdrawal—*(DOD, NATO)* An operation involving the withdrawal of land forces by sea in naval ships or craft from a hostile shore.

amplifying report—See **contact report.**

analysis—*(DOD, IADB)* A stage in the intelligence cycle in which information is subjected to review in order to identify significant facts and derive conclusions therefrom. See also **intelligence cycle.**

analysis staff—See **central analysis team.**

anchor—See **sinker.**

anchor cable—*(DOD, NATO, IADB)* In air transport, a cable in an aircraft to which the parachute static lines or strops are attached.

anchored—*(DOD)* In air intercept, a code meaning, "Am orbiting a visible orbit point."

28

anchor line extension kit—*(DOD, NATO)* A device fitted to an aircraft equipped with removable clamshell doors to enable paratroopers to exit from the rear.

ancillary facilities—*(DOD, NATO)* Those facilities required to supplement existing facilities at any particular location to provide specific minimum requirements for support of the reinforcing forces.

angels—*(DOD, IADB)* In air intercept and close air support, a code meaning aircraft altitude (in thousands of feet).

angle of convergence—*(DOD, NATO)* The angle subtended by the eyebase of an observer at the point of focus. Also called **angular parallax; parallactic angle.**

angle of depression—*(DOD, NATO)* 1. The angle in a vertical plane between the horizontal and a descending line. 2. In air photography, the angle between the optical axis of an obliquely mounted air camera and the horizontal. See also **tilt angle.**

angle of safety—*(DOD, NATO, IADB)* The minimal permissible angular clearance, at the gun, of the path of a projectile above the friendly troops. It is the angle of clearance corrected to insure the safety of the troops.

angle of view—*(DOD, NATO)* 1. The angle between two rays passing through the perspective cgnter (rear nodal point) of a camera lens to two opposite corners of the format. 2. In photogrammetry, twice the angle whose tangent is one-half the length of the diagonal of the format divided by the calibrated focal length.

angle T—*(DOD, NATO)* In artillery and naval gunfire support, the angle formed by the intersection of the gun-target line and the observer-target line.

angular parallax—See **angle of convergence.**

angular velocity sight—See **bomb sighting systems.**

annex—*(DOD, IADB)* A document appended to an operation order or other document to make it clearer or to give further details.

annotated print—*(NATO)* A photograph on which interpretation details are indicated by words or symbols.

annotation—*(DOD, NATO)* A marking placed on imagery or drawings for explanatory purposes or to indicate items or areas of special importance.

annual training—*(DOD)* The minimal period of annual active duty for training or annual field training a member performs each year to satisfy the annual training requirement associated with a Reserve component assignment. It may be performed during one consecutive period or in increments of one or more days depending upon mission requirements.

antenna mine—*(DOD, NATO)* In naval mine warfare, a contact mine fitted with antennae which, when touched by a steel ship, set up galvanic action to fire the mine. See also **mine.**

antiaircraft operations center—*(NATO, IADB)* The tactical headquarters of an antiaircraft commander. The agency provided to collect and evaluate information, and disseminate intelligence for the antiaircraft defense, and through which operational control over subordinate units is exercised.

antiaircraft weapon—See **Duster (antiaircraft weapon).**

antiair warfare—*(DOD)* A US Navy/US Marine Corps term used to indicate that action required to destroy or reduce to an acceptable level the enemy air and missile threat. It includes such measures as the use of interceptors, bombers, antiaircraft guns, surface-to-air and air-to-air missiles, electronic countermeasures, and destruction of the air or missile threat both before and after it is launched. Other measures which are taken to minimize the effects of hostile air action are cover, concealment, dispersion, deception (including electronic), and mobility. See also **counter air.**

anticountermining device—*(DOD, NATO)* A device fitted in an influence mine designed to prevent its actuation by shock.

anticrop agent—*(DOD, NATO, IADB)* A living organism or chemical used to cause disease or damage to selected food or industrial crops.

anticrop operation—*(DOD, NATO, IADB)* The employment of anticrop agents in military operations to destroy the enemy's source of selected food or industrial crops. See also **antiplant agent; herbicide.**

anti-G suit—*(DOD, IADB)* A device worn by aircrew to counteract the effects on the human body of positive acceleration.

antilift device—*(DOD, NATO, IADB)* A device arranged to detonate the mine to which it is attached, or to detonate another mine or charge nearby, if the mine is disturbed.

antimateriel agent—*(DOD, NATO, IADB)* A living organism or chemical used to cause deterioration of, or damage to, selected materiel.

antimateriel operation—*(DOD, NATO, IADB)* The employment of antimateriel weapons or agents in military operations.

antipersonnel mine (land mine warfare)—*(DOD, IADB)* A mine designed to cause casualties to personnel. See also **mine.**

antiplant agent—*(DOD, IADB)* A microorganism or chemical that will kill, disease, or damage plants. See also **anticrop agent; herbicide.**

antiradiation missile—*(DOD, NATO, IADB)* A missile which homes passively on a radiation source.

antirecovery device—*(DOD, NATO)* In naval mine warfare, any device in a mine designed to prevent an enemy discovering details of the working of the mine mechanism.

antisubmarine action—*(DOD, NATO, IADB)* An operation by one or more antisubmarine ships or aircraft, or a combination of both, against a particular enemy submarine.

antisubmarine air close support—*(DOD, IADB)* Air operations for the antisubmarine warfare protection of a supported force. These operations are normally carried out within 80 nautical miles of the force, but this limit may be varied at the discretion of the controlling officer in tactical command.

antisubmarine air distant support—*(DOD, IADB)* Antisubmarine air support at a distance from, but directly related to, specific convoys or forces.

antisubmarine air search attack unit—*(DOD, IADB)* The designation given to one or more aircraft separately organized as a tactical unit to search for and destroy submarines.

antisubmarine barrier—*(DOD, NATO, IADB)* The line formed by a series of static devices or mobile units arranged for the purpose of detecting, denying passage to, or destroying hostile submarines. See also **antisubmarine patrol.**

antisubmarine carrier group—*(NATO, IADB)* A formed group of ships consisting of one or more antisubmarine carriers and a number of escort vessels whose primary mission is to detect and destroy submarines. Such groups may be employed in convoy support or hunter/killer roles.

antisubmarine minefield—*(NATO)* A field laid specifically against submarines. It may be laid shallow and be unsafe for all craft, including submarines, or laid deep with the aim of being safe for surface ships.

antisubmarine operation—*(DOD, IADB)* Operation contributing to the conduct of antisubmarine warfare.

antisubmarine patrol—*(DOD, NATO, IADB)* The systematic and continuing investigation of an area or along a line to detect or hamper submarines, used when the direction of submarine movement can be established.

antisubmarine rocket—*(DOD, IADB)* A surface ship-launched, rocket-propelled, nuclear depth charge or homing torpedo. Designated as RUR–5A. Popular name is ASROC.

antisubmarine screen—*(DOD, NATO, IADB)* An arrangement of ships and/or aircraft for the protection of a screened unit against attack by a submarine.

antisubmarine search—*(DOD, NATO, IADB)* Systematic investigation of a particular area for the purpose of locating a submarine known or suspected to be somewhere in the area. Some types of search are also used in locating the position of a distress incident.

antisubmarine support operation—*(DOD, NATO, IADB)* An operation conducted by an antisubmarine force in the area around a force or convoy, in areas through which the force or convoy is passing, or in defense of geographic areas. Support operations may be completely coordinated with those of the force or convoy, or they may be independent operations coordinated only to the extent of providing operational intelligence and information.

antisubmarine torpedo—*(DOD, IADB)* A submarine-launched, long-range, high-speed, wire-guided, deep-diving, wakeless torpedo capable of carrying a nuclear warhead for use in antisubmarine and antisurface ship operations. Also called ASTOR.

antisubmarine warfare—*(DOD, NATO, IADB)* Operations conducted with the intention of denying the enemy the effective use of his submarines.

antisubmarine warfare forces—*(DOD, IADB)* Forces organized primarily for antisubmarine action. May be composed of surface ships, aircraft, submarines, or any combination of these, and their supporting systems.

antisurface air operation—*(DOD, NATO)* An air operation conducted in an air/sea environment against enemy surface forces.

antisweep device—*(DOD, NATO)* Any device incorporated in the mooring of a mine or obstructor, or in the mine circuits to make the sweeping of the mine more difficult.

antisweeper mine—*(DOD, NATO)* A mine which is laid or whose mechanism is designed or adjusted, with the specific object of damaging mine countermeasure vehicles. See also **mine**.

antitank helicopter—*(NATO)* A helicopter armed for use in the antitank role.

antitank mine—*(DOD, NATO, IADB)* A mine designed to immobilize or destroy a tank. See also **mine**.

antivignetting filter—*(DOD, NATO)* A filter bearing a deposit which is graduated in density to correct for the uneven illumination given by certain lenses, particularly wide-angle types.

antiwatching device—*(DOD, NATO)* A device fitted in a moored mine which causes it to sink should it watch, so as to prevent the position of the mine or minefield being disclosed. See also **watching mine**.

apogee—*(DOD, IADB)* The point at which a missile trajectory or a satellite orbit is farthest from the center of the gravitational field of the controlling body or bodies.

apparent horizon—*(DOD, NATO, IADB)* The visible line of demarcation between land/sea and sky.

apparent precession—*(DOD, NATO)* The apparent deflection of the gyro axis, relative to the earth, due to the rotating effect of the earth and not due to any applied force. Also called **apparent wander.**

apparent wander—See **apparent precession.**

appendix—*(DOD, IADB)* A subsidiary addition to a main paper. Details essential to the main paper but too bulky or numerous to include therein are usually embodied in appendices.

applicable materiel assets—*(DOD)* That portion of the total acceptable materiel assets that meets the military or other characteristics as defined by the responsible Military Service and that is in the right condition and location to satisfy a specific military requirement.

application—*(DOD, IADB)* The system or problem to which a computer is applied. Reference is often made to an application as being either of the computational type, wherein arithmetic computations predominate, or of the data processing type, wherein data handling operations predominate.

applied research—*(DOD, IADB)* Research concerned with the practical application of knowledge, material, and/or techniques directed toward a solution to an existent or anticipated military requirement. See also **basic research; research.**

apportionment—*(DOD, NATO)* The determination and assignment of the total expected effort by percentage and/or by priority that should be devoted to the various air operations and/or geographic areas for a given period of time.

appreciation of the situation—See **estimate of the situation.**

appreciations—*(DOD)* Assumptions, estimates, and facts about an opponent's intentions and military capabilities used in planning and decision making:

a. **desired appreciations**—Adversary estimates that result in adversary intentions and military capabilities to friendly advantage.
b. **essential secrecy**—Specific unknowns or uncertainities that prevent or hinder adversary derivation of accurate estimates or knowledge of facts, and effective planning and decision making.
c. **harmful appreciations**—Adversary assumptions or estimates to provide for unknowns or uncertainties, or necessary and sufficient known facts, that result in adversary intentions and military capabilities to friendly disadvantage.

approach clearance—*(DOD)* Authorization for a pilot conducting flight in accordance with instrument flight rules to commence an approach to an airport.

approach end—*(DOD, NATO)* That end of a runway nearest to the direction from which the final approach is made.

approach lane—*(DOD, NATO, IADB)* An extension of a boat lane from the line of departure toward the transport area. It may be terminated by marker ships, boats or buoys.

approach march—*(DOD, NATO)* Advance of a combat unit when direct contact with the enemy is imminent. Troops are fully or partially deployed. The approach march ends when ground contact with the enemy is made or when the attack position is occupied. See also **advance to contact.**

approach route—*(NATO)* A route which joins a port to a coastal or transit route.

approach schedule—*(DOD, NATO, IADB)* The schedule which indicates, for each scheduled wave, the time of departure from the rendezvous area, from the line of departure, and from other control points and the time of arrival at the beach.

approach sequence—*(DOD, NATO)* The order in which two or more aircraft are cleared for an approach.

approach time—*(DOD, IADB)* The time at which an aircraft is expected to commence approach procedure.

approach time—*(NATO)* The time at which an aircraft commences its final approach preparatory to landing.

apron—*(DOD, NATO, IADB)* A defined area, on an airfield, intended to accommodate aircraft for purposes of loading or unloading passengers or cargo, refueling, parking, or maintenance.

area—See also **advisory area; aircraft dispersal area; aircraft marshalling area; air defense action area; alighting area; amphibious vehicle launching area; area control center; assembly area; caution area; closed area; concentration area; control area; danger area; defensive coastal area; embarkation area; fire support area; homogeneous area; impact area; initial approach area; key areas; landing area; maneuvering area; maritime area; naval support area; objective area; prohibited area; run-up area; signal area; staging area; submarine patrol areas; terminal control area; transit area.** See also **zone.**

area air defense commander—*(DOD)* Within an overseas unified command, subordinate unified command, or joint task force, the commander will assign overall responsibility for air defense to a single commander. Normally, this will be the Air Force component commander. Representation from the other Service components involved will be provided, as appropriate, to the area air defense commander's headquarters.

area bombing—*(DOD, NATO, IADB)* Bombing of a target which is in effect a general area rather than a small or pinpoint target.

area command—*(DOD, NATO, IADB)* A command which is composed of those organized elements of one or more of the armed services, designated to operate in a specific geographical area, which are placed under a single commander, e.g.; Commander of a Unified Command, Area Commander. See also **command.**

area control center—*(DOD, NATO, IADB)* A unit established to provide air traffic control service to controlled flights in control areas under its jurisdiction. See also **air traffic control center; flight information region.**

area coordination group—*(DOD, IADB)* A composite organization, including representatives of local military, paramilitary, and other governmental agencies and their US counterparts, responsible for planning and coordinating internal defense and development operations. (Note: IADB does not use the words "and their United States counterparts".)

area damage control—*(DOD, NATO, IADB)* Measures taken before, during or after hostile action or natural or man-made disasters, to reduce the probability of damage and minimize its effects. See also **damage control; disaster control; rear area security.**

area of influence—*(DOD, NATO)* A geographical area wherein a commander is directly capable of influencing operations, by maneuver or fire support systems normally under his command or control.

area of intelligence responsibility—*(DOD, NATO)* An area allocated to a commander, in which he is responsible for the provision of intelligence, within the means at his disposal. See also **area of responsibility.**

area of interest—*(DOD, NATO, IADB)* That area of concern to the commander, including the area of influence, areas adjacent thereto, and extending into enemy territory to the objectives of current or planned operations. This area also includes areas occupied by enemy forces who could jeopardize the accomplishment of the mission.

area of militarily significant fallout—*(DOD, NATO, IADB)* The area in which radioactive fallout affects the ability of military units to carry out their normal mission.

area of northern operations—*(DOD)* A region of variable width in the Northern Hemisphere that lies north of the 50 degrees isotherm—a line along which the average temperature of the warmest 4-month period of the year does not exceed 50 degrees Fahrenheit. Mountain regions located outside of this area are included in this category of operations provided these same temperature conditions exist.

area of operational interest—*(NATO)* In air defense, an area in which automatic cross-telling of tracks of interest is provided to an adjacent site based on established criteria, such as identity and location.

area of operations—*(DOD, NATO)* That portion of an area of war necessary for military operations and for the administration of such operations.

area of responsibility—*(DOD, NATO, IADB)* 1. A defined area of land in which responsibility is specifically assigned to the commander of the area for the development and maintenance of installations, control of movement and the conduct of tactical operations involving troops under his control along with parallel authority to exercise these functions. 2. In naval usage, a predefined area of enemy terrain for which supporting ships are responsible for covering by fire on known targets or targets of opportunity and by observation.

area of war—*(DOD, IADB)* That area of land, sea, and air which is, or may become, directly involved in the operations of war.

area operations—*(DOD, NATO)* In maritime usage, operations conducted in a geographical area and not related to the protection of a specific force.

area radar prediction analysis—*(DOD)* Radar target intelligence study designed to provide radar significant data for use in the preparation of radar target predictions.

area search—*(DOD, IADB)* Visual reconnaissance of limited or defined areas.

area search—*(NATO)* Reconnaissance or search of a specific area to provide new or updated information on general or specific situations and/or activities.

area target—*(DOD, NATO, IADB)* A target consisting of an area rather than a single point.

areodesy—*(DOD)* The branch of mathematics which determines, by observation and measurement, the exact positions of points and the figures and areas of large portions of the surface of the planet Mars, or the shape and size of the planet Mars.

areodetic—*(DOD)* Of, pertaining to, or determined by areodesy.

armed forces—*(DOD, IADB)* The military forces of a nation or a group of nations. See also **force(s)**.

armed forces censorship—*(DOD)* The examination and control of personal communications to or from persons in the Armed Forces of the United States and persons accompanying or serving with the Armed Forces of the United States. See also **censorship**.

armed forces courier—*(DOD, IADB)* An officer or enlisted member in the grade of E-7 or above, of the US Armed Forces, assigned to perform Armed Forces Courier Service duties and identified by possession of an Armed Forces Courier Service Identification Card (ARF-COS Form 9). See also **courier**.

Armed Forces Courier Service—*(DOD)* A joint service of the Departments of the Army, the Navy, and the Air Force, with the Chief of Staff, US Army, as Executive Agent. The courier service provides one of the available methods for the secure and expeditious transmission of material requiring protected handling by military courier.

armed forces courier station—*(DOD)* An Army, Navy, or Air Force activity, approved by the respective military department and officially designated by Headquarters, Armed Forces Courier Service, for the acceptance, processing, and dispatching of Armed Forces Courier Service material.

Armed Forces of the United States—*(DOD)* A term used to denote collectively all components of the Army, Navy, Air Force, Marine Corps, and Coast Guard. See also **United States Armed Forces.**

armed helicopter—*(DOD, NATO)* A helicopter fitted with weapons or weapon systems.

armed mine—*(DOD, NATO)* A mine from which all safety devices have been withdrawn and, after laying, all automatic safety features and/or arming delays have operated. Such a mine is ready to receive a target signal, influence or contact. See also **mine.**

armed mine—*(IADB)* A mine ready for actuation. See also **mine.**

armed reconnaissance—*(DOD, IADB)* A mission with the primary purpose of locating and attacking targets of opportunity, i.e., enemy materiel, personnel, and facilities, in assigned general areas or along assigned ground communications routes, and not for the purpose of attacking specific briefed targets.

armed reconnaissance—*(NATO)* An air mission flown with the primary purpose of locating and attacking targets of opportunity, i.e., enemy materiel, personnel, and facilities, in assigned general areas or along assigned ground communications routes, and not for the purpose of attacking specific briefed targets.

armed sweep—*(DOD, NATO)* A sweep fitted with cutters or other devices to increase its ability to cut mine moorings.

arming—*(DOD, NATO, IADB)* As applied to explosives, weapons, and ammunition, the changing from a safe condition to a state of readiness for initiation.

arming delay device—*(DOD, NATO)* A device fitted in a mine to prevent it being actuated for a present time after laying.

arming lanyard—See **arming wire.**

arming pin—*(DOD, NATO)* A safety device which is inserted into a fuze to prevent the arming cycle from starting until its removal.

arming system—*(DOD, IADB)* That portion of a weapon which serves to ready (arm), safe, or re-safe (disarm) the firing system and fuzing system and which may actuate devices in the nuclear system.

arming wire—*(DOD, NATO)* A cable, wire, or lanyard attached to the aircraft (usually at the arming unit) and routed to a weapon system (i.e. fuze fin, parachute pack, etc.) to prevent arming initiation prior to weapon release. Also called "safety wire"; "arming lanyard"; "safety lanyard."

armored personnel carrier—*(DOD)* A lightly armored, highly mobile, full-tracked vehicle, amphibious and air-droppable, used primarily for transporting personnel and their individual equipment during tactical operations. Production modifications or application of special kits permit use as a mortar carrier, command post, flame thrower, antiaircraft artillery chassis, or limited recovery vehicle.

armored reconnaissance airborne assault vehicle—*(DOD, IADB)* A lightly armored, mobile, full-tracked vehicle serving as the main reconnaissance vehicle in infantry and airborne operations, and as the principal assault weapon of airborne troops.

arms control—*(DOD, IADB)* A concept that connotes: a. any plan, arrangement, or process, resting upon explicit or implicit international agreement, governing any aspect of the following: the numbers, types, and performance characteristics of weapon systems (including the command and control, logistics support arrangements, and any related intelligence-gathering mechanism); and the numerical strength, organization, equipment, deployment or employment of the armed forces retained by the parties. (It encompasses "disarmament.") and **b.** on some occasions, those measures taken for the purpose of reducing instability in the military environment.

arms control agreement—*(DOD, IADB)* The written or unwritten embodiment of the acceptance of one or more arms control measures by two or more nations.

arms control agreement verification—*(DOD, IADB)* A concept that entails the collection, processing, and reporting of data indicating testing or employment of proscribed weapon systems, including country of origin and location, weapon and payload identification, and event type.

arms control measure—*(DOD, IADB)* Any specific arms control course of action.

armstrong—*(DOD)* The term, peculiar to the Air Support Radar Team, indicating both the command and response for arming and fuzing circuit activation.

army—*(NATO)* 1. A formation larger than an army corps but smaller than an army group. It usually consists of two or more army corps. 2. In certain nations "army" is the land component of the armed forces. 3. In certain nations "armée" covers all the armed forces.

Army Air Defense Command Post—*(DOD, IADB)* The tactical headquarters of an Army air defense commander.

Army air-ground system—*(DOD, IADB)* The Army system which provides for interface between Army and tactical air support agencies of other Services in the planning, evaluating, processing, and coordinating of air support requirements and operations. It is composed of appropriate staff members, including G-2 air and G-3 air personnel, and necessary communication equipment.

Army base—*(DOD)* A base or group of installations for which a local commander is responsible, consisting of facilities necessary for support of Army activities including security, internal lines of communication, utilities, plants and systems, and real property for which the Army has operating responsibility. See also **base complex.**

Army corps—*(DOD, IADB)* A tactical unit larger than a division and smaller than a field army. A corps usually consists of two or more divisions together with auxiliary arms and services.

army corps—*(NATO)* A formation larger than a division but smaller than an army or army group. It usually consists to two or more divisions together with supporting arms and services. Also called **corps.**

Army group—*(DOD, IADB)* Several field armies under a designated commander.

army group—*(NATO)* The largest formation of land forces, normally comprising two or more armies or army corps under a designated commander.

Army service area—*(DOD, IADB)* The territory between the corps rear boundary and the combat zone rear boundary. Most of the Army administrative establishment and service troops are usually located in this area. See also **rear area.**

arresting barrier—See **aircraft arresting barrier.**

arresting gear—See **aircraft arresting gear.**

artificial daylight—*(NATO, IADB)* Illumination of an intensity greater than the light of a full moon on a clear night. (The optimum illumination is the equivalent of daylight.) See also **battlefield illumination.**

artificial horizon—See **attitude indicator.**

artificial moonlight—*(NATO, IADB)* Illumination of an intensity between that of starlight and that of a full moon on a clear night. See also **battlefield illumination.**

artillery fire plan table—*(DOD, NATO)* A presentation of planned targets giving data for engagement. Scheduled targets are fired in a definite time sequence. The starting time may be on call, at a prearranged time or at the occurrence of a specific event.

artillery preparation—*(NATO)* Artillery fire delivered before an attack to disrupt communications and disorganize the enemy's defense.

artillery survey control point—*(DOD, NATO)* A point at which the coordinates and the altitude are known and from which the bearings/azimuths to a number of reference objects are also known.

aspect angle—*(DOD)* The angle between the longitudinal axis of the target (projected rearward) and the line-of-sight to the interceptor measured from the tail of the target.

aspect change—*(NATO)* The different appearance of a reflecting object viewed by radar from varying directions. It is caused by the change in the effective reflecting area of the target.

ASROC—See **antisubmarine rocket.**

assault—*(DOD, IADB)* 1. The climax of an attack; closing with the enemy in hand-to-hand fighting. 2. In an amphibious operation, the period of time between the arrival of the major assault forces of the amphibious task force in the objective area and the accomplishment of the amphibious task force mission. 3. To make a short, violent, but well-ordered attack against a local objective, such as a gun emplacement, a fort, or a machine gun nest. 4. A phase of an airborne operation beginning with delivery by air of the assault echelon of the force into the objective area

and extending through attack of assault objectives and consolidation of the initial airhead. See also **assault phase; landing attack.**

assault—*(NATO)* 1. The climax of an attack; closing with the enemy in hand-to-hand fighting. 2. See **amphibious assault.** 3. A short, violent, but well-ordered attack against a local objective, such as a gun emplacement, a fort or a machine gun nest. See also **assault phase.**

assault aircraft—*(DOD, NATO, IADB)* Powered aircraft, including helicopters, which move assault troops and cargo into an objective area and which provide for their resupply.

assault area diagram—*(DOD, IADB)* A graphic means of showing, for amphibious operations, the beach designations, boat lanes, organization of the line of departure, scheduled waves, landing ship area, transport areas, and the fire support areas in the immediate vicinity of the boat lanes.

assault craft—*(DOD, NATO)* A landing craft or amphibious vehicle primarily employed for landing troops and equipment in the assault waves of an amphibious operation.

assault echelon—*(DOD, NATO)* The element of a force that is scheduled for initial assault on the objective area.

assault echelon (air transport)—*(IADB)* The element of a force that is scheduled for initial assault on the objective area.

assault fire—*(DOD)* 1. That fire delivered by attacking troops as they close with the enemy. 2. In artillery, extremely accurate, short-range destruction fire at point targets.

assault phase—*(DOD, NATO)* 1. In an amphibious operation, the period of time between the arrival of the major assault forces of the amphibious task force in the objective area and the accomplishment of their mission. 2. In an airborne operation, a phase beginning with delivery by air of the assault echelon of the force into the objective area and extending through attack of assault objectives and consolidation of the initial airhead. See also **assault**.

assault schedule—See **landing schedule**.

assault shipping—*(DOD, NATO, IADB)* Shipping assigned to the amphibious task force and utilized for transporting assault troops, vehicles, equipment, and supplies to the objective area.

assault wave—See **wave**.

assembly—*(DOD, NATO)* An item forming a portion of an equipment, that can be provisioned and replaced as an entity and which normally incorporates replaceable parts or groups of parts. See also **part; sub-assembly**.

assembly anchorage—*(DOD, NATO)* An anchorage intended for the assembly and onward routing of ships.

assembly area—*(DOD, NATO, IADB)* 1. An area in which a command is assembled preparatory to further action. 2. In a supply installation, the gross area used for collecting and combining components into complete units, kits, or assemblies.

assessment—*(DOD, IADB)* 1. Analysis of the security, effectiveness, and potential of an existing or planned intelligence activity. 2. Judgment of the motives, qualifications, and characteristics of present or prospective employees or "agents."

asset (intelligence)—*(DOD, IADB)* Any resource—person, group, relationship, instrument, installation, or supply—at the disposition of an intelligence organization for use in an operational or support role. Often used with a qualifying term such as agent asset or propaganda asset.

assign—*(DOD, NATO)* 1. To place units or personnel in an organization where such placement is relatively permanent, and/or where such organization controls and administers the units or personnel for the primary function, or greater portion of the functions, of the unit or personnel. 2. To detail individuals to specific duties or functions where such duties or functions are primary and/or relatively permanent. See also **attach**.

assign—*(IADB)* 1. The placement of units or personnel in an organization where such placement is relatively permanent and/or where such organization controls and administers the units or personnel for the primary function, or greater portion of the functions of the unit or personnel. 2. The detailing of individuals to specific duties or functions where such duties or functions are primary and/or relatively permanent. See also **attach**.

assigned forces—*(IADB)* Forces in being that have been placed under the operational command or operational control of a commander. See also **force(s)**.

assumed azimuth—*(DOD)* The assumption of azimuth origins as a field expedient until the required data are available.

assumed grid—*(DOD)* A grid constructed using an arbitrary scale superimposed on a map, chart, or photograph for use in point designation without regard to actual geographic location. See also **grid**.

assumption—*(DOD, IADB)* A supposition on the current situation or a presupposition on the future course of events, either or both assumed to be true in the absence of positive proof, necessary to enable the commander in the process of planning to complete an estimate of the situation and make a decision on the course of action.

astern fueling—*(DOD, NATO)* The transfer of fuel at sea during which the receiving ship(s) keep(s) station astern of the delivering ship.

ASTOR—See **antisubmarine torpedo**.

astro altitude—*(NATO)* The arc of the vertical circle measured from the celestial horizon to the body.

astro compass—*(NATO)* An instrument used primarily to obtain true heading or true bearing by reference to celestial bodies.

astronomical twilight—See **twilight**.

astro-tracker—*(NATO)* A navigation equipment which automatically acquires and continuously tracks a celestial body in azimuth and altitude.

asymmetrical sweep—*(DOD, NATO)* A sweep whose swept path under conditions of no wind or cross-tide is not equally spaced either side of the sweeper's track.

atmosphere—*(DOD, IADB)* The air surrounding the earth. See also **ionosphere**; **stratosphere**; **tropopause**; **troposphere**.

atmospheric environment—*(DOD, IADB)* The envelope of air surrounding the earth, including its interfaces and interactions with the earth's solid or liquid surface.

at my command—*(DOD, NATO)* In artillery and naval gunfire support, the command used when it is desired to control the exact time of delivery of fire.

atomic air burst—See **airburst**.

atomic defense—See **nuclear defense**.

atomic demolition munition—*(DOD, IADB)* A nuclear device designed to be detonated on or below the ground surface, or under water as a demolition munition against material-type targets to block, deny, and/or canalize the enemy.

atomic demolition munition—*(NATO)* A nuclear device designed or adapted for use as a demolition munition.

atomic underground burst—See **nuclear underground burst**.

atomic underwater burst—See **nuclear underwater burst**.

atomic warfare—See **nuclear warfare**.

atomic weapon—See **nuclear weapon**.

at priority call—*(DOD, NATO)* A precedence applied to the task of an artillery unit to provide fire to a formation/unit on a guaranteed basis. Normally observer, communications and liaison are not provided. An artillery unit in "direct support" or "in support" may simultaneously be placed "at priority call" to another unit or agency for a particular task and/or for a specific period of time.

attach—*(DOD, NATO)* 1. To place units or personnel in an organization where such placement is relatively temporary. Subject to limitations imposed in the attachment order, the commander of the formation, unit, or organization receiving the attachment will exercise the same degree of command and control thereover as he does over the units and persons organic to his command. However, the responsibility for transfer and promotion of personnel will normally be retained by the parent formation, unit, or organization. 2. To detail individuals to specific functions where such functions are secondary or relatively temporary, i.e., attach for quarters and rations, attach for flying duty. See also **assign**.

attach—*(IADB)* 1. The placement of units or personnel in an organization where such placement is relatively temporary. Subject to limitations imposed by the attachment order, the commander of the formation, unit, or organization receiving the attachment will exercise the same degree of command and control thereover as he does over units and persons organic to his command. However, the responsibility for transfer and promotion of personnel will normally be retained by the parent formation, unit, or organization. 2. The detailing of individuals to specific functions where such functions are secondary or relatively temporary; e.g., attach for quarters and rations; attach for flying duty. See also **assign**.

attached airlift service—*(DOD)* The airlift service provided to an organization or command by an airlift unit attached to that organization.

attack aircraft carrier—*(DOD, IADB)* A warship designed to support and operate aircraft, engage in attacks on targets afloat or ashore, and engage in sustained operations in support of other forces. *(DOD)* Designated as CV or CVN. CVN is nuclear powered.

attack altitude—*(DOD)* The altitude at which the interceptor will maneuver during the attack phase of an air intercept.

attack assessment—*(DOD)* An evaluation of information to determine the potential or actual nature and objectives of an attack for the purpose of providing information for timely decisions. See also **damage estimation.**

attack cargo ship—*(DOD, IADB)* A naval ship designed or converted to transport combat-loaded cargo in an assault landing. Capabilities as to carrying landing craft, speed of ship, armament, and size of hatches and booms are greater than those of comparable cargo ship types. Designated as LKA.

attack carrier striking forces—*(DOD, IADB)* Naval forces, the primary offensive weapon of which is carrier-based aircraft. Ships, other than carriers, act primarily to support and screen against submarine and air threat and secondarily against surface threat.

attack condition alpha—*(DOD)* Considers there is inadequate warning of attack, and the command post or headquarters of a decision authority becomes ineffective prior to the performance of essential functions.

attack condition bravo—*(DOD)* Considers there is sufficient effective warning of impending attack to relocate personnel required to perform essential functions to alternate command facilities.

attack group—*(DOD, NATO, IADB)* A subordinate task organization of the navy forces of an amphibious task force. It is composed of assault shipping and supporting naval units designated to transport, protect, land and initially support a landing group.

attack heading—*(DOD)* 1. The interceptor heading during the attack phase that will achieve the desired track-crossing angle. 2. The assigned magnetic compass heading to be flown by aircraft during the delivery phase of an air strike.

attack helicopter—*(DOD, NATO)* A helicopter designed to search out, attack and destroy enemy targets.

attacking—*(DOD)* In air intercept, a term meaning, "Am commencing attacking run with weapon indicated" (size may be given).

attack origin—*(DOD)* 1. The location or source from which an attack was initiated. 2. The nation initiating an attack. See also **attack assessment.**

attack pattern—*(DOD)* The type and distribution of targets under attack. See also **attack assessment; target pattern.**

attack position—*(DOD, IADB)* The last position occupied by the assault echelon before crossing the line of departure. See also **forming up place.**

attack position—*(NATO)* See **forming up place.**

attack size—*(DOD)* The number of weapons involved in an attack. See also **attack assessment.**

attack speed—*(DOD)* The speed at which the interceptor will maneuver during the attack phase of an air intercept.

attack timing—*(DOD)* The predicted or actual time of bursts, impacts, or arrival of weapons at their intended targets.

attack transport—*(DOD, IADB)* A naval ship designed for combat loading a battalion landing team with its equipment and supplies, and having the facilities, including landing craft, for landing them on a hostile beach. Designated as APA.

attenuation—*(DOD, NATO, IADB)* 1. Decrease in intensity of a signal, beam, or wave as a result of absorption of energy and of scattering out of the path of a detector, but not including the reduction due to geometric spreading, i.e., the inverse square of distance effect. 2. In mine warfare, the reduction in intensity of an influence as distance from the source increases.

attenuation factor—*(DOD, NATO, IADB)* The ratio of the incident radiation dose or dose rate to the radiation dose or dose rate transmitted through a shielding material. This is the reciprocal of the transmission factor.

attitude—*(DOD, NATO, IADB)* 1. The position of a body as determined by the inclination of the axes to some frame of reference. If not otherwise specified, this frame of reference is fixed to the earth. *(NATO)* 2. The grid bearing of the long axis of a target area.

attitude director indicator—*(DOD, NATO)* An attitude indicator which displays command signals from the flight director computer.

attitude indicator—*(DOD, NATO)* An instrument which displays the attitude of the aircraft by reference to sources of information which may be contained within the instrument or be external to it. When the sources of information are self-contained, the instrument may be referred to as an artificial horizon.

attrition—*(DOD, NATO, IADB)* The reduction of the effectiveness of a force caused by loss of personnel and materiel.

attrition minefield—*(DOD, NATO)* In naval mine warfare, a field intended primarily to cause damage to enemy ships.

attrition rate—*(DOD, NATO, IADB)* A factor, normally expressed as a percentage, reflecting the degree of losses of personnel or materiel due to various causes within a specified period of time.

attrition reserve aircraft—*(DOD)* Aircraft procured for the specific purpose of replacing the anticipated losses of aircraft because of peacetime and/or wartime attrition.

attrition sweeping—*(DOD, NATO)* The continuous sweeping of minefields to keep the risk of mines to all ships as low as possible.

augmentation forces—*(DOD)* Forces to be transferred to the operational command of a supported commander during the execution of an operation.

authenticate—*(DOD, IADB)* A challenge given by voice or electrical means to attest to the authenticity of a message or transmission.

authentication—*(DOD, IADB)* 1. A security measure designed to protect a communications system against acceptance of a fraudulent transmission or simulation by establishing the validity of a transmission, message, or originator. 2. A means of identifying individuals and verifying their eligibility to receive specific categories of information. 3. Evidence by proper signature or seal that a document is genuine and official.

authentication—*(NATO)* 1. Evidence by proper signature or seal that a document is genuine and official. 2. A security measure designed to protect a communication system against fraudulent transmissions.

authenticator—*(DOD)* A symbol or group of symbols, or a series of bits, selected or derived in a prearranged manner and usually inserted at a predetermined point within a message or transmission for the purpose of attesting to the validity of the message or transmission.

authenticator—*(NATO, IADB)* A letter, numeral, or group of letters or numerals, or both, attesting to the authenticity of a message or transmission.

authentic document—*(NATO, IADB)* A document bearing a signature or seal attesting that it is genuine and official. If it is an enemy document, it may have been prepared for purposes of deception and the accuracy of such document, even though authenticated, must be confirmed by other information, e.g., conditions of capture.

autocode format—*(DOD)* An abbreviated and formatted message header used in conjunction with the Mobile Cryptologic Support Facility (MCSF) to energize the automatic communications relay functions of the MCSF providing rapid exchange of data through the system.

automated data handling—See **automatic data handling.**

automatic approach and landing—*(DOD, NATO, IADB)* A control mode in which the aircraft's speed and flight path are automatically controlled for approach, flare-out, and landing. See also **ground controlled approach procedure.**

automatic data handling—*(DOD, NATO)* A generalization of automatic data processing to include the aspect of data transfer.

automatic data processing—*(DOD, NATO)* 1. Data processing largely performed by automatic means. 2. That branch of science and technology concerned with methods and techniques relating to data processing largely performed by automatic means.

automatic flight control system—*(DOD, NATO, IADB)* A system which includes all equipment to control automatically the flight of an aircraft or missile to a path or attitude described by references internal or external to the aircraft or missile.

automatic levelling—*(DOD, NATO)* A flight control system feature which returns an aircraft to level flight attitude in roll and pitch.

automatic message processing system—*(DOD)* Any organized assembly of resources and methods used to collect, process, and distribute messages largely by automatic means.

automatic pilot—*(DOD, NATO)* That part of an automatic flight control system which provides attitude stabilization with respect to internal references.

automatic search jammer—*(DOD, NATO)* An intercept receiver and jamming transmitter system which searches for and jams signals automatically which have specific radiation characteristics.

Automatic Secure Voice Communications Network—*(DOD)* A worldwide, switched, secure voice network developed to fulfill DOD long-haul, secure voice requirements. Also called AUTOSEVOCOM.

automatic supply—*(DOD, IADB)* A system by which certain supply requirements are automatically shipped or issued for a predetermined period of time without requisition by the using unit. It is based upon estimated or experience-usage factors.

automatic throttle—*(DOD, NATO)* A flight control system feature which actuates an aircraft throttle system based on its own computation and feedback from appropriate data sources.

automatic toss—*(DOD, NATO)* In a flight control system, a control mode in which the toss bombing maneuver of an aircraft is controlled automatically.

automatic trim—*(DOD, NATO)* A flight control system feature which adjusts the trim of an aircraft in flight.

Automatic Voice Network—*(DOD)* The principal long-haul, unsecure voice communications network within the Defense Communications System. Also called AUTOVON.

automation—*(DOD, IADB)* 1. The implementation of processes by automatic means. 2. The conversion of a procedure, a process, or equipment to automatic operation.

autonomous operation—*(DOD, IADB)* In air defense, the mode of operation assumed by a unit after it has lost all communications with higher echelons. The unit commander assumes full responsibility for control of weapons and engagement of hostile targets.

autonomous operation—*(NATO)* One mode of operation of a unit in which the unit commander assumes full responsibility for control of weapons and engagement of hostile targets. This mode may be either directed by higher authority or result from a loss of all means of communication.

auxiliary contours—*(NATO)* Additional contours used to portray unique ground forms not adequately portrayed by the selected contour interval.

AV-8—See **Harrier.**

available payload—*(DOD, IADB)* The passenger and/or cargo capacity expressed in weight and/or space available to the user.

available supply rate—*(NATO)* The rate of consumption that can be allocated considering the supplies and facilities available for a planned operation or a given period.

avenue of approach—*(DOD)* An air or ground route of attacking force of a given size leading to its objective or to key terrain in its path.

average heading—*(NATO)* The arithmetic mean of the different values of the headings maintained over a certain period of time.

average speed—*(DOD, NATO, IADB)* The average distance traveled per hour, calculated over the whole journey, excluding specifically ordered halts.

aviation life support equipment—See **life support equipment.**

aviation medicine—*(DOD, NATO, IADB)* The special field of medicine which is related to the biological and psychological problems of flight.

AWACS—See **Airborne Early Warning and Control System.**

axial route—*(DOD, NATO)* A route running through the rear area and into the forward area. See also **route.**

axis of advance—*(DOD, IADB)* A line of advance assigned for purposes of control; often a road or a group of roads, or a designated series of locations, extending in the direction of the enemy.

axis of control—*(DOD, NATO)* In an automatic flight control system, that section of the system which controls an aircraft in one plane.

azimuth—*(DOD, IADB)* Quantities may be expressed in positive quantities increasing in a clockwise direction, or in X, Y coordinates where south and west are negative. They may be referenced to true north or magnetic north depending on the particular weapon system used.

azimuth angle—*(DOD, NATO)* An angle measured clockwise in the horizontal plane between a reference direction and any other line.

azimuth guidance—*(DOD, NATO)* Information which will enable the pilot or autopilot of an aircraft to follow the required track.

azimuth resolution—*(DOD, NATO)* The ability of radar equipment to separate two reflectors at similar ranges but different bearings from a reference point. Normally the minimum separation distance between the reflectors is quoted and expressed as the angle subtended by the reflectors at the reference point.

B

B-52—See Stratofortress.

background count—*(DOD, NATO, IADB)* The evidence or effect on a detector of radiation, other than that which it is desired to detect, caused by any agency. In connection with health protection, the background count usually includes radiations produced by naturally occurring radioactivity and cosmic rays.

background radiation—*(DOD, NATO, IADB)* Nuclear (or ionizing) radiations arising from within the body and from the surroundings to which individuals are always exposed.

back order—*(DOD)* The quantity of an item requisitioned by ordering activities that is not immediately available for issue but is recorded as a stock commitment for future issue.

back-scattering—*(DOD, NATO)* Radio wave propagation in which the direction of the incident and scattered waves, resolved along a reference direction (usually horizontal), are oppositely directed. A signal received by back-scattering is often referred to as "back-scatter."

back tell—*(DOD, NATO)* The transfer of information from a higher to a lower echelon of command. See also **track telling**.

back-up—*(DOD, NATO)* In cartography, an image printed on the reverse side of a map sheet already printed on one side. Also the printing of such images.

backup aircraft authorization—*(DOD)* Aircraft over and above the primary authorized aircraft to permit scheduled and unscheduled maintenance, modifications, and inspections and repair without reduction of aircraft available for the operational mission. No operating resources are allocated for these aircraft in the Defense budget. See also **primary aircraft authorization**.

backup aircraft inventory—*(DOD)* The aircraft designated to meet the backup authorization. See also **primary aircraft inventory**.

balance—*(DOD, IADB)* A concept as applied to an arms control measure that connotes: a. adjustments of armed forces and armaments in such a manner that one state does not obtain military advantage over other states agreeing to the measure; and b. internal adjustments by one state of its forces in such manner as to enable it to cope with all aspects of remaining threats to its security in a post arms control agreement era.

balanced collective forces—*(IADB)* The requirement for "balance" in any military force stems from the consideration that all elements of a force should be complementary to each other. A force should function as a combined arms team, and the term "balance" implies that the ratio of the various elements of this team is such that the force is best constituted to execute its assigned mission effectively and efficiently. Applied multinationally, the term "balanced collective force" may be defined as a force composed of one or more Services furnished by more than one nation, the total strength and composition of which are such as best to fulfill the specific mission for which designed. See also **force(s)**.

balanced stock(s)—*(DOD, IADB)* 1. That condition of supply when availability and requirements are in equilibrium for specific items. 2. An accumulation of supplies in quantities determined necessary to meet requirements for a fixed period.

balance station zero—See **reference datum**.

bale cubic capacity—*(DOD, NATO, IADB)* The space available for cargo measured in cubic feet to the inside of the cargo battens, on the frames, and to the underside of the beams. In a general cargo of mixed commodities, the bale cubic applies. The stowage of the mixed cargo comes in contact with the cargo battens and as a general rule does not extend to the skin of the ship.

balisage—*(DOD, NATO, IADB)* The marking of a route by a system of dim beacon lights enabling vehicles to be driven at near day-time speed, under blackout conditions.

ballistic missile—*(DOD, NATO, IADB)* Any missile which does not rely upon aerodynamic surfaces to produce lift and consequently follows a ballistic trajectory when thrust is terminated. See also **aerodynamic missile; guided missile.**

ballistic missile early warning system—*(DOD, IADB)* An electronic system for providing detection and early warning of attack by enemy intercontinental ballistic missiles.

ballistics—*(DOD, NATO, IADB)* The science or art that deals with the motion, behavior, appearance, or modification of missiles or other vehicles acted upon by propellants, wind, gravity, temperature, or any other modifying substance, condition, or force.

ballistic trajectory—*(DOD, NATO, IADB)* The trajectory traced after the propulsive force is terminated and the body is acted upon only by gravity and aerodynamic drag.

ballistic wind—*(DOD, IADB)* That constant wind that would have the same effect upon the trajectory of a bomb or projectile as the wind encountered in flight.

balloon barrage—See **barrage**, Part 2.

balloon reflector—*(DOD, NATO)* In electronic warfare, a balloon-supported confusion reflector to produce fraudulent echoes.

band pass—*(DOD)* The number of cycles per second expressing the difference between the limiting frequencies at which the desired fraction (usually half power) of the maximal output is obtained. Term applies to all types of amplifiers.

bank angle—*(DOD, NATO)* The angle between the aircraft's normal axis and the earth's vertical plane containing the aircraft's longitudinal axis.

barometric altimeter—See **altimeter.**

barometric altimeter reversionary—See **altimeter.**

barometric altitude—*(DOD, NATO)* The aircraft altitude given by the difference between the heights corresponding to the pressure at aircraft level and mean sea level according to the standard atmosphere.

barometric vertical speed indicator—See **vertical speed indicator.**

barrage—*(DOD, IADB)* 1. A prearranged barrier of fire, except that delivered by small arms, designed to protect friendly troops and installations by impeding enemy movements across defensive lines or areas. 2. A protective screen of balloons that are moored to the ground and kept at given heights to prevent or hinder operations by enemy aircraft. This meaning also called **balloon barrage. 3.** A type of electronic countermeasures intended for simultaneous jamming over a wide area of frequency spectrum. See also **barrage jamming; electronic warfare; fire.**

barrage fire—*(DOD, NATO, IADB)* Fire which is designed to fill a volume of space or area rather than aimed specifically at a given target. See also **fire.**

barrage jamming—*(DOD, NATO, IADB)* Simultaneous electronic jamming over a broad band of frequencies. See also **jamming.**

barrier—*(DOD, NATO, IADB)* A coordinated series of obstacles designed or employed to canalize, direct, restrict, delay or stop the movement of an opposing force, and to impose additional losses in personnel, time and equipment on the opposing force. See also **aircraft arresting system.**

barrier combat air patrol—*(DOD, IADB)* One or more divisions or elements of fighter aircraft employed between a force and an objective area as a barrier across the probable direction of enemy attack. It is used as far from the force as control conditions permit, giving added protection against raids that use the most direct routes of approach. See also **combat air patrol.**

barrier forces—*(DOD, IADB)* Air, surface, and submarine units and their supporting systems positioned across the likely courses of expected enemy transit for early detection and providing rapid warning, blocking, and destruction of the enemy.

bar scale—See **graphic scale;** See also **scale.**

base—*(DOD, NATO, IADB)* 1. A locality from which operations are projected or supported. 2. An area or locality containing installations which provide logistic or other support. See also **emergency fleet operating base; establishment; island bases.** *(DOD, IADB)* 3. Home airfield or home carrier.

base command—*(DOD, NATO, IADB)* An area containing a military base or group of such bases organized under one commander. See also **command.**

base complex—See **Air Force base; Army base; Marine base; naval base; naval or Marine (air) base.** See also **noncontiguous facility.**

base defense—*(DOD, IADB)* The local military measures, both normal and emergency, required to nullify or reduce the effectiveness of enemy attacks on, or sabotage of, a base, so as to insure that the maximum capacity of its facilities is available to U.S. forces.

base development—*(DOD, NATO, IADB)* The improvement or expansion of the resources and facilities of an area or a location to support military operations.

base development plan—*(DOD, IADB)* A plan for the facilities, installations, and bases required to support military operations.

base ejection shell—*(NATO, IADB)* A type of shell which ejects its load from its base.

base element—See **base unit.**

base fuze—*(NATO, IADB)* Fuze located in the base of a projectile or bomb. See also **fuze.**

base line—*(DOD, NATO, IADB)* 1. (**surveying**) A surveyed line established with more than usual care, to which surveys are referred for coordination and correlation. 2. (**photo-grammetry**) The line between the principal points of two consecutive vertical air photographs. It is usually measured on one photograph after the principal point of the other has been transferred. 3. (**radio navigation systems**) The shorter arc of the great circle joining two radio transmitting stations of a navigation system. 4. (**triangulation**) The side of one of a series of coordinated triangles the length of which is measured with prescribed accuracy and precision and from which lengths of the other triangle sides are obtained by computation.

base map—*(DOD, NATO, IADB)* A map or chart showing certain fundamental information, used as a base upon which additional data of specialized nature are compiled or overprinted. Also, a map containing all the information from which maps showing specialized information can be prepared. See also **chart base; map.**

base map symbol—*(NATO)* A symbol used on a base map or chart as opposed to one used on an overprint to the base map or chart.

base of operations—*(DOD, IADB)* An area or facility from which a military force begins its offensive operations, to which it falls back in case of reverse, and in which supply facilities are organized.

base period—*(DOD, IADB)* That period of time for which factors were determined for use in current planning and programming.

base section—*(DOD, IADB)* An area within the communications zone in an area of operations organized to provide logistic support to forward areas.

base surge—*(DOD, NATO, IADB)* A cloud which rolls out from the bottom of the column produced by a subsurface burst of a nuclear weapon. For underwater bursts, the surge is, in effect, a cloud of liquid droplets which has the property of flowing almost as if it were a homogeneous fluid. For subsurface land bursts the surge is made up of small solid particles but still behaves like a fluid.

base symbol—See **base map symbol**.

base unit—*(DOD, IADB)* Unit of organization in a tactical operation around which a movement or maneuver is planned and performed; base element.

basic cover—*(DOD, IADB)* Coverage of any installation or area of a permanent nature with which later coverage can be compared to discover any changes that have taken place.

basic encyclopedia—*(DOD)* A compilation of identified installations and physical areas of potential significance as objectives for attack.

basic intelligence—*(DOD)* Fundamental intelligence concerning the general situation, resources, capabilities, and vulnerabilities of foreign countries or areas which may be used as reference material in the planning of operations at any level and in evaluating subsequent information relating to the same subject.

basic intelligence—*(NATO)* Intelligence, on any subject, which may be used as reference material for planning and in evaluating subsequent information. See also **current intelligence; information; intelligence**.

basic intelligence—*(IADB)* General intelligence concerning the capabilities, vulnerabilities, and intentions of foreign nations; used as a base for a variety of intelligence products for the support of planning, policy making, and military operations. See also **intelligence**.

basic load—*(DOD, NATO)* The quantity of supplies required to be on hand within, and which can be moved by, a unit or formation. It is expressed according to the wartime organization of the unit or formation and maintained at the prescribed levels.

basic load (ammunition)—*(IADB)* That quantity of non-nuclear ammunition that is authorized and required by each Service to be on hand within a unit or formation at all times. It is expressed in rounds, units, or units of weight as appropriate.

basic military route network—*(DOD, NATO)* Axial, lateral, and connecting routes designated in peacetime by the host nation to meet the anticipated military movements and transport requirements, both allied and national. See also **transport network**.

basic psychological operations study—*(DOD)* A document which describes succinctly the characteristics of a country, geographical area, or region which are most pertinent to psychological operations, and which can serve as an immediate reference for the planning and conduct of psychological operations.

basic research—*(DOD, IADB)* Research directed toward the increase of knowledge, the primary aim being a greater knowledge or understanding of the subject under study. See also **applied research; research**.

basic stopping power—*(DOD, NATO)* The probability, expressed as a percentage, of a single vehicle being stopped by mines while attempting to cross a minefield.

basic tactical organization—*(DOD, IADB)* The conventional organization of landing force units for combat, involving combinations of infantry, supporting ground arms, and aviation for accomplishment of missions ashore. This organizational form is employed as soon as possible following the landing of the various assault components of the landing force.

basic undertakings—*(DOD, IADB)* The essential things, expressed in broad terms, that must be done in order to implement the commander's concept successfully. These may include military, diplomatic, economic, psychological, and other measures. See also **strategic concept.**

basis of issue—*(DOD)* Authority which prescribes the number of items to be issued to an individual, a unit, a military organization, or for a unit piece of equipment.

bathymetric contour—See **depth contour.**

battalion landing team—*(DOD, IADB)* In an amphibious operation, an infantry battalion normally reinforced by necessary combat and service elements; the basic unit for planning an assault landing. Also known as BLT—*(DOD)*

battery—*(DOD, NATO, IADB)* 1. Tactical and administrative artillery unit or subunit corresponding to a company or similar unit in other branches of the Army. 2. All guns, torpedo tubes, searchlights or missile launchers of the same size or caliber or used for the same purpose, either installed in one ship or otherwise operating as an entity.

battery center—*(DOD, NATO)* A point on the ground, the coordinates of which are used as a reference indicating the location of the battery in the production of firing data. Also called **chart location of the battery.**

battery control central—*(NATO)* The operations center from which Hawk missiles are controlled at battery level.

battery left (or right)—*(NATO)* A method of fire in which weapons are discharged from the left (or right) one after the other, at five second intervals, unless otherwise specified.

battery (troop) left (right)—*(DOD)* A method of fire in which weapons are discharged from the left (right), one after the other, at five second intervals.

battle casualty—*(DOD)* Any casualty incurred in action. "In action" characterizes the casualty status as having been the direct result of hostile action, sustained in combat or relating thereto, or sustained going to or returning from a combat mission provided that the occurrence was directly related to hostile action. Included are persons killed or wounded mistakenly or accidentally by friendly fire directed at a hostile force or what is thought to be a hostile force. However, not to be considered as sustained in action and thereby not to be interpreted as battle casualties are injuries due to the elements, self-inflicted wounds, and, except in unusual cases, wounds or death inflicted by a friendly force while the individual is in absent-without-leave or dropped-from-rolls status or is voluntarily absent from a place of duty. See also **died of wounds received in action; non-battle casualty; wounded.**

battle casualty—*(IADB)* Any person lost to his organization, because of death, wound, missing, capture, or internment provided such loss is incurred in action. "In action" characterizes the casualty status as having been the direct result of hostile action sustained going to or returning from a combat mission provided that the occurrence was directly related to hostile action, or through misadventure, friendly action. However, injuries due to elements or self-inflicted wounds are not to be considered as sustained in action and are thereby not to be interpreted as battle casualties. See also **died of wounds received in action; non-battle casualty; wounded.**

battlefield illumination—*(DOD, NATO)* The lighting of the battle area by artificial light either visible or invisible to the naked eye.

See also **artificial daylight; artificial moonlight; indirect illumination.**

battlefield psychological activities—*(DOD, NATO)* Planned psychological activities conducted as an integral part of combat operations and designed to bring psychological pressure to bear on enemy forces and civilians under enemy control in the battle area, to assist in the achievement of the tactical objectives.

battlefield surveillance—*(DOD, NATO)* Systematic observation of the battle area for the purpose of providing timely information and combat intelligence. See also **surveillance.**

battle force—*(DOD)* A standing operational naval task force organization of carriers, surface combatants, and submarines assigned to numbered fleets. A battle force is subdivided into battle groups.

battle group—*(DOD)* A standing naval task group consisting of a carrier, surface combatants, and submarines as assigned in direct support, operating in mutual support with the task of destroying hostile submarine, surface, and air forces within the group's assigned area of responsibility.

battle map—*(DOD, IADB)* A map showing ground features in sufficient detail for tactical use by all forces, usually at a scale of 1:25,000. See also **map.**

battle reserves—*(DOD, IADB)* Reserve supplies accumulated by an army, detached corps, or detached division in the vicinity of the battlefield, in addition to unit and individual reserves. See also **reserve supplies.**

beach—*(DOD, IADB)* 1. The area extending from the shoreline inland to a marked change in physiographic form or material, or to the line of permanent vegetation (coastline). 2. In amphibious operations, that portion of the shoreline designated for landing of a tactical organization.

beach capacity—*(DOD, NATO, IADB)* An estimate, expressed in terms of measurement tons, or weight tons, of cargo that may be unloaded over a designated strip of shore per day. See also **clearance capacity; port capacity.**

beach group—See **naval beach group; shore party.**

beachhead—*(DOD, NATO, IADB)* A designated area on a hostile shore which, when seized and held, insures the continuous landing of troops and materiel, and provides maneuver space requisite for subsequent projected operations ashore. It is the physical objective of an amphibious operation. See also **airhead; bridgehead.**

beach marker—*(DOD, IADB)* A sign or device used to identify a beach or certain activities thereon, for incoming waterborne traffic. Markers may be panels, lights, buoys, or electronic devices.

beachmaster—*(DOD, IADB)* The naval officer in command of the beachmaster unit of the naval beach group.

beachmaster unit—*(DOD, IADB)* A commissioned naval unit of the naval beach group designed to provide to the shore party a naval component known as a beach party which is capable of supporting the amphibious landing of one division (reinforced). See also **beach party; shore party.**

beach minefield—*(DOD, NATO)* A minefield in the shallow water approaches to a possible amphibious landing beach.

beach organization—*(DOD, IADB)* In an amphibious operation, the planned arrangement of personnel and facilities to effect movement, supply, and evacuation across beaches and in the beach area for support of a landing force.

beach party—*(DOD, IADB)* The naval component of the shore party. See also **beachmaster unit; shore party.**

beach party commander—*(DOD, IADB)* The naval officer in command of the naval component of the shore party.

beach photography—*(DOD)* Vertical, oblique, ground, and periscope coverage at varying scales to provide information of offshore, shore, and inland areas. It covers terrain which provides observation of the beaches and is primarily concerned with the geological and tactical aspects of the beach.

beach reserves—*(DOD, NATO)* In an amphibious operation, an accumulation of supplies of all classes established in dumps in beachhead areas. See also **reserve supplies.**

beach support area—*(DOD, IADB)* In amphibious operations, the area to the rear of a landing force or elements thereof, established and operated by shore party units, which contains the facilities for the unloading of troops and materiel and the support of the forces ashore; it includes facilities for the evacuation of wounded, prisoners of war, and captured materiel.

beach survey—*(DOD)* The collection of data describing the physical characteristics of a beach; that is, an area whose boundaries are a shoreline, a coastline, and two natural or arbitrary assigned flanks.

beach width—*(DOD, IADB)* The horizontal dimensions of the beach measured at right angles to the shoreline from the line of extreme low water inland to the landward limit of the beach (the coastline).

beacon—*(DOD, IADB)* A light or electronic source which emits a distinctive or characteristic signal used for the determination of bearings, courses, or location. *(DOD, NATO, IADB)* See crash locator beacon; fan marker beacon; localizer; meaconing; personal locator beacon; radio beacon; Z marker beacon.

beacon double—*(DOD)* In air intercept, a code meaning, "Pilot select double pulse mode on your tracking beacon."

beacon off—*(DOD)* In air intercept, a code meaning, "Turn off your tracking beacon."

beacon on—*(DOD)* In air intercept, a code meaning, "Turn on your tracking beacon."

beam attack—*(DOD)* In air intercept, an attack by an interceptor aircraft attack which terminates with a heading crossing angle greater than 45° but less than 135°. See also **heading crossing angle.**

beam rider—*(DOD, IADB)* A missile guided by an electronic beam.

beam rider—*(NATO)* A missile guided by radar or radio beam.

beam width—*(DOD)* The angle between the directions, on either side of the axis, at which the intensity of the radio frequency field drops to one-half the value it has on the axis.

bearing—*(DOD, NATO, IADB)* The horizontal angle at a given point measured clockwise from a specific datum to a second point. See also **grid bearing; relative bearing.**

beaten zone—*(DOD)* The area on the ground upon which the cone of fire falls.

before-flight inspection—*(NATO)* Preflight check to ensure general aircraft safety and that disposable loads, e.g., fuel and armament equipment, etc., are correctly adjusted for the particular operation or sortie. Also called **preflight inspection.**

bent—*(DOD)* In air intercept and close air support, a code meaning, "Equipment indicated is inoperative (temporarily or indefinitely)." Cancelled by "Okay."

bilateral infrastructure—*(DOD, NATO)* Infrastructure which concerns only two NATO members and is financed by mutual agreement between them (e.g., facilities required for the use of forces of one NATO member in the territory of another). See also **infrastructure.**

billet—*(DOD, IADB)* 1. Shelter for troops. 2. To quarter troops. 3. A personnel position or assignment which may be filled by one person.

bi-margin format—*(NATO)* The format of a map or chart on which the cartographic detail is extended to two edges of the sheet, normally north and east, thus leaving two margins only.

binding—*(DOD, NATO)* The fastening or securing of items to a movable platform called a pallet. See also **palletized unit load**.

bingo—*(DOD)* 1. When originated by pilot, means, "I have reached minimal fuel for safe return to base or to designated alternate." 2. When originated by controlling activity, means, "Proceed to alternate airfield or carrier as specified."

bingo field—*(DOD)* Alternate airfield.

bin storage—*(DOD)* Storage of items of supplies and equipment in an individual compartment or subdivision of a storage unit in less than bulk quantities. See also **bulk storage; storage**.

biographical intelligence—*(DOD)* That component of intelligence which deals with individual foreign personalities of actual or potential importance.

biological agent—*(DOD, NATO, IADB)* A microorganism which causes disease in man, plants, or animals or causes the deterioration of materiel. See also **biological operation; biological weapon; chemical agent**.

biological ammunition—*(NATO)* A type of ammunition, the filler of which is primarily a biological agent.

biological defense—*(DOD, NATO)* The methods, plans and procedures involved in establishing and executing defensive measures against attack utilizing biological agents. See also **NBC defense**.

biological half-time—See **half-life**.

biological operation—*(DOD, NATO, IADB)* Employment of biological agents to produce casualties in man or animals and damage to plants or materiel; or defense against such employment.

biological warfare—See **biological operation**.

biological weapon—*(DOD, NATO, IADB)* An item of materiel which projects, disperses, or disseminates a biological agent including arthropod vectors.

black—*(DOD, IADB)* In intelligence handling, a term used in certain phrases (e.g., living black, black border crossing) to indicate reliance on illegal concealment rather than on cover.

black forces—*(NATO)* A term used in reporting of intelligence on Warsaw Pact exercises, to denote those units representing Warsaw Pact forces during such exercises. See also **force**(s); **white forces**.

black list—*(DOD, IADB)* An official counter-intelligence listing of actual or potential enemy collaborators, sympathizers, intelligence suspects, and other persons whose presence menaces the security of friendly forces.

black propaganda—*(DOD, I, IADB)* Propaganda which purports to emanate from a source other than the true one. See also **propaganda**.

blast—*(DOD, NATO, IADB)* The brief and rapid movement of air, vapor or fluid away from a center of outward pressure, as in an explosion or in the combustion of rocket fuel; the pressure accompanying this movement. This term is commonly used for "explosion," but the two terms may be distinguished.

blast effect—*(DOD, IADB)* Destruction of or damage to structures and personnel by the force of an explosion on or above the surface of the ground. Blast effect may be contrasted with the cratering and ground-shock effects of a projectile or charge that goes off beneath the surface.

blast line—*(DOD, IADB)* A horizontal radial line on the surface of the earth originating at ground zero on which measurements of blast from an explosion are taken.

blast wave—*(DOD, IADB)* A sharply defined wave of increased pressure rapidly propagated through a surrounding medium from a center of detonation or similar disturbance.

blast wave—*(NATO)* A shock wave that propagates through air. See also **shock wave.**

blast wave diffraction—*(DOD, NATO)* The passage around and envelopment of a structure by the nuclear blast wave.

bleeding edge—*(DOD, NATO, IADB)* That edge of a map or chart on which cartographic detail is extended to the edge of the sheet.

blind bombing zone—*(DOD, NATO, IADB)* A restricted area (air, land, or sea) established for the purpose of permitting air operations, unrestricted by the operations or possible attack of friendly forces.

blip—*(DOD, NATO, IADB)* The display of a received pulse on a cathode ray tube.

blister agent—*(DOD, NATO)* A chemical agent which injures the eyes and lungs, and burns or blisters the skin. Also called "vesicant agent."

blocking and chocking—*(DOD, NATO)* The use of wedges or chocks to prevent the inadvertent shifting of cargo in transit.

blocking position—*(DOD, NATO)* A defensive position so sited as to deny the enemy access to a given area or to prevent his advance in a given direction.

block shipment—*(DOD, IADB)* A method of shipment of supplies to overseas areas to provide balanced stocks or an arbitrary balanced

force for a specific number of days, e.g., shipment of 30 days' supply for an average force of 10,000 individuals.

block stowage loading—*(DOD, NATO, IADB)* A method of loading whereby all cargo for a specific destination is stowed together. The purpose is to facilitate rapid off-loading at the destination, with the least possible disturbance of cargo intended for other points. See also **loading.**

block time—*(NATO, IADB)* The period from the moment the chocks are withdrawn and brakes released, or moorings dropped, to the return to rest or take-up of moorings after the flight.

blood agent—*(DOD, NATO)* A chemical compound, including the cyanide group, that affects bodily functions by preventing the normal transfer of oxygen from the blood to body tissues. Also called "cyanogen agent."

blood chit—*(DOD)* A small cloth chart depicting an American Flag and a statement in several languages to the effect that anyone assisting the bearer to safety will be rewarded.

blood chit (intelligence)—See **blood chit.**

blow—*(DOD)* To expose, often unintentionally, personnel, installations, or other elements of a clandestine organization or activity.

blowback—*(DOD, NATO, IADB)* 1. Escape, to the rear and under pressure, of gases formed during the firing of the weapon. Blowback may be caused by a defective breech mechanism, a ruptured cartridge case or a faulty primer. 2. Type of weapon operation in which the force of expanding gases acting to the rear against the face of the bolt furnishes all the energy required to initiate the complete cycle of operation. A weapon which employs this method of operation is characterized by the absence of any breech-lock or bolt-lock mechanism.

blue commander—*(DOD, NATO)* The officer designated to exercise operational control over blue forces for a specific period during an exercise.

blue forces—*(NATO)* Those forces used in a friendly role during NATO exercises. See also **force(s)**.

blue key—*(NATO)* A blue image on any medium which is not reproduced when the superimposed work is reproduced, used as a guide for scribing or drawing.

boat diagram—*(DOD, IADB)* In the assault phase of an amphibious operation, a diagram showing the positions of individuals and equipment in each boat.

boat group—*(DOD, IADB)* The basic organization of landing craft. One boat group is organized for each battalion landing team (or equivalent) to be landed in the first trip of landing craft or amphibious vehicles.

boat lane—*(DOD, NATO, IADB)* A lane for amphibious assault landing craft, which extends seawards from the landing beaches to the line of departure. The width of a boat lane is determined by the length of the corresponding beach.

boat space—*(DOD, IADB)* The space and weight factor used to determine the capacity of boats, landing craft, and amphibious vehicles. With respect to landing craft and amphibious vehicles, it is based on the requirements of one person with individual equipment. The person is assumed to weigh 224 pounds and to occupy 13.5 cubic feet of space. See also **man space**.

boattail—*(DOD, NATO, IADB)* The conical section of a ballistic body that progressively decreases in diameter toward the tail to reduce overall aerodynamic drag.

boat wave—See **wave**.

body of a map or chart—*(NATO)* That area of a map or chart contained within the neatlines.

bogey—*(DOD, IADB)* An air contact which is unidentified but assumed to be enemy. (Not to be confused with **unknown**.) See also **friendly**; **hostile**.

bomb damage assessment—*(DOD, IADB)* The determination of the effect of all air attacks on targets (e.g., bombs, rockets, or strafing).

bomb disposal unit—See **explosive ordnance disposal unit**.

bomber—See **intermediate-range bomber aircraft**; **long-range bomber aircraft**; **medium-range bomber aircraft**.

bomb impact plot—*(DOD, IADB)* A graphic representation of the target area, usually a prestrike air photograph, on which prominent dots are plotted to mark the impact or detonation points of bombs dropped on a specific bombing attack.

bombing angle—*(DOD, NATO)* The angle between the vertical and a line joining the aircraft to what would be the point of impact of a bomb released from it at that instant.

bombing errors—*(NATO, IADB)*
1. **50 percent Circular Error**—The radius of a circle, with the center at a desired mean point of impact, which contains half the missiles independently aimed to hit the desired mean point of impact.
2. **50 percent Deflection Error**—Half the distance between two lines, drawn parallel to the aircraft's track and equidistant from the desired mean point of impact, which contains half the missiles independently aimed to hit the desired mean point of impact.
3. **50 percent Range Error**—Half the distance between two lines drawn perpendicular to the aircraft's track equidistant from the desired mean point of impact, which contains half the missiles independently aimed to hit the desired mean point of

impact. (Note: Above errors should imply overall errors unless otherwise stipulated by inclusion of the word "Random" or "Systematic" as necessary.)

bombing height—*(DOD, NATO)* In air operations, the height above ground level at which the aircraft is flying at the moment of ordnance release. Bombing heights are classified as follows:

very low:	below 100 feet;
low:	from 100 to 2,000 feet;
medium:	from 2,000 to 10,000 feet;
high:	from 10,000 to 50,000 feet;
very high:	50,000 feet and above.

bombing height—*(IADB)* Distance above a target at the moment of bomb release, measured vertically from the target to the level of the bombing aircraft.

bombing run—*(DOD, NATO)* In air bombing, that part of the flight that begins, normally from an initial point, with the approach to the target, includes target acquisition, and ends normally at the weapon release point.

bomb line—See **fire support coordination line.**

bomb release line—*(DOD, NATO, IADB)* An imaginary line around a defended area or objective over which an aircraft should release its bomb in order to obtain a hit or hits on an area or objective.

bomb release point—*(DOD, NATO, IADB)* The point in space at which bombs must be released to reach the desired point of detonation.

bomb sighting systems—*(NATO)* **1. vector sights**—Sighting systems using the vector principle and incorporating a mechanical representation of the vectors of the bombing triangle. **a. pre-set vector**—A sighting system in which the values for height, airspeed and wind are set manually on the bomb sight.

b. continuously set vector—A sighting system in which the values for height, airspeed and drift are automatically and continuously updated. **2. tachometric or synchronous sights**—Sighting systems which automatically release the bomb at the correct bombing angle by maintaining the sight line on the target, thus determining the speed relative to the target and in some cases the track through the target. **3. angular velocity sight**—A sighting system in which the correct release point is determined when the angular velocity of the target relative to the bomb aimer reaches a precomputed value.

bonding—*(DOD, NATO)* In electrical engineering, the process of connecting together metal parts so that they make low resistance electrical contact for direct current and lower frequency alternating currents. See also **earthing; grounding.**

booby trap—*(DOD, NATO, IADB)* An explosive or nonexplosive device or other material, deliberately placed to cause casualties when an apparently harmless object is disturbed or a normally safe act is performed.

booster—*(DOD, NATO, IADB)* **1.** A high-explosive element sufficiently sensitive so as to be actuated by small explosive elements in a fuze or primer and powerful enough to cause detonation of the main explosive filling. **2.** An auxiliary or initial propulsion system which travels with a missile or aircraft and which may or may not separate from the parent craft when its impulse has been delivered. A booster system may contain, or consist of, one or more units.

boost phase—*(DOD)* That portion of the flight of a ballistic missile or space vehicle during which the booster and sustainer engines operate. See also **midcourse phase; reentry phase; terminal phase.**

border—*(DOD, NATO)* In cartography, the area of a map or chart lying between the neatline and the surrounding framework.

border break—*(DOD, NATO)* A cartographic technique used when it is required to extend a portion of the cartographic detail of a map or chart beyond the sheetlines into the margin.

border crosser—*(DOD, NATO, IADB)* An individual, living close to a frontier, who normally has to cross the frontier frequently for legitimate purposes.

boresafe fuze—*(DOD, NATO, IADB)* Type of fuze having an interrupter in the explosive train that prevents a projectile from exploding until after it has cleared the muzzle of a weapon. See also **fuze.**

bottom mine—*(DOD, NATO)* A mine with negative buoyancy which remains on the seabed. Also called a **ground mine.** See also **mine.**

bottom sweep—*(NATO)* A sweep, either wire or chain, used either to sweep mines close to the bottom or to remove mines from a channel by dragging.

bound—*(DOD, NATO)* 1. In land warfare, a single movement, usually from cover to cover, made by troops, often under enemy fire. *(DOD)* 2. Distance covered in one movement by a unit that is advancing by bounds.

boundary—*(DOD, NATO)* In land warfare, a line by which areas of responsibility between adjacent units/formations are defined.

boundary (de facto)—*(NATO, IADB)* An international or administrative boundary whose existence and legality is not recognized but which is a practical division between separate national and provincial administering authorities.

boundary (de jure)—*(NATO, IADB)* An international or administrative boundary whose existence and legality is recognized.

boundary disclaimer—*(NATO, IADB)* A statement on a map or chart that the status and/or alignment of international or administrative boundaries is not necessarily recognized by the government of the publishing nation.

bouquet mine—*(DOD, NATO)* In naval mine warfare, a mine in which a number of buoyant mine cases are attached to the same sinker, so that when the mooring of one mine case is cut, another mine rises from the sinker to its set depth. See also **mine.**

BQM-34—See **Firebee.**

bracketing—*(DOD, NATO, IADB)* A method of adjusting fire in which a bracket is established by obtaining an over and a short along the spotting line, and then successively splitting the bracket in half until a target hit or desired bracket is obtained.

branch—*(DOD, IADB)* 1. A subdivision of any organization. 2. A geographically separate unit of an activity which performs all or part of the primary functions of the parent activity on a smaller scale. Unlike an annex, a branch is not merely an overflow addition. *(DOD)* 3. An arm or service of the Army.

breaching—*(IADB)* The employment of any available means to secure a passage through an enemy minefield or fortification.

breakaway—*(DOD, NATO)* 1. The onset of a condition in which the shock front moves away from the exterior of the expanding fireball produced by the explosion of a nuclear weapon. *(DOD)* 2. After completion of attack, turn to heading as directed.

break off—*(DOD)* In close air support, a command utilized to immediately terminate an attack.

breakoff position—*(DOD, NATO)* The position at which a leaver or leaver section breaks off from the main convoy to proceed to a different destination.

break-up—*(DOD, NATO)* **1.** In detection by radar, the separation of one solid return into a number of individual returns which correspond to the various objects or structure groupings. This separation is contingent upon a number of factors including range, beam width, gain setting, object size and distance between objects. **2.** In imagery interpretation, the result of magnification or enlargement which causes the imaged item to lose its identity and the resultant presentation to become a random series of tonal impressions.

brevity code—*(DOD, NATO, IADB)* A code which provides no security but which has as its sole purpose the shortening of messages rather than the concealment of their content.

bridgehead—*(DOD, IADB)* An area of ground held or to be gained on the enemy's side of an obstacle. See also **airhead; beachhead.**

bridgehead—*(NATO)* An area of ground, in a territory occupied or threatened by the enemy, which must be held or at least controlled, so as to permit the continuous embarkation, landing or crossing of troops and materiel, and/or to provide maneuver space requisite for subsequent operations. See also **airhead; beachhead.**

bridgehead line—*(DOD, NATO, IADB)* The limit of the objective area in the development of the bridgehead. See also **objective area.**

briefing—*(DOD, NATO, IADB)* The act of giving in advance specific instructions or information.

brigade—*(DOD, IADB)* A unit usually smaller than a division to which are attached groups and/or battalions and smaller units tailored to meet anticipated requirements.

broadcast-controlled air interception—*(DOD, NATO, IADB)* An interception in which the interceptor is given a continuous broadcast of information concerning an enemy raid and effects interception without further control. See also **air interception; close-controlled air interception.**

Bronco—*(DOD)* A light, twin turboprop, twin-seat observation and support aircraft. May be equipped with machine guns and light ordnance for close air support missions. Designated as OV-10.

buffer distance (nuclear)—*(DOD, NATO, IADB)* **1.** The horizontal distance which, when added to the radius of safety, will give the desired assurance that the specified degree of risk will not be exceeded. The buffer distance is normally expressed quantitatively in multiples of the delivery error. **2.** The vertical distance which is added to the fallout safe-height of burst in order to determine a desired height of burst which will provide the desired assurance that militarily significant fallout will not occur. It is normally expressed quantitatively in multiples of the vertical error.

bug—*(DOD, IADB)* **1.** A concealed microphone or listening device or other audiosurveillance device. **2.** To install means for audiosurveillance.

bugged—*(DOD)* Room or object which contains a concealed listening device.

buildup—*(DOD, NATO, IADB)* The process of attaining prescribed strength of units and prescribed levels of vehicles, equipment, stores and supplies. Also may be applied to the means of accomplishing this process.

bulk cargo—*(DOD, IADB)* That which is generally shipped in volume where the transportation conveyance is the only external container; such as liquids, ore, or grain.

bulk petroleum product—*(DOD, NATO)* A liquid petroleum product transported by various means and stored in tanks or containers having an individual fill capacity greater than 250 liters.

bulk petroleum product—*(IADB)* Liquid petroleum product which is normally transported by pipeline, rail tank car, road tank truck, road tank trailer, barge, harbor or coastal tanker, and ocean-going tanker and stored in a tank or container having a fill capacity greater than 55 US gallons (45 Imperial gallons or 250 liters).

bulk storage—*(DOD, IADB)* 1. Storage in a warehouse of supplies and equipment in large quantities, usually in original containers, as distinguished from bin storage. 2. Storage of liquids, such as petroleum products in tanks, as distinguished from drum or packaged storage. See also **bin storage; storage.**

burial—See **emergency burial; group burial; trench burial.** See also **graves registration.**

burn—*(DOD)* 1. Deliberately expose the true status of a person under cover. 2. The legitimate destruction and burning of classified material, usually accomplished by the custodian as prescribed in regulations.

burned—*(DOD)* Used to indicate that a clandestine operator has been exposed to the operation (especially in a surveillance) or that reliability as a source of information has been compromised.

burn notice—*(DOD)* An official statement by one intelligence agency to other agencies, domestic or foreign, that an individual or group is unreliable for any of a variety of reasons.

burnout—*(DOD, NATO, IADB)* The point in time or in the missile trajectory when combustion of fuels in the rocket engine is terminated by other than programmed cutoff.

burnout velocity—*(DOD, NATO, IADB)* The velocity attained by a missile at the point of burnout.

burn-through range—*(DOD, IADB)* The distance at which a specific radar can discern targets through the external interference being received.

buster—*(DOD)* In air intercept, a code meaning, "Fly at maximal continuous speed (or power)."

C

C3-protection—See **command, control, and communications countermeasures.**

C-5A—See **Galaxy.**

C-123—See **Provider.**

C-130—See **Hercules.**

C-140—See **Jet Star.**

C-141—See **Starlifter.**

cabin pressure altimeter—*(DOD, NATO)* See **altimeter.**

calibrated airspeed—*(NATO)* Indicated airspeed corrected for instrument and installation errors. Also called **rectified airspeed.** See also **airspeed.**

calibrated altitude—*(NATO)* Indicated altitude corrected for instrument and installation errors. See also **altitude.**

calibrated focal length—*(DOD, NATO)* An adjusted value of the equivalent focal length, so computed as to equalize the positive and negative values of distortion over the entire field used in a camera. See also **focal length.**

call fire—*(DOD, IADB)* Fire delivered on a specific target in response to a request from the supported unit. See also **fire.**

call for fire—*(DOD, NATO, IADB)* A request for fire containing data necessary for obtaining the required fire on a target.

call mission—*(DOD, NATO, IADB)* A type of air support mission which is not requested sufficiently in advance of the desired time of execution to permit detailed planning and briefing of pilots prior to take-off. Aircraft scheduled for this type of mission are on air, ground, or carrier alert, and are armed with a prescribed load.

call sign—*(DOD, NATO, IADB)* Any combination of characters or pronounceable words, which identifies a communication facility, a command, an authority, an activity, or a unit; used primarily for establishing and maintaining communications. See also **collective call sign; indefinite call sign; international call sign; net call sign; tactical call sign; visual call sign; voice call sign.**

camera axis—*(DOD, NATO, IADB)* An imaginary line through the optical center of the lens perpendicular to the negative photo plane.

camera axis direction—*(DOD, NATO)* Direction on the horizontal plane of the optical axis of the camera at the time of exposure. This direction is defined by its azimuth expressed in degrees in relation to true/magnetic north.

camera calibration—*(DOD, NATO, IADB)* The determination of the calibrated focal length, the location of the principal point with respect to the fiducial marks and the lens distortion effective in the focal plane of the camera referred to the particular calibrated focal length.

camera cycling rate—*(DOD, NATO)* The frequency with which camera frames are exposed, expressed as cycles per second.

camera magazine—*(NATO)* A removable part of a camera in which the unexposed and exposed portions of film are contained.

camera nadir—See **photo nadir.**

camera station (photogrammetry)—See **air station (photogrammetry).**

camera window—*(NATO)* A window in the camera compartment through which photographs are taken.

camouflage—*(DOD, IADB)* The use of concealment and disguise to minimize the possibility of detection and/or identification of troops, materiel, equipment and installations. It includes taking advantage of the natural environment as well as the application of natural and artificial materials. See also **concealment; cover.**

camouflage detection photography—*(DOD, NATO)* Photography utilizing a special type of film (usually infrared) designed for the detection of camouflage. See also **false color film.**

camouflet—*(DOD, NATO)* The resulting cavity in a deep underground burst when there is no rupture of the surface. See also **crater.**

camp—*(DOD, IADB)* A group of tents, huts, or other shelter set up temporarily for troops, and more permanent than a bivouac. A military post, temporary or permanent, may be called a camp.

campaign plan—*(DOD, IADB)* A plan for a series of related military operations aimed to accomplish a common objective, normally within a given time and space.

canalize—*(DOD)* To restrict operations to a narrow zone by use of existing or reinforcing obstacles or by fire or bombing.

Canberra—*(DOD, IADB)* A twin-jet, all-weather electronics intelligence aircraft. Designated as B–57. RB–57 is the reconnaissance version.

cancel—*(DOD, NATO)* In artillery and naval gunfire support, the term, cancel, when coupled with a previous order, other than an order for a quantity or type of ammunition, rescinds that order.

cancel check firing—*(DOD)* The order to rescind **check firing.**

cancel converge—*(DOD)* The command used to rescind **converge.**

cannibalize—*(DOD, NATO, IADB)* To remove serviceable parts from one item of equipment in order to install them on another item of equipment.

cannot observe—*(DOD, NATO)* A type of fire control which indicates that the observer or spotter will be unable to adjust fire, but believes a target exists at the given location and is of sufficient importance to justify firing upon it without adjustment or observation.

capability—*(DOD, IADB)* The ability to execute a specified course of action. (A capability may or may not be accompanied by an intention.)

capacity load (Navy)—*(DOD, IADB)* The maximum quantity of all supplies (ammunition, petroleum, oils, and lubricants, rations, general stores, maintenance stores, etc.) which each vessel can carry in proportions prescribed by proper authority. See also **combat load (air); wartime load.**

capsule—*(DOD, NATO, IADB)* 1. A sealed, pressurized cabin for extremely high altitude or space flight which provides an acceptable environment for man, animal or equipment. 2. An ejectable sealed cabin having automatic devices for safe return of the occupants to the surface.

captive firing—*(DOD, NATO)* A firing test of short duration, conducted with the missile propulsion system operating while secured to a test stand.

cardinal point effect—*(DOD, NATO, IADB)* The increased intensity of a line or group of returns on the radarscope occurring when the radar beam is perpendicular to the rectangular surface of a line or group of similarly aligned features in the ground pattern.

caretaker status—*(DOD, IADB)* A nonoperating condition in which the installations, materiel, and facilities are in a care and limited preservation status. Only a minimum of personnel is required to safeguard against fire, theft, and damage from the elements.

cargo—*(NATO)* Commodities and supplies in transit.
  a. **air cargo**—Stores, equipment or vehicles, which do not form part of the aircraft, and are either part or all of its payload.
  b. **dangerous cargo**—Cargo which, because of its dangerous properties, is subject to special regulations for its transport.
  c. **restricted air cargo**—Cargo which does not belong to the dangerous cargo category, but which requires, for air transport, extra precaution in packing and handling.
  d. **immediately vital cargo**—A cargo already loaded which the consignee country regards as immediately vital for the prosecution of the war or for national survival, notwithstanding the risk to the ship. If the cargo is carried in a ship of another nation, then that nation must agree to the delivery of the cargo. The use of this term is limited to the period of implementation of the shipping movement policy.
  e. **essential cargo**—See **essential supply**.
  f. **valuable cargo**—Cargo which may be of value during a later stage of the war.
  g. **wanted cargo**—In naval control of shipping, a cargo which is not immediately required by the consignee country but will be needed later.
  h. **unwanted cargo**—A cargo loaded in peacetime which is not required by the consignee country in wartime.

See also **loading; chemical ammunition cargo; flatted cargo; general cargo; heavy-lift cargo; high explosive cargo; inflammable cargo; perishable cargo; special cargo; troop space cargo; vehicle cargo.**

cargo carrier—*(DOD)* Highly mobile, air transportable, unarmored, full-tracked cargo and logistic carrier capable of swimming inland waterways and accompanying and resupplying self-propelled artillery weapons. Designated as M548.

cargo classification (combat loading)—*(DOD, IADB)* The division of military cargo into categories for combat loading aboard ships. See also **cargo.**

cargo outturn message—*(DOD, IADB)* A brief message report transmitted within 48 hours of completion of ship discharge to advise both the Military Sealift Command and the terminal of loading of the condition of the cargo, including any discrepancies in the form of overages, shortages, or damages between cargo as manifested and cargo as checked at time of discharge.

cargo outturn report—*(DOD, IADB)* A detailed report prepared by a discharging terminal to record discrepancies in the form of over, short, and damaged cargo as manifested, and cargo checked at a time and place of discharge from ship.

cargo sling—*(DOD, NATO, IADB)* A strap, chain, or other material used to hold cargo items securely which are to be hoisted, lowered, or suspended.

cargo tie-down point—*(DOD, IADB)* A point on military materiel designed for attachment of various means for securing the item for transport.

cargo transporter—*(DOD, IADB)* A reusable metal shipping container designed for worldwide surface and air movement of suitable military supplies and equipment through the cargo transporter service.

carpet bombing—*(DOD, NATO, IADB)* The progressive distribution of a mass bomb load upon an area defined by designated boundaries, in such manner as to inflict damage to all portions thereof.

carriage—See **gun carriage.**

carrier air group—*(DOD, NATO, IADB)* Two or more aircraft squadrons formed under one commander for administrative and tactical control of operations from a carrier.

carrier striking force—*(DOD, NATO, IADB)* A naval task force composed of aircraft carriers and supporting combatant ships capable of conducting strike operations.

cartesian coordinates—*(NATO, IADB)* A coordinate system in which locations of points in space are expressed by reference to three mutually perpendicular planes, called coordinate planes. The three planes intersect in three straight lines called coordinate axes. See also **coordinates.**

cascade image intensifier—*(NATO)* An opto-electronic amplifier capable of increasing the intensity of a radiant image by two or more stages.

case—*(DOD, IADB)* 1. An intelligence operation in its entirety. 2. Record of the development of an intelligence operation, including personnel, modus operandi, and objectives.

cassette—*(NATO)* In photography, a reloadable container for either unexposed or exposed sensitized materials which may be removed from the camera or darkroom equipment under lightened conditions.

casual—See **transient.**

casualty—*(DOD, IADB)* Any person who is lost to the organization by reason of having been declared dead, wounded, injured, diseased, interned, captured, retained, missing, missing in action, beleaguered, besieged or detained; See also **battle casualty; non-battle casualty; wounded.**

casualty staging unit—See **aeromedical staging unit.**

catalytic attack—*(DOD, IADB)* An attack designed to bring about a war between major powers through the disguised machinations of a third power.

catalytic war—*(DOD)* Not to be used. See **catalytic attack.**

catapult—*(DOD, NATO, IADB)* A structure which provides an auxiliary source of thrust to a missile or aircraft; must combine the functions of directing and accelerating the missile during its travel on the catapult; serves the same functions for a missile as does a gun tube for a shell.

caution area—*(NATO)* An airspace of defined dimensions within which restrictions to the flight of aircraft may exist at specified times. See also **area.**

CAVU—*(DOD, IADB)* Ceiling and visibility unlimited.

C-day—*(DOD, IADB)* The unnamed day on which a deployment operation commences or is to commence. The deployment may be movement of troops, cargo, weapon systems, or a combination of these elements utilizing any or all types of transport. The letter "C" will be the only one used to denote the above. The highest command or headquarters responsible for coordinating the planning will specify the exact meaning of C-day within the aforementioned definition. The command or headquarters directly responsible for the execution of the operation, if other than the one coordinating the planning, will do so in light of the meaning specified by the highest command or headquarters coordinating the planning. See also *(DOD)* **S-day, wartime manpower planning system;** *(NATO)* **designation of days and hours.**

cease engagement—*(DOD, NATO)* In air defense, a fire control order used to direct units to stop the firing sequence against a designated target. Guided missiles already in flight will continue to intercept. See also **engage; hold fire.**

cease engagement—*(IADB)* A command that weapons will disengage a particular target or targets and prepare to engage another target. Missiles in flight will continue to intercept. The order terminates engagement on a particular target.

cease fire—*(DOD, IADB)* A command given to air defense artillery units to refrain from firing on, but to continue to track, an airborne object. Missiles already in flight will be permitted to continue to intercept.

cease loading—*(DOD, NATO)* In artillery and naval gunfire support, the command used during firing of two or more rounds to indicate the suspension of inserting rounds into the weapon.

ceiling—*(DOD, IADB)* The height above the earth's surface of the lowest layer of clouds or obscuration phenomena that is reported as "broken," "overcast," or "obscured" and not classified as "thin" or "partial."

celestial guidance—*(DOD, IADB)* The guidance of a missile or other vehicle by reference to celestial bodies. See also **guidance.**

celestial sphere—*(DOD, NATO)* An imaginary sphere of infinite radius concentric with the earth, on which all celestial bodies except the earth are imagined to be projected.

cell—*(DOD)* Small group of individuals who work together for clandestine or subversive purposes.

cell system—See **net, chain, cell system.**

censorship—See **armed forces censorship; civil censorship; field press censorship; military censorship; national censorship; primary censorship; prisoner of war censorship; secondary censorship.**

center of burst—See **mean point of impact.**

center of gravity limits—*(NATO, IADB)* The limits within which an aircraft's center of gravity must lie to insure safe flight. The center of gravity of the loaded aircraft must be within these limits at take-off, in the air, and on landing. In some cases, take-off and landing limits may also be specified.

central air data computer—*(DOD, NATO)* A device which computes altitude, vertical speed, air speed and mach number from inputs of pitot and static pressure and temperature.

central analysis team—*(NATO)* A team composed of representatives from two or more Major NATO Commanders, responsible jointly to their superiors for the detailed analysis and reporting of a large-scale NATO exercise.

central analysis team—*(IADB)* A team composed of representatives from two or more commanders, responsible jointly to their superiors for the detailed analysis and reporting of a large-scale naval exercise. If an analysis is being done by one commander or his subordinate(s), it will be called an analysis staff.

centralized control—*(DOD, NATO, IADB)* In air defense, the control mode whereby a higher echelon makes direct target assignments to fire units. See also **decentralized control.**

centrally managed item—*(DOD)* An item of materiel subject to inventory control point (wholesale level) management.

central planning team—*(NATO)* A team composed of representatives of two or more NATO or national commands, responsible for the production of an exercise operation order in accordance with the exercise specification and/or exercise planning directive.

central planning team—*(IADB)* A team composed of representatives of two or more commanders, responsible jointly to their superiors for the production of the general instructions for the exercise in accordance with the agreed concept. Regional planning groups may be set up prior to the formulation of the central planning team in order to provide the central planning team with information on certain phases of the exercise. If exercise planning is done by a joint command, or by one commander or his subordinate(s), it will be called a planning staff. The central planning team issues "instructions," whereas the planning staffs issue "general exercise orders."

central procurement—*(DOD)* The procurement of material, supplies, or services by an officially designated command or agency with funds

63

specifically provided for such procurement for the benefit and use of the entire component, or, in the case of single managers, for the military departments as a whole.

central war—*(DOD)* Not to be used. See **general war.**

CG—See **guided missile cruiser.**

CGN—See **guided missile cruiser.**

CH-53A—See **Sea Stallion.**

chaff—*(DOD, IADB)* Radar confusion reflectors, which consist of thin, narrow metallic strips of various lengths and frequency responses, used to reflect echoes for confusion purposes. See also **rope; rope-chaff; window.**

chaff—*(NATO)* Strips of frequency-cut metal foil, wire, or metallized glass fiber used to reflect electromagnetic energy, usually dropped from aircraft or expelled from shells or rockets as a radar countermeasure. See also **rope; rope-chaff.**

chain—See **net, chain, cell system.**

chain of command—*(DOD, NATO, IADB)* The succession of commanding officers from a superior to a subordinate through which command is exercised. Also called **command channel.** See also **administrative chain of command; operational chain of command.**

chalk commander—*(NATO, IADB)* The commander of all troops embarked under one chalk number.

chalk number—*(NATO, IADB)* The number given to a complete load and to the transporting carrier.

chalk troops—*(NATO)* A load of troops defined by a particular chalk number. See also **chalk commander; chalk number.**

challenge—*(DOD, NATO, IADB)* Any process carried out by one unit or person with the object of ascertaining the friendly or hostile character or identity of another. See also **countersign; password; reply.**

change of operational control—*(DOD, NATO, IADB)* The date and time (Greenwich Mean Time/Greenwich Civil Time) at which the responsibility for operational control of a force or unit passes from one operational control authority to another.

channel—*(DOD, IADB)* Used in conjunction with a predetermined letter, number, or code word to reference a specific radio frequency.

channel airlift—*(DOD, IADB)* Common-user airlift service provided on a scheduled basis between two points.

Chaparral—*(DOD)* A short-range, low-altitude, surface-to-air, Army air defense artillery system. Designated as **MIM-72.** See also **Sidewinder.**

characteristic actuation probability—*(DOD, NATO)* The average probability of a mine of a given type being actuated by one run of the sweep within the characteristic actuation width.

characteristic actuation width—*(DOD, NATO)* The width of path over which mines can be actuated by a single run of the sweep gear.

characteristic detection probability—*(DOD, NATO)* The ratio of the number of mines detected on a single run to the number of mines which could have been detected within the characteristic detection width.

characteristic detection width—*(DOD, NATO)* The width of path over which mines can be detected on a single run.

characterization (evaluation)—*(DOD)* A biographical sketch of an individual or a statement of the nature and intent of an organization or group.

charge—*(DOD, NATO)* 1. The amount of propellant required for a fixed, semi-fixed, or separate loading projectile, round or shell. It may also refer to the quantity of explosive filling contained in a bomb, mine or the like. 2. In combat engineering, a quantity of explosive, prepared for demolition purposes.

charged demolition target—*(DOD, NATO, IADB)* A target on which all charges have been placed and which is in one of the states of readiness, i.e., safe or armed. See also **demolition target.**

charging point—*(NATO, IADB)* A connection on an aircraft, or aircraft component, through which the aircraft or aircraft component can be replenished with a specific commodity, e.g., oxygen, air or hydraulic fluid, etc.

chart base—*(DOD, NATO)* A chart used as a primary source for compilation or as a framework on which new detail is printed. Also called "topographic" base. See also **base map.**

chart index—See **map index.**

chart location of the battery—See **battery center.**

chart series—See **map; map series.**

chart sheet—See **map; map sheet.**

check firing—*(DOD, NATO)* In artillery and naval gunfire support, a command to cause a temporary halt in firing.

checkout—*(DOD, NATO, IADB)* A sequence of functional, operational, and calibrational tests to determine the condition and status of a weapon system or element thereof.

checkpoint—*(DOD, NATO, IADB)* 1. A predetermined point on the surface of the earth used as a means of controlling movement, a registration target for fire adjustment, or reference for location. 2. Center of impact; a burst center. 3. Geographical location on land or water above which the position of an aircraft in flight may be determined by observation or by electrical means. 4. A place where military police check vehicular or pedestrian traffic in order to enforce circulation control measures and other laws, orders and regulations.

check port/starboard—*(DOD, IADB)* In air intercept, a term meaning, "Alter heading _____ degrees to port/starboard momentarily for airborne radar search and then resume heading."

check sweeping—*(DOD, NATO)* In naval mine warfare, sweeping to check that no moored mines are left after a previous clearing operation.

chemical agent—*(DOD, NATO, IADB)* A chemical substance which is intended for use in military operations to kill, seriously injure, or incapacitate man through its physiological effects. Excluded from consideration are riot control agents, herbicides, smoke and flame. See also **biological agent.**

chemical agent cumulative action—*(DOD, IADB)* The building up, within the human body, of small ineffective doses of certain chemical agents to a point where eventual effect is similar to one large dose.

chemical ammunition—*(DOD, NATO, IADB)* A type of ammunition, the filler of which is primarily a chemical agent. See also **cargo.**

chemical ammunition cargo—*(DOD, IADB)* Cargo, such as white phosphorous munitions (shell and grenades). See also **cargo.**

chemical, biological, and radiological operation—*(DOD, NATO, IADB)* A collective term used only when referring to a combined chemical, biological, and radiological operation.

chemical defense—*(DOD, NATO, IADB)* The methods, plans and procedures involved in establishing and executing defensive measures against attack utilizing chemical agents. See also **NBC defense.**

chemical horn—*(DOD, NATO)* In naval mine warfare, a mine horn containing an electric battery, the electrolyte for which is in a glass tube protected by a thin metal sheet. Also called Hertz Horn.

chemical mine—*(NATO)* A mine containing a chemical agent designed to kill, injure, or incapacitate personnel or to contaminate materiel or terrain.

chemical operations—*(DOD, NATO, IADB)* Employment of chemical agents to kill, injure, or incapacitate for a significant period of time, man or animals, and deny or hinder the use of areas, facilities or material; or defense against such employment.

chemical survey—*(DOD, NATO)* The directed effort to determine the nature and degree of chemical hazard in an area and to delineate the perimeter of the hazard area.

chemical warfare—*(DOD)* All aspects of military operations involving the employment of lethal and incapacitating munitions/agents and the warning and protective measures associated with such offensive operations. Since riot control agents and herbicides are not considered to be chemical warfare agents, those two items will be referred to separately or under the broader term "chemical," which will be used to include all types of chemical munitions/agents collectively. The term "chemical warfare weapons" may be used when it is desired to reflect both lethal and incapacitating munitions/agents of either chemical or biological origin. Also called **CW**. See also **chemical operations, herbicide, riot control agent.**

chemical warfare agent—See **chemical agent.**

chicks—*(DOD)* Friendly fighter aircraft.

Chief Army, Navy, Air Force, or Marine Corps Censor—*(DOD)* An officer appointed by the commander of the Army, Navy, Air Force, or Marine Corps component of a unified command to supervise all censorship activities of that Service.

chief of staff—*(DOD, IADB)* The senior or principal member or head of a staff, or the principal assistant in a staff capacity to a person in a command capacity; the head or controlling member of a staff, for purposes of the coordination of its work; a position, that in itself is without inherent power of command by reason of assignment, except that which is invested in such a position by delegation to exercise command in another's name. In the Army and Marine Corps, the title is applied only to the staff on a brigade or division level or higher. In lower units, the corresponding title is executive officer. In the Air Force, the title is applied normally in the staff on an Air Force level and above. In the Navy, the title is applied only on the staff of a commander with rank of commodore or above. The corresponding title on the staff of a commander of rank lower than commodore is chief staff officer, and in the organization of a single ship, executive officer.

chop—See **change of operational control.**

chronic dose—*(IADB)* Radiation dose absorbed in circumstances such that biological recovery may have been possible. It is arbitrarily accepted that a chronic dose can only mean absorption occurring after 24 hours following the burst.

chronic radiation dose—*(DOD, NATO)* A dose of ionizing radiation received either continuously or intermittently over a prolonged period of time. A chronic radiation dose may be high enough to cause radiation sickness and death but if received at a low dose rate a significant portion of the acute cellular damage will be repaired. See also **acute radiation dose; radiation dose; radiation dose rate.**

chuffing—*(DOD, NATO)* The characteristic of some rockets to burn intermittently and with an irregular noise.

cipher—*(DOD, IADB)* Any cryptographic system in which arbitrary symbols or groups of symbols, represent units of plain text of regular length, usually single letters, or in which units of plain text are rearranged, or both, in accordance with certain predetermined rules. See also **cryptosystem.**

circuit—*(DOD, IADB)* 1. An electronic path between two or more points, capable of providing a number of channels. 2. A number of conductors connected together for the purpose of carrying an electrical current.

circuitry—*(DOD)* A complex of circuits describing interconnection within or between systems.

circular error probable—*(DOD, IADB)* An indicator of the delivery accuracy of a weapon system, used as a factor in determining probable damage to a target. It is the radius of a circle within which half of a missile's projectiles are expected to fall. Also called **CEP.** See also **delivery error; deviation; dispersion error; horizontal error.**

circular error probable—*(NATO)* An indicator of the accuracy of a missile/projectile, used as a factor in determining probable damage to a target. It is the radius of a circle within which half of the missiles/projectiles are expected to fall. See also **delivery error; deviation; dispersion error; horizontal error.**

cirvis—*(DOD, IADB)* Communications instructions for reporting vital intelligence sightings.

civic action—See **military civic action.**

civil affair—*(NATO)* Any question relating to relations in wartime between the commander of an armed force and the civilian populations and governments in areas where the force is employed, and which is settled on the basis of a mutual agreement, official or otherwise.

civil affairs—*(DOD, IADB)* Those phases of the activities of a commander which embrace the relationship between the military forces and civil authorities and people in a friendly country or area or occupied country or area when military forces are present. Civil affairs include, inter alia: **a.** matters concerning the relationship between military forces located in a country or area and the civil authorities and people of that country or area usually involving performance by the military forces of certain functions or the exercise of certain authority normally the responsibility of the local government. This relationship may occur prior to, during, or subsequent to military action in time of hostilities or other emergency and is normally covered by a treaty or other agreement, expressed or implied; and **b.** military government: the form of administration by which an occupying power exercises executive, legislative, and judicial authority over occupied territory. See also **phases of military government.**

civil affairs agreement—*(DOD, IADB)* An agreement which governs the relationship between allied armed forces located in a friendly country and the civil authorities and people of that country. See also **civil affairs.**

civil censorship—*(DOD, IADB)* Censorship of civilian communications, such as messages, printed matter, and films, entering, leaving, or circulating within, areas or territories occupied or controlled by armed forces. See also **censorship.**

civil damage assessment—*(DOD)* An appraisal of damage to a nation's population, industry, utilities, communications, transportation, food, water, and medical resources, to support planning for national recovery. See also **damage assessment.**

civil defense—*(DOD, IADB)* All those activities and measures designed or undertaken to: 1. minimize the effects upon the civilian population caused or which would be caused by an enemy attack upon the United States; 2. deal with the immediate emergency conditions which would be created by any such attack; and 3. effectuate emergency repairs to, or the emergency restoration of, vital utilities and facilities destroyed or damaged by any such attack.

civil defense—*(NATO)* Mobilization, organization, and direction of the civil population, designed to minimize by passive measures the effects of enemy action against all aspects of civil life.

civil defense emergency—See **domestic emergencies.**

civil defense intelligence—*(DOD, IADB)* The product resulting from the collection and evaluation of information concerning all aspects of the situation in the United States and its territories that are potential or actual targets of any enemy attack including, in the preattack phase, the emergency measures taken and estimates of the civil populations' preparedness. In the event of an actual attack, a description of conditions in the affected area with emphasis on the extent of damage, fallout levels, and casualty and resource estimates. The product is required by civil and military authorities for use in the formulation of decisions, the conduct of operations, and the continuation of the planning processes.

civil disturbance—*(DOD, NATO, IADB)* Group acts of violence and disorder prejudicial to public law and order.

civil disturbance readiness conditions—*(DOD)* Required conditions of preparedness to be attained by military forces in preparation for deployment to an objective area in response to an actual or threatened civil disturbance.

civil disturbances—See **domestic emergencies.**

civilian internee—*(DOD)* 1. A civilian who is interned during armed conflict or occupation for security reasons or for protection or because he has committed an offense against the detaining power. 2. A term used to refer to persons interned and protected in accordance with the Geneva Convention relative to the Protection of Civilian Persons in Time of War, 12 August 1949 (Geneva Convention). See also **Prisoner of War.**

civilian internee camp—*(DOD)* An installation established for the internment and administration of civilian internees.

civilian preparedness for war—*(NATO, IADB)* All measures and means taken in peacetime, by national and allied agencies, to enable a nation to survive an enemy attack and to contribute more effectively to the common war effort.

civil military cooperation—*(NATO)* All actions and measures undertaken between NATO commanders and national authorities, military or civil, in peace or war, which concern the relationship between allied armed forces and the government, civil population, or agencies in the areas where such forces are stationed, supported or employed.

civil military relations (in non-NATO countries)—*(NATO)* All activities undertaken by NATO commanders in war directly concerned with the relationship between allied armed forces and the government, civil population, or agencies of non-NATO countries where such armed forces are stationed, supported or employed.

civil nuclear power—*(DOD, IADB)* A nation which has potential to employ nuclear technology for development of nuclear weapons but has deliberately decided against doing so. See also **nuclear power.**

civil requirements—*(DOD, IADB)* The computed production and distribution of all types of services, supplies, and equipment during periods of armed conflict or occupation to insure the productive efficiency of the civilian economy and to provide civilians the treatment and protection to which they are entitled under customary and conventional international law.

civil reserve air fleet—*(DOD, IADB)* A group of commercial aircraft with crews which is allocated in time of emergency for exclusive military use in both international and domestic service.

civil transportation—*(DOD, IADB)* The movement of persons, property, or mail by civil facilities, and the resources (including storage, except that for agricultural and petroleum products) necessary to accomplish the movement. (Excludes transportation operated or controlled by the military, and petroleum and gas pipelines.)

civil twilight—See **twilight.**

clandestine operation—*(DOD, I, IADB)* An activity to accomplish intelligence, counterintelligence, and other similar activities sponsored or conducted by governmental departments or agencies, in such a way as to assure secrecy or concealment. *(DOD, I)* (It differs from covert operations in that emphasis is placed on concealment of the operation rather than on concealment of identity of sponsor.)

clandestine operation—*(NATO)* An activity to accomplish intelligence, counterintelligence, and other similar activities sponsored or conducted in such a way as to assure secrecy or concealment.

clara—*(DOD)* In air intercept, a code meaning, "Radar scope is clear of contacts other than those known to be friendly."

classification—*(DOD, IADB)* The determination that official information requires, in the interests of national security, a specific degree of protection against unauthorized disclosure, coupled with a designation signifying that such a determination has been made. See also **security classification.**

classification of bridges and vehicles—See **military load classification.**

classified contract—*(DOD)* Any contract that requires or will require access to classified information by the contractor or the employees in the performance of the contract. (A contract may be classified even though the contract document itself is not classified.)

classified information—*(DOD, IADB)* Official information which has been determined to require, in the interests of national security, protection against unauthorized disclosure and which has been so designated.

classified matter—*(DOD, NATO, IADB)* Official information or matter in any form or of any nature which requires protection in the interests of national security. See also **unclassified matter.**

clean aircraft—*(DOD, IADB)* 1. An aircraft in flight configuration, versus landing configuration, i.e., landing gear and flaps retracted etc. 2. An aircraft that does not have external stores.

cleansing station—See **decontamination station.**

clear—*(DOD)* 1. To approve or authorize, or to obtain approval or authorization for: **a.** a person or persons with regard to their actions, movements, duties, etc.; **b.** an object or group of objects, as equipment or supplies, with regard to quality, quantity, purpose, movement, disposition, etc.; and **c.** a request, with regard to correctness of form, validity, etc. 2. To give one or more aircraft a clearance. 3. To give a person a security clearance. 4. To fly over an obstacle without touching it. 5. To pass a designated point, line, or object. The end of a column must pass the designated feature before the latter is cleared. 6. **a.** To operate a gun so as to unload it or make certain no ammunition remains; and **b.** to free a gun of stoppages. 7. To clear an engine; to open the throttle of an idling engine to free it from carbon. 8. To clear the air to gain either temporary or permanent air superiority or control in a given sector.

clearance capacity—*(DOD, IADB)* An estimate expressed in terms of measurement or weight tons per day of the cargo that may be transported inland from a beach or port over the available means of inland communication, including roads, railroads, and inland waterways. The estimate is based on an evaluation of the physical characteristics of the transportation facilities in the area. See also **beach capacity; port capacity.**

clearance diving—*(DOD, NATO)* The process involving the use of divers for locating, identifying and disposing of mines.

clearance rate—*(DOD, NATO)* The area which would be cleared per unit time with a stated minimum percentage clearance, using specific minehunting and/or minesweeping procedures.

clearing operation—*(DOD, NATO)* An operation designed to clear all mines from a route or area.

clearway—*(DOD, NATO)* A defined rectangular area on the ground or water at the end of a runway in the direction of take-off and under control of the competent authority, selected or prepared as a suitable area over which an aircraft may make a portion of its initial climb to a specified height.

clear weather air defense fighter—*(DOD, NATO)* A fighter aircraft with equipment and weapons which enable it to engage airborne targets by day and by night, but in clear weather conditions only.

climb corridor—See **clearway.**

climb mode—*(DOD, NATO)* In a flight control system, a control mode in which aircraft climb is automatically controlled to a predetermined program.

clinic—*(DOD, IADB)* A medical treatment facility primarily intended and appropriately staffed and equipped to provide outpatient medical service for nonhospital type patients. Examination and treatment for emergency cases are types of services rendered. A clinic is also intended to perform certain nontherapeutic activities related to the health of the personnel served, such as physical examinations, immunizations, medical administration, and other preventive medical and sanitary measures necessary to support a primary military mission. A clinic will be equipped with the necessary supporting services to perform the assigned mission. A clinic may be equipped with beds (normally fewer than 25) for observation of patients awaiting transfer to a hospital and for care of cases which cannot be cared for on an outpatient status, but which do not require hospitalization. Patients whose expected duration of illness exceeds 72 hours will not normally occupy clinic beds for periods longer than necessary to arrange transfer to a hospital.

clock code position—*(DOD, IADB)* The position of a target in relation to an aircraft or ship with dead-ahead position considered as 12 o'clock.

close air support—*(DOD, NATO, IADB)* Air action against hostile targets which are in close proximity to friendly forces and which require detailed integration of each air mission with the fire and movement of those forces. See also **air interdiction; air support; immediate mission request; preplanned mission request.**

close air support aircraft—*(DOD)* See **Thunderbolt II.**

close-controlled air interception—*(DOD, NATO, IADB)* An interception in which the interceptor is continuously controlled to a position from which the target is within visual range or radar contact. See also **air interception; broadcast-controlled air-interception.**

closed area—*(DOD, NATO, IADB)* A designated area in or over which passage of any kind is prohibited.

close support—*(DOD, NATO, IADB)* That action of the supporting force against targets or objectives which are sufficiently near the supported force as to require detailed integration or coordination of the supporting action with the fire, movement, or other actions of the supported force. See also **support.**

close supporting fire—*(DOD, NATO, IADB)* Fire placed on enemy troops, weapons, or positions which, because of their proximity present the most immediate and serious threat to the supported unit. See also **supporting fire.**

closure minefield—*(DOD, NATO)* In naval mine warfare, a minefield which is planned to present such a threat that waterborne shipping is prevented from moving.

closure time—*(DOD)* The time at which the last element of a unit has arrived at a specific location.

cloud amount—*(DOD, NATO)* The proportion of sky obscured by cloud, expressed as a fraction of sky covered.

cloud chamber effect—See **condensation cloud.**

cloud cover—*(DOD, NATO)* See **cloud amount.**

cloud top height—*(DOD)* The maximal altitude to which a nuclear mushroom cloud rises.

cluster—*(DOD, NATO, IADB)* **1.** Fireworks signal in which a group of stars burns at the same time. **2.** Group of bombs released together. A cluster usually consists of fragmentation or incendiary bombs. **3.** Two or more parachutes for dropping light or heavy loads. **4.** In land mine warfare, a component of a pattern-laid minefield. It may be antitank, antipersonnel or mixed. It consists of one to five mines and no more than one antitank mine. **5.** Two or more engines coupled together so as to function as one power unit. **6.** In naval mine warfare, a number of mines laid in close proximity to each other as a pattern or coherent unit. They may be of mixed types. **7.** In mine-hunting, designates a group of minelike contacts.

cluster bomb unit—*(DOD, NATO)* An aircraft store composed of a dispenser and submunitions.

clutter—*(DOD, IADB)* Permanent echoes, cloud, or other atmospheric echo on radar scope; as contact has entered scope clutter. See also **radar clutter.**

coarse mine—*(DOD, NATO)* In naval mine warfare, a relatively insensitive influence mine.

coastal convoy—*(DOD, NATO)* A convoy whose voyage lies in general on the continental shelf and in coastal waters.

coastal frontier—*(DOD, IADB)* A geographic division of a coastal area, established for organization and command purposes in order to insure the effective coordination of military forces employed in military operations within the coastal frontier area.

coastal frontier defense—*(DOD)* The organization of the forces and materiel of the armed forces assigned to provide security for the coastal frontiers of the continental United States and its overseas possessions.

coastal frontier defense—*(IADB)* The organization of the forces and materiel of the armed forces assigned to provide security for coastal frontiers.

coastal refraction—*(DOD, NATO, IADB)* The change of the direction of travel of a radio ground wave as it passes from land to sea or from sea to land. Also called **land effect** or **shoreline effect.**

coast-in point—*(DOD)* The point of coastal penetration heading inbound to a target or objective.

coastwise traffic—*(DOD)* Sea traffic between continental United States ports on the Atlantic coast, Gulf coast, and Great Lakes, or between continental United States ports on the Pacific coast.

cocking circuit—*(DOD, NATO)* In mine warfare, a subsidiary circuit which requires actuation before the main circuits become alive.

cocooning—*(NATO, IADB)* The spraying or coating of an aircraft or equipment with a substance, e.g., a plastic, to form a cocoonlike seal against the effects of the atmosphere.

code—*(DOD, IADB)* 1. Any system of communication in which arbitrary groups of symbols represent units of plain text of varying length. Codes may be used for brevity or for security. 2. A cryptosystem in which the cryptographic equivalents (usually called "code groups") typically consisting of letters or digits (or both) in otherwise meaningless combinations are substituted for plain text elements which are primarily words, phrases, or sentences. See also **cryptosystem.**

code word—*(DOD, NATO, IADB)* 1. A word which has been assigned a classification and a classified meaning to safeguard intentions and information regarding a classified plan or operation. 2. A cryptonym used to identify sensitive intelligence data.

cold war—*(DOD, IADB)* A state of international tension wherein political, economic, technological, sociological, psychological, paramilitary, and military measures short of overt armed conflict involving regular military forces are employed to achieve national objectives.

collaborative purchase—*(DOD)* A method of purchase whereby, in buying similar commodities, buyers for two or more departments exchange information concerning planned purchases in order to minimize competition between them for commodities in the same market. See also **purchase.**

collapse depth—*(DOD, NATO)* The design depth, referenced to the axis of the pressure hull, beyond which the hull structure or hull penetrations are presumed to suffer catastrophic failure to the point of total collapse.

collate—*(DOD, IADB)* 1. The grouping together of related items to provide a record of events and facilitate further processing. 2. To compare critically two or more items or documents concerning the same general subject; normally accomplished in the processing phase in the intelligence cycle.

collation—See **intelligence cycle.**

collecting point—*(DOD, IADB)* A point designated for the assembly of personnel casualties, stragglers, disabled materiel, salvage, etc., for further movement to collecting stations or rear installations.

collection—See **intelligence cycle,** Subpart **b.**

collection (acquisition)—*(DOD)* The obtaining of information in any manner, including direct observation, liaison with official agencies, or solicitation from official, unofficial, or public sources.

collection agency—*(DOD)* Any individual, organization, or unit that has access to sources of information and the capability of collecting information from them. See also **agency.**

collection coordination facility line number—*(DOD)* An arbitrary number assigned to contingency intelligence reconnaissance objectives by the Defense Intelligence Agency collection coordination facility to facilitate all-source collection.

collection plan—*(DOD, NATO)* A plan for collecting information from all available sources to meet intelligence requirements and for transforming those requirements into orders and requests to appropriate agencies. See also **information; information requirements; intelligence cycle.**

collection requirement—*(DOD)* An established intelligence need considered in the allocation of intelligence resources to fulfill the essential elements of information and other intelligence needs of a commander.

collective call sign—*(DOD, NATO, IADB)* Any call sign which represents two or more facilities, commands, authorities, or units. The collective call sign for any of these includes the commander thereof and all subordinate commanders therein. See also **call sign.**

collective nuclear, biological and chemical protection—*(DOD, NATO)* Protection provided to a group of individuals in a nuclear, biological and chemical environment which permits relaxation of individual nuclear, biological and chemical protection.

collimating mark—*(NATO)* An index mark, rigidly connected with the camera body, which forms an image on the negative. This image is used to determine the position of the optical center or principal point of the imagery. Also called **fiducial marks.**

collision course interception—*(DOD, IADB)* An interception which is accomplished by the constant heading of both aircraft.

collocation—*(DOD, NATO)* The physical placement of two or more detachments, units, organizations, or facilities at a specifically defined location.

column cover—*(DOD, NATO)* Cover of a column by aircraft in radio contact therewith, providing for its protection by reconnaissance and/or attack of air or ground targets which threaten the column.

column formation—*(DOD, NATO, IADB)* A formation in which elements are placed one behind the other.

column gap—*(DOD, NATO)* The space between two consecutive elements proceeding on the same route. It can be calculated in units of length or in units of time measured from the rear of one element to the front of the following element.

column length—*(DOD, NATO)* The length of the roadway occupied by a column or a convoy in movement. Also called **length of a column.** See also **road space.**

combat air patrol—*(DOD, NATO, IADB)* An aircraft patrol provided over an objective area, over the force protected, over the critical area of a combat zone, or over an air defense area, for the purpose of intercepting and destroying hostile aircraft before they reach their target. See also **airborne alert; barrier combat air patrol; DADCAP; force combat air patrol; patrol; rescue combat air patrol; target combat air patrol.**

combat area—*(DOD, IADB)* A restricted area (air, land, or sea) which is established to prevent or minimize mutual interference between friendly forces engaged in combat operations. See also **combat zone.**

combat available aircraft—*(NATO)* An aircraft capable of fulfilling its normally assigned mission. It will have its primary weapon system serviceable but may require to be fueled, armed or have combat ready crews available.

combat cargo officer—*(DOD, IADB)* An embarkation officer assigned to major amphibious ships or naval staffs, functioning primarily as an adviser to and representative of the naval commander in matters pertaining to embarkation and debarkation of troops and their supplies and equipment. See also **embarkation officer.**

combat chart—*(DOD, NATO)* A special naval chart, at a scale of 1:50,000, designed for naval fire support and close air support during coastal or amphibious operations and showing detailed hydrography and topography in the coastal belt. See also **amphibious chart.**

combat control team—*(DOD, IADB)* A team of Air Force personnel organized, trained, and equipped to establish and operate navigational or terminal guidance aids, communications, and aircraft control facilities within the objective area of an airborne operation.

combat control team—*(NATO)* In air transport operations, a team of specially trained personnel who can be airdropped to provide local air traffic control and to advise on all aspects of landing, airdrop, and/or extraction zone requirements.

combat day of supply—*(NATO)* The total amount of supplies required to support one day of combat, calculated by applying the intensity factor to a standard day of supply. See also **one day's supply**.

combat engineer vehicle, full-tracked 165mm gun—*(DOD)* An armored, tracked vehicle that provides engineer support to other combat elements. Vehicle is equipped with a heavy-duty boom and winch, dozer blade, and 165mm demolition gun. It is also armed with a 7.62mm machine gun and a 50-caliber machine gun.

combat film—*(IADB)* A film exposed to record combat.

combat forces—*(DOD, IADB)* Those forces whose primary missions are to participate in combat. See also **operating forces**.

combat information—*(DOD)* Unevaluated data, gathered by or provided directly to the tactical commander which, due to its highly perishable nature or the criticality of the situation, cannot be processed into tactical intelligence in time to satisfy the user's tactical intelligence requirements. See also **information**.

combat information—*(NATO)* That frequently perishable data gathered in combat by or reported directly to, units which may be immediately used in battle or in assessing the situation. Relevant data will simultaneously enter intelligence reporting channels.

combat information center—*(DOD, NATO, IADB)* The agency in a ship or aircraft manned and equipped to collect, display, evaluate, and disseminate tactical information for the use of the embarked flag officer, commanding officer, and certain control agencies.

Certain control, assistance and coordination functions may be delegated by command to the combat information center. Also called "action information center". See also **air defense control center**.

combat information ship—*(DOD, IADB)* A designated ship charged with the coordination of the intership combat information center functions of the various ships in a task force so that the overall combat information available to commands will increase. This ship is normally the flagship of the task force commander. See also **fighter direction aircraft; fighter direction ship**.

combat intelligence—*(DOD, IADB)* That knowledge of the enemy, weather, and geographical features required by a commander in the planning and conduct of combat operations.

combat intelligence—*(NATO)* That intelligence concerning the enemy, weather, and geographical features required by a commander in the planning and conduct of combat operations. See also **combat information; intelligence; tactical intelligence**.

combat load—*(NATO, IADB)* The total warlike stores carried by an aircraft.

combat loading—*(DOD, NATO, IADB)* The arrangement of personnel and the stowage of equipment and supplies in a manner designed to conform to the anticipated tactical operation of the organization embarked. Each individual item is stowed so that it can be unloaded at the required time. See also **loading**.

combat patrol—*(NATO)* For ground forces, a tactical unit sent out from the main body to engage in independent fighting; detachment assigned to protect the front, flank, or rear of the main body by fighting if necessary. Also called **fighting patrol**. See also **combat air patrol; patrol; reconnaissance patrol**.

combat power—*(DOD, NATO)* The total means of destructive and/or disruptive force which a military unit/formation can apply against the opponent at a given time.

combat readiness—*(DOD, IADB)* Synonymous with **operational readiness**, with respect to missions or functions performed in combat.

combat readiness—*(NATO)* See **combat ready**.

combat ready—*(DOD, IADB)* Synonymous with **operationally ready**, with respect to missions or functions performed in combat.

combat ready—*(NATO)* 1. As applied to organization or equipment: available for combat operations. 2. As applied to personnel: qualified to carry out combat operations in the unit to which they are assigned.

combat ready aircraft—*(NATO)* A combat available aircraft which is fuelled, armed and has a combat ready aircrew available.

combat service support—*(DOD, IADB)* The assistance provided operating forces primarily in the fields of administrative services, chaplain services, civil affairs, finance, legal service, health services, military police, supply, maintenance, transportation, construction, troop construction, acquisition and disposal of real property, facilities engineering, topographic and geodetic engineering functions, food service, graves registration, laundry, dry cleaning, bath, property disposal, and other logistic services.

combat service support—*(NATO)* The support provided to combat forces, primarily in fields of administration and logistics.

combat service support elements—*(DOD, IADB)* Those elements whose primary missions are to provide service support to combat forces and which are a part, or prepared to become a part, of a theater, command, or task force formed for combat operations. See also **operating forces; service troops; troops.**

combat support elements—*(DOD, IADB)* Those elements whose primary missions are to provide combat support to the combat forces and which are a part, or prepared to become a part, of a theater, command, or task force formed for combat operations. See also **operating forces.**

combat support troops—*(DOD, IADB)* Those units or organizations whose primary mission is to furnish operational assistance for the combat elements. See also **troops.**

combat surveillance—*(DOD, IADB)* A continuous, all-weather, day-and-night, systematic watch over the battle area to provide timely information for tactical combat operations.

combat surveillance radar—*(DOD, IADB)* Radar with the normal function of maintaining continuous watch over a combat area.

combat survival—*(DOD, NATO, IADB)* Those measures to be taken by service personnel when involuntarily separated from friendly forces in combat, including procedures relating to individual survival, evasion, escape, and conduct after capture.

combat trail—*(DOD)* Interceptors in trail formation. Each interceptor behind the leader maintains position visually or with airborne radar.

combat troops—*(DOD, IADB)* Those units or organizations whose primary mission is destruction of enemy forces and/or installations. See also **troops.**

combat vehicle—*(DOD, IADB)* A vehicle, with or without armor, designed for a specific fighting function. Armor protection or armament mounted as supplemental equipment on noncombat vehicles will not change the classification of such vehicles to combat vehicles. See also **vehicle.**

combat zone—*(DOD, IADB)* 1. That area required by combat forces for the conduct of operations. 2. The territory forward of the Army rear area boundary. See also **combat area; communications zone.**

combat zone—*(NATO)* 1. That area required by combat forces for the conduct of operations. 2. The territory forward of the army group rear boundary. It is divided into:
  a. **The forward combat zone,** comprising the territory forward of the corps rear boundary.
  b. **The rear combat zone,** usually comprising the territory between the corps rear boundary and the army group rear boundary. See also **communications zone.**

combination circuit—*(DOD, NATO)* In mine warfare, a firing circuit which requires actuation by two or more influences, either simultaneously or at a pre-ordained interval, before the circuit can function. Also called **combined circuit.**

combination firing circuit—*(DOD, NATO)* An assembly comprising two independent firing systems, one non-electric and one electric, so that the firing of either system will detonate all charges. See also **dual-firing circuit.**

combination influence mine—*(DOD, NATO)* A mine designed to actuate only when two or more different influences are received either simultaneously or in a pre-determined order. Also called **combined influence mine.**

combination mission/level of effort-oriented items—*(DOD)* Items for which requirement computations are based on the criteria used for both level of effort-oriented and mission-oriented items.

combined—*(DOD, NATO, IADB)* Between two or more forces or agencies of two or more allies. (When all allies or services are not involved, the participating nations and services shall be identified; e.g., Combined Navies.) See also **joint.**

combined airspeed indicator—*(DOD, NATO)* An instrument which displays both indicated airspeed and mach number.

combined circuit—See **combination circuit.**

combined common user item—*(DOD, NATO, IADB)* An item of an interchangeable nature which is in common use by two or more nations.

combined doctrine—*(DOD)* Fundamental principles that guide the employment of forces of two or more nations in coordinated action toward a common objective. It is ratified by participating nations. See also **joint doctrine, multi-service doctrine.**

combined force—*(DOD, NATO, IADB)* A military force composed of elements of two or more allied nations. See also **force(s).**

combined influence mine—See **combination influence mine.**

combined operation—*(DOD, NATO, IADB)* An operation conducted by forces of two or more allied nations acting together for the accomplishment of a single mission.

combined rescue coordination center—See **rescue coordination center.**

combined staff—*(DOD, NATO, IADB)* A staff composed of personnel of two or more allied nations. See also **integrated staff; joint staff; parallel staff.**

combustor—*(DOD, NATO, IADB)* A name generally assigned to the combination of flame holder or stabilizer, igniter, combustion chamber, and injection system of a ramjet or gas turbine.

command—*(DOD, IADB)* 1. The authority that a commander in the military Service lawfully exercises over subordinates by virtue of rank or assignment. Command includes the authority and responsibility for effectively using available resources and for planning the employment of, organizing, directing, coordinating, and controlling military forces for the accomplishment of assigned missions. It also includes responsibility for health, welfare, morale, and discipline of assigned personnel. 2. An order given by a commander; that is, the will of the commander expressed for the purpose of bringing about a particular action. 3. A unit or units, an organization, or an area under the command of one individual. 4. To dominate by a field of weapon fire or by observation from a superior position. See also **air command; area command; base command.**

command—_(NATO)_ 1. The authority vested in an individual of the armed forces for the direction, coordination, and control of military forces. 2. An order given by a commander; that is, the will of the commander expressed for the purpose of bringing about a particular action. 3. A unit or units, an organization, or an area under the command of one individual. 4. To dominate by a field of weapon fire or by observation from a superior position. See also **area command; base command; full command; national command; operational command.**

command altitude—_(DOD)_ Altitude that must be assumed and/or maintained by the interceptor.

command and control—_(DOD, IADB)_ The exercise of authority and direction by a properly designated commander over assigned forces in the accomplishment of the mission. Command and control functions are performed through an arrangement of personnel, equipment, communications, facilities, and procedures employed by a commander in planning, directing, coordinating, and controlling forces and operations in the accomplishment of the mission.

command and control system—_(DOD, IADB)_ The facilities, equipment, communications, procedures, and personnel essential to a commander for planning, directing, and controlling operations of assigned forces pursuant to the missions assigned.

command axis—_(DOD, NATO, IADB)_ A line along which a headquarters will move.

command center—_(DOD, IADB)_ A facility from which a commander and his representatives direct operations and control forces. It is organized to gather, process, analyze, display, and disseminate planning and operational data and perform other related tasks.

command channel—See **chain of command.**

command, control, and communications countermeasures—_(DOD)_ The integrated use of operations security, military deception, jamming, and physical destruction, supported by intelligence, to deny information to, influence, degrade, or destroy adversary command, control, and communications (C3) capabilities and to protect friendly C3 against such actions. Also called **C3CM.** There are two divisions within C3CM:
   a. **counter-C3.** That division of C3CM comprising measures taken to deny adversary commanders and other decisionmakers the ability to command and control their forces effectively.
   b. **C3-protection.** That division of C3CM comprising measures taken to maintain the effectiveness of friendly C3 despite both adversary and friendly counter-C3 actions.

command, control and information system—_(NATO)_ An integrated system of doctrine, procedures, organizational structure, personnel, equipment, facilities and communications which provides authorities at all levels with timely and adequate data to plan, direct and control their activities.

command controlled stocks—_(DOD, NATO)_ Stocks which are placed at the disposal of a designated NATO commander in order to provide him with a flexibility with which to influence the battle logistically. "Placed at the disposal of" implies responsibility for storage, maintenance, accounting, rotation or turnover, physical security and subsequent transportation to a particular battle area.

command destruct signal—_(DOD, NATO)_ A signal used to operate intentionally the destruction signal in a missile.

command detonated mine—*(DOD, NATO)* A mine detonated by remotely controlled means.

command ejection system—See **ejection systems**.

commander(s)—See **executing commander (nuclear weapons)**; **exercise commander**; **Major NATO Commanders**; **national commander**; **national force commanders**; **national territorial commander**; **releasing commander (nuclear weapons)**.

commander's concept—See **concept of operations**.

commander's estimate of the situation—*(DOD, IADB)* A logical process of reasoning by which a commander considers all the circumstances affecting the military situation and arrives at a decision as to a course of action to be taken to accomplish the mission. A commander's estimate which considers a military situation so far in the future as to require major assumptions, is called a commander's long-range estimate of the situation. See also **estimate of the situation**.

command guidance—*(DOD, NATO, IADB)* A guidance system wherein intelligence transmitted to the missile from an outside source causes the missile to traverse a directed flight path.

command heading—*(DOD)* Heading that the controlled aircraft is directed to assume by the control station.

command net—*(DOD, NATO, IADB)* A communications network which connects an echelon of command with some or all of its subordinate echelons for the purpose of command control.

command post—*(DOD, NATO, IADB)* A unit's or subunit's headquarters where the commander and the staff perform their activities. In combat, a unit's or subunit's headquarters is often divided into echelons; the echelon in which the unit or subunit commander is locat-ed or from which he operates is called a command post.

command post exercise—*(DOD, NATO, IADB)* An exercise in which the forces are simulated, involving the commander, his staff, and communications within and between headquarters. See also **exercise; maneuver**.

command select ejection system—See **ejection systems**.

command speed—*(DOD)* The speed at which the controlled aircraft is directed to fly.

command-sponsored dependent—*(DOD)* A dependent entitled to travel to oversea commands at Government expense and endorsed by the appropriate military commander to be present in a dependent's status.

commercial items—*(DOD, IADB)* Articles of supply readily available from established commercial distribution sources, which the Department of Defense or inventory managers in the Military Services have designated to be obtained directly or indirectly from such sources.

commercial loading—See **administrative loading**.

commercial vehicle—*(DOD)* A vehicle which has evolved in the commercial market to meet civilian requirements and which is selected from existing production lines for military use.

commission—*(DOD, IADB)* 1. To put in or make ready for service or use, as to commission an aircraft or a ship. 2. A written order giving a person rank and authority as an officer in the armed forces. 3. The rank and the authority given by such an order. See also **activate; constitute**.

commit—*(DOD)* The process of committing one or more air interceptors or surface-to-air missiles for interception against a target track.

commodity loading—*(DOD, NATO, IADB)* A method of loading in which various types of cargoes are loaded together, such as ammunition, rations, or boxed vehicles, in order that each commodity can be discharged without disturbing the others. See also **loading.**

commodity manager—*(DOD, IADB)* An individual within the organization of an inventory control point or other such organization, assigned management responsibility for homogeneous grouping of materiel items.

commonality—*(DOD)* A quality which applies to materiel or systems: **a.** possessing like and interchangeable characteristics enabling each to be utilized, or operated and maintained, by personnel trained on the others without additional specialized training. **b.** having interchangeable repair parts and/or components. **c.** applying to consumable items interchangeably equivalent without adjustment.

commonality—*(NATO)* A state achieved when groups of individuals, organizations, or nations use common doctrine, procedures, or equipment. See also **compatibility; interchangeability; interoperability.**

common business-oriented language—*(DOD, IADB)* A specific language by which business data-processing procedures may be precisely described in a standard form. The language is intended not only as a means for directly presenting any business program to any suitable computer for which a compiler exists, but also as a means of communicating such procedures among individuals. Commonly referred to as **COBOL.**

common control (artillery)—*(DOD, NATO, IADB)* Horizontal and vertical map or chart location of points in the target area and position area, tied in with the horizontal and vertical control in use by two or more units. May be established by firing, survey, or combination of both, or by assumption. See also **control point; field control; ground control.**

common infrastructure—*(DOD, NATO)* Infrastructure essential to the training of NATO forces or to the implementation of NATO operational plans which, owing to its degree of common use or interest and its compliance with criteria laid down from time to time by the North Atlantic Council, is commonly financed by NATO members. See also **infrastructure.**

common item—*(DOD, IADB)* 1. Any item of materiel which is required for use by more than one activity. 2. Sometimes loosely used to denote any consumable item except repair parts or other technical items. 3. Any item of materiel which is procured for, owned by (Service stock), or used by any Military Department of the Department of Defense and that is also required to be furnished to a recipient country under the grant-aid Military Assistance Program. 4. Readily available commercial items. 5. Items used by two or more Military Services of similar manufacture or fabrication that may vary between the Services as to color or shape (as vehicles or clothing). 6. Any part or component which is required in the assembly of two or more complete end-items.

common servicing—*(DOD, IADB)* That function performed by one military Service in support of another military Service for which reimbursement is not required from the Service receiving support. See also **servicing.**

common supplies—*(DOD, IADB)* Those supplies common to two or more Services.

common use—*(DOD)* Services, materials, or facilities provided by a Department of Defense agency or a military department on a common basis for two or more Department of Defense agencies.

common user airlift service—*(DOD, IADB)* In military transport service usage, the airlift service provided on a common basis for all DOD agencies and, as authorized, for other agencies of the US Government. (Note: **IADB**

definition ends with **agencies of Government.**).

common-user military land transportation— *(DOD, IADB)* Point-to-point land transportation service operated by a single Service for common use by two or more Services.

common user network—*(DOD, IADB)* A system of circuits or channels allocated to furnish communication paths between switching centers to provide communication service on a common basis to all connected stations or subscribers. It is sometimes described as a General Purpose Network.

common-user ocean terminals—*(DOD)* A military installation, part of a military installation, or a commercial facility operated under contract or arrangement by the Military Traffic Management Command which regularly provides for two or more Services, terminal functions of receipt, transit storage or staging, processing, and loading and unloading of passengers or cargo aboard ships.

common-user ocean terminals—*(IADB)* A military installation, part of a military installation, or a commercial facility that regularly provides for two or more Services, terminal functions of receipt, transit storage or staging, processing, and loading and unloading of passengers or cargo aboard ships.

communication deception—*(DOD, IADB)* Use of devices, operations, and techniques with the intent of confusing or misleading the user of a communications link or a navigation system.

communication operation instructions—See **signal operation instructions.**

communications—*(DOD, IADB)* A method or means of conveying information of any kind from one person or place to another. See also **telecommunication.**

communications center—*(DOD, NATO)* An agency charged with the responsibility for handling and controlling communications traffic. The center normally includes message center, transmitting and receiving facilities. See also **telecommunications center.**

communications intelligence—*(DOD, IADB)* Technical and intelligence information derived from foreign communications by other than the intended recipients. Also called COMINT.

communications intelligence data base—*(DOD)* The aggregate of technical and intelligence information derived from the interception and analysis of foreign communications (excluding press, propaganda, and public broadcast) used in the direction and redirection of communications intelligence intercept, analysis, and reporting activities.

communications mark—*(DOD)* An electronic indicator used for directing attention to a particular object or position of mutual interest within or between command and control systems.

communications net—*(DOD, NATO)* An organization of stations capable of direct communications on a common channel or frequency.

communications network—*(DOD, IADB)* An organization of stations capable of intercommunications but not necessarily on the same channel.

communications satellite—*(DOD, NATO, IADB)* An orbiting vehicle, which relays signals between communications stations. There are two types:
a. **Active Communications Satellite—**A satellite that receives, regenerates, and retransmits signals between stations;
b. **Passive Communications Satellite—**A satellite which reflects communications signals between stations.

communications security—*(DOD, IADB)* The protection resulting from all measures designed to deny unauthorized persons information of value which might be derived from the possession and study of telecommunications, or to mislead unauthorized persons in their interpretation of the results of such possession and study. Also called **COMSEC.** Communications security includes **a.** cryptosecurity; **b.** transmission security; **c.** emission security; and **d.** physical security of communications security materials and information.

1. **cryptosecurity**—The component of communications security which results from the provision of technically sound crypto-systems and their proper use.
2. **transmission security**—The component of communications security which results from all measures designed to protect transmissions from interception and exploitation by means other than cryptanalysis.
3. **emission security**—The component of communications security which results from all measures taken to deny unauthorized persons information of value that might be derived from intercept and analysis of compromising emanations from crypto-equipment and telecommunications systems.
4. **physical security**—The component of communications security which results from all physical measures necessary to safeguard classified equipment, material, and documents from access thereto or observation thereof by unauthorized persons.

communications security equipment—*(DOD, IADB)* Equipment designed to provide security to telecommunications by converting information to a form unintelligible to an unauthorized interceptor and by reconverting such information to its original form for authorized recipients, as well as equipment designed specifically to aid in, or as an essential element of, the conversion process. Communications security equipment is cryptoequipment, cryptoancillary equipment, cryptoproduction equipment, and authentication equipment.

communications security material—*(DOD, IADB)* All documents, devices, equipment, or apparatus, including cryptomaterial, used in establishing or maintaining secure communications.

communications security monitoring—*(DOD, IADB)* The act of listening to, copying, or recording transmissions of one's own circuits (or when specially agreed, e.g., in allied exercises, those of friendly forces) to provide material for communications security analysis in order to determine the degree of security being provided to those transmissions. In particular, the purposes include providing a basis for advising commanders on the security risks resulting from their transmissions, improving the security of communications, and planning and conducting manipulative communications deception operations.

communications terminal—*(DOD)* Terminus of a communications circuit at which data can be either entered or received; located with the originator or ultimate addressee.

communications zone—*(DOD, NATO, IADB)* Rear part of theater of operations (behind but contiguous to the combat zone) which contains the lines of communications, establishments for supply and evacuation, and other agencies required for the immediate support and maintenance of the field forces. See also **combat zone; rear area.**

community relations—*(DOD, IADB)* The relationship between military and civilian communities.

community relations program—*(DOD)* That command function which evaluates public attitudes, identifies the mission of a military organization with the public interest, and executes a program of action to earn public understanding and acceptance. Community relations programs are conducted at all levels of command, both in the United States and overseas, by military organizations having a community relations area of responsibility. Community relations programs include, but are not limited to, such activities as liaison and cooperation with associations and organizations and their local affiliates at all levels; armed forces participation in international, national, regional, state, and local public events; installation open houses and tours;

embarkations in naval ships; orientation tours for distinguished civilians; people-to-people and humanitarian acts; cooperation with government officials and community leaders; and encouragement of armed forces personnel and their dependents to participate in activities of local schools, churches, fraternal, social, and civic organizations, sports, and recreation programs, and other aspects of community life to the extent feasible and appropriate, regardless of where they are located.

community relations program—*(IADB)* That command function that evaluates public attitudes, identifies the mission of a military organization with the public interest, and executes a program of action to earn public understanding and acceptance. Community relations programs include, but are not limited to, such activities as liaison and cooperation with associations and organizations and their local affiliates at all levels; armed forces participation in international, national, regional, state, and local public events; installation open houses and tours, embarkations in naval ships, orientation tours for distinguished government officials and community leaders; and encouragement of armed forces personnel and their dependents to participate in activities of civic organizations, sports and recreation programs, and other aspects of community life to the extent feasible and appropriate, regardless of where they are located.

comparative cover—*(DOD, NATO, IADB)* Coverage of the same area or object taken at different times, to show any changes in details. See also **cover.**

compartmentation—*(DOD)* 1. Establishment and management of an intelligence organization so that information about the personnel, organization, or activities of one component is made available to any other component only to the extent required for the performance of assigned duties. 2. Effects of relief and drainage upon avenues of approach so as to produce areas bounded on at least two sides by terrain features such as woods, ridges, or ravines that limit observation or observed fire into the area from points outside the area.

compartment marking—*(NATO)* In an aircraft, a system of marking a cabin into compartments for the positioning of loads in accordance with the weight and balance requirements.

compass direction—*(DOD, NATO)* The horizontal direction expressed as an angular distance measured clockwise from compass north.

compass north—*(DOD, NATO, IADB)* The uncorrected direction indicated by the north seeking end of a compass needle. See also **magnetic north.**

compass rose—*(DOD, NATO, IADB)* A graduated circle, usually marked in degrees, indicating directions and printed or inscribed on an appropriate medium.

compatibility—*(DOD, NATO, IADB)* Capability of two or more items or components of equipment or material to exist or function in the same system or environment without mutual interference. See also **interchangeability.**

compilation—*(NATO, IADB)* Selection, assembly, and graphic presentation of all relevant information required for the preparation of a map or chart. Such information may be derived from other maps or charts or from other sources.

compilation diagram—*(NATO)* A diagram giving details of the source material from which the map or chart has been compiled; this does not necessarily include reliability information. See also **reliability diagram.**

complaint-type investigation—*(DOD)* A counterintelligence investigation in which sabotage, espionage, treason, sedition, subversive activity, or disaffection is suspected.

complete round—*(DOD, IADB)* A term applied to an assemblage of explosive and nonexplosive components designed to perform a specific function at the time and under the conditions desired. Examples of complete rounds of ammunition are:

a. **separate loading**—consisting of a primer, propelling charge, and, except for blank ammunition, a projectile and a fuze.

b. **fixed or semifixed**—consisting of a primer, propelling charge, cartridge case, a projectile, and, except when solid projectiles are used, a fuze.

c. **bomb**—consisting of all component parts required to drop and function the bomb once.

d. **missile**—consisting of a complete warhead section and a missile body with its associated components and propellants.

e. **rocket**—consisting of all components necessary to function.

complete round—*(NATO)* Ammunition which contains all the components necessary for it to function.

component—*(DOD, NATO)* A part or combination of parts, having a specified function, which can only be installed or replaced as a whole, and is also generally expendable.

component life—*(NATO, IADB)* The period of acceptable usage after which the likelihood of failure sharply increases and before which the components are removed in the interests of reliability of operation.

component (materiel)—*(DOD)* An assembly or any combination of parts, subassemblies, and assemblies mounted together in manufacture, assembly, maintenance, or rebuild.

component search and rescue controller—*(DOD, IADB)* The designated search and rescue representative of a component commander of a unified command who is responsible in the name of his component commander for the control of component search and rescue forces committed to joint search and rescue operations. See also **search and rescue**.

composite air photography—*(DOD)* Air photographs made with a camera having one principal lens and two or more surrounding and oblique lenses. The several resulting photographs are corrected or transformed in printing to permit assembly as verticals with the same scale.

composite Air Strike Force—*(DOD)* A group of selected US Air Force units composed of appropriate elements of tactical air power (tactical fighters, tactical reconnaissance, tankers, airlift, and command and control elements) capable of employing a spectrum of nuclear and nonnuclear weapons. Composite Air Strike Force forces are held in readiness for immediate deployment from the continental United States to all areas of the world to meet national emergency contingency plans.

compound helicopter—*(DOD, NATO)* A helicopter with an auxiliary propulsion system which provides thrust in excess of that which the rotor(s) alone could produce, thereby permitting increased forward speeds; wings may or may not be provided to reduce the lift required from the rotor system.

compression chamber—See **hyperbaric chamber**.

compromise—*(DOD)* The known or suspected exposure of clandestine personnel, installations, or other assets or of classified information or material, to an unauthorized person.

compromised—*(DOD, NATO, IADB)* A term applied to classified matter, knowledge of which has, in whole or in part, passed to an unauthorized person or persons, or which has been subject to risk of such passing. See also **classified matter**.

computed air release point—*(DOD, NATO, IADB)* A computed air position where the first paratroop or cargo item is released to land on a specified impact point.

concealment—*(DOD, NATO)* The protection from observation or surveillance. See also **camouflage; cover; screen**.

concentrated fire—*(NATO, IADB)* 1. The fire of the batteries of two or more ships directed against a single target. 2. Fire from a number of weapons directed at a single point or small area. See also **fire; massed fire.**

concentration area—*(DOD, NATO, IADB)* 1. An area, usually in the theater of operations, where troops are assembled before beginning active operations. 2. A limited area on which a volume of gunfire is placed within a limited time.

concept—*(DOD, NATO)* A notion or statement of an idea, expressing how something might be done or accomplished, that may lead to an accepted procedure.

concept of operations—*(DOD, IADB)* A verbal or graphic statement, in broad outline, of a commander's assumptions or intent in regard to an operation or series of operations. The concept of operations frequently is embodied in campaign plans and operation plans; in the latter case, particularly when the plans cover a series of connected operations to be carried out simultaneously or in succession. The concept is designed to give an overall picture of the operation. It is included primarily for additional clarity of purpose. Frequently, it is referred to as commander's concept.

concept of operations—*(NATO)* A clear and concise statement of the line of action chosen by a commander in order to accomplish his mission.

condensation cloud—*(DOD, IADB)* A mist or fog of minute water droplets that temporarily surrounds the fireball following a nuclear (or atomic) detonation in a comparatively humid atmosphere. The expansion of the air in the negative phase of the blast wave from the explosion results in a lowering of the temperature, so that condensation of water vapor present in the air occurs and a cloud forms. The cloud is soon dispelled when the pressure returns to normal and the air warms up again. The phenomenon is similar to that used by physicists in the Wilson cloud chamber and is sometimes called the cloud chamber effect.

condensation trail—*(DOD)* A visible cloud streak, usually brilliantly white in color, which trails behind a missile or other vehicle in flight under certain conditions. Also known as **contrail.**

Condor—*(DOD)* An air-to-surface guided missile which provides standoff launch capability for attack aircraft. Designated as AGM-53.

conducting staff—See **exercise; directing staff.**

cone of silence—*(DOD, NATO, IADB)* An inverted cone-shaped space directly over the aerial towers of some forms of radio beacons in which signals are unheard or greatly reduced in volume. See also **Z marker beacon.**

confidential—See **security classification.**

confirmation of information (intelligence)—*(DOD, IADB)* An information item is said to be confirmed when it is reported for the second time, preferably by another independent source whose reliability is considered when confirming information.

confused—*(DOD)* In air intercept, a term meaning, "Individual contacts not identifiable."

confusion agent—*(DOD, IADB)* An individual who is dispatched by the sponsor for the primary purpose of confounding the intelligence or counterintelligence apparatus of another country rather than for the purpose of collecting and transmitting information.

confusion reflector—*(DOD, NATO)* A reflector of electromagnetic radiations used to create echoes for confusion purposes. Radar confusion reflectors include such devices as chaff, rope and corner reflectors.

connecting route—*(DOD, NATO)* A route connecting axial and/or lateral routes. See also **route.**

consol—*(DOD, NATO, IADB)* A long-range radio aid to navigation, the emissions of which, by means of their radio frequency modulation characteristics, enable bearings to be determined.

console—*(DOD, NATO, IADB)* A grouping of controls, indicators, and similar electronic or mechanical equipment, used to monitor readiness of, and/or control specific functions of, a system, such as missile checkout, countdown, or launch operations.

consolidated vehicle table—*(DOD, IADB)* A summary of all vehicles loaded on a ship, listed by types, and showing the units to which they belong.

consolidation—*(DOD)* The combining or merging of elements to perform a common or related function.

consolidation of position—*(DOD, NATO, IADB)* Organizing and strengthening a newly captured position so that it can be used against the enemy.

constant of the cone—*(NATO)* For Lambert Conical Orthomorphic projection, see **grid convergence factor.** See also **convergence factor.**

constitute—*(DOD, IADB)* To provide the legal authority for the existence of a new unit of the armed services. The new unit is designated and listed, but it has no specific existence until it is activated. See also **activate; commission.**

consumable supplies and material—See **expendable supplies and material.**

consumer—*(DOD)* Person or agency that uses information or intelligence produced by either its own staff or other agencies.

consumer logistics—*(DOD)* That part of logistics concerning reception of the initial product, storage, inspection, distribution, transport, maintenance (including repair and the serviceability) and disposal of materiel, and the provision of support and services. In consequence, consumer logistics includes: materiel requirements determination, follow-on support, stock control, provision or construction of facilities (excluding any materiel element and those facilities needed to support production logistics activities), movement control, codification, reliability and defect reporting, storage, transport and handling safety standards, and related training.

consumption rate—*(DOD, NATO, IADB)* The average quantity of an item consumed or expended during a given time interval, expressed in quantities by the most appropriate unit of measurement per applicable stated basis.

contact—*(DOD, IADB)* 1. In air intercept, a term meaning, "Unit has an unevaluated target." *(DOD)* 2. In health services, an unevaluated individual who is known to have been sufficiently near an infected individual to have been exposed to the transfer of infectious material.

contact burst preclusion—*(DOD)* A fuzing arrangement which prevents an unwanted surface burst in the event of failure of the air burst fuze.

contact lost—*(DOD, NATO, IADB)* A target tracking term used to signify that a target believed to be still within the area of visual, sonar or radar coverage is temporarily lost but the termination of track plotting is not warranted.

contact mine—*(DOD, NATO)* A mine detonated by physical contact. See also **mine.**

contact point—*(DOD, NATO, IADB)* 1. In land warfare, a point on the terrain, easily identifiable, where two or more units are required to make contact. 2. In air operations, the position at which a mission leader makes radio contact with an air control agency. See also **check point; control point; coordinating point.**

contact print—*(DOD, NATO)* A print made from a negative or a diapositive in direct contact with sensitized material.

contact reconnaissance—*(DOD, IADB)* Locating isolated units out of contact with the main force.

contact report—*(DOD, NATO)* A report indicating any detection of the enemy.

contain—*(DOD, NATO, IADB)* To stop, hold, or surround the forces of the enemy or to cause the enemy to center activity on a given front and to prevent his withdrawing any part of his forces for use elsewhere.

container anchorage terminal—*(DOD, NATO)* A sheltered anchorage (not a port) with the appropriate facilities for the transshipment of containerized cargo from containerships to other vessels.

contamination—(DOD, NATO) 1. The deposit and/or adsorption of radioactive material, or of biological or chemical agents on and by structures, areas, personnel, or objects. See also **induced radiation; residual radiation.** (DOD) 2. Food and/or water made unfit for consumption by humans or animals because of the presence of environmental chemicals, radioactive elements, bacteria or organisms, the byproduct of the growth of bacteria or organisms, the decomposing material (to include the food substance itself), or waste in the food or water.

contamination—*(IADB)* The deposit and/or absorption of radioactive material, biological, or chemical agents on and by structures, areas, personnel, or objects.

contamination control—*(NATO)* Procedures to avoid, reduce, remove, or render harmless, temporarily or permanently, nuclear, biological, and chemical contamination for the purpose of maintaining or enhancing the efficient conduct of military operations.

contamination control line—*(NATO)* A line established by competent authority identifying the area contaminated to a specific level of the contaminant of interest. See also **contamination.**

contamination control point—*(NATO)* That portion of the contamination control line used by personnel to control entry to and exit from the contaminated area. See also **contamination.**

Continental United States (CONUS)—*(DOD)* United States territory, including the adjacent territorial waters, located within the North American Continent between Canada and Mexico.

contingency plan—*(DOD, IADB)* A plan for major contingencies which can reasonably be anticipated in the principal geographic subareas of the command.

contingency plan—*(NATO)* A plan for contingencies which can reasonably be anticipated in an area of responsibility.

contingency planning facilities list program—*(DOD)* A joint Defense Intelligence Agency/unified and specified command program for the production and maintenance of current target documentation of all countries of contingency planning interest to US military planners.

contingency retention stock—*(DOD)* That portion of the quantity of an item excess to the approved force retention level for which there is no predictable demand or quantifiable requirement, and which normally would be allocated as potential DOD excess stock, except for a determination that the quantity will be retained for possible contingencies for United States forces. (Category C ships, aircraft, and other items being retained as contingency reserve are included in this stratum.)

contingency retention stock—*(IADB)* That portion of the quantity of an item in long supply for which no programmed requirement exists and which normally would be considered as excess stock, but which it has been determined will be retained for possible military or defense contingencies; however, no portion of any item to be retained as contingency retention stock may be retained as economic retention stock. See also **reserve supplies.**

contingent effects—*(DOD)* The effects, both desirable and undesirable, which are in addition to the primary effects associated with a nuclear detonation.

contingent zone of fire—*(DOD, IADB)* An area within which a designated ground unit or fire support ship may be called upon to deliver fire. See also **zone of fire.**

continue port/starboard—*(DOD, IADB)* In air intercept, a term meaning, "Continue turning port/starboard at present rate of turn to magnetic heading indicated," (3 figures) or "Continue turning port/starboard for number of degrees indicated."

continuity of command—*(DOD, IADB)* The degree or state of being continuous in the exercise of the authority vested in an individual of the armed forces for the direction, coordination, and control of military forces.

continuity of operations—*(DOD, IADB)* The degree or state of being continuous in the conduct of functions, tasks, or duties necessary to accomplish a military action or mission in carrying out the national military strategy. It includes the functions and duties of the commander, as well as the supporting functions and duties performed by the staff and others acting under the authority and direction of the commander.

continuous fire—*(DOD, NATO, IADB)* 1. Fire conducted at a normal rate without interruption for application of adjustment corrections or for other causes. 2. In field artillery and naval gunfire support, loading and firing at a specified rate or as rapidly as possible consistent with accuracy within the prescribed rate of fire for the weapon. Firing will continue until terminated by the command **end of mission** or temporarily suspended by the command **cease loading** or **check firing.**

continuous illumination fire—*(DOD, NATO, IADB)* A type of fire in which illuminating projectiles are fired at specified time intervals to provide uninterrupted lighting on the target or specified area. See also **coordinated illumination fire.**

continuously computed release point—*(NATO)* Solution of the weapon delivery release point by continuous prediction of the release point for a given set of ballistics, altitudes and airspeeds.

continuously set vector—See **bomb sighting systems Part 1.**

continuous processor—*(NATO)* Equipment which processes film or paper in continuous strips.

continuous strip camera—*(DOD, NATO, IADB)* A camera in which the film moves continuously past a slit in the focal plane, producing a photograph in one unbroken length by virtue of the continuous forward motion of the aircraft.

continuous strip imagery—*(DOD, NATO, IADB)* Imagery of a strip of terrain in which the image remains unbroken throughout its length, along the line of flight.

continuous strip photography—*(NATO)* Photography of a strip of terrain in which the image remains unbroken throughout its length, along the line of flight.

contour flight—See **terrain flight.**

contour interval—*(DOD, NATO, IADB)* Difference in elevation between two adjacent contour lines.

contour line—*(DOD, NATO, IADB)* A line on a map or chart connecting points of equal elevation.

contract maintenance—*(DOD)* The maintenance of materiel performed under contract by commercial organizations (including prime contractors) on a one-time or continuing basis, without distinction as to the level of maintenance accomplished.

contract termination—*(DOD)* As used in Defense procurement, refers to the cessation or cancellation, in whole or in part, of work under a prime contract, or a subcontract thereunder, for the convenience of, or at the option of, the government, or due to failure of the contractor to perform in accordance with the terms of the contract (default).

contrail—See **condensation trail.**

control—*(DOD, IADB)* 1. Authority which may be less than full command exercised by a commander over part of the activities of subordinate or other organizations. 2. In mapping, charting, and photogrammetry, a collective term for a system of marks or objects on the earth or on a map or a photograph, whose positions or elevations, or both, have been or will be determined. 3. Physical or psychological pressures exerted with the intent to assure that an agent or group will respond as directed. 4. An indicator governing the distribution and use of documents, information, or material. Such indicators are the subject of intelligence community agreement and are specifically defined in appropriate regulations. See also **administrative control; operational command.**

control—*(NATO)* 1. That authority exercised by a commander over part of the activities of subordinate organizations or other organizations not normally under his command, which encompasses the responsibility for implementing orders or directives. All or part of this authority may be transferred or delegated. See also **administrative control; operational control; tactical control.** 2. In mapping, charting, and photogrammetry, a collective term for a system of marks or objects on the earth or on a map or a photograph, whose positions or elevations, or both, have been or will be determined.

control and reporting center—*(DOD)* An element of the US Air Force tactical air control system, subordinate to the tactical air control center, from which radar control and warning operations are conducted within its area of responsibility.

control and reporting center—*(NATO, IADB)* A subordinate air control element of the tactical air control center from which radar control and warning operations are conducted within its area of responsibility.

control and reporting post—*(DOD)* An element of the US Air Force tactical air control system, subordinate to the control and reporting center, which provides radar control and surveillance within its area of responsibility.

control and reporting system—*(NATO)* An organization set up for: **a.** early warning, tracking, and recognition of aircraft and tracking of surface craft, and **b.** control of all active air defenses. It consists primarily of a chain of radar reporting stations and control centers and an observer organization, together with the necessary communications network.

control area—*(DOD, NATO)* A controlled airspace extending upwards from a specified limit above the earth. See also **airway; controlled airspace; control zone; terminal control area.**

control (intelligence)—See **control,** *(DOD, IADB)* Parts 3 and 4.

controlled airspace—*(DOD, NATO, IADB)* An airspace of defined dimensions within which air traffic control service is provided to controlled flights.

controlled effects nuclear weapons—*(DOD)* Nuclear weapons designed to achieve variation in the intensity of specific effects other than normal blast effect.

controlled exercise—*(NATO)* An exercise characterized by the imposition of constraints on some or all of the participating units by planning authorities with the principal intention of provoking types of interaction. See also **free play exercise.**

controlled firing area—*(DOD, IADB)* An area in which ordnance firing is conducted under controlled conditions so as to eliminate hazard to aircraft in flight. See also **restricted area.**

controlled forces—*(DOD, IADB)* Military or paramilitary forces under effective and sustained political and military direction.

controlled information—*(DOD)* Information conveyed to an adversary in a deception operation to evoke desired appreciations.

controlled interception—*(NATO, IADB)* An aircraft intercept action wherein the friendly aircraft are controlled from a ground, ship, or airborne station. See also **air interception.**

controlled item—See **regulated item.**

controlled map—*(DOD, IADB)* A map with precise horizontal and vertical ground control as a basis. Scale, azimuth, and elevation are accurate. See also **map.**

controlled mine—*(DOD, NATO)* A mine which after laying can be controlled by the user, to the extent of making the mine safe or live, or to fire the mine. See also **mine.**

controlled mosaic—*(DOD, NATO)* A mosaic corrected for scale, rectified and laid to ground control to provide an accurate representation of distances and direction. See also **mosaic; rectification; uncontrolled mosaic.**

controlled passing—*(DOD, NATO, IADB)* A traffic movement procedure whereby two lines of traffic travelling in opposite directions are enabled to traverse alternately a point or section of route which can take only one line of traffic at a time.

controlled port—*(DOD, NATO, IADB)* A harbor or anchorage at which entry and departure, assignment of berths, and traffic within the harbor or anchorage are controlled by military authorities.

controlled reprisal—*(DOD)* Not to be used. See **controlled response.**

controlled response—*(DOD, IADB)* The selection from a wide variety of feasible options of the one which will provide the specific military response most advantageous in the circumstances.

controlled route—*(DOD, NATO)* A route, the use of which is subject to traffic or movement restrictions which may be supervised. See also **route.**

controlled war—*(DOD)* Not to be used. See **limited war.**

control of electromagnetic radiation—*(DOD)* A national operational plan to minimize the use of electromagnetic radiation in the United States and its possessions and the Panama Canal Zone in the event of attack or imminent threat thereof, as an aid to the navigation of hostile aircraft, guided missiles, or other devices. See also **emission control orders.**

control of electromagnetic radiation—*(IADB)* An operational plan to minimize the use of electromagnetic radiation in the event of attack or imminent threat thereof, as an aid to the navigation of hostile aircraft, guided missiles, or other devices. See also **emission control orders.**

control point—*(DOD, NATO, IADB)* 1. A position along a route of march at which men are stationed to give information and instructions for the regulation of supply or traffic. 2. A position marked by a buoy, boat, aircraft, electronic device, conspicuous terrain feature, or other identifiable object which is given a name or number and used as an aid to navigation or control of ships, boats, or aircraft.

3. A point located by ground survey with which a corresponding point on a photograph is matched as a check, in making mosaics.

control stick steering—*(NATO)* Control of an aircraft through the automatic flight control system by manipulation of the control stick.

control system (missile)—*(DOD, NATO, IADB)* A system that serves to maintain attitude stability and to correct deflections. See also **guidance system (missile).**

control zone—*(DOD, NATO)* A controlled airspace extending upwards from the surface of the earth to a specified upper limit. See also **airway; control area; controlled airspace; terminal control area.**

CONUS—See **Continental United States.**

conventional forces—*(DOD, IADB)* Those forces capable of conducting operations using nonnuclear weapons.

conventional weapon—*(DOD, NATO, IADB)* A weapon which is neither nuclear, biological nor chemical.

converge—*(DOD, IADB)* A request or command used in a call for fire to indicate that the observer or spotter desires a sheaf in which the planes of fire intersect at a point.

converge—*(NATO)* In artillery and naval gunfire support, a command or request used in a call for fire to indicate that the observer/spotter desires the planes of fire to intersect at a point.

converged sheaf—*(DOD)* The lateral distribution of fire of two or more pieces so that the planes of fire intersect at a given point. See also **open sheaf; parallel sheaf; sheaf; special sheaf.**

convergence—See **convergence factor; grid convergence; grid convergence factor; map convergence; true convergence.**

convergence factor—*(DOD, NATO)* The ratio of the angle between any two meridians on the chart to their actual change of longitude. See also **convergence.**

convergence zone—*(DOD, IADB)* That region in the deep ocean where sound rays, refractured from the depths, return to the surface.

conversion angle—*(DOD, NATO)* The angle between a great circle (orthodromic) bearing and a rhumb line (loxodromic) bearing of a point, measured at a common origin.

conversion scale—*(DOD, NATO)* A scale indicating the relationship between two different units of measurement. See also **scale.**

convoy—*(DOD, NATO, IADB)* 1. A number of merchant ships or naval auxiliaries, or both, usually escorted by warships and/or aircraft, or a single merchant ship or naval auxiliary under surface escort, assembled and organized for the purpose of passage together. 2. A group of vehicles organized for the purpose of control and orderly movement with or without escort protection. See also **coastal convoy; evacuation convoy; ocean convoy.**

convoy assembly port—*(NATO, IADB)* A port from which convoys, whether ocean going or coastal, sail.

convoy commodore—*(DOD, NATO, IADB)* A naval officer, or master of one of the ships in a convoy, designated to command the convoy, subject to the orders of the Officer in Tactical Command. If no surface escort is present, he takes entire command.

convoy dispersal point—*(DOD, NATO)* The position at sea where a convoy breaks up, each ship proceeding independently thereafter.

convoy escort—*(DOD, NATO, IADB)* 1. A naval ship(s) or aircraft in company with a convoy and responsible for its protection. 2. An escort to protect a convoy of vehicles from being scattered, destroyed or captured. See also **escort.**

convoy joiner—See joiner. See also joiner convoy; joiner section.

convoy leaver—See leaver. See also leaver convoy; leaver section.

convoy loading—(DOD, NATO, IADB) The loading of troop units with their equipment and supplies in vessels of the same movement group, but not necessarily in the same vessel. See also loading.

convoy route—(DOD, NATO, IADB) The specific route assigned to each convoy by the appropriate routing authority.

convoy schedule—(DOD, NATO) Planned convoy sailings showing the shipping lanes, assembly and terminal areas, scheduled speed, and sailing interval.

convoy speed—(DOD, NATO, IADB) For ships, the speed which the convoy commodore orders the guide of the convoy to make good through the water.

convoy terminal area—(DOD, NATO) A geographical area, designated by the name of a port or anchorage on which it is centered, at which convoys or sections of convoys arrive and from which they will be dispersed to coastal convoy systems or as independents to their final destination.

convoy through escort—(DOD, NATO, IADB) Those ships of the close escort which normally remain with the convoy from its port of assembly to its port of arrival.

convoy title—(DOD, NATO) A combination of letters and numbers that gives the port of departure and arrival, speed, and serial number of each convoy.

cooperative logistics—(DOD, IADB) The logistic support provided a foreign government/agency through its participation in the US Department of Defense logistic system with reimbursement to the United States for support provided.

cooperative logistics support arrangements—(DOD, IADB) The combining term for procedural arrangements (cooperative logistics arrangements) and implementing procedures (supplementary procedures) which together support, define, or implement cooperative logistic understandings between the United States and a friendly foreign government under peacetime conditions.

coordinated attack—(NATO, IADB) A carefully planned and executed offensive action in which the various elements of a command are employed in such a manner as to utilize their powers to the greatest advantage to the command as a whole.

coordinated draft plan—(DOD, NATO) A plan for which a draft plan has been coordinated with the nations involved. It may be used for future planning and exercises and may be implemented during an emergency. See also draft plan; final plan; initial draft plan; operation plan.

coordinated exercise—See JCS-coordinated exercise.

coordinated illumination fire—(NATO) A type of fire in which the firing of illuminating and high explosive projectiles is coordinated to provide illumination of the target and surrounding area only at the time required for spotting and adjusting the high explosive fire. See also continuous illumination fire.

coordinated procurement assignee—(DOD) The agency or military Service assigned purchase responsibility for all Department of Defense requirements of a particular Federal Supply Group/class, commodity, or item.

coordinates—(DOD, NATO, IADB) Linear or angular quantities which designate the position that a point occupies in a given reference frame or system. Also used as a general term to designate the particular kind of reference frame or system such as plane rectangular coordinates or spherical coordinates. See also cartesian coordinates; geographic coordinates; georef; grid coordinates.

coordinating authority—(DOD) A commander or individual assigned responsibility for coordinating specific functions or activities involving forces of two or more Services or two or more forces of the same Service. The commander or individual has the authority to require consultation between the agencies involved, but does not have the authority to compel agreement. In the event that essential agreement cannot be obtained, the matter shall be referred to the appointing authority.

coordinating authority—(NATO) The authority granted to a commander or individual assigned responsibility for coordinating specific functions or activities involving forces of two or more countries or commands, or two or more services or two or more forces of the same service. He has the authority to require consultation between the agencies involved or their representatives, but does not have the authority to compel agreement. In case of disagreement between the agencies involved, he should attempt to obtain essential agreement by discussion. In the event he is unable to obtain essential agreement he shall refer the matter to the appropriate authority.

coordinating point—(DOD, NATO, IADB) Designated point at which, in all types of combat, adjacent units/formations must make contact for purposes of control and coordination.

copy negative—(DOD, NATO) A negative produced from an original not necessarily at the same scale.

corner reflector—(DOD, NATO) 1. A device, normally consisting of three metallic surfaces or screens perpendicular to one another, designed to act as a radar target or marker. 2. In radar interpretation, an object which, by means of multiple reflections from smooth surfaces, produces a radar return of greater magnitude than might be expected from the physical size of the object.

corps—(NATO) See **army corps**.

corps troops—(DOD, NATO, IADB) Troops assigned or attached to a corps, but not a part of one of the divisions that make up the corps.

correction—(DOD, NATO) 1. In fire control, any change in firing data to bring the mean point of impact or burst closer to the target. 2. A communication proword to indicate that an error in data has been announced and that corrected data will follow.

corrective maintenance—(NATO) Maintenance actions carried out to restore a defective item to a specified condition. See also **preventive maintenance**.

correlation—(DOD, NATO, IADB) In air defense, the determination that an aircraft appearing on a radarscope, on a plotting board, or visually is the same vehicle as that on which information is being received from another source.

correlation factor—(DOD, NATO) The ratio of a ground dose rate reading to a reading taken at approximately the same time at survey height over the same point on the ground.

Corsair II—(DOD) A single-seat, single turbofan engine, all-weather light attack aircraft designed to operate from aircraft carriers, armed with cannon and capable of carrying a wide assortment of nuclear and/or conventional ordnance and advanced air-to-air and air-to-ground missiles. Designated as A–7.

cost contract—(DOD) 1. A contract which provides for payment to the contractor of allowable costs, to the extent prescribed in the contract, incurred in performance of the contract. 2. A cost-reimbursement type contract under which the contractor receives no fee.

cost-plus a fixed-fee contract—(DOD) A cost reimbursement type contract which provides for the payment of a fixed fee to the contractor. The fixed fee, once negotiated, does not vary with actual cost but may be adjusted as a result of any subsequent changes in the scope of work or services to be performed under the contract.

cost sharing contract—*(DOD)* A cost reimbursement type contract under which the contractor receives no fee but is reimbursed only for an agreed portion of its allowable costs.

countdown—*(DOD, NATO, IADB)* The step-by-step process leading to initiation of missile testing, launching, and firing. It is performed in accordance with a pre-designated time schedule.

counter air—*(DOD, IADB)* A United States Air Force term for air operations conducted to attain and maintain a desired degree of air superiority by the destruction or neutralization of enemy forces. Both air offensive and air defensive actions are involved. The former range throughout enemy territory and are generally conducted at the initiative of the friendly forces. The latter are conducted near to or over friendly territory and are generally reactive to the initiative of the enemy air forces. See also **antiair warfare.** (Note: **IADB** definition begins with "Operations conducted.")

counter air operation—*(NATO)* An air operation directed against the enemy's air offensive and defensive capability in order to attain and maintain a desired degree of air superiority.

counterattack—*(DOD, NATO, IADB)* Attack by part or all of a defending force against an enemy attacking force, for such specific purposes as regaining ground lost or cutting off or destroying enemy advance units, and with the general objective of denying to the enemy the attainment of his purpose in attacking. In sustained defensive operations, it is undertaken to restore the battle position and is directed at limited objectives.

counterbattery fire—*(NATO)* Fire delivered for the purpose of destroying or neutralizing indirect fire weapon systems.

counter-C3—See **command, control and communications countermeasures.**

counterdeception—*(DOD)* Efforts to negate, neutralize, diminish the effects of, or gain advantage from, a foreign deception operation. Counterdeception does not include the intelligence function of identifying foreign deception operations. See also **deception.**

counterespionage—*(DOD, IADB)* That aspect of counterintelligence designed to detect, destroy, neutralize, exploit, or prevent espionage activities through identification, penetration, manipulation, deception, and repression of individuals, groups, or organizations conducting or suspected of conducting espionage activities.

counter-espionage—*(NATO)* Action designed to detect and counteract espionage. See also **counter-intelligence.**

counterfire—*(DOD, NATO, IADB)* Fire intended to destroy or neutralize enemy weapons. *(DOD, IADB)* Includes counter-battery, counterbombardment, and countermortar fire. See also **fire.**

counterforce—*(DOD, IADB)* The employment of strategic air and missile forces in an effort to destroy, or render impotent, selected military capabilities of an enemy force under any of the circumstances by which hostilities may be initiated.

counter-guerrilla warfare—*(DOD, I, NATO, IADB)* Operations and activities conducted by armed forces, paramilitary forces, or nonmilitary agencies against guerrillas.

counterinsurgency—*(DOD)* Those military, paramilitary, political, economic, psychological, and civic actions taken by a government to defeat insurgency.

counter-insurgency—*(NATO)* Those military, paramilitary, political, economic, psychological, and civic actions taken to defeat insurgency.

counterinsurgency—*(IADB)* Those military, paramilitary, political, economic, psychological, and civic actions taken by a government to defeat subversive insurgency.

counter-intelligence—*(DOD, NATO)* Those activities which are concerned with identifying and counteracting the threat to security posed by hostile intelligence services or organizations or by individuals engaged in espionage, sabotage or subversion. See also **counter-espionage; counter-sabotage; counter-subversion; protective security; security; security intelligence.**

counterintelligence—*(IADB)* That phase of intelligence covering all activity devoted to destroying the effectiveness of inimical foreign intelligence activities and to the protection of information against espionage, personnel against subversion, and installations or material against sabotage. See also **counterespionage; countersabotage; countersubversion.**

countermeasures—*(DOD, IADB)* That form of military science that by the employment of devices and/or techniques, has as its objective the impairment of the operational effectiveness of enemy activity. See also **electronic warfare.**

countermilitary—See **counterforce.**

countermine—*(DOD, NATO)* The process of exploding the main charge in a mine by shock of a nearby explosion of another mine or independent explosive charge. The explosion may be caused either by sympathetic detonation of the main charge, or through the explosive train and firing mechanism of the mine.

countermining—*(DOD, IADB)* 1. **land mine warfare**—Tactics and techniques used to detect, avoid, breach, and/or neutralize enemy mines and the use of available resources to deny the enemy the opportunity to employ mines. 2. **naval mine warfare**—The detonation of mines by nearby explosions, either accidental or deliberate.

countermove—*(DOD, NATO)* An operation undertaken in reaction to or in anticipation of a move by the enemy. See also **counterattack.**

counteroffensive—*(DOD, IADB)* A large scale offensive undertaken by a defending force to seize the initiative from the attacking force. See also **counterattack.**

counterpreparation fire—*(DOD, NATO, IADB)* Intensive prearranged fire delivered when the imminence of the enemy attack is discovered. *(DOD, IADB)* It is designed to: break up enemy formations; disorganize the enemy's systems of command, communications, and observation; decrease the effectiveness of artillery preparation; and impair the enemy's offensive spirit. See also **fire.**

counterreconnaissance—*(DOD, IADB)* All measures taken to prevent hostile observation of a force, area, or place.

countersabotage—*(DOD, IADB)* That aspect of counterintelligence designed to detect, destroy, neutralize, or prevent sabotage activities through identification, penetration, manipulation, deception, and repression of individuals, groups, or organizations conducting or suspected of conducting sabotage activities.

counter-sabotage—*(NATO)* Action designed to detect and counteract sabotage. See also **counter-intelligence.**

countersign—*(DOD, NATO, IADB)* A secret challenge and its reply. See also **challenge; password; reply.**

countersubversion—*(DOD, IADB)* That aspect of counterintelligence designed to detect, destroy, neutralize, or prevent subversive activities through the identification, exploitation, penetration, manipulation, deception, and repression of individuals, groups, or organizations conducting or suspected of conducting subversive activities.

counter-subversion—*(NATO)* Action designed to detect and counteract subversion. See also **counter-intelligence; subversion.**

countersurveillance—*(NATO)* All measures, active or passive, taken to counteract hostile surveillance. See also **surveillance.**

country cover diagram—*(DOD, NATO)* A small scale index, by country, depicting the existence of air photography for planning purposes only.

coupled mode—*(DOD, NATO)* A flight control state in which an aircraft is controlled through the automatic flight control system by signals from guidance equipment.

Courier—*(DOD, IADB)* A delayed repeater communication satellite which had the capability of storing and relaying communications using microwave frequencies. This satellite gave a limited demonstration of instantaneous microwave communications.

courier—*(DOD, IADB)* A messenger (usually a commissioned or warrant officer) responsible for the secure physical transmission and delivery of documents and material. Generally referred to as a command or local courier. See also **armed forces courier.**

course—*(DOD, NATO, IADB)* The intended direction of movement in the horizontal plane.

course of action—*(IADB)* 1. Any sequence of activities which an individual or unit may follow. 2. A possible plan open to an individual or commander which would accomplish, or is related to the accomplishment of, his mission. 3. The scheme adopted to accomplish a job or mission. 4. A line of conduct in an engagement.

cover—*(DOD, NATO)* 1. The action by land, air, or sea forces to protect by offense, defense, or threat of either or both. 2. Those measures necessary to give protection to a person, plan, operation, formation or installation from the enemy intelligence effort and leakage of infor-

mation. 3. The act of maintaining a continuous receiver watch with transmitter calibrated and available, but not necessarily available for immediate use. 4. Shelter or protection, either natural or artificial. *(DOD)* 5. Photographs or other recorded images which show a particular area of ground. 6. A code meaning, "Keep fighters between force/base and contact designated at distance stated from force/base" (e.g., "cover bogey twenty-seven to thirty miles").

cover—*(IADB)* 1. The action by land, air, or sea forces to protect by offense, defense, or threat of either or both. 2. Shelter or protection, either natural or artificial. 3. To maintain a continuous receiver watch with transmitter calibrated and available, but not necessarily available for immediate use. 4. Photographs or other recorded images which show a particular area of ground. 5. Keep fighters between force/base and contact designated at distance stated from force/base (e.g., "cover bogey twenty-seven to thirty miles.") 6. Protective guise used by a person, organization, or installation to prevent identification with clandestine activities. See also **comparative cover; concealment.**

coverage—*(DOD, NATO, IADB)* 1. The ground area represented on imagery, photomaps, mosaics, maps, and other geographical presentation systems. *(DOD, IADB)* 2. Cover or protection, as the coverage of troops by supporting fire. 3. The extent to which intelligence information is available in respect to any specified area of interest. 4. The summation of the geographical areas and volumes of aerospace under surveillance. See also **comparative cover.**

coverage index—*(DOD)* One of a series of overlays showing all photographic reconnaissance missions covering the map sheet to which the overlays refer. See also **cover trace (reconnaissance).**

covering fire—*(DOD, NATO, IADB)* 1. Fire used to protect troops when they are within range of enemy small arms. 2. In amphibious usage, fire delivered prior to the landing to cover preparatory operations such as underwater demolition or minesweeping. See also **fire**.

covering force—*(DOD, NATO, IADB)* 1. A force operating apart from the main force for the purpose of intercepting, engaging, delaying, disorganizing, and deceiving the enemy before he can attack the force covered. 2. Any body or detachment of troops which provides security for a larger force by observation, reconnaissance, attack, or defense, or by any combination of these methods. See also **force(s)**.

covering force area—*(NATO)* The area forward of the forward edge of the battle area out to the forward positions initially assigned to the covering forces. It is here that the covering forces execute assigned tasks.

covering troops—See **covering force**.

cover (intelligence)—See **cover, Part 6**.

cover search—*(DOD, NATO, IADB)* In air photographic reconnaissance, the process of selection of the most suitable existing cover for a specific requirement.

covert operations—*(DOD, I, IADB)* Operations which are so planned and executed as to conceal the identity of or permit plausible denial by the sponsor. They differ from clandestine operations in that emphasis is placed on concealment of identity of sponsor rather than on concealment of the operation.

cover trace (reconnaissance)—*(NATO)* One of a series of overlays showing all air reconnaissance sorties covering the map sheet to which the overlays refer.

crab angle—*(DOD, NATO)* The angle between the aircraft track or flight line and the fore and aft axis of a vertical camera, which is in line with the longitudinal axis of the aircraft.

crash locator beacon—*(DOD, NATO, IADB)* An automatic radio beacon which will help

searching forces to locate a crashed aircraft. See also **personal locator beacon**.

crash position indicator—See **crash locator beacon**.

crater—*(DOD, IADB)* The pit, depression, or cavity formed in the surface of the earth by an explosion. It may range from saucer shaped to conical, depending largely on the depth of burst. In the case of a deep underground burst, no rupture of the surface may occur. The resulting cavity is termed a camouflet.

crater depth—*(DOD)* The maximum depth of the crater measured from the deepest point of the pit to the original ground level.

cratering charge—*(DOD, NATO)* A charge placed at an adequate depth to produce a crater.

crater radius—*(DOD, IADB)* The average radius of the crater measured at the level corresponding to the original surface of the ground.

creeping barrage—*(DOD, NATO, IADB)* A barrage in which the fire of all units participating remains in the same relative position throughout and which advances in steps of one line at a time.

creeping mine—*(DOD, NATO)* In naval mine warfare, a buoyant mine held below the surface by a weight, usually in the form of a chain, which is free to creep along the seabed under the influence of stream or current.

crest—*(DOD, NATO, IADB)* A terrain feature of such altitude that it restricts fire or observation in an area beyond, resulting in dead space, or limiting the minimum elevation, or both.

crested—*(DOD, IADB)* A report which indicates that engagement of a target or observation of an area is not possible because of an obstacle or intervening crest.

crested—*(NATO)* In artillery and naval gunfire support, a report which indicates that engagement of a target or observation of an area is not possible because of an obstacle or intervening crest.

critical altitude—*(DOD, NATO, IADB)* The altitude beyond which an aircraft or airbreathing guided missile ceases to perform satisfactorily. See also **altitude**.

critical intelligence—*(DOD, IADB)* Intelligence which is crucial and requires the immediate attention of the commander. It is required to enable the commander to make decisions that will provide a timely and appropriate response to actions by the potential/actual enemy. It includes but is not limited to the following: **a.** strong indications of the imminent outbreak of hostilities of any type (warning of attack); **b.** aggression of any nature against a friendly country; **c.** indications or use of nuclear-biological-chemical weapons (targets); and **d.** significant events within potential enemy countries that may lead to modification of nuclear strike plans.

critical item—*(DOD, IADB)* An essential item which is in short supply or expected to be in short supply for an extended period. See also **critical supplies and materials; regulated item.**

critical mass—*(DOD, IADB)* The minimum amount of fissionable material capable of supporting a chain reaction under precisely specified conditions.

critical node—*(DOD)* An element, position, or communications entity whose disruption or destruction immediately degrades the ability of a force to command, control, or effectively conduct combat operations.

critical point—*(DOD, IADB)* 1. A key geographical point or position important to the success of an operation. 2. In point of time, a crisis or a turning point in an operation. 3. A selected point along a line of march used for reference in giving instructions. 4. A point

where there is a change of direction or change in slope in a ridge or stream. 5. Any point along a route of march where interference with a troop movement may occur.

critical speed—*(DOD, NATO)* A speed or range of speeds which a ship cannot sustain due to vibration or other similar phenomena.

critical supplies and material—*(DOD, NATO, IADB)* Those supplies vital to the support of operations, which owing to various causes are in short supply or are expected to be in short supply. See also **critical item; regulated item.**

critical zone—*(DOD, IADB)* The area over which a bombing plane engaged in horizontal or glide bombing must maintain straight flight so that the bomb sight can be operated properly and bombs dropped accurately.

critic report—See **critical intelligence.**

crossing—*(DOD)* In air intercept, a term meaning, "Passing from _____ to _____."

crossing area—*(DOD, NATO)* A number of adjacent crossing sites under the control of one commander.

cross-loading (personnel)—*(DOD, IADB)* A system of loading troops so that they may be disembarked or dropped at two or more landing or drop zones, thereby achieving unit integrity upon delivery. See also **loading.**

crossover point—*(DOD, IADB)* That range in the air warfare area at which a target ceases to be an air intercept target and becomes a surface-to-air missile target.

cross-servicing—*(DOD, IADB)* That function performed by one military service in support of another military service for which reimbursement is required from the service receiving support. See also **servicing.**

cross-servicing—*(NATO)* That servicing performed by one service or national element for other services or national elements and for

97

which the other services or national elements may be charged.

cross tell—*(DOD, NATO)* The transfer of information between facilities at the same operational level. See also **track telling.**

cruise missile—*(DOD, IADB)* Guided missile, the major portion of whose flight path to its target is conducted at approximately constant velocity; depends on the dynamic reaction of air for lift and upon propulsion forces to balance drag.

cruising altitude—*(DOD, NATO, IADB)* A level determined by vertical measurement from mean sea level, maintained during a flight or portion thereof.

cruising level—*(DOD, NATO, IADB)* A level maintained during a significant portion of a flight. See also **altitude.**

cryogenic liquid—*(DOD, IADB)* Liquefied gas at very low temperature, such as liquid oxygen, nitrogen, argon.

cryptanalysis—*(DOD, IADB)* The steps and operations performed in converting encrypted messages into plain text without initial knowledge of the key employed in the encryption.

cryptanalysis—*(NATO)* The study of encrypted texts. The steps or processes involved in converting encrypted text into plain text without initial knowledge of the key employed in the encryption.

cryptochannel—*(DOD, IADB)* A complete system of crypto-communications between two or more holders. The basic unit for naval cryptographic communication. It includes: **a.** the cryptographic aids prescribed; **b.** the holders thereof; **c.** the indicators or other means of identification; **d.** the area or areas in which effective; **e.** the special purpose, if any, for which provided; and **f.** pertinent notes as to distribution, usage, etc. A cryptochannel is analogous to a radio circuit.

cryptographic information—*(DOD)* All information significantly descriptive of cryptographic techniques and processes or of cryptographic systems and equipment, or their functions and capabilities, and all cryptomaterial.

cryptologic—*(DOD, IADB)* Of or pertaining to cryptology.

cryptology—*(DOD, IADB)* The science which treats of hidden, disguised, or encrypted communications. It embraces communications security and communications intelligence.

cryptomaterial—*(DOD, IADB)* All material including documents, devices, equipment, and apparatus essential to the encryption, decryption, or authentication of telecommunications. When classified, it is designated CRYPTO and subject to special safeguards.

cryptomaterial—*(NATO)* All material, including documents, devices or equipment that contains crypto information and is essential to the encryption, decryption or authentication of telecommunications.

cryptopart—*(DOD, NATO, IADB)* A division of a message as prescribed for security reasons. The operating instructions for certain cryptosystems prescribe the number of groups which may be encrypted in the systems, using a single message indicator. Cryptoparts are identified in plain language. They are not to be confused with message parts.

cryptosecurity—See **communications security.**

cryptosystem—*(DOD, IADB)* The associated items of cryptomaterial that are used as a unit and provide a single means of encryption and decryption. See also **cipher; code; decrypt; encipher; encrypt.**

crystal ball—*(DOD)* Radar scope.

cultivation—*(DOD)* A deliberate and calculated association with a person for the purpose of recruitment, obtaining information, or gaining control for these or other purposes.

culture—*(DOD, NATO)* A feature of the terrain that has been constructed by man. Included are such items as roads, buildings, and canals; boundary lines, and, in a broad sense, all names and legends on a map.

curb weight—*(DOD, IADB)* Weight of a ground vehicle including fuel, lubricants, coolant and on-vehicle materiel, excluding cargo and operating personnel.

currency—*(NATO)* The up-to-dateness of a map or chart as determined by comparison with the best available information at a given time.

Current Force—*(DOD)* The force that exists today. The Current Force represents actual force structure and/or manning available to meet present contingencies. It is the basis for operations and contingency plans and orders. See also **force; Intermediate Force Planning Level; Minimum Risk Force; Planning Force; Programmed Forces.**

current intelligence—*(DOD, IADB)* Intelligence of all types and forms of immediate interest which is usually disseminated without the delays necessary to complete evaluation or interpretation.

current intelligence—*(NATO)* Intelligence which reflects the current situation at either strategic or tactical level. See also **basic intelligence; intelligence.**

curve of pursuit—*(DOD, NATO, IADB)* The curved path described by a fighter plane making an attack on a moving target while holding the proper aiming allowance.

custody—*(DOD, IADB)* The responsibility for the control of, transfer and movement of, and access to, weapons and components. Custody also includes the maintenance of accountability for weapons and components.

customer ship—*(DOD, NATO)* The ship in a replenishment unit that receives the transferred personnel and/or supplies.

cut-off—*(DOD, NATO)* The deliberate shutting off of a reaction engine.

cutoff attack—*(DOD, IADB)* An attack that provides a direct vector from the interceptor's position to an intercept point with the target track.

cut-off velocity—*(DOD, NATO, IADB)* The velocity attained by a missile at the point of cutoff.

cutout—*(DOD, IADB)* An intermediary or device used to obviate direct contact between members of a clandestine organization.

cutter—*(DOD, NATO)* In naval mine warfare, a device fitted to a sweep wire to cut or part the moorings of mines or obstructors; it may also be fitted in the mooring of a mine or obstructor to part a sweep.

cutting charge—*(DOD, NATO)* A charge which produces a cutting effect in line with its plane of symmetry.

CV—See **attack aircraft carrier.**

CVN—See **attack aircraft carrier.**

cyanogen agent—See **blood agent.**

D

DADCAP—*(DOD, IADB)* Dawn and dusk combat air patrol.

daily intelligence summary—*(DOD)* A report prepared in message form at the joint force component command headquarters that provides higher, lateral, and subordinate headquarters with a summary of all significant intelligence produced during the previous 24-hour period. The "as of" time for information, content, and submission time for the report will be as specified by the joint force commander. Also called DISUM.

daily movement summary (shipping)—*(DOD, IADB)* A tabulation of departures and arrivals of all merchant shipping (including neutrals) arriving or departing ports during a 24-hour period. *(IADB)* These summaries are prepared by area commanders (or operational control authorities if designated by area commanders) and are classified confidential.

damage—See **nuclear damage (land warfare).**

damage area—*(DOD, NATO, IADB)* In naval mine warfare, the plan area around a minesweeper inside which a mine explosion is likely to interrupt operations.

damage assessment—*(DOD, NATO, IADB)* 1. The determination of the effect of attacks on targets. *(DOD, IADB)* 2. A determination of the effect of a compromise of classified information on national security. See also **civil damage assessment; military damage assessment.**

damage control—*(DOD, NATO, IADB)* In naval usage, measures necessary aboard ship to preserve and reestablish watertight integrity, stability, maneuverability and offensive power; to control list and trim; to effect rapid repairs of materiel; to limit the spread of, and provide adequate protection from, fire; to limit the spread of, remove the contamination by, and provide adequate protection from, toxic agents; and to provide for care of wounded personnel. See also **area damage control; disaster control; rear area security.**

damage criteria—*(DOD, IADB)* The critical levels of various effects, such as blast pressure and thermal radiation, required to achieve specified levels of damage.

damage estimation—*(DOD)* A preliminary appraisal of the potential effects of an attack. See also **attack assessment.**

damage radius—*(DOD, NATO)* In naval mine warfare, the average distance from a ship within which a mine containing a given weight and type of explosive must detonate if it is to inflict a specified amount of damage.

damage threat—*(DOD, NATO)* The probability that a target ship passing once through a minefield will explode one or more mines and sustain a specified amount of damage.

dan—*(DOD)* To mark a position or a sea area with dan buoys.

dan buoy—*(DOD)* A temporary marker buoy used during minesweeping operations to indicate boundaries of swept paths, swept areas, known hazards, and other locations or reference points.

danger—*(DOD, IADB)* Information in a call for fire to indicate that friendly forces are within 600 to 1,500 meters of the target.

danger area—*(DOD, IADB)* 1. A specified area above, below, or within which there may be potential danger. *(DOD, NATO)* 2. In air traffic control, an airspace of defined dimensions within which activities dangerous to the flight of aircraft may exist at specified times. See also **prohibited area; restricted area.**

danger close—*(DOD, NATO)* In artillery and naval gunfire support, information in a call for fire to indicate that friendly forces are within 600 meters of the target.

dangerous cargo—See **cargo.**

dangerous cargo—*(DOD, IADB)* Cargo which, because of its dangerous properties, is subject to special regulations for its transport.

dangerously exposed waters—*(DOD, NATO)* The sea areas adjacent to the severely threatened coastlines.

danger space—*(DOD)* That space between the weapon and the target where the trajectory does not rise 1.8 meters (the average height of a standing human). This includes the area encompassed by the beaten zone. See also **beaten zone.**

dan runner—*(DOD, NATO)* A ship running a line of dan buoys.

dart—*(DOD)* A target towed by a jet aircraft and fired at by fighter aircraft. Used for training only.

data—*(DOD)* Representation of facts, concepts, or instructions in a formalized manner suitable for communication, interpretation, or processing by humans or by automatic means. Any representations such as characters or analog quantities to which meaning is or might be assigned.

data block—*(DOD, NATO)* Information presented on air imagery relevant to the geographical position, altitude, attitude and heading of the aircraft and, in certain cases, administrative information and information on the sensors employed.

data code—*(DOD, IADB)* A number, letter, character, or any combination thereof used to represent a data element or data item. For example, the data codes "E8," "O3," and "O6" might be used to represent the data items of sergeant, captain, and colonel under the data element "military personnel grade."

data element—*(DOD, IADB)* A basic unit of information having a unique meaning and subcategories (data items) of distinct units or values. Examples of data elements are military personnel grade, sex, race, geographic location, and military unit.

data item—*(DOD, IADB)* A subunit of descriptive information or value classified under a data element. For example, the data element "military personnel grade" contains data items such as sergeant, captain, and colonel.

data link—*(DOD, NATO)* The means of connecting one location to another for the purpose of transmitting and receiving data.

data link—*(IADB)* A communication link suitable for transmission of data.

data mile—*(DOD, IADB)* A standard unit of distance—6,000 feet.

date line—See **international date line.**

date-time group—*(DOD, IADB)* The date and time, expressed in digits and zone suffix, the message was prepared for transmission. (Expressed as six digits followed by the zone suffix; first pair of digits denotes the date, second pair the hours, third pair the minutes.)

date-time group—*(NATO)* A group of six digits with a zone time suffix and the standardized abbreviation for the month. The first pair of digits represents the day; the second pair the hour; the third pair the minutes. After the month may be added the last two digits of the year.

datum—*(DOD, NATO, IADB)* Any numerical or geometrical quantity or set of such quantities which may serve as reference or base for other quantities. Where the concept is geometric, the plural form is "datums" in contrast to the normal plural "data."

datum (antisubmarine warfare)—*(DOD, IADB)* A datum is the last known position of a submarine, or suspected submarine, after contact has been lost.

datum dan buoy—*(DOD, NATO)* In naval mine warfare, a dan buoy intended as a geographic reference or check, which needs to be more visible and more securely moored than a normal dan buoy.

datum error (antisubmarine warfare)—*(DOD, IADB)* An estimate of the degree of accuracy in the reported position of datum.

datum (geodetic)—*(DOD, IADB)* A reference surface consisting of five quantities: the latitude and longitude of an initial point, the azimuth of a line from that point, and the parameters of the reference ellipsoid.

datum level—*(DOD, NATO)* A surface to which elevations, heights or depths on a map or chart are related. See also **altitude**.

datum point—*(DOD, NATO, IADB)* Any reference point of known or assumed coordinates from which calculation or measurements may be taken.

datum time (antisubmarine warfare)—*(DOD, IADB)* The datum time is the time when contact with the submarine, or suspected submarine, was lost.

day air defense fighter—*(DOD, NATO)* A fighter aircraft with equipment and weapons which enable it to engage airborne targets, but in clear weather conditions and by day only.

day fighter—*(NATO)* A fighter aircraft designed for air interception purposes, primarily in visual meteorological conditions. It may or may not carry electronic devices to assist in interception and in aiming its weapons.

day of supply—See **one day's supply**.

dazzle—*(DOD, IADB)* Temporary loss of vision or a temporary reduction in visual acuity. See also **flash blindness**.

DC-130—See **Hercules**.

DD—See **destroyer**.

D-day—*(DOD, IADB)* 1. The unnamed day on which a particular operation commences or is to commence. An operation may be the commencement of hostilities. **a.** The date of a major military effort. **b.** The execution date of an operation (as distinguished from the date the order to execute is issued); the date the operations phase is implemented, by land assault, air strike, naval bombardment, parachute assault, or amphibious assault. The highest command or headquarters responsible for coordinating the planning will specify the exact meaning of D-day within the aforementioned definition. If more than one such event is mentioned in a single plan, the secondary events will be keyed to the primary event by adding or subtracting days as necessary. The letter "D" will be the only one used to denote the above. The command or headquarters directly responsible for the execution of the operation, if other than the one coordinating the planning, will do so in light of the meanings specified by the highest planning headquarters. 2. Time in plans will be indicated by a letter that shows the unit of time employed and figures, with a minus or plus sign, to indicate the amount of time before or after the referenced event; e.g., "D" is for a particular day, "H" for an hour. Similarly, D + 7 means 7 days after D-day, H + 2 means 2 hours after H-hour. If the figure becomes unduly large, for example, D-day plus 90, the designation of D + 3 months may be employed; i.e., if the figure following a letter plus a time unit (D-day, H-hour, etc.) is intended to refer to units of time other than that which follows the letter, then the unit of time employed with the figure must be spelled out. See also **H-hour; K-day; M-day**. See also **designation of days and hours**. (NOTE: IADB definition does not use subdivision a., b., c.)

D-day consumption/production differential assets—*(DOD, IADB)* As applied to the D-to-P concept, these assets are required to compensate for the inability of the production base to meet expenditure (consumption) requirements during the D-to-P period. See also **D-to— concept.**

D–day materiel readiness gross capability— *(DOD, IADB)* As applied to the D-to-P concept, this capability represents the sum of all assets on hand on D–day and the gross production capability (funded and unfunded) between D–day and P–day. When this capability equals the D-to-P Materiel Readiness Gross Requirement, requirements and capabilities are in balance. See also **D-to-P concept.**

D–day pipeline assets—*(DOD)* As applied to the D-to-P concept, these assets represent the sum of CONUS and overseas operating and safety levels and intransit levels of supply. See also **D–to-P concept.**

DDG—See **guided missile destroyer.**

deadline—*(DOD, IADB)* To remove a vehicle or piece of equipment from operation or use for one of the following reasons: **a.** is inoperative due to damage, malfunctioning, or necessary repairs. The term does not include items temporarily removed from use by reason of routine maintenance, and repairs that do not affect the combat capability of the item; **b.** is unsafe; and **c.** would be damaged by further use.

dead mine—*(DOD, NATO)* A mine which has been neutralized, sterilized or rendered safe. See also **mine.**

dead space—*(DOD, NATO)* 1. An area within the maximum range of a weapon, radar, or observer, which cannot be covered by fire or observation from a particular position because of intervening obstacles, the nature of the ground, or the characteristics of the trajectory, or the limitations of the pointing capabilities of the weapons. 2. An area or zone which is within range of a radio transmitter, but in which a signal is not received. 3. The volume of space above and around a gun or guided missile system into which it cannot fire because of mechanical or electronic limitations.

dead zone—See **dead space.**

debarkation—*(DOD, IADB)* The unloading of troops, equipment, or supplies from a ship or aircraft.

debarkation—*(NATO)* The unloading of troops with their supplies and equipment from a ship.

debarkation net—*(DOD, IADB)* A specially prepared type of cargo net employed for the debarkation of troops over the side of a ship.

debarkation schedule—*(DOD, NATO, IADB)* A schedule which provides for the timely and orderly debarkation of troops and equipment and emergency supplies for the waterborne ship-to-shore movement.

decay curves (radioactive)—*(DOD, NATO, IADB)* Graph lines representing the decrease of radioactivity with the passage of time.

decay (radioactive)—*(DOD, NATO, IADB)* The decrease in the radiation intensity of any radioactive material with respect to time.

decay rate (radioactive)—*(DOD, IADB)* The time rate of the disintegration of radioactive material generally accompanied by the emission of particles and/or gamma radiation.

decay rate (radioactive)—*(NATO)* The rate of disintegration of radioactive material with respect to time.

Decca—*(DOD, NATO)* A radio phase-comparison system which uses a master and slave stations to establish a hyperbolic lattice and provide accurate ground position-fixing facilities.

decentralized control—*(DOD, NATO, IADB)* In air defense, the normal mode whereby a higher echelon monitors unit actions, making direct target assignments to units only when necessary to insure proper fire distribution or to prevent engagement of friendly aircraft. See also **centralized control.**

decentralized items—*(DOD, IADB)* Those items of supply for which appropriate authority has prescribed local management and procurement.

deception—*(DOD, NATO, IADB)* Those measures designed to mislead the enemy by manipulation, distortion, or falsification of evidence to induce him to react in a manner prejudicial to his interests. See also **counterdeception; military deception.**

deception means—*(DOD)* Methods, resources, and techniques that can be used to convey information to a foreign power. There are three categories of deception means:

a. **physical means**—Activities and resources used to convey or deny selected information to a foreign power. (Examples: military operations, including exercises, reconnaissance, training activities, and movement of forces; the use of dummy equipment and devices; tactics; bases, logistic actions, stockpiles, and repair activity; and test and evaluation activities).

b. **technical means**—Military materiel resources and their associated operating techniques used to convey or deny selected information to a foreign power through the deliberate radiation, reradiation, alteration absorption, or reflection of energy; the emission or suppression of chemical or biological odors; and the emission or suppression of nuclear particles.

c. **administrative means**—Resources, methods, and techniques designed to convey or deny oral, pictorial, documentary, or other physical evidence to a foreign power.

decision—*(DOD, IADB)* In an estimate of the situation, a clear and concise statement of the line of action intended to be followed by the commander as the one most favorable to the successful accomplishment of his mission.

decision altitude—*(DOD, NATO)* An altitude related to the highest elevation in the touch down zone, specified for a glide slope approach, at which a missed-approach procedure must be initiated if the required visual reference has not been established. See also **decision height.**

decision height—*(DOD, NATO)* A height above the highest elevation in the touch down zone, specified for a glide slope approach, at which a missed-approach procedure must be initiated if the required visual reference has not been established. See also **decision altitude.**

deck alert—See **ground alert.**

declared speed—*(DOD, NATO)* The continuous speed which a master declares his ship can maintain on a forthcoming voyage under moderate weather conditions having due regard to her present condition.

declared speed—*(IADB)* The continuous speed which a master declares his ship can maintain on a forthcoming voyage under moderate weather conditions (that is, moderate sea, wind force 4 on the Beaufort scale) having due regard to her present condition (trim, draft, state of bottom, state of machinery, and quality of bunkers). The declared speed is used by the naval control of shipping officer to determine whether a ship is qualified for inclusion in an x-knot convoy.

declassification—*(DOD, IADB)* The determination that in the interests of national security, classified information no longer requires any degree of protection against unauthorized disclosure, coupled with removal or cancellation of the classification designation.

declassify—*(NATO, IADB)* To cancel the security classification of an item of classified matter. See also **downgrade.**

declination—*(DOD, NATO, IADB)* The angular distance to a body on the celestial sphere measured north or south through 90° from the celestial equator along the hour circle of the body. Comparable to latitude on the terrestrial sphere. See also **magnetic declination; magnetic variation.**

decompression chamber—See **hypobaric chamber.**

decompression sickness—*(DOD, IADB)* A syndrome, including bends, chokes, neurological disturbances, and collapse, resulting from exposure to reduced ambient pressure and caused by gas bubbles in the tissues, fluids, and blood vessels.

decontamination—*(DOD, NATO, IADB)* The process of making any person, object, or area safe by absorbing, destroying, neutralizing, making harmless, or removing, chemical or biological agents, or by removing radioactive material clinging to or around it.

decontamination station—*(DOD, NATO)* A building or location suitably equipped and organized where personnel and materiel are cleansed of chemical, biological or radiological contaminants.

decontamination station—*(IADB)* A building or location suitably equipped and staffed where personnel and their clothing are decontaminated from the effects of toxic attack.

decoy—*(DOD, NATO, IADB)* An imitation in any sense of a person, object or phenomenon which is intended to deceive enemy surveillance devices or mislead enemy evaluation. See also **chaff.**

decoy ship—*(DOD, NATO)* A ship camouflaged as a noncombatant ship with its armament and other fighting equipment hidden and with special provisions for unmasking its weapons quickly. Also called **Q-ship.**

decoy ship (Q ship)—*(IADB)* A warship or other ship camouflaged as a merchantman or converted commerce raider with its armament and other fighting equipment hidden and with special provisions for unmasking its weapons quickly.

decrypt—*(DOD, IADB)* To convert encrypted text into its equivalent plain text by means of a cryptosystem. (This does not include solution by cryptanalysis.) Note: The term decrypt covers the meanings of decipher and decode. See also **cryptosystem.**

deep fording—*(DOD, IADB)* The ability of a self-propelled gun or ground vehicle equipped with built-in waterproofing and/or a special waterproofing kit, to negotiate a water obstacle with its wheels or tracks in contact with the ground. See also **flotation; shallow fording.**

deep fording capability—*(DOD, NATO)* The characteristic of self-propelled gun or ground vehicle equipped with built-in waterproofing and/or a special waterproofing kit, to negotiate a water obstacle with its wheels or tracks in contact with the ground. See also **shallow fording capability.**

deep minefield—*(DOD, NATO, IADB)* An anti-submarine minefield which is safe for surface ships to cross.

deep supporting fire—*(DOD, NATO, IADB)* Fire directed on objectives not in the immediate vicinity of our forces, for neutralizing and destroying enemy reserves and weapons, and interfering with enemy command, supply, communications and observations. See also **close supporting fire; direct supporting fire; supporting fire.**

DEFCON—See **defense readiness conditions.**

defector—*(DOD, IADB)* National of a country who has escaped from the control of such country or who, being outside such jurisdiction and control, is unwilling to return thereto and is of special value to another country.

defector—*(NATO)* A person who repudiates his or her country when beyond its jurisdiction or control.

defense area—*(DOD, NATO)* For any particular command, the area extending from the forward edge of the battle area to its rear boundary. It is here that the decisive defensive battle is fought.

defense classification—See **security classification**.

defense emergency—*(DOD)* An emergency condition that exists when: **a.** a major attack is made upon US forces overseas, or on allied forces in any theater and is confirmed by either the commander of a command established by the Secretary of Defense or higher authority; or **b.** an overt attack of any type is made upon the United States and is confirmed either by the commander of a command established by the Secretary of Defense or higher authority.

defense emergency—*(IADB)* An emergency condition that exists when: **a.** a major attack is made upon national forces overseas or on allied forces in any theater and is confirmed either by the commander of a command established by higher authority; or **b.** an overt attack of any type is made upon the country and is confirmed by the commander of a command established by higher authority.

defense in depth—*(DOD, NATO, IADB)* The siting of mutually supporting defense positions designed to absorb and progressively weaken attack, prevent initial observations of the whole position by the enemy, and to allow the commander to maneuver his reserve.

defense readiness condition—*(NATO, IADB)* A number or code word indicating the readiness posture of a unit for actual operations or exercises. Also called **state of readiness**.

defense readiness conditions—*(DOD)* A uniform system of progressive alert postures for use between the Joint Chiefs of Staff and the commanders of unified and specified commands and for use by the Services. Defense Readiness Conditions are graduated to match situations of varying military severity (status of alert). Defense Readiness Conditions are identified by the short title DEFCON (5), (4), (3), (2), and (1), as appropriate.

defense shipping authority—*(NATO)* The NATO civil wartime agency established in time of war responsible for the employment of merchant ships assigned to the allied ocean shipping pool to achieve the greatest efficiency in support of the common effort.

defensive coastal area—*(DOD, NATO, IADB)* A part of a coastal area and of the air, land, and water area adjacent to the coast-line within which defense operations may involve land, sea, and air forces.

defensive fire—*(NATO)* Fire delivered by supporting units to assist and protect a unit engaged in a defensive action.

defensive mine countermeasures—*(NATO)* Countermeasures intended to reduce the effect of enemy minelaying.

defensive minefield—*(DOD, NATO, IADB)* 1. In naval mine warfare, a minefield laid in international waters or international straits with the declared intention of controlling shipping in defense of sea communications. *(DOD, IADB)* 2. In land mine warfare, a minefield laid in accordance with an established plan to prevent a penetration between positions and to strengthen the defense of the positions themselves. See also **minefield**.

defensive sea area—*(DOD, IADB)* A sea area, usually including the approaches to and the waters of important ports, harbors, bays, or sounds, for the control and protection of shipping; for the safeguarding of defense installations bordering on waters of the areas; and for provision of other security measures required within the specified areas. It does not extend seaward beyond the territorial waters. See also **maritime control area**.

defensive zone—*(DOD)* A belt of terrain, generally parallel to the front, which includes two or more organized, or partially organized, battle positions.

deferred maintenance—*(NATO)* Maintenance specifically intended to eliminate an existing fault, which did not prevent continued successful operation of the device or program.

defilade—*(DOD, NATO, IADB)* 1. Protection from hostile observation and fire provided by an obstacle such as a hill, ridge, or bank. 2. A vertical distance by which a position is concealed from enemy observation. 3. To shield from enemy fire or observation by using natural or artificial obstacles.

defoliant operation—*(DOD, NATO, IADB)* The employment of defoliating agents on vegetated areas in support of military operations.

defoliating agent—*(DOD, NATO, IADB)* A chemical which causes trees, shrubs, and other plants to shed their leaves prematurely.

degaussing—*(DOD)* The process whereby a ship's magnetic field is reduced by the use of electromagnetic coils, permanent magnets, or other means.

degree of risk—*(DOD, NATO, IADB)* As specified by the commander, the risk to which friendly forces may be subjected from the effects of the detonation of a nuclear weapon used in the attack of a close-in enemy target; acceptable degrees of risk under differing tactical conditions are emergency, moderate, and negligible. See also **emergency risk (nuclear); moderate risk (nuclear); negligible risk (nuclear).**

delay—*(DOD, IADB)* A report from the firing ship to the observer or the spotter to inform that the ship will be unable to provide the requested fire immediately. It will normally be followed by the estimated duration of the delay.

delaying action—See **delaying operation.**

delaying operation—*(DOD, NATO)* An operation in which a force under pressure trades space for time by slowing down the enemy's momentum and inflicting maximum damage on the enemy without, in principle, becoming decisively engaged.

delay (radar)—*(NATO)* 1. The ground distance from a point directly beneath the aircraft to the beginning of the area of radar scan. 2. The electronic delay of the start of the time base used to select a particular segment of the total.

delay release sinker—*(DOD, NATO)* A sinker which holds a moored mine on the sea-bed for a pre-determined time after laying.

delegation of authority—*(DOD, NATO)* The action by which a commander assigns part of his authority commensurate with the assigned task to a subordinate commander. While ultimate responsibility cannot be relinquished, delegation of authority carries with it the imposition of a measure of responsibility. The extent of the authority delegated must be clearly stated.

deliberate attack—*(DOD, NATO)* A type of offensive action characterized by preplanned coordinated employment of firepower and maneuver to close with and destroy or capture the enemy.

deliberate breaching—*(DOD, NATO)* The creation of a lane through a minefield or a clear route through a barrier or fortification, which is systematically planned and carried out.

deliberate crossing—*(DOD, NATO, IADB)* A crossing of a river or stream that requires extensive planning and detailed preparations. See also **hasty crossing.**

deliberate defense—*(DOD, NATO, IADB)* A defense normally organized when out of contact with the enemy or when contact with the enemy is not imminent and time for organization is available. It normally includes an extensive fortified zone incorporating pillboxes, forts, and communications systems. See also **hasty defense.**

delivering ship—*(DOD, NATO)* The ship in a replenishment unit that delivers the rig(s).

delivery error—*(DOD, NATO, IADB)* The inaccuracy associated with a given weapon system resulting in a dispersion of shots about the aiming point. See also **circular error probable; deviation; dispersion; dispersion error; horizontal error.**

delivery forecasts—*(DOD, IADB)* 1. Periodic estimates of contract production deliveries used as a measure of the effectiveness of production and supply availability scheduling and as a guide to corrective actions to resolve procurement or production bottlenecks. 2. Estimates of deliveries under obligation against procurement from appropriated or other funds.

delivery requirements—*(DOD, IADB)* The stipulation which requires that an item of material must be delivered in the total quantity required by the date required and, when appropriate, overpacked as required.

Delta Dagger—*(DOD, IADB)* A single-engine turbojet interceptor employed in air defense. Its speed is supersonic and its armament is the AIM-4 series and AIM-26A (Falcon). It has an all-weather interceptor capability. Designated as F-102A.

Delta Dart—*(DOD, IADB)* A supersonic, single-engine turbojet interceptor aircraft. Its armament consists of Falcon (AIM-4 series) missiles with nonnuclear warheads and Genie (AIR-2A) rockets with nuclear warheads. The Delta Dart is similar to the earlier F-102 in appearance. It has an all-weather intercept capability. Designated as F-106.

demilitarized zone—*(DOD, NATO, IADB)* A defined area in which the stationing, or concentrating of military forces, or the retention or establishment of military installations of any description, is prohibited.

demolition—*(DOD, NATO, IADB)* The destruction of structures, facilities or material by use of fire, water, explosives, mechanical, or other means.

demolition belt—*(DOD, IADB)* A selected land area sown with explosive charges, mines and other available obstacles to deny use of the land to enemy operations, and as a protection to friendly troops. Primary. A continuous series of obstacles across the whole front, selected by the division or higher commander. The preparation of such a belt is normally a priority engineer task. Subsidiary. A supplement to the primary belt to give depth in front or behind or to protect the flanks.

demolition chamber—*(DOD, NATO)* Space intentionally provided in a structure for the emplacement of explosive charges.

demolition firing party—*(DOD, NATO, IADB)* The party at the site which is technically responsible for the demolition. See also **demolition guard.**

demolition guard—*(DOD, NATO, IADB)* A local force positioned to insure that a target is not captured by an enemy before orders are given for its demolition and before the demolition has been successfully fired. The commander of the demolition guard is responsible for the operational command of all troops at the demolition site, including the demolition firing party. He is responsible for transmitting the order to fire to the demolition firing party.

demolition kit—*(DOD, NATO)* The demolition tool kit complete with explosives. See also **demolition tool kit.**

demolition target—See also **charged demolition target; reserved demolition target; uncharged demolition target.**

demolition tool kit—*(DOD, NATO)* The tools, materials and accessories of a nonexplosive nature necessary for preparing demolition charges. See also **demolition kit.**

demonstration—*(DOD, NATO, IADB)* An attack or show of force on a front where a decision is not sought, made with the aim of deceiving the enemy. See also **amphibious demonstration; diversion; diversionary attack.**

denial measure—*(DOD, NATO, IADB)* An action to hinder or deny the enemy the use of

109

space, personnel, or facilities. It may include destruction, removal, contamination, or erection of obstructions.

density—*(DOD, NATO, IADB)* The average number of mines per meter of minefield front.

density altitude—*(DOD, NATO)* An atmospheric density expressed in terms of the altitude which corresponds with that density in the standard atmosphere.

departmental intelligence—*(DOD)* Intelligence that any department or agency of the Federal Government requires to execute its own mission.

Department of Defense Intelligence Information System—*(DOD)* The aggregation of DOD personnel, procedures, equipment, computer programs, and supporting communications that support the timely and comprehensive preparation and presentation of intelligence and intelligence information to military commanders and national-level decisionmakers. Also known as DODIIS.

Department of the Air Force—*(DOD)* The executive part of the Department of the Air Force at the seat of government and all field headquarters, forces, reserve components, installations, activities, and functions under the control or supervision of the Secretary of the Air Force. See also **Military Department.**

Department of the Army—*(DOD)* The executive part of the Department of the Army at the seat of government and all field headquarters, forces, reserve components, installations, activities, and functions under the control or supervision of the Secretary of the Army. See also **Military Department.**

Department of the Navy—*(DOD)* The executive part of the Department of the Navy at the seat of government; the headquarters, US Marine Corps; the entire operating forces of the United States Navy, including naval aviation, and of the US Marine Corps, including the reserve components of such forces; all field activities, headquarters, forces, bases, installations, activities, and functions under the control or supervision of the Secretary of the Navy; and the US Coast Guard when operating as a part of the Navy pursuant to law. See also **Military Department.**

departure airfield—*(DOD, IADB)* An airfield on which troops and/or materiel are emplaned for flight. See also **airfield.**

departure airfield—*(NATO)* 1. An airfield from which aircraft depart. 2. An airfield on which passengers or cargo are emplaned for flights.

departure end—*(DOD, NATO)* That end of a runway nearest to the direction in which initial departure is made.

departure point—*(DOD, NATO)* 1. A navigational check point used by aircraft as a marker for setting course. 2. In amphibious operations, an air control point at the seaward end of the helicopter approach lane system from which helicopter waves are dispatched along the selected helicopter approach lane to the initial point.

deployed nuclear weapons—*(DOD)* 1. When used in connection with the transfer of weapons between the Department of Energy and the Department of Defense, this term describes those weapons transferred to and in the custody of the Department of Defense. 2. Those nuclear weapons specifically authorized by the Joint Chiefs of Staff to be transferred to the custody of the storage facilities, carrying or delivery units of the armed forces.

deployment—*(DOD, IADB)* 1. Act of extending battalions and smaller units in width, in depth, or in both width and depth to increase readiness for contemplated action. 2. In naval usage, the change from a cruising approach or contact disposition to a disposition for battle. 3. In a strategic sense, the relocation of forces to desired areas of operation. 4. Designated location of troops and troop units as indicated in a troop schedule. 5. The series of functions that transpire from the time a packed parachute is placed in operation until it is fully opened and is supporting its load.

deployment—*(NATO)* 1. The extension or widening of the front of a military unit, extending from a close order to a battle formation. 2. In naval usage, the change from a cruising approach, or contact disposition to a disposition for battle. 3. In a strategic sense, the relocation of forces to desired areas of operation.

deployment data base—*(DOD)* The joint deployment system data base containing the necessary information on forces, materiel, and filler and replacement personnel movement requirements to support execution. The data base reflects information contained in the refined time-phased force and deployment data, or data developed during the various phases of the crisis action system, and the movement schedules or tables developed by the transportation operating agencies to support the deployment of required forces, personnel, and materiel.

deployment diagram—*(DOD, IADB)* In the assault phase of an amphibious operation, a diagram showing the formation in which the boat group proceeds from the rendezvous area to the line of departure and the method of deployment into the landing formation.

deployment operating base—*(NATO)* A base, other than the peace time base, having minimum essential operational and support facilities, to which a unit or part of a unit will deploy to operate from in time of tension or war. See also **base; emergency fleet operating base.**

depot—*(DOD, IADB)* 1. supply—An activity for the receipt, classification, storage, accounting, issue, maintenance, procurement, manufacture, assembly, research, salvage or disposal of material. 2. personnel—An activity for the reception, processing, training, assignment, and forwarding of personnel replacements.

depot maintenance—*(DOD, IADB)* That maintenance performed on materiel requiring major overhaul or a complete rebuild of parts, assemblies, subassemblies, and end-items, including the manufacture of parts, modifications, testing, and reclamation as required. Depot maintenance serves to support lower categories of maintenance by providing technical assistance and performing that maintenance beyond their responsibility. Depot maintenance provides stocks of serviceable equipment by using more extensive facilities for repair than are available in lower level maintenance activities.

depression angle—See **angle of depression.**

depth—*(DOD, NATO, IADB)* The vertical distance from the plane of the hydrographic datum to the bed of the sea, lake, or river.

depth contour—*(DOD, NATO, IADB)* A line connecting points of equal depth below the hydrographic datum. Also called **bathymetric contour** or **depth curve.**

depth curve—See **depth contour.**

derived information—*(NATO)* A parameter such as angle, range, position, velocity, etc. is said to be derived in the first receiver or other sensor in which that parameter exists or is capable of existing without reference to further information.

description of target—*(DOD, NATO, IADB)* In artillery and naval gunfire support, an element in the call for fire in which the observer or spotter describes the installation, personnel, equipment or activity to be taken under fire.

descriptive name—*(DOD, NATO, IADB)* Written indication on maps and charts, used to specify the nature of a feature (natural or artificial) shown by a general symbol.

designation of days and hours—*(NATO)* The following designations have the meaning shown:

D-day*—The day on which an operation commences or is due to commence. This may be the commencement of hostilities or any other operation.

E-day*—The day on which a NATO exercise commences.

K-day*—The day on which a convoy system is introduced or is due to be introduced on any particular convoy lane.

M-day*—The day on which mobilization commences or is due to commence.

H-hour*—The specific time at which an operation or exercise commences, or is due to commence.

*This term is used also as a reference for the designation of days/hours before or after the event. (DOD): See also **C-day; D-day; S-day; wartime manpower planning system.**)

desired appreciation—*(DOD)* See **appreciations.**

desired effects—*(DOD, IADB)* The damage or casualties to the enemy or material which a commander desires to achieve from a nuclear weapon detonation. Damage effects on material are classified as light, moderate or severe. Casualty effects on personnel may be immediate, prompt, or delayed.

desired ground zero—*(DOD, NATO, IADB)* The point on the surface of the earth at, or vertically below or above, the center of a planned nuclear detonation. Also known as DGZ. See also **actual ground zero; ground zero.**

despatch route—See **dispatch route.**

destination (merchant shipping)—See **final destination (merchant shipping); immediate destination (merchant shipping); original destination (merchant shipping).**

destroy (beam)—*(DOD)* In air intercept, a code meaning, "The interceptor will be vectored to a standard beam attack for interception and destruction of the target."

destroy (cutoff)—*(DOD)* In air intercept, a code meaning, "Intercept and destroy. Command vectors will produce a cutoff attack."

destroyed—*(DOD)* A condition of a target so damaged that it cannot function as intended nor be restored to a usable condition. In the case of a building, all vertical supports and spanning members are damaged to such an extent that nothing is salvageable. In the case of bridges, all spans must have dropped and all piers must require replacement.

destroyer—*(DOD, IADB)* A high-speed warship designed to operate offensively with strike forces, with hunter-killer groups, and in support of amphibious assault operations. Destroyers also operate defensively to screen support forces and convoys against submarine, air, and surface threats. Normal armament consists of 3-inch and 5-inch dual-purpose guns and various antisubmarine warfare weapons. Designated as DD.

destroy (frontal)—*(DOD)* In air intercept, a command meaning, "The interceptor will be vectored to a standard frontal attack for interception and destruction of the target."

destroy (stern)—*(DOD)* In air intercept a command meaning, "The interceptor will be vectored to a standard stern attack for interception and destruction of the target."

destruction—*(DOD)* A type of adjustment for destroying a given target.

destruction area—*(DOD, IADB)* An area in which it is planned to destroy or defeat the enemy airborne threat. The area may be further subdivided into air intercept, missile (long-medium-and short-range), or antiaircraft gun zones.

destruction fire—*(DOD, IADB)* Fire delivered for the sole purpose of destroying material objects. See also **fire.**

destruction radius—*(DOD, NATO)* In mine warfare, the maximum distance from an exploding charge of stated size and type at which a mine will be destroyed by sympathetic detonation of the main charge, with a stated probability of destruction, regardless of orientation.

destructive fire mission—*(DOD, NATO)* In artillery, fire delivered for the purpose of destroying a point target. See also **fire.**

destruct (missile)—*(DOD, NATO, IADB)* Intentional destruction of a missile or similar vehicle for safety or other reasons.

destruct system (missile)—*(DOD, NATO, IADB)* A system which, when operated by external command or preset internal means, destroys the missile or similar vehicle.

detachment—*(DOD, NATO, IADB)* 1. A part of a unit separated from its main organization for duty elsewhere. 2. A temporary military or naval unit formed from other units or parts of units.

detail—*(NATO)* The basic graphic representation of features.

detailed report (photographic interpretation)—*(DOD, NATO, IADB)* A comprehensive, analytical, intelligence report written as a result of the interpretation of photography usually covering a single subject, a target, target complex, and of a detailed nature.

detainee—*(DOD)* A term used to refer to any person captured or otherwise detained by an armed force.

detainee collecting point—*(DOD)* A facility or other location where detainees are assembled for subsequent movement to a detainee processing station.

detainee processing station—*(DOD)* A facility or other location where detainees are administratively processed, and provided custodial care, pending disposition and subsequent release, transfer, or movement to a prisoner-of-war or civilian internee camp.

detecting circuit—*(DOD, NATO)* The part of a mine firing circuit which responds to the influence of a target.

detection—*(DOD)* 1. In tactical operations, the perception of an object of possible military interest but unconfirmed by recognition. 2. In surveillance, the determination and transmission by a surveillance system that an event has occurred. *(DOD, IADB)* 3. In arms control, the first step in the process of ascertaining the occurrence of a violation of an arms-control agreement.

detection—*(NATO)* The discovery by any means of the presence of a person, object, or phenomenon of potential military significance. See also **identification; identification Friend or Foe; recognition.**

deterioration limit—*(DOD, NATO)* A limit placed on a particular product characteristic to define the minimum acceptable quality requirement for the product to retain its NATO code number.

deterrence—*(DOD, IADB)* The prevention from action by fear of the consequences. Deterrence is a state of mind brought about by the existence of a credible threat of unacceptable counteraction.

detonating cord—*(DOD, NATO)* A flexible fabric tube containing a high explosive designed to transmit the detonation wave.

detonating cord amplifier—*(NATO)* A device attached to a detonating cord which allows for the ignition of a charge and the simultaneous transmission of a detonating wave to another charge.

detonator—*(DOD, NATO)* A device containing a sensitive explosive intended to produce a detonation wave.

detour—*(DOD, NATO)* Deviation from those parts of a route, where movement has become difficult or impossible, to insure continuity of movement to the destination. The modified part of the route is known as a "detour."

deviation—*(DOD, NATO, IADB)* 1. The distance by which a point of impact or burst misses the target. See also **circular error probable; delivery error; dispersion error; horizontal error.** 2. The angular difference between magnetic and compass headings.

diaphragm—*(NATO, IADB)* The physical element of an optical system which regulates the quantity of light traversing the system. The quantity of light determines the brightness of the image without affecting the size of the image.

diapositive—*(DOD, NATO)* A positive photograph on a transparent medium. See also **transparency.**

died of wounds received in action—*(DOD, NATO)* A battle casualty who dies of wounds or other injuries received in action, after having reached a medical treatment facility. See also **killed in action.**

differential ballistic wind—*(DOD, NATO)* In bombing, a hypothetical wind equal to the difference in velocity between the ballistic wind and the actual wind at a release altitude.

diffraction loading—*(DOD, NATO)* The force (or loading) on the structure during the envelopment process.

dip—*(DOD, NATO)* In naval mine warfare, the amount by which a moored mine is carried beneath its set depth by a current or tidal stream acting on the mine casing and mooring.

diplomatic authorization—*(DOD, NATO, IADB)* Authority for overflight or landing obtained at government-to-government level through diplomatic channels.

dip needle circuit—*(DOD, NATO)* In naval mine warfare, a mechanism which responds to a change in the magnitude of the vertical component of the total magnetic field.

direct action fuze—See **impact action fuze; proximity fuze; self-destroying fuse; time fuze.**

direct action mission—*(DOD)* In special operations, a specified act involving operations of an overt, covert, clandestine or low visibility nature conducted primarily by a sponsoring power's special operations forces in hostile or denied areas.

direct air support center—*(DOD, IADB)* A subordinate operational component of a tactical air control system designed for control and direction of close air support and other tactical air support operations, and normally collocated with fire-support coordination elements. See also **direct air support center (airborne).**

direct air support center (airborne)—*(DOD, IADB)* An airborne aircraft equipped with the necessary staff personnel, communications, and operations facilities to function as a direct air support center. See also **direct air support center.**

direct damage assessment—*(NATO, IADB)* A direct examination of an actual strike area by air observation, air photography, or by direct observation.

directed exercise—See **JCS-directed exercise.**

direct exchange—*(DOD)* A supply method of issuing serviceable materiel in exchange for unserviceable materiel on an item-for-item basis.

direct fire—*(DOD, IADB)* Gunfire delivered on a target, using the target itself as a point of aim for either the gun or the director.

direct fire—*(NATO)* Fire directed at a target which is visible to the aimer. See also **fire.**

direct illumination—*(DOD, NATO)* Illumination provided by direct light from pyrotechnics or searchlights.

directing staff—See **exercise directing staff.**

direction—*(DOD, NATO)* 1. In artillery and naval gunfire support, a term used by a spotter/observer in a call for fire to indicate the bearing of the spotting line. 2. See **intelligence cycle.**

directional gyro indicator—*(DOD, NATO)* An azimuth gyro with a direct display and means for setting the datum to a specified compass heading.

directional radar prediction—*(NATO)* A prediction made for a particular heading.

direction finding—*(DOD, IADB)* A procedure for obtaining bearings of radio frequency emitters by using a highly directional antenna and a display unit on an intercept receiver or ancillary equipment.

direction of attack—*(DOD, IADB)* A specific direction or route that the main attack or center of mass of the unit will follow. The unit is restricted, required to attack as indicated, and is not normally allowed to bypass the enemy. The direction of attack is used primarily in counterattacks or to insure that supporting attacks make maximal contribution to the main attack.

directive—*(DOD, NATO, IADB)* 1. A military communication in which policy is established or a specific action is ordered. 2. A plan issued with a view to putting it into effect when so directed, or in the event that a stated contingency arises. 3. Broadly speaking, any communication which initiates or governs action, conduct, or procedure.

direct laying—*(DOD, NATO, IADB)* Laying in which the sights of weapons are aligned directly on the target.

direct support—*(DOD, IADB)* A mission requiring a force to support another specific force and authorizing it to answer directly the supported force's request for assistance.

direct support—*(NATO)* 1. The support provided by a unit or formation not attached or under command of the supported unit or formation, but required to give priority to the support required by that unit or formation. See also **at priority call.** 2. In maritime usage, operations related to the protection of a specific force by other units. See also **support.**

direct support artillery—*(DOD, NATO, IADB)* Artillery whose primary task is to provide fire requested by the supported unit.

direct supporting fire—*(DOD, NATO, IADB)* Fire delivered in support of part of a force, as opposed to general supporting fire which is delivered in support of the force as a whole. See also **close supporting fire; deep supporting fire; supporting fire.**

disaffected person—*(DOD, IADB)* A person who is alienated or estranged from those in authority or lacks loyalty to the government; a state of mind.

disarmament—*(DOD, IADB)* The reduction of a military establishment to some level set by international agreement. See also **arms control; arms control agreement; arms control measure.**

disarmed mine—*(DOD, NATO, IADB)* A mine which has been rendered inoperative by breaking a link in the firing sequence. See also **mine.**

disaster control—*(DOD, IADB)* Measures taken before, during, or after hostile action or natural or man-made disasters to reduce the probability of damage, minimize its effects, and initiate recovery. See also **area damage control; damage control.**

discriminating circuit—*(DOD, NATO)* That part of the operating circuit of a sea mine which distinguishes between the response of the detecting circuit to the passage of a ship and the response to other disturbances (e.g., influence sweep, countermining, etc.)

disembarkation schedule—See **debarkation schedule.**

disengagement—*(DOD, IADB)* In arms control, a general term for proposals that would result in the geographic separation of opposing non-indigenous forces without directly affecting indigenous military forces.

dispatch route—*(DOD, NATO)* In road traffic, a roadway over which full control, both as to priorities of use and the regulation of movement of traffic in time and space is exercised. Movement authorization is required for its use, even by a single vehicle. See also **route.**

dispensary—See **clinic.**

dispenser—*(DOD, NATO)* In air armament, a container or device which is used to carry and release submunitions. See also **cluster bomb unit.**

dispersal—*(DOD)* Relocation of forces for the purpose of increasing survivability. See also **dispersion.**

dispersal airfield—*(DOD, IADB)* An airfield, military or civil, to which aircraft might move before H–hour on either a temporary duty or permanent change of station basis and be able to conduct operations. See also **airfield.**

dispersed movement pattern—*(DOD, NATO, IADB)* A pattern for ship-to-shore movement which provides additional separation of landing craft both laterally and in depth. This pattern is used when nuclear weapon threat is a factor.

dispersion—*(DOD, NATO)* 1. A scattered pattern of hits around the mean point of impact of bombs and projectiles dropped or fired under identical conditions. 2. In antiaircraft gunnery, the scattering of shots in range and deflection about the mean point of explosion. 3. The spreading or separating of troops, materiel, establishment, or activities which are usually concentrated in limited areas to reduce vulnerability. 4. In chemical and bio-

logical operations, the dissemination of agents in liquid or aerosol form. 5. In airdrop operations, the scatter of personnel and/or cargo on the drop zone. 6. In naval control of shipping, the reberthing of a ship in the periphery of the port area or in the vicinity of the port for its own protection in order to minimize the risk of damage from attack. See also **convoy dispersal point.** See also **circular error probable; delivery error; deviation; dispersion error; horizontal error.**

dispersion error—*(DOD, NATO, IADB)* The distance from the point of impact or burst of a round to the mean point of impact or burst.

dispersion pattern—*(DOD, NATO, IADB)* The distribution of a series of rounds fired from one weapon or group of weapons under conditions as nearly identical as possible the points of bursts or impact being dispersed about a point called the **mean point of impact.**

displaced person—*(DOD, NATO, IADB)* A civilian who is involuntarily outside the national boundaries of his country. See also **evacuee; evacuees; refugee; refugees.**

displacement—*(DOD)* In air intercept, separation between target and interceptor tracks established to position the interceptor in such a manner as to provide sufficient maneuvering and acquisition space.

disposition—*(DOD, NATO, IADB)* 1. Distribution of the elements of a command within an area, usually the exact location of each unit headquarters and the deployment of the forces subordinate to it. 2. A prescribed arrangement of the stations to be occupied by the several formations and single ships of a fleet, or major subdivisions of a fleet, for any purpose, such as cruising, approach, maintaining contact, or battle. 3. A prescribed arrangement of all the tactical units composing a flight or group of aircraft. See also **deployment; dispersion.** *(DOD)* 4. The removal of a patient from a medical treatment facility by reason of return to duty, transfer to another treatment facility, death or other termination of medical case.

disruptive pattern—*(DOD, NATO)* In surveillance, an arrangement of suitably colored irregular shapes which, when applied to the surface of an object, is intended to enhance its camouflage.

dissemination—See **intelligence cycle.**

distance—*(DOD, IADB)* 1. The space between adjacent individual ships or boats measured in any direction between foremasts. 2. The space between adjacent men, animals, vehicles, or units in a formation measured from front to rear. 3. The space between known reference points or a ground observer and a target, measured in meters (artillery), in yards (naval gunfire), or in units specified by the observer. See also **interval.**

distributed fire—*(DOD, NATO, IADB)* Fire so dispersed as to engage most effectively an area target. See also **fire.**

distribution—*(DOD, IADB)* 1. The arrangement of troops for any purpose, such as a battle, march, or maneuver. 2. A planned pattern of projectiles about a point. 3. A planned spread of fire to cover a desired frontage or depth. 4. An official delivery of anything, such as orders or supplies. 5. That functional phase of military logistics that embraces the act of dispensing materiel, facilities, and services. 6. The process of assigning military personnel to activities, units, or billets.

distribution point—*(DOD, NATO, IADB)* A point at which supplies and/or ammunition, obtained from supporting supply points by a division or other unit, are broken down for distribution to subordinate units. Distribution points usually carry no stocks; items drawn are issued completely as soon as possible.

distribution system—*(DOD, IADB)* That complex of facilities, installations, methods, and procedures designed to receive, store, maintain, distribute, and control the flow of military materiel between the point of receipt into the military system and the point of issue to using activities and units.

ditching—*(DOD, IADB)* Controlled landing of a distressed aircraft on water.

diversion—*(DOD)* 1. The act of drawing the attention and forces of an enemy from the point of the principal operation; an attack, alarm, or feint that diverts attention. 2. A change made in a prescribed route for operational or tactical reasons. A diversion order will not constitute a change of destination. 3. A rerouting of cargo or passengers to a new transshipment point or destination or on a different mode of transportation prior to arrival at ultimate destination. 4. In naval mine warfare, a route or channel bypassing a dangerous area. A diversion may connect one channel to another or it may branch from a channel and rejoin it on the other side of the danger. See also **demonstration.**

diversion—*(NATO)* 1. The act of drawing the attention and forces of an enemy from the point of the principal operation; an attack, alarm, or feint which diverts attention. See also **demonstration.** 2. A change made in a prescribed route for operational or tactical reasons. Except in the case of aircraft, a diversion order will not constitute a change of destination. 3. In naval mine warfare, a route or channel bypassing a dangerous area. A diversion may connect one channel to another or it may branch from a channel and rejoin it on the other side of the danger. 4. In air traffic control, the act of proceeding to an airfield other than one at which a landing was intended. See also **alternate airfield.**

diversionary attack—*(DOD, NATO, IADB)* An attack wherein a force attacks, or threatens to attack, a target other than the main target for the purpose of drawing enemy defenses away from the main effort. See also **demonstration.**

diversionary landing—*(DOD, IADB)* An operation in which troops are actually landed for the purpose of diverting enemy reaction away from the main landing.

divert—*(DOD)* 1. "Proceed to divert field or carrier as specified." 2. To change the target, mission, or destination of an airborne flight.

diving chamber—See **hyperbaric chamber.**

division—*(DOD, NATO, IADB)* 1. A tactical unit/formation as follows: **a.** A major administrative and tactical unit/formation which combines in itself the necessary arms and services required for sustained combat, larger than a regiment/brigade and smaller than a corps. **b.** A number of naval vessels of similar type grouped together for operational and administrative command, or a tactical unit of a naval aircraft squadron, consisting of two or more sections. **c.** An air division is an air combat organization normally consisting of two or more wings with appropriate service units. The combat wings of an air division will normally contain similar type units. 2. An organizational part of a headquarters that handles military matters of a particular nature, such as personnel, intelligence, plans, and training, or supply and evacuation. 3. A number of personnel of a ship's complement grouped together for operational and administrative command.

division artillery—*(DOD, IADB)* Artillery that is permanently an integral part of a division. For tactical purposes, all artillery placed under the command of a division commander is considered division artillery.

division slice—See **slice.**

dock landing ship—*(DOD, IADB)* A naval ship designed to transport and launch loaded amphibious craft and vehicles with their crews and embarked personnel in amphibious assault, and to render limited docking and repair service to small ships and craft; and one that is capable of acting as a control ship in an amphibious assault. Designated LSD.

doctrine—*(DOD, IADB)* Fundamental principles by which the military forces or elements thereof guide their actions in support of national objectives. It is authoritative but requires judgment in application. See also **combined doctrine; joint doctrine; multi-service doctrine.**

doctrine—*(NATO)* Fundamental principles by which the military forces guide their actions in support of objectives. It is authoritative but requires judgment in application.

dolly—*(DOD)* Airborne data link equipment.

dome—See **spray dome.**

domestic air traffic—*(DOD)* Air traffic within the continental United States.

domestic air traffic—*(IADB)* Air traffic within a country.

domestic emergencies—*(DOD)* Emergencies affecting the public welfare and occurring within the 50 states, District of Columbia, Commonwealth of Puerto Rico, US possessions and territories, or any political subdivision thereof, as a result of enemy attack, insurrection, civil disturbance, earthquake, fire, flood, or other public disasters or equivalent emergencies that endanger life and property or disrupt the usual process of government. The term domestic emergency includes any or all of the emergency conditions defined below:
a. civil defense emergency—A domestic emergency disaster situation resulting from devastation created by an enemy attack and requiring emergency operations during and following that attack. It may be proclaimed by appropriate authority in anticipation of an attack.
b. civil disturbances—Riots, acts of violence, insurrections, unlawful obstructions or assemblages, or other disorders prejudicial to public law and order. The term civil disturbance includes all domestic conditions

requiring or likely to require the use of Federal Armed Forces pursuant to the provisions of Chapter 15 of Title 10, United States Code.

c. **major disaster**—Any flood, fire, hurricane, tornado, earthquake or other catastrophe which, in the determination of the President, is or threatens to be of sufficient severity and magnitude to warrant disaster assistance by the Federal Government under Public Law 606, 91st Congress (42 United States Code 58) to supplement the efforts and available resources of State and local governments in alleviating the damage, hardship, or suffering caused thereby.

d. **natural disaster**—All domestic emergencies except those created as a result of enemy attack or civil disturbance.

domestic intelligence—*(DOD, IADB)* Intelligence relating to activities or conditions within the United States that threaten internal security and that might require the employment of troops; and intelligence relating to activities of individuals or agencies potentially or actually dangerous to the security of the Department of Defense.

dominant user concept—*(DOD, IADB)* The concept that the Service which is the principal consumer will have the responsibility for performance of a support workload for all using Services.

door bundle—*(NATO, IADB)* A bundle for manual ejection in flight normally followed by parachutists.

doppler effect—*(DOD, NATO, IADB)* The phenomenon evidenced by the change in the observed frequency of a sound or radio wave caused by a time rate of change in the effective length of the path of travel between the source and the point of observation.

doppler radar—*(DOD, IADB)* A radar system that differentiates between fixed and moving targets by detecting the apparent change in frequency of the reflected wave due to motion of target or the observer.

doppler radar—*(NATO)* Any form of radar which detects motion relative to a reflecting surface by measuring the frequency shift of reflected radio energy due to the motion of the observer or of the reflecting surface.

dormant—*(DOD, NATO)* In mine warfare, the state of a mine during which a time delay feature in a mine prevents it from being actuated.

dose rate contour line—*(DOD, NATO, IADB)* A line on a map, diagram, or overlay joining all points at which the radiation dose rate at a given time is the same.

dosimetry—*(DOD, NATO, IADB)* The measurement of radiation doses. It applies to both the devices used (dosimeters) and to the techniques.

double agent—*(DOD, IADB)* Agent in contact with two opposing intelligence services, only one of which is aware of the double contact or quasi-intelligence services.

double flow route—*(DOD, NATO)* A route of at least two lanes allowing two columns of vehicles to proceed simultaneously, either in the same direction or in opposite directions. See also **limited access route; single flow route.**

doubtful—*(DOD, NATO)* In artillery and naval gunfire support, a term used by an observer or spotter to indicate that he was unable to determine the difference in range between the target and a round or rounds.

down—*(DOD, NATO)* In artillery and naval gunfire support: 1. A term used in a call for fire to indicate that the target is at a lower altitude than the reference point used in identifying the target. 2. A correction used by an observer/spotter in time fire to indicate that a decrease in height of burst is desired.

downgrade—*(DOD)* To determine that classified information requires, in the interests of national security, a lower degree of protection against unauthorized disclosure than currently provided, coupled with a changing of the classification designation to reflect such lower degree.

downgrade—*(NATO, IADB)* To reduce the security classification of a classified document or an item of classified matter or material. See also **declassify.**

down lock—*(DOD, NATO)* A device for locking retractable landing gear in the down or extended position.

draftee—See **transient.**

drafter—*(DOD, IADB)* A person who actually composes the message for release by the originator or the releasing officer. See also **originator.**

draft plan—*(DOD, NATO)* A plan for which a draft plan has been coordinated and agreed with the other military headquarters and is ready for coordination with the nations involved, that is those nations who would be required to take national actions to support the plan. It may be used for future planning and exercises and may form the basis for an operation order to be implemented in time of emergency. See also **initial draft plan; coordinated draft plan; final plan; operation plan.**

drag—*(DOD)* Force of aerodynamic resistance caused by the violent currents behind the shock front.

drag loading—*(DOD, NATO)* The force on an object or structure due to transient winds accompanying the passage of a blast wave. The drag pressure is the product of the dynamic pressure and the drag coefficient which is dependent upon the shape (or geometry) of the

structure or object. See also **dynamic pressure.**

Dragon—*(DOD)* A manportable medium antitank weapon, consisting of a round (missile and launcher) and a tracker that provides antitank/assault fire of infantry platoon level for employment against tanks and hard point targets such as emplaced weapons or fortifications.

drainage system—*(NATO, IADB)* Rivers, streams, and other inland water features.

drawing key—*(NATO)* An image or preliminary drawing used as a guide for scribing or drawing. See also **blue key.**

drift—*(DOD, NATO)* In ballistics, a shift in projectile direction due to gyroscopic action which results from gravitational and atmospherically induced torques on the spinning projectile.

drift angle—*(DOD, NATO)* The angle measured in degrees between the heading of an aircraft or ship and the track made good.

drifting mine—*(DOD, NATO, IADB)* A buoyant or neutrally buoyant mine, free to move under the influence of waves, wind, current or tide.

drill mine—*(DOD, NATO)* An inert filled mine or mine-like body, used in loading, laying or discharge practice and trials. See also **mine.**

drone—*(DOD, IADB)* A land, sea, or air vehicle that is remotely or automatically controlled. See also **remotely piloted vehicle.**

drone—*(NATO)* A land, sea, or air vehicle, normally unmanned, which is remotely or automatically controlled.

droop stop—*(DOD, NATO)* A device to limit downward vertical motion of helicopter rotor blades upon rotor shutdown.

120

drop—*(DOD, NATO)* In artillery and naval gunfire support, a correction used by an observer/spotter to indicate that a decrease in range along a spotting line is desired.

drop altitude—*(DOD, NATO, IADB)* The altitude above mean sea level at which airdrop is executed. See also **altitude; drop height.**

drop height—*(DOD, NATO, IADB)* The vertical distance between the drop zone and the aircraft. See also **altitude; drop altitude.**

dropmaster—*(DOD, IADB)* 1. An individual qualified to prepare, perform acceptance inspection, load, lash, and eject material for airdrop. 2. An aircrew member who, during parachute operations, will relay any required information between pilot and jumpmaster. See also **air dispatcher (cargo).**

drop message—*(DOD, NATO, IADB)* A message dropped from an aircraft to a ground or surface unit.

drop track—*(DOD)* In air intercept, the unit having reporting responsibility for a particular track is dropping that track and will no longer report it. Other units holding an interest in that track may continue to report it.

drop zone—*(DOD, NATO, IADB)* A specific area upon which airborne troops, equipment, or supplies are airdropped.

dry gap bridge—*(NATO, IADB)* A bridge, fixed or portable, which is used to span a gap that does not normally contain water, e.g., antitank ditches, road craters, etc.

D-to-P assets required on D-day—*(DOD, IADB)* As applied to the D-to-P concept, this asset requirement represents those stocks that must be physically available on D-day to meet initial allowance requirements, to fill the wartime pipeline between the producers and users (even if P-day and D-day occur simultaneously), and to provide any required D-to-P consumption/production differential stockage. The D-to-P assets required on D-day are also represented as the difference between the D-to-P Materiel Readiness Gross Requirements and the cumulative sum of all production deliveries during the D-to-P period. See also **D-to-P concept.**

D-to-P concept—*(DOD, IADB)* A logistic planning concept by which the gross materiel readiness requirement in support of approved forces at planned wartime rates for conflicts of indefinite duration will be satisfied by a balanced mix of assets on hand on D-day and assets to be gained from production through P-day when the planned rate of production deliveries to the users equals the planned wartime rate of expenditure (consumption). See also **D-day consumption/production differential assets; D-day pipeline assets; D-to-P assets required on D-day; D-to-P materiel readiness gross requirement.**

D-to-P materiel readiness gross requirement—*(DOD, IADB)* As applied to the D-to-P concept, the gross requirement for all supplies/materiel needed to meet all initial pipeline and anticipated expenditure (consumption) requirements between D-day and P-day. Includes initial allowances, CONUS and overseas operating and safety levels, intransit levels of supply, and the cumulative sum of all items expended (consumed) during the D-to-P period. See also **D-to-P concept.**

dual agent—*(DOD, IADB)* One who is simultaneously and independently employed by two or more intelligence agencies covering targets for both.

dual-capable forces—*(DOD, IADB)* Forces capable of employing dual-capable weapons.

dual capable unit—*(DOD, NATO)* A nuclear certified delivery unit capable of executing both conventional and nuclear missions.

dual-firing circuit—*(DOD, NATO)* An assembly comprising two independent firing systems, both electric or both non-electric, so that the firing of either system will detonate all charges. See also **combination firing circuit.**

dual (multi)-capable weapons—*(DOD, IADB)* 1. Weapons, weapon systems, or vehicles capable of selective equipage with different types or mixes of armament or firepower. 2. Sometimes restricted to weapons capable of handling either nuclear or non-nuclear munitions.

dual (multi)-purpose weapons—*(DOD, IADB)* Weapons which possess the capability for effective application in two or more basically different military functions and/or levels of conflict.

dual-purpose weapon—*(DOD, IADB)* A weapon designed for delivering effective fire against air or surface targets.

dual warning phenomenology—*(DOD)* Deriving warning information from two systems observing separate physical phenomena (e.g., radar/infrared or visible light/X-ray) associated with the same events to attain high credibility while being less susceptible to false reports or spoofing.

duck—*(DOD)* In air intercept, a code meaning, "Trouble headed your way" (usually followed by "bogey, salvos," etc.).

dud—*(DOD, NATO)* Explosive munition which has not been armed as intended or which has failed to explode after being armed. See also **absolute dud; dwarf dud; flare dud; nuclear dud.**

dud probability—*(DOD, IADB)* The expected percentage of failures in a given number of firings.

due in—*(DOD)* Quantities of materiel scheduled to be received from vendors, repair facilities, assembly operation, interdepot transfers, and other sources.

dummy—See **decoy.**

dummy message—*(DOD, NATO, IADB)* A message sent for some purpose other than its content, which may consist of dummy groups or may have a meaningless text.

dummy minefield—*(DOD, NATO)* In naval mine warfare, a minefield containing no live mines and presenting only a psychological threat.

dummy run—*(DOD, IADB)* Any simulated firing practice, particularly a dive bombing approach made without release of a bomb. Same as "dry run."

dump—*(DOD, NATO, IADB)* A temporary storage area, usually in the open, for bombs, ammunition, equipment, or supplies.

duplicate negative—*(DOD, NATO)* A negative reproduced from negative or diapositive.

durable materiel—See **non-expendable supplies and materiel.**

Duster (antiaircraft weapon)—*(DOD, IADB)* A self-propelled, twin 40-mm antiaircraft weapon for use against low-flying aircraft. Designated as M42.

dwarf dud—*(DOD)* A nuclear weapon that, when launched at or emplaced on a target, fails to provide a yield within a reasonable range of that which could be anticipated with normal operation of the weapon. This constitutes a dud only in a relative sense.

dwell at/on—*(DOD, NATO)* In artillery and naval gunfire support, this term is used when fire is to continue for an indefinite period at specified time or on a particular target or targets.

dynamic pressure—*(DOD, NATO)* Pressure resulting from some medium in motion, such as the air following the shock front of a blast wave.

E

E-1B—See **Tracer.**

E-2—See **Hawkeye.**

EA-6A—See **Intruder.**

EA-6B—See **Prowler.**

Eagle—*(DOD)* A twin-engine supersonic, turbofan, all-weather tactical fighter, capable of employing a variety of air-launched weapons in the air-to-air role. The Eagle is air refuelable and is also capable of long-range air superiority missions. Designated as F-15.

early resupply—*(NATO, IADB)* The shipping of supplies during the period between D-Day and the beginning of "planned resupply." See also **element of resupply.**

Early Spring—*(DOD, IADB)* An antireconnaissance satellite weapon system.

early time—See **span of detonation (atomic demolition munition employment).**

early warning—*(DOD, NATO, IADB)* Early notification of the launch or approach of unknown weapons or weapon carriers. See also **attack assessment; tactical warning.**

earmarked for assignment—*(NATO)* The status of forces which nations have agreed to assign to the operational command or operational control of a NATO Commander at some future date. In designating such forces, nations should specify when these forces will be available in terms currently agreed by the Military Committee.

earmarking of stocks—*(DOD, NATO)* The arrangement whereby nations agree, normally in peacetime, to identify a proportion of selected items of their war reserve stocks to be called for by specified NATO commanders.

earthing—*(DOD, NATO)* The process of making a satisfactory electrical connection between the structure, including the metal skin, of an object or vehicle, and the mass of the earth, to insure a common potential with the earth. See also **bonding; grounding.**

ease turn—*(DOD)* Decrease rate of turn.

easting—*(NATO)* Eastward (that is from left to right) reading of grid values on a map.

echelon—*(DOD, NATO, IADB)* 1. A subdivision of a headquarters, i.e., forward echelon, rear echelon. 2. Separate level of command. As compared to a regiment, a division is a higher echelon, a battalion is a lower echelon. 3. A fraction of a command in the direction of depth, to which a principal combat mission is assigned; i.e., attack echelon, support echelon, reserve echelon. 4. A formation in which its subdivisions are placed one behind another, with a lateral and even spacing to the same side.

echeloned displacement—*(DOD, NATO, IADB)* Movement of a unit from one position to another without discontinuing performance of its primary function. *(DOD, IADB)* Normally, the unit divides into two functional elements (base and advance); and, while the base continues to operate, the advance element displaces to a new site where, after it becomes operational, it is joined by the base element.

economic action—*(DOD, IADB)* The planned use of economic measures designed to influence the policies or actions of another state, e.g., to impair the war-making potential of a hostile power or to generate economic stability within a friendly power.

economic mobilization—*(DOD, NATO, IADB)* The process of preparing for and carrying out such changes in the organization and functioning of the national economy as are necessary to provide for the most effective use of resources in a national emergency.

economic order quantity—*(DOD)* That quantity derived from a mathematical technique used to determine the optimum (lowest) total variable costs required to order and hold inventory.

economic potential—*(DOD, NATO, IADB)* The total capacity of a nation to produce goods and services.

economic potential for war—*(DOD, IADB)* That share of the total economic capacity of a nation that can be used for the purposes of war.

economic retention stock—*(DOD, IADB)* That portion of the quantity of an item excess of the approved force retention level that has been determined will be more economical to retain for future peacetime issue in lieu of replacement of future issues by procurement. To warrant economic retention, items must have a reasonably predictable demand rate.

economic warfare—*(DOD, IADB)* Aggressive use of economic means to achieve national objectives.

E-day—See **designation of days and hours.**

edition—*(NATO)* In cartography, a particular issue of a map or chart which is different from other issues.

edition designation—*(NATO)* The number, letter, date, or symbol distinguishing one edition from another.

EEFI—*(DOD)* See **essential elements of friendly information.**

effective damage—*(DOD, IADB)* That damage necessary to render a target element inoperative, unserviceable, nonproductive, or uninhabitable.

ejection—*(DOD, NATO, IADB)* 1. Escape from an aircraft by means of an independently propelled seat or capsule. 2. In air armament, the process of forcefully separating an aircraft

store from an aircraft to achieve satisfactory separation.

ejection systems—*(DOD, NATO)*
  a. **command ejection system—**A system in which the pilot of an aircraft or the occupant of the other ejection seat(s) initiates ejection resulting in the automatic ejection of all occupants;
  b. **command select ejection system—**A system permitting the optional transfer from one crew station to another of the control of a command ejection system for automatic ejection of all occupants;
  c. **independent ejection system—**An ejection system which operates independently of other ejection systems installed in one aircraft;
  d. **sequenced ejection system—**A system which ejects the aircraft crew in sequence to ensure a safe minimum total time of escape without collision.

electrode sweep—*(DOD, NATO)* In naval mine warfare, a magnetic cable sweep in which the water forms part of the electric circuit.

electro-explosive device—*(DOD, NATO)* An electrically initiated device having an explosive or pyrotechnic output, or having a mechanical output resulting from an explosive or pyrotechnic action.

electromagnetic compatibility—*(DOD)* The ability of telecommunications equipment, subsystems, and systems to operate in their intended operational environments without suffering or causing unacceptable degradation because of electromagnetic radiation or response. Design compatibility is achieved by incorporation of engineering characteristics or features in all electromagnetic radiating and receiving equipment in order to eliminate or reject undesired signals and enhance operating capabilities. Operational compatibility is achieved by the equipment flexibility to insure interference-free operation. It involves the application of sound frequency management and clear concepts and doctrines to maximize operational effectiveness. Also called **EMC**.

electromagnetic compatibility—*(NATO)* See **compatibility**.

electromagnetic environment—*(DOD)* The resulting product of the power and time distribution, in various frequency ranges, of the radiated or conducted electromagnetic emission levels that may be encountered by a military force, system, or platform when performing its assigned mission in its intended operational environment. It is the sum of electromagnetic interference; electromagnetic pulse; hazards of electromagnetic radiation to personnel, ordnance, and volatile materials; and natural phenomena effects of lightning and p-static. Also called **EME**.

electromagnetic environmental effects—*(DOD)* The impact of the electromagnetic environment upon the operational capability of military forces, equipment, systems, and platforms. It encompasses all electromagnetic disciplines, including electromagnetic compatibility/electromagnetic interference; electromagnetic vulnerability; electromagnetic pulse; electronic counter-countermeasures, hazards of electromagnetic radiation to personnel, ordnance, and volatile materials; and natural phenomena effects of lightning and p-static. Also called **E³**.

electromagnetic interference—*(DOD)* Any electromagnetic disturbance that interrupts, obstructs, or otherwise degrades or limits the effective performance of electronics/electrical equipment. It can be induced intentionally, as in some forms of electronic warfare, or unintentionally, as a result of spurious emissions and responses, intermodulation products, and the like. Also called **EMI**.

electromagnetic intrusion—*(DOD)* The intentional insertion of electromagnetic energy into transmission paths in any manner, with the objective of deceiving operators or of causing confusion. See also **electronic warfare**.

electromagnetic pulse—*(DOD)* The electromagnetic radiation from a nuclear explosion caused by Compton-recoil electrons and photoelectrons from photons scattered in the materials of the nuclear device or in a surrounding medium. The resulting electric and magnetic fields may couple with electrical/electronic systems to produce damaging current and voltage surges. May also be caused by nonnuclear means. Also called **EMP**.

electromagnetic radiation—*(DOD, IADB)* Radiation made up of oscillating electric and magnetic fields and propagated with the speed of light. Includes gamma radiation, X-rays, ultraviolet, visible, and infrared radiation, and radar and radio waves.

electromagnetic radiation hazards—*(DOD)* Hazards caused by a transmitter/antenna installation that generates electromagnetic radiation in the vicinity of ordnance, personnel, or fueling operations in excess of established safe levels or increases the existing levels to a hazardous level; or a personnel, fueling, or ordnance installation located in an area that is illuminated by electromagnetic radiation at a level that is hazardous to the planned operations or occupancy. These hazards will exist when an electromagnetic field of sufficient intensity is generated to: **a.** Induce or otherwise couple currents and/or voltages of magnitudes large enough to initiate electroexplosive devices or other sensitive explosive components of weapon systems, ordnance, or explosive devices. **b.** Cause harmful or injurious effects to humans and wildlife. **c.** Create sparks having sufficient magnitude to ignite flammable mixtures of materials that must be handled in the affected area. Also called **EMR Hazards, RADHAZ, HERO**.

electromagnetic spectrum—*(DOD)* The range of frequencies of electromagnetic radiation from zero to infinity. It is divided into 26 alphabetically designated bands. See also **electronic warfare**.

electromagnetic spectrum—*(IADB)* The frequencies (or wave lengths) present in a given

125

electromagnetic radiation. A particular spectrum could include a single frequency or a wide range of frequencies.

electromagnetic vulnerability—*(DOD)* The characteristics of a system that cause it to suffer a definite degradation (incapability to perform the designated mission) as a result of having been subjected to a certain level of electromagnetic environmental effects. Also called **EMV.**

electronic counter-countermeasures—See **electronic warfare.**

electronic countermeasures—See **electronic warfare.**

electronic deception—See **electronic warfare.**

electronic deception—*(NATO)* Deliberate activity designed to mislead an enemy in the interpretation or use of information received by his electronic systems. See also **electronic imitative deception; electronic manipulative deception; electronic simulative deception.**

electronic imitative deception—*(NATO)* The introduction into the enemy electronic systems of radiations imitating the enemy's own emissions.

electronic jamming—See **electronic warfare; jamming.**

electronic line of sight—*(DOD, IADB)* The path traversed by electromagnetic waves that is not subject to reflection or refraction by the atmosphere.

electronic manipulative deception—*(NATO)* The alteration of friendly electromagnetic emission characteristics, patterns, or procedures to eliminate revealing, or convey misleading, tell-tale indicators that may be used by hostile forces.

electronic reconnaissance—*(DOD, IADB)* The detection, identification, evaluation, and location of foreign electromagnetic radiations

emanating from other than nuclear detonations or radioactive sources.

electronics intelligence—*(DOD, IADB)* Technical and intelligence information derived from foreign non-communications electromagnetic radiations emanating from other than nuclear detonations or radioactive sources. Also called ELINT. See also **intelligence; signals intelligence; telemetry intelligence.**

electronics security—*(DOD, IADB)* The protection resulting from all measures designed to deny unauthorized persons information of value that might be derived from their interception and study of noncommunications electromagnetic radiations, e.g., radar.

electronic simulative deception—*(NATO)* The creation of electromagnetic emissions to represent friendly notional or actual capabilities to mislead hostile forces.

electronic warfare—*(DOD)* Military action involving the use of electromagnetic energy to determine, exploit, reduce or prevent hostile use of the electromagnetic spectrum and action which retains friendly use of electromagnetic spectrum. Also called **EW.** There are three divisions within electronic warfare:

a. **electronic countermeasures**—That division of electronic warfare involving actions taken to prevent or reduce an enemy's effective use of the electromagnetic spectrum. Also called **ECM.** Electronic countermeasures include:

(1) **electronic jamming**—The deliberate radiation, reradiation, or reflection of electromagnetic energy for the purpose of disrupting enemy use of electronic devices, equipment, or systems. See also **jamming.**

(2) **electronic deception**—The deliberate radiation, reradiation, alteration, suppression, absorption, denial, enhancement, or reflection of electromagnetic energy in a manner intended to convey misleading information and to deny valid

information to an enemy or to enemy electronics-dependent weapons. Among the types of electronic deception are: **(a) manipulative electronic deception**—Actions to eliminate revealing, or convey misleading, telltale indicators that may be used by hostile forces. **(b) simulative electronic deception**—Actions to represent friendly notional or actual capabilities to mislead hostile forces. **(c) imitative electronic deception**—The introduction of electromagnetic energy into enemy systems that imitates enemy emissions.

b. **electronic counter-countermeasures**—That division of electronic warfare involving actions taken to insure friendly effective use of the electromagnetic spectrum despite the enemy's use of electronic warfare. Also called ECCM.

c. **electronic warfare support measures**—That division of electronic warfare involving actions taken under direct control of an operational commander to search for, intercept, identify, and locate sources of radiated electromagnetic energy for the purpose of immediate threat recognition. Thus, electronic warfare support measures provide a source of information required for immediate decisions involving electronic countermeasures (ECM), electronic counter-countermeasures (ECCM), avoidance, targeting, and other tactical employment of forces. Also called ESM. Electronic warfare support measures data can be used to produce signals intelligence (SIGINT), both communications intelligence (COMINT) and electronics intelligence (ELINT).

electronic warfare—*(NATO)* Military action involving the use of electromagnetic energy to determine, exploit, reduce, or prevent hostile use of the electromagnetic spectrum and action to retain its effective use by friendly forces. See also **electronic counter-countermeasures; electronic countermeasures; electronic warfare support measures.**

electronic warfare—*(IADB)* Military action involving the use of electromagnetic energy to determine, exploit, reduce or prevent hostile use of the electromagnetic spectrum and action that retains friendly use of the electromagnetic spectrum.

electronic warfare support measures—See **electronic warfare.**

electro-optical intelligence—*(DOD)* Intelligence information other than signals intelligence derived from the optical monitoring of the electromagnetic spectrum from ultraviolet (0.01 micrometers) through far infrared (1,000 micrometers). Also called **ELECTRO-OPTINT.**

electro-optics—*(DOD)* The interaction between optics and electronics leading to the transformation of electrical energy into light, or vice versa, with the use of an optical device.

ELECTRO-OPTINT—See **electro-optical intelligence.**

element of resupply—See **early resupply; improvised (early) resupply; initial (early) resupply; planned resupply; resupply of Europe.**

elements of national power—*(DOD, IADB)* All the means that are available for employment in the pursuit of national objectives.

elevation—*(DOD, NATO, IADB)* The vertical distance of a point or level, on, or affixed to, the surface of the earth measured from mean sea level. See also **altitude; height.**

elevation guidance—*(DOD, NATO)* Information which will enable the pilot or autopilot of an aircraft to follow the required glide path.

elevation of security—*(NATO)* Minimum elevation permissible for firing above friendly troops without endangering their safety. This concept can only be applied to certain equipment having a flat trajectory.

elevation tint—See **hypesometric tinting.**

elevator—*(DOD)* In air intercept, a code meaning, "Take altitude indicated" (in thousands of feet, calling off each 5,000-foot increment passed through).

elicitation (intelligence)—*(DOD, IADB)* Acquisition of information from a person or group in a manner that does not disclose the intent of the interview or conversation. A technique of human source intelligence collection, generally overt, unless the collector is other than he purports to be.

eligible traffic—*(DOD)* Traffic for which movement requirements are submitted and space is assigned or allocated. Such traffic must meet eligibility requirements specified in Joint Travel Regulations for the Uniformed Services and publications of the Department of Defense and military departments governing eligibility for land, sea, and air transportation, and be in accordance with the guidance of the Joint Chiefs of Staff.

embarkation—*(DOD, IADB)* The loading of troops with their supplies and equipment into ships and/or aircraft.

embarkation—*(NATO)* The loading of troops with their supplies and equipment into a ship.

embarkation and tonnage table—*(DOD, IADB)* A consolidated table showing personnel and cargo, by troop or naval units, loaded aboard a combat-loaded ship.

embarkation area—*(DOD, NATO, IADB)* An area ashore, including a group of embarkation points, in which final preparations for embarkation are completed and through which assigned personnel and loads for craft and ships are called forward to embark. See also **mounting area.**

embarkation element (unit) (group)—*(DOD, IADB)* A temporary administrative formation of personnel with supplies and equipment embarking or to be embarked (combat loaded) aboard the ships of one transport element (unit) (group). It is dissolved upon completion of the embarkation. An embarkation element normally consists of two or more embarkation teams: a unit, of two or more elements; and a group, of two or more units. See also **embarkation organization; embarkation team.**

embarkation officer—*(DOD, IADB)* An officer on the staff of units of the landing force who advises the commander thereof on matters pertaining to embarkation planning and loading ships. See also **combat cargo officer.**

embarkation order—*(DOD, NATO)* An order specifying dates, times, routes, loading diagrams and methods of movement to shipside or aircraft for troops and their equipment. See also **movement table.**

embarkation organization—*(DOD, IADB)* A temporary administrative formation of personnel with supplies and equipment embarking or to be embarked (combat loaded) aboard amphibious shipping. See also **embarkation element (unit) (group); embarkation team.**

embarkation team—*(DOD, IADB)* A temporary administrative formation of all personnel with supplies and equipment embarking or to be embarked (combat load) aboard one ship. See also **embarkation element (unit) (group); embarkation organization.**

EMCON—See **emission control.**

emergency anchorage—*(DOD, NATO, IADB)* An anchorage, which may have a limited defense organization, for naval vessels, mobile support units, auxiliaries, or merchant ships. See also **assembly anchorage; holding anchorage; working anchorage.**

emergency burial—*(DOD, NATO)* A burial, usually on the battlefield, when conditions do not permit either evacuation for interment in a cemetery or burial according to national or international legal regulations. See also **burial.**

emergency complement—See **emergency establishment.**

emergency destruction of nuclear weapons—*(NATO)* The destruction of nuclear munitions, components, and associated classified material, without significant nuclear yield, to render the weapon tactically useless, to prevent the disclosure of classified design information, and to prevent salvage of the weapon for reprocessing.

emergency establishment—*(NATO)* A table setting out the authorized redistribution of manpower for a unit, formation or headquarters under emergency conditions. Also called **emergency complement.**

emergency fleet operating base—*(NATO, IADB)* A base providing logistic support for fleet units operating in an area for limited periods of time. See also **base.**

emergency in war—*(NATO, IADB)* An operational contingency in a limited area caused by a critical aggravation of combat operations and requiring special and immediate action by National and Allied Commanders. The existence of such an emergency shall be determined by the Allied Commander responsible for the limited area involved, in consultation with the National Commander concerned.

emergency priority—*(DOD, IADB)* A category of immediate mission request that takes precedence over all other priorities, e.g., an enemy breakthrough. See also **immediate mission request; priority of immediate mission requests.**

emergency relocation site—*(DOD, IADB)* A site located where practicable outside a prime target area to which all or portions of a civilian or military headquarters may be moved. As a minimum, it is manned to provide for the maintenance of the facility, communications, and data base. It should be capable of rapid activation, of supporting the initial requirements of the relocated headquarters for a predetermined period, and of expansion to meet wartime requirements of the relocated headquarters.

emergency risk (nuclear)—*(DOD, NATO, IADB)* A degree of risk where anticipated effects may cause some temporary shock, casualties and may significantly reduce the unit's combat efficiency. See also **degree of risk; moderate risk (nuclear); negligible risk (nuclear).**

emergency scramble—*(DOD, IADB)* In air intercept, a code meaning, "Carrier(s) addressed immediately launch all available fighter aircraft as combat air patrol." If all available are not required, numerals and/or type may be added.

emergency substitute—*(NATO, DOD, IADB)* A product which may be used, in an emergency only, in place of another product, but only on the advice of technically qualified personnel of the nation using the product, who will specify the limitations. See also **acceptable product; standardized product.**

emission control—*(DOD)* The selective and controlled use of electromagnetic, acoustic, or other emitters to optimize command and control capabilities while minimizing, for operations security (OPSEC), detection by enemy sensors; to minimize mutual interference among friendly systems; and/or to execute a military deception plan. Also called **EMCON.** See also **electronic warfare.**

emission control—*(NATO)* Selective control of emitted electromagnetic or acoustic energy. The aim can be twofold—to minimize the enemy's detection of emissions and exploitation of the information so gained, or—to improve the performance of friendly sensors.

emission control orders—*(DOD, IADB)* Orders, referred to as EMCON orders, used to authorize, control, or prohibit the use of electronic emission equipment. See also **control of electromagnetic radiation.**

emission control policy—*(NATO)* The policy which states what electromagnetic and acoustic emission may be allowed.

emplacement—*(DOD, NATO, IADB)* 1. A prepared position for one or more weapons or pieces of equipment, for protection against hostile fire or bombardment, and from which they can execute their tasks. 2. The act of fixing a gun in a prepared position from which it may be fired.

encipher—*(DOD, IADB)* To convert plain text into unintelligible form by means of a cipher system.

encrypt—*(DOD, IADB)* To convert plain text into unintelligible forms by means of a cryptosystem. (Note: The term encrypt covers the meanings of encipher and encode.) See also **cryptosystem.**

end item—*(DOD, IADB)* A final combination of end-products, component parts, and/or materials that is ready for its intended use; e.g., ship, tank, mobile machine shop, aircraft.

end of mission—*(DOD, NATO)* In artillery and naval gunfire support, an order given to terminate firing on a specific target.

endurance—*(DOD, NATO, IADB)* The time an aircraft can continue flying, or a ground vehicle or ship can continue operating, under specified conditions, e.g., without refueling. See also **endurance distance.**

endurance distance—*(DOD, NATO, IADB)* Total distance that a ground vehicle or ship can be self-propelled at any specified endurance speed.

endurance loading—*(DOD, IADB)* The stocking aboard ship for a period of time, normally covering the number of months between overhauls, of items with all of the following characteristics: **a.** low price; **b.** low weight and cube; **c.** a predictable usage rate; and **d.** nondeteriorative. See also **loading.**

endurance speed—*(NATO, IADB)* The nautical miles per hour a ship will travel through the water under average conditions of hull, sea in temperate weather, and wartime readiness. Endurance speeds in each case will correspond with specific engine speeds.

endurance time—*(NATO, IADB)* The total time for which any specified endurance speed of a ship can be maintained. If this value is dependent on factors other than fuel, it shall be so indicated.

enemy capabilities—*(DOD, IADB)* Those courses of action of which the enemy is physically capable, and that, if adopted, will affect accomplishment of our mission. The term "capabilities" includes not only the general courses of action open to the enemy, such as attack, defense, or withdrawal, but also all the particular courses of action possible under each general course of action. "Enemy capabilities" are considered in the light of all known factors affecting military operations, including time, space, weather, terrain, and the strength and disposition of enemy forces. In strategic thinking, the capabilities of a nation represent the courses of action within the power of the nation for accomplishing its national objectives in peace or war.

engage—*(DOD)* In air intercept, a code meaning, "Attack designated contact."

engagement—*(DOD)* In air defense, an attack with guns or air-to-air missiles by an interceptor aircraft, or the launch of an air defense missile by air defense artillery and the missile's subsequent travel to intercept.

engagement control—*(DOD, NATO, IADB)* In air defense, that degree of control exercised over the operational functions of an air defense unit that are related to detection, identification, engagement, and destruction of hostile targets.

envelopment—*(DOD, NATO)* An offensive maneuver in which the main attacking force passes around or over the enemy's principal defensive positions to secure objectives to the enemy's rear. See also **turning movement.**

environmental services—*(DOD, IADB)* The various combinations of scientific, technical, and advisory activities (including modification processes, i.e., the influence of man-made and natural factors) required to acquire, produce, and supply information on the past, present, and future states of space, atmospheric, oceanograpic, and terrestrial surroundings for use in military planning and decision-making processes, or to modify those surroundings to enhance military operations.

ephemeris—*(DOD, IADB)* A publication giving the computed places of the celestial bodies for each day of the year or for other regular intervals.

equal area projection—*(NATO)* One in which equal areas on the ground are represented by equal areas on the map.

equipment—*(DOD, NATO)* All non-expendable items needed to outfit/equip an individual or organization. See also **supplies.**

equipment—*(IADB)* All articles needed to outfit an individual or organization. The term refers to clothing, tools, utensils, vehicles, weapons, and other similar items. As to type of authorization, equipment may be divided into special (or project) equipment, equipment prescribed by tables of allowances, and equipment prescribed by tables of organization and equipment. See also **individual equipment; materiel; organizational equipment; special (or project) equipment.**

equipment operationally ready—*(DOD)* The status of an item of equipment in the possession of an operating unit that indicates it is capable of fulfilling its intended mission and in a system configuration that offers a high assurance of an effective, reliable, and safe performance.

equivalent focal length—*(DOD, NATO)* The distance measured along the optical axis of the lens from the rear nodal point to the plane of best average definition over the entire field used in a camera. See also **focal length.**

escalation—*(DOD, IADB)* An increase in scope or violence of a conflict, deliberate or unpremeditated.

escapee—*(DOD, IADB)* Any person who has been physically captured by the enemy and succeeds in getting free. See also **evasion and escape.**

escape line—*(DOD)* A planned route to allow personnel engaged in clandestine activity to depart from a site or area when possibility of compromise or apprehension exists.

escape route—See **evasion and escape route.**

escort—*(DOD, NATO, IADB)* 1. A combatant unit(s) assigned to accompany and protect another force or convoy. 2. Aircraft assigned to protect other aircraft during a mission. 3. An armed guard that accompanies a convoy, a train, prisoners, etc. 4. An armed guard accompanying persons as a mark of honor. *(DOD, IADB)* 5. To convoy. 6. A member of the Armed Forces assigned to accompany, assist, or guide an individual or group, e.g., an escort officer.

escort forces—*(DOD, IADB)* Combat forces of various types provided to protect other forces against enemy attack.

espionage—*(DOD, IADB)* Actions directed toward the acquisition of information through clandestine operations.

espionage against the United States—*(DOD)* Overt, covert, or clandestine activity designed to obtain information relating to the national defense with intent or reason to believe that it will be used to the injury of the United States or to the advantage of a foreign nation. For espionage crimes see Chapter 37 of Title 18, United States Code.

essential cargo—See **essential supply.**

essential communications traffic—*(DOD)* Transmissions (record/voice) of any precedence which must be sent electrically in order for the command or activity concerned to avoid a serious impact on mission accomplishment or safety or life.

essential elements of friendly information—*(DOD)* Key questions about friendly intentions and military capabilities likely to be asked by opposing planners and decision-makers in competitive circumstances. Also called **EEFI.**

essential elements of information—*(DOD, IADB)* The critical items of information regarding the enemy and the environment needed by the commander by a particular time to relate with other available information and intelligence in order to assist in reaching a logical decision.

essential industry—*(DOD, IADB)* Any industry necessary to the needs of a civilian or war economy. The term includes the basic industries as well as the necessary portions of those other industries that transform the crude basic raw materials into useful intermediate or end products, e.g., the iron and steel industry, the food industry, and the chemical industry.

essential secrecy—*(DOD)* See **appreciations.**

essential supply—*(NATO, IADB)* A commodity which is essential for the prosecution of the war in the survival period, or for national survival in that period, and which should be discharged as soon as circumstances permit. This will comprise such things as food, refined petroleum, oils, and lubricants, and medical stores. See also **cargo.**

establishment—*(DOD, NATO, IADB)* 1. An installation, together with its personnel and equipment, organized as an operating entity. *(NATO)* 2. The table setting out the authorized numbers of men and major equipment in a unit/formations; sometimes called "table of organization" or "table of organization and equipment." See also **activity; base; equipment.**

estimate—*(DOD, IADB)* 1. An analysis of a foreign situation, development, or trend that identifies its major elements, interprets the significance, and appraises the future possibilities and the prospective results of the various actions that might be taken. 2. An appraisal of the capabilities, vulnerabilities, and potential courses of action of a foreign nation or combination of nations in consequence of a specific national plan, policy, decision, or contemplated course of action. 3. An analysis of an actual or contemplated clandestine operation in relation to the situation in which it is or would be conducted in order to identify and appraise such factors as available and needed assets and potential obstacles, accomplishments, and consequences. See also **intelligence estimate.** 4. In air intercept, a code meaning, "Provide a quick estimate of the height/depth/range/size of designated contact," or "I estimate height/depth/range/size of designated contact is _____."

estimate of the situation—*(NATO, IADB)* A logical process of reasoning by which a commander considers all the circumstances affecting the military situation and arrives at a decision as to the course of action to be taken in order to accomplish his mission. Also called **appreciation of the situation.** *(DOD:* See also **commander's estimate of the situation; logistic estimate of the situation.**)

evacuation—*(DOD, IADB)* 1. The process of moving any person who is wounded, injured, or ill to and/or between medical treatment facilities. 2. The clearance of personnel, animals, or materiel from a given locality. 3. The controlled process of collecting, classifying, and shipping unserviceable or abandoned materiel, United States and foreign, to appropriate reclamation, maintenance, technical intelligence, or disposal facilities.

evacuation control ship—*(DOD, NATO, IADB)* In an amphibious operation, a ship designated as a control point for landing craft, amphibious vehicles, and helicopters evacuating casualties from the beaches. Medical personnel embarked in the evacuation control ship effect distribution of casualties throughout the attack force in accordance with ship's casualty capacities and specialized medical facilities available, and also perform emergency surgery.

evacuation convoy—*(NATO)* An ocean convoy which is used for area evacuation.

evacuation policy—*(DOD, IADB)* 1. Command decision, indicating the length in days of the maximum period of noneffectiveness that patients may be held within the command for treatment. Patients who, in the opinion of responsible medical officers, cannot be returned to duty status within the period prescribed are evacuated by the first available means, provided the travel involved will not aggravate their disabilities. 2. A command decision concerning the movement of civilians from the proximity of military operations for security and safety reasons and involving the need to arrange for movement, reception, care, and control of such individuals. 3. Command policy concerning the evacuation of unserviceable or abandoned materiel and including designation of channels and destinations for evacuated materiel, the establishment of controls and procedures, and the dissemination of condition standards and disposition instructions.

evacuee—*(DOD)* A civilian removed from a place of residence by military direction for reasons of personal security or the requirements of the military situation. See also **displaced person; expellee; refugee.**

evacuees—*(NATO)* Resident or transient persons who have been ordered or authorized to move by competent authorities, and whose movement and accommodation are planned, organized and controlled by such authorities.

evader—*(DOD, IADB)* Any person isolated in hostile or unfriendly territory who eludes capture.

evaluation—*(DOD)* In intelligence usage, appraisal of an item of information in terms of credibility, reliability, pertinency, and accuracy. Appraisal is accomplished at several stages within the intelligence cycle with progressively different contexts. Initial evaluations, made by case officers and report officers, are focused upon the reliability of the source and the accuracy of the information as judged by data available at or close to their operational levels. Later evaluations, by intelligence analysts, are primarily concerned with verifying accuracy of information and may, in effect, convert information into intelligence. Appraisal or evaluation of items of information or intelligence is indicated by a standard letter-number system. The evaluation of the reliability of sources is designated by a letter from A through F, and the accuracy of the information is designated by numeral 1 through 6. These are two entirely independent appraisals, and these separate appraisals are indicated in accordance with the system indicated below. Thus, information adjudged to be "probably true" received from a "usually reliable source" is designated "B-2" or "B2," while information of which the "truth cannot be judged" received from a "usually reliable source" is designated "B-6" or "B6."

Reliability of Source	Accuracy of Information
A—Completely reliable	1—Confirmed by other sources
B—Usually reliable	2—Probably true
C—Fairly reliable	3—Possibly true
D—Not usually reliable	4—Doubtful
E—Unreliable	5—Improbable
F—Reliability cannot be judged	6—Truth cannot be judged

See also **intelligence cycle; operational evaluation; technical evaluation.**

evaluation—*(NATO)* See **intelligence cycle.**

evaluation of information (intelligence)—See evaluation (intelligence).

evasion and escape—*(DOD, I, NATO, IADB)* The procedures and operations whereby military personnel and other selected individuals are enabled to emerge from an enemy-held or hostile area to areas under friendly control.

evasion and escape intelligence—*(DOD, IADB)* Processed information prepared to assist personnel to escape if captured by the enemy or to evade capture if lost in enemy-dominated territory.

evasion and escape net—*(DOD, IADB)* The organization within enemy-held or hostile areas that operates to receive, move, and exfiltrate military personnel or selected individuals to friendly control. See also **unconventional warfare**.

evasion and escape route—*(DOD, IADB)* A course of travel, preplanned or not, that an escapee or evader uses in an attempt to depart enemy territory in order to return to friendly lines.

exaggerated stereoscopy—See **hyperstereoscopy**.

exceptional transport—*(DOD, NATO)* In railway terminology, a load whose size, weight, or preparation entail special difficulties vis-à-vis the facilities or equipment of even one of the railway systems to be used.

excess property—*(DOD)* The quantity of property in possession of any component of the Department of Defense that exceeds the quantity required or authorized for retention by that component.

excess property—*(IADB)* The quantity of property in possession of any component of the Armed Forces that exceeds the quantity required or authorized for retention by that component.

executing commander (nuclear weapons)—*(DOD, NATO, IADB)* A commander to whom nuclear weapons are released for delivery against specific targets or in accordance with approved plans. See also **commander(s)**; **releasing commander (nuclear weapons)**.

execution planning—*(DOD)* The phase of the crisis action system planning in which an approved operation plan or other National Command Authority-designated course of action is adjusted, refined, and translated into an operation order. Execution planning can proceed on the basis of prior deliberate planning, or it can take place under a no plan situation.

Executive Agent for the Joint Chiefs of Staff—*(DOD)* A member of the Joint Chiefs of Staff to whom they have assigned responsibility and delegated authority, which would otherwise be exercised by them collectively, to carry out for them certain of their duties.

exercise—*(DOD, NATO)* A military maneuver or simulated wartime operation involving planning, preparation, and execution. It is carried out for the purpose of training and evaluation. It may be a combined, joint, or single service exercise, depending on participating organizations. See also **command post exercise; field exercise; maneuver.**

exercise commander—*(NATO, IADB)* A commander taking part in the exercise who will issue appropriate operation orders to forces placed under his control. He may be allocated responsibilities regarding controlling, conducting, and/or directing the exercise in addition to that of command. See also **commander(s)**.

exercise directing staff—*(DOD, NATO)* A group of officers who by virtue of experience, qualifications, and a thorough knowledge of the exercise instructions, are selected to direct or control an exercise.

exercise filled mine—*(DOD, NATO)* In naval mine warfare, a mine containing an inert filling and an indicating device. See also **explosive filled mine; fitted mine; mine.**

exercise incident—*(DOD, NATO)* An occurrence injected by directing staffs into the exercise which will have an effect on the forces being exercised, or their facilities, and which will require action by the appropriate commander and/or staff being exercised.

exercise mine—*(DOD, NATO)* In naval mine warfare, a mine suitable for use in mine warfare exercises, fitted with visible or audible indicating devices to show where and when it would normally fire. See also **drill mine; mine; practice mine.**

exercise planning directive—*(NATO)* The exercise specification as developed by the officer scheduling the exercise, designed to provide further guidance to the planners of a particular exercise.

exercise program—*(NATO)* The specifications of the exercises programmed by a NATO commander for a particular calendar year.

exercise specification—*(DOD, NATO)* The fundamental requirements for an exercise, providing in advance an outline of the concept, form, scope, setting, aim, objectives, force requirements, political implications, analysis arrangements and costs.

exercise sponsor—*(DOD, NATO)* The commander who conceives a particular exercise and orders that it be planned and executed either by his staff or by a subordinate headquarters.

exercise study—*(DOD, NATO)* An activity which may take form of a map exercise, a war game, a series of lectures, a discussion group, or an operational analysis.

exercise term—*(DOD)* A combination of two words, normally unclassified, used exclusively to designate a test, drill, or exercise. An exercise term is employed to preclude the possibility of confusing exercise directives with actual operations directives.

exfiltration—*(DOD)* The removal of personnel or units from areas under enemy control.

existence load—*(DOD, IADB)* Consists of items other than those in the fighting load that are required to sustain or protect the combat soldier, that may be necessary for increased personal and environmental protection, and that are not normally carried by the individual. See also **fighting load.**

exoatmosphere—See **nuclear exoatmospheric burst.**

expeditionary force—*(DOD)* An armed force organized to accomplish a specific objective in a foreign country.

expellee—*(DOD, IADB)* A civilian outside the boundaries of the country of his or her nationality or ethnic origin who is being forcibly repatriated to that country or to a third country for political or other purposes. See also **displaced person; evacuee; refugee.**

expendable property—*(DOD, IADB)* Property that may be consumed in use or loses its identity in use and may be dropped from stock record accounts when it is issued or used.

expendable supplies and material—*(DOD, IADB)* Supplies that are consumed in use, such as ammunition, paint, fuel, cleaning and preserving materials, surgical dressing, drugs, medicines, etc., or that lose their identity, such as spare parts, etc. Sometimes referred to as consumable supplies and material.

expendable supplies and materials—*(NATO)* Items which are consumed in use, such as ammunition, or which lose their identity, such as certain repair parts, or which are of low intrinsic value, unworthy of full accounting procedures.

exploder—*(DOD, NATO)* A device designed to generate an electric current in a firing circuit after deliberate action by the user in order to initiate an explosive charge or charges.

exploitation—*(DOD, NATO, IADB)* 1. Taking full advantage of success in battle and following up initial gains. 2. Taking full advantage of any information that has come to hand for tactical or strategic purposes. 3. An offensive operation that usually follows a successful attack and is designed to disorganize the enemy in depth.

exploratory hunting—*(DOD, NATO)* In naval mine warfare, a parallel operation to search sweeping, in which a sample of the route or area is subjected to minehunting procedures to determine the presence or absence of mines.

explosive filled mine—*(DOD, NATO)* In mine warfare, a mine containing an explosive charge but not necessarily the firing train needed to detonate it. See also **exercise filled mine; fitted mine.**

explosive ordnance—*(DOD, NATO)* All munitions containing explosives, nuclear fission or fusion materials and biological and chemical agents. This includes bombs and warheads; guided and ballistic missiles; artillery, mortar, rocket and small arms ammunition; all mines, torpedos, and depth charges; demolition charges; pyrotechnics; clusters and dispensers; cartridge and propellant actuated devices; electro-explosive devices; clandestine and improvised explosive devices; and all similar or related items or components explosive in nature.

explosive ordnance disposal—*(DOD, NATO)* The detection, identification, field evaluation, rendering-safe, recovery and final disposal of unexploded explosive ordnance. It may also include the rendering safe and/or disposal of explosive ordnance which have become hazardous by damage or deterioration when the disposal of such explosive ordnance is beyond the capabilities of personnel normally assigned the responsibility for routine disposal.

explosive ordnance disposal incident—*(DOD, NATO)* The suspected or detected presence of unexploded explosive ordnance, or damaged explosive ordnance, which constitutes a hazard to operations, installations, personnel or material. Not included in this definition are the accidental arming or other conditions that develop during the manufacture of high explosive material, technical service assembly operations or the laying of mines and demolition charges.

explosive ordnance disposal procedures—*(DOD, NATO)* Those particular courses or modes of action taken by explosive ordnance disposal personnel for access to, diagnosis, rendering safe, recovery, and final disposal of explosive ordnance or any hazardous material associated with an explosive ordnance disposal incident.

a. **access procedures.** Those actions taken to locate exactly and to gain access to unexploded explosive ordnance.

b. **diagnostic procedures.** Those actions taken to identify and evaluate unexploded explosive ordnance.

c. **render safe procedures.** The portion of the explosive ordnance disposal procedures involving the application of special explosive ordnance disposal methods and tools to provide for the interruption of functions or separation of essential components of unexploded explosive ordnance to prevent an unacceptable detonation.

d. **recovery procedures.** Those actions taken to recover unexploded explosive ordnance.

e. **final disposal procedures.** The final disposal of explosive ordnance which may include demolition or burning in place, removal to a disposal area or other appropriate means.

explosive ordnance disposal unit—*(DOD, IADB)* Personnel with special training and equipment who render explosive ordnance safe (such as bombs, mines, projectiles, and booby traps), make intelligence reports on such ordnance, and supervise the safe removal thereof.

explosive ordnance reconnaissance—*(NATO)* Reconnaissance involving the investigation, detection, location, marking, initial identification and reporting of suspected unexploded explosive ordnance, by explosive ordnance reconnaissance agents, in order to determine further action.

explosive train—*(DOD, NATO)* A succession of initiating and igniting elements arranged to cause a charge to function.

exposure dose—*(DOD, NATO, IADB)* The exposure dose at a given point is a measurement of radiation in relation to its ability to produce ionization. The unit of measurement of the exposure dose is the roentgen.

exposure station—See **air station (photogrammetry)**.

extended communications search—*(DOD)* In search and rescue operations, consists of contacting all possible sources of information on the missing craft, including physically checking possible locations such as harbors, marinas, and airport ramps. An extended communications search is normally conducted after a preliminary communications search has yielded no results and when the mission is upgraded to the alert phase. Also called EXCOM. See also **preliminary communications search**;

search and rescue incident classification, Subpart **b**.

extent of damage—*(DOD, IADB)* The visible plan area of damage to a target element, usually expressed in units of 1,000 square feet, in detailed damage analysis and in approximate percentages in immediate-type damage assessment reports; e.g., 50 percent structural damage.

external reinforcing force—*(DOD, NATO)* A reinforcing force which is principally stationed in peacetime outside its intended Major NATO Command area of operations.

extraction parachute—*(DOD, NATO, IADB)* An auxiliary parachute designed to release and extract and deploy cargo from aircraft in flight and deploy cargo parachutes. See also **gravity extraction**.

extraction zone—*(DOD, NATO)* A specified drop zone used for the delivery of supplies and/or equipment by means of an extraction technique from an aircraft flying very close to the ground.

F

F-4—See Phantom II.

F-5A/B—See Freedom Fighter.

F-14—See Tomcat.

F-15—See Eagle.

F-16—See Air Combat Fighter.

F-100—See Super Sabre.

F-101—See Voodoo.

F-102A—See Delta Dagger.

F-104—See Starfighter.

F-105—See Thunderchief.

F-106—See Delta Dart.

F-111—*(DOD)* A twin-engine, supersonic, turbo-fan, all-weather tactical fighter. It is capable of employing nuclear and nonnuclear weapons. It also has the capability for operating from very short, relatively unprepared air strips. FB-111 is the strategic bomber version.

F-111—*(IADB)* A twin-engine-turbojet-powered tactical fighter for delivering nuclear and nonnuclear weapons and for operating from very short, relatively unprepared air strips with a minimum of ground support. The air-craft will have an all-weather attack capability. Other versions are: an all-weather interceptor version having a long-range pulse doppler fire control system and nuclear air-to-air missiles; a reconnaissance version having all-weather reconnaissance and bombing capabilities with both nuclear and nonnuclear weapons.

fabricator—*(DOD)* Individuals or groups who, without genuine resources, invent information or inflate or embroider over news for personal gain or for political purposes.

face of a map or chart—*(NATO)* The side on which the printed image of the map or chart appears.

facility—*(DOD, IADB)* A real property entity consisting of one or more of the following: a building, a structure, a utility system, pavement, and underlying land.

facility—*(NATO)* An activity which provides a specific kind of operating assistance to naval, ground, or air forces thereby facilitating any action or operation. See also **base; search and rescue.**

facsimile—*(DOD, NATO, IADB)* A system of telecommunication for the transmission of fixed images with a view to their reception in a permanent form.

faded—*(DOD)* In air intercept, a code meaning, "Contact has disappeared from reporting station's scope, and any position information given is estimated."

fair drawing—*(NATO)* A drawing complete in all respects in the style and form specified for reproduction.

faker—*(DOD)* A friendly aircraft simulating a hostile in an air defense exercise.

Falcon—*(DOD, IADB)* An air-to-air guided missile. The Falcon family (AIM-4 series, AIM-26A, and AIM-47A) can be carried either internally or externally on interceptor aircraft. The Falcon can be used on the F-101B, F-102, F-104, and F-106. Some of the Falcon family of missiles are equipped with nuclear warheads.

fallout—*(DOD, NATO, IADB)* The precipitation to earth of radioactive particulate matter from a nuclear cloud; also applied to the particulate matter itself.

fallout contours—*(DOD, NATO, IADB)* Lines joining points which have the same radiation intensity that define a fallout pattern, represented in terms of roentgens per hour.

fallout pattern—*(DOD, NATO, IADB)* The distribution of fallout as portrayed by fallout contours.

fallout prediction—*(DOD, IADB)* An estimate, made before and immediately after a nuclear detonation, of the location and intensity of militarily significant quantities of radioactive fallout.

fallout safe height of burst—*(DOD, IADB)* The height of burst at or above which no militarily significant fallout will be reproduced as a result of a nuclear weapon detonation. See also **types of burst.**

fallout wind vector plot—*(IADB)* A wind vector diagram based on the wind structure from the earth's surface to the highest altitude affecting fallout pattern.

fallout wind vector plot—*(NATO, DOD, IADB)* A wind vector diagram based on the wind structure from the surface of the earth to the highest altitude of interest.

false color film—*(NATO)* A color film with at least one emulsion layer sensitive to radiation outside the visible region of the spectrum (e.g., infra red), in which the representation of colors is deliberately altered. See also **camouflage detection photography.**

false origin—*(DOD, NATO, IADB)* A fixed point to the south and west of a grid zone from which grid distances are measured eastward and northward.

false parallax—*(NATO, IADB)* The apparent vertical displacement of an object from its true position, when viewed stereoscopically, due to movement of the object itself as well as to change in the point of observation.

famished—*(DOD)* In air intercept, a code meaning, "Have you any instructions for me?"

fan camera photography—*(DOD, NATO, IADB)* Photography taken simultaneously by an assembly of three or more cameras, systematically installed at fixed angles relative to each other so as to provide wide lateral coverage with overlapping images. See also **tri-camera photography.**

fan cameras—*(DOD, NATO, IADB)* An assembly of three or more cameras systematically disposed at fixed angles relative to each other so as to provide wide lateral coverage with overlapping images. See also **split cameras.**

fan marker beacon—*(DOD, NATO, IADB)* A type of radio beacon, the emissions of which radiate in a vertical, fan-shaped pattern. The signal can be keyed for identification purposes. See also **radio beacon; Z marker beacon.**

farm gate type operations—*(DOD, I)* Operational assistance and specialized tactical training provided a friendly foreign air force by the United States Armed Forces to include, under certain specified conditions, the flying of operational missions in combat by combined United States/foreign aircrews as a part of the training being given when such missions are beyond the capability of the foreign air force.

feasibility test—*(DOD, IADB)* A test to determine whether or not a plan is within the capacity of the resources that can be made available. See also **logistic implications test.**

feature—*(DOD, NATO)* In cartography, any object or configuration of ground or water represented on the face of the map or chart.

feature line overlap—*(DOD, NATO, IADB)* A series of overlapping air photographs which follow the line of a ground feature, e.g., river, road, railway, etc.

Federal Stock Number—*(DOD)* The Federal Stock Number of an item of supply consists of the applicable 4-digit class code number from the Federal Supply Classification plus a sequentially assigned 7-digit Federal Item Identification Number. The number shall be arranged as follows: 4210–196–5439. See also **National Stock Number**. Note: Federal Stock Numbers were replaced by National Stock Numbers effective 30 September 1974.

federal supply class management—*(DOD)* Those functions of materiel management that can best be accomplished by Federal Supply Classification, such as cataloging, characteristic screening, standardization, interchangeability and substitution grouping, multi-item specification management, and engineering support of the foregoing.

feet dry—*(DOD, IADB)* In air intercept, close air support, and air interdiction, a code meaning, "I am, or contact designated is, over land."

feet wet—*(DOD, IADB)* In air intercept, close air support, and air interdiction, a code meaning, "I am, or contact designated is, over water."

ferret—*(DOD, IADB)* An aircraft, ship, or vehicle especially equipped for the detection, location, recording, and analyzing of electromagnetic radiation.

few (raid size)—*(DOD, IADB)* In air intercept usage, seven or fewer aircraft. See also **many (raid size)**.

FF—See **frigate**.

FFG—See **guided missile frigate**.

fiducial mark—See **collimating mark**.

field army—*(DOD, IADB)* Administrative and tactical organization composed of a headquarters, certain organic Army troops, service support troops, a variable number of corps, and a variable number of divisions.

field artillery—*(DOD, IADB)* Equipment, supplies, ammunition, and personnel involved in the use of cannon, rocket, or surface-to-surface missile launchers. Field artillery cannons are classified according to caliber as:

    light—120mm and less
    medium—121–160mm
    heavy—161–210mm
    very heavy—greater than 210mm
See also **direct support artillery; general support artillery**.

field artillery observer—*(DOD, IADB)* A person who watches the effects of artillery fire, adjusts the center of impact of that fire onto a target, and reports the results to the firing agency. See also **naval gunfire spotting team; spotter**.

field control—*(DOD, NATO, IADB)* A series of points whose relative positions and elevations are known. These positions are used in basic data in mapping and charting. Normally, these positions are established by survey methods, and are sometimes referred to as "trig control" or "trigonometrical net(work)." See also **common control (artillery); control point; ground control**.

field exercise—*(DOD, NATO, IADB)* An exercise conducted in the field under simulated war conditions in which troops and armament of one side are actually present, while those of the other side may be imaginary or in outline. See also **command post exercise**.

field fortifications—*(DOD, NATO, IADB)* An emplacement or shelter of a temporary nature which can be constructed with reasonable facility by units requiring no more than minor engineer supervisory and equipment participation.

field headquarters—See **command post**.

field of fire—*(DOD, NATO, IADB)* The area which a weapon or a group of weapons may cover effectively with fire from a given position.

141

field of view—*(DOD, NATO)* 1. In photography, the angle between two rays passing through the perspective center (rear nodal point) of a camera lens to the two opposite sides of the format. Not to be confused with "angle of view." See also **angle of view.** 2. The total solid angle available to the gunner when looking through the gunsight.

field of vision—*(DOD, NATO)* The total solid angle available to the gunner from his normal position. See also **field of view.**

field press censorship—*(DOD, IADB)* The security review of news material subject to the jurisdiction of the Armed Forces of the United States, including all information or material intended for dissemination to the public. See also **censorship.**

fighter controller—See **air controller.**

fighter cover—*(DOD, NATO, IADB)* The maintenance of a number of fighter aircraft over a specified area or force for the purpose of repelling hostile air activities. See also **airborne alert.**

fighter direction aircraft—*(DOD, NATO, IADB)* An aircraft equipped and manned for directing fighter aircraft operations. See also **combat information ship.**

fighter direction ship—*(DOD, NATO, IADB)* A ship equipped and manned for directing fighter aircraft operations. See also **combat information ship.**

fighter engagement zone—See **weapon engagement zone.**

fighter interceptor—See **interceptor.**

fighter sweep—*(DOD, NATO, IADB)* An offensive mission by fighter aircraft to seek out and destroy enemy aircraft or targets of opportunity in an allotted area of operations.

fighting load—*(DOD, IADB)* Consists of items of individual clothing, equipment, weapons, and ammunition that are carried by, and are essential to, the effectiveness of the combat soldier and the accomplishment of the immediate mission of the unit when the soldier is on foot. See also **existence load.**

fighting patrol—See **combat patrol.**

filler—*(DOD)* A substance carried in an ammunition container such as a projectile, mine, bomb, or grenade. A filler may be an explosive, chemical, or inert substance.

filler personnel—*(DOD)* Individuals of suitable grade and skill initially required to bring a unit or organization to its authorized strength.

filler point—See **charging point.**

film badge—*(DOD, NATO, IADB)* A photographic film packet to be carried by personnel, in the form of a badge, for measuring and permanently recording (usually) gamma-ray dosage.

filter—*(DOD, NATO)* In electronics, a device which transmits only part of the incident energy and may thereby change the spectral distribution of energy:
   a. High pass filters transmit energy above a certain frequency;
   b. Low pass filters transmit energy below a certain frequency;
   c. Band pass filters transmit energy of a certain bandwidth;
   d. Band stop filters transmit energy outside a specific frequency band.

filter center—*(DOD, IADB)* The location in an aircraft control and warning system at which information from observation posts is filtered for further dissemination to air defense control centers and air defense direction centers.

filtering—*(NATO, IADB)* The process of interpreting reported information on movements of aircraft, ships, and submarines in order to determine their probable true tracks and, where applicable, heights or depths.

FIM-43—See **Redeye.**

final approach—*(DOD, NATO)* That part of an instrument approach procedure in which alignment and descent for landing are accomplished.
   a. In a non-precision approach it normally begins at the final approach fix or point and ends at the missed approach point or fix.
   b. In a precision approach the final approach is deemed to commence at the glide path intercept point and ends at the decision height/altitude.

final destination (merchant shipping)—*(NATO, IADB)* The final destination of a convoy or of an individual ship (whether in convoy or independent) irrespective of whether or not routing instructions have been issued. See also **destination (merchant shipping).**

final disposal procedures—See **explosive ordnance disposal procedures.**

final plan—*(DOD, NATO)* A plan for which drafts have been coordinated and approved and which has been signed by or on behalf of a competent authority. See also **operation plan.**

final protective fire—*(DOD, NATO, IADB)* An immediately available prearranged barrier of fire designed to impede enemy movement across defensive lines or areas.

financial property accounting—*(DOD)* The establishment and maintenance of property accounts in monetary terms; the rendition of property reports in monetary terms.

fire—*(DOD, NATO, IADB)* 1. The command given to discharge a weapon(s). 2. To detonate the main explosive charge by means of a firing system. 3. See also **barrage fire; call fire; close supporting fire; concentrated fire; counterfire; counter-preparation fire; covering fire; deep supporting fire; destruction fire; direct fire; direct supporting fire; distributed fire; grazing fire; harassing fire; in-**direct fire; interdiction fire; neutralization fire; observed fire; preparation fire; radar fire; registration fire; scheduled fire; searching fire; supporting fire; suppressive fire; unobserved fire; zone fire.

fireball—*(DOD, NATO, IADB)* The luminous sphere of hot gases which forms a few millionths of a second after detonation of a nuclear weapon and immediately starts expanding and cooling.

fire barrage (specify)—*(DOD, IADB)* An order to deliver a prearranged barrier of fire. Specification of the particular barrage may be by code name, numbering system, unit assignment, or other designated means.

Firebee—*(DOD)* A remotely controlled target drone powered by a turbojet engine. It achieves high subsonic speeds and is designed to be ground launched or air launched. It is used to test, train, and evaluate weapon systems employing surface-to-air and air-to-air missiles. Designated as **BQM-34.**

fire capabilities chart—*(DOD, NATO, IADB)* A chart, usually in the form of an overlay, showing the areas which can be reached by the fire of the bulk of the weapons of a unit.

fire control—*(DOD, NATO)* The control of all operations in connection with the application of fire on a target.

fire control radar—*(DOD, NATO, IADB)* Radar used to provide target information inputs to a weapon fire control system.

fire control system—*(DOD, NATO)* A group of interrelated fire control equipments and/or instruments designed for use with a weapon or group of weapons.

fire coordination—See **fire support coordination.**

fire coordination area—*(DOD, NATO, IADB)* An area with specified restraints into which fires in excess of those restraints will not be delivered without approval of the authority establishing the restraints.

fire direction center—*(DOD, NATO, IADB)* That element of a command post, consisting of gunnery and communication personnel and equipment, by means of which the commander exercises fire direction and/or fire control. The fire direction center receives target intelligence and requests for fire, and translates them into appropriate fire direction.

fire for effect—*(DOD, NATO, IADB)* 1. Fire which is delivered after the mean point of impact or burst is within the desired distance of the target or adjusting/ranging point. 2. Term in a call for fire to indicate the adjustment/ranging is satisfactory and fire for effect is desired.

fire message—See **call for fire.**

fire mission—*(DOD, NATO, IADB)* 1. Specific assignment given to a fire unit as part of a definite plan. 2. Order used to alert the weapon/battery area and indicate that the message following is a call for fire.

fire plan—*(DOD, NATO, IADB)* A tactical plan for using the weapons of a unit or formation so that their fire will be coordinated.

firepower—*(DOD, NATO, IADB)* 1. The amount of fire which may be delivered by a position, unit, or weapon system. 2. Ability to deliver fire.

firepower umbrella—*(DOD, NATO, IADB)* An area of specified dimensions defining the boundaries of the airspace over a naval force at sea within which the fire of ships' antiaircraft weapons can endanger aircraft, and within which special procedures have been established for the identification and operation of friendly aircraft. See also **air defense operations area.**

fire storm—*(DOD, NATO, IADB)* Stationary mass fire, generally in built-up urban areas, generating strong, inrushing winds from all sides; the winds keep the fires from spreading while adding fresh oxygen to increase their intensity.

fire support area—*(DOD, NATO, IADB)* An appropriate maneuver area assigned to fire support ships from which to deliver gunfire support of an amphibious operation. See also **naval support area.**

fire support coordination—*(DOD, NATO, IADB)* The planning and executing of fire so that targets are adequately covered by a suitable weapon or group of weapons.

fire support coordination center—*(DOD, NATO, IADB)* A single location in which are centralized communications facilities and personnel incident to the coordination of all forms of fire support. See also **supporting arms coordination center.**

fire support coordination line—*(DOD, NATO, IADB)* A line established by the appropriate ground commander to insure coordination of fire not under his control but which may affect current tactical operations. The fire support coordination line is used to coordinate fires of air, ground or sea weapons systems using any type of ammunition against surface targets. The fire support coordination line should follow well defined terrain features. The establishment of the fire support coordination line must be coordinated with the appropriate tactical air commander and other supporting elements. Supporting elements may attack targets forward of the fire support coordination line, without prior coordination with the ground force commander, provided the attack will not produce adverse surface effects on, or to the rear of, the line. Attacks against surface targets behind this line must be coordinated with the appropriate ground force commander. Also known as **FSCL.**

fire support group—*(DOD, NATO, IADB)* A temporary grouping of ships under a single commander charged with supporting troop operations ashore by naval gunfire. A fire support group may be further subdivided into fire support units and fire support elements.

fire support station—*(DOD, IADB)* An exact location at sea within a fire support area from which a fire support ship delivers fire.

fire task—See **fire mission.**

fire time—See **span of detonation (atomic demolition munition employment).**

firing area—*(DOD, NATO)* In a sweeper-sweep combination it is the horizontal area at the depth of a particular mine in which the mine will detonate. The firing area has exactly the same dimensions as the interception area but will lie astern of it unless the mine detonates immediately when actuated.

firing chart—*(DOD, IADB)* Map, photo map, or grid sheet showing the relative horizontal and vertical positions of batteries, base points, base point lines, check points, targets, and other details needed in preparing firing data.

firing circuit—*(DOD, NATO)* 1. In land operations, an electrical circuit and/or pyrotechnic loop designed to detonate connected charges from a firing point. 2. In naval mine warfare, that part of a mine circuit which either completes the detonator circuit or operates a ship counter.

firing mechanism—See **firing circuit.**

firing point—*(DOD, NATO)* That point in the firing circuit where the device employed to initiate the detonation of the charges is located.

firing system—*(DOD, NATO)* In demolition, a system composed of elements designed to fire the main charge or charges.

first generation negative—See **generation (photography).**

first generation positive—See **generation (photography).**

first light—*(DOD, IADB)* The beginning of morning nautical twilight; i.e., when the center of the morning sun is 12° below the horizon.

first salvo at—*(DOD)* In naval gunfire support, a portion of a ship's message to an observer or spotter to indicate that because of proximity to troops, the ship will not fire at the target but offset the first salvo a specific distance from the target.

first strike—*(DOD, IADB)* The first offensive move of a war. (Generally associated with nuclear operations.)

FISINT—See **foreign instrumentation signals intelligence.**

fission—*(DOD, NATO)* The process whereby the nucleus of a heavy element splits into (generally) two nuclei of lighter elements, with the release of substantial amounts of energy.

fission products—*(DOD, NATO)* A general term for the complex mixture of substances produced as a result of nuclear fission.

fission to yield ratio—*(DOD, NATO, IADB)* The ratio of the yield derived from nuclear fission to the total yield; it is frequently expressed in percent.

fitted mine—*(DOD, NATO)* In naval mine warfare, a mine containing an explosive charge, a primer, detonator, and firing system. See also **exercise filled mine; explosive filled mine.**

fix—*(DOD, NATO, IADB)* A position determined from terrestrial, electronic, or astronomical data.

fixed ammunition—*(DOD, NATO, IADB)* Ammunition in which the cartridge case is permanently attached to the projectile. See also **ammunition.**

fixed capital property—*(DOD)* 1. Assets of a permanent character having continuing value. 2. As used in military establishments, includes real estate and equipment installed or in use, either in productive plants or in field operations. Synonymous with fixed assets.

fixed medical treatment facility—*(DOD, NATO, IADB)* A medical treatment facility which is designed to operate for an extended period of time at a specific site.

fixed price incentive contract—*(DOD, IADB)* A fixed price type of contract with provision for the adjustment of profit and price by a formula based on the relationship that final negotiated total cost bears to negotiated target cost as adjusted by approved changes.

fixed price type contract—*(DOD, IADB)* A type of contract that generally provides for a firm price or, under appropriate circumstances, may provide for an adjustable price for the supplies or services being procured. Fixed price contracts are of several types so designed as to facilitate proper pricing under varying circumstances.

fixed station patrol—*(DOD, NATO, IADB)* One in which each scout maintains station relative to an assigned point on a barrier line while searching the surrounding area. Scouts are not stationary but remain underway and patrol near the center of their assigned stations. A scout is a surface ship, submarine, or aircraft.

fixer network—*(DOD, NATO, IADB)* A combination of radio or radar direction-finding installations which, operating in conjunction, are capable of plotting the position relative to the ground of an aircraft in flight.

fixer system—See **fixer network.**

flag days (red or green)—*(DOD)* Red flag days are those during which movement requirements cannot be met; green flag days are those during which the requisite amount or a surplus of transportation capability exists.

flag officer—*(DOD)* A term applied to an officer holding the rank of general, lieutenant general, major general, or brigadier general in the US Army, Air Force or Marine Corps or admiral, vice admiral, rear admiral or commodore in the US Navy or Coast Guard.

flame thrower—*(DOD, NATO, IADB)* A weapon that projects incendiary fuel and has provision for ignition of this fuel.

flammable cargo—See **inflammable cargo.**

flank guard—*(DOD, NATO, IADB)* A security element operating to the flank of a moving or stationary force to protect it from enemy ground observation, direct fire, and surprise attack.

flanking attack—*(DOD, NATO)* An offensive maneuver directed at the flank of an enemy. See also **frontal attack.**

flare—*(DOD, NATO)* The change in the flight path of an aircraft so as to reduce the rate of descent for touchdown.

flare dud—*(DOD)* A nuclear weapon that when launched at a target, detonates with anticipated yield but at an altitude appreciably greater than intended. This is not a dud insofar as yield is concerned, but it is a dud with respect to the effects on the target and the normal operation of the weapon.

flash blindness—*(DOD, NATO, IADB)* Impairment of vision resulting from an intense flash of light. It includes temporary or permanent loss of visual functions and may be associated with retinal burns. See also **dazzle.**

flash burn—*(DOD, NATO, IADB)* A burn caused by excessive exposure (of bare skin) to thermal radiation.

flash message—*(DOD, IADB)* A category of precedence reserved for initial enemy contact messages or operational combat messages of extreme urgency. Brevity is mandatory. See also **precedence.**

flash ranging—*(DOD, IADB)* Finding the position of the burst of a projectile or of an enemy gun by observing its flash.

flash report—*(DOD)* Not to be used. See **inflight report.**

flash suppressor—*(DOD, NATO, IADB)* Device attached to the muzzle of the weapon which reduces the amount of visible light or flash created by burning propellant gases.

flat—*(DOD, NATO)* In photography, lacking in contrast.

flatted cargo—*(DOD, IADB)* Cargo placed in the bottom of the holds, covered with planks and dunnage, and held for future use. Flatted cargo usually has room left above it for the loading of vehicles that may be moved without interfering with the flatted cargo. Frequently, flatted cargo serves in lieu of ballast. Sometimes called understowed cargo. See also **cargo.**

fleet—*(DOD, IADB)* An organization of ships, aircraft, marine forces, and shore-based fleet activities all under the command of a commander or commander in chief who may exercise operational as well as administrative control. See also **major fleet; numbered fleet.**

fleet ballistic missile submarine—*(DOD, IADB)* A nuclear-powered submarine designed to deliver ballistic missile attacks against assigned targets from either a submerged or surfaced condition. Designated as SSBN.

fleet in being—*(DOD, IADB)* A fleet (force) that avoids decisive action, but, because of its strength and location, causes or necessitates counter-concentrations and so reduces the number of opposing units available for operations elsewhere.

Fleet Marine Force—*(DOD)* A balanced force of combined arms comprising land, air, and service elements of the US Marine Corps. A Fleet Marine Force is an integral part of a US Fleet and has the status of a type command.

flexible response—*(DOD, IADB)* The capability of military forces for effective reaction to any enemy threat or attack with actions appropriate and adaptable to the circumstances existing.

flight—*(DOD)* 1. In Navy and Marine Corps usage, a specified group of aircraft usually engaged in a common mission. 2. The basic tactical unit in the Air Force, consisting of four or more aircraft in two or more elements. 3. A single aircraft airborne on a nonoperational mission.

flight—*(IADB)* 1. A specified group of aircraft usually engaged in a common mission. 2. A single aircraft airborne on a nonoperational mission.

flight advisory—*(DOD, IADB)* A message dispatched to aircraft in flight or to interested stations to advise of any deviation or irregularity.

flight deck—*(DOD, IADB)* 1. In certain airplanes, an elevated compartment occupied by the crew for operating the airplane in flight. 2. The upper deck of an aircraft carrier that serves as a runway.

flight following—*(DOD, NATO)* The task of maintaining contact with specified aircraft for the purpose of determining enroute progress and/or flight termination.

flight information center—*(DOD, NATO, IADB)* A unit established to provide flight information service and alerting service.

flight information region—*(DOD, NATO, IADB)* An airspace of defined dimensions within which flight information service and alerting service are provided. See also **air traffic control center; area control center.**

flight levels—*(DOD, NATO, IADB)* Surfaces of constant atmospheric pressure which are related to a specific pressure datum, 1013.2 mb (29.92 in), and are separated by specific pressure intervals. (Flight levels are expressed in three digits that represent hundreds of feet; e.g., flight level 250 represents a barometric altimeter indication of 25,000 feet and flight level 255 is an indication of 25,500 feet.)

flight line—*(DOD, NATO, IADB)* In air photographic reconnaissance, the prescribed ground path over which an air vehicle moves during the execution of its photo mission.

flight operations center—*(DOD, IADB)* The element of the tactical Army air traffic regulation system which provides for aircraft flight following, separation of aircraft under instrument conditions, and identification of friendly aircraft to friendly air defense agencies.

flight path—*(DOD, NATO)* The line connecting the successive positions occupied, or to be occupied, by an aircraft, missile or space vehicle as it moves through air or space.

flight plan—*(DOD, NATO, IADB)* Specified information provided to air traffic services units, relative to an intended flight or portion of a flight of an aircraft.

flight plan correlation—*(DOD, IADB)* A means of identifying aircraft by association with known flight plans.

flight profile—*(DOD, NATO)* The flight path of an aircraft expressed in terms of altitude, speed, range and maneuver.

flight readiness firing—*(DOD)* A missile system test of short duration conducted with the propulsion system operating while the missile is secured to the launcher. Such a test is performed to determine the readiness of the missile system and launch facilities prior to flight test.

flight readiness firing—*(NATO)* Short duration tests relating to a rocket system, carried out with the propulsion device in operation, the rocket being fixed on the launcher. Such tests are carried out in order to define the state of preparation of the rocket system and of the launching facilities before the flight test.

flight surgeon—*(DOD, NATO, IADB)* A physician specially trained in aviation medical practice whose primary duty is the medical examination and medical care of aircrew.

flight test—*(DOD, NATO, IADB)* Test of an aircraft, rocket, missile, or other vehicle by actual flight or launching. Flight tests are planned to achieve specific test objectives and gain operational information.

flight visibility—*(DOD, IADB)* The average forward horizontal distance from the cockpit of an aircraft in flight at which prominent unlighted objects may be seen and identified by day and prominent lighted objects may be seen and identified by night.

floating base support—*(DOD, NATO)* A form of logistic support in which supplies, repairs, maintenance and other services are provided in harbor or at an anchorage for operating forces from ships.

floating lines—*(NATO)* In photogrammetry, lines connecting the same two points of detail on each print of a stereo pair, used to determine whether or not the points are intervisible. The lines may be drawn directly on to the prints or superimposed by means of strips of transparent material.

floating mark or dot—*(NATO)* A mark seen as occupying a position in the three dimensional space formed by the stereoscopic fusion of a pair of photographs, used as a reference mark in examining or measuring a stereoscopic model.

floating mine—*(DOD, NATO)* In naval mine warfare, a mine visible on the surface. See also **drifting mine; free mine; watching mine; mine.**

floating reserve—*(DOD, NATO, IADB)* In an amphibious operation, reserve troops which remain embarked until needed. See also **general reserve.**

flooder—*(DOD, NATO)* In naval mine warfare, a device fitted to a buoyant mine which, on operation after a preset time, floods the mine case and causes it to sink to the bottom.

flotation—*(DOD, NATO, IADB)* The capability of a vehicle to float in water.

flotilla—*(IADB)* An administrative or tactical organization consisting of two or more squadrons of destroyers or smaller types, together with such additional ships as may be assigned as flagships and tenders.

fluxgate—*(NATO)* A detector which gives an electrical signal proportional to the intensity of the external magnetic field acting along its axis.

fluxvalve—See **fluxgate**.

fly(ing) at speed—*(DOD)* In air intercept, a code meaning, "Fly at (mach ____/ ____) indicated air speed," or, "My indicated air speed is (____ knots/mach ____)."

foam path—*(DOD)* A path of fire extinguisher foam laid on a runway to assist aircraft in an emergency landing.

focal length—See **calibrated focal length; equivalent focal length; nominal focal length**.

focal plane—*(DOD, NATO, IADB)* The plane, perpendicular to the optical axis of the lens, in which images of points in the object field of the lens are focused.

folded optics—*(DOD, NATO)* Any optical system containing reflecting components for the purpose of reducing the physical length of the system or for the purpose of changing the path of the optical axis.

follow-on echelon—*(DOD, NATO)* In amphibious operations, that echelon of the assault troops, vehicles, aircraft equipment, and supplies which, though not needed to initiate the assault, is required to support and sustain the assault. See also **assault; follow-up**.

follow-up—*(DOD, NATO)* In amphibious operations, the landing of reinforcements and stores after the assault and follow-on echelons have been landed. See also **assault; follow-on-echelon**.

follow-up echelon—*(DOD, NATO)* In air transport operations, elements moved into the objective area after the assault echelon.

follow-up echelon (air transport)—*(IADB)* Elements moved into the objective area after the assault echelon.

force—*(DOD, IADB)* 1. An aggregation of military personnel, weapon systems, vehicles and necessary support, or combination thereof. 2. A major subdivision of a fleet.

force combat air patrol—*(DOD, IADB)* A patrol of fighters maintained over the task force to destroy enemy aircraft that threaten the force. See also **combat air patrol**.

force list—*(DOD)* A total list of forces required by an operation plan, including assigned forces, augmentation forces, and other forces to be employed in support of the plan.

force rendezvous—*(DOD, NATO)* A checkpoint at which formations of aircraft or ships join and become part of the main force.

force requirement number—*(DOD)* The alphanumeric code used to uniquely identify force entries in a given operation plan time-phased force and deployment data. Also called **FRN**.

force(s)—See **airborne force; air transported force; armed forces, balanced collective forces; black forces; blue forces; combined force; covering force; forces allocated to NATO; garrison force; national forces for the defense of the NATO area; NATO assigned forces; NATO command forces; NATO earmarked forces; orange forces; other forces for NATO; purple forces; task force; underway replenishment force; white forces**.

forces allocated to NATO—(NATO)** Those forces made available to NATO by a nation under the categories of: **a.** NATO command forces. **b.** NATO assigned forces. **c.** NATO earmarked forces. **d.** Other forces for NATO. See also **force(s).**

forces in being—(DOD, NATO)** Forces classified as being in state of readiness "A" or "B" as prescribed in the appropriate Military Committee document.

force sourcing—(DOD)** The identification of the actual units, their origins, ports of embarkation, and movement characteristics to satisfy the time-phased force requirements of a supported commander.

force structure—See **military capability.**

force tabs—(DOD, IADB)** With reference to war plans, the statement of time-phased deployments of major combat units by major commands and geographical areas.

fordability—See **deep fording; shallow fording.**

foreign instrumentation signals intelligence—(DOD)** Intelligence information derived from electromagnetic emissions associated with the testing and operational deployment of foreign aerospace, surface, and subsurface systems. Also called **FISINT.**

foreign intelligence—See **intelligence.**

foreign internal defense—(DOD)** Participation by civilian and military agencies of a government in any of the action programs taken by another government to free and protect its society from subversion, lawlessness, and insurgency. See also **internal defense.**

foreign military sales—(DOD, IADB)** That portion of United States security assistance authorized by the Foreign Assistance Act of 1961, as amended, and the Arms Export Control Act of 1976, as amended. This assistance differs from the Military Assistance Program and the International Military Education and Training Program in that the recipient provides reimbursement for defense articles and services transferred.

foreign military sales trainees—(DOD, IADB)** Foreign nationals receiving training conducted by the Department of Defense on a reimbursable basis, at the country's request.

format—(DOD, NATO)** **1.** In photography, the size and/or shape of a negative or of the print therefrom. **2.** In cartography, the shape and size of a map or chart.

formation—(NATO, DOD)** **1.** An ordered arrangement of troops and/or vehicles for a specific purpose. **2.** An ordered arrangement of two or more ships, units, or aircraft proceeding together under a commander.

formerly restricted data—(DOD)** Information removed from the Restricted Data category upon a joint determination by the Department of Energy (or antecedent agencies) and Department of Defense that such information relates primarily to the military utilization of atomic weapons and that such information can be adequately safeguarded as classified defense information. (Section 142d, Atomic Energy Act of 1954, as amended.) See also **restricted data.**

forming up place—(NATO, IADB)** The last position occupied by the assault echelon before crossing the start line/line of departure. Also called **attack position.**

form lines—(DOD, NATO)** Lines resembling contours, but representing no actual elevations, which have been sketched from visual observation or from inadequate or unreliable map sources, to show collectively the configuration of the terrain.

forward aeromedical evacuation—(DOD, NATO, IADB)** That phase of evacuation which provides airlift for patients between points within the battlefield, from the battlefield to the initial point of treatment, and to subsequent points of treatment within the combat zone.

forward air controller—*(DOD, IADB)* An officer (aviator/pilot) member of the tactical air control party who, from a forward ground or airborne position, controls aircraft in close air support of ground troops.

forward air controller—*(NATO)* A qualified individual who, from a forward position on the ground or in the air, directs the action of combat aircraft engaged in close air support of land forces.

forward air control post—*(DOD)* A highly mobile US Air Force tactical air control system radar facility subordinate to the control and reporting center and/or post used to extend radar coverage and control in the forward combat area.

forward area—*(DOD, IADB)* An area in proximity to combat.

forward arming and refueling point—*(DOD)* A temporary facility, organized, equipped, and deployed by an aviation commander, and normally located in the main battle area closer to the area of operation than the aviation unit's combat service area, to provide fuel and ammunition necessary for the employment of aviation maneuver units in combat. The forward arming and refueling point permits combat aircraft to rapidly refuel and rearm simultaneously. Also called FARP.

forward edge of the battle area—*(DOD, NATO, IADB)* The foremost limits of a series of areas in which ground combat units are deployed, excluding the areas in which the covering or screening forces are operating, designated to coordinate fire support, the positioning of forces, or the maneuver of units.

forward line of own troops—*(NATO)* A line which indicates the most forward positions of friendly forces in any kind of military operation at a specific time.

forward motion compensation—See **image motion compensation.**

forward oblique air photograph—*(DOD)* Oblique photography of the terrain ahead of the aircraft.

forward observer—*(DOD, IADB)* An observer operating with front line troops and trained to adjust ground or naval gunfire and pass back battlefield information. In the absence of a forward air controller the observer may control close air support strikes. See also **spotter.**

forward observer—*(NATO)* An observer with forward troops trained to call for and adjust supporting fire and pass battlefield information.

forward overlap—See **overlap.**

forward recovery mission profile—*(DOD)* A mission profile that involves the recovery of an aircraft at a neutral/friendly forward area airfield or landing site.

forward slope—*(DOD, NATO, IADB)* Any slope which descends towards the enemy.

forward tell—*(DOD, NATO)* The transfer of information to a higher level of command. See also **track telling.**

found shipment—*(NATO)* Freight received but not listed or manifested.

four-round illumination diamond—*(DOD, NATO)* A method of distributing the fire of illumination shells which, by a combination of lateral spread and range spread, provides illumination of a large area.

fox away—*(DOD)* In air intercept, a code meaning, "Missile has fired or been released from aircraft."

fragmentary order—*(DOD, IADB)* An abbreviated form of an operation order, usually issued on a day-to-day basis, that eliminates the need for restating information contained

151

in a basic operation order. It may be issued in sections.

frame—*(DOD, NATO)* In photography, any single exposure contained within a continuous sequence of photographs.

freak—*(DOD)* In air intercept usage, a word meaning frequency in megacycles.

freddie—*(DOD)* In air intercept usage, a controlling unit.

free air anomaly—*(DOD)* The difference between observed gravity and theoretical gravity that has been computed for latitude and corrected for elevation of the station above or below the geoid, by application of the normal rate of change of gravity for change of elevation, as in free air.

free air overpressure—*(DOD, NATO, IADB)* The unreflected pressure, in excess of the ambient atmospheric pressure, created in the air by the blast wave from an explosion. See also **overpressure**.

Freedom Fighter—*(DOD)* A twin-engine supersonic turbojet, multipurpose tactical fighter/ bomber. This aircraft is multinational and is employed in the air-to-air/close air support roles. Some models are air refuelable and some are used for training. **Designated F-5AB.**

free drop—*(DOD, NATO, IADB)* The dropping of equipment or supplies from an aircraft without the use of parachutes. See also **airdrop; air movement; free fall; high velocity drop; low velocity drop.**

free fall—*(DOD, IADB)* A parachute maneuver in which the parachute is manually activated at the discretion of the jumper or automatically at a preset altitude. See also **airdrop; air movement; free drop; high velocity drop; low velocity drop.**

free fall—*(NATO)* A parachute maneuver in which the parachute is opened, either manu-

ally or automatically, at a predetermined altitude.

free field overpressure—See **free air overpressure.**

free issue—*(DOD)* Materiel provided for use or consumption without charge to the fund or fund subdivision that finances the activity to which issued.

free lance—*(DOD)* In air intercept, a code meaning, "Self-control of aircraft is being employed."

free mine—*(DOD, NATO)* In naval mine warfare, a moored mine whose mooring has parted or been cut.

free play exercise—*(DOD, NATO)* An exercise to test the capabilities of forces under simulated contingency and/or wartime conditions, limited only by those artificialities or restrictions required by peacetime safety regulations. See also **controlled exercise.**

free rocket—*(DOD, NATO, IADB)* A rocket not subject to guidance or control in flight.

freight consolidating activity—*(DOD)* A transportation activity that receives less than carload/truckload shipments of materiel for the purpose of assembling them into carload/ truckload lots for onward movement to the ultimate consignee or to a freight distributing activity or other break bulk point. See also **freight distributing activity.**

freight distributing activity—*(DOD)* A transportation activity that receives and unloads consolidated carloads/truckloads of less than carload/truckload shipments of material and forwards the individual shipments to the ultimate consignee. See also **freight consolidating activity.**

fresh target—*(DOD)* A request or command sent by the observer or spotter to the firing ship to indicate that fire will be shifted from the original target to a new target by spots (corrections) applied to the computer solution being generated.

friendly—*(DOD, IADB)* A contact positively identified as friendly. See also **bogey; hostile.**

frigate—*(DOD, IADB)* A warship designed to operate independently, or with strike, anti-submarine warfare, or amphibious forces against submarine, air, and surface threats. (Normal armament consists of 3-inch and 5-inch dual-purpose guns and advanced antisubmarine warfare weapons.) Designated as **FF.** See also **guided missile frigate.**

front—*(DOD, NATO, IADB)* 1. The lateral space occupied by an element measured from the extremity of one flank to the extremity of the other flank. 2. The direction of the enemy. 3. The line of contact of two opposing forces. 4. When a combat situation does not exist or is not assumed, the direction toward which the command is faced.

frontal attack—*(DOD, NATO)* 1. An offensive maneuver in which the main action is directed against the front of the enemy forces. *(DOD, IADB)* 2. In air intercept, an attack by an interceptor aircraft that terminates with a heading crossing angle greater than 135°.

frustrated cargo—*(DOD)* Any shipment of supplies and/or equipment which while en route to destination is stopped prior to receipt and for which further disposition instructions must be obtained.

full beam spread—See **indirect illumination.**

full charge—*(DOD)* The larger of the two propelling charges available for naval guns.

full command—*(NATO, IADB)* The military authority and responsibility of a superior officer to issue orders to subordinates. It covers every aspect of military operations and administration and exists only within national services. The term command, as used internationally, implies a lesser degree of authority than when it is used in a purely national sense. *(NATO)* It follows that no NATO commander has full command over the forces that are assigned to him. This is because nations, in assigning forces to NATO, assign only operational command or operational control. See also **command.**

full mobilization—See **mobilization.**

functions—*(DOD, IADB)* The appropriate or assigned duties, responsibilities, missions, or tasks of an individual, office, or organization. *(DOD)* As defined in the National Security Act of 1947, as amended, the term "function" includes functions, powers, and duties, (5 United States Code 171n (a).)

fusion—*(DOD, NATO)* The process whereby the nuclei of light elements combine to form the nucleus of a heavier element, with the release of tremendous amounts of energy.

fuze—See **base fuze; boresafe fuze; impact action fuze; proximity fuze; self-destroying fuze; shuttered fuze; time fuze.**

fuze cavity—*(DOD, NATO)* A recess in a charge for receiving a fuze.

fuze (specify)—*(DOD)* In artillery and naval gunfire support, a command or request to indicate the type of fuze action desired; i.e., delay, quick, time, proximity.

G

gadget—*(DOD, IADB)* Radar equipment. (Type of equipment may be indicated by a letter as listed in operation orders.) May be followed by a color to indicate state of jamming. Colors will be used as follows:
a. **green**—Clear of jamming.
b. **amber**—Sector partially jammed.
c. **red**—Sector completely jammed.
d. **blue**—Completely jammed.

Galaxy—*(DOD, IADB)* A large cargo transport aircraft powered by four turbofan engines, capable of carrying a very large payload (including outsize cargo and personnel) into forward area air fields. It further is capable of refueling in flight. Designated C–5A.

gamma rays—*(DOD, IADB)* High energy electromagnetic radiation emitted from atomic nuclei during a nuclear reaction. Gamma rays and very high energy X-rays differ only in origin. X-rays do not originate from atomic nuclei but are produced in other ways.

gap—*(DOD, NATO)* An area within a minefield or obstacle belt, free of live mines or obstacles, whose width and direction will allow a friendly force to pass through in tactical formation. See also **phoney minefield.**

gap filler radar—*(DOD, NATO)* A radar used to supplement the coverage of the principal radar in areas where coverage is inadequate.

gap (imagery)—*(DOD)* Any space where imagery fails to meet minimum coverage requirements. This might be a space not covered by imagery or a space where the minimum specified overlap was not obtained. See also **holiday.**

gap marker—*(DOD, NATO)* In landmine warfare, markers used to indicate a minefield gap. Gap markers at the entrance to, and exit from, the gap will be referenced to a landmark or intermediate marker. See also **marker.**

garble—*(DOD, IADB)* An error in transmission, reception, encryption, or decryption that changes the text of a message or any portion thereof in such a manner that it is incorrect or undecryptable.

garnishing—*(DOD, NATO)* In surveillance, natural or artificial material applied to an object to achieve or assist camouflage.

garrison force—*(DOD, NATO, IADB)* All units assigned to a base or area for defense, development, operation, and maintenance of facilities. See also **force(s).**

gate—*(DOD)* In air intercept, a code meaning, "Fly at maximum possible speed (or power)." (To be maintained for a limited time only, depending on type of aircraft. Use of afterburners, rockets, etc., in accordance with local doctrine.)

general and complete disarmament—*(DOD, IADB)* Reductions of armed forces and armaments by all states to levels required for internal security and for an international peace force. Connotation is "total disarmament" by all states.

general cargo—*(DOD, IADB)* Cargo which is susceptible for loading in general, nonspecialized stowage areas; e.g., boxes, barrels, bales, crates, packages, bundles, and pallets.

general map—*(DOD, IADB)* A map of small scale used for general planning purposes. See also **map.**

general orders—*(DOD, IADB)* 1. Permanent instructions, issued in order form, that apply to all members of a command, as compared with special orders, which affect only individuals or small groups. General orders are usually concerned with matters of policy or administration. 2. A series of permanent guard orders that govern the duties of a sentry on post.

155

general purchasing agents—(*DOD*) Agents who have been appointed in the principal overseas areas of operations to supervise, control, co-ordinate, negotiate, and develop the local procurement of supplies, services, and facilities by United States Armed Forces, in order that the most effective utilization may be made of local resources and production.

general purchasing agents—(*IADB*) Agents who have been appointed to supervise, control, co-ordinate, negotiate, and develop the local procurement of supplies, services, and facilities in order that the most effective utilization may be made of local resources and production.

general quarters—(*DOD, IADB*) A condition of readiness when naval action is imminent. All battle stations are fully manned and alert; ammunition is ready for instant loading; guns and guided missile launchers may be loaded.

general reserve—(*DOD, NATO, IADB*) Reserve of troops under the control of the overall commander. See also **floating reserve**.

general staff—(*DOD*) A group of officers in the headquarters of Army or Marine divisions, Marine brigades and aircraft wings, or similar or larger units that assist their commanders in planning, coordinating, and supervising operations. A general staff may consist of four or more principal functional sections: personnel (G-1), military intelligence (G-2), operations and training (G-3), logistics (G-4), and (in Army organizations) civil affairs/military government (G-5). (A particular section may be added or eliminated by the commander, dependent upon the need that has been demonstrated.) The comparable Air Force staff is found in the wing and larger units, with sections designated Personnel, Operations, etc. G-2 Air and G-3 Air are Army officers assigned to G-2 or G-3 at division, corps, and Army headquarters level who assist in planning and coordinating joint operations of ground and air units. Naval staffs ordinarily are not organized on these lines, but when they are, they are designated N-1, N-2, etc.

Similarly, a joint staff may be designated J-1, J-2, etc. In Army brigades and smaller units and in Marine Corps units smaller than a brigade or aircraft wing, staff sections are designated S-1, S-2, etc., with corresponding duties; referred to as a unit staff in the Army and as an executive staff in the Marine Corps. See also **staff**.

general staff—(*IADB*) A group of officers in the headquarters of divisions or similar larger units that assist their commanders in planning, coordinating, and supervising operations. A general staff may consist of four or more principal functional sections: personnel (G-1), military intelligence (G-2), operations and training (G-3), logistics (G-4), and civil affairs/military government (G-5). (A particular section may be added or eliminated by the commander, dependent upon the need that has been demonstrated.) In brigades and smaller units, staff sections are designated S-1, S-2, etc., with corresponding duties. See also **staff**.

general stopping power—(*DOD, NATO*) The percentage of a group of vehicles in battle formation likely to be stopped by mines when attempting to cross a minefield.

general support—(*DOD, NATO, IADB*) That support which is given to the supported force as a whole and not to any particular subdivision thereof.

general support artillery—(*DOD, NATO, IADB*) Artillery which executes the fire directed by the commander of the unit to which it organically belongs or is attached. It fires in support of the operation as a whole rather than in support of a specific subordinate unit.

general support-reinforcing—(*DOD, IADB*) A tactical artillery mission. General support-reinforcing artillery has the mission of supporting the force as a whole and of providing reinforcing fires for another artillery unit.

general support rocket system—(*DOD*) A multiple rocket launcher system that supplements cannon artillery by delivery of large quantities of firepower in a short time against critical, time-sensitive targets.

general unloading period—*(DOD, NATO)* In amphibious operations, that part of the ship-to-shore movement in which unloading is primarily logistic in character, and emphasizes speed and volume of unloading operations. It encompasses the unloading of units and cargo from the ships as rapidly as facilities on the beach permit. It proceeds without regard to class, type, or priority of cargo, as permitted by cargo handling facilities ashore. See also **initial unloading period.**

general war—*(DOD, IADB)* Armed conflict between major powers in which the total resources of the belligerents are employed, and the national survival of a major belligerent is in jeopardy.

generation (photography)—*(DOD)* The preparation of successive positive/negative reproductions from an original negative/positive (first-generation). For example, the first positive produced from an original negative is a second-generation product; the negative made from this positive is a third-generation product; and the next positive or print from that negative is a fourth-generation product.

Genie—*(DOD, IADB)* An air-to-air, unguided rocket equipped with nuclear warhead. Designed to be carried by the F-101 and F-106. Designated as **AIR-2.**

geodetic datum—See **datum (geodetic).**

geographic coordinates—*(DOD, NATO, IADB)* The quantities of latitude and longitude which define the position of a point on the surface of the earth with respect to the reference spheroid. See also **coordinates.**

geographic reference points—*(DOD, IADB)* A means of indicating position, usually expressed either as double letters or as code words that are established in operation orders or by other means.

georef—*(DOD, NATO, IADB)* A worldwide position reference system that may be applied to any map or chart graduated in latitude and longitude regardless of projection. It is a method of expressing latitude and longitude in a form suitable for rapid reporting and plotting. (This term is derived from the words "The World Geographic Reference System.")

glide bomb—*(DOD, IADB)* A bomb fitted with airfoils to provide lift, carried and released in the direction of a target by an airplane.

glide mode—*(DOD, NATO)* In a flight control system, a control mode in which an aircraft is automatically positioned to the center of the glide slope course.

go around—See **overshoot.**

go around mode—*(DOD, NATO)* In an automatic flight control system, a control mode which terminates an aircraft approach and programs a climb. See also **overshoot.**

goldie—*(DOD)* The term, peculiar to air support radar team operations, indicating that the aircraft automatic flight-control system and ground-control bombing system are engaged and awaiting electronic ground control commands.

goldie lock—*(DOD)* The term, peculiar to air support radar team operations, indicating ground controller has electronic control of the aircraft.

go no-go—*(DOD, NATO)* The condition or state of operability of a component or system: "go," functioning properly; or "no-go," not functioning properly.

gradient circuit—*(DOD, NATO)* In mine warfare, a circuit which is actuated when the rate of change, with time, of the magnitude of the influence is within predetermined limits.

grand slam—*(DOD)* All enemy aircraft originally sighted are shot down.

graphic—*(DOD, NATO)* Any and all products of the cartographic and photogrammetric art. A graphic may be a map, chart, or mosaic or even a film strip that was produced using cartographic techniques.

graphic scale—*(DOD, NATO, IADB)* A graduated line by means of which distances on the map, chart, or photograph may be measured in terms of ground distance. See also **scale**.

grapnel—*(DOD, NATO)* In naval mine warfare, a device fitted to a mine mooring designed to grapple the sweep wire when the mooring is cut.

graticule—*(DOD, NATO)* 1. In cartography, a network of lines representing the earth's parallels of latitude and meridians of longitude. 2. In imagery interpretation, see **reticle**.

graticule ticks—*(DOD, NATO)* In cartography, short lines indicating where selected meridians and parallels intersect.

graves registration—*(DOD, IADB)* Supervision and execution of matters pertaining to the identification, removal, and burial of the dead, and collection and processing of their effects. See also **burial**.

gravity extraction—*(DOD, NATO, IADB)* The extraction of cargoes from the aircraft by influence of their own weight. See also **extraction parachute**.

graze—*(DOD, NATO)* In artillery and naval gunfire support, a spotting, or an observation, by a spotter or an observer to indicate that all bursts occurred on impact.

grazing fire—*(DOD, NATO, IADB)* Fire approximately parallel to the ground where the center of the cone of fire does not rise above one meter from the ground. See also **fire**.

great circle—*(IADB)* A circle on the surface of the earth, the plane of which passes through the center of the earth.

great circle route—*(NATO, IADB)* The route which follows the shortest arc of a great circle between two points.

Greenwich Mean Time—*(DOD, IADB)* Mean solar time at the meridian of Greenwich, England, used as a basis for standard time throughout the world. Normally expressed in four numerals 0001 through 2400. Also called **zulu time**.

grey propaganda—*(DOD, I, IADB)* Propaganda that does not specifically identify any source. See also **propaganda**.

grid—*(DOD, IADB)* 1. Two sets of parallel lines intersecting at right angles and forming squares; the grid is superimposed on maps, charts, and other similar representations of the earth's surface in an accurate and consistent manner to permit identification of ground locations with respect to other locations and the computation of direction and distance to other points. 2. A term used in giving the location of a geographic point by grid coordinates. See also **military grid; military grid reference system**.

grid—*(NATO)* See **military grid**.

grid bearing—*(DOD, IADB)* Bearing measured from grid north.

grid bearing—*(NATO)* The direction of an object from a point, expressed as a horizontal angle, measured clockwise with reference to grid north. See also **bearing**.

grid convergence—*(DOD, IADB)* The horizontal angle at a place between true north and grid north. It is proportional to the longitude difference between the place and the central meridian. See also **convergence**.

grid convergence—*(NATO)* The horizontal angle at a point between true north and grid north. See also **convergence**.

grid convergence factor—*(DOD, NATO)* The ratio of the grid convergence angle to the longitude difference. In the Lambert Conical Orthomorphic projection this ratio is constant for all charts based on the same two standard parallels. See also **constant of the cone; convergence; grid convergence.**

grid convergence factor—*(IADB)* The ratio of the grid convergence angle to the longitude difference. In the Lambert Conical Orthomorphic projection this is constant and is sometimes called the constant of the cone. See also **convergence; grid convergence.**

grid coordinates—*(DOD, NATO)* Coordinates of a grid coordinate system to which numbers and letters are assigned for use in designating a point on a gridded map, photograph, or chart. See also **coordinates.**

grid coordinate system—*(DOD, NATO)* A plane-rectangular coordinate system usually based on, and mathematically adjusted to, a map projection in order that geographic positions (latitudes and longitudes) may be readily transformed into plane coordinates and the computations relating to them may be made by the ordinary method of plane surveying. See also **coordinates.**

grid interval—*(DOD, NATO, IADB)* The distance represented between the lines of a grid.

grid magnetic angle—*(DOD, NATO, IADB)* Angular difference in direction between grid north and magnetic north. It is measured east or west from grid north. Grid magnetic angle is sometimes called **grivation** and/or **grid variation.**

grid navigation—*(DOD, NATO)* A method of navigation using a grid overlay for direction reference. See also **navigational grid.**

grid north—*(DOD, NATO, IADB)* The northerly or zero direction indicated by the grid datum of directional reference.

grid ticks—*(DOD, NATO)* Small marks on the neatline of a map or chart indicating additional grid reference systems included on that sheet. Grid ticks are sometimes shown on the interior grid lines of some maps for ease of referencing.

grid variation—See **grid magnetic angle.**

gripper edge—*(NATO)* The edge by which paper or other printing material is drawn into the printing machine.

grivation—See **grid magnetic angle.**

gross error—*(DOD)* A nuclear weapon detonation at such a distance from the desired ground zero as to cause no nuclear damage to the target.

gross weight—*(DOD, NATO)* 1. Weight of a vehicle, fully equipped and serviced for operation, including the weight of the fuel, lubricants, coolant, vehicle tools and spares, crew, personal equipment and load. 2. Weight of a container or pallet including freight and binding. See also **net weight.**

ground alert—*(DOD, NATO, IADB)* That status in which aircraft on the ground/deck are fully serviced and armed, with combat crews in readiness to take off within a specified short period of time (usually 15 minutes) after receipt of a mission order. See also **alert.**

ground control—*(DOD, NATO, IADB)* A system of accurate measurements used to determine the distances and directions or differences in elevation between points on the earth. See also **common control (artillery); control point; field control; traverse.**

ground control (geodetic)—See **ground control.**

ground controlled approach procedure—*(DOD, NATO, IADB)* The technique for talking down, through the use of both surveillance and precision approach radar, an aircraft during its approach so as to place it in a position for landing; optical landing system. See also **automatic approach and landing; optical landing system.**

159

ground controlled interception—*(DOD, NATO)* A technique which permits control of friendly aircraft or guided missiles for the purpose of effecting interception. See also **air interception.**

ground effect machine—*(NATO)* A machine which normally flies within the zone of the ground effect or ground cushion.

ground fire—*(DOD, IADB)* Small arms ground-to-air fire directed against aircraft.

grounding—*(DOD, NATO)* The bonding of an equipment case, frame or chassis, to an object or vehicle structure to insure a common potential. See also **bonding; earthing.**

ground liaison officer—*(DOD, IADB)* An officer trained in offensive air support activities. Ground liaison officers are normally organized into parties under the control of the appropriate Army commander to provide liaison to Air Force and naval units engaged in training and combat operations.

ground liaison officer—*(NATO)* An officer especially trained in air reconnaissance and/or offensive air support activities. These officers are normally organized into teams under the control of the appropriate ground force commander to provide liaison to air force and navy units engaged in training and combat operations. See also **air liaison officer.**

ground liaison party—*(DOD, IADB)* An army unit consisting of a variable number of personnel responsible for liaison with a tactical air support agency.

ground liaison section—*(DOD, IADB)* An army unit consisting of a variable number of army officers, other ranks, and vehicles responsible for army/air liaison, under control of army headquarters.

ground liaison section—*(NATO)* A ground unit responsible for ground-air liaison under control of the ground headquarters.

ground mine—See bottom mine.

ground nadir—*(DOD, NATO)* The point on the ground vertically beneath the perspective center of the camera lens. On a true vertical photograph this coincides with the principal point.

ground observer center—*(DOD, IADB)* A center to which ground observer teams report and which in turn will pass information to the appropriate control and/or reporting agency.

ground observer organization—*(NATO, IADB)* A corps of ground watchers deployed at suitable points throughout an air defense system to provide visual and aural information of aircraft movements.

ground observer team—*(DOD, IADB)* Small units or detachments deployed to provide information of aircraft movements over a defended area, obtained either by aural or visual means.

ground position—*(DOD, NATO, IADB)* The position on the earth vertically below an aircraft.

ground position indicator—*(NATO)* An instrument which determines and displays automatically the ground position of an aircraft.

ground readiness—*(DOD, IADB)* That status wherein aircraft can be armed and serviced and personnel alerted to take off within a specified length of time after receiving orders.

ground return—*(DOD, NATO, IADB)* The reflection from the terrain as displayed and/or recorded as an image.

ground signals—*(DOD, NATO)* A visual signal displayed on an airfield to give local air traffic rules information to flight crews in the air. See also **signal area.**

ground speed—*(DOD, NATO)* The horizontal component of the speed of an aircraft relative to the earth's surface.

ground speed mode—*(DOD, NATO)* In a flight control system, a control mode in which the ground speed of an aircraft is automatically controlled to a computed value.

ground visibility—*(DOD, IADB)* Prevailing horizontal visibility near the earth's surface as reported by an accredited observer.

ground zero—*(DOD, NATO, IADB)* The point on the surface of the earth at, or vertically below or above, the center of a planned or actual nuclear detonation. See also **actual ground zero; desired ground zero.**

group—*(DOD, IADB)* 1. A flexible administrative and tactical unit composed of either two or more battalions or two or more squadrons. The term also applies to combat support and service support units. 2. A number of ships and/or aircraft, normally a subdivision of a force, assigned for a specific purpose.

group burial—*(DOD, IADB)* A burial in a common grave of two or more individually unidentified remains. See also **burial.**

group of targets—*(DOD, NATO)* Two or more targets on which fire is desired simultaneously. A group of targets is designated by a letter/number combination or a nickname.

group rendezvous—*(DOD, IADB)* A check point at which formations of the same type will join before proceeding. See also **force rendezvous.**

group rendezvous—*(NATO)* See **force rendezvous.**

guard—*(DOD, NATO)* A security element whose primary task is to protect the main force by fighting to gain time, while also observing and reporting information. See also **flank guard; screen.**

guardship—*(NATO, IADB)* A ship detailed for a specific duty for the purpose of enabling other ships in company to assume a lower degree of readiness.

guerrilla—*(DOD, IADB)* A combat participant in guerrilla warfare. See also **unconventional warfare.**

guerrilla warfare—*(DOD, I, NATO, IADB)* Military and paramilitary operations conducted in enemy held or hostile territory by irregular, predominantly indigenous forces. See also **unconventional warfare.**

guidance—*(DOD, IADB)* 1. Policy, direction, decision, or instruction having the effect of an order when promulgated by a higher echelon. 2. The entire process by which target intelligence information received by the guided missile is used to effect proper flight control to cause timely direction changes for effective target interception. See also **active homing guidance; celestial guidance; command guidance; homing guidance; inertial guidance; midcourse guidance; passive homing guidance; preset guidance; semiactive homing guidance; stellar guidance; terminal guidance; terrestrial reference guidance.**

guidance coverage—*(DOD, NATO)* That volume of space in which guidance information (azimuth and/or elevation and/or distance) is provided to aircraft to the specified performance and accuracy. This may be specified either with relation to airfield/airstrip geometry, making assumptions about deployment of ground equipment, or with relation to the coverage provided by individual ground units.

guidance station equipment—*(DOD, NATO, IADB)* The ground-based portion of the missile guidance system necessary to provide guidance during missile flight.

guidance system (missile)—*(DOD, NATO, IADB)* A system which evaluates flight information, correlates it with target data, determines the desired flight path of the missile and communicates the necessary commands to the missile flight control system. See also **control system (missile).**

guided missile—*(DOD, IADB)* An unmanned vehicle moving above the surface of the earth whose trajectory or flight path is capable of being altered by an external or internal mechanism. See also **aerodynamic missile; ballistic missile.**

guided missile—*(NATO)* An unmanned self-propelled vehicle whose trajectory or course, while in flight, is controlled.

guided missile (air-to-air)—*(NATO, IADB)* An air-launched guided missile for use against air targets.

guided missile (air-to-surface)—*(NATO)* An air-launched guided missile for use against surface targets.

guided missile cruiser—*(DOD, IADB)* A warship designed to operate with strike and amphibious forces against air, surface, and subsurface threats. Normal armaments consist of 3-inch or 5-inch guns, an advanced area-defense antiair-warfare missile system, and anti-submarine-warfare weapons. Designed as **CGN.**

guided missile destroyer—*(DOD, IADB)* For mission, see **destroyer.** This destroyer type is equipped with Terrier/Tartar guided missiles, improved naval gun battery, long-range sonar, and antisubmarine warfare weapons, including **ASROC.** Designated as **DDG.**

guided missile equipment carrier—*(DOD)* A self-propelled, full-tracked, amphibious, air-transportable, unarmored carrier for various guided missile systems and their equipment.

guided missile frigate—*(DOD, IADB)* Equipped with Tartar or SM-1 missile launchers. 5"/54 or 70-mm gun battery. Designated as **FFG.** See also **Frigate.**

guided missile submarine—*(DOD, IADB)* A submarine designed to have an additional capability to launch guided missile attacks. Designated as SSG and SSGN. The SSGN is nuclear powered.

guided missile (surface-to-air)—*(NATO, IADB)* A surface-launched guided missile for use against air targets.

guided missile (surface-to-surface)—*(NATO)* A surface-launched guided missile for use against surface targets.

guide signs—*(NATO, IADB)* Signs used to indicate locations, distances, directions, routes, and similar information. (Note: IADB term is **guide signs (road transport)**.)

guide specification—*(DOD, NATO)* Minimum requirements to be used as a basis for the evaluation of a national specification covering a fuel, lubricant or associated product proposed for standardization action.

guinea-pig—*(DOD, NATO)* In naval mine warfare, a ship used to determine whether an area can be considered safe from influence mines under certain conditions, or, specifically, to detonate pressure mines.

gull—*(DOD, NATO)* In electronic warfare, a floating radar reflector used to simulate a surface target at sea for deceptive purposes.

gun—*(DOD, IADB)* 1. A cannon with relatively long barrel, operating with relatively low angle of fire, and having a high muzzle velocity. 2. A cannon with tube length 30 calibers or more. See also **howitzer; mortar.**

gun carriage—*(DOD, NATO, IADB)* A mobile or fixed support for a gun. It sometimes includes the elevating and traversing mechanisms. Sometimes called **carriage.**

gun direction—*(NATO, IADB)* The distribution and direction of the gunfire of a ship.

guns/weapons free—*(DOD)* In air intercept, means fire may be opened on all aircraft not recognized as friendly.

guns/weapons tight—*(DOD)* In air intercept, means do not open fire, or cease firing on any aircraft (or on bogey specified, or in section indicated) unless target(s) known to be hostile.

gun-target line—*(DOD, NATO, IADB)* An imaginary straight line from the gun(s) to the target. See also **spotting line.**

gun-type weapon—*(DOD, IADB)* A device in which two or more pieces of fissionable mate-rial, each less than a critical mass, are brought together very rapidly so as to form a supercritical mass that can explode as the result of a rapidly expanding fission chain.

gyro-magnetic compass—*(DOD)* A directional gyroscope whose azimuth scale is maintained in alignment with the magnetic meridian by a magnetic detector unit.

H

H–2—See Sea Sprite.

H–3—See Sea King.

H–46—See Sea Knight.

hachuring—*(DOD, NATO)* A method of representing relief upon a map or chart by shading in short disconnected lines drawn in the direction of the slopes.

half-life—*(DOD, NATO, IADB)* The time required for the activity of a given radioactive species to decrease to half of its initial value due to radioactive decay. The half-life is a characteristic property of each radioactive species and is independent of its amount or condition. The effective half-life of a given isotope is the time in which the quantity in the body will decrease to half as a result of both radioactive decay and biological elimination.

half-residence time—*(DOD, NATO, IADB)* As applied to delayed fallout, it is the time required for the amount of weapon debris deposited in a particular part of the atmosphere to decrease to half of its initial value.

half thickness—*(DOD, NATO, IADB)* Thickness of absorbing material necessary to reduce by one-half the intensity of radiation which passes through it.

halftone—*(DOD, NATO)* Any photomechanical printing surface or the impression therefrom in which detail and tone values are represented by a series of evenly spaced dots in varying size and shape, varying in direct proportion to the intensity of the tones they represent. See also **halftone screen**.

halftone screen—*(DOD, NATO)* A series of regular spaced opaque lines on glass, crossing at right angles, producing transparent apertures between intersections. Used in a process camera to break up a solid or continuous tone image into a pattern of small dots. See also **halftone**.

handover—*(DOD, IADB)* The passing of control authority of an aircraft from one control agency to another control agency. Handover action may be accomplished between control agencies of separate Services when conducting joint operations or between control agencies within a single command and control system. Handover action is complete when the receiving controller acknowledges assumption of control authority.

handover line—*(DOD, NATO)* A control feature, preferably following easily defined terrain features, at which responsibility for the conduct of combat operations is passed from one force to another.

hang fire—*(DOD, NATO)* An undesired delay in the functioning of a firing system.

harassing (air)—*(DOD, IADB)* The attack of any target within the area of land battle not connected with interdiction or close air support. It is designed to reduce the enemy's combat effectiveness.

harassing fire—*(DOD, NATO, IADB)* Fire designed to disturb the rest of the enemy troops, to curtail movement and, by threat of losses, to lower morale. See also **fire**.

harassment—*(DOD, IADB)* An incident in which the primary objective is to disrupt the activities of a unit, installation, or ship, rather than to inflict serious casualties or damage.

harbor—*(DOD, IADB)* A restricted body of water, an anchorage, or other limited coastal water area and its mineable water approaches, from which shipping operations are projected or supported. Generally, a harbor is part of a base, in which case the harbor defense force forms a component element of the base defense force established for the local defense of the base and its included harbor.

harbor defense—*(DOD, NATO, IADB)* The defense of a harbor or anchorage and its water approaches against external threats such as: **a.** submarine, submarine-borne, or small surface craft attack; **b.** enemy minelaying operations; and **c.** sabotage. The defense of a harbor from guided or dropped missiles while such missiles are airborne is considered to be a part of air defense. See also **port security.**

hard beach—*(DOD, IADB)* A portion of a beach especially prepared with a hard surface extending into the water, employed for the purpose of loading or unloading directly into or from landing ships or landing craft.

hardened site—*(DOD, NATO)* A site constructed to provide protection against the effects of conventional and nuclear explosions. It may also be equipped to provide protection against a chemical or biological attack.

hard missile base—*(DOD, NATO)* A launching base that is protected against a nuclear explosion.

hard port—*(DOD)* After heading to magnetic heading indicated, turning to the port in a tight turn (three digit group), or alter heading indicated number of degrees to the port in a tight turn (one or two digit group with word "degrees".)

hardstand—*(DOD, NATO, IADB)* 1. A paved or stabilized area where vehicles are parked. 2. Open ground area having a prepared surface and used for the storage of materiel.

hard starboard—*(DOD)* Alter heading to magnetic heading indicated, turning to the starboard in a tight turn (three digit group), or alter heading indicated number of degrees to the starboard in a tight turn (one or two digit group with word "degrees").

hardware—*(DOD)* 1. The generic term dealing with physical items as distinguished from its capability or function such as equipment, tools, implements, instruments, devices, sets, fittings, trimmings, assemblies, subassemblies, components, and parts. The term is often used in regard to the stage of development, as in the passage of a device or component from the design stage into the hardware stage as the finished object. 2. In data automation, the physical equipment or devices forming a computer and peripheral components. See also **software.**

harmful appreciations—*(DOD)* See **appreciations.**

harmonization—*(DOD)* The process and/or results of adjusting differences or inconsistencies to bring significant features into agreement.

Harpoon—*(DOD)* An all-weather, anti-ship cruise missile capable of being employed from surface ships (RGM–84), aircraft (AGM–84A) or submarines (UGM–84). The missile is turbojet powered and employs a low level cruise trajectory. Terminal guidance is active radar. A 500-pound conventional warhead is employed.

Harrier—*(DOD)* A single-engine, vectored thrust, turbojet, vertical and/or short take-off-and-landing light attack aircraft, designed to operate from land bases and naval vessels in a close air support role. Capable of carrying a variety of conventional and/or nuclear weapons. Designated as AV–8.

hasty attack—*(DOD, NATO)* In land operations, an attack in which preparation time is traded for speed in order to exploit an opportunity. See also **deliberate attack.**

hasty breaching—*(DOD, NATO, IADB)* The rapid creation of a route through a minefield, barrier or fortification by any expedient method.

hasty breaching (land mine warfare)—*(DOD, IADB)* The creation of lanes through enemy minefields by expedient methods such as blasting with demolitions, pushing rollers or disabled vehicles through the minefields when the time factor does not permit detailed reconnaissance, deliberate breaching, or bypassing the obstacle. See also **breaching**.

hasty crossing—*(DOD, NATO, IADB)* A crossing of a river or stream using crossing means at hand or readily available, without pausing to make elaborate preparations. See also **deliberate crossing**.

hasty defense—*(DOD, NATO, IADB)* A defense normally organized while in contact with the enemy or when contact is imminent and time available for the organization is limited. It is characterized by improvement of the natural defensive strength of the terrain by utilization of foxholes, emplacements, and obstacles. See also **deliberate defense**.

hatch list—*(DOD, IADB)* A list showing, for each hold section of a cargo ship, a description of the items stowed, their volume and weight, the consignee of each, and the total volume and weight of materiel in the hold.

havens (moving)—See **moving havens**.

Hawk—*(DOD, IADB)* A mobile air defense artillery, surface-to-air missile system that provides non-nuclear, low to medium altitude air defense coverage for ground forces. Designated as **MIM-23**.

Hawkeye—*(DOD)* A twin turboprop, multicrew airborne early warning and interceptor control aircraft designed to operate from aircraft carriers. It carries a long range radar and integrated computer system for the detection and tracking of airborne targets at all altitudes. Designated as **E-2**.

hazard sign (road transport)—*(NATO, IADB)* A sign used to indicate traffic hazards. Military hazard signs should be used in a communications zone area only in accordance with existing agreements with national authorities.

HC-130—See **Hercules.**

heading—*(DOD)* In air intercept, a code meaning, "My, or bogey's, magnetic course is _____."

heading—*(NATO)* The direction in which the longitudinal axis of an aircraft or ship is pointed, usually expressed in degrees clockwise from north (true, magnetic, compass, or grid).

heading crossing angle—*(DOD, IADB)* In air intercept, the angular difference between interceptor heading and target heading at the time of intercept.

heading hold mode—*(DOD, NATO)* In a flight control system, a control mode which automatically maintains an aircraft heading that exists at the instant of completion of a maneuver.

heading indicator—*(DOD, NATO)* An instrument which displays heading transmitted electrically from a remote compass system.

heading select feature—*(DOD, NATO)* A flight control system feature which permits selection or preselection of desired automatically controlled heading or headings of an aircraft.

heads up—*(DOD)* In air intercept, a code meaning, "Enemy got through (part or all)," or, "I am not in position to engage target."

head-up display—*(DOD, NATO)* A display of flight, navigation, attack, or other information superimposed upon the pilot's forward field of view. See also **horizontal situation display.**

heavy artillery—See **field artillery.**

heavy antitank weapon—*(DOD, IADB)* A weapon capable of operating from ground or vehicle, used to defeat armor and other material targets.

heavy drop—*(DOD)* A system of delivery of heavy supplies and equipment by parachute.

heavy-lift cargo—*(DOD, IADB)* 1. Any single cargo lift, weighing over 5 long tons, and to be handled aboard ship. *(DOD)* 2. In Marine Corps usage, individual units of cargo that exceed 800 pounds in weight or 100 cubic feet in volume. See also **cargo.**

heavy-lift ship—*(DOD, NATO, IADB)* A ship specially designed and capable of loading and unloading heavy and bulky items. It has booms of sufficient capacity to accommodate a single lift of 100 tons.

height—*(DOD, IADB)* The vertical distance of an object, point, or level above the ground or other established reference plane. Height may be indicated as follows:
   very low—Less than 500 feet.
   low—500 to 2,000 feet (above ground level).
   medium—2,000 to 25,000 feet.
   high—25,000 to 50,000 feet.
   very high—More than 50,000 feet.

height—*(NATO)* 1. The vertical distance of a level, a point, or an object considered as a point, measured from a specified datum. 2. The vertical dimension of an object. See also **altitude; elevation.**

height datum—See altitude datum.

height delay—See altitude.

height hole—See altitude hole.

height of burst—*(DOD, NATO, IADB)* The vertical distance from the earth's surface or target to the point of burst. See also **optimum height of burst; safe burst height; types of burst.**

helicopter approach route—*(DOD, NATO)* The track or series of tracks along which helicopters move to a specific landing site or landing zone. See also **helicopter lane; helicopter retirement route.**

helicopter assault force—*(DOD, NATO, IADB)* A task organization combining helicopters, supporting units, and helicopter-borne troop units for use in helicopter-borne assault operations.

helicopter break-up point—*(DOD, IADB)* A control point at which helicopters returning from a landing zone break formation and are released to return to base or are dispatched for other employment.

helicopter departure point—See **departure point.**

helicopter direction center—*(DOD, NATO)* In amphibious operations, the primary direct control agency for the helicopter group/unit commander operating under the overall control of the tactical air control center.

helicopter drop point—*(DOD, IADB)* A designated point within a landing zone where helicopters are unable to land because of the terrain, but in which they can discharge cargo or troops while hovering.

helicopter landing site—*(DOD, IADB)* A designated subdivision of a helicopter landing zone in which a single flight or wave of assault helicopters land to embark or disembark troops and/or cargo.

helicopter landing zone—*(DOD, IADB)* A specified ground area for landing assault helicopters to embark or disembark troops and/or cargo. A landing zone may contain one or more landing sites.

helicopter lane—*(DOD, NATO, IADB)* A safety air corridor in which helicopters fly to or from their destination during helicopter operations. See also **helicopter approach route; helicopter retirement route.**

helicopter retirement route—*(DOD, NATO)* The track or series of tracks along which helicopters move from a specific landing site or landing zone. See also **helicopter approach route; helicopter lane.**

helicopter support team—*(DOD, NATO)* A task organization formed and equipped for employment in a landing zone to facilitate the landing and movement of helicopter-borne troops, equipment and supplies, and to evacuate selected casualties and prisoners of war.

helicopter team—*(DOD, IADB)* The combat-equipped troops lifted in one helicopter at one time.

helicopter transport area—*(DOD, IADB)* Areas to the seaward and on the flanks of the outer transport and landing ship areas, but preferably inside the area screen, to which helicopter transports proceed for launching or recovering helicopters. See also **transport area**.

helicopter wave—See **wave**.

helipad—*(DOD, NATO, IADB)* A prepared area designated and used for takeoff and landing of helicopters. (Includes touchdown or hover point.)

heliport—*(DOD, NATO, IADB)* A facility designated for operating, basing, servicing, and maintaining helicopters.

herbicide—*(DOD, IADB)* A chemical compound that will kill or damage plants. See also **anticrop agent; antiplant agent**.

Hercules—*(DOD, IADB)* A medium range troop and cargo transport designed for air-drop or air-land delivery into a combat zone as well as conventional airlift. This aircraft is equipped with four turbo-prop engines, and integral ramp and cargo door. The D model is ski equipped. The E model has additional fuel capacity for extended range. Designated as C-130. The inflight tanker configuration is designated HC-130, which is also used for the aerial rescue mission. The gunship version is designated AC-130; the drone control version is designated DC-130.

H-hour—*(DOD, IADB)* The specific hour on D-day at which a particular operation commences. The operation may be the commencement of hostilities; the hour at which an operation plan is executed or to be executed (as distinguished from the hour the order to execute is issued); the hour that the operations phase is implemented, either by land assault, parachute assault, amphibious assault, air or naval bombardment. The highest command or headquarters coordinating the planning will specify the exact meaning of H-hour within the aforementioned definition. Normally, the letter "H" will be the only one used to denote the above. However, when several operations or phases of an operation are being conducted in the same area on D-day, and confusion may arise through the use of the same hour designation for two or more of them, any letter of the alphabet may be used except A, C, D, E, J, M, or others that may be reserved for exclusive use. See also **D-day**.

H-hour—*(NATO)* See **designation of days and hours**.

high—*(DOD, IADB)* A height between 25,000 and 50,000 feet.

high airburst—*(DOD, IADB)* The fallout safe height of burst for a nuclear weapon that increases damage to or casualties on soft targets, or reduces induced radiation contamination at actual ground zero. See also **types of burst**.

high altitude—*(DOD, NATO, IADB)* Conventionally, an altitude above 10,000 meters (33,000 feet). See also **altitude**.

high altitude bombing—*(DOD, IADB)* Horizontal bombing with the height of release over 15,000 feet.

high altitude burst—*(DOD, NATO, IADB)* The explosion of a nuclear weapon which takes place at a height in excess of 100,000 feet (30,000 meters). See also **types of burst**.

high angle—*(DOD, NATO)* In artillery and naval gunfire support, an order or request to obtain high angle fire.

high angle fire—*(DOD, NATO, IADB)* Fire delivered at angles of elevation greater than the elevation that corresponds to the maximum range of the gun and ammunition concerned; fire, the range of which decreases as the angle of elevation is increased.

high density airspace control zone—*(DOD, NATO)* Airspace of defined dimensions, designated by the airspace control authority, in which there is a concentrated employment of numerous and varied weapons/airspace users.

high explosive cargo—*(DOD, IADB)* Cargo such as artillery ammunition, bombs, depth charges, demolition material, rockets, and missiles. See also **cargo**.

high oblique—See **oblique air photograph**.

high speed submarine—*(DOD, IADB)* A submarine capable of submerged speeds of 20 knots or more.

high value asset control items—*(DOD)* Items of supply identified for intensive management control under approved inventory management techniques designed to maintain an optimum inventory level of high investment items. Also known as hi-value asset control items.

high velocity drop—*(DOD, NATO, IADB)* A drop procedure in which the drop velocity is greater than 30 feet per second (low velocity drop) and lower than free drop velocity. See also **airdrop**.

hill shading—*(DOD, NATO)* A method of representing relief on a map by depicting the shadows that would be cast by high ground if light were shining from a certain direction.

hoist—*(DOD, NATO)* In helicopters, the mechanism by which external loads may be raised or lowered vertically.

hold—*(DOD, NATO, IADB)* 1. A cargo stowage compartment aboard ship. 2. To maintain or retain possession of by force, as a position or an area. 3. In an attack, to exert sufficient pressure to prevent movement or redisposi-

tion of enemy forces. 4. As applied to air traffic, to keep an aircraft within a specified space or location which is identified by visual or other means in accordance with Air Traffic Control instructions.

holdee—See **transient**.

hold fire—*(DOD, IADB)* Do not open fire, or cease firing on raid/track designated. Missiles in flight must not be permitted to continue to intercept raid/track designated. (Note: This is an emergency order that temporarily terminates the active status of antiair warfare weapons on raid/track designated.)

hold fire—*(NATO)* In air defense, an emergency order to stop firing. Guided missiles already in flight must not be permitted to continue to intercept. See also **cease engagement; engage**.

holding anchorage—*(DOD, NATO)* An anchorage where ships may lie: **a.** if the assembly or working anchorage, or port, to which they have been assigned is full; **b.** when delayed by enemy threats or other factors from proceeding immediately on their next voyage; **c.** when dispersed from a port to avoid the effects of a nuclear attack. See also **assembly anchorage; emergency anchorage; working anchorage**.

holding attack—*(DOD, NATO, IADB)* An attack designed to hold the enemy in position, to deceive him as to where the main attack is being made, to prevent him from reinforcing the elements opposing the main attack and/or to cause him to commit his reserves prematurely at an indecisive location.

holding pattern mode—*(DOD, NATO)* Automatic control of an aircraft to fly the programmed holding pattern.

holding point—*(DOD, NATO)* A geographically or electronically defined location used in stationing aircraft in flight in a predetermined pattern in accordance with air traffic control clearance. See also **orbit point**.

holding position—*(DOD, NATO)* A specified location on the airfield, close to the active runway and identified by visual means, at which the position of a taxiing aircraft is maintained in accordance with air traffic control instructions.

holiday—*(DOD)* An unintentional omission in imagery coverage of an area. See also **gap (imagery)**.

holiday—*(NATO)* In naval mine warfare, a gap left unintentionally during sweeping or minehunting arising from errors in navigation, station-keeping, dan laying, breakdowns or other causes.

hollow charge—*(DOD, NATO)* A shaped charge producing a deep cylindrical hole of relatively small diameter in the direction of its axis of rotation.

home recovery mission profile—*(DOD)* A mission profile that involves the recovery of an aircraft at its permanent or temporarily assigned operating base.

homing—*(DOD, NATO)* The technique whereby a mobile station directs itself, or is directed, towards a source of primary or reflected energy, or to a specified point.

homing adaptor—*(DOD, NATO)* A device which when used with an aircraft radio receiver, produces aural and/or visual signals which indicate the direction of a transmitting radio station with respect to the heading of the aircraft.

homing guidance—*(DOD, NATO, IADB)* A system by which a missile steers itself towards a target by means of a self-contained mechanism which is activated by some distinguishing characteristics of the target. See also **active homing guidance; guidance; passive homing guidance; semi-active homing guidance**.

homing mine—*(DOD, NATO)* In naval mine warfare, a mine fitted with propulsion equipment that homes on to a target. See also **mine.**

homogeneous area—*(DOD, NATO, IADB)* An area which has uniform radar reflecting power at all points. See also **inserted grouping (radar)**.

hook—*(DOD)* A procedure used by an air controller to electronically direct the data processing equipment of a semi-automatic command and control system to take a specified action on a specific radar blip or symbol.

horizon—*(DOD, IADB)* In general, the apparent or visible junction of the earth and sky, as seen from any specific position. Also called the apparent, visible, or local horizon. A horizontal plane passing through a point of vision or perspective center. The apparent or visible horizon approximates the true horizon only when the point of vision is very close to sea level.

horizontal action mine—*(DOD, NATO)* In land mine warfare, a mine designed to produce a destructive effect in a plane approximately parallel to the ground.

horizontal action mine—*(IADB)* A mine designed to produce a destructive effect in a plane approximately parallel to the ground.

horizontal error—*(DOD, NATO, IADB)* The error in range, deflection, or in radius, which a weapon may be expected to exceed as often as not. Horizontal error of weapons making a nearly vertical approach to the target is described in terms of circular error probable. Horizontal error of weapons producing elliptical dispersion pattern is expressed in terms of probable error. See also **circular error probable; delivery error; deviation; dispersion error.**

horizontal loading—*(DOD, NATO, IADB)* Loading of items of like character in horizontal layers throughout the holds of a ship. See also **loading.**

horizontal situation display—*(DOD, NATO)* An electronically generated display on which navigation information and stored mission and procedural data can be presented. Radar information and television picture can also be displayed either as a map overlay or as a separate image. See also **head-up display.**

horizontal situation indicator—*(DOD, NATO)* An instrument which may display bearing and distance to a navigation aid, magnetic heading, track/course and track/course deviation.

horn—*(DOD, NATO)* In naval mine warfare, a projection from the mine shell of some contact mines which, when broken or bent by contact, causes the mine to fire.

horse collar—See **rescue strop.**

hospital—*(DOD, IADB)* A medical treatment facility capable of providing inpatient care. It is appropriately staffed and equipped to provide diagnostic and therapeutic services, as well as the necessary supporting services required to perform its assigned mission and functions. A hospital may, in addition, discharge the functions of a clinic.

hostage—*(DOD, IADB)* A person held as a pledge that certain terms or agreements will be kept. (The taking of hostages is forbidden under the Geneva Conventions, 1949.)

host country—*(DOD, IADB)* A nation in which representatives or organizations of another state are present because of government invitation and/or international agreement.

hostile—*(DOD, IADB)* A contact positively identified as enemy. See also **bogey; friendly.**

hostile acts—*(DOD, IADB)* Basic rules established by higher authority for defining and recognizing hostile acts by aircraft, submarines, surface units, and ground forces, will be promulgated by the commanders of unified or specified commands, and by other appropriate commanders when so authorized.

hostile track (air defense)—*(DOD, NATO)* The classification assigned to a track which, based upon established criteria, is determined to be an enemy airborne, ballistic, and/or orbiting threat.

host nation—*(DOD, NATO)* A nation which receives the forces and/or supplies of allied nations and/or NATO organizations to be located on, or to operate in, or to transit through its territory.

host nation assistance—See **host nation support.**

host nation post—*(NATO)* A post which has been agreed by the local national authorities and should be permanently filled by them in view of its administrative/national nature.

host nation support—*(NATO)* Civil and military assistance rendered in peace and war by a host nation to allied forces and NATO organizations which are located on or in transit through the host nation's territory. The basis of such assistance is commitments arising from the NATO Alliance or from bilateral or multilateral agreements concluded between the host nation, NATO organizations and (the) nation(s) having forces operating on the host nation's territory.

hot photo interpretation report—Not to be used. See **Joint Tactical Air Reconnaissance/ Surveillance Mission Report.**

hot report—Not to be used. See **Joint Tactical Air Reconnaisance/Surveillance Mission Report.**

hot spot—*(DOD, NATO, IADB)* Region in a contaminated area in which the level of radioactive contamination is considerably greater than in neighboring regions in the area.

Hound Dog—*(DOD, IADB)* A turbojet-propelled, air-to-surface missile designed to be carried externally on the B-52. It is equipped with a nuclear warhead and can be launched for either high or low altitude attacks against enemy targets, supplementing the internally carried firepower of the B-52. Designated as **AGM-28B.**

hovercraft—See **ground effect machine.**

hovering—*(DOD, NATO, IADB)* A self-sustaining maneuver whereby a fixed, or nearly fixed, position is maintained relative to a spot on the surface of the earth or underwater.

hovering ceiling—*(DOD, NATO, IADB)* The highest altitude at which the helicopter is capable of hovering in standard atmosphere. It is usually stated in two figures: hovering in ground effect and hovering out of ground effect.

howitzer—*(DOD, IADB)* 1. A cannon which combines certain characteristics of guns and mortars. The howitzer delivers projectiles with medium velocities, either by low or high trajectories. 2. Normally a cannon with a tube length of 20 to 30 calibers; however, the tube length can exceed 30 calibers and still be considered a howitzer when the high angle fire zoning solution permits range overlap between charges. See also **gun; mortar.**

human intelligence—*(DOD, NATO)* A category of intelligence derived from information collected and provided by human sources. Also called **HUMINT.**

human resources intelligence—*(DOD)* The intelligence information derived from the intelligence collection discipline that uses human beings as both sources and collectors, and where the human being is the primary collection instrument. Also called **HUMINT.**

HUMINT—See **human resources intelligence.**

hunter-killer group—See **antisubmarine carrier group.**

hunter track—*(DOD, NATO)* In naval mine warfare, the track to be followed by the hunter (or sweeper) to ensure that the hunt-ing (or sweeping) gear passes over the lap track.

hydrofoil patrol craft—*(DOD, IADB)* A patrol combatant, missile, fast surface patrol craft, capable of quick reaction and offensive operations against major enemy surface combatants. Designated as **PHM.**

hydrogen bomb—See **thermonuclear weapon.**

hydrographic chart—*(DOD, NATO, IADB)* A nautical chart showing depths of water, nature of bottom, contours of bottom and coastline, and tides and currents in a given sea or sea and land area.

hydrographic reconnaissance—*(DOD, IADB)* Reconnaissance of an area of water to determine depths, beach gradients, the nature of the bottom, and the location of coral reefs, rocks, shoals, and man-made obstacles.

hydrographic section (beach party)—*(DOD, IADB)* A section of a beach party whose duties are to clear the beach of damaged boats, conduct hydrographic reconnaissance, assist in removing underwater obstructions, act as stretcher bearers and furnish relief boat crews.

hydrography—*(DOD, NATO)* The science which deals with the measurements and description of the physical features of the oceans, seas, lakes, rivers, and their adjoining coastal areas, with particular reference to their use for navigational purposes.

hyperbaric chamber—*(DOD, NATO)* A chamber used to induce an increase in ambient pressure as would occur in descending below sea level, in a water or air environment. It is the only type of chamber suitable for use in the treatment of decompression sickness in flying or diving. Also called **compression chamber; diving chamber; recompression chamber.**

hyperbolic navigation system—*(DOD, NATO)* A radio navigation system which enables the position of an aircraft equipped with a suitable receiver to be fixed by two or more intersecting hyperbolic position lines. The system employs either a time difference measurement of pulse transmissions or a phase difference measurement of phase-locked continuous wave transmissions. See also **Decca; loran.**

hyperfocal distance—(DOD, NATO) The distance from the lens to the nearest object in focus when the lens is focused at infinity.

hypergolic fuel—(DOD, NATO, IADB) Fuel which will spontaneously ignite with an oxidizer, such as aniline with fuming nitric acid. It is used as the propulsion agent in certain missile systems.

hypersonic—(DOD, NATO, IADB) Of or pertaining to speeds equal to, or in excess of, five times the speed of sound. See also **speed of sound.**

hyperstereoscopy—(DOD, NATO) Stereoscopic viewing in which the relief effect is noticeably exaggerated, caused by the extension of the camera base. Also called **exaggerated stereoscopy.**

hypobaric chamber—(DOD, NATO) A chamber used to induce a decrease in ambient pressure as would occur in ascending to altitude. This type of chamber is primarily used for training and experimental purposes. Also called **altitude chamber; decompression chamber.**

hypsometric tinting—(DOD, NATO, IADB) A method of showing relief on maps and charts by coloring in different shades those parts which lie between selected levels. Sometimes referred to as **elevation tint; altitude tint; layer tint.**

I

identification—*(DOD, IADB)* 1. The process of determining the friendly or hostile character of an unknown detected contact. 2. In arms control, the process of determining which nation is responsible for the detected violations of any arms control measure. 3. In ground combat operations, discrimination between recognizable objects as being friendly or enemy, or the name that belongs to the object as a member of a class.

identification—*(NATO)* 1. The indication by any act or means of your own friendly character or individuality. See also **recognition**. 2. In imagery interpretation, the discrimination between objects within a particular type or class.

Identification friend or foe—*(IADB)* A system using radar transmissions to which equipment carried by friendly forces automatically responds, for example, by emitting pulses, thereby distinguishing themselves from enemy forces. It is the primary method of determining the friendly or unfriendly character of aircraft and ships by other aircraft or ships and by ground forces employing radar detection equipment and associated identification friend or foe units. See also **selective identification feature**.

identification, friend or foe (IFF)—*(NATO, DOD)* A system using electromagnetic transmissions to which equipment carried by friendly forces automatically responds, for example, by emitting pulses, thereby distinguishing themselves from enemy forces.

Identification Friend or Foe personal identifier—*(DOD, IADB)* The discrete Identification Friend or Foe code assigned to a particular aircraft, ship, or other vehicle for identification by electronic means.

identification maneuver—*(DOD, IADB)* A maneuver performed for identification purposes.

identify—*(DOD)* A code meaning, "Identify the contact designated by any means at your disposal." See also **identification, recognition**.

identify—*(NATO)* See **identification; recognition**.

identity—See **identification; recognition**.

igloo space—*(DOD, IADB)* Area in an earth-covered structure of concrete and/or steel designed for the storage of ammunition and explosives. See also **storage**.

igniter—*(DOD, NATO)* A device designed to produce a flame or a flash which is used to initiate a firing circuit.

ignition system—See **firing system**.

I go—*(DOD)* A code meaning, "I am leaving my patrol/mission in ___ minutes." See also **I stay**.

illumination by diffusion—See **indirect illumination**.

illumination by reflection—See **indirect illumination**.

illumination fire—*(NATO)* Fire designed to illuminate an area.

image degradation—*(NATO)* The reduction of the inherent optimum potential of individual sensor systems caused by error in sensor operations, processing procedures or incorrect film handling. Reduction in quality caused by unavoidable factors not associated with the sensor system, i.e. atmospherics, snow, cover, etc., is not associated with the term.

image displacement—*(NATO)* In a photograph, any dimensional or positional error.

image format—*(DOD)* Actual size of negative, scope, or other medium on which image is produced.

image motion compensation—*(DOD, NATO)* Movement intentionally imparted to film at such a rate as to compensate for the forward motion of an air or space vehicle when photographing ground objects.

imagery—*(DOD, NATO, IADB)* Collectively, the representations of objects reproduced electronically or by optical means on film, electronic display devices, or other media.

imagery collateral—*(DOD, NATO)* The reference materials which support the imagery interpretation function.

imagery correlation—*(DOD, NATO)* The mutual relationship between the different signatures on imagery from different types of sensors in terms of position and the physical characteristics signified.

imagery data recording—*(DOD, NATO)* The transposing of information relating to the airborne vehicle, and sensor, such as speed, height, tilt, position and time, to the matrix block on the sensor record at the moment of imagery acquisition.

imagery exploitation—*(DOD, NATO)* The cycle of processing and printing imagery to the positive or negative state, assembly into imagery packs, identification, interpretation, mensuration, information extraction, the preparation of reports and the dissemination of information.

imagery intelligence—*(DOD)* Intelligence information derived from the exploitation of collection by visual photography, infrared sensors, lasers, electro-optics and radar sensors such as synthetic aperture radar wherein images of objects are reproduced optically or electronically on film, electronic display devices or other media. Also called **IMINT**. See also **photographic intelligence**.

imagery interpretation—*(DOD, NATO, IADB)* 1. The process of location, recognition, identification, and description of objects, activities, and terrain represented on imagery. *(NATO)* 2. The extraction of information from photographs or other recorded images.

imagery interpretation key—*(DOD, NATO)* Any diagram, chart, table, list, or set of examples, etc., which is used to aid imagery interpreters in the rapid identification of objects visible on imagery.

imagery pack—*(DOD, NATO)* An assembly of the records from different imagery sensors covering a common target area.

imagery sortie—*(DOD, NATO)* One flight by one aircraft for the purpose of recording air imagery.

IMINT—See **imagery intelligence**.

imitative deception—See **electronic warfare**.

imitative electronic deception (IED)—See **electronic warfare**.

immediate air support—*(DOD, NATO, IADB)* Air support to meet specific requests which arise during the course of a battle and which by their nature cannot be planned in advance. See also **air support**.

immediate destination (merchant shipping)—*(NATO, IADB)* The next destination of a ship or convoy, irrespective of whether or not onward routing instructions have been issued to it. See also **destination (merchant shipping)**.

immediately vital cargo—See **cargo**.

immediately vital cargo—*(IADB)* A cargo already loaded, which the consignee country regards as immediately vital for the prosecution of the war or for national survival, and delivery of which may be authorized by the national authorities of the flag or ship carrying the cargo, notwithstanding the risk to the ship.

immediate message—*(DOD, IADB)* A category of precedence reserved for messages relating to situations that gravely affect the security of national/allied forces or populace and which require immediate delivery to the addressee(s). See also **precedence**.

immediate mission request—*(DOD, IADB)* A request for an air strike on a target which, by its nature, could not be identified sufficiently in advance to permit detailed mission coordination and planning. See also **preplanned mission request**.

immediate mission request (reconnaissance)—*(DOD, IADB)* A request for a mission on a target which, by its nature, could not be identified sufficiently in advance to permit detailed mission coordination and planning.

immediate nuclear support—*(DOD, IADB)* Nuclear support to meet specific requests which arise during the course of a battle, and which, by their nature, cannot be planned in advance. See also **preplanned nuclear support; nuclear support**.

immediate operational readiness—*(DOD, IADB)* Those operations directly related to the assumption of an alert or quick-reaction posture. Typical operations include strip alert, airborne alert/indoctrination, no-notice launch of an alert force, and the maintenance of missiles in an alert configuration. See also **nuclear weapon exercise; nuclear weapon maneuver**.

immediate operational readiness—*(NATO)* The state in which an armed force is ready in all respects for instant combat.

impact action fuze—*(DOD, NATO, IADB)* A fuze that is set in action by the striking of a projectile or bomb against an object, e.g., percussion fuze, contact fuze. Synonymous with **direct action fuze**. See also **fuze**.

impact area—*(DOD, IADB)* An area having designated boundaries within the limits of which all ordnance will detonate or impact.

impact area—*(NATO)* An area having designated boundaries within the limits of which all ordnance is to make contact with the ground.

impact point—See **point of impact**.

impact pressure—*(DOD, NATO)* The difference between pitot pressure and static pressure.

implosion weapon—*(DOD, IADB)* A weapon in which a quantity of fissionable material, less than a critical mass at ordinary pressure, has its volume suddenly reduced by compression (a step accomplished by using chemical explosives) so that it becomes supercritical, producing a nuclear explosion.

implosion weapon—*(NATO)* A device in which a quantity of fissionable material, less than a critical mass, has its volume suddenly decreased by compression, so that it becomes supercritical and an explosion can take place. The compression is achieved by means of a spherical arrangement of specially fabricated shapes of ordinary high explosive which produce an inwardly-directed implosion wave, the fissionable material being at the center of the sphere.

imprest fund—*(DOD)* A cash fund of a fixed amount established through an advance of funds, without appropriation change, to an authorized imprest fund cashier to effect immediate cash payments of relatively small amounts for authorized purchases of supplies and nonpersonal services.

imprint—*(DOD, NATO)* Brief note in the margin of a map giving all or some of the following: date of publication, printing, name of publisher, printer, place of publication, number of copies printed, and related information.

improved conventional munitions—*(DOD)* Munitions characterized by the delivery of two or more antipersonnel or antimateriel and/or antiarmor submunitions by an artillery warhead or projectile.

improvised (early) resupply—*(NATO, IADB)* The onward movement of commodities which are available on land and which can be readily loaded into ships. See also **element of resupply.**

improvised explosive devices—*(DOD, NATO)* Those devices placed or fabricated in an improvised manner incorporating destructive, lethal, noxious, pyrotechnic or incendiary chemicals, designed to destroy, disfigure, distract or harass. They may incorporate military stores, but are normally devised from non-military components.

improvised mine—*(DOD)* A mine fabricated from available materials at or near its point of use.

inactive aircraft inventory—*(DOD)* Aircraft in storage, bailment, government-furnished equipment on loan or lease outside of the Defense establishment or otherwise not available to the Military Services.

inactive duty training—*(DOD)* Authorized training performed by a member of a Reserve Component not on active duty or active duty for training and consisting of regularly scheduled unit training assemblies, additional training assemblies, periods of appropriate duty or equivalent training, and any special additional duties authorized for Reserve Component personnel by an authority designated by the Secretary concerned, and performed by them in connection with the prescribed activities of the organization in which they are assigned.

inbound traffic—*(DOD)* Traffic originating in an area outside continental United States destined for or moving in the general direction of continental United States.

incapacitating agent—*(DOD, IADB)* An agent that produces temporary physiological or mental effects, or both, which will render individuals incapable of concerted effort in the performance of their assigned duties.

incapacitating agent—*(NATO)* A chemical agent which produces temporary disabling conditions which (unlike those caused by riot control agents) can be physical or mental and persist for hours or days after exposure to the agent has ceased. Medical treatment, while not usually required, facilitates a more rapid recovery. See also **chemical agent; riot control agent.**

incentive type contract—*(DOD, IADB)* A contract that may be of either a fixed price or cost reimbursement nature, with a special provision for adjustment of the fixed price or fee. It provides for a tentative target price and a maximum price or maximum fee, with price or fee adjustment after completion of the contract for the purpose of establishing a final price or fee based on the contractor's actual costs plus a sliding scale of profit or fee that varies inversely with the cost but which in no event shall permit the final price or fee to exceed the maximum price or fee stated in the contract. See also **fixed price type contract.**

incident classification—See **search and rescue incident classification.**

incident (exercise)—*(IADB)* An occurrence injected by directing staffs into the exercise which will have an effect on the forces being exercised or their facilities and which will require action by the appropriate commander and/or staff being exercised. See also **exercise incident *(NATO).***

incidents—*(DOD, IADB)* Brief clashes or other military disturbances generally of a transitory nature and not involving protracted hostilities.

inclination angle—See **pitch angle.**

indefinite call sign—*(DOD, NATO, IADB)* A call sign which does not represent a specific facility, command, authority, activity, or unit, but which may represent any one or any group of these. See also **call sign.**

indefinite delivery type contract—*(DOD, IADB)* A type of contract used for procurements where the exact time of delivery is not known at time of contracting.

independent—*(DOD, NATO)* A merchant ship under naval control sailed singly and unescorted by a warship. See also **military independent**.

independent ejection system—See **ejection systems**.

independent mine—*(DOD, NATO)* A mine which is not controlled by the user after laying. See also **mine**.

index contour line—*(NATO)* A contour line accentuated by a heavier line weight to distinguish it from intermediate contour lines. Index contours are usually shown as every fifth contour with their assigned values, to facilitate reading elevations.

index to adjoining sheets—See **inter-chart relationship diagram**.

indicated airspeed—See **airspeed**.

indicated airspeed hold mode—*(DOD, NATO)* In a flight control system, a control mode in which desired indicated airspeed of an aircraft is maintained automatically.

indicating—*(DOD)* In air intercept, a code meaning, "Contact speed, by plot, is ____."

indications and warning—*(DOD)* Those intelligence activities intended to detect and report time-sensitive intelligence information on foreign developments that could involve a threat to the United States or allied military, political, or economic interests or to US citizens abroad. It includes forewarning of enemy actions or intentions; the imminence of hostilities; insurgency; nuclear/non-nuclear attack on the United States, its overseas forces, or allied nations; hostile reactions to United States reconnaissance activities; terrorists' attacks; and other similar events.

indications (intelligence)—*(DOD)* Information in various degrees of evaluation, all of which bears on the intention of a potential enemy to adopt or reject a course of action.

indicator—*(DOD, NATO)* In intelligence usage, an item of information which reflects the intention or capability of a potential enemy to adopt or reject a course of action.

indirect air support—*(DOD, IADB)* All forms of air support provided to land or naval forces which do not immediately assist those forces in the tactical battle.

indirect air support—*(NATO)* Support given to land or sea forces by air action against objectives other than enemy forces engaged in tactical battle. It includes the gaining and maintaining of air superiority interdiction, and harassing. See also **air support**.

indirect damage assessment—See **poststrike damage estimation**.

indirect fire—*(DOD, IADB)* Fire delivered on a target that is not itself used as a point of aim for the weapons or the director.

indirect fire—*(NATO)* Fire delivered at a target which cannot be seen by the aimer. See also **fire**.

indirect illumination—*(DOD, NATO)* Battlefield illumination provided by employing searchlight or pyrotechnic illuminants using diffusion or reflection. **a. Illumination by diffusion:** Illumination of an area beneath and to the flanks of a slightly elevated searchlight or of pyrotechnic illuminants, by the light scattered from atmospheric particles. **b. Illumination by reflection:** Illumination of an area by reflecting light from low cloud. Either or both of these effects are present when a searchlight is used in defilade or with its beam spread to maximum width.

indirect laying—*(DOD, NATO, IADB)* Aiming a gun either by sighting at a fixed object, called the aiming point, instead of the target or by using a means of pointing other than a sight, such as a gun director, when the target cannot be seen from the gun position.

individual equipment—*(DOD, IADB)* Referring to method of use, signifies personal clothing and equipment, for the personal use of the individual. See also **equipment.**

individual nuclear, biological and chemical protection—*(NATO)* Protection provided to the individual in a nuclear, biological and chemical environment by protective clothing and/or personal equipment.

individual ready reservist—*(DOD)* A member of the Ready Reserve not assigned to the Selected Reserve and not on active duty.

individual reserves—*(DOD, IADB)* The supplies carried on a soldier, animal, or vehicle for individual use in an emergency. See also **reserve supplies.**

individual sponsored dependent—*(DOD)* A dependent not entitled to travel to the overseas command at Government expense or who enters the command without endorsement of the appropriate oversea commander.

induced environment—*(DOD, IADB)* Any man-made or equipment-made environment which directly or indirectly affects the performance of man or materiel.

induced precession—*(DOD, NATO)* A precession resulting from a torque, deliberately applied to a gyro.

induced radiation—*(DOD, NATO, IADB)* Radiation produced as a result of exposure to radioactive materials, particularly the capture of neutrons. See also **contamination; initial radiation; residual radiation; residual radioactivity.**

induction circuit—*(DOD, NATO)* In naval mine warfare, a circuit actuated by the rate of change in a magnetic field due to the move-

ment of the ship or the changing current in the sweep.

industrial mobilization—*(DOD, IADB)* The transformation of industry from its peacetime activity to the industrial program necessary to support national military objectives. It includes the mobilization of materials, labor, capital, production facilities, and contributory items and services essential to the industrial program. See also **mobilization.**

industrial preparedness—*(DOD, IADB)* The state of preparedness of industry to produce essential materiel to support the national military objectives.

industrial preparedness program—*(DOD)* Plans, actions, or measures for the transformation of the industrial base, both government-owned and civilian-owned, from its peacetime activity to the emergency program necessary to support the national military objectives. It includes industrial preparedness measures such as modernization, expansion, and preservation of the production facilities and contributory items and services for planning with industry.

industrial property—*(DOD)* As distinguished from military property, means any contractor-acquired or government-furnished property, including materials, special tooling, and industrial facilities, furnished or acquired in the performance of a contract or subcontract.

industrial readiness—See **industrial preparedness.**

inert filling—*(DOD, NATO)* A prepared non-explosive filling of the same weight as the explosive filling.

inertial guidance—*(DOD, IADB)* A guidance system designed to project a missile over a predetermined path, wherein the path of the missile is adjusted after launching by devices wholly within the missile and independent of outside information. The system measures and converts accelerations experienced to distance traveled in a certain direction. See also **guidance**.

inertial navigation system—*(DOD, NATO)* A self-contained navigation system using inertial detectors, which automatically provides vehicle position, heading and velocity.

inert mine—*(DOD, NATO, IADB)* An inert replica of a standard mine. It is used for instructional purposes. See also **mine**.

infill—*(NATO)* In cartography, the filling of an area or feature with color, e.g., roads, town shapes, lakes, etc.

infiltration—*(DOD, IADB)* 1. The movement through or into an area or territory occupied by either friendly or enemy troops or organizations. The movement is made, either by small groups or by individuals, at extended or irregular intervals. When used in connection with the enemy, it infers that contact is avoided. 2. In intelligence usage, placing an agent or other person in a target area in hostile territory. Usually involves crossing a frontier or other guarded line. Methods of infiltration are: black (clandestine); grey (through legal crossing point but under false documentation); white (legal).

infiltration—*(NATO)* A technique and process in which a force moves as individuals or small groups over, through or around enemy positions without detection.

inflammable cargo—*(DOD, IADB)* Cargo such as drummed gasoline and oils. See also **cargo**.

inflight phase—*(DOD)* The flight of a missile or space vehicle from launch to detonation or impact.

inflight report—*(DOD, IADB)* The transmission from the airborne system of information obtained both at the target and en route.

inflight report—*(NATO)* A standard form of message whereby aircrews report mission results while in flight. It is also used for report-

ing any other tactical information sighted of such importance and urgency that the delay, if reported by normal debriefing, would negate the usefulness of the information.

influence field—*(DOD, NATO)* The distribution in space of the influence of a ship or minesweeping equipment.

influence mine—*(DOD, NATO)* A mine actuated by the effect of a target on some physical condition in the vicinity of the mine or on radiations emanating from the mine. See also **mine**.

influence release sinker—*(DOD, NATO)* A sinker which holds a moored or rising mine at the sea-bed and releases it when actuated by a suitable ship influence.

influence sweep—*(DOD, NATO)* A sweep designed to produce an influence similar to that produced by a ship and thus actuate mines.

informant—*(DOD, IADB)* 1. A person who, wittingly or unwittingly, provides information to an agent, a clandestine service, or the police. 2. In reporting, a person who has provided specific information and is cited as a source.

information—*(DOD)* 1. In intelligence usage, unevaluated material of every description that may be used in the production of intelligence. 2. The meaning that a human assigns to data by means of the known conventions used in their representation.

information—*(NATO)* In intelligence usage, unprocessed data of every description which may be used in the production of intelligence. See also **intelligence cycle**.

information box—*(NATO)* A space on an annotated overlay, mosaic, map, etc., which is used for identification, reference, and scale information.

information (intelligence)—*(IADB)* Unevaluated material of every description, including that derived from observations, reports, rumors, imagery, and other sources that, when processed, may produce intelligence.

information processing—See **intelligence cycle.**

information report—*(DOD, IADB)* Report used to forward raw information collected to fulfill intelligence requirements.

information requirements—*(DOD, NATO)* Those items of information regarding the enemy and his environment which need to be collected and processed in order to meet the intelligence requirements of a commander. See also **priority intelligence requirements.**

informer—*(DOD, IADB)* Person who intentionally discloses to police or to a security service information about persons or activities considered suspect, usually for a financial reward.

infrared film—*(DOD, IADB)* Film carrying an emulsion especially sensitive to "near-infrared." Used to photograph through haze, because of the penetrating power of infrared light; and in camouflage detection to distinguish between living vegetation and dead vegetation or artificial green pigment.

infrared film—*(NATO)* Film carrying an emulsion especially sensitive to the near infrared portion of the electromagnetic spectrum.

infrared imagery—*(DOD, IADB)* That imagery produced as a result of sensing electromagnetic radiations emitted or reflected from a given target surface in the infrared position of the electromagnetic spectrum (approximately 0.72 to 1,000 microns).

infrared linescan system—*(DOD, NATO)* A passive airborne infrared recording system which scans across the ground beneath the flight path, adding successive lines to the record as the vehicle advances along the flight path.

infrared photography—*(DOD)* Photography employing an optical system and direct image recording on film sensitive to near-infrared

wavelength (infrared film). Note: Not to be confused with infrared imagery.

infrared radiation—*(DOD, NATO)* Radiation emitted or reflected in the infrared portion of the electromagnetic spectrum.

infrastructure—*(DOD, NATO, IADB)* A term generally applicable to all fixed and permanent installations, fabrications, or facilities for the support and control of military forces. See also **bilateral infrastructure; common infrastructure; national infrastructure.**

initial active duty training—*(DOD)* The first period of active duty for training prescribed by law or regulation for non-prior-service enlistees which, when satisfactorily completed, produces a trained member in a military specialty. See also **active duty for training.**

initial approach—*(DOD, NATO, IADB)* **a.** That part of an instrument approach procedure in which the aircraft has departed an initial approach fix or point and is maneuvering to enter the intermediate or final approach. It ends at the intermediate fix or point or, where no intermediate segment is established, at the final approach fix or point. **b.** That part of a visual approach of an aircraft immediately prior to arrival over the airfield of destination, or over the reporting point from which the final approach to the airfield is commenced.

initial approach area—*(DOD, NATO, IADB)* An area of defined width lying between the last preceding navigational fix or dead reckoning position and either the facility to be used for making an instrument approach or a point associated with such a facility that is used for demarcating the termination of initial approach.

initial contact report—See **contact report.**

initial draft plan—*(NATO)* A plan which has been drafted and coordinated by the originating headquarters, and is ready for external coordination with other military headquarters.

It cannot be directly implemented by the issuing commander, but it may form the basis for an operation order issued by the commander in the event of an emergency. See also **draft plan; coordinated draft plan; final plan; operation plan.**

initial (early) resupply—*(NATO, IADB)* The onward movement of ships which are already loaded with cargoes which will serve the requirements after D-day. This includes such shipping evacuation from major ports/major water terminals and subsequently dispersed to secondary ports/alternate water terminals and anchorages. See also **element of resupply.**

initial entry into Military Service—*(DOD)* Entry for the first time into military status (active duty or reserve) by induction, enlistment, or appointment in any Service of the Armed Forces of the United States. Appointment may be as a commissioned or warrant officer; as a cadet or midshipman at the Service academy of one of the armed forces; or as a midshipman, US Naval Reserve, for US Naval Reserve Officers' Training Corps training at a civilian institution.

initial issues—*(DOD)* The issue of materiel not previously furnished to an individual or organization, including new inductees and newly activated organizations and the issue of newly authorized items of materiel.

initial operational capability—*(DOD, IADB)* The first attainment of the capability to employ effectively a weapon, item of equipment, or system of approved specific characteristics, and which is manned or operated by an adequately trained, equipped, and supported military unit or force.

initial path sweeping—*(DOD, NATO)* In naval mine warfare, initial sweeping to clear a path through a mined area dangerous to the following mine sweepers. See also **precursor sweeping.**

initial photo interpretation report—*(DOD)* A first-phase interpretation report, subsequent

to the Joint Tactical Air Reconnaissance/Surveillance Mission Report, presenting the results of the initial readout of new imagery to answer the specific requirements for which the mission was requested.

initial point—*(DOD, IADB)* 1. The first point at which a moving target is located on a plotting board. 2. A well-defined point, easily distinguishable visually and/or electronically, used as a starting point for the bomb run to the target. 3. **airborne**—A point close to the landing area where serials (troop carrier air formations) make final alterations in course to pass over individual drop or landing zones. 4. **helicopter**—An air control point in the vicinity of the landing zone from which individual flights of helicopters are directed to their prescribed landing sites. 5. Any designated place at which a column or element thereof is formed by the successive arrival of its various subdivisions, and comes under the control of the commander ordering the move. See also **target approach point.**

initial point—*(NATO)* 1. A well-defined point, easily distinguishable visually and/or electronically, used as a starting point for the run to the target. 2. The first point at which a moving target is located on a plotting board. 3. (Airborne) A point close to the landing area where serials (troop carrier air formations) make final alterations in course to pass over individual drop or landing zones. 4. (Helicopter) An air control point in the vicinity of the landing zone from which individual flights of helicopters are directed to their prescribed landing sites. 5. A pre-selected point on the surface of the earth which is used as a reference. See also **target approach point.**

initial programmed interpretation report (IPIR)—*(DOD, NATO)* A standardized imagery interpretation report providing information on programmed mission objectives or other vital intelligence information which can be readily identified near these objectives, and which has not been reported elsewhere.

initial provisioning—*(DOD, IADB)* The process of determining the range and quantity of items (i.e., spares and repair parts, special tools, test equipment, and support equipment) required to support and maintain an item for an initial period of service. Its phases include the identification of items of supply, the establishment of data for catalog, technical manual, and allowance list preparation, and the preparation of instructions to assure delivery of necessary support items with related end articles.

initial radiation—*(DOD, NATO, IADB)* The radiation, essentially neutrons and gamma rays, resulting from a nuclear burst and emitted from the fireball within one minute after burst. See also **induced radiation; residual radiation.**

initial reserves—*(DOD, IADB)* In an amphibious operation, those supplies which normally are unloaded immediately following the assault waves; usually the supplies for the use of the beach organization, battalion landing teams, and other elements of regimental combat teams for the purpose of initiating and sustaining combat until higher supply installations are established. See also **reserve supplies.**

initial unloading period—*(DOD, NATO)* In amphibious operations, that part of the ship-to-shore movement in which unloading is primarily tactical in character and must be instantly responsive to landing force requirements. All elements intended to land during this period are serialized. See also **general unloading period.**

initial vector—*(DOD, IADB)* The initial command heading to be assumed by an interceptor after it has been committed to intercept an airborne object.

initial velocity—See **muzzle velocity.**

initiation—*(NATO)* 1. The action of a device used as the first element of an explosive train which, upon receipt of the proper impulse, causes the detonation or burning of an explosive item. 2. **(nuclear)** The action which sets off a chain reaction in a fissile mass which has reached the critical state (generally by the emission of a "spurt" of neutrons).

initiation of procurement action—*(DOD)* That point in time when the approved document requesting procurement and citing funds is forwarded to the procuring activity. See also **procurement lead time.**

injury—*(DOD, IADB)* A term comprising such conditions as fractures, wounds, sprains, strains, dislocations, concussions, and compressions. In addition, it includes conditions resulting from extremes of temperature or prolonged exposure. Acute poisonings, except those due to contaminated food, resulting from exposure to a toxic or poisonous substance are also classed as injuries. See also **battle casualty; casualty; nonbattle casualty; wounded.**

inland search and rescue region—*(DOD)* The inland areas of continental United States, except waters under the jurisdiction of the United States. See also **search and rescue region.**

inner transport area—*(DOD)* In amphibious operations, an area as close to the landing beach as depth of water, navigational hazards, boat traffic, and enemy action permit, to which transports may move to expedite unloading. See also **outer transport area; transport area.**

in-place force—*(DOD, NATO)* A NATO assigned force which, in peacetime, is principally stationed in the designated combat zone of the NATO Command to which it is committed.

inserted grouping (radar)—*(DOD, NATO)* The inclusion of one area of homogeneous surface material in an area of different material. See also **homogeneous area.**

inset—*(NATO)* In cartography, a separate map positioned within the neatline of a larger map. Three forms are recognized: **a.** An area geographically outside a sheet but included therein for convenience of publication, usually at the same scale; **b.** A portion of the map or chart at an enlarged scale; **c.** A smaller scale map or chart of surrounding areas, included for location purposes.

inshore patrol—*(DOD, NATO, IADB)* A naval defense patrol operating generally within a naval defense coastal area and comprising all elements of harbor defenses, the coastal lookout system, patrol craft supporting bases, aircraft, and Coast Guard stations. (Note: **IADB** definition ends with the word "aircraft.")

inspection—*(DOD, IADB)* In arms control, physical process of determining compliance with arms control measures.

installation—*(DOD, IADB)* A grouping of facilities, located in the same vicinity, which support particular functions. Installations may be elements of a base. See also **base; base complex.**

instantaneous vertical speed indicator—See **vertical speed indicator.**

instructional mine—*(DOD, NATO)* An inert mine used for instruction and normally sectionalized for this purpose. See also **inert mine.**

instrument approach procedure—*(DOD, NATO)* A series of predetermined maneuvers for the orderly transfer of an aircraft under instrument flight conditions from the beginning of the initial approach to a landing or to a point from which a landing may be made visually or the missed approach procedure is initiated.

instrument flight—*(DOD, NATO, IADB)* Flight in which the path and attitude of the aircraft are controlled solely by reference to instruments.

instrument landing system—*(DOD, NATO, IADB)* A system of radio navigation intended to assist aircraft in landing which provides lateral and vertical guidance, which may include indications of distance from the optimum point of landing.

instrument recording photography—*(NATO)* Photography of the presentation of instrument data.

in support—*(DOD, NATO)* An expression used to denote the task of providing artillery supporting fire to a formation or unit. Liaison and observation are not normally provided. See also **at priority call; direct support.**

in support of—*(DOD, NATO, IADB)* Assisting or protecting another formation, unit, or organization while remaining under original control.

insurgency—*(DOD, NATO, I, IADB)* An organized movement aimed at the overthrow of a constituted government through use of subversion and armed conflict.

integrated fire control system—*(DOD, IADB)* A system which performs the functions of target acquisition, tracking, data computation, and engagement control, primarily using electronic means assisted by electromechanical devices.

integrated logistics support—*(DOD)* A composite of all the support considerations necessary to assure the effective and economical support of a system for its life cycle. It is an integral part of all other aspects of system acquisition and operation.

integrated logistic support—*(NATO, IADB)* The pooling of specified resources by nations for use by the same nations as decided by coordinating agency or authority to which the subscribing nations have agreed. See also **logistic assistance; mutual aid; reallocation of resources.**

integrated material management—*(DOD)* The exercise of total Department of Defense management responsibility for a Federal Supply Group/Class, commodity, or item by a single agency. It normally includes computation of requirements, funding, budgeting, storing, issuing, cataloging, standardizing, and procuring functions.

integrated staff—*(DOD, NATO, IADB)* A staff in which one officer only is appointed to each post on the establishment of the headquarters, irrespective of nationality and Service. See also **combined staff; joint staff; parallel staff; staff.**

integrated warfare—*(DOD)* The conduct of military operations in any combat environment wherein opposing forces employ non-conventional weapons in combination with conventional weapons.

integrating circuit—*(DOD, NATO)* A circuit whose actuation is dependent on the time integral of a function of the influence.

integration—*(DOD)* 1. A stage in the intelligence cycle in which a pattern is formed through the selection and combination of evaluated information. 2. In photography, a process by which the average radar picture seen on several scans of the time base may be obtained on a print, or the process by which several photographic images are combined into a single image.

integration—*(NATO)* In photography, a process by which the average radar picture seen on several scans of the time base may be obtained on a print, or the process by which several photographic images are combined into a single image.

integration—*(IADB)* The process of forming an intelligence pattern through selection and combination of evaluated information.

intelligence—*(DOD)* The product resulting from the collection, processing, integration, analysis, evaluation and interpretation of available information concerning foreign countries or areas.

intelligence—*(NATO)* The product resulting from the processing of information concerning foreign nations, hostile or potentially hostile forces or elements, or areas of actual or potential operations. The term is also applied to the activity which results in the product and to the organizations engaged in such activity. See also **basic intelligence; combat intelligence; current intelligence; security intelligence; strategic intelligence; tactical intelligence; target intelligence; technical intelligence.**

intelligence annex—*(DOD, IADB)* A supporting document of an operation plan or order that provides detailed information on the enemy situation, assignment of intelligence tasks, and intelligence administrative procedures.

intelligence collection plan—*(DOD, IADB)* A plan for gathering information from all available sources to meet an intelligence requirement. Specifically, a logical plan for transforming the essential elements of information into orders or requests to sources within a required time limit. See also **intelligence cycle.**

intelligence contingency funds—*(DOD)* Appropriated funds to be used for intelligence activities when the use of other funds is not applicable or would either jeopardize or impede the mission of the intelligence unit.

intelligence cycle—*(DOD, IADB)* The steps by which information is converted into intelligence and made available to users. There are five steps in the cycle:
a. **planning and direction**—Determination of intelligence requirements, preparation of a collection plan, issuance of orders and requests to information collection agencies, and a continuous check on the productivity of collection agencies.
b. **collection**—Acquisition of information and the provision of this information to processing and/or production elements.
c. **processing**—Conversion of collected information into a form suitable to the production of intelligence.

d. production—Conversion of information into intelligence through the integration, analysis, evaluation, and interpretation of all source data and the preparation of intelligence products in support of known or anticipated user requirements.

e. dissemination—Conveyance of intelligence to users in a suitable form.

intelligence cycle—*(NATO)* The sequence of activities whereby information is obtained, assembled, converted into intelligence and made available to users. This sequence comprises the following four phases:

a. direction—Determination of intelligence requirements, planning the collection effort, issuance of orders and requests to collection agencies and maintenance of a continuous check on the productivity of such agencies.

b. collection—The exploitation of sources by collection agencies and the delivery of the information obtained to the appropriate processing unit for use in the production of intelligence.

c. processing—The conversion of information into intelligence through collation, evaluation, analysis, integration and interpretation.

d. dissemination—The timely conveyance of intelligence, in an appropriate form and by any suitable means, to those who need it.

intelligence data base—*(DOD, IADB)* The sum of holdings of intelligence data and finished intelligence products at a given organization.

intelligence data handling systems—*(DOD, IADB)* Information systems that process and manipulate raw information and intelligence data as required. They are characterized by the application of general purpose computers, peripheral equipment, and automated storage and retrieval equipment for documents and photographs. While automation is a distinguishing characteristic of intelligence data handling systems, individual system components may be either automated or manually operated.

intelligence estimate—*(DOD, NATO)* The appraisal, expressed in writing or orally, of available intelligence relating to a specific situation or condition with a view to determining the courses of action open to the enemy or potential enemy and the order of probability of their adoption.

intelligence journal—*(DOD, IADB)* A chronological log of intelligence activities covering a stated period, usually 24 hours. It is an index of reports and messages that have been received and transmitted, and of important events that have occurred, and actions taken. The journal is a permanent and official record.

intelligence-related activities—*(DOD)* 1. Those activities outside the consolidated defense intelligence program which: **a.** Respond to operational commanders' tasking for time-sensitive information on foreign entities; **b.** Respond to national intelligence community tasking of systems whose primary mission is support to operating forces; **c.** Train personnel for intelligence duties; **d.** Provide an intelligence reserve; or **e.** Are devoted to research and development of intelligence or related capabilities. 2. Specifically excluded are programs which are so closely integrated with a weapon system that their primary function is to provide immediate-use targeting data.

intelligence report—*(DOD, IADB)* A specific report of information, usually on a single item, made at any level of command in tactical operations and disseminated as rapidly as possible in keeping with the timeliness of the information. Also called **INTREP**.

intelligence reporting—*(DOD, IADB)* The preparation and conveyance of information by any means. More commonly, the term is restricted to reports as they are prepared by the collector and as they are transmitted by him to his headquarters and by this component of the intelligence structure to one or more intelligence-producing components. Thus, even in this limited sense, reporting embraces both collection and dissemination. The term is applied to normal and specialist intelligence reports. See also **normal intelligence reports; specialist intelligence reports.**

intelligence requirement—*(DOD, IADB)* Any subject, general or specific, upon which there is a need for the collection of information, or the production of intelligence. See also **essential elements of information.**

intelligence subject code—*(DOD)* A system of subject and area references to index the information contained in intelligence reports as required by a general intelligence document reference service.

intelligence summary—*(DOD)* A specific report providing a summary of items of intelligence at frequent intervals. See also **intelligence.**

intensity factor—*(DOD, NATO)* A multiplying factor used in planning activities to evaluate the foreseeable intensity or the specific nature of an operation in a given area for a given period of time. It is applied to the standard day of supply in order to calculate the combat day of supply.

intensity mine circuit—*(DOD, NATO)* A circuit whose actuation is dependent on the field strength reaching a level differing by some pre-set minimum from that experienced by the mine when no ships are in the vicinity.

intention—*(DOD, IADB)* An aim or design (as distinct from capability) to execute a specified course of action.

intercepting search—*(DOD, NATO, IADB)* A type of search designed to intercept an enemy whose previous position is known and the limits of whose subsequent course and speed can be assumed.

interceptor—*(DOD, NATO, IADB)* A manned aircraft utilized for identification and/or engagement of airborne objects.

interceptor controller—*(NATO, IADB)* An officer who controls fighter aircraft allotted to him for interception purposes.

intercept point—*(DOD, NATO, IADB)* The point to which an airborne vehicle is vectored or guided to complete an interception.

intercept receiver—*(DOD, NATO)* A receiver designed to detect and provide visual and/or aural indication of electromagnetic emissions occurring within the particular portion of the electro-magnetic spectrum to which it is tuned.

interchangeability—*(DOD, NATO, IADB)* A condition which exists when two or more items possess such functional and physical characteristics as to be equivalent in performance and durability, and are capable of being exchanged one for the other without alteration of the items themselves, or of adjoining items, except for adjustment, and without selection for fit and performance. See also **compatibility.**

inter-chart relationship diagram—*(NATO)* A diagram on a map or chart showing names and/or numbers of adjacent sheets in the same (or related) series. Also called "index to adjoining sheets." See also **map index.**

intercoastal traffic—*(DOD)* Sea traffic between Atlantic, Gulf, and Great Lakes continental United States ports and Pacific Continental United States ports.

intercom—*(DOD, IADB)* A telephone apparatus by means of which personnel can talk to each other within an aircraft, tank, ship, or activity.

inter-command exercise—*(NATO)* An exercise involving two or more Major NATO Commanders and/or their subordinates.

interconnection—*(DOD)* The linking together of interoperable systems.

intercontinental ballistic missile—*(DOD, IADB)* A ballistic missile with a range capability from about 3,000 to 8,000 nautical miles.

intercount dormant period—*(DOD, NATO, IADB)* In naval mine warfare, the period after the actuation of a ship counter before it is ready to receive another actuation.

interdepartmental/agency support—*(DOD)* Provision of logistic and/or administrative support in services or materiel by one or more Military Services to one or more departments or agencies of the United States Government (other than military) with or without reimbursement. See also **international logistic support; inter-Service support; support.**

interdepartmental intelligence—*(DOD)* Integrated departmental intelligence that is required by departments and agencies of the United States Government for the execution of their missions but which transcends the exclusive competence of a single department or agency to produce.

interdict—*(IADB)* To prevent or hinder, by any means, enemy use of an area or route.

interdiction—*(DOD)* An action to divert, disrupt, delay or destroy the enemy's surface military potential before it can be used effectively against friendly forces.

interdiction fire—*(NATO, IADB)* Fire placed on an area or point to prevent the enemy from using the area or point. See also **fire.**

interface—*(DOD)* A boundary or point common to two or more similar or dissimilar command and control systems, sub-systems, or other entities against which or at which necessary information flow takes place.

interim financing—*(DOD, IADB)* Advance payments, partial payments, loans, discounts, advances, and commitments in connection therewith; and guarantees of loans, discounts, advances, and commitments in connection therewith; and any other type of financing necessary for both performance and termination of contracts.

interim overhaul—*(DOD, IADB)* An availability for the accomplishment of necessary repairs and urgent alterations at a naval shipyard or other shore-based repair activity, normally scheduled halfway through the established regular overhaul cycle.

inter-look dormant period—*(DOD, NATO)* In mine warfare, the time interval after each look in a multi-look mine, during which the firing mechanism will not register.

intermediate approach—*(DOD, NATO)* That part of an instrument approach procedure in which aircraft configuration, speed and positioning adjustments are made. It blends the initial approach segment into the final approach segment. It begins at the intermediate fix or point and ends at the final approach fix or point.

intermediate area illumination—*(NATO)* Illumination in the area, extending in depth from the far boundary of the close-in (about 2,000 meters) to the maximum effective range of the bulk of division artillery weapons (about 10,000 meters).

intermediate contour line—*(NATO)* A contour line drawn between index contours. Depending on the contour interval there are three or four intermediate contours between the index contours. See also **index contour line.**

Intermediate Force Planning Level—*(DOD)* The force level established during Planning Force development to depict the buildup from the Current Force to the Planning Force. The Intermediate Force Planning Level is insufficient to carry out strategy with a reasonable assurance of success and consequently cannot be referred to as the Planning Force. See also **Current Force; force; Minimum Risk Force; Planning Force; Programmed Forces.**

intermediate maintenance (field)—*(DOD, IADB)* That maintenance which is the respon-

189

sibility of and performed by designated maintenance activities for direct support of using organizations. Its phases normally consist of **a.** calibration, repair, or replacement of damaged or unserviceable parts, components, or assemblies; **b.** the emergency manufacture of nonavailable parts; and **c.** providing technical assistance to using organizations. (NOTE: IADB definition does not use subdivisions **a., b., c.**)

intermediate marker (land mine warfare)— *(DOD, NATO, IADB)* A marker, natural, artificial or specially installed, which is used as a point of reference between the landmark and the minefield. See also **marker (land mine warfare).**

intermediate-range ballistic missile—*(DOD, IADB)* A ballistic missile with a range capability from about 1,500 to 3,000 nautical miles.

intermediate-range bomber aircraft—*(DOD)* A bomber designed for a tactical operating radius of between 1,000 to 2,500 nautical miles at design gross weight and design bomb load.

intermittent arming device—*(DOD, NATO)* A device included in a mine so that it will be armed only at set times.

intermittent illumination—*(DOD, NATO)* A type of fire in which illuminating projectiles are fired at irregular intervals.

internal defense—*(DOD, I, IADB)* The full range of measures taken by a government to free and protect its society from subversion, lawlessness, and insurgency. See also **foreign internal defense.**

internal development—*(DOD)* Actions taken by a nation to promote its growth by building viable institutions (political, military, economic, and social) that respond to the needs of its society.

internal radiation—*(DOD, NATO, IADB)* Nuclear radiation (alpha and beta particles and

gamma radiation) resulting from radioactive substances in the body.

internal security—*(DOD, I, IADB)* The state of law and order prevailing within a nation.

international actual strength—*(NATO)* The total number of military and civilian personnel currently filling international posts.

international arms control organization— *(DOD, I, IADB)* An appropriately constituted organization established to supervise and verify the implementation of arms control measures.

international call sign—*(DOD, NATO, IADB)* A call sign assigned in accordance with the provisions of the International Telecommunications Union to identify a radio station. The nationality of the radio station is identified by the first or the first two characters. (When used in visual signaling, international call signs are referred to as "signal letters.") See also **call sign.**

international civilian personnel with NATO status—*(NATO)* Civilian persons assigned or appointed to authorized NATO international civilian posts.

international cooperative logistics—*(DOD, NATO)* Cooperation and mutual support in the field of logistics through the coordination of policies, plans, procedures, development activities and the common supply and exchange of goods and services arranged on the basis of bilateral and multilateral agreements with appropriate cost reimbursement provisions.

international date line—*(DOD, NATO)* The line coinciding approximately with the anti-meridian of Greenwich, modified to avoid certain habitable land. In crossing this line there is a date change of one day. Also called **date line.**

international identification code—*(DOD, NATO)* In railway terminology, a code which identifies a military train from point of origin to final destination. The code consists of a series of figures, letters, or symbols indicating the priority, country of origin, day of departure, national identification code number and country of destination of the train.

international job description—*(NATO)* A delineation of the specific duties, responsibilities and qualifications pertaining to a specific international post.

international loading gauge (GIC)—*(DOD, NATO)* The loading gauge upon which international railway agreements are based. A load whose dimensions fall within the limits of this gauge may move without restriction on most of the railways of Continental Western Europe. GIC is an abbreviation for "gabarit international de chargement," formerly called **PPI.**

international logistics—*(DOD, IADB)* The negotiating, planning, and implementation of supporting logistics arrangements between nations, their forces, and agencies. It includes furnishing logistic support (major end items, materiel, and/or services) to, or receiving logistic support from, one or more friendly foreign governments, international organizations, or military forces, with or without reimbursement. It also includes planning and actions related to the intermeshing of a significant element, activity, or component of the military logistics systems or procedures of the United States with those of one or more foreign governments, international organizations, or military forces on a temporary or permanent basis. It includes planning and actions related to the utilization of United States logistics policies, systems, and/or procedures to meet requirements of one or more foreign governments, international organizations, or forces.

international logistic support—*(DOD, IADB)* The provision of military logistic support by one participating nation to one or more participating nations, either with or without reimbursement. See also **interdepartmental/ agency support; inter-Service support; support.**

international manpower ceiling—*(NATO)* The total number of international posts, military and civilian, which has been authorized for each international organization.

international map of the world—*(NATO, IADB)* A map series at 1:1,000,000 scale published by a number of countries to common internationally agreed specifications.

international military education and training—*(DOD, IADB)* Formal or informal instruction provided to foreign military students, units, and forces on a nonreimbursable (grant) basis by offices or employees of the United States, contract technicians, and contractors. Instruction may include correspondence courses; technical, educational or informational publications; and media of all kinds. See also **United States Military Service Funded Foreign Training.**

international military personnel—*(NATO)* Military persons assigned or appointed to authorized international military posts.

international military post—*(NATO)* An international post authorized to be filled by a military person whose pay and allowances remain the responsibility of the parent nation.

International Peace Force—*(DOD)* An appropriately constituted organization established for the purpose of preserving world peace.

international personnel—*(NATO)* Military and civilian persons assigned or appointed to authorized international posts.

international post—*(NATO)* A post, position, job or billet, authorized in a peacetime establishment or emergency establishment which carries a specific international job description, whose incumbent is responsible to international authority.

interocular distance—*(DOD)* The distance between the centers of rotation of the eyeballs of an individual or between the oculars of optical instruments.

191

interoperability—*(DOD, NATO)* 1. The ability of systems, units or forces to provide services to and accept services from other systems, units or forces and to use the services so exchanged to enable them to operate effectively together. *(DOD)* 2. The condition achieved among communications-electronics systems or items of communications-electronics equipment when information or services can be exchanged directly and satisfactorily between them and/or their users. The degree of interoperability should be defined when referring to specific cases.

interoperation—*(DOD)* The use of interoperable systems, units, or forces.

interphone—See **intercom**.

interpretability—*(DOD, NATO, IADB)* Suitability of imagery for interpretation with respect to answering adequately requirements on a given type of target in terms of quality and scale.
  a. **poor**—Imagery is unsuitable for interpretation to answer adequately requirements on a given type of target.
  b. **fair**—Imagery is suitable for interpretation to answer requirements on a given type of target but with only average detail.
  c. **good**—Imagery is suitable for interpretation to answer requirements on a given type of target in considerable detail.
  d. **excellent**—Imagery is suitable for interpretation to answer requirements on a given type of target in complete detail.

interpretation—*(DOD)* A stage in the intelligence cycle in which the significance of information is judged in relation to the current body of knowledge.

interpretation—*(NATO)* See **intelligence cycle**.

interrogation (intelligence)—*(DOD, IADB)* Systematic effort to procure information by direct questioning of a person under the control of the questioner.

interrupted line—*(NATO)* A broken, dashed or pecked line usually used to indicate the indefinite alignment or area of a feature on the chart.

inter-Service education—*(DOD, IADB)* Military education which is provided by one Service to members of another Service. See also **military education; military training**.

inter-Service support—*(DOD, IADB)* Action by one Military Service or element thereof to provide logistic and/or administrative support to another Military Service or element thereof. Such action can be recurring or nonrecurring in character on an installation, area, or worldwide basis. See also **interdepartmental/ agency support; international logistic support; support**.

inter-Service training—*(DOD, IADB)* Military training which is provided by one Service to members of another Service. See also **military education; military training**.

intertheater traffic—*(DOD)* Traffic between theaters exclusive of that between the continental United States and theaters.

interval—*(DOD, NATO, IADB)* 1. The space between adjacent groups of ships or boats measured in any direction between the corresponding ships or boats in each group. 2. The space between adjacent individuals, ground vehicles, or units in a formation that are placed side by side, measured abreast. 3. The space between adjacent aircraft measured from front to rear in units of time or distance. 4. The time lapse between photographic exposures. 5. At battery right or left, an interval ordered in seconds is the time between one gun firing and the next gun firing. Five seconds is the standard interval. 6. At rounds of fire for effect the interval is the time in seconds between successive rounds from each gun.

interview (intelligence)—*(DOD, IADB)* To gather information from a person who is aware that information is being given although there is ignorance of the true connection and purposes of the interviewer. Generally overt unless the collector is other than purported to be.

in the dark—*(DOD)* In air intercept, a code meaning, "Not visible on my scope."

intracoastal sealift—*(DOD, IADB)* Shipping used primarily for the carriage of personnel and/or cargo along a coast or into river ports to support operations within a given area.

intra-command exercise—*(DOD, NATO)* An exercise which involves an identified part of one Major NATO Command or subordinate command.

intransit aeromedical evacuation facility—*(DOD, IADB)* A medical facility, on or in the vicinity of an air base, that provides limited medical care for intransit patients awaiting air transportation. This type of medical facility is provided to obtain effective utilization of transport airlift within operating schedules. It includes "remain overnight" facilities, intransit facilities at aerial ports of embarkation and debarkation, and casualty staging facilities in an overseas combat area. See also **aeromedical evacuation unit.**

intransit inventory—*(DOD, IADB)* That materiel in the military distribution system that is in the process of movement from point of receipt from procurement and production (either contractor's plant or first destination, depending upon point of delivery) and between points of storage and distribution.

intransit stock—See **intransit inventory.**

intratheater traffic—*(DOD, IADB)* Traffic within a theater.

Intruder—*(DOD, IADB)* A twin-engine, turbojet, two-place, long-range, all-weather, aircraft carrier-based, low-altitude attack aircraft, possessing an integrated attack-navigation and central digital computer system to locate, track, and destroy small moving targets, and large fixed targets. The armament system consists of an assortment of nuclear and/or non-nuclear weapons, Sidewinder, Bullpup, napalm, and all standard Navy rockets. This aircraft can be air refueled. Designated as A-6.

intruder—*(DOD, NATO)* An individual, unit, or weapon system, in or near an operational or exercise area, which presents the threat of intelligence gathering or disruptive activity.

intruder operation—*(DOD, NATO, IADB)* An offensive operation by day or night over enemy territory with the primary object of destroying enemy aircraft in the vicinity of their bases.

intrusion—See **electromagnetic intrusion.**

invasion currency—See **military currency.**

inventory control—*(DOD, NATO, IADB)* That phase of military logistics which includes managing, cataloging, requirements determinations, procurement, distribution, overhaul, and disposal of materiel. Synonymous with **materiel control, materiel management, inventory management,** and **supply management.**

inventory control point—*(DOD)* An organizational unit or activity within a DOD supply system that is assigned the primary responsibility for the materiel management of a group of items either for a particular Service or for the Defense Department as a whole. Materiel inventory management includes cataloging direction, requirements computation, procurement direction, distribution management, disposal direction, and, generally, rebuild direction.

inventory management—See **inventory control.**

inventory managers—See **inventory control point.**

inverter—*(DOD, NATO)* In electrical engineering, a device for converting direct current into alternating current. See also **rectifier.**

investigation—*(DOD)* A duly authorized, systematized, detailed examination or inquiry to uncover facts and determine the truth of a matter. This may include collecting, processing, reporting, storing, recording, analyzing, evaluating, producing and disseminating the authorized information.

investment costs—*(DOD)* Those program costs required beyond the development phase to introduce into operational use a new capability; to procure initial, additional, or replacement equipment for operational forces; or to provide for major modifications of an existing capability. They exclude research, development, test and evaluation, military personnel, and Operation and Maintenance appropriation costs.

ionization—*(DOD, NATO, IADB)* The process of producing ions by the removal of electrons from, or the addition of electrons to, atoms or molecules.

ionosphere—*(DOD)* That part of the atmosphere, extending from about 70 to 500 kilometers, in which ions and free electrons exist in sufficient quantities to reflect electromagnetic waves.

Iroquois—*(DOD)* A light single-rotor helicopter utilized for cargo/personnel transport and attack helicopter support. Some versions are armed with machine guns and light air-to-ground rockets. Designated as **UH-1.**

irregular forces—*(DOD, IADB)* Armed individuals or groups who are not members of the regular armed forces, police, or other internal security forces.

irregular outer edge (land mine warfare)—*(DOD, IADB)* Short mine strips laid in an irregular manner in front of a minefield facing the enemy to deceive the enemy as to the type or extent of the minefield. Generally, the irregular outer edge will only be used in minefields with buried mines.

irregular outer edge—*(NATO)* In land mine warfare, short mine rows or strips laid in an irregular manner in front of a minefield facing the enemy, to deceive the enemy as to the type or extent of the minefield. Generally, the irregular outer edge will only be used in minefields with buried mines.

isobar—*(IADB)* A line along which the atmospheric pressure is, or is assumed to be, the same or constant.

isocentre—*(NATO)* The point on a photograph intersected by the bisector of the angle between the plumbline and the photograph perpendicular.

isoclinal—*(IADB)* A line drawn on a map or chart joining points of equal magnetic dip.

isodose rate line—See **dose rate contour line.**

isogonal—*(IADB)* A line drawn on a map or chart joining points of equal magnetic declination for a given time.

isogonic line—See **isogonal.**

isogriv—*(NATO, IADB)* A line on a map or chart which joins points of equal angular difference between grid north and magnetic north. See also **grid magnetic angle.**

isotopes—*(DOD, IADB)* Forms of the same element having identical chemical properties but differing in their atomic masses due to different numbers of neutrons in their respective nuclei and in their nuclear properties.

issue priority designator—See **priority designator.**

I stay—*(DOD)* In air intercept, a code meaning, "Am remaining with you on patrol/mission _____ hours." See also **I go.**

item manager—*(DOD)* An individual within the organization of an inventory control point or other such organization assigned management responsibility for one or more specific items of materiel.

J

jamming—See **barrage jamming; electronic countermeasures; electronic jamming; selective jamming; spot jamming.**

JCS-coordinated exercise—*(DOD)* A minor exercise, the scheduling of which requires coordination by the Joint Chiefs of Staff because it involves the units or forces of more than one commander in chief or agency. See also **exercise.**

JCS-directed exercise—*(DOD)* A strategic mobility or major commander in chief directed exercise of considerable interest to the Joint Chiefs of Staff. See also **exercise.**

jet advisory service—*(DOD, IADB)* The service provided certain civil aircraft while operating within radar and nonradar jet advisory areas. Within radar jet advisory areas, civil aircraft receiving this service are provided radar flight following, radar traffic information, and vectors around observed traffic. In nonradar jet advisory areas, civil aircraft receiving this service are afforded standard instrument flight rules separation from all other aircraft known to air traffic control to be operating within these areas.

jet conventional low-altitude bombing system—*(DOD, IADB)* A maneuver used by jet aircraft to loft conventional ordnance by means of a low-altitude bombing system.

jet propulsion—*(DOD, IADB)* Reaction propulsion in which the propulsion unit obtains oxygen from the air, as distinguished from rocket propulsion in which the unit carries its own oxygen-producing material. In connection with aircraft propulsion, the term refers to a gasoline or other fuel turbine jet unit, which discharges hot gas through a tail pipe and a nozzle, affording a thrust which propels the aircraft. See also **rocket propulsion.**

Jet Star—*(DOD, IADB)* A small, fast, support-type transport aircraft powered by four turbo-jet engines which are podded two on either side of the fuselage. Designated as C-140.

jet stream—*(DOD, IADB)* A narrow band of high velocity wind in the upper troposphere or in the stratosphere.

jettison—*(DOD, IADB)* The selective release of stores from an aircraft other than normal attack.

jettison—*(NATO)* Deliberate release of an aircraft store from an aircraft to effect aircraft safety or prepare for air combat.

jettisoned mines—*(DOD, NATO)* Mines which are laid as quickly as possible in order to empty the minelayer of mines, without regard to their condition or relative positions.

joiner—*(DOD, NATO)* An independent merchant ship sailed to join a convoy. See also **joiner convoy; joiner section.**

joiner convoy—*(DOD, NATO)* A convoy sailed to join the main convoy. See also **joiner; joiner section.**

joiner section—*(DOD, NATO)* A joiner or joiner convoy, after rendezvous, and while maneuvering to integrate with the main convoy.

joint—*(DOD, NATO)* Connotes activities, operations, organizations, etc., in which elements of more than one service of the same nation participate. (When all services are not involved, the participating services shall be identified, e.g., Joint Army-Navy.) See also **combined.**

joint airborne training—*(DOD, IADB)* Training operations or exercises involving airborne and appropriate troop carrier units. This training includes: **a.** air delivery of personnel and equipment; **b.** assault operations by airborne troops and/or air transportable units; **c.** loading exercises and local orientation

195

flights of short duration; and **d.** maneuvers/exercises as agreed upon by Services concerned and/or as authorized by the Joint Chiefs of Staff. (Note: **IADB** definition does not use the words "and/or as authorized by the Joint Chiefs of Staff.")

joint amphibious operation—*(DOD, NATO, IADB)* An amphibious operation conducted by significant elements of two or more Services.

joint amphibious task force—*(DOD, IADB)* A temporary grouping of units of two or more Services under a single commander, organized for the purpose of engaging in an amphibious landing for assault on hostile shores.

joint amphibious task force—*(NATO)* A temporary grouping of units of two or more services under a single commander, organized for the purpose of engaging in an amphibious operation.

joint Army-Navy-Air Force publications—*(DOD)* A series of publications produced by supporting agencies of the Joint Chiefs of Staff and intended for distribution through the approved offices of distribution within the Army, Navy, and Air Force.

joint chiefs of staff—*(DOD)* See **Organization of the Joint Chiefs of Staff.**

joint common user item—*(NATO, IADB)* An item of an interchangeable nature which is in common use by two or more services of a nation.

joint communications network—*(DOD)* The aggregation of all the joint communications systems in a theater. The joint communications network includes the Joint Multi-channel Trunking and Switching System and the Joint Command and Control Communications Systems(s).

Joint Deployment Agency—*(DOD)* The activity that supports the Joint Chiefs of Staff and supported commanders in planning for and executing deployments. Also called **JDA.**

joint deployment community—*(DOD)* Those headquarters, commands, and agencies involved in the training, preparation, movement, reception, employment, support, and sustainment of military forces assigned or commited to a theater of operations or objective area. The joint deployment community usually consists of the Organization of the Joint Chiefs of Staff, Services, certain Service major commands (including the Service wholesale logistic commands), unified and specified commands (and their Service component commands), transportation operating agencies, Joint Deployment Agency, joint task forces (as applicable), Defense Logistics Agency, and other Defense agencies (e.g., Defense Intelligence Agency) as may be appropriate to a given scenario. Also called **JDC.**

joint deployment system—*(DOD)* A system that consists of personnel, procedures, directives, communications systems, and electronic data processing systems to directly support time-sensitive planning and execution, and to complement peacetime deliberate planning. Also called **JDS.**

joint doctrine—*(DOD)* Fundamental principles that guide the employment of forces of two or more Services of the same nation in coordinated action toward a common objective. It is ratified by all four Services and may be promulgated by the Joint Chiefs of Staff. See also **multi-service doctrine; combined doctrine.**

joint force—*(DOD, IADB)* A general term applied to a force which is composed of significant elements of the Army, the Navy or the Marine Corps, and the Air Force, or two or more of these Services, operating under a single commander authorized to exercise unified command or operational control over joint forces.

joint intelligence—*(DOD, IADB)* Intelligence produced by elements of more than one Service of the same nation.

joint intelligence liaison element—*(DOD)* A liaison element provided by the Central Intelligence Agency in support of a unified command or joint task force.

joint manpower program—*(DOD)* The document which reflects an activity's mission, functions, organization, current and projected manpower needs, and, when applicable, its required mobilization augmentation. A recommended joint manpower program also identifies and justifies any changes proposed by the commander/director of a joint activity for the next five fiscal years. Also called **JMP.**

joint multichannel trunking and switching system—*(DOD)* That composite multichannel trunking and switching system formed from assets of the Services, the Defense Communications System, other available systems, and/or assets controlled by the Joint Chiefs of Staff to provide an operationally responsive, survivable communication system, preferably in a mobile/transportable/recoverable configuration, for the joint force commander in an area of operations.

joint nuclear accident coordinating center—*(DOD)* A combined Defense Nuclear Agency and Department of Energy centralized agency for exchanging and maintaining information concerned with radiological assistance capabilities and coordinating assistance activities, when called upon, in connection with accidents involving radioactive materials.

joint operational intelligence agency—*(DOD, IADB)* An intelligence agency in which the efforts of two or more Services are integrated to furnish that operational intelligence essential to the commander of a joint force and to supplement that available to subordinate forces of the command. The agency may or may not be part of such joint force commander's staff.

joint operations area—*(DOD)* That portion of an area of conflict in which a joint force commander conducts military operations pursuant to an assigned mission and the administration incident to such military operations. Also called **JOA.**

joint operations center—*(DOD, IADB)* A jointly manned facility of a joint force commander's headquarters established for planning, monitoring, and guiding the execution of the commander's decisions.

joint purchase—*(DOD, IADB)* A method of purchase whereby purchases of a particular commodity for two or more departments are made by an activity established, staffed, and financed by them jointly for that purpose. See also **purchase.**

joint rescue coordination center—*(DOD)* See **rescue coordination center.**

joint rescue coordination center—*(IADB)* An installation staffed by supervisory personnel from all participating Services and possessing sufficient facilities to direct and coordinate all available search and rescue facilities within a specified area. See also **search and rescue.**

joint servicing—*(DOD)* That function performed by a jointly staffed and financed activity in support of two or more military Services. See also **servicing.**

joint staff—*(DOD)* 1. The staff of a commander of a unified or specified command, or of a joint task force, which includes members from the several Services comprising the force. These members should be assigned in such a manner as to insure that the commander understands the tactics, techniques, capabilities, needs, and limitations of the component parts of the force. Positions on the staff should be divided so that Service representation and influence generally reflect the Service composition of the force. 2. The staff of the Joint Chiefs of Staff as provided for under the National Security Act of 1947, as amended. See also **Organization of the Joint Chiefs of Staff; staff.**

joint staff—*(NATO, IADB)* A staff formed of two or more of the services of the same country. See also **combined staff; integrated staff; parallel staff.**

joint table of allowances—*(DOD)* A document which authorizes end-items of materiel for units operated jointly by two or more military assistance advisory groups and missions. Also called **JTA**.

joint table of distribution—*(DOD)* A manpower document which identifies the positions and enumerates the spaces that have been approved for each organizational element of a joint activity for a specific fiscal year (authorization year), and those spaces which have been accepted for planning and programming purposes for the four subsequent fiscal years (program years). Also called **JTD**. See also **joint manpower program**.

Joint Tactical Air Reconnaissance/Surveillance Mission Report—*(DOD)* A preliminary report of information from tactical reconnaissance aircrews rendered by designated debriefing personnel immediately after landing and dispatched prior to compilation of the Initial Photo Interpretation Report. It provides a summary of the route conditions, observations, and aircrew actions and identifies sensor products. If available, items of significant interest obtained from initial readout of the sensor record are also included. Also called **MISREP**.

joint target list—*(DOD)* A consolidated list of selected targets considered to have military significance in the joint operations area.

joint task force—*(DOD)* A force composed of assigned or attached elements of the Army, the Navy or the Marine Corps, and the Air Force, or two or more of these Services, which is constituted and so designated by the Secretary of Defense or by the commander of a unified command, a specified command, or an existing joint task force.

joint task force—*(IADB)* A force composed of assigned or attached elements of the Army, Navy and Air Force, or two or more of these Services.

joint zone (air, land, or sea)—*(DOD, IADB)* An area established for the purpose of permitting friendly surface, air, and subsurface forces to operate simultaneously.

join-up—*(NATO)* To form separate aircraft or groups of aircraft into a specific formation. See also **rendezvous**.

judy—*(DOD)* In air intercept, a code meaning, "I have contact and am taking over the intercept."

jumpmaster—*(DOD, IADB)* The assigned airborne-qualified individual who controls parachutists from the time they enter the aircraft until they exit. See also **stick commander (air transport)**.

jump-off line—See **line of departure**.

jump speed—*(DOD, NATO)* The airspeed at which parachute troops can jump with comparative safety from an aircraft.

K

KA–6—See **Intruder.**

KC–97L—See **Stratofreighter.**

KC–135—See **Stratotanker.**

K-day—*(DOD, IADB)* The basic date for the introduction of a convoy system on any particular convoy lane. See also **D-day; M-day.**

K-day—*(NATO)* See **designation of days and hours.**

key—*(NATO)* In cartography, a term sometimes loosely used as a synonym for "legend." See also **blue key; drawing key; legend.**

key facilities list—*(DOD)* A register of selected command installations and industrial facilities of primary importance to the support of military operations or military production programs. It is prepared under the policy direction of the Joint Chiefs of Staff.

key point—*(DOD, NATO, IADB)* A concentrated site or installation, the destruction or capture of which would seriously affect the war effort or the success of operations.

key symbol—*(NATO)* In psychological operations, a simple, suggestive, repetitive element (rhythm, sign, color, etc.) which has an immediate impact on a target audience and which creates a favorable environment for the acceptance of a psychological theme.

key terrain—*(DOD, NATO, IADB)* Any locality, or area, the seizure or retention of which affords a marked advantage to either combatant. See also **key area.**

killed in action—*(DOD, NATO, IADB)* A battle casualty who is killed outright or who dies as a result of wounds or other injuries before reaching a medical treatment facility. See also **died of wounds received in action.**

killing zone—*(DOD)* An area in which a commander plans to force the enemy to concentrate so as to destroy him with conventional weapons or the tactical employment of nuclear weapons.

kill probability—*(DOD, NATO, IADB)* A measure of the probabilty of destroying a target.

kiloton weapon—*(DOD, NATO, IADB)* A nuclear weapon, the yield of which is measured in terms of thousands of tons of trinitrotoluene explosive equivalents, producing yields from 1 to 999 kilotons. See also **megaton weapon; nominal weapon; subkiloton weapon.**

kite—*(DOD, NATO)* In naval mine warfare, a device which when towed, submerges and planes at a predetermined level without sideways displacement.

L

Lance—(DOD) A mobile, storable, liquid propellant, surface-to-surface guided missile, with nuclear and nonnuclear capability; designed to support the Army corps with long-range fires. Designated as XMGM-52.

land arm mode—(DOD, NATO) A mode of operation in which automatic sequence is used to engage and disengage appropriate modes of an aircraft automatic flight control system in order to execute the various flight phases in the terminal area necessary for completing an automatic approach and landing.

land control operations—(DOD, IADB) The employment of ground forces, supported by naval and air forces, as appropriate, to achieve military objectives in vital land areas. Such operations include destruction of opposing ground forces, securing key terrain, protection of vital land lines of communication, and establishment of local military superiority in areas of land operations.

landing aid—(DOD, NATO, IADB) Any illuminating light, radio beacon, radar device, communicating device, or any system of such devices for aiding aircraft in an approach and landing.

landing approach—(DOD, NATO) The continuously changing position of an aircraft in space directed toward effecting a landing on a predetermined area.

landing area—(DOD, NATO, IADB) 1. That part of the objective area within which are conducted the landing operations of an amphibious force. It includes the beach, the approaches to the beach, the transport areas, the fire support areas, the air occupied by close supporting aircraft, and the land included in the advance inland to the initial objective. 2. (**Airborne**) The general area used for landing troops and materiel either by airdrop or air landing. This area includes one or more drop zones or landing strips. 3. Any specially prepared or selected surface of land, water, or deck designated or used for take-off and landing of aircraft. See also **airfield.**

landing attack—(DOD, IADB) An attack against enemy defenses by troops landed from ships, aircraft, boats, or amphibious vehicles. See also **assault.**

landing beach—(DOD, NATO, IADB) That portion of a shoreline usually required for the landing of a battalion landing team. However, it may also be that portion of a shoreline constituting a tactical locality (such as the shore of a bay) over which a force larger or smaller than a battalion landing team may be landed.

landing craft—(DOD, NATO, IADB) A craft employed in amphibious operations, specifically designed for carrying troops and equipment and for beaching, unloading, and retracting. Also used for logistic cargo resupply operations.

landing craft and amphibious vehicle assignment table—(DOD, IADB) A table showing the assignment of personnel and materiel to each landing craft and amphibious vehicle and the assignment of the landing craft and amphibious vehicles to waves for the ship-to-shore movement.

landing craft availability table—(DOD, IADB) A tabulation of the type and number of landing craft that will be available from each ship of the transport group. The table is the basis for the assignment of landing craft to the boat groups for the ship-to-shore movement.

landing diagram—(DOD, NATO, IADB) A graphic means of illustrating the plan for the ship-to-shore movement.

landing force—(DOD, NATO, IADB) A task organization of troop units, aviation and ground, assigned to an amphibious assault. It is the highest troop echelon in the amphibious operation. See also **amphibious force.**

landing group—*(NATO)* A subordinate task organization of the landing force capable of conducting landing operations, under a single tactical command, against a position or group of positions.

landing mat—*(DOD, NATO, IADB)* A prefabricated, portable mat so designed that any number of planks (sections) may be rapidly fastened together to form surfacing for emergency runways, landing beaches, etc.

landing point—*(DOD, NATO)* A point within a landing site where one helicopter or vertical take-off and landing aircraft can land. See also **airfield.**

landing roll—*(DOD, NATO)* The movement of an aircraft from touchdown through deceleration to taxi speed or full stop.

landing schedule—*(DOD, IADB)* In an amphibious operation, a schedule which shows the beach, hour, and priorities of landing of assault units, and which coordinates the movements of landing craft from the transports to the beach in order to execute the scheme of maneuver ashore.

landing ship—*(DOD, NATO, IADB)* An assault ship which is designed for long sea voyages and for rapid unloading over and on to a beach.

landing ship dock—*(NATO, IADB)* A ship designed to transport and launch loaded amphibious craft and/or amphibian vehicles with their crews and embarked personnel and/or equipment and to render limited docking and repair services to small ships and craft.

landing site—*(DOD, NATO)* 1. A site within a landing zone containing one or more landing points. See also **airfield.** 2. In amphibious operations, a continuous segment of coastline over which troops, equipment and supplies can be landed by surface means.

landing threshold—*(DOD, IADB)* The beginning of that portion of a runway usable for landing.

landing vehicle, tracked, engineer, model 1—*(DOD, IADB)* A lightly armored amphibious vehicle designed for minefield and obstacle clearance in amphibious assaults and operations inland. Equipped with line charges for projection in advance of the vehicle and bulldozer-type blade with scarifier teeth. Designated as LVTE-1.

landing zone—*(DOD, NATO)* Any specified zone used for the landing of aircraft. See also **airfield.**

landing zone control—See **pathfinder drop zone control.**

landing zone control party—*(DOD, NATO)* Personnel specially trained and equipped to establish and operate communications devices from the ground for traffic control of aircraft/helicopters for a specific landing zone.

landmark—*(DOD, NATO, IADB)* A feature, either natural or artificial, that can be accurately determined on the ground from a grid reference.

land mine warfare—See **mine warfare.**

land projection operations—See **land, sea, or aerospace projection operations.**

land, sea, or aerospace projection operations—*(DOD)* The employment of land, sea, or air forces, or appropriate combinations thereof, to project United States military power into areas controlled or threatened by enemy forces. Operations may include penetration of such areas by amphibious, airborne, or land-transported means, as well as air combat operations by land-based and/or carrier air.

land search—*(DOD)* The search of terrain by earth-bound personnel.

lane marker—*(DOD, NATO)* In land mine warfare, sign used to mark a minefield lane. Lane markers, at the entrance to and exit from the lane, may be referenced to a landmark or intermediate marker. See also **marker; minefield lane.**

lap—*(DOD, NATO)* In naval mine warfare, that section or strip of an area assigned to a single sweeper or formation of sweepers for a run through the area.

lap course—*(DOD, NATO)* In naval mine warfare, the true course desired to be made good during a run along a lap.

lap track—*(DOD, NATO)* In naval mine warfare, the center line of a lap; ideally, the track to be followed by the sweep or detecting gear.

lap turn—*(DOD, NATO)* In naval mine warfare, the maneuver a minesweeper carries out during the period between the completion of one run and the commencement of the run immediately following.

lap width—*(DOD, NATO)* In naval mine warfare, the swept path of the ship or formation divided by the percentage coverage being swept to.

large-lot storage—*(DOD, IADB)* A quantity of material which will require four or more pallet columns stored to maximum height. Usually accepted as stock stored in carload or greater quantities. See also **storage.**

large-scale map—*(DOD, IADB)* A map having a scale of 1:75,000 or larger. See also **map.**

large ship—*(NATO)* A ship of over 450 feet (or 137 meters) in length. See also **small ship.**

large spread—*(DOD)* A report by an observer or a spotter to the ship to indicate that the distance between the bursts of a salvo is excessive.

laser designator—*(DOD, NATO)* A device that emits a beam of laser energy which is used to mark a specific place or object.

laser guidance unit—*(DOD, NATO)* A device which incorporates a laser seeker to provide guidance commands to the control system of a missile, projectile or bomb.

laser guided weapon—*(DOD, NATO)* A weapon which utilizes a seeker to detect laser energy reflected from a laser marked/designated target and through signal processing provides guidance commands to a control system which guides the weapon to the point from which the laser energy is being reflected.

laser illuminator—*(DOD, NATO)* A device for enhancing the illumination in a zone of action by irradiating with a laser beam.

laser intelligence—*(DOD)* Technical and intelligence information derived from laser systems; a subcategory of electro-optical intelligence. Also called **LASINT.**

laser linescan system—*(DOD, NATO)* An active airborne imagery recording system which uses a laser as the primary source of illumination to scan the ground beneath the flight path, adding successive across-track lines to the record as the vehicle advances. See also **infrared linescan system.**

laser pulse duration—*(DOD, NATO)* The time during which the laser output pulse power remains continuously above half its maximum value.

laser rangefinder—*(DOD, NATO)* A device which uses laser energy for determining the distance from the device to a place or object.

laser seeker—*(DOD, NATO)* A device based on a direction sensitive receiver which detects the energy reflected from a laser designated target and defines the direction of the target relative to the receiver. See also **laser guided weapon.**

laser target designating system—*(DOD, NATO)* A system which is used to direct (aim or point) laser energy at a target. The system consists of the laser designator or laser target marker with its display and control components necessary to acquire the target and direct the beam of laser energy thereon.

laser target marker—See **laser designator.**

laser target marking system—See **laser target designating system.**

laser tracker—*(DOD, NATO)* A device which locks on to the reflected energy from a laser marked/designated target and defines the direction of the target relative to itself.

lashing—*(DOD, NATO)* See **tie down.** See also **restraint of loads.**

lashing point—See **tie down point.**

LASINT—See **laser intelligence.**

late—*(DOD, NATO)* In artillery and naval gunfire support, a report made to the observer or spotter, whenever there is a delay in reporting "shot" by coupling a time in seconds with the report.

lateral gain—*(DOD, NATO)* The amount of new ground covered laterally by successive photographic runs over an area.

lateral route—*(DOD, NATO)* A route generally parallel to the forward edge of the battle area, which crosses, or feeds into, axial routes. See also **route.**

lateral spread—*(DOD)* A technique used to place the mean point of impact of two or more units 100 meters apart on a line perpendicular to the gun-target line.

lateral tell—See **cross tell; track telling.**

late time—See **span of detonation (atomic demolition munition employment).**

latitude band—*(DOD, NATO)* Any latitudinal strip, designated by accepted units of linear or angular measurement, which circumscribes the earth. Also called **latitudinal band.**

lattice—*(DOD, NATO, IADB)* A network of intersecting positional lines printed on a map or chart from which a fix may be obtained.

launch—*(DOD, IADB)* The transition from static repose to dynamic flight of a missile.

launcher—*(DOD, NATO, IADB)* A structural device designed to support and hold a missile in position for firing.

launching site—*(NATO, IADB)* Any site or installation with the capability of launching missiles from surface to air or surface to surface.

launch pad—*(DOD, NATO, IADB)* A concrete or other hard surface area on which a missile launcher is positioned.

launch time—*(DOD, IADB)* The time at which an aircraft or missile is scheduled to be airborne. See also **airborne order.**

launch under attack—*(DOD)* Execution by National Command Authorities of Single Integrated Operational Plan forces subsequent to tactical warning of strategic nuclear attack against the United States and prior to first impact. Also called **LUA.**

law of armed conflict—See **law of war.**

law of war—*(DOD)* That part of international law that regulates the conduct of armed hostilities. It is often termed the **law of armed conflict.** See also **rules of engagement.**

lay—*(DOD, IADB)* 1. Direct or adjust the aim of a weapon. 2. Setting of a weapon for a given range, or for a given direction, or both. 3. To drop one or more aerial bombs or aerial mines onto the surface from an aircraft. 4. To spread a smoke screen on the ground from an aircraft. 5. To calculate or project a course.

6. To lay on: **a.** to execute a bomber strike; **b.** to set up a mission.

laydown bombing—*(DOD, NATO, IADB)* A very low level bombing technique wherein delay fuzes and/or devices are used to allow the attacker to escape the effects of his bomb.

layer depth—*(DOD, IADB)* The depth from the surface of the sea to the point above the first major negative thermocline at which sound velocity is maximum.

layer tint—See **hypsometric tinting.**

laying-up position—*(NATO)* Any suitable position where naval units can berth, camouflage and replenish in preparation for forthcoming operations. See also **waiting position.**

lay reference number—*(DOD, NATO)* In naval mine warfare, a number allocated to an individual mine by the minefield planning authority to provide a simple means of referring to it.

lazy—*(DOD)* In air intercept, a code meaning, "Equipment indicated at standby."

LCC—See **amphibious command ship.**

lead aircraft—*(DOD, IADB)* **1.** The airborne aircraft designated to exercise command of other aircraft within the flight. **2.** An aircraft in the van of two or more aircraft.

lead aircraft—*(NATO)* **1.** An airborne aircraft designated to provide certain command and air control functions. **2.** An aircraft in the van of two or more aircraft.

lead collision course—*(DOD, NATO)* A vector which, if maintained by an interceptor aircraft, will result in collision between the interceptor's fixed armament and the target.

lead pursuit—*(DOD, NATO)* An interceptor vector designed to maintain a course of flight at a predetermined point ahead of a target.

leapfrog—*(DOD, NATO, IADB)* Form of movement in which like supporting elements are moved successively through or by one another along the axis of movement of supported forces.

leaver—*(DOD, NATO)* An independent merchant ship which breaks off from the main convoy. See also **leaver convoy; leaver section.**

leaver convoy—*(DOD, NATO)* A convoy which has broken off from the main convoy and is proceeding to a different destination.

leaver section—*(DOD, NATO)* A group of ships forming part of the main convoy which will subsequently break off to become leavers or a leaver convoy.

left (or right)—*(DOD, NATO, IADB)* **1.** Terms used to establish the relative position of a body of troops. The person using the terms "left" or "right" is assumed to be facing in the direction of the enemy regardless of whether the troops are advancing towards or withdrawing from the enemy. **2.** Correction used in adjusting fire to indicate that a lateral shift of the mean point of impact perpendicular to the reference line or spotting line is desired.

left (right) bank—*(DOD, IADB)* That bank of a stream or river on the left (right) of the observer when he is facing in the direction of flow or downstream.

legend—*(NATO)* An explanation of symbols used on a map, chart, sketch, etc., commonly printed in tabular form at the side of the map, etc.

lens coating—*(NATO)* A thin transparent coating applied to a surface of a lens element.

lens distortion—*(NATO)* Image displacement caused by lens irregularities and aberrations.

level—*(DOD)* In air intercept, a word meaning, "Contact designated is at your angels."

level of effort-oriented items—*(DOD)* Items for which requirements computations are based on such factors as equipment and personnel density and time and rate of use. See also **combination mission/level of effort-oriented items; mission-oriented items.**

level of supply—*(DOD, NATO, IADB)* The quantity of supplies or materiel authorized or directed to be held in anticipation of future demands. See also **operating level of supply; order and shipping time; procurement lead time; requisitioning objective; safety level of supply; stockage objective; strategic reserve.**

LGM–25C—See **Titan II.**

LGM–30—See **Minuteman.**

LHA—See **amphibious assault ship (general purpose).**

liaison—*(DOD, NATO, IADB)* That contact or intercommunication maintained between elements of military forces to insure mutual understanding and unity of purpose and action.

liberated territory—*(DOD, NATO IADB)* Any area, domestic, neutral or friendly, which, having been occupied by an enemy, is retaken by friendly forces.

life cycle—*(DOD)* The total phases through which an item passes from the time it is initially developed until the time it is either consumed in use or disposed of as being excess to all known materiel requirements.

lifeguard submarine—*(DOD, NATO, IADB)* A submarine employed for rescue in an area which cannot be adequately covered by air or surface rescue facilities because of enemy opposition, distance from friendly bases, or other reasons. It is stationed near the objective and sometimes along the route to be flown by the strike aircraft.

life support equipment—*(DOD)* Equipment designed to sustain aircrew members and passengers throughout the flight environment, optimizing their mission effectiveness and affording a means of safe and reliable escape, descent, survival, and recovery in emergency situations.

light artillery—See **field artillery.**

light damage—See **nuclear damage (land warfare).**

lightening—*(DOD, NATO)* The operation (normally carried out at anchor) of transferring crude oil cargo from a large tanker to a smaller tanker, so reducing the draft of the larger tanker to enable it to enter port.

light filter—*(DOD, NATO)* An optical element such as a sheet of glass, gelatine or plastic dyed in a specific manner to absorb selectively light of certain colors.

light line—*(DOD, NATO, IADB)* A designated line forward of which vehicles are required to use black-out lights at night.

limited access route—*(DOD, NATO)* A one way route with one or more restrictions which preclude its use by the full range of military traffic. See also **double flow route; single flow route.**

limited denied war—*(DOD)* Not to be used. No substitute recommended.

limited production type item—*(DOD, IADB)* An item under development, commercially available or available from other Government agencies, for which an urgent operational requirement exists and for which no other existing item is substitutable; which appears to fulfill an approved materiel requirement or other Military Department-approved requirements, and to be promising enough operationally to warrant initiating procurement and/or production for service issue prior to completion of development and/or test or adoption as a standard item.

limited standard item—*(DOD, IADB)* An item of supply determined by standardization action as authorized for procurement only to support in-Service military materiel requirements.

limited war—*(DOD, IADB)* Armed conflict short of general war, exclusive of incidents, involving the overt engagement of the military forces of two or more nations.

limit of fire—*(DOD, NATO, IADB)* 1. The boundary marking off the area on which gunfire can be delivered. 2. Safe angular limits for firing at aerial targets.

line—*(DOD, NATO)* In artillery and naval gunfire support, a spotting, or an observation, used by a spotter or an observer to indicate that a burst(s) occurred on the spotting line.

linear scale—See **graphic scale; scale.**

line astern—See **trail formation.**

line gauge—*(NATO)* A measurement of line width.

line of arrival—See **line of impact.**

line of departure—*(DOD, NATO, IADB)* 1. A line designated to coordinate the departure of attack or scouting elements. Also called **jump-off line.** 2 A suitably marked offshore coordinating line to assist assault craft to land on designated beaches at scheduled times.

line of impact—*(NATO, IADB)* A line tangent to the trajectory at the point of impact or burst.

line of position—*(DOD)* In air intercept, a reference which originates at a target and extents outward at a predetermined angle.

line overlap—See **overlap 1.**

liner—*(DOD)* In air intercept, a code meaning, "Fly at speed giving maximum cruising range."

line-route map—*(DOD, IADB)* A map or overlay for signal communications operations that shows the actual routes and types of construction of wire circuits in the field. It also gives the locations of switchboards and telegraph stations. See also **map.**

line search—*(DOD, NATO)* Reconnaissance along a specific line of communications, such as a road, railway or waterway, to detect fleeting targets and activities in general.

lines of communications—*(DOD, IADB)* All the routes, land, water, and air, which connect an operating military force with a base of operations and along which supplies and military forces move.

lines of communications—*(NATO)* All the land, water, and air routes that connect an operating military force with one or more bases of operations, and along which supplies and reinforcements move.

line weight—See **line gauge.**

link—*(DOD, NATO, IADB)* 1. In communications, a general term used to indicate the existence of communications facilities between two points. 2. A maritime route, other than a coastal or transit route, which links any two or more routes.

link encryption—*(DOD, IADB)* The application of on-line crypto-operation to a link of a communications system so that all information passing over the link is encrypted in its entirety.

link-lift vehicle—*(DOD)* The conveyance, together with its operating personnel, used to satisfy a movement requirement between nodes.

link-route segments—*(DOD)* Route segments that connect nodes wherein link-lift vehicles perform the movement function.

liquid explosive—*(DOD, NATO)* Explosive which is fluid at normal temperatures.

liquid propellant—*(DOD, IADB)* Any liquid combustible fed to the combustion chamber of a rocket engine.

listening watch—*(DOD, IADB)* A continuous receiver watch established for the reception of traffic addressed to, or of interest to, the unit maintaining the watch, with complete log optional.

list of targets—*(DOD, IADB)* A tabulation of confirmed or suspect targets maintained by any echelon for informational and fire support planning purposes. See also **target list**.

litter—*(DOD, IADB)* A basket or frame utilized for the transport of injured persons.

litter patient—*(DOD, IADB)* A patient requiring litter accommodations while in transit.

live exercise—*(NATO)* An exercise using real forces and units.

LKA—See **attack cargo ship**.

load—See **airlift capability**; **airlift requirement**; **allowable load**; **combat load**; **payload** (parts 1 and 4); **standard load**.

load control group—*(DOD, NATO)* Personnel who are concerned with organization and control of loading within the pick-up zone.

loading—*(DOD, NATO, IADB)* The process of putting troops, equipment, and supplies into ships, aircraft, trains, road transport, or other means of conveyance. See also **administrative loading**; **block stowage loading**; **cargo; combat loading**; **commodity loading**; **convoy loading**; **cross loading (personnel)**; **endurance loading**; **horizontal loading**; **preload loading**; **selective loading**; **unit loading**; **vertical loading**.

loading chart (aircraft)—*(DOD, IADB)* Any one of a series of charts carried in an aircraft which shows the proper location for loads to be transported and which pertains to check-lists, balance records, and clearances for weight and balance.

loading plan—*(DOD, NATO, IADB)* All of the individually prepared documents which, taken together, present in detail all instructions for the arrangement of personnel, and the loading of equipment for one or more units or other special grouping of personnel or material moving by highway, water, rail, or air transportation. See also **ocean manifest**.

loading point—*(DOD, NATO)* A point where one aircraft can be loaded or unloaded.

loading site—*(DOD, NATO, IADB)* An area containing a number of loading points.

load spreader—*(DOD, NATO, IADB)* Material used to distribute the weight of a load over a given floor area to avoid exceeding designed stress.

localizer—*(DOD, NATO)* A directional radio beacon which provides to an aircraft an indication of its lateral position relative to a predetermined final approach course. See also **beacon; instrument landing system**.

localizer mode—*(DOD, NATO)* In a flight control system, a control mode in which an aircraft is automatically positioned to, and held at, the center of the localizer course.

local mean time—*(DOD, NATO)* The time interval elapsed since the mean sun's transit of the observer's anti-meridian.

local procurement—*(DOD, IADB)* The process of obtaining personnel, services, supplies, and equipment from local or indigenous sources.

local purchase—*(DOD)* The function of acquiring a decentralized item of supply from sources outside the Department of Defense.

local purchase—*(IADB)* The function of acquiring a decentralized item of supply from sources outside the military establishment.

local wage rate NATO civilian employee— *(NATO)* Civilian employee who does not occupy a NATO international civilian post and who does not enjoy NATO status.

local war—*(DOD)* Not to be used. See **limited war.**

LOCAP—*(DOD)* Low combat air patrol.

location diagram—*(NATO)* On a map or chart, a diagram shown in the margin to indicate the position of the sheet in relation to the surrounding country, or to adjoining sheets of the same or adjacent map series. See **map index.**

lock on—*(DOD, NATO, IADB)* Signifies that a tracking or target-seeking system is continuously and automatically tracking a target in one or more coordinates (e.g., range, bearing, elevation).

lodgment area—See **airhead; beachhead.**

loft bombing—*(DOD, IADB)* A method of bombing in which the delivery plane approaches the target at a very low altitude, makes a definite pullup at a given point, releases the bomb at predetermined point during the pullup, and tosses the bomb onto the target. See also **over-the-shoulder bombing; toss bombing.**

logair—*(DOD)* Long-term contract airlift service within continental United States for the movement of cargo in support of the logistics systems of the Military Services (primarily the Army and Air Force) and Department of Defense agencies. See also **quicktrans.**

logistic assessment—*(DOD, NATO, IADB)* An evaluation of: **a.** The logistic support required to support particular military operations in a theater of operations, country, or area. **b.** The actual and/or potential logistics support available for the conduct of military operations either within the theater, country, or area, or located elsewhere.

logistic assistance—*(NATO, IADB)* A generic term used to denote types of assistance between and within military commands both in peace and war. See also **integrated logistic support; mutual aid; reallocation of resources.**

logistic estimate of the situation—*(DOD, IADB)* An appraisal resulting from an orderly examination of the logistic factors influencing contemplated courses of action to provide conclusions concerning the degree and manner of that influence. See also **estimate of the situation.**

logistic implications test—*(DOD, IADB)* An analysis of the major logistic aspects of a joint strategic war plan and the consideration of the logistic implications resultant therefrom as they may limit the acceptability of the plan. The logistic analysis and consideration are conducted concurrently with the development of the strategic plan. The objective is to establish whether the logistic requirements generated by the plan are in balance with availabilities, and to set forth those logistic implications that should be weighed by the Joint Chiefs of Staff in their consideration of the plan. See also **feasibility test.**

logistic routes—See **lines of communication.**

logistics—*(DOD, NATO, IADB)* The science of planning and carrying out the movement and maintenance of forces. In its most comprehensive sense, those aspects of military operations which deal with: **a.** design and development, acquisition, storage, movement, distribution, maintenance, evacuation, and disposition of materiel; **b.** movement, evacuation, and hospitalization of personnel; **c.** acquisition or construction, maintenance, operation, and disposition of facilities; and **d.** acquisition or furnishing of services.

logistics over the shore operations—*(DOD, IADB)* The loading and unloading of ships without the benefit of fixed port facilities, in friendly or nondefended territory, and, in time of war, during phases of theater development in which there is no opposition by the enemy.

logistics sourcing—*(DOD)* The identification of the origin and determination of the availability of the time-phased force and deployment data nonunit logistics requirements.

logistic support (medical)—*(DOD, IADB)* Medical care, treatment, hospitalization, evacuation, furnishing of medical services, supplies, materiel, and adjuncts thereto.

long-range bomber aircraft—*(DOD)* A bomber designed for a tactical operating radius over 2,500 nautical miles at design gross weight and design bomb load.

long-range transport aircraft—See **transport aircraft.**

look—*(DOD, NATO)* In mine warfare, a period during which a mine circuit is receptive of an influence.

loran—*(DOD, NATO, IADB)* A long-range radio navigation position fixing system using the time difference of reception of pulse type transmissions from two or more fixed stations. This term is derived from the words *lo*ng-*ra*nge electronic *n*avigation.

lost—*(DOD, NATO)* In artillery and naval gunfire support, a spotting, or an observation used by a spotter or an observer to indicate that rounds fired by a gun or mortar were not observed.

lot—*(DOD, IADB)* Specifically, a quantity of material all of which was manufactured under identical conditions and assigned an identifying lot number.

low—*(DOD, IADB)* A height between five hundred and two thousand feet.

low airburst—*(DOD, NATO, IADB)* The fallout safe height of burst for a nuclear weapon which maximizes damage to or casualties on surface targets. See also **types of burst.**

low-altitude bombing—*(DOD, IADB)* Horizontal bombing with the height of release between 900 and 8,000 feet.

low altitude bombing system mode—*(DOD, NATO)* In a flight control system, a control mode in which the low altitude bombing maneuver of an aircraft is controlled automatically.

low angle—*(DOD, NATO)* In artillery and naval gunfire support, an order or request to obtain low-angle fire.

low angle fire—*(DOD, NATO, IADB)* Fire delivered at angles of elevation below the elevation that corresponds to the maximum range of the gun and ammunition concerned.

low angle loft bombing—*(DOD, NATO, IADB)* Type of loft bombing of free fall bombs wherein weapon release occurs at an angle less than 35 degrees above the horizontal. See also **loft bombing.**

low dollar value item—*(DOD)* An item which normally requires considerably less management effort than those in the other management intensity groupings.

low level flight—See **terrain flight.**

low level transit route—*(DOD, NATO)* A temporary corridor of defined dimensions which facilitates the low level passage of friendly aircraft through friendly air defenses and controlled or restricted airspace.

low oblique—See **oblique air photograph.**

low velocity drop—*(DOD, NATO, IADB)* A drop procedure in which the drop velocity does not exceed 30 feet per second.

low visibility operations—*(DOD)* Sensitive operations wherein the political/military restrictions inherent in covert and clandestine operations are either not necessary or not feasible; actions are taken as required to limit exposure of those involved and/or their activities.

Execution of these operations is undertaken with the knowledge that the action and/or sponsorship of the operation may preclude plausible denial by the initiating power.

LPA—See attack transport.

LPD—See amphibious transport dock.

LSD—See dock landing ship.

LST—See tank landing ship.

LVTE–1—See landing vehicle, tracked, engineer, model 1.

M

M-42—See Duster (antiaircraft weapon).

M48A3—See tank, combat, full-tracked, 90–mm gun.

M-60—See tank, combat, full-tracked, 105–mm gun.

M88A1—See recovery vehicle.

M548—See cargo carrier.

Mace—*(DOD, IADB)* An improved version of the MGM–1C Matador, differing primarily in its improved guidance system, longer-range, low-level attack capability and higher yield warhead. The MGM–13A is guided by a self-contained radar guidance system. The CGM–13B is guided by an inertial guidance system. Designated as **MGM–13.**

mach front—See mach stem.

mach hold mode—*(DOD, NATO)* In a flight control system, a control mode in which a desired flight (flying) speed of an aircraft expressed as a mach number is maintained automatically.

machmeter—*(DOD, NATO)* An instrument which displays the mach number of the aircraft derived from inputs of pitot and static pressures.

mach no/yes—*(DOD)* In air intercept, a code meaning, "I have reached maximum speed and am not/am closing my target."

mach number—*(DOD, IADB)* The ratio of the velocity of a body to that of sound in the surrounding medium.

mach number indicator—See machmeter.

mach stem—*(DOD, NATO)* The shock front formed by the fusion of the incident and reflected shock fronts from an explosion. The term is generally used with reference to a blast wave, propagated in the air, reflected at the surface of the earth. In the ideal case, the mach stem is perpendicular to the reflecting surface and slightly convex (forward). Also called **mach front.**

mach trim compensator—*(DOD, NATO)* In a flight control system, an automatic control sub-system which provides pitch trim of an aircraft as a function of mach number.

mach wave—See mach stem.

magnetic bearing—See bearing.

magnetic circuit—See magnetic mine.

magnetic compass—*(DOD, NATO, IADB)* An instrument containing a freely suspended magnetic element which displays the direction of the horizontal component of the earth's magnetic field at the point of observation.

magnetic declination—*(DOD, NATO, IADB)* The angle between the magnetic and geographical meridians at any place, expressed in degrees east or west to indicate the direction of magnetic north from true north. In nautical and aeronautical navigation, the term magnetic variation is used instead of magnetic declination and the angle is termed variation of the compass or magnetic variation. Magnetic declination is not otherwise synonymous with magnetic variation which refers to regular or irregular change with time of the magnetic declination, dip, or intensity. See also **magnetic variation.**

magnetic equator—*(DOD, NATO)* A line drawn on a map or chart connecting all points at which the magnetic inclination (dip) is zero for a specified epoch. Also called "**aclinic line.**"

magnetic mine—*(DOD, NATO)* A mine that responds to the magnetic field of a target.

magnetic minehunting—*(DOD)* The process of using magnetic detectors to determine the presence of mines or minelike objects.

magnetic minehunting—*(NATO)* The process of using magnetic detectors to determine the presence of mines or minelike objects which may be either on or protruding from the seabed, or buried.

magnetic north—*(DOD, NATO, IADB)* The direction indicated by the north-seeking pole of a freely suspended magnetic needle, influenced only the earth's magnetic field.

magnetic tape—*(DOD, IADB)* A tape or ribbon of any material impregnated or coated with magnetic or other material on which information may be placed in the form of magnetically polarized spots.

magnetic variation—*(DOD, NATO, IADB)* The horizontal angle at a place between the true north and magnetic north measured in degrees and minutes east or west according to whether magnetic north lies east or west of true north. See also **magnetic declination.**

main airfield—*(DOD, NATO, IADB)* An airfield planned for permanent occupation in peacetime, at a location suitable for wartime utilization, and with operational facilities of a standard adequate to develop full use of its war combat potential. See also **alternative airfield; departure airfield; redeployment airfield.**

main armament—*(DOD)* The request of the observer or spotter to obtain fire from the largest guns installed on the fire support ship.

main attack—*(DOD, NATO, IADB)* The principal attack or effort into which the commander throws the full weight of the offensive power at his disposal. An attack directed against the chief objective of the campaign or battle.

main battle tank—See **tank, main battle.**

main convoy—*(DOD, NATO)* The convoy as a whole which sails from the convoy assembly port/anchorage to its destination. It may be supplemented by joiners or joiner convoys, and leavers or leaver convoys may break off.

main detonating line—*(DOD, NATO)* In demolition, a line of detonating cord used to transmit the detonation wave to two or more branches.

mainguard—*(NATO, IADB)* Element of an advanced guard. See also **advanced guard.**

main line of resistance—*(DOD, IADB)* A line at the forward edge of the battle position, designated for the purpose of coordinating the fire of all units and supporting weapons, including air and naval gunfire. It defines the forward limits of a series of mutually supporting defensive areas, but it does not include the areas occupied or used by covering or screening forces.

main road—*(DOD, IADB)* A road capable of serving as the principal ground line of communication to an area or locality. Usually it is wide enough and suitable for two-way, all-weather traffic at high speeds.

main supply route—*(DOD, NATO, IADB)* The route or routes designated within an area of operations upon which the bulk of traffic flows in support of military operations.

maintenance—*(NATO)* 1. All action taken to retain materiel in or to restore it to a specified condition. It includes: inspection, testing, servicing, classification as to serviceability, repair, rebuilding, and reclamation. 2. All supply and repair action taken to keep a force in condition to carry out its mission. 3. The routine recurring work required to keep a facility (plant, building, structure, ground facility, utility system, or other real property) in such condition that it may be continuously utilized, at its original or designed capacity and efficiency, for its intended purpose.

maintenance and operations support set— *(DOD)* A US Air Force grouping of reusable lightweight, air transportable shelters designed to provide deployable maintenance and operations facilities to support a specific weapon system, i.e., F-4, F-15, A-7, C-130. The expandable shelters are configured to allow rapid installation of unit equipment, tools, and other organic equipment for such functions as command post, life support, inertial navigation, and fire control. Units deploying with these sets can conduct sustained operations at any location which possesses the necessary base operating/housekeeping facilities.

maintenance area— *(DOD, IADB)* A general locality in which are grouped a number of maintenance activities for the purpose of retaining or restoring materiel to a serviceable condition.

maintenance engineering— *(DOD, IADB)* The application of techniques, engineering skills, and effort, organized to insure that the design and development of weapon systems and equipment provide adequately for their effective and economical maintenance.

maintenance (materiel) *(DOD, IADB)* 1. All action taken to retain materiel in a serviceable condition or to restore it to serviceability. It includes inspection, testing, servicing, classification as to serviceability, repair, rebuilding, and reclamation. 2. All supply and repair action taken to keep a force in condition to carry out its mission. 3. The routine recurring work required to keep a facility (plant, building, structure, ground facility, utility system, or other real property) in such condition that it may be continuously utilized, at its original or designed capacity and efficiency, for its intended purpose.

maintenance status— *(DOD, IADB)* 1. A nonoperating condition, deliberately imposed, with adequate personnel to maintain and preserve installations, materiel, and facilities in such a condition that they may be readily restored to operable condition in a minimum time by the assignment of additional personnel and without extensive repair or overhaul. 2. That condition of materiel which is in fact, or is administratively classified as, unserviceable, pending completion of required servicing or repairs.

major disaster—See **domestic emergencies.**

major fleet— *(DOD, IADB)* A principal, permanent subdivision of the operating forces of the Navy with certain supporting shore activities. Presently there are two such fleets: the Pacific Fleet and the Atlantic Fleet. See also **fleet.**

Major NATO Commanders— *(NATO)* Major NATO Commanders are Supreme Allied Commander Atlantic, Supreme Allied Commander Europe and Allied Commander-in-Chief Channel. See also **commander(s); Major Subordinate Commanders; Principal Subordinate Commanders; Subordinate Area Commanders.**

major nuclear power— *(DOD, NATO, IADB)* Any nation that possesses a nuclear striking force capable of posing a serious threat to every other nation.

major port— *(DOD, NATO, IADB)* Any port with two or more berths and facilities and equipment capable of discharging 100,000 tons of cargo per month from ocean-going ships. Such ports will be designated as probable nuclear targets. See also **port.**

Major Subordinate Commanders— *(NATO)* The designation assigned to NATO commanders operationally responsible to Supreme Allied Commander Europe and Supreme Allied Commander Atlantic for an allocated geographical area or function. See also **Major NATO Commanders; Principal Subordinate Commanders; Subordinate Area Commanders.**

major water terminal— *(DOD, NATO, IADB)* A water terminal with facilities for berthing numerous ships simultaneously at wharves and/or working anchorages, located within sheltered coastal waters adjacent to rail, highway, air and/or inland water transportation nets. It covers a relatively large area, and its scope of operation is such that it is designated as a probable nuclear target. See also **water terminal.**

major weapon system—*(DOD)* One of a limited number of systems or subsystems which, for reasons of military urgency, criticality, or resource requirements, is determined by the Department of Defense as being vital to the national interest.

make safe—*(DOD)* One or more actions necessary to prevent or interrupt complete function of the system (traditionally synonymous with "dearm," "disarm," and "disable"). Among the necessary actions are: (1) install (safety devices such as pins or locks); (2) disconnect (hoses, linkages, batteries); (3) bleed (accumulators, reservoirs); (4) remove (explosive devices such as initiators, fuzes, detonators); (5) intervene (as in welding, lockwiring).

management—*(DOD, IADB)* A process of establishing and attaining objectives to carry out responsibilities. Management consists of those continuing actions of planning, organizing, directing, coordinating, controlling, and evaluating the use of men, money, materials, and facilities to accomplish missions and tasks. Management is inherent in command, but it does not include as extensive authority and responsibility as command.

management and control system (mobility)—*(DOD)* Those elements of organizations and/or activities which are part of, or are closely related to, the mobility system, and which authorize requirements to be moved, to obtain and allocate lift resources, or to direct the operation of linklift vehicles.

maneuver—*(IADB)* 1. A movement to place ships, troops, materiel, or fire in a better location with respect to the enemy. 2. A tactical exercise carried out at sea, in the air, on the ground, or on a map in imitation of war. 3. The operation of a ship, aircraft, or vehicle to cause it to perform desired movements. See

also **command post exercise; exercise; field exercise.**

maneuver—*(DOD, NATO)* 1. A movement to place ships or aircraft in a position of advantage over the enemy. 2. A tactical exercise carried out at sea, in the air, on the ground, or on a map in imitation of war. 3. The operation of a ship, aircraft, or vehicle, to cause it to perform desired movements. 4. Employment of forces on the battlefield through movement in combination with fire, or fire potential, to achieve a position of advantage in respect to the enemy in order to accomplish the mission.

maneuverable reentry vehicle—*(DOD)* A reentry vehicle capable of performing preplanned flight maneuvers during the reentry phase. See also **multiple independently targetable reentry vehicle; multiple reentry vehicle; reentry vehicle.**

maneuvering area—*(DOD, IADB)* That part of an airfield used for takeoffs, landings, and associated maneuvers. See also **aircraft marshalling area.**

maneuvering area—*(NATO)* That part of an airfield to be used for the take-off and landing of aircraft and for the surface movement of aircraft associated with take-off and landing, excluding aprons. See also **aircraft marshalling area.**

manifest—*(DOD, IADB)* A document specifying in detail the passengers or items carried for a specific destination.

manipulative deception—See **electronic warfare.**

manipulative electronic deception (MED)—See **electronic warfare.**

man portable—*(DOD, NATO)* Capable of being carried by one man. Specifically, the term may be used to qualify: 1. Items designed to be carried as an integral part of individual, crew served or team equipment of the dis-

mounted soldier in conjunction with his assigned duties. Upper weight limit: approximately 14 kilograms (31 pounds.) 2. In land
warfare, equipment which can be carried by
one man over long distance without serious
degradation of the performance of his normal
duties.

manpower—See **manpower requirements; manpower resources.**

manpower management—*(DOD, NATO)* The
means of manpower control to ensure the
most efficient and economical use of available
manpower.

manpower management survey—*(DOD, NATO)*
Systematic evaluation of a functional area,
utilizing expert knowledge, manpower scaling
guides, experience and other practical considerations in determining the validity and managerial efficiency of the function's present or
proposed manpower establishment.

manpower requirements—*(DOD)* Human resources needed to accomplish specified work
loads of organizations.

manpower resources—*(DOD)* Human resources
available to the Services which can be applied
against manpower requirements.

manpower scaling guide—*(NATO)* Manpower
management standards or guide lines which
express a manpower requirement as a variable dependant upon workload encountered.

man space—*(DOD, IADB)* The space and weight
factor used to determine the combat capacity
of vehicles, craft, and transport aircraft, based
on the requirements of one person with individual equipment. The person is assumed to
weigh between 222–250 pounds and to occupy
13.5 cubic feet of space. See also **boat space.**

man transportable—*(DOD)* Items which are
usually transported on wheeled, tracked, or
air vehicles, but have integral provisions to
allow periodic handling by one or more individuals for limited distances (100–500 meters).

Upper weight limit: approximately 65 pounds
per individual.

many (raid size)—*(DOD)* In air intercept usage,
8 or more aircraft. See also **few (raid size).**

map—*(DOD, NATO, IADB)* A graphic representation, usually on a plane surface, and at an
established scale, of natural or artificial features on the surface of a part or the whole of
the earth or other planetary body. The features are positioned relative to a coordinate
reference system. See also **administrative
map; battle map; chart index; chart series;
chart sheet; controlled map; general map;
large-scale map; line route map; map chart;
map index; map series; map sheet; medium-
scale map; operation map; planimetric map;
situation map; small-scale map; strategic
map; tactical map; topographic map; traffic
circulation map; weather map.**

map chart—*(DOD, IADB)* A representation of a
land-sea area, using the characteristics of a
map to represent the land area and the characteristics of a chart to represent the sea
area, with such special characteristics as to
make the map-chart most useful in military
operations, particularly amphibious operations. See also **map.**

map convergence—*(DOD, NATO)* The angle at
which one meridian is inclined to another on
a map or chart. See also **convergence.**

map exercise—*(DOD, IADB)* An exercise in
which a series of military situations is stated
and solved on a map.

map index—*(DOD, NATO, IADB)* Graphic key
primarily designed to give the relationship between sheets of a series, their coverage, availability, and further information on the series.
See also **map.**

mapping camera—See **air cartographic camera.**

map reference—*(DOD, NATO, IADB)* A means
of identifying a point on the surface of the

earth by relating it to information appearing on a map, generally the graticule or grid.

map reference code—*(DOD, NATO, IADB)* A code used primarily for encoding grid coordinates and other information pertaining to maps. This code may be used for other purposes where the encryption of numerals is required.

map series—*(DOD, NATO, IADB)* A group of maps or charts usually having the same scale and cartographic specifications, and with each sheet appropriately identified by producing agency as belonging to the same series.

map sheet—*(DOD, NATO, IADB)* An individual map or chart either complete in itself or part of a series. See also **map.**

margin—*(DOD, NATO)* In cartography, the area of a map or chart lying outside the border.

marginal data—*(DOD, NATO)* All explanatory information given in the margin of a map or chart which clarifies, defines, illustrates, and/or supplements the graphic portion of the sheet.

marginal information—See **marginal data.**

marginal weather—*(DOD, IADB)* Weather which is sufficiently adverse to a military operation so as to require the imposition of procedural limitations. See also **adverse weather.**

Marine air command and control system—*(DOD)* A US Marine Corps tactical air command and control system which provides the tactical air commander with the means to command, coordinate, and control all air operations within an assigned sector and to coordinate air operations with other Services. It is composed of command and control agencies with communications-electronics equipment that incorporates a capability from manual through semiautomatic control.

Marine Air Control Squadron—*(DOD, IADB)* The component of the Marine Air Control

Group which provides and operates ground facilities for the detection and interception of hostile aircraft and for the the navigational direction of friendly aircraft in the conduct of support missions.

Marine Air-Ground Task Force—*(DOD)* A Marine Air-Ground Task Force is a task organization of Marine forces (Division, Aircraft Wing and Service Support Groups) under a single command and structured to accomplish a specific mission. The Marine Air-Ground Task Force components will normally include command, ground combat, aviation combat, and combat service support elements (including Navy Support Elements). Three types of Marine Air-Ground Task Forces which can be task organized are the Marine Amphibious Unit, Marine Amphibious Brigade, Marine Amphibious Force. Also called **MAGTF.**

Marine Air Support Squadron—*(DOD, IADB)* The component of the Marine Air Control Group which provides and operates facilities for the control of support aircraft operating in direct support of ground forces.

Marine Amphibious Brigade—*(DOD)* A Marine Amphibious Brigade is a task organization which is normally built around a regimental landing team, a provisional Marine aircraft group, and a logistics support group. It is capable of conducting amphibious assault operations of a limited scope. During potential crisis situations, a Marine Amphibious Brigade may be forward deployed afloat for an extended period in order to provide an immediate combat response. Also called **MAB.**

Marine Amphibious Force—*(DOD)* The Marine Amphibious Force, the largest of the Marine air-ground task forces, is normally built around a division/wing team, but can include several divisions and aircraft wings, together with an appropriate combat service support organization. The Marine Amphibious Force is capable of conducting a wide range of amphibious assault operations and sustained operations ashore. It can be tailored for a wide variety of combat missions in any geographic environment. Also called **MAF.**

Marine Amphibious Unit—*(DOD)* The Marine Amphibious Unit is a task organization which is normally built around a battalion landing team, composite squadron, and logistic support unit. It fulfills routine forward afloat deployment requirements, provides an immediate reaction capability for crisis situations, and is capable of relatively limited combat operations. Also called **MAU.**

Marine base—*(DOD)* A base for support of Marine ground forces, consisting of activities or facilities for which the Marine Corps has operating responsibilities, together with interior lines of communication and the minimum surrounding area necessary for local security. (Normally, not greater than an area of 20 square miles.) See also **base complex.**

Marine division/wing team—*(DOD, IADB)* A Marine Corps air-ground team consisting of one division and one aircraft wing, together with their normal reinforcements.

marine environment—*(DOD)* The oceans, seas, bays, estuaries, and other major water bodies, including their surface interface and interaction with the atmosphere and with the land seaward of the mean high water mark.

maritime area—*(NATO, IADB)* A maritime theater of operations can be divided for the purposes of decentralization of command into maritime areas and sub-areas, e.g., Atlantic theater, which is divided into maritime area and sub-area commands.

maritime control area—*(DOD, IADB)* An area generally similar to a defensive sea area in purpose except that it may be established any place on the high seas. Maritime control areas are normally established only in time of war. See also **defensive sea area.**

maritime operation—*(NATO, IADB)* An action performed by forces on, under, or over the sea

to gain or exploit control of the sea or to deny its use to the enemy.

maritime search and rescue region—*(DOD)* The waters subject to the jurisdiction of the United States; the territories and possessions of the United States (except Canal Zone and the inland area of Alaska) and designated areas of the high seas. See also **search and rescue region.**

mark—*(DOD, NATO)* 1. In artillery and naval gunfire support: **a.** a call for fire on a specified location to orient the observer/spotter or to indicate targets; **b.** a report made by the observer or spotter in firing illumination shells to indicate the instant of optimum light on the target. 2. In close air support and air interdiction, an air control agency's term utilized to indicate the point of weapon release. It is usually preceded by the word "standby" as a preparatory command.

marker—*(DOD, NATO, IADB)* 1. A visual or electronic aid used to mark a designated point. 2. In land mine warfare: See **gap marker; intermediate marker; lane marker; row marker; strip marker.** 3. In naval operations during a period of tension, a maritime unit which has an immediate offensive or obstructive capability. See also **beacon; shadower.**

marker ship—*(DOD, NATO, IADB)* In an amphibious operation, a ship which takes accurate station on a designated control point. It may fly identifying flags by day and show lights to seaward by night.

marking error—*(DOD, NATO)* In naval mine warfare, the distance and bearing of a marker from a target.

marking fire—*(DOD, NATO)* Fire placed on a target for the purpose of identification.

marking panel—*(DOD, NATO, IADB)* A sheet of material displayed for visual communication usually between friendly units. See also **panel code.**

marking team—*(NATO, IADB)* Personnel landed in the landing area with the task of establishing navigational aids. See also **pathfinder aircraft; pathfinders.**

mark mark—*(DOD)* Command from ground controller for aircraft to release bombs; may indicate electronic ground-controlled release or voice command to aircrew.

married failure—*(DOD, NATO)* In naval mine warfare, a moored mine lying on the seabed connected to its sinker from which it has failed to release owing to defective mechanism.

marshalling—*(DOD, NATO, IADB)* 1. The process by which units participating in an amphibious or airborne operation, group together or assemble when feasible or move to temporary camps in the vicinity of embarkation points, complete preparations for combat or prepare for loading. 2. The process of assembling, holding, and organizing supplies and/or equipment, especially vehicles of transportation, for onward movement. See also **stage; staging area.**

masking—*(DOD, NATO)* In electronic warfare, the use of additional transmitters to hide a particular electromagnetic radiation as to location of source and/or purpose of the radiation.

mass—*(DOD, NATO, IADB)* 1. The concentration of combat power. 2. The military formation in which units are spaced at less than the normal distances and intervals.

mass casualties—*(NATO)* Any large numbers of casualties produced in a relatively short period of time which far exceed local logistical support capabilities.

massed fire—*(DOD, IADB)* 1. The fire of the batteries of two or more ships directed against a single target. 2. Fire from a number of weapons directed at a single point or small area. See also **concentrated fire.**

master film—*(DOD, NATO)* The earliest generation of imagery (negative or positive) from which subsequent copies are produced.

master force list—*(DOD)* A file which contains the current status of each requirement for a given operation plan. The master force list is made available for file transfer service (FTS) transfer to other Worldwide Military Command and Control System activities from a file produced from the joint deployment system data base. Also called **MFL.**

master plot—*(DOD, NATO)* A portion of a map or overlay on which are drawn the outlines of the areas covered by an air photographic sortie. Latitude and longitude, map, and sortie information are shown. See also **sortie plot.**

materials handling—*(DOD, NATO, IADB)* The movement of materials (raw materials, scrap, semi-finished, and finished) to, through, and from productive processes; in warehouses and storage; and in receiving and shipping areas.

materials handling equipment—*(DOD)* Mechanical devices for handling of supplies with greater ease and economy.

materiel—*(DOD)* All items (including ships, tanks, self-propelled weapons, aircraft, etc., and related spares, repair parts, and support equipment, but excluding real property, installations, and utilities) necessary to equip, operate, maintain, and support military activities without distinction as to its application for administrative or combat purposes. See also **equipment; personal property.**

materiel cognizance—*(DOD, IADB)* Denotes responsibility for exercising supply management over items or categories of materiel.

materiel control—See **inventory control.**

materiel inventory objective—*(DOD)* The quantity of an item required to be on hand and on order on M-day in order to equip, provide a materiel pipeline, and sustain the approved

US force structure (active and reserve) and those Allied forces designated for US materiel support, through the period prescribed for war materiel planning purposes. It is the quantity by which the war materiel requirement exceeds the war materiel procurement capability and the war materiel requirement adjustment. It includes the M-day force materiel requirement and the war reserve materiel requirement.

materiel management—See **inventory control.**

materiel pipeline—*(DOD, IADB)* The quantity of an item required in the worldwide supply system to maintain an uninterrupted replacement flow.

materiel readiness—*(DOD, IADB)* The availability of materiel required by a military organization to support its wartime activities or contingencies, disaster relief (flood, earthquake, etc.), or other emergencies.

materiel release confirmation—*(DOD)* A notification from a shipping/storage activity advising the originator of a materiel release order of the positive action taken on the order. It will also be used with appropriate shipment status document identifier codes as a reply to a followup initiated by the inventory control point.

materiel release order—*(DOD)* An order issued by an accountable supply system manager (usually an inventory control point or accountable depot/stock point) directing a non-accountable activity (usually a storage site or materiel drop point) within the same supply distribution complex to release and ship materiel.

materiel requirements—*(DOD, IADB)* Those quantities of items of equipment and supplies necessary to equip, provide a materiel pipeline, and sustain a service, formation, organization, or unit in the fulfillment of its purposes or tasks during a specified period.

Maverick—*(DOD)* An air-to-surface missile with launch and leave capability. It is designed for use against stationary or moving small, hard targets such as tanks, armored vehicles, and field fortifications. Designated as AGM-65.

maximum aircraft arresting hook load—*(DOD)* The maximum load experienced by an aircraft arresting hook assembly during an arrestment.

maximum effective range—*(DOD, NATO)* The maximum distance at which a weapon may be expected to be accurate and achieve the desired result.

maximum effective range—*(IADB)* The maximum distance at which a weapon may be expected to deliver its destructive charge with the accuracy specified to inflict prescribed damage.

maximum landing weight—*(DOD, NATO, IADB)* The maximum gross weight due to design or operational limitations at which an aircraft is permitted to land.

maximum operating depth—*(DOD, NATO)* The depth which a submarine is not to exceed during operations. This depth is determined by the submarine's national naval authority. See also **test depth.**

maximum ordinate—*(DOD, NATO, IADB)* In artillery and naval gunfire support: **a.** the highest point along the trajectory of a projectile; **b.** the difference in altitude (vertical interval) between the origin and the summit of the trajectory of a projectile.

maximum permissible concentration—See **radioactivity concentration guide.**

maximum permissible dose—*(DOD, NATO, IADB)* That radiation dose which a military commander or other appropriate authority may prescribe as the limiting cumulative radiation dose to be received over a specific period of time by members of his command,

221

consistent with current operational military considerations.

maximum range—*(DOD, NATO, IADB)* The greatest distance a weapon can fire without consideration of dispersion.

maximum sustained speed (transport vehicles)—*(DOD, NATO, IADB)* The highest speed at which a vehicle, with its rated payload, can be driven for an extended period on a level first-class highway without sustaining damage.

maximum take-off weight—*(DOD, NATO, IADB)* The maximum gross weight due to design or operational limitations at which an aircraft is permitted to take off.

mayday—*(DOD, IADB)* Distress call.

M-day—*(DOD, IADB)* The term used to designate the day on which mobilization is to begin. See also **D-day; K-day.**

M-day—See **designation of days and hours.**

M-day force materiel requirement—*(DOD)* The quantity of an item required to be on hand and on order (on M-day minus one day) to equip and provide a materiel pipeline for the approved peacetime US force structure, both active and reserve.

meaconing—*(DOD, NATO, IADB)* A system of receiving radio beacon signals and rebroadcasting them on the same frequency to confuse navigation. The meaconing stations cause inaccurate bearings to be obtained by aircraft or ground stations. See also **beacon.**

mean line of advance—*(DOD)* In naval usage, the direction expected to be made good over a sustained period.

mean point of burst—See **mean point of impact.**

mean point of impact—*(DOD, NATO, IADB)* The point whose coordinates are the arithmetic means of the coordinates of the separate points of impact/burst of a finite number of projectiles fired or released at the same aiming point under a given set of conditions.

mean sea level—*(DOD, IADB)* The average height of the surface of the sea for all stages of the tide, used as a reference for elevations.

mean sea level—*(NATO)* The average sea level for a particular geographical location, obtained from numerous observations, at regular intervals, over a long period of time.

means of transport—See **mode of transport.**

measurement and signature intelligence—*(DOD)* Scientific and technical intelligence information obtained by quantitative and qualitative analysis of data (metric, angle, spatial, wavelength, time dependence, modulation, plasma, and hydromagnetic) derived from specific technical sensors for the purpose of identifying any distinctive features associated with the source, emitter, or sender and to facilitate subsequent identification and/or measurement of the same. Also called **MASINT.**

measuring magnifier—*(NATO)* A magnifying instrument incorporating a graticule for measuring small distances.

mechanical sweep—*(DOD, NATO)* In naval mine warfare, any sweep used with the object of physically contacting the mine or its appendages.

median incapacitating dose—*(DOD, NATO)* The amount or quantity of chemical agent which when introduced into the body will incapacitate 50 percent of exposed, unprotected personnel.

median lethal dose—*(DOD, NATO, IADB)* 1. (**Nuclear**) The amount of radiation over the whole body which would be fatal to 50 percent of the exposed personnel in a given period of time. 2. (**Chemical**) The dose of chemical agent that would kill 50 percent of exposed, unprotected and untreated personnel. It is expressed in milligram minutes per cubic meter.

medical evacuees—*(DOD)* Personnel who are wounded, injured, or ill and must be moved to or between medical facilities.

medical intelligence—*(DOD)* That category of intelligence resulting from collection, evaluation, analysis, and interpretation of foreign medical, bio-scientific, and environmental information which is of interest to strategic planning and to military medical planning and operations for the conservation of the fighting strength of friendly forces and the formation of assessments of foreign medical capabilities in both military and civilian sectors.

medical officer—*(DOD, NATO)* Physician with officer rank.

medical treatment facility—*(DOD, IADB)* A facility established for the purpose of furnishing medical and/or dental care to eligible individuals.

medium—*(DOD)* As used in air intercept, a height between 2,000 and 25,000 feet.

medium-altitude bombing—*(DOD, IADB)* Horizontal bombing with the height of release between 8,000 and 15,000 feet.

medium-angle loft bombing—*(DOD, IADB)* Type of loft bombing wherein weapon release occurs at an angle between 35 and 75 degrees above the horizontal.

medium artillery—See **field artillery**.

medium atomic demolition munition—*(DOD, IADB)* A low-yield, team-portable, atomic demolition munition which can be detonated either by remote control or a timer device.

medium-lot storage—*(DOD, IADB)* Generally defined as a quantity of material which will require one to three pallet stacks, stored to

maximum height. Thus, the term refers to relatively small lots as distinguished from definitely large or small lots. See also **storage**.

medium-range ballistic missile—*(DOD, IADB)* A ballistic missile with a range capability from about 600 to 1,500 nautical miles.

medium-range bomber aircraft—*(DOD)* A bomber designed for a tactical operating radius of under 1,000 nautical miles at design gross weight and design bomb load.

medium-range transport aircraft—See **transport aircraft**.

medium-scale map—*(DOD, IADB)* A map having a scale larger than 1:600,000 and smaller than 1:75,000. See also **map**.

meeting engagement—*(DOD, NATO)* A combat action that occurs when a moving force, incompletely deployed for battle, engages an enemy at an unexpected time and place.

megaton weapon—*(DOD, NATO, IADB)* A nuclear weapon, the yield of which is measured in terms of millions of tons of trinitrotoluene explosive equivalents. See also **kiloton weapon; nominal weapon; subkiloton weapon**.

memory—See **storage**.

mercantile convoy—*(DOD, NATO)* A convoy consisting primarily of merchant ships controlled by the naval control of shipping organization.

mercast system—See **merchant ship broadcast system**.

merchant intelligence—*(DOD)* In intelligence handling, communication instructions for reporting by merchant vessels of vital intelligence sightings. Also called **MERINT**.

merchant ship—*(DOD, NATO)* A vessel engaged in mercantile trade except river craft, estuarial craft, or craft which operate solely within harbor limits.

merchant ship broadcast system—*(DOD, NATO)* A system of radio broadcasts to allied merchant ships which may be activated to provide for the transmission of official messages to merchant ships in any part of the world.

merchant ship casualty report—*(DOD, IADB)* A report by message, or other means, of a casualty to a merchant ship at sea or in port. Merchant ship casualty reports are sent by the escort force commander or other appropriate authority to the operational control authority in whose area the casualty occurred.

merchant ship control zone—*(DOD, NATO)* A defined area of sea or ocean inside which it may be necessary to offer guidance, control and protection to allied shipping.

merchant ship reporting and control message system—*(DOD, NATO)* A worldwide message system for reporting the movements of and information relating to the control of merchant ships.

merged—*(DOD)* In air intercept, a code meaning, "Tracks have come together."

message—*(DOD, IADB)* Any thought or idea expressed briefly in a plain or secret language, prepared in a form suitable for transmission by any means of communication.

message—*(NATO)* Any thought or idea expressed briefly in a plain, coded, or secret language, prepared in a form suitable for transmission by any means of communication.

message center—See **telecommunications center**.

message (telecommunications)—*(DOD)* Record information expressed in plain or encrypted language and prepared in a format specified for intended transmission by a telecommunications system.

meteorological data—*(DOD, IADB)* Meteorological facts pertaining to the atmosphere, such as wind, temperature, air density, and other phenomena which affect military operations.

metrology—*(DOD)* The science of measurement, including the development of measurement standards and systems for absolute and relative measurements.

MGM-13—See **Mace**.

MGM-29A—See **Sergeant**.

MGM-31A—See **Pershing**.

MGM-51—See **Shillelagh**.

microform—*(DOD, NATO)* A generic term for any form, whether film, video tape, paper or other medium, containing miniaturized or otherwise compressed images which cannot be read without special display devices.

midcourse guidance—*(DOD)* The guidance applied to a missile between termination of the boost phase and the start of the terminal phase of flight. See also **guidance**.

midcourse guidance—*(NATO)* The guidance applied to a missile between termination of the launching phase and the start of the terminal phase of flight.

midcourse phase—*(DOD)* That portion of the trajectory of a ballistic missile between the boost phase and the reentry phase. See also **ballistic trajectory; boost phase; reentry phase; terminal phase**.

middleman—*(DOD)* In air intercept, a code meaning, "Very high frequency or ultra-high frequency radio relay equipment."

midnight—*(DOD)* In air intercept, a code meaning, "Changeover from close to broadcast control."

militarily significant fallout—*(DOD, IADB)* Radioactive contamination capable of inflicting radiation doses on personnel which may result in a reduction of their combat effectiveness.

Military Affiliate Radio System—*(DOD)* A program conducted by the Departments of the Army, Navy, and Air Force in which amateur radio stations and operators participate in and contribute to the mission of providing auxiliary and emergency communications on a local, national, or international basis as an adjunct to normal military communications. Also referred to as **MARS**.

Military Airlift Command—*(DOD)* The single manager operating agency for designated airlift service. Also referred to as **MAC**.

military assistance advisory group—*(DOD, IADB)* A joint Service group, normally under the military command of a commander of a unified command and representing the Secretary of Defense, which primarily administers the US military assistance planning and programming in the host country. Also called **MAAG**.

Military Assistance Articles and Services List—*(DOD, IADB)* A Department of Defense publication listing source, availability, and price of items and services for use by the unified commands and Military Departments in preparing military assistance plans and programs. (Note: IADB uses the words "United States" before Department of Defense.)

Military Assistance Program—*(DOD, IADB)* That portion of the US security assistance authorized by the Foreign Assistance Act of 1961, as amended, which provides defense articles and services to recipients on a nonreimbursable (grant) basis.

Military Assistance Program Training—See **international military education and training**.

military capability—*(DOD)* The ability to achieve a specified wartime objective (win a war or battle, destroy a target set). It includes four major components: force structure, modernization, readiness, and sustainability.

a. **force structure**—Numbers, size, and composition of the units that comprise our Defense forces; e.g., divisions, ships, airwings.

b. **modernization**—Technical sophistication of forces, units, weapon systems, and equipments.

c. **readiness**—The ability of forces, units, weapon systems, or equipments to deliver the outputs for which they were designed (includes the ability to deploy and employ without unacceptable delays).

d. **sustainability**—The "staying power" of our forces, units, weapon systems, and equipments, often measured in numbers of days. (Note: This is the part 2. definition of **sustainability**, which is published alphabetically.)

military censorship—*(DOD, IADB)* All types of censorship conducted by personnel of the Armed Forces of the United States, to include armed forces censorship, civil censorship, prisoner of war censorship, and field press censorship. See also **censorship**. (Note: IADB does not use the words **"of the United States."**)

military characteristics—*(DOD, IADB)* Those characteristics of equipment upon which depends its ability to perform desired military functions. Military characteristics include physical and operational characteristics but not technical characteristics.

military civic action—*(DOD, I, IADB)* The use of preponderantly indigenous military forces on projects useful to the local population at all levels in such fields as education, training, public works, agriculture, transportation, communications, health, sanitation, and others contributing to economic and social development, which would also serve to improve the standing of the military forces with the population. *(DOD, I)* (US forces may at times advise or engage in military civic actions in overseas areas.)

military convoy—*(DOD, NATO)* A land or maritime convoy that is controlled and reported as a military unit. A maritime convoy can consist of any combination of merchant ships, auxiliaries or other military units.

military currency—*(DOD, NATO, IADB)* Currency prepared by a power and declared by its military commander to be legal tender for use by civilian and/or military personnel as prescribed in the areas occupied by its forces. It should be of distinctive design to distinguish it from the official currency of the countries concerned, but may be denominated in the monetary unit of either.

military damage assessment—*(DOD)* An appraisal of the effects of an attack on a nation's military forces to determine residual military capability and to support planning for recovery and reconstitution. See also **damage assessment.**

military deception—*(DOD)* Actions executed to mislead foreign decisionmakers, causing them to derive and accept desired appreciations of military capabilities, intentions, operations, or other activities that evoke foreign actions that contribute to the originator's objectives. There are three categories of military deception:
a. **strategic military deception**—Military deception planned and executed to result in foreign national policies and actions which support the originator's national objectives, policies, and strategic military plans.
b. **tactical military deception**—Military deception planned and executed by and in support of operational commanders against the pertinent threat, to result in opposing operational actions favorable to the originator's plans and operations.
c. **Department/Service military deception**—Military deception planned and executed by Military Services about military systems, doctrine, tactics, techniques, personnel or service operations, or other activities to result in foreign actions which increase or maintain the originator's capabilities relative to adversaries. See also **deception.**

Military Department—*(DOD)* One of the departments within the Department of Defense cre-

ated by the National Security Act of 1947, as amended. See also **Department of the Army; Department of the Navy; Department of the Air Force.**

military designed vehicle—*(DOD)* A vehicle having military characteristics resulting from military research and development processes, designed primarily for use by forces in the field in direct connection with, or support of, combat or tactical operations.

military education—*(DOD, IADB)* The systematic instruction of individuals in subjects which will enhance their knowledge of the science and art of war. See also **military training.**

military geographic documentation—*(DOD, IADB)* Military geographic information which has been evaluated, processed, summarized, and published.

military geographic documentation—*(NATO)* Military geographic information which has been evaluated, processed, summarized and published in standardized format in order to meet a military requirement.

military geographic information—*(DOD, IADB)* Comprises the information concerning physical aspects, resources, and artificial features which is necessary for planning and operations.

military geographic information—*(NATO)* Geographic information which is necessary for planning and operations.

military geography—*(DOD, IADB)* The specialized field of geography dealing with natural and man-made physical features that may affect the planning and conduct of military operations.

military government—See **civil affairs.**

military government ordinance—*(DOD, IADB)* An enactment, on the authority of a military governor, promulgating laws or rules regulating the occupied territory under his control.

military governor—*(DOD, NATO, IADB)* The military commander or other designated person who, in an occupied territory, exercises supreme authority over the civil population subject to the laws and usages of war and to any directive received from his government or his superior.

military grid—*(DOD, NATO, IADB)* Two sets of parallel lines intersecting at right angles and forming squares; the grid is superimposed on maps, charts, and other similar representations of the surface of the earth in an accurate and consistent manner to permit identification of ground locations with respect to other locations and the computation of direction and distance to other points. See also **military grid reference system.**

military grid reference system—*(DOD, NATO, IADB)* A system which uses a standard-scaled grid square, based on a point of origin on a map projection of the surface of the earth in an accurate and consistent manner to permit either position referencing or the computation of direction and distance between grid positions. See also **military grid.**

military independent—*(DOD, NATO)* A merchant ship or auxiliary sailed singly but controlled and reported as a military unit. See also **independent.**

military intelligence—*(DOD)* Intelligence on any foreign military or military-related situation or activity which is significant to military policymaking or the planning and conduct of military operations and activities.

military intervention—*(DOD, IADB)* The deliberate act of a nation or a group of nations to introduce its military forces into the course of an existing controversy.

military land transportation resources—*(DOD, IADB)* All military-owned transportation resources, designated for common-user, over the ground, point-to-point use.

military load classification—*(DOD, NATO, IADB)* A standard system in which a route, bridge or raft is assigned class number(s) representing the load it can carry. Vehicles are also assigned number(s) indicating the minimum class of route, bridge or raft they are authorized to use. See also **route classification.**

military necessity—*(DOD, NATO, IADB)* The principle whereby a belligerent has the right to apply any measures which are required to bring about the successful conclusion of a military operation and which are not forbidden by the laws of war.

military nuclear power—*(DOD, NATO, IADB)* A nation which has nuclear weapons and the capability for their employment. See also **nuclear power.**

military occupation—*(DOD, IADB)* A condition in which territory is under the effective control of a foreign armed force. See also **occupied territory; phases of military government.**

military platform—*(DOD)* A side-loading platform generally at least 300 meters/1000 feet long for military trains.

military posture—*(DOD, IADB)* The military disposition, strength, and condition of readiness as it affects capabilities.

military projection operations—See **land, sea, or aerospace projection operations.**

military requirement—*(DOD, NATO, IADB)* An established need justifying the timely allocation of resources to achieve a capability to accomplish approved military objectives, missions, or tasks. See also **objective force level.**

military resources—*(DOD)* Military and civilian personnel, facilities, equipment, and supplies under the control of a DOD component.

Military Sealift Command—*(DOD)* The single manager operating agency for designated sealift service. Also referred to as **MSC.**

Military Service—*(DOD)* A branch of the Armed Forces of the United States, established by act of Congress, in which persons are appointed, enlisted, or inducted for military service, and which operates and is administered within a military or executive department. The military services are: the United States Army, the United States Navy, the United States Air Force, the United States Marine Corps, and the United States Coast Guard.

military standard requisitioning and issue procedure—*(DOD)* A uniform procedure established by the Department of Defense for use within the Department of Defense to govern requisition and issue of materiel within standardized priorities. Also referred to as MIL-STRIP.

military standard transportation and movement procedures—*(DOD)* Uniform and standard transportation data, documentation, and control procedures applicable to all cargo movements in the Department of Defense transportation system. Also referred to as **MILSTAMP.**

military strategy—*(DOD, IADB)* The art and science of employing the armed forces of a nation to secure the objectives of national policy by the application of force or the threat of force. See also **strategy.**

military strategy—*(NATO)* That component of national or multinational strategy, presenting the manner in which military power should be developed and applied to achieve national objectives or those of a group of nations.

military symbol—*(DOD, NATO)* A graphic sign used, usually on map, display or diagram, to represent a particular military unit, installation, activity or other item of military interest.

military traffic—*(DOD, IADB)* Department of Defense personnel, mail, and cargo to be, or being, transported.

Military Traffic Management Command—*(DOD, IADB)* The single manager operating agency for military traffic, land transportation, and common-user ocean terminals. Also referred to as **MTMC.**

military training—*(DOD, IADB)* The instruction of personnel to enhance their capacity to perform specific military functions and tasks; the exercise of one or more military units conducted to enhance their combat readiness. See also **military education.**

MILVAN—*(DOD, IADB)* Military-owned demountable container, conforming to United States and international standards, operated in a centrally controlled fleet for movement of military cargo.

MILVAN chassis—*(DOD, IADB)* The compatible chassis to which the milvan is attached by coupling the lower four standard corner fittings of the container to compatible mounting blocks in the chassis to permit road movement.

MIM–14—See **Nike Hercules.**

MIM–23—See **Hawk.**

MIM–72—See **Chaparral.**

mine—*(DOD, NATO, IADB)* 1. In land mine warfare, an explosive or other material, normally encased, designed to destroy or damage ground vehicles, boats, or aircraft, or designed to wound, kill, or otherwise incapacitate personnel. It may be detonated by the action of its victim, by the passage of time, or by controlled means. 2. In naval mine warfare, an explosive device laid in the water with the intention of damaging or sinking ships or of deterring shipping from entering an area. The term does not include devices attached to the bottoms of ships or to harbor installations by personnel operating underwater, nor does it include devices which explode immediately on expiration of a predetermined time after laying.

mineable waters—*(DOD, NATO)* Waters where naval mines of any given type may be effective against any given target.

mine clearance—*(DOD, NATO, IADB)* The process of detecting and/or removing land mines by manual or mechanical means.

mine countermeasures—*(DOD, IADB)* All methods for preventing or reducing damage or danger from mines.

mined area—*(DOD, NATO)* An area declared dangerous due to the presence or suspected presence of mines.

mine defense—*(DOD, NATO, IADB)* The defense of a position, area, etc., by land or underwater mines. A mine defense system includes the personnel and equipment needed to plant, operate, maintain, and protect the minefields that are laid.

mine disposal—*(DOD, NATO)* The operation by suitably qualified personnel designed to render safe, neutralize, recover, remove or destroy mines.

minefield—*(DOD, NATO)* 1. In land warfare, an area of ground containing mines laid with or without a pattern. See also **defensive minefield; mixed minefield; nuisance minefield; phoney minefield; protective minefield.** 2. In naval warfare, an area of water containing mines laid with or without a pattern. See also **dummy minefield.**

minefield lane—*(DOD, NATO, IADB)* A marked lane, unmined, or cleared of mines, leading through a minefield.

minefield marking—*(DOD, IADB)* Visible marking of all points required in laying a minefield and indicating the extent of such minefields.

minefield marking—*(NATO)* A standardized system of marking to indicate the location and extent of a minefield.

minefield record—*(DOD, NATO, IADB)* A complete written record of all pertinent information concerned on a minefield, submitted on a standard form by the officer in charge of the laying operations.

minehunting—*(DOD, NATO, IADB)* The employment of ships, airborne equipment and/or divers to locate and dispose of individual mines.

mine row—*(DOD, NATO, IADB)* A single row of mines or clusters. See also **mine strip.**

mine spotting—*(DOD, NATO)* In naval mine warfare, the process of visually observing a mine or minefield.

mine strip—*(DOD, NATO, IADB)* In land mine warfare, two parallel mine rows laid simultaneously six meters or six paces apart. See also **mine row.**

minesweeping—*(DOD, NATO, IADB)* The technique of searching for, or clearing mines using mechanical or explosion gear, which physically removes or destroys the mine, or produces, in the area, the influence fields necessary to actuate it.

mine warfare—*(DOD, NATO, IADB)* The strategic and tactical use of mines and their countermeasures.

mine warfare chart—*(DOD, NATO)* A special naval chart, at a scale of 1:50,000 or larger (preferably 1:25,000 or larger) designed for planning and executing mine warfare operations, either based on an existing standard nautical chart, or produced to special specifications.

mine warfare forces (naval)—*(DOD, IADB)* Navy forces charged with the strategic and tactical use of naval mines and their countermeasures. Such forces are capable of offensive and defensive measures in connection with laying and clearing mines.

mine warfare group—*(DOD, NATO)* A task organization of mine warfare units for the conduct of minelaying and/or mine countermeasures in maritime operations.

minewatching—*(DOD, NATO, IADB)* In naval mine warfare, the mine countermeasures procedure which detects, finds the position of, and/or identifies mines during the act of mine laying.

mine weapons—*(DOD, NATO)* The collective term for all weapons which may be used in mine warfare.

minimize—*(DOD, IADB)* A condition wherein normal message and telephone traffic is drastically reduced in order that messages connected with an actual or simulated emergency shall not be delayed.

minimum aircraft operating surface—*(DOD, NATO)* A surface on an airfield which is essential for the movement of aircraft between their dispersal areas and the minimum operating strip itself. See also **minimum operating strip.**

minimum-altitude bombing—*(DOD, IADB)* Horizontal or glide bombing with the height of release under 900 feet. It includes masthead bombing, which is sometimes erroneously referred to as "skip bombing." See also **skip bombing.**

minimum attack altitude—*(DOD)* The lowest altitude determined by the tactical use of weapons, terrain consideration, and weapons effects which permits the safe conduct of an air attack and/or minimizes effective enemy counteraction.

minimum crossing altitude—*(DOD, IADB)* The lowest altitude at certain radio fixes at which an aircraft must cross when proceeding in the direction of a higher minimum en route instrument flight rules altitude.

minimum descent altitude—*(DOD, NATO)* The lowest altitude to which descent shall be authorized in procedures not using a glide slope, until the required visual reference has been established. See also **minimum descent height.**

minimum descent height—*(DOD, NATO)* The lowest height to which descent shall be authorized in procedures not using a glide slope, until the required visual reference has been established. See also **minimum descent altitude.**

minimum essential equipment—*(DOD, IADB)* That part of authorized allowances of Army equipment, clothing, and supplies needed to preserve the integrity of a unit during movement without regard to the peformance of its combat or service mission. Items common within this category will normally be carried by, or accompany troops to the port and will be placed aboard the same ships with the troops. As used in movement directives, minimum essential equipment refers to specific items of both organizational and individual clothing and equipment.

minimum normal burst altitude—*(DOD)* The altitude above terrain below which air defense nuclear warheads are not normally detonated.

minimum obstruction clearance altitude—*(DOD)* The specified altitude in effect between radio fixes on very high frequency omnirange airways, off-airway routes, or route segments, which meets obstruction clearance requirements for the entire route segment, and that assures acceptable navigational signal coverage only within 22 miles of a very high frequency omnirange.

minimum operating strip—*(DOD, NATO)* A runway which meets the minimum requirements for operating assigned and/or allocated aircraft types on a particular airfield at maximum or combat gross weight. See also **minimum aircraft operating surface.**

minimum quality surveillance—*(NATO, IADB)* The minimum measures to be applied to determine and maintain the quality of bulk and packaged petroleum products in order that these products will be in a condition suitable for immediate use.

minimum range—*(DOD, IADB)* 1. Least range setting of a gun at which the projectile will clear an obstacle or friendly troops between the gun and the target. 2. Shortest distance to which a gun can fire from a given position.

minimum reception altitude—*(DOD, IADB)* The lowest altitude required to receive adequate signals to determine specific very high frequency omnirange/tactical air navigation fixes.

minimum residual radioactivity weapon—*(DOD, NATO, IADB)* A nuclear weapon designed to have optimum reduction of unwanted effects from fallout, rainout, and burst site radioactivity. See also **salted weapon**.

Minimum Risk Force—*(DOD)* The force, developed in Part II of the Joint Strategic Planning Document Supporting Analysis, that achieves national objectives with Minimum risk. The Minimum Risk Force level represents the collective judgment of the Joint Chiefs of Staff. Minimum Risk Forces are not constrained by fiscal, manpower, logistic, mobility, basing, or other limitations and can be described as "the forces to which, if you were to add additional forces, you would not realize a measurable decrease in risk." See also **Current Force; force; Intermediate Force Planning Level; Planning Force; Programmed Force**.

minimum safe altitude—*(DOD, NATO, IADB)* The altitude below which it is hazardous to fly owing to presence of high ground or other obstacles.

minimum safe distance (nuclear)—*(DOD, NATO, IADB)* The sum of the radius of safety and the buffer distance.

minimum warning time (nuclear)—*(DOD, NATO, IADB)* The sum of system reaction time and personnel reaction time.

minor control—See **photogrammetric control**.

minor port—*(DOD, NATO, IADB)* A port having facilities for the discharge of cargo from coasters or lighters only. See also **port**.

Minuteman—*(DOD, IADB)* A three-stage, solid propellant, ballistic missile which is guided to its target by an all-inertial guidance and control system. The missiles are equipped with nuclear warheads and designed for deployment in hardened and dispersed underground silos. With the improved third stage and the post-boost vehicle, the Minuteman III missile can deliver multiple independently targetable reentry vehicles and their penetration aids to multiple targets. Designated as LGM–30.

misfire—*(DOD, NATO, IADB)* 1. Failure to fire or explode properly. 2. Failure of a primer or the propelling charge of a round or projectile to function wholly or in part.

missed approach—*(DOD, NATO)* An approach which is not completed by landing.

missed approach procedure—*(DOD, NATO)* The procedures to be followed if, after an instrument approach, a landing is not effected and occurring normally: **a.** when the aircraft has descended to the decision height/altitude and has not established visual contact; or **b.** when directed by air traffic control to pull up or to go around again.

missile assembly-checkout facility—*(DOD, IADB)* A building, van, or other type structure located near the operational missile launching location and designed for the final assembly and checkout of the missile system.

missile engagement zone—*(NATO)* See **weapon engagement zone**.

missile intercept zone—*(DOD, IADB)* That geographical division of the destruction area where surface-to-air missiles have primary responsibility for destruction of airborne objects. See also **destruction area.**

missile monitor—*(DOD, IADB)* A mobile, electronic, air defense fire-distribution system for use at Army air defense group, battalion, and battery levels. It employs digital data to exchange information within the system and provides means for the Army air defense commander to monitor actions of the units and take corrective action when necessary. It automatically exchanges information with adjacent missile monitor systems when connected with them by data links.

missile release line—*(DOD)* The line at which an attacking aircraft could launch an air-to-surface missile against a specific target.

mission—*(DOD, IADB)* 1. The task, together with the purpose, which clearly indicates the action to be taken and the reason therefor. 2. In common usage, especially when applied to lower military units, a duty assigned to an individual or unit; a task. 3. The dispatching of one or more aircraft to accomplish one particular task.

mission—*(NATO)* 1. A clear, concise statement of the task of the command and its purpose. 2. One or more aircraft ordered to accomplish one particular task.

mission-essential materiel—*(DOD)* 1. That materiel which is authorized and available to combat, combat support, combat service support, and combat readiness training forces to accomplish their assigned missions. 2. For the purpose of sizing organic industrial facilities, that Service-designated materiel authorized to combat, combat support, combat service support, and combat readiness training forces and activities, including Reserve and National Guard activities, which is required to support approved emergency and/or war plans, and where the materiel is used to: **a.** destroy the enemy or his capacity to continue war; **b.** provide battlefield protection of personnel; **c.** communicate under war conditions;

d. detect, locate, or maintain surveillance over the enemy; **e.** provide combat transportation and support of men and materiel; and **f.** support training functions, but is suitable for employment under emergency plans to meet purposes enumerated above.

mission-oriented items—*(DOD)* Items for which requirements, computations are based upon the assessment of enemy capabilities expressed as a known or estimated quantity of total targets to be destroyed. See also **combination mission/level-of-effort-oriented items; level-of-effort-oriented items.**

mission report—*(DOD, NATO)* A standard report containing the results of a mission and significant sightings along the flight route.

mission review report (photographic interpretation)—*(DOD)* An intelligence report containing information on all targets covered by one photographic sortie.

mission type order—*(DOD, IADB)* 1. Order issued to a lower unit that includes the accomplishment of the total mission assigned to the higher headquarters. 2. Order to a unit to perform a mission without specifying how it is to be accomplished.

mixed—*(DOD, NATO)* In artillery and naval gunfire support, a spotting, or an observation, by a spotter or an observer to indicate that the rounds fired resulted in an equal number of air and impact bursts.

mixed air—*(DOD, NATO)* In artillery and naval gunfire support, a spotting, or an observation, by a spotter or an observer to indicate that the rounds fired resulted in both air and impact bursts with a majority of the bursts being airbursts.

mixed bag—*(DOD, NATO)* In naval mine warfare, a collection of mines of various types, firing systems, sensitivities, arming delays and ship counter settings.

mixed graze—*(DOD, NATO)* In artillery and naval gunfire support, a spotting, or an observation, by a spotter or an observer to indicate that the rounds fired resulted in both air and impact bursts with a majority of the bursts being impact bursts.

mixed minefield—*(DOD, NATO, IADB)* A minefield containing both antitank and antipersonnel mines. See also **minefield.**

mixup, caution—*(DOD)* In air intercept, a term meaning mixture of friendly and hostile aircraft.

mobile air movements team—*(NATO, IADB)* An air force team trained for operational deployment on air movement/traffic section duties.

mobile defense—*(DOD, IADB)* Defense of an area or position in which maneuver is used with organization of fire and utilization of terrain to seize the initiative from the enemy.

mobile mine—*(DOD, NATO)* In naval mine warfare, a mine designed to be propelled to its proposed laying position by propulsion equipment like a torpedo. It sinks at the end of its run and then operates like a mine. See also **mine.**

mobile support group (naval)—*(DOD, IADB)* Provides logistic support to ships at an anchorage; in effect, a naval base afloat although certain of its supporting elements may be located ashore.

mobile support group—*(NATO)* A group which provides logistic support to ships at an anchorage; in effect, a naval base afloat although certain of its supporting elements may be located ashore.

mobile training team—*(DOD, IADB)* A mobile training team consists of one or more US personnel drawn from Service resources and sent on temporary duty to a foreign nation to give instruction. The mission of the team is to provide, by training instructor personnel, a military service of the foreign nation with a self-training capability in a particular skill.

mobility—*(DOD, NATO, IADB)* A quality or capability of military forces which permits them to move from place to place while retaining the ability to fulfill their primary mission.

mobility system support resources—*(DOD, IADB)* Those resources that are required to: a. complement the airlift and sealift forces, and/or b. perform those work functions directly related to the origination, processing, or termination of a movement requirement.

mobilization—*(DOD)* 1. The act of assembling and organizing national resources to support national objectives in time of war or other emergencies. See also **industrial mobilization.** 2. The process by which the Armed Forces or part of them are brought to a state of readiness for war or other national emergency. This includes activating all or part of the Reserve components as well as assembling and organizing personnel, supplies, and materiel. Mobilization of the Armed Forces includes but is not limited to the following categories:
a. **selective mobilization**—Expansion of the active Armed Forces resulting from action by Congress and/or the President to mobilize Reserve component units, individual ready reservists, and the resources needed for their support to meet the requirements of a domestic emergency that is not the result of an enemy attack.
b. **partial mobilization**—Expansion of the active Armed Forces resulting from action by Congress (up to full mobilization) or by the President (not more than 1,000,000) to mobilize Ready Reserve component units, individual reservists, and the resources needed for their support to meet the requirements of a war or other national emergency involving an external threat to the national security.
c. **full mobilization**—Expansion of the active Armed Forces resulting from action by Congress and the President to mobilize all

Reserve component units in the existing approved force structure, all individual reservists, retired military personnel, and the resources needed for their support to meet the requirements of a war or other national emergency involving an external threat to the national security.

d. **total mobilization**—Expansion of the active Armed Forces resulting from action by Congress and the President to organize and/or generate additional units or personnel, beyond the existing force structure, and the resources needed for their support, to meet the total requirements of a war or other national emergency involving an external threat to the national security.

mobilization—*(NATO, IADB)* 1. The act of preparing for war or other emergencies through assembling and organizing national resources. 2. The process by which the armed forces or part of them are brought to a state of readiness for war or other national emergency. This includes assembling and organizing personnel, supplies, and material for active military service.

mobilization augmentee—See **mobilization designee.**

mobilization base—*(DOD, IADB)* The total of all resources available, or which can be made available, to meet foreseeable wartime needs. Such resources include the manpower and material resources and services required for the support of essential military, civilian, and survival activities, as well as the elements affecting their state of readiness, such as (but not limited to) the following: manning levels, state of training, modernization of equipment, mobilization materiel reserves and facilities, continuity of government, civil defense plans and preparedness measures, psychological preparedness of the people, international agreements, planning with industry, dispersion, and standby legislation and controls.

mobilization designee—*(DOD)* A member of the Individual Ready Reserve who is preselected, pretrained, and assigned to occupy an authorized active duty position not filled by active duty personnel, in a Military Department or a position in the Federal Emergency Management Agency, as required, during early mobilization.

mobilization exercise—*(DOD, IADB)* An exercise involving, either completely or in part, the implementation of mobilization plans.

mobilization reserves—*(DOD)* Not to be used. See **war reserves.**

mock-up—*(DOD, NATO)* A model, built to scale, of a machine, apparatus, or weapon, used in studying the construction of, and in testing a new development, or in teaching personnel how to operate the actual machine, apparatus, or weapon.

mode (identification friend or foe)—*(DOD, IADB)* The number or letter referring to the specific pulse spacing of the signals transmitted by an interrogator.

mode of transport—*(DOD, IADB)* The various modes used for a movement. For each mode, there are several means of transport. They are: **a.** inland surface transportation (rail, road, and inland waterway); **b.** sea transport (coastal and ocean); **c.** air transportation; and **d.** pipelines.

moderate damage—See **nuclear damage (land warfare).**

moderate risk (nuclear)—*(DOD, NATO, IADB)* A degree of risk where anticipated effects are tolerable, or at worst a minor nuisance. See also **degree of risk; emergency risk (nuclear); negligible risk (nuclear).**

modernization—See **military capability.**

modification center—*(DOD, IADB)* An installation consisting of an airfield and of facilities for modifying standard production aircraft to meet certain requirements which were not anticipated at the time of manufacture.

modify—*(DOD, NATO)* In artillery, an order by the person authorized to make modifications to a fire plan.

moment—*(DOD, NATO)* In air transport, the weight of a load multiplied by its distance from a reference point in the aircraft.

monitoring—*(DOD, NATO)* 1. The act of listening, carrying out surveillance on, and/or recording the emissions of one's own or allied forces for the purposes of maintaining and improving procedural standards and security, or for reference, as applicable. 2. The act of listening, carrying out surveillance on, and/or recording of enemy emissions for intelligence purposes.

monitoring—*(IADB)*. 1. The act of detecting the presence of radiation and the measurement thereof with radiation measuring instruments. 2. The act of listening to, reviewing, and/or recording enemy, one's own, or other friendly forces' communications for the purpose of maintaining standards, improving communications, or for reference, as applicable. 3. The act of detecting the presence of radiation and the measurement thereof with radiation measuring instruments. See also **communications security monitoring.**

monitoring service—*(DOD)* The general surveillance of known air traffic movements by reference to a radar scope presentation or other means, for the purpose of passing advisory information concerning conflicting traffic or providing navigational assistance. Direct supervision or control is not exercised, nor is positive separation provided.

moored mine—*(DOD, NATO)* A contact or influence-operated mine of positive buoyancy held below the surface by a mooring attached to a sinker or anchor on the bottom. See also **mine.**

mopping up—*(DOD, NATO, IADB)* The liquidation of remnants of enemy resistance in an area that has been surrounded or isolated, or through which other units have passed without eliminating all active resistance.

mortar—*(DOD, IADB)* A muzzle-loading, indirect fire weapon with either a rifled or smooth bore. It usually has a shorter range than a howitzer, employs a higher angle of fire, and has a tube length of 10 to 20 calibers. See also **gun; howitzer.**

mosaic—*(DOD, NATO, IADB)* An assembly of overlapping photographs that have been matched to form a continuous photographic representation of a portion of the surface of the earth. See also **controlled mosaic; semi-controlled mosaic; uncontrolled mosaic.**

motorized unit—*(DOD, NATO, IADB)* A unit equipped with complete motor transportation that enables all of its personnel, weapons, and equipment to be moved at the same time without assistance from other sources.

mounting—*(DOD, NATO, IADB)* 1. All preparations made in areas designated for the purpose, in anticipation of an operation. It includes the assembly in the mounting area, preparation and maintenance within the mounting area, movement to loading points, and subsequent embarkation into ships, craft, or aircraft if applicable. 2. A carriage or stand upon which a weapon is placed.

mounting area—*(DOD, IADB)* A general locality where assigned forces of an amphibious or airborne operation, with their equipment, are assembled, prepared, and loaded in shipping and/or aircraft preparatory to an assault. See also **embarkation area.**

movement control—*(DOD, NATO, IADB)* The planning, routing, scheduling and control of personnel and freight movements over lines of communication; also an organization responsible for these functions.

movement control officer—*(NATO, IADB)* An officer of the movement control organization responsible for the executive control of movement of military personnel and cargo by all means of transport.

movement control post—*(DOD, NATO)* The post through which the control of movement is exercised by the commander, depending on operational requirements.

movement credit—*(DOD, NATO)* The allocation granted to one or more vehicles in order to move over a controlled route in a fixed time according to movement instructions.

movement directive—*(DOD)* The basic document published by the Department of the Army or the Department of the Air Force, or jointly, which authorizes a command to take action to move a designated unit from one location to another.

movement directive—*(IADB)* The basic document published by competent authority which authorizes a command to take action to move a designated unit from one location to another.

movement order—*(DOD, IADB)* An order issued by a commander covering the details for a move of his command.

movement priority—*(NATO, IADB)* The relative precedence given to each movement requirement.

movement report control center—*(DOD, IADB)* The controlling agency for the entire movement report system. It has available all information relative to the movements of naval ships and other ships under naval control.

movement report system—*(DOD, IADB)* A system established to collect and make available to certain commands vital information on the status, location, and movement of flag commands, commissioned fleet units, and ships under operational control of the Navy.

movement requirement—*(DOD, IADB)* A stated movement mode and time-phased need for the transport of units, personnel, and/or materiel from a specified origin to a specified destination.

movement restriction—*(DOD, NATO, IADB)* A restriction temporarily placed on traffic into and/or out of areas to permit clearance of, or prevention of congestion.

movement schedule—*(DOD)* A schedule developed to monitor or track a separate entity whether it is a force requirement, cargo or personnel increment, or lift asset. The schedule reflects the assignment of specific lift resources (such as an aircraft or ship) that will be used to move the personnel and cargo included in a specific movement increment. Arrival and departure times at ports of embarkation, etc., are detailed to show a flow and workload at each location. Movement schedules are detailed enough to support plan implementation.

movement table—*(DOD, NATO, IADB)* A table giving detailed instructions or data for a move. When necessary it will be qualified by the words road, rail, sea, air, etc., to signify the type of movement. Normally issued as an annex to a movement order or instruction.

moving havens—*(DOD, IADB)* Restricted areas established to provide a measure of security to submarines and surface ships in transit through areas in which the existing attack restrictions would be inadequate to prevent attack by friendly forces. See also **moving submarine haven; moving surface ship haven.**

moving map display—*(DOD, NATO)* A display in which a symbol, representing the vehicle, remains stationary while the map or chart image moves beneath the symbol so that the display simulates the horizontal movement of the vehicle in which it is installed. Occasionally the design of the display is such that the map or chart image remains stationary while the symbol moves across a screen. See also **projected map display.**

moving mine—*(DOD, NATO)* The collective description of mines, such as drifting, oscillating, creeping, mobile, rising, homing and bouquet mines.

moving submarine haven—*(DOD, IADB)* Established by Submarine Notices, surrounding submarines in transit, extending 50 miles ahead, 100 miles behind, and 15 miles on each side of the estimated position of the submarine along its stated track. See also **moving havens.**

moving surface ship haven—*(DOD, IADB)* Established by Surface Ship Notices, and will normally be a circle with a specified radius centered on the estimated position of the ship or the guide of a group of ships. See also **moving havens.**

moving target indicator—*(DOD, NATO, IADB)* A radar presentation which shows only targets which are in motion. Signals from stationary targets are subtracted out of the return signal by the output of a suitable memory circuit.

multi-modal—*(DOD, NATO)* In transport operations, a term applied to the movement of passengers and cargo by more than one method of transport.

multiple drill—See **multiple unit training assemblies.**

multiple independently targetable reentry vehicle—*(DOD)* A reentry vehicle carried by a delivery system which can place one or more reentry vehicles over each of several separate targets. See also **maneuverable reentry vehicle; multiple reentry vehicle; reentry vehicle.**

multiple reentry vehicle—*(DOD)* The reentry vehicle of a delivery system which places more than one reentry vehicle over an individual target. See also **maneuverable reentry vehicle; multiple independently targetable reentry vehicle; reentry vehicle.**

multiple unit training assemblies—*(DOD)* Two or more unit training assemblies executed during one or more consecutive days. No more than two unit training assemblies may be performed in one calendar day.

multiple warning phenomenology—*(DOD)* Deriving warning information from two or more systems observing separate physical phenomena associated with the same events to attain high credibility while being less susceptible to false reports or spoofing.

multi-service doctrine—*(DOD)* Fundamental principles that guide the employment of forces of two or three Services of the same nation in coordinated action toward a common objective. It is ratified by two or three Services, and is normally promulgated in joint Service publications that identify the participating Services, e.g., Army-Navy doctrine. See also **joint doctrine; combined doctrine.**

multi-spectral imagery—*(DOD, NATO)* The image of an object obtained simultaneously in a number of discrete spectral bands.

music—*(DOD)* In air intercept, a term meaning electronic jamming.

mutual aid—*(NATO, IADB)* Arrangements made at government level between one nation and one or more other nations to assist each other. See also **integrated logistic support; logistic assistance; reallocation of resources.**

mutual support—*(DOD, NATO, IADB)* That support which units render each other against an enemy, because of their assigned tasks, their position relative to each other and to the enemy, and their inherent capabilities. See also **cross-servicing; support.**

muzzle brake—*(DOD)* A device attached to the muzzle of a weapon which utilizes escaping gas to reduce recoil.

muzzle compensator—*(DOD)* A device attached to the muzzle of a weapon which utilizes escaping gas to control muzzle movement.

muzzle velocity—*(DOD, IADB)* The velocity of a projectile with respect to the muzzle at the instant the projectile leaves the weapon.

N

nadir—*(NATO)* That point on the celestial sphere directly beneath the observer and directly opposite the zenith.

nadir point—See **nadir**.

napalm—*(DOD, IADB)* 1. Powdered aluminum soap or similar compound used to gelatinize oil or gasoline for use in napalm bombs or flame throwers. 2. The resultant gelatinized substance.

nap-of-the-earth flight—See **terrain flight**.

national censorship—*(DOD)* The examination and control under civil authority of communications entering, leaving, or transiting the borders of the United States, its territories, or its possessions. See also **censorship**.

national command—*(NATO)* A command that is organized by, and functions under the authority of, a specific nation. It may or may not be placed under a NATO commander. See also **command**.

National Command Authorities—*(DOD)* The President and the Secretary of Defense or their duly deputized alternates or successors. Commonly referred to as NCA.

national commander—*(NATO, IADB)* A national commander, territorial or functional, who is normally not in the allied chain of command.

national component—*(NATO)* Any national forces of one or more services under the command of a single national commander, assigned to any NATO commander.

national component—*(IADB)* Any national forces of one or more services under the command of a single national commander.

national defense area—*(DOD)* An area established on non-Federal lands located within the United States, its possessions or territories, for the purpose of safeguarding classified defense information or protecting DOD equipment and/or material. Establishment of a national defense area temporarily places such non-Federal lands under the effective control of the Department of Defense and results only from an emergency event. The senior DOD representative at the scene will define the boundary, mark it with a physical barrier, and post warning signs. The landowner's consent and cooperation will be obtained whenever possible; however, military necessity will dictate the final decision regarding location, shape and size of the national defense area. Also called NDA.

national emergency—*(DOD)* A condition declared by the President or the Congress by virtue of powers previously vested in them which authorize certain emergency actions to be undertaken in the national interest. Action to be taken may include partial, full, or total mobilization of national resources. See also **mobilization**.

national force commanders—*(NATO)* Commanders of national forces assigned as separate elements of subordinate allied commands. See also **commander(s)**.

national forces for the defense of the NATO area—*(NATO)* Non-allocated forces whose mission involves the defense of an area within the NATO area of responsibility. See also **forces**.

national infrastructure—*(DOD, NATO)* Infrastructure provided and financed by a NATO member in its own territory solely for its own forces (including those forces assigned to or designated for NATO). See also **infrastructure**.

national intelligence—*(DOD, IADB)* Integrated departmental intelligence that covers the broad aspects of national policy and national security, is of concern to more than one department or agency, and transcends the exclusive competence of a single department or agency.

national intelligence estimate—*(DOD, IADB)* A strategic estimate of the capabilities, vulnerabilities, and probable courses of action of foreign nations which is produced at the national level as a composite of the views of the intelligence community.

national intelligence surveys—*(DOD, IADB)* Basic intelligence studies produced on a coordinated interdepartmental basis and concerned with characteristics, basic resources, and relatively unchanging natural features of a foreign country or other area.

nationality undetermined post—*(NATO)* An international military post which has not been accepted by any nation.

national military authority—*(NATO, IADB)* The government agency, such as Ministry of Defense or Service Ministry, empowered to make decisions on military matters on behalf of its country. This authority may be delegated to a military or civilian group or individual at any level appropriate for dealing with allied commanders or their subordinates.

national objectives—*(DOD, IADB)* Those fundamental aims, goals, or purposes of a nation— as opposed to the means for seeking these ends—toward which a policy is directed and efforts and resources of the nation are applied.

national policy—*(DOD, IADB)* A broad course of action or statements of guidance adopted by the government at the national level in pursuit of national objectives.

national security—*(DOD)* A collective term encompassing both national defense and foreign relations of the United States. Specifically, the condition provided by: **a.** a military or defense advantage over any foreign nation or group of nations, or **b.** a favorable foreign relations position, or **c.** a defense posture capa-

ble of successfully resisting hostile or destructive action from within or without, overt or covert. See also **security**.

national shipping authority—*(NATO)* The organization within each allied government responsible in time of war for the direction of its own merchant shipping.

National Stock Number—*(DOD)* The 13-digit stock number replacing the 11-digit Federal Stock Number. It consists of the 4-digit Federal Supply Classification code and the 9-digit National Item Identification Number. The National Item Identification Number consists of a 2-digit National Codification Bureau number designating the central cataloging office of the NATO or other friendly country which assigned the number and a 7-digit (xxx-xxxx) nonsignificant number. The number shall be arranged as follows: 9999-00-999-9999. See also **Federal Stock Number**.

national strategy—*(DOD, IADB)* The art and science of developing and using the political, economic, and psychological powers of a nation, together with its armed forces, during peace and war, to secure national objectives. See also **strategy**.

national territorial commander—*(NATO, IADB)* A national commander who is responsible for the execution of purely national functions in a specific geographical area. He remains a national territorial commander regardless of any allied status which may be assigned to him. See also **commander(s)**.

NATO airspace—*(NATO)* The airspace above any NATO nation and its territorial waters.

NATO assigned forces—*(NATO)* Forces in being which nations agree to place under the operational command or operational control of a NATO commander at a specified stage, state or measure in the NATO alert system or as prescribed in special agreements. See also **force(s)**.

NATO code number—*(NATO)* An identifying letter and number allocated to a product when it meets a specification which has been accepted under a NATO Standardization Agreement.

NATO commander—*(NATO)* A military commander in the NATO chain of command. Also called **allied commander.**

NATO command forces—*(NATO)* Forces in being which nations have placed under the operational command or operational control of a NATO commander. See also **force(s).**

NATO earmarked forces—*(NATO)* Forces which nations agree to place under the operational command or operational control of a NATO commander at some future time. See also **force(s).**

NATO forces—See **force(s).**

NATO intelligence subject code—*(NATO)* A numerical framework developed for indexing the subject matter of intelligence documents. In addition to the subject outline, it includes a system of alphabetical or numerical symbols for geographic areas which are used with the subject classification.

NATO international civilian post—*(NATO)* A permanent international post of NATO grade A, L, B, or C authorized to be filled by a civilian whose pay and allowances are established by the North Atlantic Council and provided from the international budget.

NATO military authority—*(NATO)* Any international military headquarters or organization covered by the Protocol on the Status of International Military Headquarters set up pursuant to the North Atlantic Treaty, (called the Paris Protocol) and any other military authority to which the NATO Council has applied the provisions of the Agreement on the Status of the North Atlantic Treaty Organization, National Representatives and International Staff (called the Ottawa Agreement) by virtue of the said Agreement.

NATO preparation time—*(NATO)* The time between the receipt of authorization from NATO political authorities for Major NATO Commanders to implement military measures to counter an impending attack and the start of the attack. See also **NATO warning time.**

NATO warning time—*(NATO)* The time between recognition by a Major NATO Commander, or higher NATO authority that an attack is impending and the start of the attack. See also **NATO preparation time.**

NATO-wide exercise—*(NATO)* An exercise involving all three Major NATO Commanders with a majority of subordinate commanders and national defense staffs concerned.

natural disaster—See **domestic emergencies.**

nautical chart—See **hydrographic chart.**

nautical mile—*(DOD, IADB)* A measure of distance equal to one minute of arc on the earth's surface. *(DOD)* The United States has adopted the international nautical mile equal to 1,852 meters or 6,076.11549 feet.

nautical plotting chart—*(DOD, NATO)* An outline chart, devoid of hydrographic information, of a specific scale and projection, usually portraying a graticule and compass rose, designed to be ancillary to standard nautical charts, and produced either as an individual chart or a part of a coordinated series.

nautical twilight—See **twilight.**

naval augmention group—*(NATO, IADB)* A formed group of escort ships employed to augment the through escort of convoys when passing through areas known or suspected to be threatened by enemy forces. See also **convoy through escort.**

naval base—*(DOD, IADB)* A naval base primarily for support of the forces afloat, contiguous to a port or anchorage, consisting of activities or facilities for which the Navy has operating responsibilities, together with interior lines of communication and the minimum surrounding area necessary for local security. (Normally, not greater than an area of 40 square miles.) See also **base complex.**

naval beach group—*(DOD, NATO, IADB)* A permanently organized naval command, within an amphibious force, comprised of a commander, his staff, a beachmaster unit, an amphibious construction battalion, and an assault craft unit, designed to provide an administrative group from which required naval tactical components may be made available to the attack force commander and to the amphibious landing force commander to support the landing of one division (reinforced). See also **shore party.**

naval beach unit—See **naval beach group.**

naval campaign—*(DOD, NATO, IADB)* An operation or a connected series of operations conducted essentially by naval forces including all surface, subsurface, air and amphibious troops, for the purpose of gaining, extending, or maintaining control of the sea.

naval construction force—*(DOD, IADB)* The combined construction units of the Navy, including primarily the mobile construction battalions and the amphibious construction battalions. These units are part of the operating forces and represent the Navy's capability for advanced base construction.

naval control of shipping—*(DOD, NATO)* Control exercised by naval authorities of movement, routing, reporting, convoy organization and tactical diversion of allied merchant shipping. It does not include the employment or active protection of such shipping.

naval control of shipping liaison officer—*(NATO)* A naval officer designated for duty on the staff of an allied naval control of shipping organization.

naval control of shipping officer—*(DOD, NATO, IADB)* A naval officer appointed to form merchant convoys; control and coordinate the routing and movements of such convoys, independently sailed merchant ships, and hospital ships in and out of a port or base, subject to the directions of the Operational Control Authority.

naval control of shipping organization—*(DOD)* The organization within the Navy which carries out the specific responsibilities of the Chief of Naval Operations to provide for the control and protection of movements of merchant ships in time of war.

naval district—*(DOD)* A geographically defined area in which one naval officer, designated commandant, is the direct representative of the Secretary of the Navy and the Chief of Naval Operations. The commandant has the responsibility for local naval defense and security and for the coordination of naval activities in the area.

naval gunfire liaison team—*(DOD, NATO, IADB)* Personnel and equipment required to coordinate and advise ground/landing forces on naval gunfire employment.

naval gunfire operations center—*(DOD, NATO, IADB)* The agency established in a ship to control the execution of plans for the employment of naval gunfire, process requests for naval gunfire support, and to allot ships to forward observers. Ideally located in the same ship as the Supporting Arms Coordination Center.

naval gunfire spotting team—*(DOD, IADB)* The unit of a shore fire control party which designates targets; controls commencement, cessation, rate, and types of fire; and spots fire on the target. See also **field artillery observer; spotter.**

naval operation—*(DOD, IADB)* A naval action, or the performance of a naval mission, which may be strategic, tactical, logistic, or training; the process of carrying on or training for naval combat to gain the objectives of any battle or campaign.

naval or marine (air) base—*(DOD)* An air base for support of naval or marine air units, consisting of landing strips, seaplane alighting areas, and all components of related facilities for which the Navy or Marine Corps has operating responsibilities, together with interior lines of communication and the minimum surrounding area necessary for local security. (Normally, not greater than an area of 20 square miles.) See also **base complex.**

naval port control office—*(DOD, IADB)* The authority established at a port or port complex to coordinate arrangements for logistic support and harbor services to ships under naval control and to otherwise support the naval control of shipping organization.

naval stores—*(DOD, NATO, IADB)* Any articles or commodities used by a naval ship or station, such as equipment, consumable supplies, clothing, petroleum, oils, and lubricants, medical supplies, and ammunition.

naval support area—*(DOD, NATO, IADB)* A sea area assigned to naval ships detailed to support an amphibious operation. See also **fire support area.**

naval tactical data system—*(DOD, IADB)* A complex of data inputs, user consoles, converters, adapters, and radio terminals interconnected with high-speed general purpose computers and its stored programs. Combat data is collected, processed, and composed into a picture of the overall tactical situation which enables the force commander to make rapid, accurate evaluations and decisions.

navigational grid—*(DOD, NATO, IADB)* A series of straight lines, superimposed over a conformal projection and indicating grid north, used as an aid to navigation. The interval of the grid lines is generally a multiple of 60 or 100 nautical miles. See also **military grid.**

navigation head—*(DOD, NATO, IADB)* A transshipment point on a waterway where loads are transferred between water carriers and land carriers. A navigation head is similar in function to a railhead or truckhead.

navigation mode—*(DOD, NATO)* In a flight control system, a control mode in which the flight path of an aircraft is automatically maintained by signals from navigation equipment.

NBC defense—*(DOD)* Nuclear defense, biological defense, and chemical defense, collectively. The term may not be used in the context of US offensive operations.

near miss—*(DOD, NATO)* Any circumstances in flight when the degree of separation between two aircraft might constitute a hazardous situation. Also called "**airmiss.**"

near miss (aircraft)—*(DOD, IADB)* Any circumstance in flight where the degree of separation between two aircraft is considered by either pilot to have constituted a hazardous situation involving potential risk of collision.

near real time—*(DOD)* Delay caused by automated processing and display between the occurrence of an event and reception of the data at some other location. See also **real time; reporting time interval.**

neatlines—*(DOD, NATO)* The lines that bound the body of a map, usually parallels and meridians. See also **graticule.**

need to know—*(DOD, IADB)* A criterion used in security procedures which requires the custodians of classified information to establish, prior to disclosure, that the intended recipient must have access to the information to perform his official duties.

negative—*(DOD)* As used in air intercept, means cancel or no.

negative phase of the shock wave—*(DOD)* The period during which the pressure falls below ambient and then returns to the ambient value. See also **positive phase of the shock wave; shock wave.**

negative photo plane—*(DOD, NATO)* The plane in which a film or plate lies at the moment of exposure.

neglect—*(DOD, NATO)* In artillery and naval gunfire support, a report to the observer/spotter to indicate that the last round(s) was fired with incorrect data and that the round(s) will be fired again using correct data.

negligible risk—*(NATO)* A degree of risk where personnel are reasonably safe from a nuclear burst, with the exception of dazzle or temporary loss of night vision. See also **degree of risk**.

negligible risk (nuclear)—*(DOD, IADB)* A degree of risk where personnel are reasonably safe, with the exceptions of dazzle or temporary loss of night vision. See also **degree of risk (nuclear); emergency risk (nuclear); moderate risk (nuclear)**.

nerve agent—*(DOD, NATO)* A lethal agent which causes paralysis by interfering with the transmission of nerve impulses.

net call sign—*(DOD, NATO, IADB)* A call sign which represents all stations within a net. See also **call sign**.

net, chain, cell system—*(DOD, IADB)* Patterns of clandestine organization, especially for operational purposes. Net is the broadest of the three; it usually involves: **a.** a succession of echelons; and **b.** such functional specialists as may be required to accomplish its mission. When it consists largely or entirely of non-staff employees, it may be called an agent net. Chain focuses attention upon the first of these elements; it is commonly defined as a series of agents and informants who receive instructions from and pass information to a principal agent by means of cutouts and couriers. Cell system emphasizes a variant of the first element of net; its distinctive feature is the grouping of personnel into small units that are relatively isolated and self-contained. In the interest of maximum security for the organization as a whole, each cell has contact with the rest of the organization only through an agent of the organization and a single member of the cell. Others in the cell do not know the agent, and nobody in the cell knows the identities or activities of members of other cells.

net (communications)—*(DOD, IADB)* An organization of stations capable of direct communications on a common channel or frequency.

net control station—*(DOD)* A communications station designated to control traffic and enforce circuit discipline within a given net. Also called NCS.

net inventory assets—*(DOD)* That portion of the total materiel assets which is designated to meet the materiel inventory objective. It consists of the total materiel assets less the peacetime materiel consumption and losses through normal appropriation and procurement leadtime periods.

net sweep—*(DOD, NATO)* In naval mine warfare, a two-ship sweep, using a netlike device, designed to collect drifting mines or scoop them up from the sea bottom.

net weight—*(DOD, IADB)* Weight of a ground vehicle without fuel, engine oil, coolant, on-vehicle materiel, cargo, or operating personnel.

net weight—*(NATO)* 1. Weight of a vehicle, fully equipped and serviced for operation, including the weight of the fuel, lubricants, coolant, vehicle tools and spares, but not including the weight of the crew, personal equipment and load. 2. Weight of a container or pallet without freight and binding. See also **gross weight**.

neutrality—*(DOD, IADB)* In international law, the attitude of impartiality, during periods of war, adopted by third states toward belligerents and recognized by the belligerents, which creates rights and duties between the impartial states and the belligerents. In a United Nations enforcement action, the rules of neutrality apply to impartial members of the United Nations except so far as they are excluded by the obligation of such members under the United Nations Charter.

neutralization—*(DOD, NATO)* In mine warfare, a mine is said to be neutralized when it has been rendered, by external means, incapable of firing on passage of a target, although it may remain dangerous to handle.

neutralization fire—*(DOD, IADB)* Fire which is delivered to render the target ineffective or unusable. See also **fire**.

neutralization fire—*(NATO)* Fire which is delivered to hamper and interrupt movement and/or the firing of weapons. See also **fire**.

neutralize—*(DOD, IADB)* As pertains to military operations, to render ineffective or unusable.

neutralize track—*(DOD)* As used in air intercept, to render the target being tracked ineffective or unusable.

neutral state—*(DOD, IADB)* In international law, a state which pursues a policy of neutrality during war. See also **neutrality**.

neutron induced activity—*(DOD, NATO)* Radioactivity induced in the ground or an object as a result of direct irradiation by neutrons.

nickname—*(DOD)* A combination of two separate unclassified words which is assigned an unclassified meaning and is employed only for unclassified administrative, morale, or public information purposes.

nickname—*(NATO)* Two short separate words which may be formally or informally assigned by any appropriate authority to an event, project, activity, placename, topographical feature, or item of equipment for convenience of reference but not for the security of information.

night cap—*(DOD, IADB)* Night combat air patrol (written NCAP).

night effect—*(DOD, NATO)* An effect mainly caused by variations in the state of polarization of reflected waves, which sometimes result in errors in direction finding bearings. The effect is most frequent at nightfall.

Nike Hercules—*(DOD, IADB)* An Army air defense artillery surface-to-air guided missile system which provides nuclear or conventional, medium- to high-altitude air defense coverage against manned bombers and air breathing missiles. The system is designed to operate in either a mobile or fixed-site configuration and has a capability of performing surface-to-surface missions. Designated as MIM-14.

node—*(DOD)* A location in a mobility system where a movement requirement is originated, processed for onward movement, or terminated.

no-fire line—*(DOD, NATO)* A line short of which artillery or ships do not fire except on request or approval of the supported commander, but beyond which they may fire at any time without danger to friendly troops.

no joy—*(DOD)* In air intercept, a code meaning, "I have been unsuccessful," or, "I have no information."

nominal filter—*(DOD, NATO)* A filter capable of cutting off a nominated minimum percentage by weight of solid particles greater than a stated micron size.

nominal focal length—*(DOD, NATO)* An approximate value of the focal length, rounded off to some standard figure, used for the classification of lenses, mirrors, or cameras.

nominal scale—See **principal scale**; also **scale**.

nominal weapon—*(DOD, NATO, IADB)* A nuclear weapon producing a yield of approximately 20 kilotons. See also **kiloton weapon; megaton weapon; subkiloton weapon.**

nonair transportable—*(DOD, IADB)* That which is not transportable by air by virtue of dimension, weight, and/or special characteristics or restrictions.

nonaligned state—*(DOD, IADB)* A state which pursues a policy of nonalignment.

nonalignment—*(DOD, IADB)* The political attitude of a state which does not associate, or identify itself with the political ideology or objective espoused by other states, groups of states, or international causes, or with the foreign policies stemming therefrom. It does not preclude involvement, but expresses the attitude of no precommitment to a particular state (or block) or policy before a situation arises.

nonappropriated funds—*(DOD)* Funds generated by DOD military and civilian personnel and their dependents and used to augment funds appropriated by the Congress to provide a comprehensive, morale-building welfare, religious, educational, and recreational program, designed to improve the well-being of military and civilian personnel and their dependents.

non-battle casualty—*(DOD, NATO, IADB)* A person who is not a battle casualty, but who is lost to his organization by reason of disease or injury, including persons dying from disease or injury, or by reason of being missing where the absence does not appear to be voluntary or due to enemy action or to being interned. See also **battle casualty; wounded.**

noncontiguous facility—*(DOD)* A facility for which the Service indicated has operating responsibility, but which is not located on, or in the immediate vicinity of, a base complex of that Service. Its area includes only that actually occupied by the facility, plus the minimum surrounding area necessary for close-in security. See also **base complex.**

nondeferrable issue demand—*(DOD)* Issue demand related to specific periods of time which will not exist after the close of those periods, even though not satisfied during the period.

noneffective sortie—*(DOD, IADB)* Any aircraft dispatched which for any reason fails to carry out the purpose of the mission. Abortive sorties are included.

nonexpendable supplies and material—*(DOD, IADB)* Supplies which are not consumed in use and which retain their original identity during the period of use, such as weapons, machines, tools, and equipment.

non-expendable supplies and material—*(NATO)* Items which are not consumed in use and which retain their original identity during the period of use, such as weapons, and which normally require further accounting.

nonfixed medical treatment facility—*(DOD, IADB)* A medical treatment facility designed to be moved from place to place, including medical treatment facilities afloat.

non-linear approach—*(DOD, NATO)* In approach and landing systems, a final approach in which the nominal flight path is not a straight line.

non-permissive environment—See **operational environment.**

nonprior service personnel—*(DOD)* Individuals without any prior military service, who receive a commission in or enlist directly into an Armed Force of the United States.

nonprogram aircraft—*(DOD, IADB)* All aircraft, other than active and reserve categories, in the total aircraft inventory, including X-models; aircraft for which there is no longer a requirement either in the active or reserve category; and aircraft in the process of being dropped from the total aircraft inventory. See also **aircraft.**

non-quota post—*(NATO)* An international post which is open to all nations and which is filled by an individual who is selected by a defined process from among nominees from nations.

nonrecurring demand—*(DOD)* A request by an authorized requisitioner to satisfy a materiel requirement known to be a one-time occurrence. This materiel is required to provide initial stockage allowances, to meet planned program requirements, or to satisfy a one-time project or maintenance requirement. Nonrecurring demands normally will not be considered by the supporting supply system in the development of demand-based elements of the requirements computation.

non-registered publication—*(DOD, NATO, IADB)* A publication which bears no register number and for which periodic accounting is not required.

nonscheduled units—*(DOD, IADB)* Units of the landing force held in readiness for landing during the initial unloading period, but not included in either scheduled or on-call waves. This category usually includes certain of the combat support units and most of the combat service support units with higher echelon (division and above) reserve units of the landing force. Their landing is directed when the need ashore can be predicted with a reasonable degree of accuracy.

nonstandard item—*(DOD)* An item of supply determined by standardization action as not authorized for procurement.

nonstocked item—*(DOD)* An item that does not meet the stockage criteria for a given activity and, therefore, is not stocked at the particular activity.

non-submarine contact chart—*(DOD, NATO)* A special naval chart, at a scale of 1:100,000 to 1:1,000,000, showing bathymetry, bottom characteristics, wreck data and non-submarine contact data for coastal and off-shore waters. It is designed for use in conducting submarine and anti-submarine warfare operations. Also called **non-sub contact chart.**

non-unit-related cargo—*(DOD)* All equipment and supplies requiring transportation to an area of operations, other than those identified as the equipment or accompanying supplies of a specific unit (e.g., resupply, military support for allies, and support for nonmilitary programs, such as civil relief).

non-unit-related personnel—*(DOD)* All personnel requiring transportation to or from an area of operations, other than those assigned to a specific unit (e.g., filler personnel, replacements, temporary duty/temporary additional duty, (TDY/TAD) personnel, civilians, medical evacuees, and retrograde personnel).

normal charge—*(DOD)* Charge employing a standard amount of propellant to fire a gun under ordinary conditions, as compared with a reduced charge. See also **reduced charge.**

normal impact effect—See **cardinal point effect.**

normal intelligence reports—*(DOD, IADB)* A category of reports used in the dissemination of intelligence, which is conventionally used for the immediate dissemination of individual items of intelligence. See also **intelligence reporting; specialist intelligence reports.**

normal lighting—*(DOD, NATO)* Lighting of vehicles as prescribed or authorized by the law of a given country without restrictions for military reasons. See also **reduced lighting.**

normal operations—*(DOD, IADB)* Generally and collectively, the broad functions which the commander of a unified combatant command undertakes when he is assigned responsibility for a given geographic or functional area. Except as otherwise qualified in certain unified command plan paragraphs which relate to particular commands, "normal operations" of a unified command commander include: planning for and execution of operations in contingencies, limited war and gen-

247

eral war; planning and conduct of cold war activities; planning for and administration of military assistance; and maintaining the relationships and exercising the directive or coordinating authority prescribed in JCS Pubs 2, 3, and 4.

northing—*(NATO, IADB)* Northward, that is, from bottom to top, reading of grid values on a map.

no-strike target list—*(DOD)* A list designated by a commander containing targets not to be destroyed. Destruction of targets on the list would interfere with or unduly hamper projected friendly military operations, or friendly relations with indigenous personnel or governments.

NOTAM—See **notice to airmen.**

notice to airmen—*(DOD, NATO)* A notice, containing information concerning the establishment, condition or change in any aeronautical facility, service, procedures or hazard, the timely knowledge of which is essential to personnel concerned with flight operations. Also called **NOTAM.**

notional ship—*(DOD, IADB)* A theoretical or average ship of any one category used in transportation planning (e.g., a Liberty ship for dry cargo; a T–2 tanker for bulk petroleum, oils, and lubricants; a personnel transport of 2,400 troop spaces.)

not operationally ready, maintenance—*(DOD)* A condition status of an item of equipment or a system, in the possession of an operational unit, indicating that it is not operationally ready because maintenance work must be accomplished at organizational and/or intermediate levels of maintenance. Also called **NORM.**

not operationally ready, supply—*(DOD)* A condition status of an item of equipment or a system, in the possession of an operational unit, indicating that it is not operationally ready nor can maintenance work be performed to return it to an operationally ready status until the required items of supply become available at the work site. Also called **NORS.**

no-wind position—See **air position.**

Nth country—*(DOD)* A reference to additions to the group of powers possessing nuclear weapons—the next country of a series to acquire nuclear capabilities.

NUCINT—See **nuclear intelligence.**

nuclear accident—See **nuclear weapon(s) accident.**

nuclear airburst—*(DOD, NATO, IADB)* The explosion of a nuclear weapon in the air, at a height greater than the maximum radius of the fireball. See also **types of burst.**

nuclear, biological, chemical area of observation—*(NATO)* A geographical area consisting of several nuclear, biological, chemical zones of observation, comparable to the area of responsibility of an Army or Army Group or an Allied Tactical Air Force.

nuclear, biological, chemical collection center—*(NATO)* An agency responsible for the receipt, collation and evaluation of reports of nuclear detonations, biological and chemical attacks and resultant contamination within the zone of observation and for the production and dissemination of appropriate reports and warnings.

nuclear, biological, chemical control center—*(NATO)* The agency responsible for coordinating the activities of all nuclear, biological and chemical collection centers in a given area of observation. This agency may also assume the function of a collection center for the area in which it is located.

nuclear, biological, chemical zone of observation—*(NATO)* A geographical area which defines the responsibility for collecting and reporting information on enemy or unidentified nuclear detonations, biological or chemical attacks, and resultant contamination. Boundaries of nuclear, biological, chemical zones of observation, which may overlap, will be determined by the organization of the forces concerned.

nuclear bonus effects—*(DOD, NATO)* Desirable damage or casualties produced by the effects from friendly nuclear weapons that cannot be accurately calculated in targeting as the uncertainties involved preclude depending on them for a militarily significant result.

nuclear burst—See **types of burst.**

nuclear cloud—*(DOD, NATO, IADB)* An all-inclusive term for the volume of hot gases, smoke, dust, and other particulate matter from the nuclear bomb itself and from its environment, which is carried aloft in conjunction with the rise of the fireball produced by the detonation of the nuclear weapon.

nuclear collateral damage—*(DOD, NATO)* Undesired damage or casualties produced by the effects from friendly nuclear weapons.

nuclear column—*(DOD, NATO, IADB)* A hollow cylinder of water and spray thrown up from an underwater burst of a nuclear weapon, through which the hot, high-pressure gases formed in the explosion are vented to the atmosphere. A somewhat similar column of dirt is formed in an underground explosion.

nuclear commitment—*(DOD, NATO)* A statement by a NATO member that specific forces have been committed or will be committed to NATO in a nuclear only or dual capable role.

nuclear coordination—*(DOD, IADB)* A broad term encompassing all the actions involved with planning nuclear strikes, including liaison between commanders, for the purpose of satisfying support requirements or because of the extension of weapons effects into the territory of another.

nuclear damage assessment—*(DOD, NATO)* The determination of the damage effect to the population, forces and resources resulting from actual nuclear attack. It is performed during and after an attack. The operational significance of the damage is not evaluated in this assessment.

nuclear damage (land warfare)—*(DOD, NATO, IADB)*
1. **Light Damage**—Damage which does not prevent the immediate use of equipment or installations for which it was intended. Some repair by the user may be required to make full use of the equipment or installations.
2. **Moderate Damage**—Damage which prevents the use of equipment or installations until extensive repairs are made.
3. **Severe Damage**—Damage which prevents use of equipment or installations permanently.

nuclear defense—*(DOD, NATO, IADB)* The methods, plans, and procedures involved in establishing and exercising defensive measures against the effects of an attack by nuclear weapons or radiological warfare agents. It encompasses both the training for, and the implementation of, these methods, plans, and procedures. See also **NBC defense; radiological defense.**

nuclear delivery unit—*(DOD, NATO)* Any level of organization capable of employing a nuclear weapon system or systems when the weapon or weapons have been released by proper authority.

nuclear delivery vehicle—*(DOD, NATO)* That portion of the weapon system which provides the means of delivery of a nuclear weapon to the target.

nuclear detonation detection and reporting system—*(DOD, NATO, IADB)* A system deployed to provide surveillance coverage of critical friendly target areas, and indicate place, height of burst, yield, and ground zero of nuclear detonations.

nuclear dud—*(DOD)* A nuclear weapon which, when launched at or emplaced on a target, fails to provide any explosion of that part of the weapon designed to produce the nuclear yield.

nuclear energy—*(DOD, IADB)* All forms of energy released in the course of a nuclear fission or nuclear transformation.

nuclear equipoise—*(DOD)* Not to be used. See **nuclear stalemate**.

nuclear exoatmospheric burst—*(DOD, IADB)* The explosion of a nuclear weapon above the sensible atmosphere (above 120 kilometers) where atmospheric interaction is minimal. See also **types of burst**.

nuclear incident—*(DOD, IADB)* An unexpected event involving a nuclear weapon, facility, or component, resulting in any of the following, but not constituting a nuclear weapon(s) accident: **a.** an increase in the possibility of explosion or radioactive contamination; **b.** errors committed in the assembly, testing, loading, or transportation of equipment, and/or the malfunctioning of equipment and materiel which could lead to an unintentional operation of all or part of the weapon arming and/or firing sequence, or which could lead to a substantial change in yield, or increased dud probability; and **c.** any act of God, unfavorable environment or condition resulting in damage to the weapon, facility, or component.

nuclear incident—*(NATO)* An unexpected event involving a nuclear weapon, facility, or component, but not constituting a nuclear weapon(s) accident.

nuclear intelligence—*(DOD)* Intelligence information derived from the collection and analysis of radiation and other effects resulting from radioactive sources. Also called NUCINT.

nuclear logistic movement—*(DOD, IADB)* The transport of nuclear weapons in connection with supply or maintenance operations.

Under certain specified conditions, combat aircraft may be used for such movements.

nuclear logistic movement—*(NATO)* The transport of nuclear weapons or components of nuclear weapons in connection with supply or maintenance operations.

nuclear nation—*(DOD, NATO, IADB)* Military nuclear powers and civil nuclear powers. See also **nuclear power**.

nuclear parity—*(DOD, IADB)* A condition at a given point in time when opposing forces possess nuclear offensive and defensive systems approximately equal in overall combat effectiveness.

nuclear power—*(DOD, NATO, IADB)* Not to be used without appropriate modifier. See also **civil nuclear power; major nuclear power; military nuclear power; nuclear nation; nuclear weapons state**.

nuclear radiation—*(DOD, NATO, IADB)* Particulate and electromagnetic radiation emitted from atomic nuclei in various nuclear processes. The important nuclear radiations, from the weapon standpoint, are alpha and beta particles, gamma rays, and neutrons. All nuclear radiations are ionizing radiations, but the reverse is not true; X-rays for example, are included among ionizing radiations, but they are not nuclear radiations since they do not originate from atomic nuclei.

nuclear reactor—*(DOD, IADB)* A facility in which fissile material is used in a self-supporting chain reaction (nuclear fission) to produce heat and/or radiation for both practical application and research and development.

nuclear round—See **complete round**.

nuclear safety line—*(DOD, NATO, IADB)* A line selected, if possible, to follow well-defined topographical features and used to delineate levels of protective measures, degrees of damage or risk to friendly troops, and/or to prescribe limits to which the effects of friendly weapons may be permitted to extend.

nuclear stalemate—*(DOD, IADB)* A concept which postulates a situation wherein the relative strength of opposing nuclear forces results in mutual deterrence against employment of nuclear forces.

nuclear strike warning—*(DOD, NATO, IADB)* A warning of impending friendly or suspected enemy nuclear attack.

nuclear support—*(DOD)* The use of nuclear weapons against hostile forces in support of friendly air, land, and naval operations. See also **immediate nuclear support; preplanned nuclear support.**

nuclear surface burst—*(DOD, NATO, IADB)* An explosion of a nuclear weapon at the surface of land or water; or above the surface, at a height less than the maximum radius of the fireball. See also **types of burst.**

nuclear transmutation—*(DOD, IADB)* Artificially induced modification (nuclear reaction) of the constituents of certain nuclei, thus giving rise to different nuclides.

nuclear underground burst—*(DOD, NATO, IADB)* The explosion of a nuclear weapon in which the center of the detonation lies at a point beneath the surface of the ground. See also **types of burst.**

nuclear underwater burst—*(DOD, NATO, IADB)* The explosion of a nuclear weapon in which the center of the detonation lies at a point beneath the surface of the water. See also **types of burst.**

nuclear vulnerability assessment—*(DOD, NATO, IADB)* The estimation of the probable effect on population, forces, and resources from a hypothetical nuclear attack. It is performed predominantly in the preattack period; however, it may be extended to the transattack or postattack periods.

nuclear warfare—*(DOD, NATO, IADB)* Warfare involving the employment of nuclear weapons. See also **postattack period; transattack period.**

nuclear warning message—*(DOD, IADB)* A warning message which must be disseminated to all affected friendly forces any time a nuclear weapon is to be detonated if effects of the weapon will have impact upon those forces.

nuclear weapon—*(DOD, NATO)* A complete assembly (i.e., implosion type, gun type, or thermonuclear type), in its intended ultimate configuration which, upon completion of the prescribed arming, fusing and firing sequence, is capable of producing the intended nuclear reaction and release of energy.

nuclear weapon—*(IADB)* A device in which the explosion results from the energy released by reactions involving atomic nuclei, either fission or fusion, or both.

nuclear weapon(s) accident—*(DOD)* An unexpected event involving nuclear weapons or radiological nuclear weapon components that results in any of the following; **a.** accidental or unauthorized launching, firing, or use by United States forces or United States supported allied forces, of a nuclear-capable weapon system which could create the risk of an outbreak of war; **b.** nuclear detonation; **c.** nonnuclear detonation or burning of a nuclear weapon or radiological nuclear weapon component; **d.** radioactive contamination; **e.** seizure, theft, loss or destruction of a nuclear weapon or radiological nuclear weapon component, including jettisoning; **f.** public hazard, actual or implied.

nuclear weapon(s) accident—*(NATO)* Any unplanned occurrence involving loss or destruction of, or serious damage to, nuclear weapons or their components which results in an actual or potential hazard to life or property.

nuclear weapon degradation—*(DOD, IADB)* The degeneration of a nuclear warhead to

251

such an extent that the anticipated nuclear yield is lessened.

nuclear weapon employment time—*(DOD, NATO, IADB)* The time required for delivery of a nuclear weapon after the decision to fire has been made.

nuclear weapon exercise—*(DOD, NATO, IADB)* An operation not directly related to immediate operational readiness. It includes removal of a weapon from its normal storage location, preparing for use, delivery to an employment unit, the movement in a ground training exercise to include loading aboard an aircraft or missile and return to storage. It may include any or all of the operations listed above, but does not include launching or flying operations. Typical exercises include aircraft generation exercises, ground readiness exercises, ground tactical exercises, and various categories of inspections designed to evaluate the capability of the unit to perform its prescribed mission. See also **immediate operational readiness; nuclear weapon manuever.**

nuclear weapon maneuver—*(DOD, NATO)* An operation not directly related to immediate operational readiness. It may consist of all those operations listed for a nuclear weapon exercise and is extended to include flyaway in combat aircraft, but does not include expenditure of the weapon. Typical maneuvers include nuclear operational readiness maneuvers and tactical air operations. See also **immediate operational readiness; nuclear weapon exercise.**

nuclear weapon maneuver—*(IADB)* An operation not directly related to immediate operational readiness. It may consist of all those operations listed for a nuclear weapon exercise but is extended to include flyaway in combat aircraft not to include expenditure of the weapon. Typical maneuvers include nuclear operational readiness maneuvers and tactical air operations. See also **immediate operational readiness; nuclear weapon exercise.**

nuclear weapons state—See **military nuclear power.**

nuclear weapons surety—*(DOD)* Materiel, personnel, and procedures which contribute to the security, safety, and reliability of nuclear weapons and to the assurance that there will be no nuclear weapon accidents, incidents, unauthorized weapon detonations, or degradation in performance at the target.

nuclear yield—*(NATO)* The energy released in the detonation of a nuclear weapon, measured in terms of the kilotons or megatons of trinitrotoluene required to produce the same energy release.

nuclear yields—*(DOD, IADB)* The energy released in the detonation of a nuclear weapon, measured in terms of the kilotons or megatons of trinitrotoluene required to produce the same energy release. Yields are categorized as:

very low—less than 1 kiloton.
low—1 kiloton to 10 kilotons.
medium—over 10 kilotons to 50 kilotons.
high—over 50 kilotons to 500 kilotons.
very high—over 500 kilotons.
See also **nominal weapon; subkiloton weapon.**

nucleon—*(DOD, IADB)* The common name for a constituent particle of the atomic nucleus. It is applied to protons and neutrons, but it is intended to include any other particle that is found to exist in the nucleus.

nuclide—*(DOD)* All nuclear species, both stable (about 270) and unstable (about 500), of the chemical elements, as distinguished from the two or more nuclear species of a single chemical element which are called isotopes.

nudets—See **nuclear detonation detection and reporting system.**

nuisance minefield—*(DOD, NATO, IADB)* A minefield laid to delay and disorganize the enemy and to hinder his use of an area or route. See also **minefield.**

numbered fleet—*(DOD)* A major tactical unit of the Navy immediately subordinate to a major fleet command and comprising various task forces, elements, groups, and units for the purpose of prosecuting specific naval operations. See also **fleet.**

numbered wave—See **wave.**

number . . . in (out)—*(DOD, NATO)* In artillery, term used to indicate a change in status of weapon number ————.

(number of) rounds—*(DOD, NATO)* In artillery and naval gunfire support, a command or request used to indicate the number of projectiles per tube to be fired on a specified target.

numerical scale—See **scale.**

O

objective—*(DOD, NATO, IADB)* The physical object of the action taken, e.g., a definite tactical feature, the seizure and/or holding of which is essential to the commander's plan. See also **target**.

objective area—*(DOD, NATO, IADB)* 1. A defined geographical area within which is located an objective to be captured or reached by the military forces. This area is defined by competent authority for purposes of command and control. *(DOD)* 2. The city or other geographical location where a civil disturbance is occurring or is anticipated, and where Federal Armed Forces are, or may be, employed.

objective force level—*(DOD, IADB)* The level of military forces that needs to be attained within a finite time frame and resource level to accomplish approved military objectives, missions, or tasks. See also **military requirement**.

obligated reservist—*(DOD)* An individual who has a statutory requirement imposed by the Military Selective Service Act of 1967 or Section 651, Title 10 United States Code to serve on active duty in the armed forces or to serve while not on active duty in a reserve component for a period not to exceed that prescribed by the applicable statute.

oblique air photograph—*(DOD, NATO)* An air photograph taken with the camera axis directed between the horizontal and vertical planes. Commonly referred to as an "oblique": **a. High Oblique.** One in which the apparent horizon appears, and **b. Low Oblique.** One in which the apparent horizon does not appear.

oblique air photograph strip—*(DOD)* Photographic strip composed of oblique air photographs.

obliquity—*(DOD)* The characteristic in wide-angle or oblique photography which portrays the terrain and objects at such an angle and range that details necessary for interpretation are seriously masked or are at a very small scale, rendering interpretation difficult or impossible.

observation helicopter—*(DOD, NATO)* Helicopter used primarily for observation and reconnaissance but which may be used for other roles.

observation post—*(DOD, NATO, IADB)* A position from which military observations are made, or fire directed and adjusted, and which possesses appropriate communications; may be airborne.

observed fire—*(DOD, NATO, IADB)* Fire for which the point of impact or burst can be seen by an observer. The fire can be controlled and adjusted on the basis of observation. See also **fire**.

observed fire procedures—*(DOD, NATO, IADB)* A standardized procedure for use in adjusting indirect fire on a target.

observer identification—*(DOD, NATO)* In artillery and naval gunfire support, the first element of a call for fire to establish communication and to identify the observer/spotter.

observers (exercise)—*(IADB)* Representatives from nations who are invited to attend as observers at exercises.

observer-target distance—*(NATO)* The distance along an imaginary straight line from the spotter or observer to the target.

observer-target line—*(DOD, NATO, IADB)* An imaginary straight line from the observer/spotter to the target. See also **spotting line**.

observer-target range—*(DOD, IADB)* The distance along an imaginary straight line from the observer/spotter to the target.

obstruction—*(NATO)* 1. Any object which rises far enough above the surrounding surface or above a specified height to create a hazard to aircraft in flight. 2. Any object which rises far enough above the surrounding sea bed to create a hazard to navigation.

obstructor—*(DOD, NATO)* In naval mine warfare, a device laid with the sole object of obstructing or damaging mechanical minesweeping equipment.

occupation currency—See **military currency.**

occupation of position—*(NATO, IADB)* Movement into and proper organization of an area to be used as a battle position.

occupied territory—*(DOD, IADB)* Territory under the authority and effective control of a belligerent armed force. The term is not applicable to territory being administered pursuant to peace terms, treaty, or other agreement, express or implied, with the civil authority of the territory. See also **civil affairs agreement.**

ocean convoy—*(DOD, NATO)* A convoy whose voyage lies, in general, outside the continental shelf. See also **convoy.**

ocean manifest—*(DOD, NATO, IADB)* A detailed listing of the entire cargo loaded into any one ship showing all pertinent data which will readily identify such cargo and where and how the cargo is stowed.

oceanography—*(DOD)* The study of the sea, embracing and integrating all knowledge pertaining to the sea and its physical boundaries, the chemistry and physics of seawater, and marine biology.

ocean station ship—*(DOD, NATO, IADB)* A ship assigned to operate within a specified area to provide several services including search and rescue, meteorological information, navigational aid, and communications facilities.

offensive counter air operation—*(DOD, NATO)* An operation mounted to destroy, disrupt or limit enemy air power as close to its source as possible.

offensive mine countermeasures—*(DOD, NATO)* Measures intended to prevent the enemy from successfully laying mines.

offensive minefield—*(DOD, NATO)* In naval mine warfare, a minefield laid in enemy territorial water or waters under enemy control.

officer conducting the exercise—*(NATO)* The officer responsible for the conduct of an allocated part of the exercise from the Blue, Orange and Purple aspects. He will issue necessary supplementary instructions. In addition, he may be an exercise commander.

officer conducting the serial—*(NATO)* The officer designated to exercise tactical control over assigned forces for a specific exercise serial.

officer in tactical command—*(DOD, NATO)* In maritime usage, the senior officer present eligible to assume command, or the officer to whom he has delegated tactical command.

officer scheduling the exercise—*(NATO)* The officer who originates the exercise and orders it to take place. He will issue basic instructions which will include the designation of exercise areas, the allocation of forces, and the necessary coordinating instructions. He will also designate the officers conducting the exercise.

official information—*(DOD)* Information which is owned by, produced for or by, or is subject to the control of the United States Government.

offset bombing—*(DOD, NATO)* Any bombing procedure which employs a reference or aiming point other than the actual target.

offset distance (nuclear)—*(DOD, NATO, IADB)* The distance the desired ground zero or actual ground zero is offset from the center of an area target or from a point target.

offset point—*(DOD, NATO)* In air interception, a point in space relative to a target's flight path toward which an interceptor is vectored and from which the final or a preliminary turn to attack heading is made.

offset post—*(NATO)* A post identified for elimination or disestablishment when establishing a newly authorized post. The disestablished post may be within or outside the organization receiving the new post.

offshore patrol—*(DOD, NATO, IADB)* A naval defense patrol operating in the outer areas of navigable coastal waters. It is a part of the naval local defense forces consisting of naval ships and aircraft and operates outside those areas assigned to the inshore patrol.

off-the-shelf item—*(DOD)* An item which has been developed and produced to military or commercial standards and specifications, is readily available for delivery from an industrial source, and may be procured without change to satisfy a military requirement.

oiler—*(DOD, NATO, IADB)* A naval or merchant tanker specially equipped and rigged for replenishing other ships at sea.

on berth—*(DOD, IADB)* Said of a ship when it is properly moored to a quay, wharf, jetty, pier, or buoy or when it is at anchor and available for loading or discharging passengers and cargo.

on call—*(DOD, NATO, IADB)* A term used to signify that a prearranged concentration, air strike, or final protective fire may be called for. See also **call for fire; call mission.**

on-call target—*(DOD, NATO)* In artillery and naval gunfire support, a planned target other than a scheduled target on which fire is delivered when requested.

on-call target (nuclear)—*(DOD, IADB)* A planned nuclear target other than a scheduled nuclear target for which a need can be anticipated but which will be delivered upon request rather than at a specific time. Coordination and warning of friendly troops and aircraft are mandatory.

on-call wave—See **wave.**

one day's supply—*(DOD, NATO, IADB)* A unit or quantity of supplies adopted as a standard of measurement, used in estimating the average daily expenditure under stated conditions. It may also be expressed in terms of a factor, e.g., rounds of ammunition per weapon per day. See also **standard day of supply; combat day of supply.**

one-look circuit—*(DOD, NATO)* A mine circuit which requires actuation by a given influence once only.

on hand—*(DOD)* The quantity of an item that is physically available in a storage location and contained in the accountable property book records of an issuing activity.

on-scene commander—*(DOD, IADB)* The person designated to coordinate the rescue efforts at the rescue site.

on station—*(DOD, IADB)* 1. In air intercept usage, a code meaning, "I have reached my assigned station." 2. In close air support and air interdiction, means airborne aircraft are in position to attack targets or to perform the mission designated by control agency.

on station time—*(DOD, IADB)* The time an aircraft can remain on station. May be determined by endurance or orders.

on target—*(DOD)* In air intercept, a code meaning, "My fire control director(s)/system(s) have acquired the indicated contact and is (are) tracking successfully."

on the deck—*(DOD)* At minimum altitude.

O-O line—*(NATO)* A line for the coordination of field artillery observation, designated by the corps or force artillery commander and dividing primary responsibility for observation between the corps or force artillery and division artillery.

open—*(DOD)* Term used in a call for fire to indicate that the spotter or observer desires bursts to be separated by the maximum effective width of the burst of the shell fired.

open improved storage space—*(DOD, IADB)* Open area which has been graded and hard surfaced or prepared with topping of some suitable material so as to permit effective material handling operations. See also **storage.**

open route—*(DOD, NATO)* A route not subject to traffic or movement control restrictions.

open sheaf—*(DOD, IADB)* The lateral distribution of the fire of two or more pieces so that adjoining points of impact or points of burst are separated by the maximum effective width of burst of the type shell being used. See also **converged sheaf; parallel sheaf; sheaf; special sheaf.**

open source information—*(DOD)* Information of potential intelligence value (i.e., intelligence information) which is available to the general public.

open unimproved wet space—*(DOD, IADB)* That water area specifically allotted to and usable for storage of floating equipment. See also **storage.**

operating forces—*(DOD, IADB)* Those forces whose primary missions are to participate in combat and the integral supporting elements thereof. See also **combat forces; combat service support elements; combat support elements.**

operating level of supply—*(DOD, IADB)* The quantities of materiel required to sustain operations in the interval between requisitions or the arrival of successive shipments. These quantities should be based on the established replenishment period (monthly, quarterly, etc.) See also **level of supply.**

operation—*(DOD, NATO, IADB)* A military action or the carrying out of a strategic, tactical, service, training, or administrative military mission; the process of carrying on combat, including movement, supply, attack, defense and maneuvers needed to gain the objectives of any battle or campaign.

operational chain of command—*(DOD, NATO, IADB)* The chain of command established for a particular operation or series of continuing operations. See also **administrative chain of command; chain of command.**

operational characteristics—*(DOD, IADB)* Those military characteristics which pertain primarily to the functions to be performed by equipment, either alone or in conjunction with other equipment; e.g., for electronic equipment, operational characteristics include such items as frequency coverage, channeling, type of modulation, and character of emission.

operational characteristics—*(NATO)* The specific military qualities required of an item of equipment to enable it to meet an agreed operational need.

operational command—*(DOD, IADB)* Those functions of command involving the composition of subordinate forces, the assignment of tasks, the designation of objectives, and the authoritative direction necessary to accomplish the mission. Operational command should be exercised by the use of the assigned normal organizational units through their responsible commanders or through the commanders of subordinate forces established by the commander exercising operational command. It does not include such matters as administration, discipline, internal organization, and unit training, except when a subordinate commander requests assistance. *(DOD)* (The term is synonymous with "operational control" and is uniquely applied to the operational control exercised by the commanders of unified and specified commands over assigned forces in accordance with the National Security Act of 1947, as amended and revised (10 United States Code 124.) See also **administrative control; control.**

operational command—*(NATO)* The authority granted to a commander to assign missions or tasks to subordinate commanders, to deploy units, to reassign forces, and to retain or delegate operational and/or tactical control as may be deemed necessary. It does not of itself include responsibility for administration or logistics. May also be used to denote the forces assigned to a commander.

operational control—For DOD, synonymous with **operational command.**

operational control—*(NATO)* The authority delegated to a commander to direct forces assigned so that the commander may accomplish specific missions or tasks which are usually limited by function, time, or location; to deploy units concerned, and to retain or assign tactical control of those units. It does not include authority to assign separate employment of components of the units concerned. Neither does it, of itself, include administrative or logistic control. See also **operational command.**

operational control authority—*(DOD, NATO)* The naval commander responsible within a specified geographical area for the operational control of all maritime forces assigned to him and for the control of movement and protection of all merchant shipping under allied naval control.

operational environment—*(DOD)* A composite of the conditions, circumstances, and influences which affect the employment of military forces and bear on the decisions of the unit commander. Some examples are: **a. permissive environment**—Operational environment in which host country military and law enforcement agencies have control and the intent and capability to assist operations that a unit intends to conduct. **b. semi-permissive**

environment—Operational environment in which host government forces, whether opposed to or receptive to operations that a unit intends to conduct do not have totally effective control of the territory and population in the intended area of operations. **c. non-permissive environment**—Operational environment that is under control of hostile forces that have the intent and capability to effectively oppose or react to the operations a unit intends to conduct.

operational environment—*(IADB)* As pertains to the military, it is a composite of the conditions, circumstances, and influences which affect the employment of military forces and which bear on the decisions of the commander.

operational evaluation—*(DOD, IADB)* The test and analysis of a specific end item or system, insofar as practicable under Service operating conditions, in order to determine if quantity production is warranted considering: **a.** the increase in military effectiveness to be gained; and **b.** its effectiveness as compared with currently available items or systems, consideration being given to: (1) personnel capabilities to maintain and operate the equipment; (2) size, weight, and location considerations; and (3) enemy capabilities in the field. See also **technical evaluation.**

operational intelligence—*(DOD, IADB)* Intelligence required for planning and executing all types of operations. See also **intelligence.**

operational interchangeability—*(NATO)* Ability to substitute one item for another of different composition or origin without loss in effectiveness, accuracy, and safety of performance.

operationally ready—*(DOD, IADB)* **1. as applied to a unit, ship, or weapon system**—Capable of performing the missions or functions for which organized or designed. Incorporates both equipment readiness and personnel readiness. **2. as applied to personnel**—Available and qualified to perform assigned missions or functions. *(IADB)* **3. as applied to equip-**

259

ment—Available and in condition for serving the functions for which designed. See also **equipment operationally ready.**

operational missile—*(DOD, NATO, IADB)* A missile which has been accepted by the using services for tactical and/or strategic use.

operational procedures—*(DOD, NATO)* The detailed methods by which headquarters and units carry out their operational tasks.

operational readiness—*(DOD, NATO, IADB)* The capability of a unit/formation, ship, weapon system or equipment to perform the missions or functions for which it is organized or designed. May be used in a general sense or to express a level or degree of readiness.

operational readiness evaluation—*(DOD, NATO, IADB)* An evaluation of the operational capability and effectiveness of a unit or any portion thereof.

operational requirement—See **military requirement.**

operational reserve—*(DOD, NATO, IADB)* An emergency reserve of men and/or material established for the support of a specific operation. See also **reserve supplies.**

operational route—*(DOD, NATO)* Land route allocated to a command for the conduct of a specific operation, derived from the corresponding basic military route network.

operational stocks—*(NATO)* Those stocks held to meet possible operational requirements over and above holdings/allowances. See also **theater operational stocks; war reserves.**

operational testing—*(DOD, IADB)* A continuing process of evaluation which may be applied to either operational personnel or situations to determine their validity or reliability.

operational training—*(DOD, NATO)* Training that develops, maintains or improves the operational readiness of individuals or units.

operation annexes—*(DOD, IADB)* Those amplifying instructions which are of such a nature, or are so voluminous or technical, as to make their inclusion in the body of the plan or order undesirable.

operation exposure guide—*(DOD)* The maximum amount of nuclear radiation which the commander considers his unit may be permitted to receive while performing a particular mission or missions.

operation map—*(DOD, IADB)* A map showing the location and strength of friendly forces involved in an operation. It may indicate predicted movement and location of enemy forces. See also **map.**

operation order—*(DOD, IADB)* A directive issued by a commander to subordinate commanders for the purpose of effecting the coordinated execution of an operation.

operation order—*(NATO)* A directive, usually formal, issued by a commander to subordinate commanders for the purpose of effecting the coordinated execution of an operation. See also **operation plan.**

operation plan—*(DOD, NATO, IADB)* A plan for a single or series of connected operations to be carried out simultaneously or in succession. It is usually based upon stated assumptions and is the form of directive employed by higher authority to permit subordinate commanders to prepare supporting plans and orders. The designation "plan" is usually used instead of "order" in preparing for operations well in advance. An operation plan may be put into effect at a prescribed time, or on signal, and then becomes the operation order. See also **coordinated draft plan; draft plan; final plan; initial draft plan; operation order.**

operations center—See **command center.**

operations research—*(DOD, IADB)* The analytical study of military problems undertaken to provide responsible commanders and staff agencies with a scientific basis for decision on action to improve military operations. Also known as **operational research; operations analysis.**

operations security—*(DOD)* The process of denying adversaries information about friendly capabilities and intentions by identifying, controlling, and protecting indicators associated with planning and conducting military operations and other activities. Also called **OPSEC.**

operations security indicators—*(DOD)* Actions or information, classified or unclassified, obtainable by an adversary that would result in adversary appreciations, plans, and actions harmful to achieving friendly intentions and preserving friendly military capabilities.

opportune lift—*(DOD)* That portion of lift capability available for use after planned requirements have been met.

opportunity target—See **target of opportunity.**

opposite numbers—*(DOD)* Officers (including foreign) having corresponding duty assignments within their respective military Services or establishments.

OPSEC—See **operations security.**

optical axis—*(DOD, NATO)* In a lens element, the straight line which passes through the centers of curvature of the lens surfaces. In an optical system, the line formed by the coinciding principal axes of the series of optical elements.

optical landing system—*(DOD, IADB)* A shipboard gyrostabilized or shore-based device which indicates to the pilot his displacement from a preselected glide path. See also **ground controlled approach procedure.**

optical minehunting—*(DOD, NATO)* The use of an optical system (e.g., television or towed diver) to detect and classify mines or minelike objects on or protruding from the seabed.

optimum height—*(DOD, NATO, IADB)* The height of an explosion which will produce the maximum effect against a given target.

optimum height of burst—*(DOD, NATO, IADB)* For nuclear weapons, the optimum height of burst for a particular target (or area) is that at which it is estimated a weapon of a specified energy yield will produce a certain desired effect over the maximum possible area.

orange commander—*(DOD, NATO)* The officer designated to exercise operational control over orange forces for a specific period during an exercise.

orange forces—*(NATO)* Those forces used in an enemy role during NATO exercises. See also **force(s).**

oranges (sour)—*(DOD)* In air intercept, a code meaning, "Weather is unsuitable for aircraft mission."

oranges (sweet)—*(DOD)* In air intercept, a code meaning, "Weather is suitable for aircraft mission."

orbital injection—*(DOD)* The process of providing a space vehicle with sufficient velocity to establish an orbit.

orbit determination—*(DOD)* The process of describing the past, present, or predicted position of a satellite in terms of orbital parameters.

orbiting—*(DOD)* In air intercept, means circling, or circle and search.

orbit point—*(DOD, NATO, IADB)* A geographically or electronically defined location used in stationing aircraft in flight during tactical operations when a predetermined pattern is not established. See also **holding point.**

order—*(DOD, NATO, IADB)* A communication, written, oral, or by signal, which conveys instructions from a superior to a subordinate. *(DOD, IADB)* In a broad sense, the terms "order" and "command" are synonymous. However, an order implies discretion as to the details of execution whereas a command does not.

order and shipping time—*(DOD, IADB)* The time elapsing between the initiation of stock replenishment action for a specific activity and the receipt by that activity of the materiel resulting from such action. Order and shipping time is applicable only to materiel within the supply system, and it is composed of the distinct elements, order time, and shipping time. See also **level of supply**.

order of battle—*(DOD, NATO, IADB)* The identification, strength, command structure, and disposition of the personnel, units, and equipment of any military force.

order time—*(DOD, IADB)* 1. The time elapsing between the initiation of stock replenishment action and submittal of requisition or order. 2. The time elapsing between the submittal of requisition or order and shipment of materiel by the supplying activity. See also **order and shipping time**.

ordinary priority—*(DOD, IADB)* A category of immediate mission request which is lower than "urgent priority" but takes precedence over "search and attack priority," e.g., a target which is delaying a unit's advance but which is not causing casualties. See also **immediate mission request; priority of immediate mission requests**.

ordinary transport—*(DOD, NATO)* In railway terminology, a load whose size, weight or preparation does not entail special difficulties vis-a-vis the facilities or equipment of the railway systems to be used. See also **exceptional transport**.

ordnance—*(DOD, IADB)* Explosives, chemicals, pyrotechnic and similar stores, e.g., bombs, guns and ammunition, flares, smoke, napalm.

organic—*(DOD, IADB)* Assigned to and forming an essential part of a military organization.

(DOD) Organic parts of a unit are those listed in its table of organization for the Army, Air Force, and Marine Corps, and are assigned to the administrative organizations of the operating forces for the Navy.

organic—*(NATO)* Forming an integral part of a military organization.

organizational equipment—*(DOD, IADB)* Referring to method of use, signifies that equipment, other than individual equipment, which is used in furtherance of the common mission of an organization or unit. See also **equipment**.

organizational maintenance—*(DOD, IADB)* That maintenance which is the responsibility of and performed by a using organization on its assigned equipment. Its phases normally consist of inspecting, servicing, lubricating, adjusting, and the replacing of parts, minor assemblies, and subassemblies.

organization of the ground—*(DOD, NATO, IADB)* The development of a defensive position by strengthening the natural defenses of the terrain and by assignment of the occupying troops to specific localities.

Organization of the Joint Chiefs of Staff—*(DOD)* The Organization of the Joint Chiefs of Staff is an element within the Department of Defense that includes the Joint Chiefs of Staff, the Office of the Chairman of the Joint Chiefs of Staff, and the directorates and agencies designated as Joint Staff, or as supporting agencies or special offices of the Organization of the Joint Chiefs of Staff. Also known as OJCS. See also **joint staff**.

original destination (merchant shipping)—*(NATO)* The original final destination of a convoy or an individual ship (whether in convoy or independent). This is particularly applicable to the original destination of a voyage begun in peacetime. See also **final destination (merchant shipping); immediate destination (merchant shipping)**.

original negative—See generation (photography).

original positive—See generation (photography).

originating medical facility—(DOD, NATO, IADB) A medical facility that initially transfers a patient to another medical facility.

originator—(DOD, IADB) The command by whose authority a message is sent. The responsibility of the originator includes the responsibility for the functions of the drafter and the releasing officer. See also drafter; releasing officer.

Orion—(DOD, IADB) A four-engine, turboprop, all-weather, long-range, land-based antisubmarine aircraft. It is capable of carrying a varied assortment of search radar, nuclear depth charges, and homing torpedoes. It can be used for search, patrol, hunter-killer, and convoy escort operations. Designated as P-3. Electronic countermeasures version is designated EP-3.

oropesa sweep—(DOD, NATO) In naval mine warfare, a form of sweep in which a length of sweep wire is towed by a single ship, lateral displacement being caused by an otter and depth being controlled at the ship end by a kite and at the other end by a float and float wire.

orthomorphic projection—(DOD, NATO) A projection in which the scale, although varying throughout the map, is the same in all directions at any point, so that very small areas are represented by correct shape and bearings are correct.

oscillating mine—(DOD, NATO) A mine, hydrostatically controlled, which maintains a pre-set depth below the surface of the water independently of the rise and fall of the tide. See also mine.

other forces for NATO—(NATO) Forces not assigned or earmarked for a NATO command, but which might cooperate with NATO forces or be placed under the operational command or operational control of a NATO commander in certain circumstances which should be specified. See also force(s).

other war reserve materiel requirement—(DOD) This level consists of the war reserve materiel requirement less the pre-positioned war reserve materiel requirement.

other war reserve materiel requirement, balance—(DOD) That portion of the other war reserve materiel requirement which has not been acquired or funded. This level consists of the other war reserve materiel requirement less the other war reserve materiel requirement, protectable.

other war reserve materiel requirement, protectable—(DOD) The portion of the other war reserve materiel requirement which is protected for purposes of procurement, funding, and inventory management.

other war reserve stock—(DOD) The quantity of an item acquired and placed in stock against the other war reserve materiel requirement.

otter—(DOD, NATO) In naval mine warfare, a device which, when towed, displaces itself sideways to a predetermined distance.

outbound traffic—(DOD) Traffic originating in continental United States destined for overseas or overseas traffic moving in a general direction away from continental United States.

outer fix—(DOD, IADB) A fix in the destination terminal area, other than the approach fix, to which aircraft are normally cleared by an air route traffic control center or a terminal area traffic control facility, and from which aircraft are cleared to the approach fix or final approach course.

outer transport area—(DOD) In amphibious operations, an area inside the antisubmarine screen to which assault transports proceed initially after arrival in the objective area. See also **inner transport area; transport area.**

outline map—*(DOD, NATO)* A map which represents just sufficient geographic information to permit the correlation of additional data placed upon it.

outline plan—*(DOD, NATO, IADB)* A preliminary plan which outlines the salient features or principles of a course of action prior to the initiation of detailed planning.

OV–10—See **Bronco.**

over—*(DOD, NATO)* In artillery and naval gunfire support, a spotting, or an observation, used by a spotter or an observer to indicate that a burst(s) occurred beyond the target in relation to the spotting line.

overhaul—*(DOD)* The restoration of an item to a completely serviceable condition as prescribed by maintenance serviceability standards. See also **rebuild; repair.**

overhead clearance—*(DOD, NATO, IADB)* The vertical distance between the route surface and any obstruction above it.

overlap—*(DOD)* 1. In photography, the amount by which one photograph includes the same area covered by another, customarily expressed as a percentage. The overlap between successive air photographs on a flight line is called "forward overlap." The overlap between photographs in adjacent parallel flight lines is called "side overlap." 2. In cartography, which portion of a map or chart that overlaps the area covered by another of the same series. 3. In naval mine warfare, the width of which part of the swept path of a ship or formation that is also swept by an adjacent sweeper or formation or is reswept on the next adjacent lap.

overlap—*(NATO)* 1. In photography, the amount by which one photograph includes the same area covered by another, customarily

expressed as a percentage. The overlap between successive air photographs on a flight line is called "forward overlap." The overlap between photographs in adjacent parallel flight lines is called "side overlap." The overlap of successive lines of a linescan is called "line overlap." 2. In cartography, that portion of a map or chart which overlaps the area covered by another of the same series. 3. In naval mine warfare, the width of that part of the swept path of a ship or formation which is also swept by an adjacent sweeper or formation or is re-swept on the next adjacent lap.

overlap tell—*(DOD, NATO)* The transfer of information to an adjacent facility concerning tracks detected in the adjacent facility's area of responsibility. See also **track telling.**

overlap zone—*(DOD, IADB)* A designated area on each side of a boundary between adjacent tactical air control systems wherein coordination and interaction between the systems is required.

overlay—*(DOD, NATO, IADB)* A printing or drawing on a transparent or semi-transparent medium at the same scale as a map, chart, etc., to show details not appearing or requiring special emphasis on the original.

overpressure—*(DOD, NATO, IADB)* The pressure resulting from the blast wave of an explosion. It is referred to as "positive" when it exceeds atmospheric pressure and "negative" during the passage of the wave when resulting pressures are less than atmospheric pressure.

overprint—*(DOD, NATO, IADB)* Information printed or stamped upon a map or chart, in addition to that originally printed, to show data of importance or special use.

overrun control—*(NATO)* Equipment enabling a camera to continue operating for a predetermined number of frames or seconds after normal cut-off.

overseas—*(DOD)* All locations, including Alaska and Hawaii, outside the continental United States.

overseas search and rescue region—*(DOD)* Overseas unified command areas (or portions thereof not included within the inland region or the maritime region). See also **search and rescue region.**

overshoot—*(NATO)* A phase of flight wherein a landing approach of an aircraft is not continued to touch-down. See also **go around mode.**

over the beach operations—See **logistics over the shore operations.**

over-the-horizon radar—*(DOD)* A radar system that makes use of the atmospheric reflection and refraction phenomena to extend its range of detection beyond line of sight. Over-the-horizon radars may be either forward scatter or back scatter systems.

over-the-shoulder bombing—*(DOD, IADB)* A special case of loft bombing where the bomb is released past the vertical in order that the bomb may be thrown back to the target. See also **loft bombing; toss bombing.**

overt operation—*(DOD, IADB)* The collection of intelligence openly, without concealment.

P

P-3—See **Orion.**

pace—*(DOD, NATO)* For ground forces, the speed of a column or element regulated to maintain a prescribed average speed.

pace setter—*(DOD, NATO, IADB)* An individual, selected by the column commander, who travels in the lead vehicle or element to regulate the column speed and establish the pace necessary to meet the required movement order.

packaged forces—*(DOD)* Forces of varying size and composition preselected for specific missions in order to facilitate planning and training.

packaged petroleum product—*(DOD, IADB)* A petroleum product (generally a lubricant, oil, grease or specialty item) normally packaged by a manufacturer and procured, stored, transported, and issued in containers having a fill capacity of 55 United States gallons (or 45 Imperial gallons, or 205 liters) or less.

packaged petroleum product—*(NATO)* A petroleum product, generally a lubricant, oil, grease or speciality item normally packaged by the manufacturer and subsequently stored, transported and issued in containers having an individual fill capacity of 250 liters or less.

padding—*(DOD, IADB)* Extraneous text added to a message for the purpose of concealing its beginning, ending, or length.

pallet—*(DOD, NATO, IADB)* A flat base for combining stores or carrying a single item to form a unit load for handling, transportation, and storage by materials handling equipment.

palletized unit load—*(DOD, NATO, IADB)* Quantity of any item, packaged or unpackaged, which is arranged on a pallet in a specified manner and securely strapped or fastened thereto so that the whole is handled as a unit.

pan—*(DOD)* In air intercept, a code meaning the calling station has a very urgent message to transmit concerning the safety of a ship, aircraft, or other vehicle, or of some person on board or within sight.

pancake—*(DOD)* In air intercept, a code meaning, "Land," or, "I wish to land" (reason may be specified; e.g., "pancake ammo," "pancake fuel").

panel code—*(DOD, NATO, IADB)* A prearranged code designed for visual communications, usually between friendly units, by making use of marking panels. See also **marking panel.**

panoramic air camera—*(DOD, NATO)* An air camera which, through a system of moving optics or mirrors, scans a wide area of the terrain, usually from horizon to horizon. The camera may be mounted vertically or obliquely within the aircraft, to scan across or along the line of flight.

panoramic ground camera—*(DOD, NATO)* A camera which photographs a wide expanse of terrain by rotating horizontally about the vertical axis through the center of the camera lens.

parachute deployment height—*(DOD, NATO, IADB)* The height above the intended impact point at which the parachute or parachutes are fully deployed.

paradrop—*(NATO)* Delivery by parachute of personnel or cargo from an aircraft in flight.

parallactic angle—See **angle of convergence.**

parallax—*(NATO)* In photography, the apparent displacement of the position of an object in relation to a reference point, due to a change in the point of observation.

parallax difference—*(DOD, NATO)* The difference in displacement of the top of an object in relation to its base, as measured on the two images of the object on a stereo pair of photographs.

parallel classification—*(DOD, NATO)* In railway terminology, the classification of ordinary transport military vehicles and equipment, based on a comparative study of the main characteristics of those vehicles and equipment and of those of the ordinary flat wagons of a corresponding category onto which they can be loaded.

parallel sheaf—*(DOD, IADB)* In artillery and naval gunfire support, a sheaf in which the planes (lines) of fire of all pieces are parallel. See also **converged sheaf; open sheaf; special sheaf.**

parallel staff—*(DOD, NATO, IADB)* A staff in which one officer from each nation, or service, working in parallel is appointed to each post. See also **combined staff; integrated staff; joint staff.**

paramilitary forces—*(DOD, I, IADB)* Forces or groups which are distinct from the regular armed forces of any country, but resembling them in organization, equipment, training, or mission.

paraphrase—*(DOD, IADB)* To change the phraseology of a message without changing its meaning.

pararescue team—*(DOD, IADB)* Specially trained personnel qualified to penetrate to the site of an incident by land or parachute, render medical aid, accomplish survival methods, and rescue survivors.

parlimentaire—*(DOD, IADB)* An agent employed by a commander of belligerent forces in the field to go in person within the enemy lines for the purpose of communicating or negotiating openly and directly with the enemy commander.

parrot—*(DOD)* Identification Friend or Foe transponder equipment.

part—*(NATO)* An item forming part of an assembly or sub-assembly, which is not normally further broken down.

partial mobilization—See **mobilization.**

partial storage monitoring—*(DOD, IADB)* A periodic inspection of major assemblies or components for nuclear weapons, consisting mainly of external observation of humidity, temperatures, and visual damage or deterioration during storage. This type of inspection is also conducted prior to and upon completion of a movement.

partisan warfare—*(DOD, IADB)* Not to be used. See **guerrilla warfare.**

part number—*(DOD)* A combination of numbers, letters and symbols assigned by a designer, a manufacturer or vendor to identify a specific part or item of materiel.

pass—*(DOD, IADB)* A short tactical run or dive by an aircraft at a target; a single sweep through or within firing range of an enemy air formation.

passage of lines—*(DOD, NATO)* An operation in which a unit attacks through another unit which is in contact with the enemy.

passenger mile—*(DOD, IADB)* One passenger transported one mile. For air and ocean transport, use nautical miles; for rail, highway, and inland waterway transport in the continental United States, use statute miles.

passive—*(DOD, NATO)* In surveillance, an adjective applied to actions or equipments which emit no energy capable of being detected.

passive air defense—*(DOD, NATO, IADB)* All measures, other than active defense, taken to minimize the effects of hostile air action. These include the use of cover, concealment, camouflage, dispersion, and protective construction. See also **air defense.**

passive communications satellite—See **communications satellite.**

passive defense—*(DOD, IADB)* Measures taken to reduce the probability of and to minimize the effects of damage caused by hostile action without the intention of taking the initiative.

passive homing guidance—*(DOD, NATO, IADB)* A system of homing guidance wherein the receiver in the missile utilizes radiation from the target. See also **guidance.**

passive mine—*(DOD, NATO)* 1. A mine whose anticountermining device has been operated preventing the firing mechanism from being actuated. The mine will usually remain passive for a comparatively short time. 2. A mine which does not emit a signal to detect the presence of a target, in contrast to an active mine. See also **active mine.**

pass time (road)—*(DOD, NATO, IADB)* The time that elapses between the moment when the leading vehicle of a column passes a given point and the moment when the last vehicle passes the same point.

password—*(DOD, NATO, IADB)* A secret word or distinctive sound used to reply to a challenge. See also **challenge; countersign; reply.**

pathfinder aircraft—*(NATO, IADB)* An aircraft with a specially trained crew carrying drop zone/landing zone marking teams, target markers, or navigational aids, which precedes the main force to the drop zone/landing zone or target.

pathfinder drop zone control—*(DOD, IADB)* The communication and operation center from which pathfinders exercise aircraft guidance.

pathfinder landing zone control—See **pathfinder drop zone control.**

pathfinders—*(DOD, IADB)* 1. Experienced aircraft crews who lead a formation to the drop zone, release point, or target. 2. Teams dropped or air landed at an objective to establish and operate navigational aids for the purpose of guiding aircraft to drop and landing zones. 3. A radar device used for navigating or homing to an objective when visibility precludes accurate visual navigation. 4. Teams air delivered into enemy territory for the purpose of determining the best approach and withdrawal lanes, landing zones, and sites for helicopter-borne forces.

pathfinder team—*(NATO)* A team dropped or air landed at an objective to establish and operate navigational aids for the purpose of guiding aircraft to drop and landing zones.

patient—*(DOD)* A sick, injured, wounded or other person requiring medical/dental care or treatment.

patrol—*(DOD, NATO, IADB)* A detachment of ground, sea, or air forces sent out for the purpose of gathering information or carrying out a destructive, harassing, mopping-up, or security mission. See also **combat air patrol; combat patrol; reconnaissance patrol; standing patrol.**

pattern bombing—*(DOD, IADB)* The systematic covering of a target area with bombs uniformly distributed according to a plan.

pattern laying—*(DOD, NATO, IADB)* In land mine warfare, the laying of mines in a fixed relationship to each other.

payload—*(DOD, NATO, IADB)* 1. The sum of the weight of passengers and cargo that an aircraft can carry. See also **load.** 2. The warhead, its container, and activating devices in a military missile. 3. The satellite or research vehicle of a space probe or research missile. 4. The load (expressed in tons of cargo or equipment, gallons of liquid, or number of passengers) which the vehicle is designed to transport under specified conditions of operation, in addition to its unladen weight.

payload build-up (missile and space)—(DOD, IADB) The process by which the scientific instrumentation (sensors, detectors, etc.) and necessary mechanical and electronic subassemblies are assembled into a complete operational package capable of achieving the scientific objectives of the mission.

payload integration (missile and space)—(DOD, IADB) The compatible installation of a complete payload package into the spacecraft and space vehicle.

payload (missile)—See **payload**, Part 2.

P-day—(DOD, IADB) That point in time at which the rate of production of an item available for military consumption equals the rate at which the item is required by the armed forces.

peacetime complement—See **peacetime establishment.**

peacetime establishment—(NATO) A table setting out the authorized peacetime manpower requirement for a unit, formation or headquarters. Also called "peacetime complement."

peacetime force materiel assets—(DOD, IADB) That portion of total materiel assets which is designated to meet the peacetime force materiel requirement. See also **war reserves.**

peacetime force materiel requirement—(DOD) The quantity of an item required to equip, provide a materiel pipeline and sustain the United States force structure (active and reserve) and those allied forces designated for United States peacetime support in current Secretary of Defense guidance including approved supply support arrangements with foreign military sales countries, and support the scheduled establishment through normal appropriation and procurement leadtime periods.

peacetime materiel consumption and losses—(DOD) The quantity of an item consumed, lost or worn-out beyond economical repair through normal appropriation and procurement leadtime periods.

peak overpressure—(DOD, NATO, IADB) The maximum value of overpressure at a given location which is generally experienced at the instant the shock (or blast) wave reaches that location. See also **shock wave.**

pecked line—(NATO) A symbol consisting of a line broken at regular intervals.

pecuniary liability—(DOD) A personal, joint, or corporate monetary obligation to make good any lost, damaged, or destroyed property resulting from fault or neglect. It may also result under conditions stipulated in a contract or bond.

pencil beam—(DOD, NATO) A searchlight beam reduced to, or set at, its minimum width.

penetration—(DOD, NATO, IADB) In land operations, a form of offensive which seeks to break through the enemy's defense and disrupt the defensive system.

penetration aids—(DOD) Techniques and/or devices employed by offensive aerospace weapon systems to increase the probability of penetration of enemy defenses. See also **attack assessment.**

penetration (air traffic control)—(DOD, IADB) That portion of a published high altitude instrument approach procedure which prescribes a descent path from the fix on which the procedure is based to a fix or altitude from which an approach to the airport is made.

penetration (intelligence)—(DOD, IADB) The recruitment of agents within, or the infiltration of agents or technical monitoring devices in an organization or group for the purpose of acquiring information or of influencing its activities.

percentage clearance—*(DOD, NATO)* In mine warfare, the estimated percentage of mines of specified characteristics which have been cleared from an area or channel.

perigee—*(IADB)* The point at which a satellite orbit is the least distance from the center of the gravitational field of the controlling body or bodies.

perimeter defense—*(DOD, IADB)* A defense without an exposed flank, consisting of forces deployed along the perimeter of the defended area.

periodic intelligence summary—*(DOD, IADB)* A report of the intelligence situation in a tactical operation, normally produced at corps level or its equivalent, and higher, usually at intervals of 24 hours, or as directed by the commander. Also called PERINTSUM.

peripheral war—*(DOD)* Not to be used. See **limited war.**

perishable cargo—*(DOD, IADB)* Cargo requiring refrigeration, such as meat, fruit, and fresh vegetables, and medical department biologicals. See also **cargo.**

permafrost—*(DOD, IADB)* Permanently frozen subsoil.

permanent echo—*(DOD, NATO)* Any dense and fixed radar return caused by reflection of energy from the earth's surface. Distinguished from "ground clutter" by being from definable locations rather than large areas.

permissive action link—*(DOD)* A device included in or attached to a nuclear weapon system to preclude arming and/or launching until the insertion of a prescribed discrete code or combination. It may include equipment and cabling external to the weapon or weapon system to activate components within the weapon or weapon system.

permissive environment—See **operational environment.**

Pershing—*(DOD, IADB)* A mobile surface-to-surface inertially guided missile of a solid propellant type. It possesses a nuclear warhead capability and is designed to support the ground forces with the attack of long range ground targets. Designated as MGM-31A.

personal locator beacon—*(DOD, NATO, IADB)* A locator beacon capable of providing homing signals to help search and rescue operations. See also **crash locator beacon.**

personal property—*(DOD)* Property of any kind or any interest therein, except real property, records of the Federal Government, and naval vessels of the following categories: aircraft carriers, battleships, cruisers, destroyers, and submarines.

personnel—*(DOD, IADB)* Those individuals required in either a military or civilian capacity to accomplish the assigned mission.

personnel reaction time (nuclear)—*(DOD, NATO, IADB)* The time required by personnel to take prescribed protective measures after receipt of a nuclear strike warning.

personnel security investigation—*(DOD)* An inquiry into the activities of an individual which is designed to develop pertinent information pertaining to trustworthiness and suitability for a position of trust as related to loyalty, character, emotional stability, and reliability.

perspective grid—*(DOD, NATO)* A network of lines, drawn or superimposed on a photograph, to represent the perspective of a systematic network of lines on the ground or datum plane.

petroleum intersectional service—*(DOD, NATO, IADB)* An intersectional or interzonal service in a theater of operations that operates pipelines and related facilities for the supply of bulk petroleum products to theater Army elements and other forces as directed.

petroleum, oils, and lubricants—*(DOD, NATO, IADB)* A broad term which includes all petroleum and associated products used by the armed forces.

Phalanx—*(DOD)* A close-in weapons system providing automatic, autonomous terminal defense against the anti-ship cruise missile threat. The system includes self-contained search and track radars, weapons control and 20-mm M61 gun firing sub-caliber penetrators.

Phantom II—*(DOD, IADB)* A twin-engine, supersonic, multipurpose, all-weather jet fighter/bomber. It operates from land and aircraft carriers and employs both air-to-air and air-to-surface weapons. The Phantom is a prime air interdiction/close air support and fleet defense vehicle. Special missions such as laser bombing, electronic bombing, and radar bombing are considered routine capabilities. It is capable of employing nuclear and nonnuclear weapons. Designated as **F-4**. RF-4 is the photo-reconnaissance version.

phantom order—*(DOD, IADB)* A draft contract with an industrial establishment for wartime production of a specific product with provisions for necessary preplanning in time of peace and for immediate execution of the contract upon receipt of proper authority.

phase line—*(DOD, NATO, IADB)* A line utilized for control and coordination of military operations, usually a terrain feature extending across the zone of action. See also **report line.**

phases of military government—*(DOD, IADB)*
1. **assault**—That period which commences with first contact with civilians ashore and extends to the establishment of military government control ashore by the landing force.
2. **consolidation**—That period which commences with the establishment of military government control ashore by the landing force and extends to the establishment of control by occupation forces.
3. **occupation**—That period which commences when an area has been occupied in fact, and the military commander within that area is in a position to enforce public safety and order. See also **civil affairs; military occupation.**

Phoenix—*(DOD)* A long-range air-to-air missile with electronic guidance/homing. Designated as AIM-54A.

phonetic alphabet—*(DOD)* A list of standard words used to identify letters in a message transmitted by radio or telephone. The following are the authorized words, listed in order, for each letter in the alphabet: Alfa, Bravo, Charlie, Delta, Echo, Foxtrot, Golf, Hotel, India, Juliet, Kilo, Lima, Mike, November, Oscar, Papa, Quebec, Romeo, Sierra, Tango, Uniform, Victor, Whiskey, X-ray, Yankee, and Zulu.

phoney minefield—*(DOD, NATO)* An area free of live mines used to simulate a minefield, or section of a minefield, with the object of deceiving the enemy. See also **gap, minefield.**

photoflash bomb—*(DOD, NATO, IADB)* A bomb designed to produce a brief and intense illumination for medium altitude night photography.

photoflash cartridge—*(DOD, NATO, IADB)* A pyrotechnic cartridge designed to produce a brief and intense illumination for low altitude night photography.

photogrammetric control—*(DOD, NATO)* Control established by photogrammetric methods as distinguished from control established by ground methods. Sometimes called "minor control."

photogrammetry—*(DOD, NATO)* The science or art of obtaining reliable measurements from photographic images.

photographic coverage—*(DOD)* The extent to which an area is covered by photography from one mission or a series of missions or in a period of time. Coverage, in this sense, conveys the idea of availability of photography and is not a synonym for the word "photography."

photographic filter—*(NATO)* A layer of glass, gelatine, or other material used to modify the spectrum of the incidental light.

photographic intelligence—*(DOD, IADB)* The collected products of photographic interpretation, classified and evaluated for intelligence use.

photographic interpretation—See **imagery interpretation.**

photographic panorama—*(DOD)* A continuous photograph or an assemblage of overlapping oblique or ground photographs which have been matched and joined together to form a continuous photographic representation of the area.

photographic reading—*(DOD, NATO)* The simple recognition of natural or man-made features from photographs not involving imagery interpretation techniques.

photographic scale—*(DOD, NATO)* The ratio of a distance measured on a photograph or mosaic to the corresponding distance on the ground, classified as follows:
a. **very large scale**—1:4,999 and larger
b. **large scale**—1:5,000 to 1:9,999
c. **medium scale**—1:10,000 to 1:24,999
d. **small scale**—1:25,000 to 1:49,999
e. **very small scale**—1:50,000 and smaller
See also **scale.**

photographic sortie—See **imagery sortie.**

photographic strip—*(DOD, NATO)* Series of successive overlapping photographs taken along a selected course or direction.

photo interpretation key—See **imagery interpretation key.**

photomap—*(DOD, NATO)* A reproduction of a photograph or photomosaic upon which the grid lines, marginal data, contours, place names, boundaries, and other data may be added.

photo nadir—*(DOD, NATO)* The point at which a vertical line through the perspective center of the camera lens intersects the photo plane.

physical characteristics—*(DOD, IADB)* Those military characteristics of equipment which are primarily physical in nature, such as weight, shape, volume, water-proofing, and sturdiness.

physical security—*(DOD, NATO, IADB)* That part of security concerned with physical measures designed to safeguard personnel, to prevent unauthorized access to equipment, installations, material and documents, and to safeguard them against espionage, sabotage, damage, and theft. See also **communications security; protective security; security.**

pictomap—*(DOD)* A topographic map in which the photographic imagery of a standard mosaic has been converted into interpretable colors and symbols by means of a pictomap process.

pictorial symbolization—*(DOD, NATO, IADB)* The use of symbols which convey the visual character of the features they represent.

piece part—See **part.**

pigeon—*(DOD)* In air intercept, a code meaning, "The magnetic bearing and distance of base (or unit indicated) from you is ____ degrees ____ miles."

pillbox—*(DOD, NATO, IADB)* A small, low fortification that houses machine guns, antitank weapons, etc. A pillbox is usually made of concrete, steel, or filled sandbags.

pilot's trace—*(DOD, NATO)* A rough overlay to a map made by the pilot of a photographic reconnaissance aircraft during or immediately after a sortie. It shows the location, direction, number, and order of photographic runs made, together with the camera(s) used on each run.

pinpoint—*(DOD, NATO, IADB)* 1. A precisely identified point, especially on the ground, that locates a very small target, a reference point for rendezvous or for other purposes; the coordinates that define this point. 2. The ground position of aircraft determined by direct observation of the ground.

pinpoint photograph—*(DOD, NATO)* A single photograph or a stereo pair of a specific object or target.

pinpoint target—*(DOD, NATO)* In artillery and naval gunfire support, a target less than 50 meters in diameter.

pipeline—*(DOD, NATO, IADB)* In logistics, the channel of support or a specific portion thereof by means of which materiel or personnel flow from sources of procurement to their point of use.

pitch—*(DOD, NATO)* 1. The rotation of an aircraft or ship about its lateral axis. 2. In air photography, the camera rotation about the transverse axis of the aircraft. Also called **tip.**

pitch angle—*(DOD, NATO)* The angle between the aircraft's longitudinal axis and the earth's horizontal plane. Also called **inclination angle.**

plan for landing—*(NATO)* In amphibious operations, a collective term referring to all individually prepared naval and landing force documents which, taken together, present in detail all instructions for execution of the ship-to-shore movement. See also **landing diagram; ship-to-shore movement.**

planimetric map—*(DOD, IADB)* A map representing only the horizontal position of features. Sometimes called a line map. See also **map.**

planned resupply—*(NATO, IADB)* The shipping of supplies in a regular flow as envisaged by existing preplanned schedules and organizations, which will usually include some form of planned procurement. See also **element of resupply.**

planned target—*(DOD, NATO)* In artillery and naval gunfire support, a target on which fire is prearranged.

planned target (nuclear)—*(DOD, IADB)* A nuclear target planned on an area or point in which a need is anticipated. A planned nuclear target may be scheduled or on call. Firing data for a planned nuclear target may or may not be determined in advance. Coordination and warning of friendly troops and aircraft are mandatory.

planning factor—*(DOD, NATO)* A multiplier used in planning to estimate the amount and type of effort involved in a contemplated operation. Planning factors are often expressed as rates, ratios, or lengths of time.

planning factor (logistics)—*(IADB)* A properly selected multiplier, used in planning to estimate the amount and type of effort involved in a contemplated operation. Planning factors are often expressed as rates, ratios, or lengths of time.

Planning Force—*(DOD)* The force level required to provide reasonable assurance of successful execution of the national strategy. It is sized for a specific scenario presented in the Joint Strategic Planning Document Supporting Analysis Part I and is keyed to the projected threat in the last year of the planning period (i.e., the Five-Year Defense Program plus four years). The Planning Force is developed from the Minimum Risk Force by prioritizing missions, sequencing force employment, and accepting a higher level of risk. It is not constrained by fiscal, manpower, logistics, mobility, basing, or similar limitations. See also **Current Force; force; Intermediate Force Planning Level; Minimum Risk Force; Programmed Forces.**

planning staff—See **central planning team.**

planograph—*(DOD, IADB)* A scale drawing of a storage area showing the approved layout of the area, location of bulk, bin, rack, and box pallet areas, aisles, assembly areas, walls, doorways, directions of storage, office space, wash rooms, and other support and operational areas.

plan position indicator—*(DOD, NATO)* A cathode ray tube on which radar returns are so displayed as to bear the same relationship to the transmitter as the objects giving rise to them.

plan range—*(NATO)* In air photographic reconnaissance, the horizontal distance from the point below the aircraft to an object on the ground.

plant equipment—*(DOD, IADB)* Personal property of a capital nature, consisting of equipment, furniture, vehicles, machine tools, test equipment, and accessory and auxiliary items, but excluding special tooling and special test equipment, used or capable of use in the manufacture of supplies or for any administrative or general plant purpose.

plastic explosive—*(NATO)* Explosive which is malleable at normal temperatures.

plastic range—*(DOD, NATO)* The stress range in which a material will not fail when subjected to the action of a force, but will not recover completely so that a permanent deformation results when the force is removed.

plastic spray packaging—See **cocooning.**

plastic zone—*(DOD, NATO)* The region beyond the rupture zone associated with crater formation resulting from an explosion in which there is no visible rupture, but in which the soil is permanently deformed and compressed to a high density. See also **rupture zone.**

plate—*(DOD, NATO)* 1. In cartography: **a.** a printing plate of zinc, aluminum, or engraved copper; **b.** collective term for all "states" of an engraved map reproduced from the same engraved printing plate; **c.** all detail to appear on a map or chart which will be reproduced from a single printing plate (e.g., the "blue plate" or the "contour plate"). 2. In photography, a transparent medium, usually glass, coated with a photographic emulsion. See also **diapositive; transparency.**

platform drop—*(DOD, NATO, IADB)* The airdrop of loaded platforms from rear loading aircraft with roller conveyors. See also **airdrop; airdrop platform.**

plot—*(DOD, NATO)* 1. Map, chart, or graph representing data of any sort. 2. Representation on a diagram or chart of the position or course of a target in terms of angles and distances from positions; location of a position on a map or a chart. 3. The visual display of a single location of an airborne object at a particular instant of time. 4. A portion of a map or overlay on which are drawn the outlines of the areas covered by one or more photographs. See also **master plot.**

pogo—*(DOD)* In air intercept, a code meaning, "Switch to communications channel number preceding 'pogo.' If unable to establish communications, switch to channel number following 'pogo.' "

point designation grid—*(DOD, NATO, IADB)* A system of lines, having no relation to the actual scale, or orientation, drawn on a map, chart, or air photograph dividing it into squares so that points can be more readily located.

point of impact—*(DOD, NATO, IADB)* 1. The point on the drop zone where the first parachutist or air dropped cargo item lands or is expected to land. 2. The point at which a projectile, bomb, or re-entry vehicle impacts or is expected to impact.

point of no return—*(DOD, NATO, IADB)* A point along an aircraft track beyond which its endurance will not permit return to its own or some other associated base on its own fuel supply.

point target—*(DOD, IADB)* 1. A target of such small dimension that it requires the accurate placement of ordnance in order to neutralize or destroy it. 2. **nuclear**—A target in which the ratio of radius of damage to target radius is equal to or greater than 5.

point target—*(NATO)* A target which requires the accurate placement of bombs or fire.

point target (nuclear)—See **point target**, Part 2.

point to point sealift—*(DOD, IADB)* The movement of troops and/or cargo in Military Sealift Command nucleus or commercial shipping between established ports, in administrative landings or logistics over the shore operations. See also **administrative landing; administrative movement; logistics over the shore operations.** (Note: IADB does not use the words "Military Sealift Command.")

poised mine—*(DOD, NATO)* A mine in which the ship counter setting has been run down to "one" and which is ready to detonate at the next actuation. See also **mine.**

polar coordinates—*(DOD, NATO)* 1. In artillery and naval gunfire support, the direction, distance and vertical correction (shift) from the observer/spotter position to the target. *(DOD, IADB)* 2. The location of a point in a plane by the length of a radius vector, from a fixed origin in the plane, and the angle the radius vector makes with a fixed line in the plane. See also **coordinates.**

Polaris—*(DOD, IADB)* An underwater/surface-launched, surface-to-surface, solid-propellant ballistic missile with inertial guidance and nuclear warhead. Designated as UGM-27.
  UGM-27A—1,200 nautical mile range.
  UGM-27B—1,500 nautical mile range.
  UGM-27C—2,500 nautical mile range.

polar plot—*(DOD, NATO, IADB)* The method of locating a target or point on the map by means of polar coordinates.

political intelligence—*(DOD, IADB)* Intelligence concerning foreign and domestic policies of governments and the activities of political movements.

political warfare—*(DOD, IADB)* Aggressive use of political means to achieve national objectives.

politico-military gaming—*(DOD, IADB)* Simulation of situations involving the interaction of political, military, sociological, psychological, economic, scientific, and other appropriate factors.

pool—*(DOD, IADB)* 1. To maintain and control a supply of resources or personnel upon which other activities may draw. The primary purpose of a pool is to promote maximum efficiency of use of the pooled resources or personnel, e.g., a petroleum pool, a labor and equipment pool. 2. Any combination of resources which serves a common purpose.

popeye—*(DOD)* In air intercept, a code meaning, "In clouds or area of reduced visibility."

port—*(DOD, IADB)* A place at which ships may discharge or receive their cargoes. It includes any port accessible to ships on the seacoast, navigable rivers or inland waterways. The term "ports" should not be used in conjunction with air facilities which are designated as aerial ports, airports, etc. See also **control port; indoctrination port; major port; minor port; secondary port; water terminal.**

port capacity—*(DOD, NATO, IADB)* The estimated capacity of a port or an anchorage to clear cargo in 24 hours usually expressed in tons. See also **beach capacity; clearance capacity.**

port complex—*(DOD, NATO, IADB)* A port complex comprises one or more port areas of varying importance whose activities are geographically linked either because these areas are dependent on a common inland transport system or because they constitute a common initial destination for convoys.

port designator—*(DOD, NATO)* A group of letters identifying ports in convoy titles or messages.

port evacuation of shipping—*(DOD, NATO)* The movement of merchant ships from a threatened port for their own protection.

port security—*(DOD, NATO)* The safeguarding of vessels, harbors, ports, waterfront facilities and cargo from internal threats such as: destruction, loss, or injury from sabotage or other subversive acts; accidents; thefts; or other causes of similar nature. See also **harbor defense; physical security; security.**

Poseidon—*(DOD, IADB)* A two-stage, solid propellant ballistic missile capable of being launched from a specially configured submarine operating in either its surface or submerged mode. Designated as **UGM-73A.** The missile is equipped with inertial guidance, nuclear warheads and a maneuverable bus that has the capability to carry up to 14 reentry bodies which can be directed to as many as 14 separate targets.

positional defense—See **position defense.**

position defense—*(NATO, IADB)* The type of defense in which the bulk of the defending force is disposed in selected tactical localities where the decisive battle is to be fought. Principal reliance is placed on the ability of the forces in the defended localities to maintain their positions and to control the terrain between them. The reserve is used to add depth, to block, or restore the battle position by counterattack.

positive control—*(DOD, NATO, IADB)* A method of airspace control which relies on positive identification, tracking, and direction of aircraft within an airspace, conducted with electronic means by an agency having the authority and responsibility therein.

positive identification and radar advisory zone—*(DOD, IADB)* A specified area established for identification and flight following of aircraft in the vicinity of a fleet-defended area.

positive phase of the shock wave—*(DOD)* The period during which the pressure rises very sharply to a value that is higher than ambient and then decreases rapidly to the ambient pressure. See also **negative phase of the shock wave; shock wave.**

possible—*(DOD, IADB)* A term used to qualify a statement made under conditions wherein some evidence exists to support the statement. This evidence is sufficient to warrant mention, but insufficient to warrant assumption as true. See also **probable.**

postattack period—*(DOD)* In nuclear warfare, that period which extends from the termination of the final attack until political authorities agree to terminate hostilities. See also **post-hostilities period; transattack period.**

post-flight inspection—See **after-flight inspection.**

post hostilities period—*(DOD, IADB)* That period subsequent to the date of ratification by political authorities of agreements to terminate hostilities.

poststrike damage estimation—*(NATO)* A revised target analysis based on new data such as actual weapon yield, burst height, and ground zero obtained by means other than direct assessment.

277

poststrike reconnaissance—*(DOD, IADB)* Missions undertaken for the purpose of gathering information used to measure results of a strike.

pounce—*(DOD)* In air intercept, a code meaning, "I am in position to engage target."

PPI gauge—See **International Loading Gauge.**

practice mine—*(DOD, NATO, IADB)* 1. In land mine warfare, a replica of a standard mine, having the same features and weight as the mine it represents. It is constructed to emit a puff of smoke or make a noise to simulate detonation. See also **mine.** 2. In naval mine warfare, an inert-filled mine but complete with assembly, suitable for instruction and for practice in preparation. See also **drill mine.**

prearranged fire—*(DOD, NATO, IADB)* Fire that is formally planned and executed against targets or target areas of known location. Such fire is usually planned well in advance and is executed at a predetermined time or during a predetermined period of time. See also **fire; on call; scheduled fire.**

preassault operation—*(DOD, NATO, IADB)* An operation conducted in the objective area prior to the assault. It includes reconnaissance, minesweeping, bombardment, bombing, underwater demolition, and destruction of beach obstacles.

precautionary launch—*(DOD)* The launching of nuclear loaded aircraft under imminent nuclear attack so as to preclude friendly aircraft destruction and loss of weapons on the ground/carrier.

precedence—*(DOD, IADB)* 1. **communications**—A designation assigned to a message by the originator to indicate to communications personnel the relative order of handling and to the addressee the order in which the message is to be noted. 2. **reconnaissance**—A letter designation, assigned by a unit requesting several reconnaissance missions, to indicate the relative order of importance, within an established priority, of the mission requested. See also **flash message; immediate message; priority message; routine message.**

precedence—*(NATO)* A designation assigned to a message by the originator to indicate to communication personnel the relative order of handling and to the addressee the order in which the message is to be noted.

precession—See **apparent precession; induced precession; real precession.**

precision bombing—*(DOD, IADB)* Bombing directed at a specific point target.

precursor—*(IADB)* An air pressure wave that moves ahead of the main blast wave for some distance as a result of a nuclear explosion of appropriate yield and low burst height over a heat absorbing (or dusty) surface. The pressure at the precursor front increases more gradually than in a true (or ideal) shock wave, so that the behavior in the precursor region is said to be nonideal.

precursor front—*(DOD, NATO)* An air pressure wave which moves ahead of the main blast wave for some distance as a result of a nuclear explosion of appropriate yield and low burst height over a heat-absorbing (or dusty) surface. The pressure at the precursor front increases more gradually than in a true (or ideal) shock wave, so that the behavior in the precursor region is said to be nonideal.

precursor sweeping—*(DOD, NATO)* The sweeping of an area by relatively safe means in order to reduce the risk to mine countermeasures vessels in subsequent operations.

predicted fire—*(DOD, NATO)* Fire that is delivered without adjustment.

predominant height—*(DOD, NATO)* In air reconnaissance, the height of 51 percent or more of the structures within an area of similar surface material.

preemptive attack—*(DOD, IADB)* An attack initiated on the basis of incontrovertible evidence that an enemy attack is imminent.

preemptive war—*(DOD)* Not to be used. See **preemptive attack.**

preflight inspection—See **before-flight inspection.**

preinitiation—*(DOD)* The initiation of the fission chain reaction in the active material of a nuclear weapon at any time earlier than that at which either the designed or the maximum compression or degree of assembly is attained.

pre-launch survivability—*(DOD, IADB)* The probability that a delivery and/or launch vehicle will survive an enemy attack under an established condition of warning.

preliminary communications search—*(DOD)* In search and rescue operations, consists of contacting and checking major facilities within the areas where the craft might be or might have been seen. A preliminary communications search is normally conducted during the uncertainty phase. Also called PRECOM. See also **extended communications search; search and rescue incident classification,** Subpart a.

preliminary demolition—*(IADB)* A target prepared for demolition preliminary to a withdrawal, the demolition of which can be executed as soon after preparation as convenient on the orders of the officer to whom the responsibility for such demolitions has been delegated.

preliminary demolition target—*(DOD, NATO)* A target, other than a reserved demolition target, which is earmarked for demolition and which can be executed immediately after preparation, provided that prior authority has been granted. See also **reserved demolition target.**

preload loading—*(DOD, NATO, IADB)* The loading of selected items aboard ship at one port prior to the main loading of the ship at another. See also **loading.**

premature dud—See **flare dud.**

preparation fire—*(DOD, NATO, IADB)* Fire delivered on a target preparatory to an assault. See also **fire.**

preplanned air support—*(DOD, NATO, IADB)* Air support in accordance with a program, planned in advance of operations. See also **air support.**

preplanned mission request—*(DOD, IADB)* A request for an air strike on a target which can be anticipated sufficiently in advance to permit detailed mission coordination and planning.

preplanned mission request (reconnaissance)—*(DOD, IADB)* A request for a mission on a target or in support of a maneuver which can be anticipated sufficiently in advance to allow detailed mission coordination and planning.

preplanned nuclear support—*(DOD, IADB)* Nuclear support planned in advance of operations. See also **immediate nuclear support; nuclear support.**

pre-position—*(DOD, NATO, IADB)* To place military units, equipment, or supplies at or near the point of planned use or at a designated location to reduce reaction time, and to insure timely support of a specific force during initial phases of an operation.

pre-positioned war reserve materiel requirement, balance—*(DOD)* That portion of the pre-positioned war reserve materiel requirement which has not been acquired or funded. This level consists of the pre-positioned war reserve materiel requirement, less the pre-positioned war reserve requirement, protectable.

pre-positioned war reserve materiel requirement, protectable—*(DOD)* That portion of the pre-positioned war reserve materiel requirement which is protected for purposes of procurement, funding and inventory management.

pre-positioned war reserve requirement— *(DOD)* That portion of the war reserve materiel requirement which the current Secretary of Defense guidance dictates be reserved and positioned at or near the point of planned use or issue to the user prior to hostilities, to reduce reaction time and to assure timely support of a specific force/project until replenishment can be effected.

pre-positioned war reserve stock—*(DOD)* The assets that are designated to satisfy the pre-positioned war reserve materiel requirement.

prescribed nuclear load—*(DOD, NATO, IADB)* A specified quantity of nuclear weapons to be carried by a delivery unit. The establishment and replenishment of this load after each expenditure is a command decision and is dependent upon the tactical situation, the nuclear logistical situation, and the capability of the unit to transport and utilize the load. It may vary from day to day and among similar delivery units.

prescribed nuclear stockage—*(DOD, NATO, IADB)* A specified quantity of nuclear weapons, components of nuclear weapons, and warhead test equipment to be stocked in special ammunition supply points or other logistical installations. The establishment and replenishment of this stockage is a command decision and is dependent upon the tactical situation, the allocation, the capability of the logistical support unit to store and maintain the nuclear weapons, and the nuclear logistical situation. The prescribed stockage may vary from time to time and among similar logistical support units.

preset guidance—*(DOD, IADB)* A technique of missile control wherein a predetermined flight path is set into the control mechanism and cannot be adjusted after launching. See also **guidance.**

pre-set vector—See **bomb sighting systems.**

pressure-altitude—*(DOD, NATO, IADB)* An atmospheric pressure expressed in terms of altitude which corresponds to that pressure in the standard atmosphere. See also **altitude.**

pressure breathing—*(DOD, NATO, IADB)* The technique of breathing which is required when oxygen is supplied direct to an individual at a pressure higher than the ambient barometric pressure.

pressure front—See **shock front.**

pressure mine—*(DOD, NATO)* 1. In land mine warfare, a mine whose fuze responds to the direct pressure of a target. 2. In naval mine warfare, a mine whose circuit responds to the hydrodynamic pressure field of a target. See also **mine.**

pressure mine circuit—See **pressure mine.**

pressure suit—*(DOD, NATO, IADB)* 1. **Partial.** A skin tight suit which does not completely enclose the body but which is capable of exerting pressure on the major portion of the body in order to counteract an increased intrapulmonary oxygen pressure. 2. **Full.** A suit which completely encloses the body and in which a gas pressure, sufficiently above ambient pressure for maintenance of function, may be sustained.

pressurized cabin—*(DOD, IADB)* The occupied space of an aircraft in which the air pressure has been increased above that of the ambient atmosphere by compression of the ambient atmosphere into the space.

prestrike reconnaissance—*(DOD, IADB)* Missions undertaken for the purpose of obtaining complete information about known targets for use by the strike force.

prevention of stripping equipment—See **antirecovery device.**

preventive maintenance—*(DOD, IADB)* The care and servicing by personnel for the purpose of maintaining equipment and facilities in satisfactory operating condition by providing for systematic inspection, detection, and correction of incipient failures either before they occur or before they develop into major defects.

preventive maintenance—*(NATO)* Systematic and/or prescribed maintenance intended to reduce the probability of failure. See also **corrective maintenance.**

preventive war—*(DOD, IADB)* A war initiated in the belief that military conflict, while not imminent, is inevitable, and that to delay would involve greater risk.

prewithdrawal demolition target—*(DOD, IADB)* A target prepared for demolition preliminary to a withdrawal, the demolition of which can be executed as soon after preparation as convenient on the orders of the officer to whom the responsibility for such demolitions has been delegated.

primary aircraft authorization—*(DOD)* Aircraft authorized to a unit for performance of its operational mission. The primary authorization forms the basis for the allocation of operating resources to include manpower, support equipment, and flying hours funds. See also **backup aircraft authorization.**

primary aircraft inventory—*(DOD)* The aircraft assigned to meet the primary aircraft authorization.

primary censorship—*(DOD, IADB)* Armed forces censorship performed by personnel of a company, battery, squadron, ship, station, base, or similar unit on the personal communications of persons assigned, attached, or otherwise under the jurisdiction of a unit. See also **censorship.**

primary interest—*(DOD, IADB)* Principal, although not exclusive, interest and responsibility for accomplishment of a given mission, including responsibility for reconciling the activities of other agencies that possess collateral interest in the program.

primed charge—*(DOD, NATO)* A charge ready in all aspects for ignition.

prime mover—*(DOD, IADB)* A vehicle, including heavy construction equipment, possessing military characteristics, designed primarily for towing heavy, wheeled weapons and frequently providing facilities for the transportation of the crew of, and ammunition for, the weapon.

priming charge—*(NATO)* An initial charge which transmits the detonation wave to the whole of the charge.

principal items—*(DOD)* End items and replacement assemblies of such importance that management techniques require centralized individual item management throughout the supply system to include depot level, base level and items in the hands of using units. These specifically include the items where, in the judgment of the Services, there is a need for central inventory control including centralized computation of requirements, central procurement, central direction of distribution and central knowledge and control of all assets owned by the Services.

principal operational interest—*(DOD, IADB)* When used in connection with an established facility operated by one Service for joint use by two or more Services, the term indicates a requirement for the greatest use of, or the greatest need for, the services of that facility. The term may be applied to a Service, but is more applicable to a command.

principal parallel—*(DOD, NATO)* On an oblique photograph, a line parallel to the true horizon and passing through the principal point.

principal plane—*(DOD, NATO)* A vertical plane which contains the principal point of an oblique photograph, the perspective center of the lens and the ground nadir.

principal point—*(DOD, NATO)* The foot of the perpendicular to the photo plane through the perspective center. Generally determined by intersection of the lines joining opposite collimating or fiducial marks.

principal scale—*(DOD, NATO)* In cartography, the scale of a reduced or generating globe representing the sphere or spheroid, defined by the fractional relation of their respective radii. Also called **nominal scale.**" See also **scale.**

Principal Subordinate Commanders—*(NATO)* The designation assigned to NATO commanders operationally responsible to Major Subordinate Commanders for an allocated geographical area or function. See also **Major NATO Commanders; Major Subordinate Commanders; Subordinate Area Commanders.**

principal vertical—*(DOD, NATO)* On an oblique photograph, a line perpendicular to the true horizon and passing through the principal point.

printing size of a map or chart—*(DOD, NATO)* The dimensions of the smallest rectangle which will contain a map or chart including all the printed material in its margin.

print reference—*(DOD, NATO)* A reference to an individual print in an air photographic sortie.

priority—*(DOD, IADB)* With reference to war plans and the tasks derived therefrom, an indication of relative importance rather than an exclusive and final designation of the order of accomplishment.

priority designator—*(DOD)* A two-digit issue and priority code (01 through 15) placed in military standard requisitioning and issue procedure requisitions, based upon a combination of factors which relate the mission of the requisitioner and the urgency of need or the end use, used to provide a means of assigning relative rankings to competing demands placed on the Department of Defense supply system.

priority intelligence requirements—*(DOD, NATO)* Those intelligence requirements for which a commander has an anticipated and stated priority in his task of planning and decision making. See also **information requirements; intelligence cycle.**

priority message—*(DOD, IADB)* A category of precedence reserved for messages which require expeditious action by the addressee(s) and/or furnish essential information for the conduct of operations in progress when routine precedence will not suffice. See also **precedence.**

priority national intelligence objectives—*(DOD)* A guide for the coordination of intelligence collection and production in response to requirements relating to the formulation and execution of national security policy. They are compiled annually by the Washington Intelligence Community and flow directly from the intelligence mission as set forth by the National Security Council. They are specific enough to provide a basis for planning the allocation of collection and research resources but not so specific as to constitute in themselves research and collection requirements.

priority national intelligence objectives—*(IADB)* A guide for the coordination of intelligence collection and production in response to requirements relating to the formulation and execution of national security policy. They are specific enough to provide a basis for planning the allocation of collection and research resources but not so specific as to constitute in themselves research and collection requirements.

priority of immediate mission requests—See **emergency priority; ordinary priority; search and attack priority; urgent priority.**

priority of preplanned mission requests—*(DOD, IADB)* 1. Targets capable of preventing the execution of the plan of action. 2. Targets capable of immediate serious interference with the plan of action. 3. Targets capable of ultimate serious interference with the execution of the plan of action. 4. Targets capable of limited interference with the execution of the plan of action.

priority system for mission requests for tactical reconnaissance—*(DOD, IADB)* Priority I—Takes precedence over all other requests except previously assigned priorities I. The results of these requests are of paramount importance to the immediate battle situation or objective. **Priority II**—The results of these requirements are in support of the general battle situation and will be accomplished as soon as possible after priorities I. These are requests to gain current battle information. **Priority III**—The results of these requests update the intelligence data base but do not affect the immediate battle situation. **Priority IV**—The results of these requests are of a routine nature. These results will be fulfilled when the reconnaissance effort permits. See also **precedence.**

prior permission—*(DOD, NATO, IADB)* Permission granted by the appropriate authority prior to the commencement of a flight or a series of flights landing in or flying over the territory of the nation concerned.

prisoner of war—*(DOD)* A detained person as defined in Articles 4 and 5 of the Geneva Convention Relative to the Treatment of Prisoners of War of August 12, 1949. In particular, one who, while engaged in combat under orders of his government, is captured by the armed forces of the enemy. As such, he is entitled to the combatant's privilege of immunity from the municipal law of the capturing state for warlike acts which do not amount to breaches of the law of armed conflict. For example, a prisoner of war may be, but is not limited to, any person belonging to one of the following categories who has fallen into the power of the enemy: a member of the armed forces, organized militia or volunteer corps; a person who accompanies the armed forces without actually being a member thereof; a member of a merchant marine or civilian aircraft crew not qualifying for more favorable treatment; or individuals who, on the ap-

proach of the enemy, spontaneously take up arms to resist the invading forces.

prisoner of war branch camp—*(DOD, NATO)* A subsidiary camp under the supervision and administration of a prisoner of war camp.

prisoner of war camp—*(DOD, IADB)* An installation established for the internment and administration of prisoners of war.

prisoner of war camp—*(NATO)* A camp of a semi-permanent nature established in the communication zone or zone of interior (home country) for the internment and complete administration of prisoners of war. It may be located on, or independent of, other military installations.

prisoner of war censorship—*(DOD)* The censorship of the communications to and from enemy prisoners of war and civilian internees held by the United States Armed Forces. See also **censorship.**

prisoner of war collecting point—*(NATO)* A designated locality in a forward battle area where prisoners are assembled pending local examination for information of immediate tactical value and subsequent evacuation.

prisoner of war compound—*(DOD, NATO, IADB)* A subdivision of a prisoner of war enclosure.

prisoner of war enclosure—*(DOD, NATO, IADB)* A subdivision of a prisoner of war camp.

prisoner of war personnel record—*(DOD, NATO, IADB)* A form for recording the photograph, fingerprints, and other pertinent personal data concerning the prisoner of war, including that required by the Geneva Convention.

prisoners of war—*(IADB)* Persons as defined in the Geneva Convention relative to the Treatment of Prisoners of War, 12 August 1949 (GPW).

probability of damage—*(DOD, NATO, IADB)* The probability that damage will occur to a target expressed as a percentage or as a decimal.

probability of detection—*(DOD)* The probability that the search object will be detected under given conditions if it is in the area searched.

probable—*(DOD, IADB)* A term used to qualify a statement made under conditions wherein the available evidence indicates that the statement is factual until there is further evidence in confirmation or denial. See also **possible**.

probable error—See **horizontal error**.

probable error deflection—*(DOD)* Error in deflection which is exceeded as often as not.

probable error height of burst—*(DOD)* Error in height of burst which projectile/missile fuzes may be expected to exceed as often as not.

probable error range—*(DOD)* Error in range which is exceeded as often as not.

probably destroyed (aircraft)—*(DOD, NATO, IADB)* A damage assessment on an enemy aircraft seen to break-off combat in circumstances which lead to the conclusion that it must be a loss although it is not actually seen to crash.

procedural control—*(DOD, NATO)* A method of airspace control which relies on a combination of previously agreed and promulgated orders and procedures.

procedure turn—*(DOD, NATO)* An aircraft maneuver in which a turn is made away from a designated track followed by a turn in the opposite direction, both turns being executed at a constant rate so as to permit the aircraft to intercept and proceed along the reciprocal of the designated track.

procedure word—*(DOD)* A word or phrase limited to radio telephone procedure used to facilitate communication by conveying information in a condensed standard form. Usually called **proword**.

processing—*(DOD, NATO)* 1. In photography, the operations necessary to produce negatives, diapositives, or prints from exposed films, plates or paper. 2. See **intelligence cycle**.

proclamation—*(DOD, IADB)* A document published to the inhabitants of an area which sets forth the basis of authority and scope of activities of a commander in a given area and which defines the obligations, liabilities, duties, and rights of the population affected.

procurement—*(DOD, IADB)* The process of obtaining personnel, services, supplies, and equipment. See also **central procurement**.

procurement lead time—*(DOD, IADB)* The interval in months between the initiation of procurement action and receipt into the supply system of the production model (excludes prototypes) purchased as the result of such actions, and is composed of two elements, production lead time and administrative lead time. See also **initiation of procurement action; level of supply; receipt into the supply system**.

production—*(DOD, IADB)* The conversion of raw materials into products and/or components thereof, through a series of manufacturing processes. It includes functions of production engineering, controlling, quality assurance, and the determination of resources requirements.

production base—*(DOD, IADB)* The total national industrial production capacity available for the manufacture of items to meet materiel requirements.

production lead time—*(DOD, IADB)* The time interval between the placement of a contract and receipt into the supply system of materiel purchased. Two entries are provided:

a. initial—The time interval if the item is not under production as of the date of contract placement.

b. reorder—The time interval if the item is under production as of the date of contract placement. See also **procurement lead time.**

production logistics—*(DOD)* That part of logistics concerning research, design, development, manufacture and acceptance of materiel. In consequence, production logistics includes: standardization and interoperability, contracting, quality assurance, initial provisioning, transportability, reliability and defect analysis, safety standards, specifications and production processes, trials and testing (including provision of necessary facilities), equipment documentation, configuration control and modifications.

production loss appraisal—*(DOD, IADB)* An estimate of damage inflicted on an industry in terms of quantities of finished products denied the enemy from the moment of attack, through the period of reconstruction, and to the point when full production is resumed.

proficiency training aircraft—*(DOD, IADB)* Aircraft required to maintain the proficiency of pilots and other aircrew members who are assigned to nonflying duties.

profile—See **flight profile.**

proforma—*(DOD, NATO)* A standard form. See also **standard NATO data message.**

proforma—*(IADB)* 1. A message, the nature of the successive elements of which is understood by prearrangement. 2. A standard form.

program aircraft—*(DOD, IADB)* The total of the active and reserve aircraft. See also **aircraft.**

program manager—See **system manager.**

Programmed Forces—*(DOD)* The forces that exist for each year of the Five-Year Defense Program. They contain the major combat and tactical support forces that are expected to execute the national strategy within manpower, fiscal, and other constraints. See also **Current Force; force; Intermediate Force Planning Level; Minimum Risk Force; Planning Force.**

program of nuclear cooperation—*(DOD, NATO)* Presidentially approved bilateral proposals for the United States to provide nuclear weapons, and specified support to user nations who desire to commit delivery units to NATO in nuclear only or dual capable roles. After presidential approval in principle, negotiations will be initiated with the user nation to develop detailed support arrangements.

progress payment—*(DOD, IADB)* Payment made as work progresses under a contract, upon the basis of costs incurred, of percentage of completion accomplished, or of a particular stage of completion. The term does not include payments for partial deliveries accepted by the Government under a contract, or partial payments on contract termination claims.

prohibited area—*(DOD, IADB)* A specified area within the land areas of a state or territorial waters adjacent thereto over which the flight of aircraft is prohibited. May also refer to land or sea areas to which access is prohibited. See also **danger area; restricted area.**

prohibited area—*(NATO)* 1. An airspace of defined dimensions, above the land areas or territorial waters of a state, within which the flight of aircraft is prohibited. 2. An area shown on charts within which navigation and/or anchoring is prohibited except as authorized by appropriate authority. See also **danger area; restricted area.**

project—*(DOD)* A planned undertaking of something to be accomplished, produced, or constructed, having a finite beginning and a finite ending.

projected map display—*(DOD, NATO)* The displayed image of a map or chart projected

285

through an optical or electro-optical system onto a viewing surface.

projectile—*(DOD, IADB)* An object projected by an applied exterior force and continuing in motion by virtue of its own inertia, as a bullet, shell, or grenade. Also applied to rockets and to guided missiles.

projectile—*(NATO)* An object capable of being propelled by a force normally from a gun, and continuing in motion by virtue of its kinetic energy.

projection—*(DOD, NATO)* In cartography, any systematic arrangement of meridians and parallels portraying the curved surface of the sphere or spheroid upon a plane.

projection print—*(DOD)* An enlarged or reduced photographic print made by projection of the image of a negative or a transparency onto a sensitized surface.

projection print—*(NATO)* A photographic print obtained by projection of the image of a negative or a transparency on to a sensitized surface.

project manager—See **system manager.**

proliferation (nuclear weapons)—*(DOD)* The process by which one nation after another comes into possession of, or into the right to determine the use of nuclear weapons, each potentially able to launch a nuclear attack upon another nation.

prompt radiation—*(DOD)* The gamma rays produced in fission and as a result of other neutron reactions and nuclear excitation of the weapon materials appearing within a second or less after a nuclear explosion. The radiations from these sources are known either as prompt or instantaneous gamma rays. See also **induced radiation; initial radiation; residual radiation.**

pronto—*(DOD)* As quickly as possible.

propaganda—*(DOD, I, IADB)* Any form of communication in support of national objectives designed to influence the opinions, emotions, attitudes, or behavior of any group in order to benefit the sponsor, either directly or indirectly. See also **black propaganda; grey propaganda; white propaganda.**

propaganda—*(NATO)* Any information, ideas, doctrines, or special appeals disseminated to influence the opinion, emotions, attitudes, or behavior of any specified group in order to benefit the sponsor either directly or indirectly. **a. Black.** Propaganda which purports to emanate from a source other than the true one. **b. Grey.** Propaganda which does not specifically identify any source. **c. White.** Propaganda disseminated and acknowledged by the sponsor or by an accredited agency thereof.

propellant—*(DOD, IADB)* That source which provides the energy required for propelling a projectile. Specifically, an explosive charge for propelling a projectile; also a fuel, either solid or liquid, for propelling a rocket or missile.

propelled mine—See **mobile mine.**

property—*(DOD, IADB)* 1. Anything that may be owned. 2. As used in the military establishment, this term is usually confined to tangible property, including real estate and materiel. 3. For special purposes and as used in certain statutes, this term may exclude such items as the public domain, certain lands, certain categories of naval vessels and records of the Federal Government.

property account—*(DOD)* A formal record of property and property transactions in terms of quantity and/or cost, generally by item. An official record of Government property required to be maintained.

proportional navigation—*(DOD, IADB)* A method of homing navigation in which the missile turn rate is directly proportional to the turn rate in space of the line of sight.

protective clothing—*(DOD, NATO)* Clothing especially designed, fabricated, or treated to protect personnel against hazards caused by extreme changes in physical environment, dangerous working conditions, or enemy action.

protective minefield—*(DOD, NATO, IADB)* 1. In land mine warfare, a minefield employed to assist a unit in its local, close-in protection. 2. In naval mine warfare, a minefield laid in friendly territorial waters to protect ports, harbors, anchorages, coasts and coastal routes. See also **minefield**.

protective security—*(NATO)* The organized system of defensive measures instituted and maintained at all levels of command with the aim of achieving and maintaining security. See also **physical security; security**.

prototype—*(DOD, IADB)* A model suitable for evaluation of design, performance, and production potential.

Provider—*(DOD, IADB)* An assault, twin-engine transport which can operate from short, unprepared landing strips to transport troops and assorted equipment. Twin jets are installed to supplement the takeoff capability. Designated as C–123. AC–12K is the gunship version.

provisional unit—*(NATO, IADB)* An assemblage of personnel and equipment temporarily organized for a limited period of time for the accomplishment of a specific mission.

provisioning—See **initial provisioning**.

Prowler—*(DOD)* A twin turbojet engine, quadruple crew, all-weather, electronic countermeasures aircraft designed to operate from aircraft carriers. It contains a wide assortment of integrated, computer-controlled, active and passive electronic countermeasures equipment. Designated as EA–6B.

proword—See **procedure word**.

proximity fuze—*(DOD, NATO)* A fuze wherein primary initiation occurs by remotely sensing the presence, distance, and/or direction of a target or its associated environment by means of a signal generated by the fuze or emitted by the target, or by detecting a disturbance of a natural field surrounding the target.

prudent limit of endurance—*(DOD, NATO, IADB)* The time during which an aircraft can remain airborne and still retain a given safety margin of fuel.

prudent limit of patrol—*(DOD, NATO)* The time at which an aircraft must depart from its operational area in order to return to its base and arrive there with a given safety margin (usually 20 percent) of fuel reserve for bad weather diversions.

pseudopursuit navigation—*(DOD, IADB)* A method of homing navigation in which the missile is directed toward the instantaneous target position in azimuth, while pursuit navigation in elevation is delayed until more favorable angle of attack on the target is achieved.

psychological consolidation activities—*(DOD, NATO)* Planned psychological activities in peace and war directed at the civilian population located in areas under friendly control in order to achieve a desired behavior which supports the military objectives and the operational freedom of the supported commanders.

psychological media—*(NATO)* The media, technical or non-technical, which establish any kind of communication with a target audience.

psychological operations—*(DOD, NATO)* Planned psychological activities in peace and war directed to enemy, friendly, and neutral audiences in order to influence attitudes and behavior affecting the achievement of political and military objectives. They include strategic psychological activities, consolidation psychological operations and battlefield psychological activities.

psychological operations—*(IADB)* These operations include psychological warfare and, in addition, encompass those political, military, economic, and ideological actions planned and conducted to create in neutral or friendly foreign groups the emotions, attitudes, or behavior to support the achievement of national objectives.

psychological operations approach—*(NATO)* The technique adopted to induce a desired reaction on the part of the target audience.

psychological situation—*(NATO)* The current emotional state, mental disposition or other behavioral motivation of a target audience, basically founded on its national political, social, economic, and psychological peculiarities but also subject to the influence of circumstances and events.

psychological theme—*(NATO)* An idea or topic on which a psychological operation is based.

psychological warfare—*(DOD, IADB)* The planned use of propaganda and other psychological actions having the primary purpose of influencing the opinions, emotions, attitudes, and behavior of hostile foreign groups in such a way as to support the achievement of national objectives. See also **psychological warfare consolidation.**

psychological warfare consolidation—*(DOD, IADB)* Psychological warfare directed toward populations in friendly rear areas or in territory occupied by friendly military forces with the objective of facilitating military operations and promoting maximum cooperation among the civil populace. See also **psychological warfare.**

public affairs—*(DOD, IADB)* Those public information and community relations activities directed toward the general public by the various elements of the Department of Defense.

public information—*(DOD, IADB)* Information of a military nature, the dissemination of which through public news media is not inconsistent with security, and the release of which is considered desirable or nonobjectionable to the responsible releasing agency.

public information—*(NATO)* Information which is released or published for the primary purpose of keeping the public fully informed, thereby gaining their understanding and support.

pull-up point—*(DOD, NATO, IADB)* The point at which an aircraft must start to climb from a low-level approach in order to gain sufficient height from which to execute the attack or retirement. See also **contact point; turn-in point.**

pulse duration—*(DOD, IADB)* In radar, measurement of pulse transmission time in microseconds, that is, the time the radar's transmitter is energized during each cycle. Also called pulse length and pulse width.

pulsejet—*(DOD, NATO, IADB)* A jet-propulsion engine containing neither compressor nor turbine. Equipped with valves in the front which open and shut, it takes in air to create thrust in rapid periodic bursts rather than continuously.

pulse repetition frequency—*(DOD, IADB)* In radar, the number of pulses that occur each second. Not to be confused with transmission frequency which is determined by the rate at which cycles are repeated within the transmitted pulse.

pulsing—*(DOD, NATO)* In naval mine warfare, a method of operating magnetic and acoustic sweeps in which the sweep is energized by current which varies or is intermittent in accordance with a predetermined schedule.

punch—*(DOD)* In air intercept, a code meaning, "You should very soon be obtaining a contact on the aircraft that is being intercepted." (Use only with "air intercept" interceptions.)

purchase—*(DOD, IADB)* To procure property or services for a price; includes obtaining by barter. See also **collaborative purchase; joint purchase; single department purchase.**

purchase description—*(DOD)* A statement outlining the essential characteristics and functions of an item, service, or material required to meet the minimum needs of the Government. It is used when a specification is not available or when specific procurement specifications are not required by the individual Military Departments or the Department of Defense.

purchase description—*(IADB)* A statement outlining the essential characteristics and functions of an item, service, or material required to meet the minimum needs of the purchaser.

purchase notice agreements—*(DOD)* Agreements concerning the purchase of brand-name items for resale purposes established by each military Service under the control of the Defense Logistics Agency.

purchasing office—*(DOD, IADB)* Any installation or activity, or any division, office, branch, section, unit, or other organizational element of an installation or activity charged with the functions of procuring supplies or services.

purple—*(DOD)* In air intercept, a code meaning, "The unit indicated is suspected of carrying nuclear weapons" (i.e., "purple VB").

purple commander—*(DOD, NATO)* The officer designated to exercise operational control over purple forces for a specific period during an exercise.

purple forces—*(NATO)* Those forces used to oppose both blue and orange forces in NATO exercises. This is most usually applicable to submarines and aircraft. See also **force(s).**

pursuit—*(DOD, NATO)* An offensive operation designed to catch or cut off a hostile force attempting to escape, with the aim of destroying it.

pyrotechnic—*(DOD, NATO)* A mixture of chemicals which when ignited is capable of reacting exothermically to produce light, heat, smoke, sound or gas, and may also be used to introduce a delay into an explosive train because of its known burning time. The term excludes propellants and explosives.

pyrotechnic delay—*(DOD, NATO)* A pyrotechnic device added to a firing system which transmits the ignition flame after a predetermined delay.

Q

q-message—(DOD, NATO) A classified message relating to navigational dangers, navigational aids, mined areas, and searched or swept channels.

Q-ship—See **decoy ship.**

quadrant elevation—(DOD, NATO) The angle between the level base of the trajectory/horizontal and the axis of the bore when laid. (DOD) It is the algebraic sum of the elevation, angle of site, and complementary angle of site.

Quail—(DOD, IADB) An air-launched decoy missile carried internally in the B-52 and used to degrade the effectivenes of enemy radar, interceptor aircraft, air defense missiles, etc. Designated as **ADM-20.**

quick search procedure—(NATO) A method of search done as quickly as possible by searching the entire area on the outbound leg and by using twice as many aircraft as are normally used.

quicktrans—(DOD) Long term contract airlift service within continental United States for the movement of cargo in suport of the logistic system for the military Services (primarily the Navy and Marine Corps) and Department of Defense agencies. See also **logair.**

quota post—(NATO) An international post which a particular nation has accepted to fill indefinitely.

R

radar—*(DOD, IADB)* A radio detection device which provides information on range, azimuth and/or elevation of objects.

radar advisory—*(DOD, IADB)* The term used to indicate that the provision of advice and information is based on radar observation.

radar altimeter—See altimeter.

radar altimetry area—*(DOD, NATO)* A large and comparatively level terrain area with a defined elevation which can be used in determining the altitude of airborne equipment by the use of radar.

radar altitude control mode—*(DOD, NATO)* In an automatic flight control system, a control mode in which the height of an aircraft is maintained by reference to signals from a radar altimeter.

radar beacon—*(DOD, IADB)* A receiver-transmitter combination which sends out a coded signal when triggered by the proper type of pulse, enabling determination of range and bearing information by the interrogating station or aircraft.

radar camouflage—*(DOD, NATO)* The use of radar absorbent or reflecting materials to change the radar echoing properties of a surface of an object.

radar clutter—*(DOD, NATO, IADB)* Unwanted signals, echoes, or images on the face of the display tube, which interfere with observation of desired signals.

radar countermeasures—See electronic warfare; chaff.

radar coverage—*(DOD, NATO, IADB)* The limits within which objects can be detected by one or more radar stations.

radar danning—*(DOD, NATO)* In naval mine warfare, a method of navigating by using radar to keep the required distance from a line of dan buoys.

radar deception—See electronic deception.

radar echo—*(NATO)* 1. The electromagnetic energy received after reflection from an object. 2. The deflection or change of intensity on a cathode ray tube display produced by a radar echo.

radar fire—*(DOD, NATO, IADB)* Gunfire aimed at a target which is tracked by radar. See also fire.

radar guardship—*(DOD, NATO)* Any ship which has been assigned the task by the officer in tactical command of maintaining the radar watch.

radar horizon—*(DOD, NATO)* The locus of points at which the rays from a radar antenna become tangential to the earth's surface. On the open sea this locus is horizontal but on land it varies according to the topographical features of the terrain.

radar imagery—*(DOD, IADB)* Imagery produced by recording radar waves reflected from a given target surface.

radar intelligence—*(DOD)* Intelligence information derived from data collected by radar. Also called RADINT.

radar netting—*(DOD, NATO, IADB)* The linking of several radars to a single center to provide integrated target information.

radar netting station—*(DOD, NATO, IADB)* A center which can receive data from radar tracking stations and exchange this data among other radar tracking stations, thus forming a radar netting system. See also radar netting unit; radar tracking station.

radar netting unit—*(DOD, IADB)* Optional electronic equipment which converts the operations central of certain air defense fire distribution systems to a radar netting station. See also **radar netting station.**

radar picket—*(DOD, NATO, IADB)* Any ship, aircraft, or vehicle, stationed at a distance from the force protected, for the purpose of increasing the radar detection range.

radar picket CAP—*(DOD)* Radar picket combat air patrol.

radar reconnaissance—*(DOD, IADB)* Reconnaissance by means of radar to obtain information on enemy activity and to determine the nature of terrain.

radar return—See **radar echo.**

radarscope overlay—*(DOD, NATO)* A transparent overlay for placing on the radarscope for comparison and identification of radar returns.

radarscope photography—*(DOD, NATO)* A film record of the returns shown by a radar screen.

radar signal film—*(DOD)* The film on which is recorded all the reflected signals acquired by a coherent radar, and which must be viewed or processed through an optical correlator to permit interpretation.

radar silence—*(DOD, NATO, IADB)* An imposed discipline prohibiting the transmission by radar of electromagnetic signals on some or all frequencies.

radar tracking station—*(DOD, IADB)* A radar facility which has the capability of tracking moving targets.

radiac—*(DOD, NATO)* An acronym derived from the words "*ra*dioactivity, *d*etection, *i*ndication *a*nd *c*omputation" and used as an all-encompassing term to designate various types of radiological measuring instruments or equipment. (This word is normally used as an adjective.)

radiac dosimeter—*(DOD, IADB)* An instrument used to measure the ionizing radiation absorbed by that instrument.

radial—*(DOD, IADB)* A magnetic bearing extending from a very high frequency omni-range/tactical air navigation station.

radial displacement—*(DOD, NATO)* On vertical photographs, the apparent "leaning out," or the apparent displacement of the top of any object having height in relation to its base. The direction of displacement is radial from the principal point on a true vertical, or from the isocentre on a vertical photograph distorted by tip or tilt.

radiant exposure—See **thermal exposure.**

radiation dose—*(DOD, NATO)* The total amount of ionizing radiation absorbed by material or tissues, expressed in centigrays. *(DOD)* The term radiation dose is often used in the sense of the exposure dose expressed in roentgens, which is a measure of the total amount of ionization that the quantity of radiation could produce in air. This could be distinguished from the absorbed dose, also given in rads, which represents the energy absorbed from the radiation per gram of specified body tissue. Further, the biological dose, in rems, is a measure of the biological effectiveness of the radiation exposure.

radiation dose—*(IADB)* The total amount of ionizing radiation absorbed by material or tissues, commonly expressed in rads

radiation dose rate—*(DOD, NATO, IADB)* The radiation dose (dosage) absorbed per unit of time. *(DOD, IADB)* A radiation dose rate can be set at some particular unit of time (e.g., H + 1 hour) and would be called H + 1 radiation dose rate.

radiation exposure state—*(DOD, NATO)* The condition of a unit, or exceptionally an individual, deduced from the cumulative whole body radiation dose(s) received. It is expressed as a symbol which indicates the potential for future operations and the degree of risk if exposed to additional nuclear radiation.

radiation intelligence—*(DOD)* Intelligence derived from the collection and analysis of non-information-bearing elements extracted from the electromagnetic energy unintentionally emanated by foreign devices, equipments, and systems, excluding those generated by the detonation of atomic/nuclear weapons.

radiation intensity—*(DOD, NATO, IADB)* The radiation dose rate at a given time and place. It may be used, coupled with a figure, to denote the radiation intensity used at a given number of hours after a nuclear burst, e.g., RI-3 is a radiation intensity 3 hours after the time of burst.

radiation scattering—*(DOD, NATO, IADB)* The diversion of radiation (thermal, electromagnetic, or nuclear) from its original path as a result of interaction or collisions with atoms, molecules, or larger particles in the atmosphere or other media between the source of the radiation (e.g., a nuclear explosion) and a point at some distance away. As a result of scattering, radiation (especially gamma rays and neutrons) will be received at such a point from many directions instead of only from the direction of the source.

radiation sickness—*(NATO, IADB)* An illness resulting from excessive exposure to ionizing radiation. The earliest symptoms are nausea, vomiting, and diarrhea, which may be followed by loss of hair, hemorrhage, inflammation of the mouth and throat, and general loss of energy.

radiation situation map—*(NATO, IADB)* A map showing the actual and/or predicted radiation situation in the area of interest.

RADINT—See radar intelligence.

radioactivity—*(DOD, IADB)* The spontaneous emission of radiation, generally alpha or beta particles, often accompanied by gamma rays, from the nuclei of an unstable isotope.

radioactivity concentration guide—*(DOD, NATO, IADB)* The amount of any specified radioisotope that is acceptable in air and water for continuous consumption.

radio altimeter—See altimeter.

radio and wire integration—*(DOD)* The combining of wire circuits with radio facilities.

radio approach aids—*(DOD, NATO, IADB)* Equipment making use of radio to determine the position of an aircraft with considerable accuracy from the time it is in the vicinity of an airfield or carrier until it reaches a position from which landing can be carried out.

radio beacon—*(DOD, NATO, IADB)* A radio transmitter which emits a distinctive, or characteristic, signal used for the determination of bearings, courses, or location. See also **beacon.**

radio countermeasures—See electronic warfare.

radio deception—*(DOD, IADB)* The employment of radio to deceive the enemy. Radio deception includes sending false dispatches, using deceptive headings, employing enemy call signs, etc. See also **electronic warfare.**

radio detection—*(DOD, NATO, IADB)* The detection of the presence of an object by radiolocation without precise determination of its position.

radio direction finding—*(DOD, NATO, IADB)* Radio-location in which only the direction of a station is determined by means of its emissions.

radio direction finding data base—*(DOD, IADB)* The aggregate of information, acquired by both airborne and surface means, necessary to provide support to radio direction finding operations to produce fixes on target transmitters/emitters. The resultant bearings and fixes serve as a basis for tactical decisions concerning military operations, including exercises, planned or underway.

radio fix—*(DOD, NATO, IADB)* 1. The locating of a radio transmitter by bearings taken from two or more direction finding stations, the site of the transmitter being at the point of intersection. 2. The location of a ship or aircraft by determining the direction of radio signals coming to the ship or aircraft from two or more sending stations, the locations of which are known.

radio guard—*(DOD, IADB)* A ship, aircraft, or radio station designated to listen for and record transmissions, and to handle traffic on a designated frequency for a certain unit or units.

radiological defense—*(DOD, NATO, IADB)* Defensive measures taken against the radiation hazards resulting from the employment of nuclear and radiological weapons.

radiological monitoring—See **monitoring.**

radiological operation—*(DOD, NATO, IADB)* The employment of radioactive materials or radiation producing devices to cause casualties or restrict the use of terrain. It includes the intentional employment of fallout from nuclear weapons.

radiological survey—*(DOD, NATO, IADB)* The directed effort to determine the distribution and dose rates of radiation in an area.

radiological survey flight altitude—*(DOD, IADB)* The altitude at which an aircraft is flown during an aerial radiological survey.

radio magnetic indicator—*(DOD, NATO)* An instrument which displays aircraft heading and bearing to selected radio navigation aids.

radio navigation—*(DOD, NATO, IADB)* Radio-location intended for the determination of po-sition or direction or for obstruction warning in navigation.

radio range finding—*(DOD, NATO, IADB)* Radio-location in which the distance of an object is determined by means of its radio emissions, whether independent, reflected, or retransmitted on the same or other wave length.

radio range station—*(DOD, NATO, IADB)* A radio navigation land station in the aeronautical radio navigation service providing radio equi-signal zones. (In certain instances a radio range station may be placed on board a ship.)

radio recognition—*(DOD, NATO, IADB)* The determination by radio means of the friendly or enemy character, or the individuality, of another.

radio recognization and identification—See **Identification Friend or Foe.**

radio silence—*(DOD, NATO)* A condition in which all or certain radio equipment capable of radiation is kept inoperative. *(DOD)* (Note: In combined or United States Joint or intra-Service communications the frequency bands and/or types of equipment affected will be specified.)

radio sonobuoy—See **sonobuoy.**

radio telegraphy—*(DOD, NATO, IADB)* The transmission of telegraphic codes by means of radio.

radio telephony—*(DOD, NATO, IADB)* The transmission of speech by means of modulated radio waves.

radius of action—*(DOD, NATO, IADB)* The maximum distance a ship, aircraft, or vehicle can travel away from its base along a given course with normal combat load and return without refueling, allowing for all safety and operating factors.

radius of damage—*(DOD, IADB)* The distance from ground zero at which there is a 0.50 probability of achieving the desired damage.

radius of integration—*(DOD, IADB)* The distance from ground zero which indicates the area within which the effects of both the nuclear detonation and conventional weapons are to be integrated.

radius of safety—*(DOD, NATO, IADB)* The horizontal distance from ground zero beyond which the weapon effects on friendly troops are acceptable.

raid—*(DOD, NATO, IADB)* An operation, usually small scale, involving a swift penetration of hostile territory to secure information, confuse the enemy, or to destroy his installations. It ends with a planned withdrawal upon completion of the assigned mission.

raid report—*(DOD, NATO)* In air defense, one of a series of related reports that are made for the purpose of developing a plot to assist in the rapid evaluation of a tactical situation.

railhead—*(DOD, NATO)* A point on a railway where loads are transferred between trains and other means of transport. See also **navigation head.**

railway line capacity—*(DOD, NATO)* The maximum number of trains which can be moved in each direction over a specified section of track in a 24 hour period. See also **route capacity.**

railway loading ramp—*(DOD, NATO)* A sloping platform situated at the end or beside a track and rising to the level of the floor of the rail cars or wagons.

rainfall (nuclear)—*(DOD, IADB)* The water that is precipitated from the base surge clouds after an underwater burst of a nuclear weapon. This rain is radioactive and presents an important secondary effect of such a burst.

rainout—*(DOD, NATO, IADB)* Radioactive material in the atmosphere brought down by precipitation.

ramjet—*(DOD, NATO, IADB)* A jet-propulsion engine containing neither compressor nor turbine which depends for its operation on the air compression accomplished by the forward motion of the engine. See also **pulsejet.**

random minelaying—*(DOD, NATO)* In land mine warfare, the laying of mines without regard to pattern.

range—*(DOD, IADB)* 1. The distance between any given point and an object or target. 2. Extent or distance limiting the operation or action of something, such as the range of an aircraft, ship, or gun. 3. The distance which can be covered over a hard surface by a ground vehicle, with its rated payload, using the fuel in its tank and its cans normally carried as part of the ground vehicle equipment. 4. Area equipped for practice in shooting at targets. In this meaning, also called target range.

range—*(NATO)* 1. The distance between any given point and an object or target. 2. Extent or distance limiting the operation or action of something, such as the range of an aircraft, ship, or gun. 3. The distance which can be covered over a hard suface by a ground vehicle, with its rated payload, using the fuel in its tank and its cans normally carried as part of the ground vehicle equipment. 4. An area reserved and normally equipped for practice in weapons delivery and/or shooting at targets. Also called "target range."

range marker—*(DOD, NATO)* A single calibration blip fed onto the time base of a radial display. The rotation of the time base shows the single blips as a circle on the plan position indicator scope. It may be used to measure range.

range markers—*(DOD, IADB)* Two upright markers which may be lighted at night, placed so that when aligned, the direction indicated assists in piloting. They may be used in amphibious operations to aid in beaching landing ships or craft.

range resolution—*(NATO)* The ability of the radar equipment to separate two reflecting objects on a similar bearing, but at different ranges from the antenna. The ability is determined primarily by the pulse length in use.

range spread—*(DOD, IADB)* The technique used to place the mean point of impact of two or more units 100 meters apart on the gun-target line.

ranging—*(DOD, NATO, IADB)* The process of establishing target distance. Types of ranging include echo, intermittent, manual, navigational, explosive echo, optical, radar, etc. See also **spot**.

rated load—*(DOD, NATO)* The designed safe operating load for the equipment under prescribed conditions.

rate of fire—*(DOD, NATO, IADB)* The number of rounds fired per weapon per minute.

rate of march—*(DOD, NATO, IADB)* The average number of miles or kilometers to be travelled in a given period of time, including all ordered halts. It is expressed in miles or kilometers in the hour. See also **pace**.

rationalization—*(DOD)* Any action that increases the effectiveness of allied forces through more efficient or effective use of defense resources committed to the alliance. Rationalization includes consolidation, reassignment of national priorities to higher alliance needs, standardization, specialization, mutual support or improved interoperability, and greater cooperation. Rationalization applies to both weapons/materiel resources and non-weapons military matters.

ration dense—*(DOD, IADB)* Foods which, through processing, have been reduced in volume and quantity to a small compact package without appreciable loss of food value,

quality, or acceptance, with a high yield in relation to space occupied, such as dehydrates and concentrates.

ratio print—*(DOD)* A print the scale of which has been changed from that of the negative by photographic enlargement or reduction.

ratline—*(DOD, IADB)* An organized effort for moving personnel and/or material by clandestine means across a denied area or border.

reaction time—*(DOD, IADB)* 1. The elapsed time between the initiation of an action and the required response. 2. The time required between the receipt of an order directing an operation and the arrival of the initial element of the force concerned in the designated area.

readiness—See **military capability**.

readiness condition—See **operational readiness**.

ready—*(DOD, NATO, IADB)* The term used to indicate that a weapon(s) is loaded, aimed, and prepared to fire.

ready CAP—*(DOD, IADB)* Fighter aircraft in condition of "standby."

ready position—*(DOD, NATO)* In helicopter operations, a designated place where a helicopter load of troops and/or equipment waits for pick-up.

ready reserve—*(DOD)* The Selected Reserve and Individual Ready Reserve liable for active duty as prescribed by law. (10 U.S.C. 268, 672 and 673.)

reallocation authority—*(DOD, NATO)* The authority given to NATO commanders and normally negotiated in peacetime, to reallocate in an "emergency in war" national logistic resources controlled by the combat forces under their command, and made available by nations, in order to influence the battle logistically. See also **reallocation of resources**.

reallocation of resources—*(NATO)* The provision of logistic resources by the military forces of one nation from those deemed "made available" under the terms incorporated in appropriate NATO documents, to the military forces of another nation or nations as directed by the appropriate military authority. See also **integrated logistic support; logistic assistance; mutual aid.**

real precession—*(DOD, NATO)* Precession resulting from an applied torque such as friction and dynamic imbalance.

real property—*(DOD, IADB)* Lands, buildings, structures, utilities systems, improvements and appurtenances thereto. Includes equipment attached to and made part of buildings and structures (such as heating systems) but not movable equipment (such as plant equipment).

real time—*(DOD)* The absence of delay, except for the time required for the transmission by electromagnetic energy, between the occurrence of an event or the transmission of data, and the knowledge of the event, or reception of the data at some other location. See also **near real time; reporting time interval.**

real wander—See **real precession.**

rear area—*(DOD, NATO)* For any particular command, the area extending forward from its rear boundary to the rear of the area of responsibility of the next lower level of command. This area is provided primarily for the performance of combat service support functions.

rear area—*(IADB)* The area in the rear of the combat and forward areas. See also **Army service area; communications zone.**

rear area security—*(IADB)* The measures taken prior to, during, and/or after an enemy airborne attack, sabotage action, infiltration, guerrilla action, and/or initiation of psychological or propaganda warfare to minimize the effects thereof. See also **area damage control; damage control; disaster control.**

rear echelon—*(DOD, NATO, IADB)* Elements of a force which are not required in the objective area.

rear guard—*(DOD, IADB)* Security detachment that protects the rear of a column from hostile forces. During a withdrawal, it delays the enemy by armed resistance, destroying bridges, and blocking roads.

rear guard—*(NATO)* 1. The rearmost elements of an advancing or withdrawing force. It has the following functions: **a.** To protect the rear of a column from hostile forces. **b.** During the withdrawal, to delay the enemy. **c.** During the advance, to keep supply routes open. 2. Security detachment which a moving ground force details to the rear to keep it informed and covered.

rearming—*(DOD, IADB)* 1. An operation that replenishes the prescribed stores of ammunition, bombs, and other armament items for an aircraft, naval ship, tank, or armored vehicle, including replacement of defective ordnance equipment, in order to make it ready for combat service. 2. Resetting the fuze on a bomb, or on an artillery, mortar, or rocket projectile, so that it will detonate at the desired time.

rebuild—*(DOD)* The restoration of an item to a standard as nearly as possible to its original condition in appearance, performance, and life expectancy. See also **overhaul; repair.**

recce—See **reconnaissance.**

RECCEXREP—See **reconnaissance exploitation report.**

receipt—*(DOD, NATO)* A transmission made by a receiving station to indicate that a message has been satisfactorily received.

receipt into the supply system—*(DOD, IADB)* That point in time when the first item or first

299

quantity of the item of the contract has been received at or is en route to point of first delivery after inspection and acceptance. See also **procurement lead time.**

receiving ship—*(DOD, NATO)* The ship in a replenishment unit that receives the rig(s).

reception—*(DOD, IADB)* 1. All ground arrangements connected with the delivery and disposition of air or sea drops. Includes selection and preparation of site, signals for warning and approach, facilitation of secure departure of agents, speedy collection of delivered articles, and their prompt removal to storage places having maximum security. When a group is involved, it may be called a reception committee. 2. Arrangements to welcome and provide secure quarters or transportation for defectors, escapees, evaders, or incoming agents.

receptivity—*(DOD, NATO)* The vulnerability of a target audience to particular psychological operations media.

reciprocal jurisdiction—*(DOD)* The exercise of court-martial jurisdiction by one armed force over personnel of another armed force, pursuant to specific authorization by the President or by the Secretary of Defense.

reclama—*(DOD, IADB)* A request to duly constituted authority to reconsider its decision or its proposed action.

recognition—*(DOD, IADB)* 1. The determination by any means of the individuality of persons, or of objects such as aircraft, ships, or tanks, or of phenomena such as communications-electronics patterns. 2. In ground combat operations, the determination that an object is similar within a category of something already known; e.g., tank, truck, man.

recognition—*(NATO)* The determination by any means of the friendly or enemy character or of the individuality of another, or of objects such as aircraft, ships, or tanks, or of phe-

nomena such as communications-electronics patterns.

recognition signal—*(DOD, IADB)* Any prearranged signal by which individuals or units may identify each other.

recoilless rifle (heavy)—*(DOD, IADB)* A weapon capable of being fired from either a ground mount or from a vehicle, and capable of destroying tanks.

recompression chamber—See **hyperbaric chamber.**

reconnaissance—*(DOD, NATO, IADB)* A mission undertaken to obtain, by visual observation or other detection methods, information about the activities and resources of an enemy or potential enemy; or to secure data concerning the meteorological, hydrographic, or geographic characteristics of a particular area.

reconnaissance exploitation report—*(DOD, NATO)* The proforma used to report the results of a tactical air reconnaissance mission. Whenever possible the report should include the interpretation of sensor imagery. Also called **RECCEXREP.**

reconnaissance by fire—*(DOD, NATO, IADB)* A method of reconnaissance in which fire is placed on a suspected enemy position to cause the enemy to disclose his presence by movement or return of fire.

reconnaissance in force—*(DOD, NATO)* An offensive operation designed to discover and/or test the enemy's strength or to obtain other information.

reconnaissance patrol—*(DOD)* See **patrol.**

reconnaissance patrol—*(NATO)* For ground forces, a patrol used to gain tactical information preferably without the knowledge of the enemy. See also **combat air patrol; combat patrol; patrol.**

reconnaissance photography—*(DOD, IADB)* Photography taken primarily for purposes other than making maps, charts, or mosaics. It is used to obtain information on the results of bombing, or on enemy movements, concentrations, activities and forces.

reconstitution site—*(DOD, IADB)* A location selected by the surviving command authority as the site at which a damaged or destroyed headquarters can be reformed from survivors of the attack and/or personnel from other sources, predesignated as replacements.

record as target—*(DOD, NATO)* In artillery and naval gunfire support, the order used to denote that the target is to be recorded for future engagement or reference.

recorded—*(DOD, NATO)* In artillery and naval gunfire support, the response used to indicate that the action taken to "record as target" has been completed.

record information—*(DOD)* All forms (e.g., narrative, graphic, data, computer memory) of information registered in either temporary or permanent form so that it can be retrieved, reproduced, or preserved.

recoverable item—*(DOD)* An item which normally is not consumed in use and is subject to return for repair or disposal. See also **reparable item.**

recovery—*(DOD, NATO)* 1. In air operations, that phase of a mission which involves the return of an aircraft to a base. 2. In naval mine warfare, salvage of a mine as nearly intact as possible to permit further investigation for intelligence and/or evaluation purposes. See also **salvage procedure.** 3. *(DOD)* In amphibious reconnaissance, the physical extraction of landed forces or their link-up with friendly forces.

recovery airfield—*(DOD, IADB)* Any airfield, military or civil, at which aircraft might land post-H-hour. It is not expected that combat missions would be conducted from a recovery airfield. See also **airfield.**

recovery and reconstitution—*(DOD, IADB)* Those actions taken by one nation prior to, during, and following an attack by an enemy nation to minimize the effects of the attack, rehabilitate the national economy, provide for the welfare of the populace, and maximize the combat potential of remaining forces and supporting activities.

recovery controller—*(DOD, NATO)* The air controller responsible for the correct execution of recovering aircraft to the appropriate terminal control agency.

recovery procedures—See **explosive ordnance disposal procedures.**

recovery site—*(DOD)* In evasion and escape usage, an area from which an evader or an escaper can be evacuated.

recovery vehicle, medium—*(DOD)* A full tracked vehicle designed for crew rescue and recovery of tanks and other vehicles under battlefield conditions. Designated as M88A1.

rectification—*(DOD, NATO, IADB)* In photogrammetry, the process of projecting a tilted or oblique photograph on to a horizontal reference plane.

rectified airspeed—See **calibrated airspeed.**

rectifier—*(DOD, NATO)* A device for converting alternating current into direct current. See also **inverter.**

recuperation—*(DOD, IADB)* Not to be used. See **recovery and reconstitution.**

recurring demand—*(DOD)* A request by an authorized requisitioner to satisfy a materiel requirement for consumption or stock replenishment that is anticipated to recur periodically. Demands for which the probability of future occurrence is unknown will be considered as recurring. Recurring demands will be considered by the supporting supply system in order to procure, store and distribute materiel to meet similar demands in the future.

redeployment—*(DOD, IADB)* The transfer of a unit, an individual, or supplies deployed in one area to another area, or to another location within the area, or to the zone of interior for the purpose of further employment.

redeployment airfield—*(DOD, NATO, IADB)* An airfield not occupied in its entirety in peacetime, but available immediately upon outbreak of war for use and occupation by units redeployed from their peacetime locations. It must have substantially the same standard of operational facilities as a main airfield. See also **alternative airfield; departure airfield; main airfield.**

redesignated site—*(DOD)* A surviving facility that maybe redesignated as the command center to carry on the functions of an incapacitated alternate headquarters and/or facility.

Redeye—*(DOD, IADB)* A lightweight manportable, shoulder-fired air defense artillery weapon for low altitude air defense of forward combat area troops. Designated as **FIM-43.**

redistribution—*(DOD, IADB)* The act of effecting transfer in control, utilization, or location of material between units or activities within or among the military Services or between the military Services and other Federal agencies. (Note: **IADB** definition uses the words "governmental agencies" instead of "Federal agencies.")

reduced charge—*(DOD, IADB)* 1. The smaller of the two propelling charges available for naval guns. 2. Charge employing a reduced amount of propellant to fire a gun at short ranges as compared to a normal charge. See also **normal charge.**

reduced lighting—*(DOD, NATO)* The reduction in brightness of ground vehicle lights by either reducing power or by screening in such a way that any visible light is limited in output. See also **normal lighting.**

reduction (photographic)—*(DOD)* The production of a negative, diapositive, or print at a scale smaller than the original.

reefer—*(DOD, IADB)* 1. A refrigerator. 2. A motor vehicle, railroad freight car, ship, aircraft, or other conveyance, so constructed and insulated as to protect commodities from either heat or cold.

reentry phase—*(DOD)* That portion of the trajectory of a ballistic missile or space vehicle where there is a significant interaction of the vehicle and the earth's atmosphere. See also **boost phase; midcourse phase; terminal phase.**

re-entry vehicle—*(DOD, NATO, IADB)* That part of a space vehicle designed to re-enter the earth's atmosphere in the terminal portion of its trajectory. See also **maneuverable reentry vehicle; multiple reentry vehicle.**

reference box—*(DOD, NATO)* The identification box placed in the margin of a map or chart which contains the series designation, sheet number and edition number in a readily identified form. Also called **refer to box.** See also **information box.**

reference datum—*(DOD, NATO, IADB)* As used in the loading of aircraft, an imaginary vertical plane at or near the nose of the aircraft from which all horizontal distances are measured for balance purposes. Diagrams of each aircraft show this reference datum as "balance station zero."

reference diversion point—*(DOD, NATO)* One of a number of positions selected by the routing authority on both sides of the route of a convoy or independent to facilitate diversion at sea.

reference line—*(DOD, NATO, IADB)* A convenient and readily identifiable line used by the observer or spotter as the line to which spots will be related. One of three types of spotting lines. See also **spotting line.**

reference point—*(DOD, NATO, IADB)* A prominent, easily located point in the terrain.

reflected shock wave—*(DOD, IADB)* When a shock wave traveling in a medium strikes the interface between this medium and a denser medium, part of the energy of the shock wave induces a shock wave in the denser medium and the remainder of the energy results in the formation of a reflected shock wave that travels back through the less dense medium. See also **shock wave.**

reflection—*(DOD, NATO)* Energy diverted back from the interface of two media. The reflection may be specular (i.e. direct) or diffuse according to the nature of the contact surfaces.

reflex force—*(DOD)* As applied to Air Force units, that part of the alert force maintained overseas or at zone of interior forward bases by scheduled rotations.

reflex sight—*(DOD, NATO)* An optical or computing sight that reflects a reticle image (or images) onto a combining glass for superimposition on the target.

refuge area—*(DOD, NATO)* A coastal area considered safe from enemy attack to which merchant ships may be ordered to proceed when the shipping movement policy is implemented. See also **safe anchorage.**

refugee—*(DOD, IADB)* A civilian who by reason of real or imagined danger has left home to seek safety elsewhere. See also **displaced person; evacuee; expellee.**

refugees—*(NATO)* Persons who, because of real or imagined danger, move of their own volition, spontaneously or in violation of stay-put policy, irrespective of whether they move within their own country (national refugees) or across international boundaries (international refugees).

regimental landing team—*(DOD, IADB)* A task organization for landing, comprised of an infantry regiment reinforced by those elements which are required for initiation of its combat function ashore.

regional reinforcing force—*(DOD, NATO)* A reinforcing force made available to a Major NATO Commander which is further allocated by him to a specific Major Subordinate Commander for employment.

regional reserve—*(DOD, NATO)* A reinforcing force, made available through a Major NATO Commander to a Major Subordinate Commander, that is not yet committed to a specific task, but is available as required for employment or engagement on order within the Major Subordinate Commander's area of responsibility.

register—*(DOD, NATO)* In cartography, the correct position of one component of a composite map image in relation to the other components, at each stage of production.

registered matter—*(NATO)* Any classified matter registered, usually by number, and accounted for periodically.

registered publication—*(NATO)* A classified publication bearing a register number as well as a long and short title, and for which periodic accounting is required.

register glass—*(NATO)* In photography, a glass plate at the focal plane against which the film is pressed during exposure.

register marks—*(DOD, NATO)* In cartography, designated marks, such as small crosses, circles, or other patterns applied to original copy prior to reproduction to facilitate registration of plates and to indicate the relative positions of successive impressions.

registration—*(DOD)* The adjustment of fire to determine firing data corrections.

registration fire—*(DOD, NATO, IADB)* Fire delivered to obtain accurate data for subsequent effective engagement of targets. See also **fire.**

registration point—*(DOD, NATO)* Terrain feature or other designated point on which fire is adjusted for the purpose of obtaining corrections to firing data.

regrade—*(DOD, IADB)* To determine that certain classified information requires, in the interests of national defense, a higher or a lower degree of protection against unauthorized disclosure than currently provided, coupled with a changing of the classification designation to reflect such higher or lower degree.

regroup airfield—*(DOD, IADB)* Any airfield, military or civil, at which post-H-hour reassembling of aircraft is planned for the express purpose of rearming, recocking, and resumption of armed alert, overseas deployment, or conducting further combat missions. See also **airfield.**

regular drill—See **unit training assembly.**

regulated item—*(DOD, NATO, IADB)* Any item over which proper authority exercises close supervision of distribution to individual units or commands because the item is scarce, costly, or of a highly technical or hazardous nature. See also **critical item; critical supplies and material.**

regulating station—*(DOD, IADB)* A command agency established to control all movements of personnel and supplies into or out of a given area.

regulatory sign—*(NATO, IADB)* A sign used by competent authority to regulate and control traffic.

rehabilitation—*(DOD, NATO, IADB)* 1. The processing, usually in a relatively quiet area, of units or individuals recently withdrawn from combat or arduous duty, during which units recondition equipment and are rested, furnished special facilities, filled up with replacements, issued replacement supplies and equipment, given training, and generally made ready for employment in future operations. 2. The action performed in restoring an installation to authorized design standards.

reimbursable NATO military personnel—*(NATO)* A category of military personnel provided by the receiving state to NATO and for which reimbursement to the nation concerned is made from the NATO international budget.

reinforcing—*(DOD, NATO, IADB)* In artillery usage, tactical mission in which one artillery unit augments the fire of another artillery unit.

relateral tell—*(DOD, NATO)* The relay of information between facilities through the use of a third facility. This type of telling is appropriate between automated facilities in a degraded communications environment. See also **track telling.**

relative altitude—See **vertical separation.**

relative aperture—*(DOD)* The ratio of the equivalent focal length to the diameter of the entrance pupil of photographic lens expressed f:4.5, etc. Also called f-number; stop; aperture stop; or diaphragm stop.

relative bearing—*(DOD, NATO)* The direction expressed as a horizontal angle normally measured clockwise from the forward point of the longitudinal axis of the vehicle to an object or body. See also **bearing; grid bearing.**

relative biological effectiveness—*(DOD)* The ratio of the number of rads of gamma (or X) radiation of a certain energy which will produce a specified biological effect to the number of rads of another radiation required to produce the same effect is the relative biological effectiveness of the latter radiation.

relative biological effectiveness—*(NATO)* The ratio of the absorbed dose of gamma or X-rays of a certain energy to the absorbed dose of another ionizing radiation which produces the same biological effect.

release—*(DOD, NATO)* In air armament, the intentional separation of a free-fall aircraft store, from its suspension equipment, for purposes of employment of the store.

release altitude—*(DOD, IADB)* Altitude of an aircraft above the ground at the time of release of bombs, rockets, missiles, tow targets, etc.

released—*(NATO)* In air defense, weapons and crews which have been released from commitments and states of readiness. When so released, they are given a time at which a state of readiness will be resumed.

release point—*(NATO, IADB)* 1. In road movements, a well-defined point on a route at which the elements composing a column return under the authority of their respective commanders, each one of these elements continuing its movement towards its own appropriate destination. 2. In air transport, a point on the ground directly above which the first paratroop or cargo item is airdropped. See also **computed air release point.**

release point (road)—*(DOD)* A well defined point on a route at which the elements composing a column return under the authority of their respective commanders, each one of these elements continuing its movement towards its own appropriate destination.

releasing commander (nuclear weapons)—*(DOD, NATO, IADB)* A commander who has been delegated authority to approve the use of nuclear weapons within prescribed limits. See also **commander(s); executing commander (nuclear weapons).**

releasing officer—*(DOD, IADB)* A properly designated individual who may authorize the sending of a message for and in the name of the originator. See also **originator.**

reliability—*(NATO)* The ability of an item to perform a required function under stated conditions for a specified period of time.

reliability diagram—*(DOD, NATO)* In cartography, a diagram showing the dates and quality of the source material from which a map or chart has been compiled. See also **information box.**

reliability of source—See **evaluation.**

relief—*(DOD, NATO, IADB)* Inequalities of evaluation and the configuration of land features on the surface of the earth which may be represented on maps or charts by contours, hypsometric tints, shading, or spot elevations.

relief in place—*(DOD, NATO, IADB)* An operation in which, by direction of higher authority, all or part of a unit is replaced in an area by the incoming unit. The responsibilities of the replaced elements for the mission and the assigned zone of operations are transferred to the incoming unit. The incoming unit continues the operation as ordered.

remaining forces—*(DOD)* The total surviving United States forces at any given stage of combat operations.

remote delivery—*(DOD, NATO)* In mine warfare, the delivery of mines to a target area by any means other than direct emplacement. The exact position of mines so laid may not be known.

remotely piloted vehicle—*(DOD, NATO)* An unmanned air vehicle capable of being controlled by a person from a distant location through a communications link. It is normally designed to be recoverable. See also **drone.**

rem (roentgen equivalent mammal)—*(DOD, IADB)* One rem is the quantity of ionizing radiation of any type which, when absorbed by man or other mammal, produces a physiological effect equivalent to that produced by the absorption of 1 roentgen of X-ray or gamma radiation.

305

render safe procedures—See **explosive ordance disposal procedures.**

rendezvous—*(DOD, NATO)* A pre-arranged meeting at a given time and location from which to begin an action or phase of an operation, or to which to return after an operation. See also **join-up.**

rendezvous area—*(DOD, IADB)* In an amphibious operation, the area in which the landing craft and amphibious vehicles rendezvous to form waves after being loaded, and prior to movement to the line of departure.

reorder cycle—*(DOD, IADB)* The interval between successive reorder (procurement) actions.

reorder point—*(DOD, IADB)* 1. That point at which time a stock replenishment requisition would be submitted to maintain the predetermined or calculated stockage objective. 2. The sum of the safety level of supply plus the level for order and shipping time equals the reorder point. See also **level of supply.**

repair—*(DOD)* The restoration of an item to serviceable condition through correction of a specific failure or unserviceable condition. See also **overhaul; rebuild.**

repair cycle—*(DOD)* The stages through which a reparable item passes from the time of its removal or replacement until it is reinstalled or placed in stock in a serviceable condition.

repair cycle aircraft—*(DOD)* Aircraft in the active inventory that are in or awaiting depot maintenance, including those in transit to or from depot maintenance.

reparable item—*(DOD)* An item that can be reconditioned or economically repaired for reuse when it becomes unserviceable. See also **recoverable item.**

repatriate—*(DOD)* A person who returns to his country or citizenship, having left his native country, either against his will or as one of a group who left for reason of politics, religion, or other pertinent reasons.

repeat—*(DOD, NATO)* In artillery and naval gunfire support, an order or request to fire again the same number of rounds with the same method of fire.

repeater-jammer—*(DOD, NATO)* A receiver transmitter device which amplifies, multiplies and retransmits the signals received, for purposes of deception or jamming.

replacement demand—*(DOD, IADB)* A demand representing replacement of items consumed or worn out.

replacement factor—*(DOD, NATO, IADB)* The estimated percentage of equipment or repair parts in use that will require replacement during a given period due to wearing out beyond repair, enemy action, abandonment, pilferage, and other causes except catastrophes.

replacements—*(DOD)* Personnel required to take the place of others who depart a unit.

replenishment at sea—*(DOD, NATO)* Those operations required to make a transfer of personnel and/or supplies when at sea.

reply—*(DOD, NATO, IADB)* An answer to a challenge. See also **challenge; countersign; password.**

reported unit—*(DOD)* A unit designation that has been mentioned in an agent report, captured document, or interrogation report, but for which available information is insufficient to include the unit in accepted order of battle holdings.

reporting post—*(DOD, NATO, IADB)* An element of the control and reporting system used to extend the radar coverage of the control and reporting center. It does not undertake the control of aircraft.

reporting time interval—*(DOD, IADB)* 1. In surveillance, the time interval between the detection of an event and the receipt of a report by the user. 2. In communications, the time for transmission of data or a report from the originating terminal to the end receiver. See also **near real time.**

report line—*(NATO)* A line at which troops, after having reached it, must report to their command echelon.

representative fraction—*(DOD)* The scale of a map, chart, or photograph expressed as a fraction or ratio. See also **scale.**

representative fraction—*(NATO)* See **scale.**

reproduction material—*(NATO)* Material, generally in the form of positive or negative copies on film or glass for each color plate, from which a map or chart may be directly reproduced.

request modify—*(DOD, NATO)* In artillery and naval gunfire support, a request by any person, other than the person authorized to make modifications to a fire plan, for a modification.

required delivery date—*(DOD)* A calendar date that specifies when materiel is actually required to be delivered to the requisitioner and it is always a date that is earlier or later than the computed standard delivery date, i.e., a required delivery date cannot exactly equal a computed standard delivery date.

required military force—*(NATO, IADB)* The armed forces necessary to carry out a military mission over a specified period of time.

required supply rate—*(NATO)* The amount of ammunition expressed in rounds per weapon per day for those items fired by weapons, and of all other items of supply expressed in terms of appropriate unit of measure per day, estimated to sustain operations of any designated force without restriction for a specified period.

required supply rate (ammunition)—*(DOD)* In Army usage, the amount of ammunition expressed in terms of rounds per weapon per day for ammunition items fired by weapons, and in terms of other units of measure per day for bulk allotment and other items, estimated to be required to sustain operations of any designated force without restriction for a specified period. Tactical commanders use this rate to state their requirements for ammunition to support planned tactical operations at specified intervals. The required supply rate is submitted through command channels. It is consolidated at each echelon and is considered by each commander in subsequently determining the controlled supply rate within the command.

requirements—See **military requirement.**

requisition—*(DOD, NATO, IADB)* 1. An authoritative demand or request especially for personnel, supplies, or services authorized but not made available without specific request; to make such a demand or request. *(DOD, IADB)* 2. To demand or require services from an invaded or conquered nation.

requisitioning objective—*(DOD, IADB)* The maximum quantities of materiel to be maintained on hand and on order to sustain current operations. It will consist of the sum of stocks represented by the operating level, safety level, and the order and shipping time or procurement lead time, as appropriate. See also **level of supply.**

rescue combat air patrol—*(DOD)* An aircraft patrol provided over a combat search and rescue objective area for the purpose of intercepting and destroying hostile aircraft. Its primary mission is to protect the Search and Rescue Task Force during recovery operations. See also **combat air patrol.**

rescue coordination center—*(DOD)* A primary search and rescue facility suitably staffed by supervisory personnel and equipped for coordinating and controlling search and rescue operations. The facility may be operated unilaterally by personnel of a single Service (**rescue coordination center**), jointly by personnel of two or more Services (**joint rescue coordination center**), or it may have a combined staff of personnel from two or more allied nations (**combined rescue coordination center**). Formerly called **Search and Rescue Coordination Center.**

rescue ship—*(DOD, NATO)* In shipping control, a ship of a convoy stationed at the rear of a convoy column to rescue survivors.

rescue strop—*(NATO)* A piece of rescue equipment which is placed around a person's chest to secure that person to a rescue line or helicopter hoist cable. Also called **horse collar.**

research—*(DOD, IADB)* All effort directed toward increased knowledge of natural phenomena and environment and toward the solution of problems in all fields of science. This includes basic and applied research.

reseau—*(DOD, NATO)* A grid system of a standard size in the image plane of a photographic system used for mensuration purposes.

reserve—*(DOD, IADB)* 1. Portion of a body of troops which is kept to the rear, or withheld from action at the beginning of an engagement, available for a decisive movement. 2. Members of the military Services who are not in active service but who are subject to call to active duty. 3. Portion of an appropriation or contract authorization held or set aside for future operations or contingencies and in respect to which administrative authorization to incur commitments or obligations has been withheld. See also **general reserve; operational reserve; reserve supplies.**

reserve aircraft—*(DOD, IADB)* Those aircraft which have been accumulated in excess of immediate needs for active aircraft and are retained in the inventory against possible future needs. See also **aircraft.**

Reserve Components—*(DOD)* Reserve Components of the Armed Forces of the United States are: **a.** the Army National Guard of the United States; **b.** the Army Reserve; **c.** the Naval Reserve; **d.** the Marine Corps Reserve; **e.** the Air National Guard of the United States; **f.** the Air Force Reserve; and **g.** the Coast Guard Reserve. In each reserve component there are three reserve categories, namely: a Ready Reserve, a Standby Reserve, and a Retired Reserve. Each reservist shall be placed in one of these categories. (10 United States Code 261 and 267.)

reserved demolition target—*(DOD, NATO, IADB)* A target for demolition, the destruction of which must be controlled at a specific level of command because it plays a vital part in the tactical or strategical plan, or because of the importance of the structure itself, or because the demolition may be executed in the face of the enemy. See also **demolition target.**

reserved route—*(DOD, NATO)* In road traffic, a specific route allocated exclusively to an authority or formation. See also **route.**

reserved route—*(IADB)* A route, the use of which is: **a.** allocated exclusively to a particular authority or formation, or **b.** intended to meet a particular requirement. See also **route.**

reserve supplies—*(DOD, IADB)* Supplies accumulated in excess of immediate needs for the purpose of insuring continuity of an adequate supply. Also called **reserves.** See also **battle reserves; beach reserves; contingency retention stock; economic retention stock; individual reserves; initial reserves; unit reserves.**

residual contamination—*(DOD, NATO, IADB)* Contamination which remains after steps have been taken to remove it. These steps may consist of nothing more than allowing the contamination to decay normally.

residual forces—*(DOD)* Unexpended portions of the remaining United States forces that have an immediate combat potential for continued military operations, and that have been deliberately withheld from utilization.

residual radiation—*(NATO, IADB)* Nuclear radiation caused by fallout, radioactive material dispersed artificially, or irradiation which results from a nuclear explosion and persists longer than one minute after burst. See also **contamination; induced radiation; initial radiation.**

residual radioactivity—*(DOD)* Nuclear radiation that results from radioactive sources and which persists for longer than one minute. Sources of residual radioactivity created by nuclear explosions include fission fragments and radioactive matter created primarily by neutron activation, but also by gamma and other radiation activation. Other possible sources of residual radioactivity include radioactive material created and dispersed by means other than nuclear explosion. See also **contamination; induced radiation; initial radiation.**

resistance movement—*(DOD, IADB)* An organized effort by some portion of the civil population of a country to resist the legally established government or an occupying power and to disrupt civil order and stability.

resolution—*(DOD, NATO)* A measurement of the smallest detail which can be distinguished by a sensor system under specific conditions.

responsibility—*(DOD, IADB)* 1. The obligation to carry forward an assigned task to a successful conclusion. With responsibility goes authority to direct and take the necessary action to insure success. 2. The obligation for the proper custody, care, and safekeeping of property or funds entrusted to the possession or supervision of an individual. See also **accountability.**

responsor—*(DOD, NATO, IADB)* An electronic device used to receive an electronic challenge and display a reply thereto.

rest—*(DOD, NATO)* In artillery, a command that indicates that the unit(s) or gun(s) to which it is addressed shall not follow up fire orders during the time that the order is in force.

rest and recuperation—*(DOD, IADB)* The withdrawal of individuals from combat or duty in a combat area for short periods of rest and recuperation. This is commonly referred to as R&R. See also **rehabilitation.**

restart at . . .—*(DOD, NATO)* In artillery, a term used to restart a fire plan after "dwell at . . ." or "check firing" or "cease loading" has been ordered.

restitution—*(DOD, NATO)* The process of determining the true planimetric position of objects whose images appear on photographs.

restitution factor—See **correlation factor.**

restraint factor—*(NATO, IADB)* A factor, normally expressed in multiples of the force of gravity, which determines the required strength of lashings and tie-downs to secure a particular load.

restraint of loads—*(DOD)* The process of binding, lashing, and wedging items into one unit or into its transporter in a manner that will insure immobility during transit.

restricted air cargo—See **cargo.**

restricted area—*(DOD, IADB)* 1. An area (land, sea, or air) in which there are special restrictive measures employed to prevent or minimize interference between friendly forces. 2. An area under military jurisdiction in which special security measures are employed to prevent unauthorized entry. See also **air surface zones; controlled firing area; restricted areas (air).**

restricted area—*(NATO)* 1. An airspace of defined dimensions, above the land areas or territorial waters of a state, within which the flight of aircraft is restricted in accordance with certain specified conditions. 2. An area in which there are special restrictive measures employed to prevent or minimize interference between friendly forces. 3. An area under military jurisdiction in which special security measures are employed to prevent unauthorized entry.

restricted areas (air)—(DOD, IADB) Designated areas established by appropriate authority over which flight of aircraft is restricted. They are shown on aeronautical charts and published in notices to airmen, and publications of aids to air navigation. See also restricted area.

restricted data—(DOD) All data (information) concerning: a. design, manufacture, or utilization of atomic weapons; b. the production of special nuclear material; or c. the use of special nuclear material in the production of energy, but shall not include data declassified or removed from the restricted data category pursuant to Section 142 of the Atomic Energy Act. (Section 11w, Atomic Energy Act of 1954, as amended.) See also formerly restricted data.

restricted operations area—(DOD, NATO) Airspace of defined dimensions, designated by the airspace control authority, in response to specific operational situations/requirements within which the operation of one or more airspace users is restricted.

restrictive fire plan—(DOD, NATO, IADB) A safety measure for friendly aircraft which establishes airspace that is reasonably safe from friendly surface delivered non-nuclear fires.

resume—(DOD) In air intercept usage a code meaning, "Resume last patrol ordered."

resupply—(DOD, NATO, IADB) The act of replenishing stocks in order to maintain required levels of supply.

resupply of Europe—(NATO) The shipping of supplies to Europe during the period from the outbreak of war until the end of such a requirement. These supplies to exclude any material already located upon land in Europe, but to include other supplies irrespective of

their origin or location. See also element of resupply.

retard—(DOD) A request from a spotter to indicate that the illuminating projectile burst is desired later in relation to the subsequent bursts of high explosive projectiles.

reticle—(DOD, NATO) A mark such as a cross or a system of lines lying in the image plane of a viewing apparatus. It may be used singly as a reference mark on certain types of monocular instruments or as one of a pair to form a floating mark as in certain types of stereoscopes. See also graticule.

retirement—(DOD, NATO) An operation in which a force out of contact moves away from the enemy.

retirement route—(DOD) The track or series of tracks along which helicopters move from a specific landing site or landing zone. See also approach route; helicopter lane.

retrofit action—(DOD) Action taken to modify inservice equipment.

retrograde movement—(DOD, IADB) Any movement of a command to the rear, or away from the enemy. It may be forced by the enemy or may be made voluntarily. Such movements may be classified as withdrawal, retirement, or delaying action.

retrograde operation—See retrograde movement.

retrograde personnel—(DOD) Personnel evacuated from a theater of operations, may include noncombatants and civilians.

return load—(DOD, NATO, IADB) Personnel and/or cargo to be transported by a returning carrier.

return to base—(DOD) Proceed to the point indicated by the displayed information. This point is being used to return the aircraft to a place at which the aircraft can land. Command heading, speed and altitude may be used, if desired.

reverse slope—*(NATO, IADB)* Any slope which descends away from the enemy.

revolving fund—*(DOD)* A fund established to finance a cycle of operations to which reimbursements and collections are returned for reuse in a manner such as will maintain the principal of the fund, e.g., working capital funds, industrial funds, and loan funds.

RF-4—See **Phantom II.**

RGM-66D—See **Standard SSM (ARM).**

RGM-84—See **Harpoon.**

RH-53—See **Sea Stallion.**

right (left) bank—See **left (right) bank.**

right (or left)—See **left (or right).**

RIM-66—See **Standard Missile.**

RIM-67—See **Standard Missile.**

riot control agent—*(DOD, IADB)* A chemical that produces temporary irritating or disabling effects when in contact with the eyes or when inhaled.

riot control agent—*(NATO)* A substance which produces temporary irritating or disabling physical effects that disappear within minutes of removal from exposure. There is no significant risk of permanent injury, and medical treatment is rarely required. See also **incapacitating agent.**

riot control operations—*(DOD)* The employment of riot control agents and/or special tactics, formations and equipment in the control of violent disorders.

ripe—*(NATO)* In mine warfare, a word once used to mean "armed." See also **armed mine.**

rising mine—*(DOD, NATO)* In naval mine warfare, a mine having positive buoyancy which is released from a sinker by a ship influence or by a timing device. The mine may fire by contact, hydrostatic pressure or other means.

risk—See **degree of risk (nuclear).**

riverine area—*(DOD, IADB)* An inland or coastal area comprising both land and water, characterized by limited land lines of communication, with extensive water surface and/or inland waterways that provide natural routes for surface transportation and communications.

riverine operations—*(DOD, IADB)* Operations conducted by forces organized to cope with and exploit the unique characteristics of a riverine area, to locate and destroy hostile forces, and/or to achieve, or maintain control of the riverine area. Joint riverine operations combine land, naval, and air operations, as appropriate, and are suited to the nature of the specific riverine area in which operations are to be conducted.

road block—*(DOD, NATO, IADB)* A barrier or obstacle (usually covered by fire) used to block, or limit the movement of, hostile vehicles along a route.

road capacity—*(DOD, IADB)* The maximum traffic flow obtainable on a given roadway, using all available lanes, usually expressed in vehicles per hour or vehicles per day.

road clearance time—*(DOD, NATO, IADB)* The total time a column requires to travel over and clear a section of the road.

road net—*(DOD, IADB)* The system of roads available within a particular locality or area.

road space—*(DOD, NATO, IADB)* The length of roadway allocated to, and/or actually occupied by, a column on a route, expressed in miles or kilometers.

roamer—*(NATO)* Grids constructed to common map scales used for determination of map coordinates.

rocket—*(NATO)* A self-propelled vehicle whose trajectory or course, while in flight, cannot be controlled.

rocket propulsion—*(DOD, IADB)* Reaction propulsion wherein both the fuel and the oxidizer, generating the hot gases expended through a nozzle, are carried as part of the rocket engine. Specifically, rocket propulsion differs from jet propulsion in that jet propulsion utilizes atmospheric air as an oxidizer whereas rocket propulsion utilizes nitric acid or a similar compound as an oxidizer. See also **jet propulsion.**

roentgen—*(DOD, NATO)* A unit of exposure dose of gamma (or X-) radiation. In field dosimetry, one roentgen is essentially equal to one rad.

Roland—See **US Roland.**

role number—*(DOD, NATO)* In the medical field, the classification of treatment facilities according to their different capabilities.

roll—*(NATO)* 1. The rotation of an aircraft or ship about its longitudinal axis. 2. In air photography, the camera rotation about the longitudinal axis of the aircraft. Also called "tilt." See also **tilt angle.**

roll back—*(DOD, IADB)* The process of progressive destruction and/or neutralization of the opposing defenses, starting at the periphery and working inward, to permit deeper penetration of succeeding defense positions.

roller conveyor—*(NATO)* A materials handling aid containing rollers over which cargo is moved.

roll-in-point—*(DOD, IADB)* The point at which aircraft enter the final leg of the attack, e.g., dive, glide.

roll-up—*(DOD, IADB)* The process for orderly dismantling of facilities no longer required in support of operations and available for transfer to other areas.

romper—*(DOD, NATO)* A ship which has moved more than 10 nautical miles ahead of its convoy, and is unable to rejoin it. See also **straggler.**

rope—*(DOD, NATO, IADB)* An element of chaff consisting of a long roll of metallic foil or wire which is designed for broad, low-frequency responses. See also **chaff.**

rope-chaff—*(IADB)* Chaff which contains one or more rope elements. See also **chaff.**

rotational post—*(NATO)* A manpower post filled on a rotational basis. Within NATO, it may be confined to specified nations.

rotor governing mode—*(DOD, NATO)* A control mode in which helicopter rotor speed is maintained automatically.

roundout—See **flare.**

rounds complete—*(DOD, NATO)* In artillery and naval gunfire support, the term used to report that the number of rounds specified in fire for effect have been fired. See also **shot.**

rounds (number of)—See **(number of) rounds.**

route—*(DOD, NATO, IADB)* The prescribed course to be traveled from a specific point of origin to a specific destination. See also **axial route; controlled route; dispatch route; lateral route; reserved route; signed route; supervised route.**

route capacity—*(DOD, NATO)* 1. The maximum traffic flow of vehicles in one direction at the most restricted point on the route. 2. The maximum number of metric tons which can be moved in one direction over a particular route in one hour. It is the product of the maximum traffic flow and the average payload of the vehicles using the route. See also **railway line capacity.**

route classification—*(DOD, NATO, IADB)* Classification assigned to a route using factors of minimum width, worst route type, least bridge, raft or culvert military load classification, and obstructions to traffic flow. See also **military load classification.**

route lanes—*(DOD, NATO)* A series of parallel tracks for the routing of independently sailed ships.

route reconnaissance—*(NATO)* Reconnaissance along a specific line of communications, such as road, railway or waterway, to provide new or updated information on route conditions and activities along the route.

routine message—*(DOD, IADB)* A category of precedence to be used for all types of messages that justify transmission by rapid means unless of sufficient urgency to require a higher precedence. See also **precedence.**

routing indicator—*(DOD, IADB)* A group of letters assigned to indicate: **a.** the geographic location of a station; **b.** a fixed headquarters of a command, activity, or unit at a geographic location; and **c.** the general location of a tape relay or tributary station to facilitate the routing of traffic over the tape relay networks.

row marker—*(DOD, NATO)* In land mine warfare, a natural, artificial, or specially installed marker, located at the start and finish of a mine row where mines are laid by individual rows.

rules of engagement—*(DOD)* Directives issued by competent military authority which delineate the circumstances and limitations under which United States forces will initiate and/or continue combat engagement with other forces encountered. See also **law of war.**

rules of engagement—*(NATO)* Directives issued by competent military authority which specify the circumstances and limitations under which forces will initiate and/or continue combat engagement with other forces encountered.

run—*(DOD)* 1. That part of a flight of one photographic reconnaissance aircraft during which photographs are taken. 2. The transit of a sweeper-sweep combination or of a mine-hunter operating its equipment through a lap. This term may also be applied to a transit of any formation of sweepers.

run—*(NATO)* 1. That part of a flight of one reconnaissance aircraft during which sensor imagery is taken. 2. The transit of a sweeper-sweep combination or of a mine-hunter operating its equipment through a lap. This term may also be applied to a transit of any formation of sweepers.

running fix—*(DOD, NATO, IADB)* The intersection of two or more position lines, not obtained simultaneously, adjusted to a common time.

run-up area—*(NATO, IADB)* A zone within the maneuvering area reserved for testing aircraft engines prior to take-off.

runway—*(DOD, NATO)* A defined rectangular area of an airfield, prepared for the landing and take-off run of aircraft along its length.

runway visual range—*(DOD, NATO)* The maximum distance in the direction of takeoff or landing at which the runway, or specified lights or markers delineating it, can be seen from a position above a specified point on its center line at a height corresponding to the average eye level of pilots at touch-down.

rupture zone—*(DOD, NATO, IADB)* The region immediately adjacent to the crater boundary in which the stresses produced by the explosion have exceeded the ultimate strength of the medium. It is characterized by the appearance of numerous radial cracks of various sizes. See also **plastic zone.**

RUR-5A—See **antisubmarine rocket.**

S

S-2—See **Tracker.**

S-3—See **Viking.**

sabot—*(DOD, NATO, IADB)* Lightweight carrier in which a subcaliber projectile is centered to permit firing the projectile in the larger caliber weapon. The carrier fills the bore of the weapon from which the projectile is fired; it is normally discarded a short distance from the muzzle.

sabotage—*(DOD, IADB)* An act or acts with intent to injure, interfere with, or obstruct the national defense of a country by willfully injuring or destroying, or attempting to injure or destroy, any national defense or war material, premises or utilities, to include human and natural resources.

sabotage alert team—See **security alert team.**

safe anchorage—*(DOD, NATO)* An anchorage considered safe from enemy attack to which merchant ships may be ordered to proceed when the shipping movement policy is implemented. See also **refuge area.**

safe area—*(DOD, IADB)* A designated area in hostile territory that offers the evader or escapee a reasonable chance of avoiding capture and of surviving until he can be evacuated.

safe burst height—*(DOD, NATO, IADB)* The height of burst at or above which the level of fallout, or damage to ground installations is at a predetermined level acceptable to the military commander. See also **types of burst.**

safe current—*(DOD, NATO)* In naval mine warfare, the maximum current that can be supplied to a sweep in a given waveform and pulse cycle which does not produce a danger area with respect to the mines being swept for.

safe depth—*(DOD, NATO)* In naval mine warfare, the shallowest depth of water in which a ship will not actuate a bottom mine of the type under consideration. Safe depth is usually quoted for conditions of ship upright, calm sea and a given speed.

safe distance—*(DOD, NATO)* In naval mine warfare, the horizontal range from the edge of the explosion damage area to the center of the sweeper.

Safeguard—*(DOD)* A ballistic missile defense system.

safe haven—*(DOD)* 1. Designated area(s) to which noncombatants of the United States Government's responsibility, and commercial vehicles and materiel, may be evacuated during a domestic or other valid emergency. 2. Temporary storage provided Department of Energy classified shipment transporters at Department of Defense facilities in order to assure safety and security of nuclear material and/or non-nuclear classified material. Also includes parking for commercial vehicles containing Class A or Class B explosives.

safe house—*(DOD)* An innocent-appearing house or premises established by an organization for the purpose of conducting clandestine or covert activity in relative security.

safe separation distance—*(DOD, NATO)* The minimum distance between the delivery system and the weapon beyond which the hazards associated with functioning (detonation) are acceptable.

safe speed—*(DOD, NATO)* In naval mine warfare, the speed at which a particular ship can proceed without actuating a given influence mine, at the depth under consideration, within the damage area.

safety angle—See **angle of safety.**

315

safety device—*(DOD, NATO)* A device which prevents unintentional functioning.

safety distance (road)—*(DOD, NATO)* The distance between vehicles traveling in column specified by the command in light of safety requirements.

safety fuze—*(DOD, NATO)* A pyrotechnic contained in a flexible and weather-proof sheath burning at a timed and constant rate, used to transmit a flame to the detonator.

safety height—See **altitude; minimum safe altitude.**

safety lanes—*(DOD, NATO, IADB)* Specified sea lanes designated for use in transit by submarine and surface ships to prevent attack by friendly forces.

safety lanyard—See **arming wire.**

safety level of supply—*(DOD, IADB)* The quantity of materiel, in addition to the operating level of supply, required to be on hand to permit continuous operations in the event of minor interruption of normal replenishment or unpredictable fluctuations in demand. See also **level of supply.**

safety line—*(DOD, NATO)* In land mine warfare, demarcation line for trip wire or wire-actuated mines in a minefield. It serves to protect the laying personnel. After the minefield is laid this line is neither marked on the ground nor plotted on the minefield record.

safety pin—See **arming wire.**

safety wire—See **arming wire.**

safety zone—*(DOD, NATO, IADB)* An area (land, sea, or air) reserved for noncombat operations of friendly aircraft, surface ships, submarines or ground forces. (Note: **DOD and IADB** do not use the word submarines.)

safe working load—*(DOD, NATO)* In sea operations, the maximum load that can be safely applied to a fitting, and normally shown on a label plate adjacent to the fitting. See also **static test load.**

safing—*(DOD)* As applied to weapons and ammunition, the changing from a state of readiness for initiation to a safe condition.

safing and arming mechanism—*(DOD, NATO)* A mechanism whose primary purpose is to prevent an unintended functioning of the main charge of the ammunition prior to completion of the arming delay and, in turn, allow the explosive train of the ammunition to function after arming.

Saint—*(DOD)* A satellite inspector system designed to demonstrate the feasibility of intercepting, inspecting, and reporting on the characteristics of satellites in orbit.

salted weapon—*(DOD, NATO, IADB)* A nuclear weapon which has, in addition to its normal components, certain elements or isotopes which capture neutrons at the time of the explosion and produce radioactive products over and above the usual radioactive weapon debris. See also **minimum residual radioactivity weapon.**

salvage—*(DOD, IADB)* 1. Property that has some value in excess of its basic material content but which is in such condition that it has no reasonable prospect of use for any purpose as a unit and its repair or rehabilitation for use as a unit is clearly impractical. 2. The saving or rescuing of condemned, discarded, or abandoned property, and of materials contained therein for reuse, refabrication, or scrapping.

salvage group—*(DOD, IADB)* In an amphibious operation, a naval task organization designated and equipped to rescue personnel and to salvage equipment and material.

salvage procedure—*(DOD, NATO, IADB)* 1. The recovery, evacuation, and reclamation of damaged, discarded, condemned, or abandoned allied or enemy materiel, ships, craft, and floating equipment for reuse, repair, refabrication, or scrapping. 2. Naval salvage operations include harbor and channel clearance, diving, hazardous towing and rescue tug services and the recovery of materiel, ships, craft, and floating equipment sunk offshore or elsewhere stranded.

salvo—*(DOD, IADB)* 1. In naval gunfire support, a method of fire in which a number of weapons are fired at the same target simultaneously. 2. In close air support/air interdiction operations, a method of delivery in which the release mechanisms are operated to release or fire all ordnance of a specific type simultaneously.

Sam-D—*(DOD)* An Army air defense artillery, surface-to-air missile system under development to replace Nike Hercules and the improved Hawk systems.

sanctuary—*(DOD, IADB)* A nation or area near or contiguous to the combat area which by tacit agreement between the warring powers is exempt from attack and therefore serves as a refuge for staging, logistic, or other activities of the combatant powers.

sanitize—*(DOD)* Revise a report or other document in such a fashion as to prevent identification of sources, or of the actual persons and places with which it is concerned, or of the means by which it was acquired. Usually involves deletion or substitution of names and other key details.

satellite and missile surveillance—*(DOD, IADB)* The systematic observation of aerospace for the purpose of detecting, tracking, and characterizing objects, events, and phenomena associated with satellites and inflight missiles, friendly and enemy. See also **surveillance.**

saunter—*(DOD)* In air intercept, a term meaning, "Fly at best endurance."

S-bend distortion—See **S-curve distortion.**

scale—*(DOD, NATO)* The ratio or fraction between the distance on a map, chart or photograph and the corresponding distance on the surface of the earth. See also **conversion scale; graphic scale; photographic scale; principal scale.**

scale of an exercise—*(NATO)* The size of an exercise in terms of resources required or allocated. It may be categorized as large, medium or small, viewed in the context of NATO as a whole.

scale (photographic)—See **photographic scale.**

scaling law—*(DOD, NATO)* A mathematical relationship which permits the effects of a nuclear explosion of given energy yield to be determined as a function of distance from the explosion (or from ground zero) provided the corresponding effect is known as a function of distance for a reference explosion, e.g., of 1-kiloton energy yield.

scan—*(DOD)* 1. In air intercept, a term meaning: "Search sector indicated and report any contacts." 2. The patch periodically followed by a radiation beam.

scan—*(NATO)* In electro-magnetic or acoustic search, one complete rotation of the antenna. It may determine a time base.

scan (elint)—*(DOD)* The motion of an electronic beam through space searching for a target. Scanning is produced by the motion of the antenna or by lobe switching.

scan line—*(DOD, NATO)* The line produced on a recording medium frame by a single sweep of a scanner.

scan period—*(DOD)* The period taken by a radar, sonar, etc., to complete a scan pattern and return to a starting point.

scan rate—*(DOD, NATO)* The rate at which individual scans are recorded.

317

scan type—*(DOD)* The path made in space by a point on the radar beam; for example, circular, helical, conical, spiral, or sector.

scatterable mine—*(NATO)* A mine laid without regard to classical pattern that is designed to be delivered by aircraft, artillery, missile, ground dispenser or hand thrown.

scene of action commander—*(DOD, NATO, IADB)* In antisubmarine warfare, the commander at the scene of contact. He is usually in a ship, or may be in a fixed wing aircraft, helicopter, or submarine.

scheduled fire—*(DOD, NATO, IADB)* A type of prearranged fire executed at a predetermined time.

scheduled maintenance—*(DOD, IADB)* Periodic prescribed inspection and/or servicing of equipment accomplished on a calendar, mileage, or hours of operation basis. See also **organizational maintenance.**

scheduled service (air transport)—*(DOD, IADB)* A routine air transport service operated in accordance with a timetable.

scheduled speed—*(DOD, NATO)* The planned sustained speed of a convoy through the water which determines the speed classification of that convoy. See also **convoy speed; critical speed; declared speed.**

scheduled target—*(DOD, NATO)* In artillery and naval gunfire support, a planned target on which fire is to be delivered at a specific time.

scheduled target (nuclear)—*(DOD, IADB)* A planned target on which a nuclear weapon is to be delivered at a specific time during the operation of the supported force. The time is specified in terms of minutes before or after a designated time or in terms of the accomplishment of a predetermined movement or task. Coordination and warning of friendly troops and aircraft are mandatory.

scheduled wave—See **wave.**

schedule of fire—*(DOD, IADB)* Groups of fires or series of fires fired in a definite sequence according to a definite program. The time of starting the schedule may be ON CALL. For identification purposes schedules may be referred to by a code name or other designation.

schedule of targets—*(DOD, NATO)* In artillery and naval gunfire support, individual targets, groups or series of targets to be fired on, in a definite sequence according to a definite program.

scheme of maneuver—*(DOD, IADB)* The tactical plan to be executed by a force in order to seize assigned objectives.

scientific and technical intelligence—*(DOD, IADB)* The product resulting from the collection, evaluation, analysis, and interpretation of foreign scientific and technical information which covers: **a.** foreign developments in basic and applied research and in applied engineering techniques; and **b.** scientific and technical characteristics, capabilities, and limitations of all foreign military systems, weapons, weapon systems, and materiel, the research and development related thereto, and the production methods employed for their manufacture.

scientific intelligence—See **scientific and technical intelligence.**

scram—*(DOD)* In air intercept usage, a code meaning, "Am about to open fire. Friendly units keep clear or get clear of indicated contact, bogey or area." Direction of withdrawal may be indicated. Type of fire may be indicated (e.g., **scram proximity:** "Am about to open fire with proximity-fuzed ammuntion" **scram mushroom:** "Am about to fire a special weapon.").

scramble—*(DOD, NATO)* An order directing takeoff of aircraft as quickly as possible, usually followed by mission instructions.

scramble—*(IADB)* Take-off accomplished as quickly as possible (usually followed by course and altitude instructions).

scram mushroom—See **scram**.

scram proximity—See **scram**.

screen—*(DOD, NATO)* 1. An arrangement of ships, aircraft and/or submarines to protect a main body or convoy. 2. In cartography, a sheet of transparent film, glass or plastic carrying a "ruling" or other regularly repeated pattern which may be used in conjunction with a mask, either photographically or photomechanically, to produce areas of the pattern. See also **halftone screen**. 3. In surveillance, camouflage and concealment, any natural or artificial material, opaque to surveillance sensor(s), interposed between the sensor(s) and the object to be camouflaged or concealed. See also **concealment**. 4. A security element whose primary task is to observe, identify and report information, and which only fights in self-protection. See also **flank guard; guard**.

screen coordinator—*(NATO)* In naval usage, an officer appointed by the officer in tactical command to exercise specific command functions relating to the screen. See also **screen**.

scribing—*(NATO)* In cartography, a method of preparing a map or chart by cutting the lines into a prepared coating.

S-curve distortion—*(DOD, NATO)* The distortion in the image produced by a scanning sensor which results from the forward displacement of the sensor during the time of lateral scan.

S-Day—*(DOD)* A date used in the WARMAPS (wartime manpower planning system) data base to denote the first mobilization manpower action in the scenario (e.g., the 100,000 call-up), when this first action does not coincide with M-day. See also **wartime manpower planning system**.

sea-air-land team—*(DOD, IADB)* A group of officers and individuals specially trained and equipped for conducting unconventional and paramilitary operations and to train personnel of allied nations in such operations including surveillance and reconnaissance in and from restricted waters, rivers, and coastal areas. Commonly referred to as SEAL team.

Sea Cobra—*(DOD)* A single-rotor, dual-crew, light attack helicopter armed with a variety of machine guns, rockets, grenade launchers, and anti-tank missiles. It is utilized for attack helicopter support. Designated as AH-1J.

sea control operations—*(DOD, IADB)* The employment of naval forces, supported by land and air forces, as appropriate, to achieve military objectives in vital sea areas. Such operations include destruction of enemy naval forces, suppression of enemy sea commerce, protection of vital sea lanes, and establishment of local military superiority in areas of naval operations.

sea echelon—*(DOD, NATO, IADB)* A portion of the assault shipping which withdraws from, or remains out of, the transport area during an amphibious landing and operates in designated areas to seaward in an on-call or unscheduled status.

sea frontier—*(DOD, IADB)* The naval command of a coastal frontier, including the coastal zone in addition to the land area of the coastal frontier and the adjacent sea areas.

Sea King—*(DOD)* A single-rotor, medium-lift helicopter utilized for air/sea rescue and personnel/cargo transport in support of aircraft carrier operations. Some versions are equipped for antisubmarine operations. Designated as **H-3**.

Sea Knight—*(DOD)* A twin-rotor, medium-lift helicopter utilized for personnel and cargo transport. Designated as **H-46**.

sea-launched ballistic missile—*(DOD, IADB)* A ballistic missile launched from a submarine or surface ship.

sealed cabin—*(DOD, NATO, IADB)* The occupied space of an aircraft characterized by walls which do not allow any gaseous exchange between the ambient atmosphere and the inside atmosphere and containing its own ways of regenerating the inside atmosphere.

sea projection operations—See **land, sea, or aerospace projection operations.**

search—*(DOD, IADB)* 1. An operation to locate an enemy force known or believed to be at sea. 2. A systematic reconnaissance of a defined area, so that all parts of the area have passed within visibility. 3. To distribute gunfire over an area in depth by successive changes in gun elevation.

search and attack priority—*(DOD, IADB)* The lowest category of immediate mission request involving suspected targets related to the enemy tactical or logistical capabilities, e.g., those which are not inhibiting a unit's advance but by their fleeting nature and tactical importance should be located and destroyed. See also **immediate mission request; priority of immediate mission requests.**

search and rescue—*(DOD, NATO, IADB)* The use of aircraft, surface craft, submarines, specialized rescue teams and equipment to search for and rescue personnel in distress on land or at sea. See also **component search and rescue controller; joint rescue coordination center.**

search and rescue alert notice—*(DOD)* An alerting message used for United States domestic flights. It corresponds to the declaration of the alert phase. Also called ALNOT. See also **search and rescue incident classification, subpart b.**

search and rescue coordination center—*(IADB)* A primary search and rescue facility suitably staffed by supervisory personnel and equipped for coordinating and controlling search and rescue operations. It may be operated jointly or unilaterally. See also **rescue coordination center.**

search and rescue coordinator—*(DOD, IADB)* The designated search and rescue representative of the area commander with overall responsibility and authority for operation of the joint rescue coordination center, and for joint search and rescue operations within the geographical area assigned.

search and rescue incident classification—*(DOD)* Three emergency phases into which an incident may be classified or progress, according to the seriousness of the incident and its requirement for rescue service:
   a. **uncertainty phase**—Doubt exists as to the safety of a craft or person because of knowledge of possible difficulties or because of lack of information concerning progress or position.
   b. **alert phase**—Apprehension exists for the safety of a craft or person because of definite information that serious difficulties exist that do not amount to a distress or because of a continued lack of information concerning progress or position.
   c. **distress phase**—Immediate assistance is required by a craft or person because of being threatened by grave or imminent danger or because of continued lack of information concerning progress or position after procedures for the alert phase have been executed.

search and rescue mission coordinator—*(DOD, IADB)* A search and rescue controller selected by the search and rescue coordinator to direct a specific mission.

search and rescue region—See **inland search and rescue region; maritime search and rescue region; overseas search and rescue region.**

search attack unit—*(DOD, IADB)* The designation given to one or more ships separately organized or detached from a formation as a tactical unit to search for and destroy submarines.

searched channel—*(DOD, NATO)* In naval mine warfare, the whole or part of a route or a path which has been searched, swept or hunted, the width of the channel being specified.

searching fire—*(DOD, NATO, IADB)* Fire distributed in depth by successive changes in the elevation of a gun. See also **fire.**

search jammer—See **automatic search jammer.**

search mission (air)—*(DOD, NATO, IADB)* An air reconnaissance by one or more aircraft dispatched to locate an object or objects known or suspected to be in a specific area.

search radius—*(DOD)* In search and rescue operations, a radius centered on a datum point having a length equal to the total probable error plus an additional safety length to insure a greater than 50 percent probability that the target is in the search area.

search sweeping—*(DOD, NATO)* In naval mine warfare, the operation of sweeping a sample of route or area to determine whether poised mines are present.

sea skimmer—*(NATO)* A missile designed to transit at less than 50 feet (or 15 meters) above the surface of the sea.

Sea Sprite—*(DOD)* A single rotor light lift helicopter utilized for air/sea rescue, personnel/cargo transport and antisubmarine operations from naval vessels. Designated as **H-2.**

Sea Stallion—*(DOD)* A single-rotor heavy-lift helicopter utilized for personnel/cargo transport. Designated as **CH-53.** A mine countermeasures-equipped version is designated as **RH-53.**

sea superiority—*(DOD, IADB)* That degree of dominance in the sea battle of one force over another that permits the conduct of operations by the former and its related land, sea, and air forces at a given time and place without prohibitive interference by the opposing force.

sea supremacy—*(DOD, IADB)* That degree of sea superiority wherein the opposing force is incapable of effective interference.

sea surveillance—*(DOD, NATO, IADB)* The systematic observation of surface and subsurface sea areas by all available and practicable means primarily for the purpose of locating, identifying and determining the movements of ships, submarines, and other vehicles, friendly and enemy, proceeding on or under the surface of the world's seas and oceans. See also **surveillance.**

sea surveillance system—*(DOD, NATO, IADB)* A system for collecting, reporting, correlating and presenting information supporting and derived from the task of sea surveillance.

seavan—*(DOD, IADB)* Commercial or Government-owned (or leased) shipping containers which are moved via ocean transportation without bogey wheels attached, i.e., lifted on and off the ship.

secondary armament—*(DOD, IADB)* In ships with multiple-size guns installed, that battery consisting of guns next largest to those of the main battery.

secondary censorship—*(DOD)* Armed forces censorship performed on the personal communications of officers, civilian employees, and accompanying civilians of the Armed Forces of the United States, and on those personal communications of enlisted personnel of the armed forces not subject to armed forces primary censorship or those requiring reexamination. See also **censorship.**

secondary port—*(DOD, NATO, IADB)* A port with one or more berths, normally at quays, which can accommodate ocean-going ships for discharge. See also **port.**

321

secondary rescue facilities—*(DOD, IADB)* Local airbase-ready aircraft, crash boats, and other air, surface, subsurface, and ground elements suitable for rescue missions including government and privately operated units and facilities.

secondary road—*(DOD, IADB)* A road supplementing a main road, usually wide enough and suitable for two-way all-weather traffic at moderate or slow speeds.

secondary water terminal—*(DOD, NATO, IADB)* A coastal area with no facility for placing deep draft ships alongside a wharf. Secondary water terminals are established on beaches that desirably are adjacent to rail lines and/or good coastal highways. At secondary water terminals, shipping is unloaded at anchorages located from one to five miles offshore, and the cargo and personnel unloaded are landed in the terminal area by ship-to-shore lighters. The scope of operation is so limited that it is not designated as a probable primary nuclear target. See also **water terminal.**

second strike—*(DOD, IADB)* The first counterblow of a war. (Generally associated with nuclear operations.)

second strike capability—*(NATO, IADB)* The ability to survive a first strike with sufficient resources to deliver an effective counterblow (generally associated with nuclear weapons).

secret—See **security classification.**

section—*(DOD)* 1. As applied to ships or naval aircraft, a tactical subdivision of a division. It is normally one-half of a division in the case of ships, and two aircraft in the case of aircraft. 2. A subdivision of an office, installation, territory, works, or organization; especially a major subdivision of a staff. 3. A tactical unit of the Army and Marine Corps. A section is smaller than a platoon and larger than a squad. In some organizations the section, rather than the squad, is the basic tactical unit. 4. An area in a warehouse extending

from one wall to the next; usually the largest subdivision of one floor.

sector—*(DOD, NATO, IADB)* 1. An area designated by boundaries within which a unit operates, and for which it is responsible. 2. One of the subdivisions of a coastal frontier. See also **area of influence; zone of action.**

sector commander—*(NATO)* An officer responsible for the tactical control of air defense forces and the operations of facilities within a specified sector of an air defense area.

sector controller—*(NATO)* An officer appointed to act on behalf of a sector commander in a sector operations center. He is responsible for operational control of all active air defenses in the sector area in coordination with those of adjacent sectors. In these tasks he is subject to overall direction by the group or command controller.

sector of fire—*(DOD, NATO, IADB)* An area which is required to be covered by fire by an individual, a weapon, or a unit.

sector scan—*(DOD, NATO)* Scan in which the antenna oscillates through a selected angle.

secure—*(DOD, NATO)* In an operational context, to gain possession of a position or terrain feature, with or without force, and to make such disposition as will prevent, as far as possible, its destruction or loss by enemy action. See also **denial measure.**

secure (operations)—*(IADB)* To gain possession of a position or terrain feature, with or without force, and to make such disposition as will prevent, as far as possible, its destruction or loss by enemy action.

security—*(DOD, IADB)* 1. Measures taken by a military unit, an activity or installation to protect itself against all acts designed to, or which may, impair its effectiveness. 2. A condition that results from the establishment and maintenance of protective measures that insure a state of inviolability from hostile acts

322

or influences. 3. With respect to classified matter, it is the condition that prevents unauthorized persons from having access to official information that is safeguarded in the interests of national security. See also **national security.**

security—*(NATO)* The condition achieved when designated information, materiel, personnel, activities and installations are protected against espionage, sabotage, subversion and terrorism, as well as against loss or unauthorized disclosure. The term is also applied to those measures necessary to achieve this condition and to the organizations responsible for those measures. See also **counterintelligence; physical security; port security; protective security; security intelligence; subversion.**

security alert team—*(DOD, IADB)* Two or more security force members who form the initial reinforcing element responding to security alarms, emergencies, or irregularities.

security assistance—*(DOD)* Group of programs authorized by the Foreign Assistance Act of 1961, as amended, and the Arms Export Control Act of 1976, as amended, or other related statutes by which the United States provides defense articles, military training, and other defense-related services, by grant, credit, or cash sales, in furtherance of national policies and objectives.

security certification—*(DOD, NATO, IADB)* A certification issued by competent national authority to indicate that a person has been investigated and is eligible for access to classified matter to the extent stated in the certification. (Note: Neither the DOD nor the IADB definition uses the word "national.")

security classification—*(DOD)* A category to which national security information and material is assigned to denote the degree of damage that unauthorized disclosure would cause to national defense or foreign relations of the United States and to denote the degree of protection required. There are three such categories:

a. **top secret—**National security information or material which requires the highest degree of protection and the unauthorized disclosure of which could reasonably be expected to cause exceptionally grave damage to the national security. Examples of "exceptionally grave damage" include armed hostilities against the United States or its allies; disruption of foreign relations vitally affecting the national security; the compromise of vital national defense plans or complex cryptologic and communications intelligence systems; the revelation of sensitive intelligence operations; and the disclosure of scientific or technological developments vital to national security.

b. **secret—**National security information or material which requires a substantial degree of protection and the unauthorized disclosure of which could reasonably be expected to cause serious damage to the national security. Examples of "serious damage" include disruption of foreign relations significantly affecting the national security; significant impairment of a program or policy directly related to the national security; revelation of significant military plans or intelligence operations; and compromise of significant scientific or technological developments relating to national security.

c. **confidential—**National security information or material which requires protection and the unauthorized disclosure of which could reasonably be expected to cause damage to the national security. See also **classification; security.**

security classification—*(NATO)* A category or grade assigned to defense information or materiel to indicate the degree of danger to NATO/national security that would result from its unauthorized disclosure and the standard of protection required to guard against unauthorized disclosure.

security clearance—*(DOD, NATO, IADB)* An administrative determination by competent national authority that an individual is eligible, from a security stand-point, for access to

323

classified information. (Note: Neither the DOD nor the IADB definition uses the word "national.")

security countermeasures—(IADB) Measures designed to impair the effectiveness of an unfriendly or hostile attack upon security.

security intelligence—(DOD, NATO) Intelligence on the indentity, capabilities and intentions of hostile organizations or individuals who are or may be engaged in espionage, sabotage, subversion or terrorism. See also **counterintelligence; intelligence; security.**

security supporting assistance—(DOD) Program by which economic assistance is provided on a loan or grant basis, to selected foreign governments having unique security problems. The funds are used to finance imports of commodities, capital, or technical assistance in accordance with terms of a bilateral agreement; counterpart funds thereby generated may be used as budgetary support. These funds enable a recipient to devote more of its own resources to defense and security purposes than it otherwise could do without serious economic or political consequences.

Selected Reserve—(DOD) That portion of the Ready Reserve consisting of units and, as designated by the Secretary concerned, of individual Reservists required to participate in inactive duty training periods and annual training, both of which are in a pay status. The Selected Reserve also includes persons performing initial active duty for training. (10 U.S.C. 268(b).)

selective identification feature—(DOD, IADB) A capability which, when added to the basic Identification Friend or Foe system, provides the means to transmit, receive, and display selected coded replies.

selective identification feature—(NATO) Airborne pulse-type transponder which provides automatic selective identification of aircraft in which it is installed, to friend-or-foe identi-fication installations, whether ground, shipboard, or airborne.

selective jamming—See **spot jamming.**

selective loading—(DOD, NATO, IADB) The arrangement and stowage of equipment and supplies aboard ship in a manner designed to facilitate issues to units. See also **loading.**

selective mobilization—See **mobilization.**

selective unloading—(DOD, NATO) In an amphibious operation, the controlled unloading from assault shipping, and movement ashore, of specific items of cargo at the request of the landing force commander. See also **combat loading; loading; selective loading.**

selenodesy—(DOD, IADB) That branch of applied mathematics that determines, by observation and measurement, the exact positions of points and the figures and areas of large portions of the moon's surface, or the shape and size of the moon.

selenodetic—(DOD, IADB) Of or pertaining to, or determined by selenodesy.

self-destroying fuze—(DOD, NATO, IADB) A fuze designed to burst a projectile before the end of its flight. See also **fuze.**

self-protection depth—(DOD, NATO) The depth of water where the aggregate danger width relative to mines affected by a minesweeping technique is zero. Safe depth is a particular self-protection depth.

semi-active homing guidance—(DOD, NATO, IADB) A system of homing guidance wherein the receiver in the missile utilizes radiations from the target which has been illuminated by an outside source.

semi-controlled mosaic—(DOD, NATO) A mosaic composed of corrected or uncorrected prints laid so that major ground features match their geographical coordinates. See also **mosaic.**

semi-fixed ammunition—(DOD, NATO, IADB) Ammunition in which the cartridge case is not permanently attached to the projectile. See also **ammunition.**

semi-permissive environment—See **operational environment.**

senior officer present afloat—(DOD, IADB) The senior line officer of the Navy, on active service, eligible for command at sea, who is present and in command of any unit of the operating forces afloat in the locality or within an area prescribed by competent authority. This officer is responsible for the administration of matters which collectively affect naval units of the operating forces afloat in the locality prescribed.

sensitive—(DOD, IADB) Requiring special protection from disclosure which could cause embarrassment, compromise, or threat to the security of the sponsoring power. May be applied to an agency, installation, person, position, document, material, or activity.

sensitive compartmented information—(DOD) All information and materials bearing special community controls indicating restricted handling within present and future community intelligence collection programs and their end products for which community systems of compartmentation have been or will be formally established. (These controls are over and above the provisions of DOD 5200.1-R, Information Security Program Regulation.) Also called **SCI.**

sensor—(DOD, NATO) An equipment which detects, and may indicate, and/or record objects and activities by means of energy or particles emitted, reflected, or modified by objects.

separate loading ammunition—(DOD, NATO, IADB) Ammunition in which the projectile and charge are loaded into a gun separately See also **ammunition.**

separation zone—(NATO) An area between two adjacent horizontal or vertical areas into which units are not to proceed unless certain safety measures can be fulfilled.

sequence circuit—(DOD, NATO, IADB) In mine warfare, a circuit which requires actuation by a predetermined sequence of influences of predetermined magnitudes.

sequenced ejection system—See **ejection systems.**

Sergeant—(DOD, IADB) A mobile, inertially guided, solid-propellant, surface-to-surface missile, with nuclear warhead capability, designed to attack targets up to a range of 75 nautical miles. Designated as **MGM-29A.**

serial—(DOD, NATO, IADB) An element or a group of elements within a series which is given a numerical or alphabetical designation for convenience in planning, scheduling, and control.

serial assignment table—(DOD, IADB) A table that is used in amphibious operations and shows the serial number, the title of the unit, the approximate number of personnel; the material, vehicles, or equipment in the serial; the number and type of landing craft and/or amphibious vehicles required to boat the serial; and the ship on which the serial is embarked.

series of targets—(NATO) In artillery and naval gunfire support, a number of targets and/or group(s) of targets planned to support a maneuver phase. A series of targets may be indicated by a nickname.

seriously ill—(DOD, NATO, IADB) A patient is seriously ill when his illness is of such severity that there is cause for immediate concern but there is no imminent danger to life. See also **very seriously ill.**

seriously wounded—(DOD, IADB) A stretcher case. See also **wounded.**

325

service ammunition—*(DOD, IADB)* Ammunition intended for combat, rather than for training purposes.

service force—*(DOD, IADB)* A naval task organization that performs missions for the logistic support of operations.

service group—*(DOD, IADB)* A major naval administration and/or tactical organization, consisting of the commander and the staff, designed to exercise operational control and administrative command of assigned squadrons and units in executing their tasks of providing logistic support of fleet operations.

service mine—*(DOD, NATO)* A mine capable of a destructive explosion.

service squadron—*(DOD, IADB)* An administrative and/or tactical subdivision of a naval service force or service group, consisting of the commander and the staff, organized to exercise operational control and administrative command of assigned units in providing logistic support of fleet units as directed.

service test—*(DOD, IADB)* A test of an item, system of materiel, or technique conducted under simulated or actual operational conditions to determine whether the specified military requirements or characteristics are satisfied. See also **troop test**.

service troops—*(DOD, IADB)* Those units designed to render supply, maintenance, transportation, evacuation, and hospitalization, and other services required by air and ground combat units to carry out effectively their mission in combat. See also **combat service support elements; troops**.

servicing—See **common servicing; cross-servicing; joint servicing**. See also **inter-Service support**.

severe damage—See **nuclear damage (land warfare)**.

severely threatened coastline—*(NATO)* A coastline already specified within the NATO area which should be evacuated under threat of nuclear attack.

shaded relief—*(DOD, NATO)* A cartographic technique that provides an apparent three-dimensional configuration of the terrain on maps and charts by the use of graded shadows that would be cast by high ground if light were shining from the northwest. Shaded relief is usually used in combination with contours. See also **hill shading**.

shadow—See **trailer aircraft**.

shadower—*(NATO)* A maritime unit observing and (not necessarily continuously) maintaining contact with an object; shadowing may be carried out either overtly or covertly. See also **trailer aircraft; marker**.

shadow factor—*(NATO)* A multiplication factor derived from the sun's declination, the latitude of the target and the time of photography, used in determining the heights of objects from shadow length. Also called **tangent altitude (tan alt)**.

shallow fording—*(DOD, IADB)* The ability of a self-propelled gun or ground vehicle equipped with built-in waterproofing, with its wheels or tracks in contact with the ground, to negotiate a water obstacle without the use of a special waterproofing kit. See also **deep fording; flotation**.

shallow fording capability—*(NATO)* The characteristic of a self-propelled gun or ground vehicle equipped with built-in waterproofing, with its wheels or tracks in contact with the ground, to negotiate a water obstacle without the use of a special waterproofing kit.

shaped charge—*(DOD, NATO)* A charge shaped so as to concentrate its explosive force in a particular direction.

sheaf—*(DOD, IADB)* In artillery and naval gunfire support, planned planes (lines) of fire that produce a desired pattern of bursts with rounds fired by two or more weapons.

shear link assembly—*(DOD, NATO)* A device designed to break at a specified mechanical load.

sheet explosive—*(DOD, NATO)* Plastic explosive provided in a sheet form.

sheetlines—*(DOD)* Those lines defining the geographic limits of the map or chart detail.

shelf life—*(DOD, NATO)* The length of time during which an item of supply, subject to deterioration or having a limited life which cannot be renewed, is considered serviceable while stored. See also **storage life.**

shelling report—*(DOD, NATO, IADB)* Any report of enemy shelling containing information on caliber, direction, time, density and area shelled.

shell (specify)—*(DOD, NATO)* A command or request indicating the type of projectile to be used.

shielding—*(DOD, NATO, IADB)* 1. Material of suitable thickness and physical characteristics used to protect personnel from radiation during the manufacture, handling, and transportation of fissionable and radioactive materials. 2. Obstructions which tend to protect personnel or materials from the effects of a nuclear explosion.

shift—*(NATO)* The ability to move the origin of a radial display away from the center of the cathode ray tube.

shifting fire—*(DOD, IADB)* Fire delivered at constant range at varying deflections; used to cover the width of a target that is too great to be covered by an open sheaf.

Shillelagh—*(DOD, IADB)* A missile system mounted on the main battle tank and assault reconnaissance vehicle for employment against enemy armor, troops, and field fortifications. Designated as **MGM-51.**

ship combat readiness—See **combat ready.**

ship counter—*(DOD, NATO)* In naval mine warfare, a device in a mine which prevents the mine from detonating until a preset number of actuations has taken place.

ship haven—See **moving havens.**

ship influence—*(DOD, NATO)* In naval mine warfare, the magnetic, acoustic and pressure effects of a ship, or a minesweep simulating a ship, which is detectable by a mine or other sensing devices.

shipping—*(IADB)* A term applied collectively to those ships which are used to transport personnel or cargo, or both; often modified to denote type, use, or force to which assigned.

shipping control—See **naval control of shipping.**

shipping designator—*(DOD, IADB)* A code word assigned to a particular overseas base, port, or area, for specific use as an address on shipments to the overseas location concerned. The code word is usually four letters and may be followed by a number to indicate a particular addressee.

shipping lane—*(DOD, NATO)* A term used to indicate the general flow of merchant shipping between two departure/terminal areas.

shipping movement policy—*(NATO)* The policy for the movement of merchant ships in the early days of war laid down in Military Committee documents.

shipping time—*(DOD, IADB)* The time elapsing between the shipment of materiel by the supplying activity and receipt of materiel by the requiring activity. See also **order and shipping time.**

ship-to-shore movement—*(DOD, NATO, IADB)* That portion of the assault phase of an amphibious operation which includes the deployment of the landing force from the assault shipping to designated landing areas.

ship will adjust—*(DOD)* In naval gunfire support, a method of control in which the ship can see the target and, with the concurrence of the spotter, will adjust.

shock front—*(DOD, NATO, IADB)* The boundary between the pressure disturbance created by an explosion (in air, water, or earth) and the ambient atmosphere, water, or earth.

shock wave—*(DOD, NATO)* The continuously propagated pressure pulse formed by the blast from an explosion in air, under water or under ground. See also **blast wave.**

shoran—*(DOD, IADB)* A precise short-range electronic navigation system which uses the time of travel of pulse-type transmission from two or more fixed stations to measure slant-range distance from the stations. Also, in conjunction with a suitable computer, used in precision bombing. (This term is derived from the words "*sho*rt-*ra*nge *n*avigation.")

shore bombardment line—*(NATO, IADB)* A ground line establishd to delimit bombardment by friendly surface ships.

shore fire control party—*(DOD, IADB)* A specially trained unit for control of naval gunfire in support of troops ashore, consisting of a spotting team to adjust fire and a naval gunfire liaison team to perform liaison functions for the supported battalion commander.

shore party—*(DOD, NATO, IADB)* A task organization of the landing force, formed for the purpose of facilitating the landing and movement off the beaches of troops, equipment, and supplies; for the evacuation from the beaches of casualties and prisoners of war; and for facilitating the beaching, retraction, and salvaging of landing ships and craft. It comprises elements of both the naval and landing forces. Also called **beach group.** See also **beachmaster unit; beach party; naval beach group.**

shore-to-shore movement—*(DOD, IADB)* The assault movement of personnel and materiel directly from a shore staging area to the objective, involving no further transfers between types of craft or ships incident to the assault movement.

short—*(DOD, NATO)* In artillery and naval gunfire support, a spotting, or an observation, used by an observer to indicate that a burst(s) occurred short of the target in relation to the spotting line.

short distance navigational aid—*(NATO, IADB)* An equipment or system that provides navigational assistance to a range not exceeding 200 statute miles (320 kilometers).

shortfall—*(DOD)* The lack of forces, equipment, personnel, materiel, or capability, apportioned to and identified as a plan requirement, that would adversely affect the command's ability to accomplish its mission.

short range air defense engagement zone—See **weapon engagement zone.**

short range attack missile—*(DOD)* An air-to-surface missile, armed with a nuclear warhead, launched from the B-52 and the FB-111 aircraft. The missile range, speed, and accuracy allow the carrier aircraft to "standoff" from its intended targets and launch missiles outside enemy defenses. Designated as **AGM-69.**

short-range ballistic missile—*(DOD, IADB)* A ballistic missile with a range capability up to about 600 nautical miles.

short-range transport aircraft—See **transport aircraft.**

short round—*(DOD, IADB)* 1. The unintentional or inadvertent delivery of ordnance on friendly troops, installations, or civilians by a friendly weapon system. 2. A defective cartridge in which the projectile has been seated too deeply.

short scope buoy—*(DOD, NATO)* A buoy used as a navigational reference which remains nearly vertical over its sinker.

short supply—*(DOD, IADB)* An item is in short supply when the total of stock on hand and anticipated receipts during a given period are less than the total estimated demand during that period.

short take-off and landing—*(DOD, NATO, IADB)* The ability of an aircraft to clear a 50-foot (15 meters) obstacle within 1,500 feet (500 meters) of commencing take-off or in landing, to stop within 1,500 feet (500 meters) after passing over a 50-foot (15 meters) obstacle.

short title—*(DOD, NATO, IADB)* A short, identifying combination of letters, and/or numbers assigned to a document or device for purposes of brevity and/or security.

shot—*(DOD, NATO)* In artillery and naval gunfire support, a report that indicates a gun, or guns, have been fired. See also **rounds complete**.

Shrike—*(DOD)* An air-launched antiradiation missile designed to home on and destroy radar emitters. Designated as AGM-45.

shuttered fuze—*(DOD, NATO, IADB)* A fuze in which inadvertent initiation of the detonator will not initiate either the booster or the burst charge. See also **fuze**.

shuttle bombing—*(DOD, IADB)* Bombing of objectives, utilizing two bases. By this method, a bomber formation bombs its target, flies on to its second base, reloads, and returns to its home base, again bombing a target if required.

sick—*(DOD)* In air intercept, a code meaning, "Equipment indicated is operating at reduced efficiency."

sidelay—*(DOD, NATO)* Device on the feed board of a printing machine for controlling the lateral alignment of the printing paper.

side looking airborne radar—*(DOD, NATO, IADB)* An airborne radar, viewing at right angles to the axis of the vehicle, which produces a presentation of terrain or moving targets. *(DOD, IADB)* Commonly referred to as SLAR.

side oblique air photograph—*(DOD)* An oblique photograph taken with the camera axis at right angles to the longitudinal axis of the aircraft.

side overlap—See **overlap**.

Sidewinder—*(DOD, IADB)* A solid-propellant, air-to-air missile with non-nuclear warhead and infrared, heat-seeking homer. Designated as AIM-9. The ground-to-air version is designated as **Chaparral** (MIM-72).

sighting—*(DOD, IADB)* Actual visual contact. Does not include other contacts, which must be reported by type, e.g., radar and sonar contacts. See also **contact report**.

sighting angle—*(NATO)* In bombing, the angle between the line-of-sight to the aiming point and the vertical.

SIGINT direct service—*(DOD)* A reporting procedure to provide signals intelligence (SIGINT) to a military commander or other authorized recipient in response to SIGINT requirements. The product may vary from recurring, serialized reports produced by the National Security Agency/Central Security Service to instantaneous aperiodic reports provided to the command or other recipient, usually from a fixed SIGINT activity engaged in collection and processing. See also **signals intelligence**.

SIGINT direct service activity—*(DOD)* A signals intelligence (SIGINT) activity composed of collection and associated resources that normally performs in a direct service role

329

under the SIGINT operational control of the Director, National Security Agency/Chief, Central Security Service. See also **signals intelligence.**

SIGINT direct support—*(DOD)* The provision of signals intelligence (SIGINT) information to a military commander by a SIGINT direct support unit in response to SIGINT operational tasking levied by that Commander. See also **signals intelligence.**

SIGINT direct support unit—*(DOD)* A signals intelligence (SIGINT) unit, usually mobile, designed to perform a SIGINT direct support role for a military commander under delegated authority from the Director, National Security Agency/Chief, Central Security Service. See also **signals intelligence.**

SIGINT operational control—*(DOD)* The authoritative direction of signals intelligence (SIGINT) activities, including tasking and allocation of effort, and the authoritative prescription of those uniform techniques and standards by which SIGINT information is collected, processed, and reported. See also **signals intelligence.**

SIGINT operational tasking—*(DOD)* The authoritative operational direction of and direct levying of signals intelligence (SIGINT) requirements by a military commander on designated SIGINT resources. These requirements are directive, irrespective of other priorities, and are conditioned only by the capability of those resources to produce such information. Operational tasking includes authority to deploy and redeploy all or part of the SIGINT resources for which SIGINT operational tasking authority has been delegated. See also **signals intelligence.**

SIGINT operational tasking authority—*(DOD)* A military commander's authority to operationally direct and levy signals intelligence (SIGINT) requirements on designated SIGINT resources; includes authority to deploy and redeploy all or part of the SIGINT resources for which SIGINT operational tasking authority

has been delegated. Also called SOTA. See also **signals intelligence.**

SIGINT resources—*(DOD)* Personnel and equipment of any unit, activity, or organizational element engaged in signals intelligence (SIGINT) activities. See also **signals intelligence.**

SIGINT support plans—*(DOD)* Plans prepared by the National Security Agency/Central Security Service, in coordination with concerned elements of the United States SIGINT system, which specify how the resources of the system will be aligned in crisis or war to support military operations covered by certain JCS and unified and specified command operation plans. See also **signals intelligence.**

signal—*(DOD, NATO, IADB)* 1. As applied to electronics, any transmitted electrical impulse. 2. Operationally, a type of message, the text of which consists of one or more letters, words, characters, signal flags, visual displays, or special sounds with prearranged meaning, and which is conveyed or transmitted by visual, acoustical, or electrical means.

signal area—*(NATO)* An area on an airfield used for the display of ground signals.

signal center—*(DOD, IADB)* A combination of signal communication facilities operated by the Army in the field and consisting of a communications center, telephone switching central and appropriate means of signal communications. See also **communications center.**

signal letters—See **international call sign.**

signal operation instructions—*(DOD, IADB)* A series of orders issued for technical control and coordination of the signal communication activities of a command. *(DOD)* In Marine Corps usage, these instructions are designated communication operation instructions.

signal security—*(DOD, IADB)* A generic term that includes both communications security and electronic security. See also **security.**

signals intelligence—*(DOD, IADB)* A category of intelligence information comprising all communications intelligence, electronics intelligence, and telemetry intelligence. Also called SIGINT. See also **electronics intelligence; intelligence; telemetry intelligence.**

signals support—*(NATO)* The provision of personnel and equipment from other forces for the establishment of a special or supplementary communications system.

signal-to-noise ratio—*(DOD, IADB)* The ratio of the amplitude of the desired signal to the amplitude of noise signals at a given point in time.

signature equipment—*(DOD, NATO)* Any item of equipment which reveals the type and nature of the unit or formation to which it belongs.

signature (target)—*(DOD, NATO)* 1. The characteristic pattern of the target displayed by detection and identification equipment. 2. In naval mine warfare, the variation in the influence field produced by the passage of a ship or sweep.

signed route—*(DOD, IADB)* A route along which a unit has placed directional signs bearing its unit identification symbol. The signs are for the unit's use only and must comply with movement regulations.

significant tracks (air defense)—*(DOD, NATO, IADB)* Tracks of aircraft or missiles which behave in an unusual manner which warrants attention and could pose a threat to a defended area.

simulative electronic deception (SED)—See **electronic warfare.**

simultaneous engagement—*(DOD, IADB)* The concurrent engagement of hostile targets by combination of interceptor aircraft and surface-to-air missiles.

single department purchase—*(DOD)* A method of purchase whereby one department buys particular commodities for another department or departments. See also **purchase.**

single flow route—*(DOD, NATO)* A route at least one-and-a-half lanes wide allowing the passage of a column of vehicles, and permitting isolated vehicles to pass or travel in the opposite direction at predetermined points. See also **limited access route; double flow route.**

single manager—*(DOD)* A Military Department or Agency designated by the Secretary of Defense to be responsible for management of specified commodities or common service activities on a Department of Defense-wide basis.

sinker—*(DOD, NATO, IADB)* In naval mine warfare, a heavy weight to which a buoyant mine is moored. The sinker generally houses the mooring rope drum and depth-setting mechanism and for mines laid by ships, it also serves as a launching trolley.

situation map—*(DOD, NATO, IADB)* A map showing the tactical or the administrative situation at a particular time. See also **map.**

situation report—*(DOD, NATO, IADB)* A report giving the situation in the area of a reporting unit or formation.

skim sweeping—*(DOD, NATO)* In naval mine warfare, the technique of wire sweeping to a fixed depth over deep-laid moored mines to cut any shallow enough to endanger surface shipping.

skin paint—*(DOD, IADB)* A radar indication caused by the reflected radar signal from an object.

skin tracking—*(DOD, IADB)* The tracking of an object by means of a skin paint.

skip bombing—*(DOD, IADB)* A method of aerial bombing in which a bomb is released from such a low altitude that it slides or glances along the surface of the water or ground and strikes the target at or above water level or ground level. See also **minimum-altitude bombing.**

skip it—*(DOD)* In air intercept, a code meaning, "Do not attack"; "Cease attack"; "Cease interception."

Skyhawk—*(DOD, IADB)* A single-engine, turbo-jet attack aircraft designed to operate from aircraft carriers, and capable of delivering nuclear and/or non-nuclear weapons, providing troop support, or conducting reconnaissance missions. It can act as a tanker, and can itself be air refueled. It possesses a limited all-weather attack capability, and can operate from short, unprepared fields. Designated as A-4.

slant range—*(DOD, NATO)* The line of sight distance between two points, not at the same level relative to a specific datum.

slated items—*(DOD)* Bulk petroleum and packaged bulk petroleum items that are requisitioned for overseas use by means of a consolidated requirement document, prepared and submitted through joint petroleum office channels. Packaged petroleum items are requisitioned in accordance with normal requisitioning procedures.

slice—*(DOD, IADB)* An average logistic planning factor used to obtain estimates of requirements for personnel and materiel. A personnel slice, e.g., generally consists of the total strength of the stated basic combatant elements, plus its proportionate share of all supporting and higher headquarters personnel.

slightly wounded—*(DOD, IADB)* A casualty that is a sitting or a walking case. See also **wounded.**

slip indicator—*(DOD, NATO)* An instrument which displays a measure of the resultant of

the inertial and gravity forces in the lateral and normal plane of aircraft.

small arms—*(DOD, IADB)* All arms, including automatic weapons, up to and including 20 millimeters (.787 inches).

small arms ammunition—*(DOD, IADB)* Ammunition for small arms, i.e., all ammunition up to and including 20 millimeters (.787 inches).

small circle—*(IADB)* A circle on the surface of the earth, the plane of which does not pass through the earth's center.

small-lot storage—*(DOD, IADB)* Generally considered to be a quantity of less than one pallet stack, stacked to maximum storage height. Thus, the term refers to a lot consisting of from one container to two or more pallet loads, but is not of sufficient quantity to form a complete pallet column. See also **storage.**

small-scale map—*(DOD, IADB)* A map having a scale smaller than 1:600,000. See also **map.**

small ship—*(NATO)* A ship of 450 feet (or 137 meters) or less in length. See also **large ship.**

smoke screen—*(DOD, NATO, IADB)* Cloud of smoke used to mask either friendly or enemy installations or maneuvers.

snagline mine—*(DOD, NATO)* A contact mine with a buoyant line attached to one of the horns or switches which may be caught up and pulled by the hull or propellers of a ship.

snake mode—*(NATO)* A control mode in which the pursuing aircraft flies a programmed weaving flight path to allow time to accomplish identification functions.

snap report—*(DOD)* Not to be used. See **Joint Tactical Air Reconnaissance/Surveillance Mission Report.**

snow—*(DOD)* In air intercept, a term meaning sweep jamming.

sofar—*(DOD, IADB)* The technique of fixing an explosion at sea by time difference of arrival of sound energy at several separate geographical locations. (The term is derived from the word "*so*und, *f*ixing *a*nd *r*anging.")

soft missile base—*(DOD, NATO, IADB)* A launching base that is not protected against a nuclear explosion.

software—*(DOD)* A set of computer programs, procedures and associated documentation concerned with the operation of a data processing system, e.g., compilers, library routines, manuals, circuit diagrams.

soil shear strength—*(DOD)* The maximum resistance of a soil to shearing stresses.

solenoid sweep—*(DOD, NATO)* In naval mine warfare, a magnetic sweep consisting of a horizontal axis coil wound on a floating iron tube.

sonar—*(DOD, IADB)* A sonic device used primarily for the detection and location of underwater objects. (This term is derived from the words "*so*und *n*avigation *a*nd *r*anging.")

sonic—*(DOD, IADB)* Of or pertaining to sound or the speed of sound. See also **speed of sound.**

sonobuoy—*(DOD, IADB)* A sonar device used to detect submerged submarines which when activated relays information by radio. It may be active directional or nondirectional, or it may be passive directional or nondirectional.

sonobuoy—*(NATO)* An acoustic device, used mainly for the detection of submarines which, when activated, transmits information by radio.

sortie—*(DOD, IADB)* 1. A sudden attack made from a defensive position. In this meaning, it is sometimes called a sally. 2. An operational flight by one aircraft. 3. To depart from a port or anchorage, with an implication of departure for operations or maneuver. See also **mission.**

sortie (air)—*(NATO)* An operational flight by one aircraft.

sortie allotment message—*(DOD)* The means by which the joint force commander allots excess sorties to meet requirements of his subordinate commanders which are expressed in their air employment/allocation plan.

sortie number—*(DOD, NATO)* A reference used to identify the images taken by all the sensors during one air reconnaissance sortie.

sortie plot—*(DOD)* An overlay representing the area on a map covered by imagery taken during one sortie. *(NATO)*—See **master plot.**

sortie reference—See **sortie number.**

sorting—See **triage.**

source—*(DOD, IADB)* 1. A person, thing, or activity from which intelligence information is obtained. 2. In clandestine activities, a person (agent), normally a foreign national, in the employ of an intelligence activity for intelligence purposes. 3. In interrogation activities, any person who furnishes intelligence information, either with or without the knowledge that the information is being used for intelligence purposes. In this context, a controlled source is in the employment or under the control of the intelligence activity and knows that the information is to be used for intelligence purposes. An uncontrolled source is a voluntary contributor of information and may or may not know that the information is to be used for intelligence purposes. See also **agent; collection agency.**

source—*(NATO)* In intelligence usage, a person from whom or thing from which information can be obtained. See also **agency; agent.**

space assignment—*(DOD)* An assignment to the individual Departments/Services by the appropriate transportation operating agency of

333

movement capability which completely or partially satisfies the stated requirements of the Departments/Services for the operating month and that has been accepted by them without the necessity for referral to the Joint Transportation Board for allocation.

space control operations—*(DOD)* Operations that provide freedom of action in space for friendly forces while, when directed, denying it to an enemy, and include the broad aspects of protection of US and US allied space systems and negation of enemy space systems. Space control operations encompass all elements of the space defense mission.

space defense—*(DOD, IADB)* All defensive measures designed to destroy attacking enemy vehicles (including missiles) while in space, or to nullify or reduce the effectiveness of such attack. See also **aerospace defense.**

space support operations—*(DOD)* Operations required to ensure that space control and support of terrestrial forces are maintained. They include activities such as launching and deploying space vehicles, maintaining and sustaining space vehicles while on orbit, and recovering space vehicles if required.

Spacetrack—*(DOD)* A global system of radar, optical and radiometric sensors linked to a computation and analysis center in the North American Air Defense Command combat operations center complex. The Spacetrack mission is detection, tracking, and cataloging of all man-made objects in orbit of the earth. It is the Air Force portion of the North American Air Defense Command Space Detection and Tracking system. See also **Spadats; Spasur.**

Spadats—*(DOD, IADB)* A *space* *d*etection *a*nd *t*racking *s*ystem capable of detecting and tracking space vehicles from the earth, and reporting the orbital characteristics of these vehicles to a central control facility. See also **Spacetrack; Spasur.**

span of detonation (atomic demolition munition employment)—*(DOD)* That total period of time, resulting from a timer error, between the earliest and the latest possible detonation time. **1. early time**—The earliest possible time that an atomic demolition munition can detonate; **2. fire time**—That time the atomic demolition munition will detonate should the timers function precisely without error; **3. late time**—The latest possible time that an atomic demolition munition can detonate.

spare—*(NATO)* An individual part, subassembly or assembly supplied for the maintenance or repair of systems or equipment.

Sparrow—*(DOD, IADB)* An air-to-air solid-propellant missile with nonnuclear warhead and electronic-controlled homing. Designated as **AIM-7.** The ship-launched surface-to-air version is designated as **Sea Sparrow (RIM-7).**

Spartan—*(DOD, IADB)* A nuclear surface-to-air guided missile formerly deployed as part of the Safeguard ballistic missile defense weapon system. It is designed to intercept strategic ballistic reentry vehicles in the exoatmosphere.

spasm war—*(DOD)* Not to be used. See **general war.**

Spasur—*(DOD)* An operational space surveillance system with the mission to detect and determine the orbital elements of all man-made objects in orbit of the earth. The mission is accomplished by means of a continuous fan of continuous wave energy beamed vertically across the continental United States and an associated computational facility. It is the Navy portion of the North American Air Defense Command Space Detection and Tracking System. See also **Spacetrack; Spadats.**

special agent—*(DOD, IADB)* A person, either United States military or civilian, who is a specialist in military security or the collection of intelligence or counterintelligence information. (Note: IADB does not use the words United States.)

special air operation—*(DOD, NATO)* An operation, conducted at any level of conflict, in support of unconventional warfare and clandestine, covert and psychological activities.

special ammunition supply point—*(DOD, IADB)* A mobile supply point where special ammunition is stored and issued to delivery units.

special assignment airlift requirements—*(DOD, IADB)* Airlift requirements, including JCS-directed/coordinated exercises, that require special consideration due to the number of passengers involved, weight or size of cargo, urgency of movement, sensitivity, or other valid factors that preclude the use of channel airlift.

special atomic demolition munition—*(DOD, IADB)* A very low-yield, man-portable, atomic demolition munition that is detonated by a timer device.

special cargo—*(DOD, IADB)* Cargo that requires special handling or protection, such as pyrotechnics, detonators, watches, and precision instruments. See also **cargo.**

special-equipment vehicle—*(DOD, IADB)* A vehicle consisting of a general-purpose chassis with special-purpose body and/or mounted equipments designed to meet a specialized requirement. See also **vehicle.**

special flight—*(DOD, NATO, IADB)* An air transport flight, other than a scheduled service, set up to move a specific load.

Special Forces—See **United States Army Special Forces.**

special hazard—*(DOD, NATO)* In aircraft crash rescue and fire-fighting activities: fuels, materials, components or situations that could increase the risks normally associated with military aircraft accidents and could require special procedures, equipment or extinguishing agents.

specialist intelligence report—*(DOD, IADB)* A category of specialized, technical reports used in the dissemination of intelligence. See also **intelligence reporting.**

specialization—*(DOD)* An arrangement within an alliance wherein a member or group of members most suited by virtue of technical skills, location, or other qualifications assume(s) greater responsibility for a specific task or significant portion thereof for one or more other members.

special job cover map—*(NATO)* A small scale map used to record progress on photographic reconnaissance tasks covering very large areas. As each portion of the task is completed, the area covered is outlined on the map.

special operations—*(DOD)* Operations conducted by specially trained, equipped, and organized DOD forces against strategic or tactical targets in pursuit of national military, political, economic, or psychological objectives. These operations may be conducted during periods of peace or hostilities. They may support conventional operations, or they may be prosecuted independently when the use of conventional forces is either inappropriate or infeasible.

special operations—*(IADB)* Secondary or supporting operations that may be adjuncts to various other operations and for which no one Service is assigned primary responsibility.

special (or project) equipment—*(DOD, IADB)* Equipment not authorized in standard equipment publications but determined as essential in connection with a contemplated operation, function, or mission. See also **equipment.**

special-purpose vehicle—*(DOD, IADB)* A vehicle incorporating a special chassis and designed to meet a specialized requirement. See also **vehicle.**

special sheaf—*(DOD, IADB)* In artillery and naval gunfire support, any sheaf other than parallel, converged, or open.

335

special staff—*(DOD, IADB)* All staff officers having duties at a headquarters and not included in the general (coordinating) staff group or in the personal staff group. The special staff includes certain technical specialists and heads of services, e.g., quartermaster officer, antiaircraft officer, transportation officer, etc. See also **staff**.

special weapons—*(DOD, IADB)* A term sometimes used to indicate weapons grouped for special procedures, for security, or other reasons. Specific terminology, e.g., nuclear weapons, guided missiles, is preferable.

specific intelligence collection requirement—*(DOD, IADB)* An identified gap in intelligence holdings that may be satisfied only by collection action, and that has been validated by the appropriate requirements control authority. Commonly referred to as SICR.

specific search—*(DOD, IADB)* Reconnaissance of a limited number of points for specific information.

specified command—*(DOD)* A command that has a broad continuing mission and that is established and so designated by the President through the Secretary of Defense with the advice and assistance of the Joint Chiefs of Staff. It normally is composed of forces from but one Service.

spectrozonal photography—*(DOD, NATO)* A photographic technique whereby the natural spectral emissions of all objects are selectively filtered in order to image only those objects within a particular spectral band or zone and eliminate the unwanted background.

spectrum of war—*(DOD, IADB)* A term which encompasses the full range of conflict; cold, limited, and general war.

speed—See **airspeed; convoy speed; critical speed; declared speed; endurance speed; maximum sustained speed (transport vehicle); scheduled speed; speed of advance; speed of sound.**

speed of advance—*(DOD, NATO)* In naval usage, the speed expected to be made good over the ground. See also **pace; rate of march.**

speed of advance—*(IADB)* In naval usage, the speed expected to be made good over the distance along a route. See also **mean line of advance.**

speed of sound—*(DOD, NATO, IADB)* The speed at which sound travels in a given medium under specified conditions. The speed of sound at sea level in the International Standard Atmosphere is 1108 ft/second, 658 knots, 1215 km/hour. See also **hypersonic; sonic; subsonic; supersonic; transonic.**

spigot—See **sprag.**

spin stabilization—*(DOD, IADB)* Directional stability of a projectile obtained by the action of gyroscopic forces that result from spinning of the body about its axis of symmetry.

spitting—*(DOD)* In air antisubmarine warfare operations, a code meaning, "I am about to lay, or am laying, sonobuoys. I may be out of radio contact for a few minutes." If transmitted from the submarine it indicates that the submarine has launched a sonobuoy.

splash—*(DOD, NATO)* 1. In artillery and naval gunfire support, word transmitted to an observer or spotter five seconds before the estimated time of the impact of a salvo or round. 2. In air interception, target destruction verified by visual or radar means.

splashed—*(DOD)* In air intercept, a code meaning, "Enemy aircraft shot down," (followed by number and type).

split cameras—*(DOD, NATO, IADB)* An assembly of two cameras disposed at a fixed overlapping angle relative to each other.

split pair—See **split vertical photography.**

split-up—See **break-up.**

split vertical photography—*(DOD, NATO)* Photographs taken simultaneously by two cameras mounted at an angle from the vertical, one tilted to the left and one to the right, to obtain a small side overlap.

spoiling attack—*(DOD, IADB)* A tactical maneuver employed to seriously impair a hostile attack while the enemy is in the process of forming or assembling for an attack. Usually employed by armored units in defense by an attack on enemy assembly positions in front of a main line of resistance or battle position.

spoiling attack—*(NATO)* A tactical maneuver employed to impair seriously a hostile attack while the enemy is in the process of forming up or assembling for an attack.

spoking (radar)—*(DOD, NATO)* Periodic flashes of the rotating time base on a radial display. Sometimes caused by mutual interference.

sponsor—*(DOD)* Military member or civilian employee with dependents.

spoofer—*(DOD)* In air intercept, a code meaning, "A contact employing electronic or tactical deception measures."

spot—*(DOD, NATO, IADB)* 1. To determine by observation, deviations of ordnance from the target for the purpose of supplying necessary information for the adjustment of fire. 2. To place in a proper location. See also **adjustment of fire**.

spot elevation—*(DOD, NATO, IADB)* A point on a map or chart whose elevation is noted.

spot jamming—*(DOD, NATO, IADB)* The jamming of a specific channel or frequency. See also **barrage jamming; electronic warfare; jamming**.

spot net—*(DOD, IADB)* Radio communication net used by a spotter in calling fire.

spot report—*(DOD, IADB)* A concise narrative report of essential information covering events or conditions that may have an immediate and significant effect on current planning and operations that is afforded the most expeditious means of transmission consistent with requisite security. (Note: In reconnaissance and surveillance usage, **spot report** is not to be used. See **Joint Tactical Air Reconnaissance/Surveillance Mission Report**.)

spot size—*(DOD, NATO)* The size of the electron spot on the face of the cathode ray tube.

spotter—*(DOD, IADB)* An observer stationed for the purpose of observing and reporting results of naval gunfire to the firing agency and who also may be employed in designating targets. See also **field artillery observer; naval gunfire spotting team**.

spotting—*(DOD, NATO, IADB)* A process of determining by visual or electronic observation, deviations of artillery or naval gunfire from the target in relation to a spotting line for the purpose of supplying necessary information for the adjustment or analysis of fire.

spotting line—*(DOD, NATO, IADB)* Either the gun-target line, the observer-target line, or a reference line used by the spotter or observer in making spot corrections. See also **gun target line; observer-target line; reference line**.

sprag—*(NATO)* A projection preventing the movement of platforms or pallets in the side guidance rails in an aircraft cabin.

spray dome—*(DOD, NATO)* The mound of water spray thrown up into the air when the shock wave from an underwater detonation of a nuclear weapon reaches the surface.

spreading fire—*(DOD)* A notification by the spotter or the naval gunfire ship, depending on who is controlling the fire, to indicate that fire is about to be distributed over an area.

Sprint—*(DOD, IADB)* A high acceleration, nuclear surface-to-air guided missile formerly deployed as part of the Safeguard ballistic missile defense weapon system. It is designed to intercept strategic ballistic reentry vehicles in the endoatmosphere.

sprocket—*(DOD, NATO)* In naval mine warfare, an anti-sweep device included in a mine mooring to allow a sweep wire to pass through the mooring without parting the mine from its sinker.

squadron—*(DOD, IADB)* 1. An organization consisting of two or more divisions of ships, or two or more divisions (Navy) or flights of aircraft. It is normally, but not necessarily, composed of ships or aircraft of the same type. 2. The basic administrative aviation unit of the Army, Navy, Marine Corps, and Air Force.

squawk—*(DOD)* A code meaning, "Switch Identification Friend or Foe master control to 'normal' (Mode and Code as directed) position."

squawk flash—*(DOD)* A code meaning, "Actuate Identification Friend or Foe I/P switch."

squawking—*(DOD)* A code meaning, "Showing Identification Friend or Foe in Mode (and Code) indicated."

squawk low—*(DOD)* A code meaning, "Switch Identification Friend or Foe master control to 'low' position."

squawk may day—*(DOD)* A code meaning, "Switch Identification Friend or Foe master control to 'emergency' position."

squawk mike—*(DOD)* A code meaning, "Actuate Identification Friend or Foe MIC switch and key transmitter as directed."

squawk standby—*(DOD)* A code meaning, "Switch Identification Friend or Foe master control to 'standby' position."

squib—*(DOD, IADB)* A small pyrotechnic device that may be used to fire the igniter in a rocket or for some similar purpose. Not to be confused with a detonator that explodes.

squirt—*(DOD, NATO)* In air-to-air refuelling, a means of providing visual detection of a nearby aircraft. In practice this is achieved by the donor aircraft dumping fuel and/or the receiver aircraft selecting afterburners, if so equipped.

SS—See **submarine.**

SSBN—See **fleet ballistic missile submarine.**

SSG—See **guided missile submarine.**

SSGN—See **guided missile submarine.**

SSN—See **submarine.**

staballoy—*(DOD)* Designates metal alloys made from high-density depleted uranium with other metals for use in kinetic energy penetrators for armor-piercing munitions. Several different metals such as titanium or molybdenum can be used for the purpose. The various staballoy metals have low radioactivity that is not considered to be a significant health hazard.

stability augmentation feature—*(NATO)* In a flight control system, an automatic device which operates to augment the short term stability characteristics of an aircraft.

stable base film—*(DOD, NATO)* A particular type of film having a high stability in regard to shrinkage and stretching.

staff—See **combined staff; general staff; integrated staff; joint staff; parallel staff; special staff.**

staff supervision—*(DOD, IADB)* The process of advising other staff officers and individuals subordinate to the commander of the commander's plans and policies, interpreting those plans and policies, assisting such subordinates in carrying them out, determining the extent to which they are being followed, and advising the commander thereof.

stage—*(DOD, NATO)* 1. An element of the missile or propulsion system that generally separates from the missile at burnout or cut-off. Stages are numbered chronologically in order of burning. 2. To process, in a specified area, troops which are in transit from one locality to another. See also **marshalling; staging area.** 3. *(NATO)* The part of an air route from one air staging unit to the next.

staged crew—*(NATO)* Aircrew prepositioned at specific points along an air route to allow the continuous operation of the aircraft.

staged crews—*(DOD, IADB)* Aircrews specifically positioned at intermediate airfields to take over aircraft operating on air routes, thus relieving complementary crews of flying fatigue and speeding up the flow rate of the aircraft concerned.

staging area—*(DOD, NATO, IADB)* 1. **Amphibious or airborne**—A general locality between the mounting area and the objective of an amphibious or airborne expedition, through which the expedition or parts thereof pass after mounting, for refueling, regrouping of ships, and/or exercise, inspection, and redistribution of troops. 2. **Other movements**—A general locality established for the concentration of troop units and transient personnel between movements over the lines of communication. See also **marshalling; stage.**

staging base—*(DOD, IADB)* 1. An advanced naval base for the anchoring, fueling, and refitting of transports and cargo ships, and for replenishing mobile service squadrons. 2. A landing and takeoff area with minimum servicing, supply, and shelter provided for the temporary occupancy of military aircraft during the course of movement from one location to another.

standard—*(DOD, NATO)* An exact value, a physical entity, or an abstract concept, established and defined by authority, custom, or common consent to serve as a reference, model, or rule in measuring quantities or qualities, establishing practices or procedures, or evaluating results. A fixed quantity or quality.

standard advanced base units—*(DOD, IADB)* Personnel and materiel organized to function as advanced base units, including the functional components which are employed in the establishment of naval advanced bases. Such advanced base units may establish repair bases, supply bases, supply depots, airfields, air bases, or other naval shore establishments at overseas locations; e.g., Acorns, Cubs, Gropacs, and Lions. (Note: IADB definition stops with the words "naval shore establishments.")

Standard Arm—*(DOD)* An air-launched antiradiation missile designed to home on and destroy radar emitters. Designated as **AGM-78.**

standard day of supply—*(NATO)* The total amount of supplies required for an average day based on Standing Group NATO rates and/or on national rates as appropriate. See also **one day's supply.**

standardization—*(DOD)* The process by which the Department of Defense achieves the closest practicable cooperation among the Services and Defense agencies for the most efficient use of research, development, and production resources, and agrees to adopt on the broadest possible basis the use of: **a.** common or compatible operational, administrative, and logistic procedures; **b.** common or compatible technical procedures and criteria; **c.** common, compatible, or interchangeable supplies, components, weapons, or equipment; and **d.** common or compatible tactical doctrine with corresponding organizational compatibility.

standardization—*(NATO)* Within NATO, the process of developing concepts, doctrines, procedures and designs to achieve and maintain the most effective levels of compatibility, interoperability, interchangeability and commonality in the fields of operations, administration and materiel.

standardization agreement—(NATO) The record of an agreement among several or all the member nations to adopt like or similar military equipment, ammunition, supplies, and stores; and operational, logistic, and administrative procedures. National acceptance of a NATO allied publication issued by the Military Agency for Standardization may be recorded as a Standardization Agreement. Also called **STANAG**.

standardization agreement—(IADB) The record of an agreement among several or all of the member nations to adopt like or similar military equipment, ammunition, supplies and stores; and operational, logistic and administrative procedures.

standardized product—(NATO) A product that conforms to specifications resulting from the same or equivalent technical requirements. NATO standardized products are identified by a NATO code number.

standard load—(NATO) A load which has been pre-planned as to dimensions, weight and balance, and designated by a number or some classification.

Standard Missile—(DOD) A shipboard, surface-to-surface/air missile with solid propellant rocket engine. It is equipped with non-nuclear warhead, semi-active or passive homing. Designated **RIM-66** Medium Range (Tartar replacement) and **RIM-67** Extended Range (Terrier replacement).

standard NATO data message—(NATO) NATO message formats and codes prescribed by a Standardization Agreement and used to exchange information between participating national and/or international units or facilities.

standard operating procedure—See **standing operating procedure.**

standard parallel—(DOD, NATO, IADB) A parallel on a map or chart along which the scale is as stated for that map or chart.

standard pattern—(DOD, NATO, IADB) In land-mine warfare, the agreed pattern to which mines are normally laid.

standard route—(DOD, NATO) In naval control of shipping, a pre-planned single track, assigned a code name, connecting positions within the main shipping lanes.

Standard SSM (ARM)—(DOD) A surface-to-surface anti-radiation missile equipped with a conventional warhead. It is planned for anti-ship missions and is carried by the FFG-1 class, 8 DDG-2 class units and the PG 98 and 100. Designated as **RGM-66D**.

standby reserve—(DOD) Those units and members of the Reserve Components (other than those in the Ready Reserve or Retired Reserve) who are liable for active duty only as provided in 10 U.S.C. 273, 672 and 674.
1. **active status, standby reserve—**Reservists who (a) are completing their statutory military service obligation, or (b) are being retained in an active status under 10 U.S.C. 1006, or (c) were screened from the Ready Reserve as being key personnel and request assignment to the Active Status List, or (d) may be temporarily assigned to the Standby Reserve for hardship or other cogent reason determined by the Secretary concerned, with the expectation of their being returned to the Ready Reserve.
2. **inactive status, standby reserve—**Individuals who are not required by law or regulation to remain members of an active status program but who (a) desire to retain their Reserve affiliation in a non-participating status, and (b) have skills that may be of possible future use to the Military Department concerned.

stand fast—(DOD, NATO) In artillery, the order at which all action on the position ceases immediately.

standing operating procedure—*(DOD, NATO)* A set of instructions covering those features of operations which lend themselves to a definite or standardized procedure without loss of effectiveness. The procedure is applicable unless ordered otherwise. Also called **standard operating procedure.**

standing order—*(DOD, NATO)* A promulgated order which remains in force until amended or cancelled.

standing patrol—*(NATO)* A patrol which will be of a strength decided by the commander allotting the task. Its task may be recce, listening, fighting, or a combination of these. It differs from a recce, fighting, or listening patrol in that, having taken up its allotted position, it is not free to maneuver in the performance of its task without permission. See also **patrol.**

Starfighter—*(DOD, IADB)* A supersonic, single-engine, turbojet, air superiority fighter. It is capable of employing nuclear and nonnuclear weapons. It is used by other nations as a prime air interceptor. Designated as **F-104.**

Starlifter—*(DOD, IADB)* A large cargo transport powered by four turbofan engines, capable of intercontinental range with heavy payloads and airdrops. Designated as **C-141.**

start line—See **line of departure.**

start point—*(NATO)* A well defined point on a route at which a movement of vehicles begins to be under the control of the commander of this movement. It is at this point that the column is formed by the successive passing, at an appointed time, of each of the elements composing the column. In addition to the principal start point of a column there may be secondary start points for its different elements.

state and regional defense airlift—*(DOD)* The program for use during an emergency of civil aircraft other than air carrier aircraft.

state chicken—*(DOD)* In air intercept, a code meaning, "I am at a fuel state requiring recovery, tanker service, or diversion to an airfield."

state lamb—*(DOD)* In air intercept, a code meaning, "I do not have enough fuel for an intercept plus reserve required for carrier recovery."

state of readiness—See **defense readiness conditions; weapons readiness state.**

state of readiness—state 1 (safe)—*(DOD, IADB)* The state of a demolition target upon or within which the demolition charge has been placed and secured. The firing or initiating circuits have been installed, but not connected to the demolition charge. Detonators or initiators have not been connected nor installed.

state of readiness—state 1—safe—*(NATO)* The state of a demolition target in which charges are in place. The firing circuit may be in place, but the detonators are not installed and the means of firing are not connected. See also **state of readiness—state 2—armed.**

state of readiness—state 2—armed—*(DOD, NATO)* The state of a demolition target in which the demolition charges are in place, the firing and priming circuits are installed and complete, ready for immediate firing. See also **state of readiness—state 1—safe.**

state of readiness—state 2—armed—*(IADB)* The state of a target whose demolition is ready for immediate firing.

state tiger—*(DOD)* In air intercept, a code meaning, "I have sufficient fuel to complete my mission as assigned."

static air temperature—*(DOD, NATO)* The temperature at a point at rest relative to the ambient air.

static line (air transport)—*(DOD, IADB)* A line attached to a parachute pack and to a strop or anchor cable in an aircraft so that when the load is dropped the parachute is deployed automatically.

static line cable—See **anchor cable.**

static marking—*(DOD, NATO)* Marks on photographic negatives and other imagery caused by unwanted discharges of static electricity.

static test load—*(DOD, NATO)* In sea operations, twice the safe working load. See also **safe working load.**

station—*(DOD, IADB)* 1. A general term meaning any military or naval activity at a fixed land location. 2. A particular kind of activity to which other activities or individuals may come for a specific service, often of a technical nature, e.g., aid station. 3. An assigned or prescribed position in a naval formation or cruising disposition; or an assigned area in an approach, contact, or battle disposition. 4. Any place of duty or post or position in the field to which an individual, or group of individuals, or a unit may be assigned. 5. One or more transmitters or receivers or a combination of transmitters and receivers, including the accessory equipment necessary at one location, for carrying on radio communication service. Each station will be classified by the service in which it operates permanently or temporarily.

station authentication—*(DOD, IADB)* A security measure designed to establish the authenticity of a transmitting or receiving station.

station time—*(DOD, NATO)* In air transport operations, the time at which crews, passengers, and cargo are to be on board and ready for the flight.

staybehind—*(DOD)* Agent or agent organization established in a given country to be activated in the event of hostile overrun or other circumstances under which normal access would be denied.

stay behind force—*(DOD, NATO)* A force which is left in position to conduct a specified mission when the remainder of the force withdraws or retires from the area.

steady—*(DOD)* In air intercept, a code meaning, "Am on prescribed heading," or, "Straighten out immediately on present heading or heading indicated."

steer—*(DOD)* In air intercept, close air support and air interdiction, a code meaning, "Set magnetic heading indicated to reach me (or _____)."

stellar guidance—*(DOD, IADB)* A system wherein a guided missile may follow a predetermined course with reference primarily to the relative position of the missile and certain preselected celestial bodies. See also **guidance.**

stepped-up separation—*(DOD, NATO)* The vertical separation in a formation of aircraft measured from an aircraft ahead upward to the next aircraft behind or in echelon.

step-up—*(NATO)* An element of a headquarters which provides a leapfrog capability.

stereogram—*(NATO)* A stereoscopic set of photographs or drawings correctly oriented and mounted for stereoscopic viewing.

stereographic coverage—*(DOD)* Photographic coverage with overlapping air photographs to provide a three-dimensional presentation of the picture; 60 percent overlap is considered normal and 53 percent is generally regarded as the minimum.

stereoscopic cover—*(NATO)* Photographs taken with sufficient overlap to permit complete stereoscopic examinations.

stereoscopic model—*(NATO)* The mental impression of an area or object seen as being in three dimensions when viewed stereoscopically on photographs.

stereoscopic pair—*(NATO)* Two photographs with sufficient overlap of detail to make possible stereoscopic examination of an object or an area common to both.

sterilize—*(DOD, NATO)* 1. In naval mine warfare, to permanently render a mine incapable of firing by means of a device (e.g., sterilizer) within the mine. *(DOD, IADB)* 2. To remove from material to be used in covert and clandestine operations, marks or devices which can identify it as emanating from the sponsoring nation or organization.

sterilizer—*(DOD, NATO)* In mine warfare, a device included in mines to render the mine permanently inoperative on expiration of a pre-determined time after laying.

stern attack—*(DOD)* In air intercept, an attack by an interceptor aircraft that terminates with a heading crossing angle of 45° or less. See also **heading crossing angle.**

stick (air transport)—*(DOD, IADB)* A number of paratroopers who jump from one aperture or door of an aircraft during one run over a drop zone.

stick—*(NATO)* A number of paratroopers who jump from one aperture or door of an aircraft during one run over a drop zone.

stick commander (air transport)—*(DOD, IADB)* A designated individual who controls parachutists from the time they enter the aircraft until their exit. See also **jumpmaster.**

Stinger—*(DOD)* A lightweight, man-portable, shoulder-fired, air defense artillery missile weapon for low altitude air defense of forward area combat troops.

stockage objective—*(DOD, IADB)* The maximum quantities of materiel to be maintained on hand to sustain current operations. It will consist of the sum of stocks represented by the operating level and the safety level. See also **level of supply.**

stock control—*(DOD, NATO, IADB)* Process of maintaining inventory data on the quantity,

location, and condition of supplies and equipment due-in, on-hand, and due-out, to determine quantities of material and equipment available and/or required for issue and to facilitate distribution and management of materiel. See also **inventory control.**

stock coordination—*(DOD, IADB)* A supply management function exercised usually at department level that controls the assignment of material cognizance for items or categories of material to inventory managers.

stock fund—*(DOD)* A revolving fund established to finance costs of inventories of supplies. It is authorized by specific provision of law to finance a continuing cycle of operations. Reimbursements and collections derived from such operations are available for use by the fund without further action by the Congress.

stock level—See **level of supply.**

Stock Number—See **National Stock Number.**

stockpile to target sequence—*(DOD, IADB)* 1. The order of events involved in removing a nuclear weapon from storage, and assembling, testing, transporting, and delivering it on the target. 2. A document that defines the logistical and employment concepts and related physical environments involved in the delivery of a nuclear weapon from the stockpile to the target. It may also define the logistical flow involved in moving nuclear weapons to and from the stockpile for quality assurance testing, modification and retrofit, and the recycling of limited life components.

stockpile to target sequence—*(NATO)* The order and permutations of events involved in removing a nuclear weapon from storage, and assembling, testing, transporting, and delivering it on the target.

stock record account—*(DOD, IADB)* A basic record showing by item the receipt and issuance of property, the balances on hand and such other identifying or stock control data as may be required by proper authority.

stocks—*(NATO)* The quantity of supplies and material on hand ready for use. See also **operational stocks; theater operational stocks.**

stop squawk—*(DOD)* A code meaning, "Turn identification friend or foe master control to 'off.' "

stopway—*(DOD, NATO)* A defined rectangular area on the ground at the end of a runway in the direction of take-off designated and prepared by the competent authority as a suitable area in which an aircraft can be stopped in the case of an interrupted take-off. It must be capable of supporting aircraft of approximately 23,000 kilograms (50,000 lbs.).

storage—*(DOD)* 1. The retention of data in any form, usually for the purpose of orderly retrieval and documentation. 2. A device consisting of electronic, electrostatic, electrical, hardware or other elements into which data may be entered, and from which data may be obtained as desired. See also **ammunition and toxic material open space; bin storage; bulk storage; igloo space; large-lot storage; medium-lot storage; open improved storage space; open unimproved wet space; small-lot storage.**

storage life—*(DOD, NATO)* The length of time for which an item of supply including explosives, given specific storage conditions, may be expected to remain serviceable and, if relevant, safe. See also **shelf life.**

stores—See **naval stores; supplies.**

stowage diagram—*(DOD, NATO)* A scaled drawing included in the loading plan of a vessel for each deck or platform showing the exact location of all cargo. See also **stowage plan.**

stowage factor—*(DOD, IADB)* The number which expresses the space, in cubic feet, occupied by a long ton of any commodity as prepared for shipment, including all crating or packaging.

stowage plan—*(DOD, IADB)* A completed stowage diagram showing what materiel has been loaded and its stowage location in each hold, between-deck compartment, or other space in a ship, including deck space. Each port of discharge is indicated by colors or other appropriate means. Deck and between-deck cargo normally is shown in perspective, while cargo stowed in the lower hold is shown in profile, except that vehicles usually are shown in perspective regardless of stowage. See also **stowage diagram.**

strafing—*(DOD, IADB)* The delivery of automatic weapons fire by aircraft on ground targets.

straggler—*(DOD, NATO)* 1. Any personnel, vehicles, ships or aircraft which, without apparent purpose or assigned mission, become separated from their unit, column or formation. *(NATO)* 2. A ship separated from its convoy by more than 5 nautical miles, through inability to keep up, and unable to rejoin before dark, or over 10 nautical miles from its convoy whether or not it can rejoin before dark. See also **romper.**

stranger (bearing, distance, altitude)—*(DOD)* In air intercept, a code meaning, "An unidentified aircraft, bearing, distance, and altitude as indicated relative to you."

strangle—*(DOD)* A code meaning, "Switch off equipment indicated."

strangle parrot—*(DOD)* A code meaning, "Switch off Identification Friend or Foe equipment."

strapping—*(DOD, IADB)* 1. An operation by which supply containers, such as cartons or boxes, are reinforced by bands, metal straps, or wire, placed at specified intervals around them, drawn taut, and then sealed or clamped by a machine. 2. Measurement of storage tanks and calculation of volume to provide tables for conversion of depth of product in linear units of measurement to volume of contents.

strategic advantage—*(DOD, IADB)* The overall relative power relationship of opponents that enables one nation or group of nations effectively to control the course of a military/political situation.

strategic air transport—*(DOD)* The movement of personnel and materiel by air in accordance with a strategic plan.

strategic air transport operations—*(DOD, NATO, IADB)* The carriage of passengers and cargo between theaters by means of: **a.** scheduled services; **b.** special flights; **c.** air logistic support; **d.** aeromedical evacuation.

strategic air warfare—*(DOD, IADB)* Air combat and supporting operations designed to effect, through the systematic application of force to a selected series of vital targets, the progressive destruction and disintegration of the enemy's war-making capacity to a point where the enemy no longer retains the ability or the will to wage war. Vital targets may include key manufacturing systems, sources of raw material, critical material, stockpiles, power systems, transportation systems, communication facilities, concentration of uncommitted elements of enemy armed forces, key agricultural areas, and other such target systems.

strategic air warfare—*(NATO)* Air operations designed to effect the progressive destruction and disintegration of the enemy's war-making capacity.

Strategic Army Forces—See **United States Strategic Army Forces.**

strategic concentration—*(DOD, NATO, IADB)* The assembly of designated forces in areas from which it is intended that operations of the assembled force shall begin so that they are best disposed to initiate the plan of campaign.

strategic concept—*(DOD, NATO, IADB)* The course of action accepted as the result of the estimate of the strategic situation. It is a statement of what is to be done in broad terms sufficiently flexible to permit its use in framing the military, diplomatic, economic, psychological and other measures which stem from it. See also **basic undertakings.**

strategic intelligence—*(DOD)* Intelligence that is required for the formation of policy and military plans at national and international levels. Strategic intelligence and tactical intelligence differ primarily in level of application but may also vary in terms of scope and detail.

strategic intelligence—*(NATO)* Intelligence which is required for the formation of policy and military plans at national and international levels. See also **tactical intelligence.**

strategic map—*(DOD, IADB)* A map of medium scale, or smaller, used for planning of operations, including the movement, concentration, and supply of troops. See also **map.**

strategic material (critical)—*(DOD, IADB)* A material required for essential uses in a war emergency, the procurement of which in adequate quantity, quality, or time, is sufficiently uncertain, for any reason, to require prior provision of the supply thereof.

strategic mining—*(NATO)* A long term mining campaign designed to deny the enemy the use of specific sea routes or sea areas.

strategic mission—*(DOD, IADB)* A mission directed against one or more of a selected series of enemy targets with the purpose of progressive destruction and disintegration of the enemy's war-making capacity and his will to make war. Targets include key manufacturing systems, sources of raw material, critical material, stockpiles, power systems, transportation systems, communication facilities, and other such target systems. As opposed to tactical operations, strategic operations are designed to have a long-range, rather than immediate, effect on the enemy and its military forces.

strategic mobility—*(DOD)* The capability to deploy and sustain military forces worldwide in support of national strategy. See also **mobility**.

strategic plan—*(DOD, IADB)* A plan for the overall conduct of a war.

strategic psychological activities—*(DOD, NATO)* Planned psychological activities in peace and war which normally pursue objectives to gain the support and cooperation of friendly and neutral countries and to reduce the will and the capacity of hostile or potentially hostile countries to wage war.

strategic reserve—*(DOD, NATO)* An external reinforcing force which is not committed in advance to a specific Major Subordinate Command, but which can be deployed to any region for a mission decided at the time by the Major NATO Commander.

strategic reserve—*(IADB)* That quantity of material that is placed in a particular geographic location due to strategic considerations or in anticipation of major interruptions in the supply distribution system. It is over and above the stockage objective. See also **level of supply**.

strategic transport aircraft—*(DOD, NATO, IADB)* Aircraft designed primarily for the carriage of personnel and/or cargo over long distances.

strategic vulnerability—*(DOD, IADB)* The susceptibility of vital elements of national power to being seriously decreased or adversely changed by the application of actions within the capability of another nation to impose. Strategic vulnerability may pertain to political, geographic, economic, scientific, sociological, or military factors.

strategic warning—*(DOD, NATO, IADB)* A notification that enemy-initiated hostilities may be imminent. This notification may be received from minutes to hours, to days, or longer, prior to the initiation of hostilities. See also **attack assessment; strategic warning lead time; strategic warning post-decision time; strategic warning pre-decision time; tactical warning**.

strategic warning lead time—*(DOD, IADB)* That time between the receipt of strategic warning and the beginning of hostilities. This time may include two action periods: strategic warning pre-decision time and strategic warning post-decision time. See also **commander's estimate of the situation; strategic concept; strategic warning**.

strategic warning post-decision time—*(DOD, IADB)* That time which begins after the decision, made at the highest levels of government(s) in response to strategic warning, is ordered executed and ends with the start of hostilities or termination of the threat. It is that part of strategic warning lead time available for executing pre-hostility actions to strengthen the national strategic posture; however, some preparatory actions may be initiated in the pre-decision period. See also **strategic warning; strategic warning lead time**.

strategic warning pre-decision time—*(DOD, IADB)* That time which begins upon receipt of strategic warning and ends when a decision is ordered executed. It is that part of strategic warning lead time available to the highest levels of government(s) to determine that strategic course of action to be executed. See also **strategic warning; strategic warning lead time**.

strategy—*(DOD, IADB)* The art and science of developing and using political, economic, psychological, and military forces as necessary during peace and war, to afford the maximum support to policies, in order to increase the probabilities and favorable consequences of victory and to lessen the chances of defeat. See also **military strategy; national strategy**.

Stratofortress—*(DOD, IADB)* An all-weather, intercontinental, strategic heavy bomber powered by eight turbojet engines. It is capable of delivering nuclear and non-nuclear bombs, air-to-surface missiles and decoys. Its range is extended by in-flight refueling. Designated as B-52.

Stratofreighter—*(DOD, IADB)* A strategic aerial tanker-freighter powered by four reciprocating engines. It is equipped for in-flight refueling of bombers and fighters. Designated as KC-97L.

stratosphere—*(DOD)* The layer of the atmosphere above the troposphere in which the change of temperature with height is relatively small. See also **atmosphere**.

Stratotanker—*(DOD, IADB)* A multipurpose aerial tanker-transport powered by four turbojet engines. It is equipped for high-speed, high-altitude refueling of bombers and fighters. Designated as KC-135.

stream—*(DOD)* Dispensing of chaff (solid/random interval/bursts).

stream takeoff—*(DOD, NATO, IADB)* Aircraft taking off in trail/column formation.

strength—See **economic potential; unit strength.**

strength group—*(DOD)* A surface action group (unit) (element) composed of the heaviest combatant ships available with their aircraft and assigned screen.

stretcher—See **litter**.

stretch out—*(DOD)* A reduction in the delivery rate specified for a program without a reduction in the total quantity to be delivered.

strike—*(DOD, NATO, IADB)* An attack which is intended to inflict damage on, seize, or destroy an objective.

strike cruiser—*(DOD)* A warship designed to operate offensively with carrier strike forces or surface action groups against surface, air and subsurface threats. Planned armaments include the Aegis missile system, a major caliber gun, surface-to-surface missiles and advanced antisubmarine warfare weapons and sensors. Capability to operate helicopters or vertical takeoff and landing aircraft is planned.

strike force—*(DOD, IADB)* A force composed of appropriate units necessary to conduct strikes, attack or assault operations. See also **task force**.

strike photography—*(DOD, NATO)* Air photographs taken during an air strike.

strip marker—*(DOD, NATO)* In land mine warfare, a marker, natural, artificial, or specially installed, located at the start and finish of a mine strip. See also **marker**.

strip plot—*(DOD, NATO)* A portion of a map or overlay on which a number of photographs taken along a flight line is delineated without defining the outlines of individual prints.

strip search—*(NATO)* Reconnaissance along a straight line between two given reference points.

strong point—*(DOD, NATO, IADB)* A key point in a defensive position, usually strongly fortified and heavily armed with automatic weapons, around which other positions are grouped for its protection.

strop—*(IADB)* In air transport, a length of webbing connecting the static line to the anchor cable.

subassembly—*(DOD, NATO)* A portion of an assembly, consisting of two or more parts, that can be provisioned and replaced as an entity. See also **assembly; component; part.**

sub-collection center—See **nuclear, biological, chemical collection center.**

subgravity—*(DOD, NATO, IADB)* A condition in which the resultant ambient acceleration is between 0 and 1 G.

subkiloton weapon—*(DOD, NATO, IADB)* A nuclear weapon producing a yield below one kiloton. See also **kiloton weapon; megaton weapon; nominal weapon.**

sublimited war—Not to be used. No substitute recommended.

submarine—*(DOD, IADB)* A warship designed for under-the-surface operations with primary mission of locating and destroying ships, including other submarines. It is capable of various other naval missions. SSNs are nuclear powered. Designated as SS and SSN. See also **fleet ballistic missile submarine.**

submarine base—*(NATO)* A base providing logistic support for submarines.

submarine exercise area coordinator—*(NATO)* An authority who publishes permanently established national submarine exercise areas and lanes which have been agreed to by the nations concerned.

submarine havens—*(NATO)* Specified sea areas for submarine non-combat operations including: **a.** Submarine sanctuaries announced by the area, fleet, or equivalent commander. **b.** Areas reserved for submarine operations and training in noncombat zones. **c.** Moving areas, established by "Submarine Notices," surrounding submarines in transit, extending 50 nautical miles ahead, 100 nautical miles behind, and 15 nautical miles on each side of the estimated position of the submarine along the stated track. See also **moving havens.**

submarine launched missile—See **sea-launched ballistic missile.**

submarine movement advisory authority—*(NATO)* The authority who monitors movements of submarines and ships operating variable depth sonar or towed arrays within his area of responsibility and advises the submarine operating authorities and, if necessary, units concerned, of possible mutual interference.

submarine notice—*(NATO)* A message report originated by a submarine operating authority providing operational and movement instructions for submarines in peace and war, including transit and patrol area information.

submarine operating authority—*(NATO)* The naval commander exercising operational control of submarines.

submarine patrol area—*(DOD, NATO)* A restricted area established to allow submarine operations:
a. unimpeded by the operation of, or possible attack from, friendly forces in wartime;
b. without submerged mutual interference in peacetime.

submarine rocket—*(DOD, IADB)* Submerged, submarine-launched, surface-to-surface rocket with nuclear depth charge or homing torpedo payload, primarily antisubmarine. Popular name is Subroc. Designated as UUM-44A.

submarine safety lanes—See **safety lanes.**

submarine sanctuaries—*(DOD, IADB)* Restricted areas that are established for the conduct of non-combat submarine or antisubmarine exercises. They may be either stationary or moving and are normally designated only in rear areas. See also **moving havens.**

submarine striking forces—*(DOD, IADB)* Submarines having guided or ballistic missile launching and/or guidance capabilities formed to launch offensive nuclear strikes.

Subordinate Area Commanders—*(NATO)* The designation assigned to NATO commanders operationally responsible to Allied Commander-in Chief Channel for an allocated geographical area. See also **Major NATO Commanders, Major Subordinate Commanders; Principal Subordinate Commanders.**

Subroc—See **submarine rocket.**

subsidiary landing—*(DOD, NATO)* In an amphibious operation, a landing usually made outside the designated landing area, the purpose of which is to support the main landing.

subsonic—*(DOD, IADB)* Of or pertaining to speeds less than the speed of sound. See also **speed of sound.**

substitute transport-type vehicle—*(DOD, IADB)* A wheeled vehicle designed to perform, within certain limitations, the same military function as military transport vehicles, but not requiring all the special characteristics thereof. They are developed from civilian designs by addition of certain features, or from military designs by deletion of certain features. See also **vehicle.**

subversion—*(DOD, I, IADB)* Action designed to undermine the military, economic, psychological, political strength or morale of a regime. See also **unconventional warfare.**

subversion—*(NATO)* Action designed to weaken the military, economic or political strength of a nation by undermining the morale, loyalty or reliability of its citizens.

subversion of DOD personnel—*(DOD)* Actions designed to undermine the loyalty, morale or discipline of Department of Defense military and civilian personnel.

subversive activity—*(DOD, IADB)* Anyone lending aid, comfort, and moral support to individuals, groups or organizations that advocate the overthrow of incumbent governments by force and violence is subversive and is engaged in subversive activity. All willful acts that are intended to be detrimental to the best interests of the government and that do not fall into the categories of treason, sedition, sabotage, or espionage will be placed in the category of subversive activity.

subversive political action—*(DOD, IADB)* A planned series of activities designed to accomplish political objectives by influencing, dominating, or displacing individuals or groups who are so placed as to affect the decisions and actions of another government.

summit—*(DOD, IADB)* The highest altitude above mean sea level that a projectile reaches in its flight from the gun to the target; the algebraic sum of the maximum ordinate and the altitude of the gun.

superimposed—*(NATO)* A term used in fire planning to indicate that an artillery unit is augmenting fire on a target and its fire may be lifted from that target by the authority implicit in its fire support role.

supernumerary civilian personnel (NATO)—*(NATO)* International civilian personnel, previously assigned to an international civilian post who are on extended sick leave in accordance with article 45.65 of the NATO civilian personnel regulations and who continue to enjoy NATO status.

Super Sabre—*(DOD, IADB)* A supersonic, single-engine, turbojet, tactical fighter/bomber. It is capable of employing nuclear and non-nuclear weapons. It is also refuelable and performs a variety of close air support tasks. Designated as **F-100.**

supersonic—*(DOD, IADB)* Of or pertaining to speed in excess of the speed of sound. See also **speed of sound.**

supervised route—*(DOD, NATO)* In road traffic, a roadway over which limited control is exercised by means of traffic control posts, traffic patrols or both. Movement authorization is required for its use by a column of vehicles or a vehicle of exceptional size or weight. See also **route.**

supplement—*(NATO, IADB)* A supplement is a separate publication, related to a basic publication and prepared for purposes of promulgating additional information or summaries, and may include extracts from the basic publication.

supplemental programmed interpretation report—*(NATO)* A standardized imagery interpretation report providing information, which has not previously been included in other reports, on significant targets covered by the mission; or when supplemental information is required.

supplies—*(DOD, IADB)* All items necessary for the equipment, maintenance, and operation of a military command, including food, clothing, equipment, arms, ammunition, fuel, materials, and machinery of all kinds. See also **naval stores**. For planning and administrative purposes supplies are divided as noted below. The subclassification materiel designators (A through T) may be used in combination with the designated subclassifications to further define a portion of a class of supply for planning purposes, e.g., use of Class V AL to designate ammunition, air missile. Additional codes may be utilized by the Services to satisfy a specific requirement. This additional permissive coding is not to be utilized in lieu of that designated for the major classification and subclassification.

a. **Class I**—Subsistence including gratuitous health and welfare items. Subclassifications for Class I are : A—Air (inflight rations); R—Refrigerated subsistence; S—Nonrefrigerated subsistence (less combat rations); C—Combat rations (including gratuitous health and welfare items).

b. **Class II**—Clothing, individual equipment, tentage, organization tool sets and tool kits, hand tools, administrative, and housekeeping supplies and equipment. Subclassifications for Class II are: B—Ground support materiel (includes power generators and construction, barrier, bridging, firefighting, petroleum, and mapping equipment); E—General supplies; F—Clothing and textiles; M—Weapons; and T—Industrial supplies (includes bearings, block and tackle, cable, chain, wire rope, screws, bolts, studs, steel rods, plates and bars).

c. **Class III**—Petroleum, oils, and lubricants: Petroleum, oils, and lubricants, hydraulic and insulating oils, preservatives, liquid and compressed gases, bulk chemical products, coolants, de-icing and antifreeze compounds, together with components and additives of such products, and coal. Subclassifications for Class III are: A—Air; and W—Ground (surface).

d. **Class IV**—Construction: Construction materials to include installed equipment, and all fortification/barrier materials. (No subclassifications.)

e. **Class V**—Ammunition: Ammunition of all types (including chemical, biological, radiological, and special weapons), bombs, explosives, mines, fuzes, detonators, pyrotechnics, missiles, rockets, propellants, and other associated items. Subclassifications for Class V are: A—Air; and W—Ground.

f. **Class VI**—Personal Demand Items (Nonmilitary Sales Items). (No subclassifications.)

g. **Class VII**—Major End Items: A final combination of end products that is ready for its intended use; e.g., launchers, tanks, mobile machine shops, vehicles. Subclassifications for Class VII are: A—Air; B—Ground support materiel (includes power generators and construction, barrier, bridging, fire fighting, petroleum, and mapping equipment); D—Administrative vehicles (commercial vehicles utilized in administrative motor pools); G—Electronics; K—Tactical vehicles; L—Missiles; M—Weapons; and N—Special weapons.

h. **Class VIII**—Medical Materiel Including Medical Peculiar Repair Parts. (No subclassifications.)

i. **Class IX**—Repair Parts and Components: Includes kits, assemblies, and sub-assemblies, reparable and nonreparable, required for maintenance support of all equipment. Subclassifications for Class IX are the same as Class VII with addition of T—Industrial supplies (includes bearings, block and tackle, cable, chain, wire rope, screws, bolts, studs, steel rods, plates and bars).

j. Class X—Materiel to Support Nonmilitary Programs, e.g., Agricultural and Economic Development, not included in Classes I-IX. (No subclassifications.)

supplies—*(NATO)* All items necessary for the equipment, maintenance and operation of military forces.

supply—*(DOD, IADB)* The procurement, distribution, maintenance while in storage, and salvage of supplies, including the determination of kind and quantity of supplies.
  a. producer phase—That phase of military supply which extends from determination of procurement schedules to acceptance of finished supplies by the military Services.
  b. consumer phase—That phase of military supply which extends from receipt of finished supplies by the military Services through issue for use or consumption.

supply by air—See **airdrop; air movement.**

supply control—*(DOD, IADB)* The process by which an item of supply is controlled within the supply system, including requisitioning, receipt, storage, stock control, shipment, disposition, identification, and accounting.

supplying ship—*(DOD, NATO)* The ship in a replenishment unit that provides the personnel and/or supplies to be transferred.

supply management—See **inventory control.**

supply point—*(DOD, NATO, IADB)* Any point where supplies are issued in detail.

supply transaction reporting—*(DOD)* Reporting on individual transactions affecting the stock status of materiel to the appropriate supply accounting activity as they occur.

support—*(DOD, IADB)* 1. The action of a force which aids, protects, complements, or sustains another force in accordance with a directive requiring such action. 2. A unit which helps another unit in battle. Aviation, artillery, or naval gunfire may be used as a support for in-fantry. 3. A part of any unit held back at the beginning of an attack as a reserve. 4. An element of a command which assists, protects, or supplies other forces in combat. See also **interdepartmental/agency support; international logistic support; inter-Service support.**

support—*(NATO)* The action of a force, or portion thereof, which aids, protects, complements, or sustains any other force.

support helicopter—See **assault aircraft; utility helicopter (maneuver); assault aircraft.**

supporting aircraft—*(DOD, IADB)* All active aircraft other than unit aircraft. See also **aircraft.**

supporting arms—*(DOD, IADB)* Air, sea, and land weapons of all types employed to support ground units.

supporting arms coordination center—*(DOD, IADB)* A single location on board an amphibious command ship in which all communication facilities incident to the coordination of fire support of the artillery, air, and naval gunfire are centralized. This is the naval counterpart to the fire support coordination center utilized by the landing force. See also **fire support coordination center.**

supporting artillery—*(DOD, IADB)* Artillery which executes fire missions in support of a specific unit, usually infantry, but remains under the command of the next higher artillery commander.

supporting attack—*(DOD, NATO)* An offensive operation carried out in conjunction with a main attack and designed to achieve one or more of the following:
  a. deceive the enemy;
  b. destroy or pin down enemy forces which could interfere with the main attack;
  c. control ground whose occupation by the enemy will hinder the main attack; or
  d. force the enemy to commit reserves prematurely or in an indecisive area.

supporting fire—*(DOD, NATO, IADB)* Fire delivered by supporting units to assist or protect a unit in combat. See also **close supporting fire; deep supporting fire; direct supporting fire.**

supporting forces—*(DOD)* Forces stationed in, or to be deployed to, an area of operations to provide support for the execution of an operation order. Operational command of supporting forces is not passed to the supported commander.

supporting operations—*(DOD, NATO)* In amphibious operations, those operations conducted by forces other than those assigned to the amphibious task force. They are ordered by higher authority at the request of the amphibious task force commander and normally are conducted outside the area for which the amphibious task force commander is responsible at the time of their execution.

support items—*(DOD)* Items subordinate to, or associated with an end item (i.e., spares, repair parts, tools, test equipment and sundry materiels) and required to operate, service, repair or overhaul an end item.

suppression—*(DOD)* Temporary or transient degradation of the performance of a weapons system, below the level needed to fulfill its mission objectives, by an opposing force.

suppression mission—*(DOD)* A mission to suppress an actual or suspected weapons system for the purpose of degrading its performance below the level needed to fulfill its mission objectives at a specific time for a specified duration.

suppression of enemy air defenses—*(DOD, NATO)* That activity which neutralizes, destroys or temporarily degrades enemy air defenses in a specific area by physical attack and/or electronic warfare.

suppressive fire—*(DOD)* Fires on or about a weapons system to degrade its performance below the level needed to fulfill its mission ob-

jectives, during the conduct of the fire mission. See also **fire.**

surface burst—See **nuclear surface burst.**

surface code—See **panel code.**

surface striking forces (naval)—*(DOD, IADB)* Forces that are organized primarily to do battle with enemy forces or to conduct shore bombardment. Units comprising such a force are generally incorporated in and operate as part of another force, but with provisions for their formation into a surface striking force should such action appear likely and/or desirable.

surface-to-air missile—*(DOD, IADB)* A surface-launched missile designed to operate against a target above the surface.

surface-to-air missile envelope—*(DOD, IADB)* That air space within the kill capabilities of a specific surface-to-air missile system.

surface-to-air missile installation—*(DOD, IADB)* A surface-to-air missile site with the surface-to-air missile system hardware installed.

surface-to-air missile site—*(DOD, IADB)* A plot of ground prepared in such a manner that it will readily accept the hardware used in surface-to-air missile system.

surface-to-surface missile—*(DOD, IADB)* A surface-launched missile designed to operate against a target on the surface.

surface zero—See **ground zero.**

surplus property—*(DOD)* Any excess property not required for the needs and for the discharge of the responsibilities of all federal agencies, including the Department of Defense, as determined by the General Services Administration.

surprise dosage attack—*(DOD, NATO)* A chemical operation which establishes on target a dosage sufficient to produce the desired casualties before the troops can mask or otherwise protect themselves.

surveillance—*(DOD, NATO, IADB)* The systematic observation of aerospace, surface or subsurface areas, places, persons, or things, by visual, aural, electronic, photographic, or other means. See also **air surveillance; satellite and missile surveillance; sea surveillance.**

surveillance approach—*(DOD, IADB)* An instrument approach conducted in accordance with directions issued by a controller referring to the surveillance radar display.

survey control point—*(DOD)* A survey station used to coordinate survey control.

survey information center—*(DOD)* A place where survey data are collected, correlated, and made available to subordinate units.

survey photography—See **air cartographic photography.**

susceptibility—*(DOD, NATO)* The vulnerability of a target audience to particular forms of psychological operations approach.

suspension equipment—*(DOD, NATO)* All aircraft devices such as racks, adapters, missile launchers and pylons used for carriage, employment and jettison of aircraft stores.

suspension strop—*(DOD, NATO, IADB)* A length of webbing or wire rope between the helicopter and cargo sling.

sustainability—*(DOD)* 1. The ability to maintain the necessary level and duration of combat activity to achieve national objectives. Sustainability is a function of providing and maintaining those levels of force, materiel, and consumables necessary to support a military effort. 2. See **military capability.**

sustained attrition minefield—*(DOD, NATO)* In naval mine warfare, a minefield which is re-

plenished to maintain its danger to the enemy in the face of countermeasures.

sustained rate of fire—*(DOD, NATO)* Actual rate of fire that a weapon can continue to deliver for an indefinite length of time without seriously overheating.

sweep—*(DOD)* To employ technical means to uncover planted microphones or other surveillance devices. See also **technical survey.**

sweeper track—See **hunter track.**

sweep jamming—*(DOD, NATO)* A narrow band of jamming that is swept back and forth over a relatively wide operating band of frequencies.

swept path—*(DOD, NATO)* In naval mine warfare, the width of the lane swept by the mechanical sweep at all depths less than the sweep depth.

switch horn—*(DOD, NATO)* In naval mine warfare, a switch in a mine operated by a projecting spike. See also **horn.**

sympathetic detonation—*(DOD, NATO)* Detonation of a charge by exploding another charge adjacent to it.

synthesis—*(DOD, IADB)* In intelligence usage, the examining and combining of processed information with other information and intelligence for final interpretation.

synthetic exercise—*(DOD, NATO)* An exercise in which enemy and/or friendly forces are generated, displayed and moved by electronic or other means on simulators, radar scopes or other training devices.

system—*(DOD)* Any organized assembly of resources and procedures united and regulated by interaction or interdependence to accomplish a set of specific functions.

system manager—*(DOD, IADB)* A general term of reference to those organizations directed by

353

individual managers, exercising authority over the planning, direction, and control of tasks and associated functions essential for support of designated weapons or equipment systems. The authority vested in this organization may include such functions as research, development, procurement, production, materiel distribution, and logistic support, when so assigned. When intended to relate to a specific system manager, this term will be preceded by the appropriate designation (e.g., Chinook System Manager, Sonar System Manager, F-4 System Manager). This term will normally be used in lieu of system support manager, weapon system manager, program manager, and project manager when such organizations perform these functions.

systems design—*(DOD, NATO)* The preparation of an assembly of methods, procedures, or techniques united by regulated interaction to form an organized whole.

system support manager—See **system manager.**

T

table of allowance—*(DOD)* An equipment allowance document which prescribes basic allowances of organizational equipment, and provides the control to develop, revise, or change equipment authorization inventory data.

table of organization—See **establishment.**

table of organization and equipment—See **establishment.**

tacan—*(DOD, NATO)* An ultra-high frequency electronic air navigation system which provides a continuous indication of bearing and distance (slant range) to the tacan station, common components being used in distance and bearing determination. The term is derived from *tac*tical *a*ir *n*avigation.

tachometric or synchronous sights—See **bomb sighting systems.**

tacit arms control agreement—*(DOD, IADB)* An arms control course of action in which two or more nations participate without any formal agreement having been made.

tac-log group—*(DOD, IADB)* Representatives designated by troop commanders to assist Navy control officers aboard control ships in the ship-to-shore movement of troops, equipment, and supplies.

tactical aeromedical evacuation—*(DOD, NATO, IADB)* That phase of evacuation which provides airlift for patients from the combat zone to points outside the combat zone, and between points within the communications zone.

tactical air command—*(DOD, IADB)* 1. An Air Force organization designed to conduct offensive and defensive air operations in conjunction with land or sea forces. 2. A designation of one of the subordinate commands of the Air Force.

tactical air command center—*(DOD)* The principal United States Marine Corps air operation installation from which aircraft and air warning functions of tactical air operations are directed. It is the senior agency of the Marine Corps Air Command and Control System from which the Marine Corps tactical air commander can direct and control tactical air operations and coordinate such air operations with other Services.

tactical air commander (ashore)—*(DOD, IADB)* The officer (aviator) responsible to the landing force commander for control and coordination of air operations within the landing force commander's area of responsibility when control of these operations is passed ashore.

tactical air control center—*(DOD, NATO, IADB)* The principal air operations installation (land or ship based) from which all aircraft and air warning functions of tactical air operations are controlled.

tactical air control group—*(DOD, IADB)* 1. **land-based**—A flexible administrative and tactical component of a tactical air organization which provides aircraft control and warning functions ashore for offensive and defensive missions within the tactical air zone of responsibility. 2. **ship-based**—An administrative and tactical component of an amphibious force which provides aircraft control and warning facilities afloat for offensive and defensive missions within the tactical air command area of responsibility.

tactical air controller—*(DOD, IADB)* The officer in charge of all operations of the tactical air control center (afloat). This officer is responsible to the tactical air officer for the control of all aircraft and air warning facilities within the area of responsibility. See also **air controller.**

tactical air controller—*(NATO)* The officer in charge of all operations of the tactical air con-

355

trol center. He is responsible to the tactical air commander for the control of all aircraft and air warning facilities within his area of responsibility. See also **air controller.**

tactical air control operations team—(*DOD*) A team of ground environment personnel assigned to certain allied tactical air control units/elements.

tactical air control party—(*DOD, NATO, IADB*) A subordinate operational component of a tactical air control system designed to provide air liaison to land forces and for the control of aircraft.

tactical air control party support team—(*DOD, IADB*) An Army team organized to provide armored combat and/or special purpose vehicles and crews to certain tactical air control parties.

tactical air control squadron—(*DOD, IADB*) **1. land-based—**A flexible administrative component of a tactical air control group, known as TACRON, which provides the control mechanism for a land-based tactical air control center, a tactical air direction center, or tactical air control parties. **2. ship-based—**An administrative and tactical component of the tactical air control group, known as TACRON, which provides the control mechanism for the ship-based tactical air direction center or the ship-based tactical air control center.

tactical air control system—(*DOD, NATO, IADB*) The organization and equipment necessary to plan, direct, and control tactical air operations and to coordinate air operations with other Services. It is composed of control agencies and communications-electronics facilities which provide the means for centralized control and decentralized execution of missions.

tactical air coordinator (airborne)—(*DOD, IADB*) An officer who coordinates, from an aircraft, the action of combat aircraft engaged in close support of ground or sea forces. See also **forward observer.**

tactical air direction center—(*DOD, IADB*) An air operations installation under the overall control of the tactical air control center (afloat)/tactical air command center, from which aircraft and air warning service functions of tactical air operations in an area of responsibility are directed. See also **tactical air director.**

tactical air director—(*DOD, IADB*) The officer in charge of all operations of the tactical air direction center. This officer is responsible to the tactical air controller for the direction of all aircraft and air warning facilities assigned to the area of responsibility. When operating independently of a tactical air control center (afloat), the tactical air director assumes the functions of the tactical air controller. See also **tactical air direction center.**

tactical air doctrine—(*DOD, NATO*) Fundamental principles designed to provide guidance for the employment of air power in tactical air operations to attain established objectives.

tactical air force—(*DOD, NATO, IADB*) An air force charged with carrying out tactical air operations in coordination with ground or naval forces.

tactical air observer—(*DOD, IADB*) An officer trained as an air observer whose function is to observe from airborne aircraft and report on movement and disposition of friendly and enemy forces, on terrain, weather, and hydrography and to execute other missions as directed.

tactical air officer (afloat)—(*DOD, IADB*) The officer (aviator) under the amphibious task force commander who coordinates planning of all phases of air participation of the amphibious operation and air operations of supporting forces en route to and in the objective area. Until control is passed ashore, this officer exercises control over all operations of the tactical air control center (afloat) and is charged with: **a.** control of all aircraft in the objective area assigned for tactical air operations, including offensive and defensive air; **b.** control of all other aircraft entering or passing through the objective area; and **c.** control of all air warning facilities in the objective area.

tactical air operation—*(DOD, IADB)* An air operation involving the employment of air power in coordination with ground or naval forces to: **a.** gain and maintain air superiority; **b.** prevent movement of enemy forces into and within the objective area and to seek out and destroy these forces and their supporting installations; **c.** join with ground or naval forces in operations within the objective area, in order to assist directly in attainment of their immediate objective.

tactical air operation—*(NATO)* The employment of air power in coordination with ground or naval forces to:
  a. attain and maintain air superiority;
  b. prevent movement of enemy forces into and within the combat zone and to seek out and destroy these forces and their supporting installations; and
  c. assist in attaining ground or naval forces objectives by combined/joint operations.

tactical air operations center—*(DOD, IADB)* A subordinate operational component of the Marine Air Command and Control System designed for direction and control of all en route air traffic and air defense operations, to include manned interceptors and surface-to-air weapons, in an assigned sector. It is under the operational control of the Tactical Air Command Center.

tactical air reconnaissance—*(DOD, IADB)* The use of air vehicles to obtain information concerning terrain, weather, and the disposition, composition, movement, installations, lines of communications, electronic and communication emissions of enemy forces. Also included are artillery and naval gunfire adjustment, and systematic and random observation of ground battle areas, targets, and/or sectors of airspace.

tactical air support—*(DOD, NATO, IADB)* Air operations carried out in co-ordination with surface forces and which directly assist land or maritime operations. See also **air support**.

tactical air support element—*(DOD)* An element of a United States Army division, corps, or field army tactical operations center consisting of G-2 and G-3 air personnel who coordinate and integrate tactical air support with current tactical ground operations.

tactical air transport operations—*(DOD, NATO, IADB)* The carriage of passengers and cargo within a theater by means of: **a.** Airborne operations: (1) Parachute assault, (2) Helicopter borne assault, (3) Air landing; **b.** Air logistic support; **c.** Special missions; **d.** Aeromedical evacuation missions.

tactical area of responsibility—*(DOD, IADB)* A defined area of land for which responsibility is specifically assigned to the commander of the area as a measure for control of assigned forces and coordination of support. Commonly referred to as TAOR.

tactical call sign—*(DOD, NATO, IADB)* A call sign which identifies a tactical command or tactical communication facility. See also **call sign**.

tactical command—*(NATO)* The authority delegated to a commander to assign tasks to forces under his command for the accomplishment of the mission assigned by higher authority.

tactical command ship—*(IADB)* A warship converted from a light cruiser, and designed to serve as a command ship for a fleet/force commander. It is equipped with extensive communication equipment. Designated as CC.

tactical concept—*(NATO)* A statement, in broad outline, which provides a common basis for future development of tactical doctrine.

tactical control—*(NATO)* The detailed and, usually, local direction and control of movements or maneuvers necessary to accomplish missions or tasks assigned.

tactical data information link—A—(DOD) A netted link in which one unit acts as a net control station and interrogates each unit by roll call. Once interrogated, that unit transmits its data to the net. This means that each unit receives all the information transmitted. This is a direct transfer of data and no relaying is involved. Also called **TADIL-A.**

tactical data information link—B—(DOD) A point-to-point data link between two units which provides for simultaneous transmission and reception of data (duplex). Also called **TADIL-B.**

tactical diversion—See diversion.

tactical information processing and interpretation system—(DOD, IADB) A tactical, mobile, land-based, automated information-handling system designed to store and retrieve intelligence information and to process and interpret imagery or nonimagery data. Also called **TIPI.**

tactical intelligence—(DOD, NATO) Intelligence which is required for the planning and conduct of tactical operations. (DOD) Tactical intelligence and strategic intelligence differ primarily in level of application but may also vary in terms of scope and detail. See also **combat intelligence; intelligence; strategic intelligence.**

tactical intelligence and related activities—(DOD) Those activities outside the National Foreign Intelligence Program that: a. respond to operational commanders' tasking for time-sensitive information on foreign entities; b. respond to national intelligence community tasking of systems whose primary mission is support to operating forces; c. train personnel for intelligence duties; d. provide an intelligence reserve; or e. are devoted to research and development of intelligence or related capabilities. Specifically excluded are programs which are so closely integrated with a weapon system that their primary function is to provide immediate-use targeting data. Also called **TIARA.**

tactical loading—See combat loading; unit loading.

tactical locality—(DOD, NATO, IADB) An area of terrain which, because of its location or features, possesses a tactical significance in the particular circumstances existing at a particular time.

tactical map—(DOD, IADB) A large-scale map used for tactical and administrative purposes. See also **map.**

tactical minefield—(DOD, NATO) A minefield which is part of a formation obstacle plan and is laid to delay, channel or break up an enemy advance.

tactical mining—(DOD, NATO) In naval mine warfare, mining designed to influence a specific operation or to counter a known or presumed tactical aim of the enemy. Implicit in tactical mining is a limited period of effectiveness of the minefield.

tactical nuclear weapon employment—(DOD, IADB) The use of nuclear weapons by land, sea, or air forces against opposing forces, supporting installations or facilities, in support of operations which contribute to the accomplishment of a military mission of limited scope, or in support of the military commander's scheme of maneuver, usually limited to the area of military operations.

tactical operations area—(DOD) That area between the fire support coordination line and the rear operations area where maximum flexibility in the use of airspace is needed to assure mission accomplishment. The rear boundary of the tactical operations area should normally be at or near the rear boundary of the frontline divisions.

tactical operations center—(DOD, IADB) A physical groupment of those elements of an Army general and special staff concerned with the current tactical operations and the tactical support thereof.

tactical range—*(DOD, NATO)* A range in which realistic targets are in use and a certain freedom of maneuver is allowed.

tactical reserve—*(DOD, NATO)* A part of a force, held under the control of the commander as a maneuvering force to influence future action.

tactical sub-concept—*(DOD, NATO)* A statement, in broad outline, for a specific field of military capability within a tactical concept which provides a common basis both for equipment and weapon system development and for future development of tactical doctrine.

tactical transport aircraft—*(DOD, NATO, IADB)* Aircraft designed primarily for the carriage of personnel and/or cargo over short or medium distances.

tactical troops—*(DOD, IADB)* Combat troops, together with any service troops required for their direct support, who are organized under one commander to operate as a unit and engage the enemy in combat. See also **troops**.

tactical unit—*(DOD, IADB)* An organization of troops, aircraft, or ships which is intended to serve as a single unit in combat. It may include service units required for its direct support.

tactical vehicle—See **military designed vehicle**.

tactical warning—*(DOD, NATO, IADB)* 1. A notification that the enemy has initiated hostilities. Such warning may be received any time from the launching of the attack until it reaches its target. See also **attack assessment; strategic warning.** *(DOD, IADB)* 2. In satellite and missile surveillance, a notification to operational command centers that a specific threat event is occurring. The component elements that describe threat events are:
Country of origin—country or countries initiating hostilities.
Event type and size—identification of the type of event and determination of the size or number of weapons.
Country under attack—determined by observing trajectory of an object and predicting its impact point.
Event time—time the hostile event occurred.

tactics—*(DOD, IADB)* 1. The employment of units in combat. 2. The ordered arrangement and maneuver of units in relation to each other and/or to the enemy in order to utilize their full potentialities.

tail hook—See **aircraft arresting hook**.

tally ho—*(DOD)* A code meaning, "Target visually sighted" (presumably the target I have been ordered to intercept). This should be followed by initial contact report as soon as possible. The sighting should be amplified if possible (e.g., "tally ho pounce," or "tally ho heads up").

Talos—*(DOD, IADB)* A shipborne, surface-to-air missile with solid-propellant rocket/ramjet engine. It is equipped with nuclear or nonnuclear warhead, and command, beam-rider homing guidance. Designated as **RIM-8**.

tan alt—See **shadow factor**.

tank, combat, full-tracked, 90-mm gun—*(DOD, IADB)* A fully armored combat vehicle providing mobile fire power and crew protection for offensive combat, armed with one 90-mm gun, one 50-caliber machine gun, and one 7.62-mm machine gun. Designated as **M48A3**.

tank, combat, full-tracked, 105-mm gun—*(DOD, IADB)* A heavy, fully armored combat vehicle providing mobile fire power and crew protection for offensive combat, armed with one 105-mm gun, one 7.62-mm gun and one 50-caliber machine gun. Designated as **M-60**.

tank, combat, full-tracked, 152-mm gun—*(DOD)* A heavily armored vehicle providing mobile firepower and crew protection for offensive combat armed with one 152-mm gun/launcher, capable of firing Shillelagh missiles or conventional combustible ammunition, one

50-caliber machine gun and one 7.62-mm machine gun.

tank landing ship—*(DOD, IADB)* A naval ship designed to transport and land amphibious vehicles, tanks, combat vehicles, and equipment in amphibious assault. Designated as **LST**.

tank, main battle—*(DOD, IADB)* A tracked vehicle providing mobile firepower and crew protection for offensive combat.

target—*(DOD, IADB)* 1. A geographical area, complex, or installation planned for capture or destruction by military forces. 2. In intelligence usage, a country, area, installation, agency, or person against which intelligence operations are directed. 3. An area designated and numbered for future firing. 4. In gunfire support usage, an impact burst which hits the target. See also **objective area**.

target—*(NATO)*
1. A geographical area, complex, or installation planned for capture or destruction by military forces. See also **objective area.**
2. In intelligence usage, a country, area, installation, agency, or person against which intelligence activities are directed.
3. An area designated and numbered for future firing.
4. In artillery and naval gunfire support, an impact burst which hits the target.
5. In radar,
   (a) generally, any discrete object which reflects or retransmits energy back to the radar equipment;
   (b) specifically, an object of radar search or surveillance.

target acquisition—*(DOD, NATO, IADB)* The detection, identification, and location of a target in sufficient detail to permit the effective employment of weapons. See also **target analysis.**

target allocation—*(NATO)* In air defense, the process, following weapon assignment, of allocating a particular target or area to a specific

surface-to-air missile unit or interceptor aircraft.

target analysis—*(DOD, NATO, IADB)* An examination of potential targets to determine military importance, priority of attack, and weapons required to obtain a desired level of damage or casualties. See also **target acquisition.**

target approach point—*(DOD, NATO, IADB)* In air transport operations, a navigational check point over which the final turn into the drop zone/landing zone is made. See also **initial point.**

target area survey base—*(DOD, NATO)* A base line used for the locating of targets or other points by the intersection of observations from two stations located at opposite ends on the line.

target array—*(DOD, IADB)* A graphic representation of enemy forces, personnel, and facilities in a specific situation, accompanied by a target analysis.

target audience—*(DOD, NATO)* An individual or group selected for influence or attack by means of psychological operations.

target base line—*(DOD)* A line connecting prime targets along the periphery of a geographic area.

target bearing—*(DOD, IADB)* 1. **true**—The true compass bearing of a target from a firing ship. 2. **relative**—The bearing of a target measured in the horizontal from the bow of one's own ship clockwise from 0° to 360°, or from the nose of one's own aircraft in hours of the clock.

target CAP—See **target combat air patrol.**

target classification—*(DOD, IADB)* A grouping of targets in accordance with their threat to the amphibious task force and its component elements: targets not to be fired upon prior to

D-day and targets not to be destroyed except on direct orders.

target combat air patrol—*(DOD, IADB)* A patrol of fighters maintained over an enemy target area to destroy enemy aircraft and to cover friendly shipping in the vicinity of the target area in amphibious operations. See also **combat air patrol.**

target complex—*(DOD, NATO, IADB)* A geographically integrated series of target concentrations. See also **target.**

target concentration—*(DOD, NATO, IADB)* A grouping of geographically proximate targets. See also **target; target complex.**

target data inventory—*(DOD, IADB)* A basic targeting program which provides a standardized target data in support of the requirements of the Joint Chiefs of Staff, military departments, and unified and specified commands for target planning coordination and weapons application.

target date—*(DOD, NATO, IADB)* The date on which it is desired that an action be accomplished or initiated.

target description—See **description of target.**

target director post—*(DOD, IADB)* A special control element of the tactical air control system. It performs no air warning service but is used to position friendly aircraft over predetermined target coordinates, or other geographical locations, under all weather conditions.

target discrimination—*(DOD, NATO, IADB)* The ability of a surveillance or guidance system to identify or engage any one target when multiple targets are present.

target dossier—*(DOD, NATO, IADB)* A file of assembled target intelligence about a specific geographic area.

target folder—*(DOD, NATO, IADB)* A folder containing target intelligence and related materials prepared for planning and executing action against a specific target.

target grid—*(NATO)* Device for converting the observer's target locations and corrections with respect to the observer target line to target locations and corrections with respect to the gun target line.

target illustration print—*(NATO)* A single contact print or enlarged portion of a selected area from a single print, providing the best available illustration of a specific installation or pin-point target.

target information sheet—*(NATO)* Brief description of the target, completing the "descriptive target data." It should include technical and physical characteristics, details on exact location, disposition, importance, and possible obstacles for an aircraft flying at low altitudes.

targeting—*(DOD, NATO)* The process of selecting targets and matching the appropriate response to them taking account of operational requirements and capabilities.

target intelligence—*(DOD, NATO, IADB)* Intelligence which portrays and locates the components of a target or target complex and indicates its vulnerability and relative importance.

target list—*(DOD, IADB)* The listing of targets maintained and promulgated by the senior echelon of command; it contains those targets which are to be engaged by supporting arms, as distinguished from a "list of targets" which may be maintained by any echelon as confirmed, suspect, or possible targets for informational and planning purposes.

target list—*(NATO)* A tabulation of confirmed or suspected targets maintained by any echelon for information and fire support planning purposes. Also called **list of targets.**

target materials—*(DOD, IADB)* Graphic, textual, tabular, or other presentations of target intelligence, primarily designed to support operations against designated targets by one or more weapon systems. Target materials are suitable for training, planning, executing, and evaluating such operations.

target number—*(NATO)* The reference number given to the target by the fire control unit.

target of opportunity—*(DOD, IADB)* 1. A target visible to a surface or air sensor or observer, which is within range of available weapons and against which fire has not been scheduled or requested. 2. **nuclear**—A nuclear target observed or detected after an operation begins that has not been previously considered, analyzed or planned for a nuclear strike. Generally fleeting in nature, it should be attacked as soon as possible within the time limitations imposed for coordination and warning of friendly troops and aircraft.

target of opportunity—*(NATO)* A target which appears during combat and which can be reached by ground fire, naval fire, or aircraft fire, and against which fire has not been scheduled. Also called **opportunity target.**

target overlay—*(DOD, NATO)* A transparent sheet which, when superimposed on a particular chart, map, drawing, tracing or other representation, depicts target locations and designations. The target overlay may also show boundaries between maneuver elements, objectives and friendly forward dispositions.

target pattern—*(DOD, IADB)* The flight path of aircraft during the attack phase. Also called **attack pattern.**

target priority—*(DOD, IADB)* A grouping of targets with the indicated sequence of attack.

target range—See **range.**

target response (nuclear)—*(DOD, NATO, IADB)* The effect on men, material, and equipment of blast, heat, light, and nuclear radiation resulting from the explosion of a nuclear weapon.

target status board—*(NATO)* A wall chart maintained by the air intelligence division of the joint operations center. It includes target lists, locations, priority and status of action taken. It may also include recommended armament and fuzing for destruction.

target system—*(DOD, NATO, IADB)* 1. All the targets situated in a particular geographic area and functionally related. *(DOD, IADB)* 2. A group of targets which are so related that their destruction will produce some particular effect desired by the attacker. See also **target complex.**

target system component—*(DOD, IADB)* A set of targets belonging to one or more groups of industries and basic utilities required to produce component parts of an end product such as periscopes, or one type of a series of interrelated commodities, such as aviation gasoline.

Tartar—*(IADB)* A shipborne, surface-to-air missile with solid-propellant rocket engine and nonnuclear warhead. Designated as RIM-24.

task component—*(DOD, IADB)* A subdivision of a fleet, task force, task group, or task unit, organized by the respective commander or by higher authority for the accomplishment of specific tasks.

task element—*(DOD, IADB)* A component of a naval task unit organized by the commander of a task unit or higher authority.

task fleet—*(DOD, IADB)* A mobile command consisting of ships and aircraft necessary for the accomplishment of a specific major task or tasks which may be of a continuing nature.

task force—*(DOD, NATO, IADB)* 1. A temporary grouping of units, under one commander, formed for the purpose of carrying out a specific operation or mission. 2. Semi-permanent organization of units, under one commander, formed for the purpose of carrying out a continuing specific task. 3. A component of a fleet organized by the commander of a task fleet or higher authority for the accomplishment of a specific task or tasks. See also **force(s)**.

task group—*(DOD, IADB)* A component of a naval task force organized by the commander of a task force or higher authority.

tasking—*(NATO)* The process of translating the allocation into orders, and passing these orders to the units involved. Each order normally contains sufficient detailed instructions to enable the executing agency to accomplish the mission successfully.

task organization—*(DOD, IADB)* 1. In the Navy, an organization which assigns to responsible commanders the means with which to accomplish their assigned tasks in any planned action. 2. An organization table pertaining to a specific naval directive.

task unit—*(DOD, IADB)* A component of a naval task group organized by the commander of a task group or higher authority.

taxiway—*(NATO, IADB)* A specially prepared or designated path on an airfield for the use of taxiing aircraft.

technical analysis—*(DOD, NATO)* In imagery interpretation, the precise description of details appearing on imagery.

technical assistance—*(DOD, IADB)* The providing of advice, assistance, and training pertaining to the installation, operation, and maintenance of equipment.

technical characteristics—*(DOD, IADB)* Those characteristics of equipment which pertain primarily to the engineering principles involved in producing equipment possessing desired military characteristics, e.g., for electronic equipment, technical characteristics include such items as circuitry, and types and arrangement of components.

technical escort—*(DOD, IADB)* Individuals technically qualified and properly equipped to accompany designated material requiring a high degree of safety and/or security during shipment.

technical evaluation—*(DOD, IADB)* The study and investigations by a developing agency to determine the technical suitability of material, equipment, or a system, for use in the military Services. See also **operational evaluation**.

technical information—*(DOD, IADB)* Information, including scientific information, which relates to research, development, engineering, test, evaluation, production, operation, use, and maintenance of munitions and other military supplies and equipment.

technical intelligence—*(DOD)* See **scientific and technical intelligence**.

technical intelligence—*(NATO)* Intelligence concerning foreign technological developments, and the performance and operational capabilities of foreign material, which have or may eventually have a practical application for military purposes.

technical specification—*(NATO)* A detailed description of technical requirements stated in terms suitable to form the basis for the actual design development and production processes of an item having the qualities specified in the operational characteristics. See also **operational characteristics**.

technical supply operations—*(DOD, IADB)* Operations performed by supply units or technical supply elements of supply and maintenance units in acquiring, accounting for, storing, and issuing Class II and IV items needed by supported units and maintenance activities.

technical survey—*(DOD, IADB)* A complete electronic and physical inspection to ascertain that offices, conference rooms, war rooms, and other similar locations where classified information is discussed are free of monitoring systems. See also **sweep.**

telebrief—*(NATO)* Direct telephone communications between an air controller and pilots in their aircraft on the ground.

telecommunication—*(DOD, NATO, IADB)* Any transmission, emission, or reception of signs, signals, writings, images, sounds, or information of any nature by wire, radio, visual, or other electro-magnetic systems.

telecommunications center—*(DOD, IADB)* A facility, normally serving more than one organization or terminal, responsible for transmission, receipt, acceptance, processing and distribution of incoming and outgoing messages.

teleconference—*(DOD, NATO, IADB)* A conference between persons remote from one another but linked by a telecommunications system.

telemetry intelligence—*(DOD)* Technical and intelligence information derived from the intercept, processing, and analysis of foreign telemetry. Also called **TELINT.** See also **electronics intelligence; intelligence; signals intelligence.**

teleprocessing—*(DOD)* The combining of telecommunications and computer operations interacting in the automatic processing, reception, and transmission of data and/or information.

teleran system—*(DOD, IADB)* A navigational system which: **a.** employs ground-based search radar equipment along an airway to locate aircraft flying near that airway; **b.** transmits, by television means, information pertaining to these aircraft and other information to the pilots of properly equipped aircraft; and **c.** provides information to the pilots appropriate for use in the landing approach.

television imagery—*(DOD)* Imagery acquired by a television camera and recorded or transmitted electronically.

telling—See **track telling.**

temperature gradient—*(DOD, IADB)* At sea, a temperature gradient is the change of temperature with depth; a positive gradient is a temperature increase with an increase in depth, and a negative gradient is a temperature decrease with an increase in depth.

temporarily filled military post—*(NATO)* A nationality undetermined post which a nation has agreed to fill for one tour of duty only.

temporary cemetery—*(DOD, NATO, IADB)* A cemetery for the purpose of: **a.** The initial burial of the remains if the circumstances permit or **b.** The reburial of remains exhumed from an emergency burial.

temporary civilian personnel—*(NATO)* Civilians engaged either to replace members of the staff who are temporarily absent or to undertake tasks temporarily in excess of the national or international manpower ceiling.

terminal clearance capacity—*(DOD, IADB)* The amount of cargo or personnel that can be moved through and out of a terminal on a daily basis.

terminal control area—*(DOD, IADB)* A control area or portion thereof normally situated at the confluence of air traffic service routes in the vicinity of one or more major airfields. See also **airway; control area; controlled airspace; control zone.**

terminal control area—*(NATO)* A control area normally established at the confluence of Air Traffic Service routes in the vicinity of one or more major airfields. See also **airway; controlled airspace; control area; control zone.**

terminal guidance—*(DOD, IADB)* 1. The guidance applied to a guided missile between midcourse guidance and arrival in the vicinity of the target. 2. Electronic, mechanical, visual, or other assistance given an aircraft pilot to facilitate arrival at, operation within or over, landing upon, or departure from an air landing or airdrop facility. See also **guidance.**

terminal guidance—*(NATO)* The guidance applied to a missile between midcourse guidance and its arrival in the vicinity of the target.

terminal operations—*(DOD, IADB)* The reception, processing, and staging of passengers, the receipt, transit storage and marshalling of cargo, the loading and unloading of ships or aircraft, and the manifesting and forwarding of cargo and passengers to destination.

terminal phase—*(DOD, IADB)* That portion of the trajectory of a ballistic missile between reentry into the atmosphere or the end of the midcourse phase and impact or arrival in the vicinity of the target. See also **boost phase; midcourse phase; reentry phase.**

terminal velocity—*(DOD, NATO, IADB)* 1. Hypothetical maximum speed a body could attain along a specified flight path under given conditions of weight and thrust if diving through an unlimited distance in air of specified uniform density. 2. Remaining speed of a projectile at the point in its downward path where it is level with the muzzle of the weapon.

terrain avoidance system—*(DOD, NATO)* A system which provides the pilot or navigator of an aircraft with a situation display of the ground or obstacles which project above either a horizontal plane through the aircraft or a plane parallel to it, so that the pilot can maneuver the aircraft to avoid the obstruction.

terrain clearance system—*(DOD, NATO)* A system which provides the pilot, or autopilot, of an aircraft with climb or dive signals such that the aircraft will maintain a selected height over flat ground and clear the peaks of undulating ground within the selected height in a vertical plane through the flight vector.

This system differs from terrain following in that the aircraft need not descend into a valley to follow the ground contour.

terrain exercise—*(DOD, IADB)* An exercise in which a stated military situation is solved on the ground, the troops being imaginary and the solution usually being in writing.

terrain flight—*(DOD, NATO)* Flight close to the earth's surface during which airspeed, height and/or altitude are adapted to the contours and cover of the ground in order to avoid enemy detection and fire.

terrain following system—*(DOD, NATO, IADB)* A system which provides the pilot or autopilot of an aircraft with climb or dive signals such that the aircraft will maintain as closely as possible, a selected height above a ground contour in a vertical plane through the flight vector.

terrain intelligence—*(DOD, IADB)* Processed information on the military significance of natural and man-made characteristics of an area.

terrain study—*(DOD, IADB)* An analysis and interpretation of natural and man-made features of an area, their effects on military operations, and the effect of weather and climate on these features.

terrestrial environment—*(DOD)* The earth's land area, including its man-made and natural surface and sub-surface features, and its interfaces and interactions with the atmosphere and the oceans.

terrestrial reference guidance—*(DOD, IADB)* The technique of providing intelligence to a missile from certain characteristics of the surface over which the missile is flown, thereby achieving flight along a predetermined path. See also **guidance.**

Terrier—*(DOD, IADB)* A surface-to-air missile with solid-fuel rocket motor. It is equipped with radar beam rider or homing guidance and nuclear or nonnuclear warhead. Designated as RIM-2.

Terrier land weapon system—*(DOD, IADB)* A surface-to-air missile system, utilizing the Terrier RIM-2B and Terrier RIM-2C missile with ground-launching and guidance equipment, developed specifically for amphibious operations. *(DOD)* This equipment is a lighter and land-mobile version of the Navy system.

terrorist threat condition—*(DOD)* A level of terrorist threat to US military facilities and personnel. Also called **THREATCON**. There are three levels of THREATCON:
  a. **THREATCON WHITE**—Nonspecific threat of terrorism against US military personnel or facilities in a general geographic area. (This threat may be based on information that terrorist elements in an area have general plans concerning military facilities.)
  b. **THREATCON YELLOW**—Specific threat of terrorism against US military personnel or facilities within a particular geographic area. (This threat may be based on information that terrorist elements are actively preparing for operations in a particular area.)
  c. **THREATCON RED**—Imminent threat of terrorist acts against specific US military personnel or facilities. (This threat may be based on information regarding plans or preparations for terrorist attacks against specific persons or facilities.)

test depth—*(DOD, NATO)* The depth to which the submarine is tested by actual or simulated submergence. See also **maximum operating depth**.

tests—See **service test; troop test**.

theater—*(DOD)* The geographical area outside the continental United States for which a commander of a unified or specified command has been assigned military responsibility.

theater of operations—See **area of operations**.

theater of war—See **area of war**.

theater operational stocks—*(NATO)* Operational stocks normally held in a theater to support that theater. See also **operational stocks; war reserves**.

thermal crossover—*(DOD)* The natural phenomenon which normally occurs twice daily when temperature conditions are such that there is a loss of contrast between two adjacent objects on infrared imagery.

thermal energy—*(DOD, IADB)* The energy emitted from the fireball as thermal radiation. The total amount of thermal energy received per unit area at a specified distance from a nuclear explosion is generally expressed in terms of calories per square centimeter.

thermal exposure—*(DOD, NATO)* The total normal component of thermal radiation striking a given surface throughout the course of a detonation; expressed in calories per square centimeter and/or megajoules per square meter.

thermal imagery—*(DOD, NATO)* Imagery produced by sensing and recording the thermal energy emitted or reflected from the objects which are imaged.

thermal pulse—*(DOD, IADB)* The radiant power versus time pulse from a nuclear weapon detonation.

thermal radiation—*(DOD, NATO, IADB)* 1. The heat and light produced by a nuclear explosion. *(DOD, IADB)* 2. Electromagnetic radiations emitted from a heat or light source as a consequence of its temperature; it consists essentially of ultraviolet, visible, and infrared radiations.

thermal shadow—*(DOD, NATO)* The tone contrast difference of infrared linescan imagery which is caused by a thermal gradient which persists as a result of a shadow of an object which has been moved.

thermal X-rays—*(DOD, NATO)* The electromagnetic radiation, mainly in the soft (low-energy) X-ray region, emitted by the debris of a nuclear weapon by virtue of its extremely high temperature.

thermonuclear—*(DOD, NATO, IADB)* An adjective referring to the process (or processes) in which very high temperatures are used to bring about the fusion of light nuclei, with the accompanying liberation of energy.

thermonuclear weapon—*(DOD, NATO, IADB)* A weapon in which very high temperatures are used to bring about the fusion of light nuclei such as those of hydrogen isotopes (e.g., deuterium and tritium) with the accompanying release of energy. The high temperatures required are obtained by means of fission.

third area conflict—*(DOD)* Not to be used. See **cold war; general war; guerrilla warfare; limited war.**

THREATCON RED—See **terrorist threat condition.**

THREATCON WHITE—See **terrorist threat condition.**

THREATCON YELLOW—See **terrorist threat condition.**

threshold—*(DOD, NATO)* The beginning of that portion of the runway usable for landing.

Thunderbolt II—*(DOD)* A twin-engine, subsonic, turbofan, tactical fighter/bomber. It is capable of employing a variety of air-to-surface-launched weapons in the close air support role. Short-field, unimproved surfaces are considered normal take-off/landing operating areas. This aircraft is also capable of long endurance in the target area and is supplemented by air refueling. An internally mounted 30-mm cannon is capable of destroying a wide variety of armor-protected vehicles. Designated as **A-10.**

Thunderchief—*(DOD, IADB)* A supersonic, single-engine, turbojet-powered tactical fighter capable of delivering nuclear weapons as well as non-nuclear bombs and rockets. It is also capable of close support for ground forces. Its range can be extended by in-flight refueling. It is equipped with the Sidewinder weapon. The aircraft is capable of all-weather attack. Designated as **F-105.**

TIARA—See **tactical intelligence and related activities.**

tied on—*(DOD)* In air intercept, a code meaning, "The aircraft indicated is in formation with me."

tie down—*(DOD, NATO)* The fastening or securing of a load to its carrier by use of ropes, cables or other means to prevent shifting during transport. Also used (as a noun) to describe the material employed to secure a load.

tie down diagram—*(DOD, NATO)* A drawing indicating the prescribed method of securing a particular item of cargo within a specific type of vehicle.

tie down point—*(DOD, NATO)* An attachment point provided on or within a vehicle for securing cargo.

tie down point pattern—*(DOD, NATO)* The pattern of tie down points within a vehicle.

tilt—See **roll.**

tilt angle—*(DOD, NATO)* The angle between the optical axis of an air camera and the vertical at the time of exposure. See also **angle of depression.**

time and material contract—*(DOD, IADB)* A contract providing for the procurement of supplies or services on the basis of: **a.** direct labor hours at specified fixed hourly rates (which rates include direct and indirect labor, overhead, and profit); and **b.** material at cost.

367

time fuze—*(DOD, NATO, IADB)* A fuze which contains a graduated time element to regulate the time interval after which the fuze will function. See also **fuze.**

time of attack—*(DOD, IADB)* The hour at which the attack is to be launched. If a line of departure is prescribed, it is the hour at which the line is to be crossed by the leading elements of the attack.

time of delivery—*(DOD, IADB)* The time at which the addressee or responsible relay agency receipts for a message.

time of flight—*(DOD, NATO, IADB)* In artillery and naval gunfire support, the time in seconds from the instant a weapon is fired, launched, or released from the delivery vehicle or weapons system to the instant it strikes or detonates.

time of origin—*(DOD, IADB)* The time at which a message is released for transmission.

time of receipt—*(DOD, IADB)* The time at which a receiving station completes reception of a message.

time on target—*(DOD)* 1. Time at which aircraft are scheduled to attack/photograph the target. 2. The actual time at which aircraft attack/photograph the target. 3. The time at which a nuclear detonation is planned at a specified desired ground zero.

time on target—*(NATO)* 1. The method of firing on a target in which various artillery units and naval gunfire support ships so time their fire as to assure the initial rounds strike the target simultaneously at the time required. 2. Time at which aircraft are scheduled to attack/photograph a target.

time on target (air)—See **time on target**—*(DOD)* Parts 1 and 2.

time over target conflict—*(DOD)* A situation wherein two or more delivery vehicles are scheduled such that their proximity violates the established separation criteria for yield, time, distance, or all three.

time over target (nuclear)—See **time on target**—*(DOD)* Part 3.

time-phased force and deployment data—*(DOD)* The computer-supported data base portion of an operation plan; it contains time-phased force data, non-unit-related cargo and personnel data, and movement data for the operation plan, including:
a. In-place units.
b. Units to be deployed to support the operation plan with a priority indicating the desired sequence for their arrival at the port of debarkation.
c. Routing of forces to be deployed.
d. Movement data associated with deploying forces.
e. Estimates of non-unit-related cargo and personnel movements to be conducted concurrently with the deployment of forces.
f. Estimate of transportation requirements that must be fulfilled by common-user lift resources as well as those requirements that can be fulfilled by assigned or attached transportation resources.
Also called **TPFDD.**

time-phased force and deployment list—*(DOD)* Appendix 1 to Annex A of the operation plan. It identifies types and/or actual units required to support the operation plan and indicates origin and ports of debarkation or ocean area. It may also be generated as a computer listing from the time-phased force and deployment data. Also called **TPFDL.**

time-sensitive targets—*(DOD)* Those targets requiring immediate response because they pose (or will soon pose) a clear and present danger to friendly forces or are highly lucrative, fleeting targets of opportunity.

time slot—*(DOD, NATO)* Period of time during which certain activities are governed by specific regulations.

time-to-go—*(DOD)* During an air intercept, the time to fly to the offset point from any given interceptor position; after passing the offset point, the time to fly to the intercept point.

tip—See **pitch.**

tips—*(DOD, IADB)* External fuel tanks.

Titan II—*(DOD, IADB)* A liquid-propellant, two-stage, rocket-powered intercontinental ballistic missile which is guided to its target by an all-inertial guidance and control system. The missile is equipped with a nuclear warhead and designed for deployment in hardened and dispersed underground silos. Designated as **LGM-25C.**

title block—See **information box.**

titling strip—*(NATO)* The information added to negatives and/or positives, in accordance with regulations to identify and provide reference information.

TNT equivalent—*(DOD, NATO, IADB)* A measure of the energy released from the detonation of a nuclear weapon, or from the explosion of a given quantity of fissionable material, in terms of the amount of TNT (Trinitrotoluene) which could release the same amount of energy when exploded.

tolerance dose—*(DOD, IADB)* The amount of radiation which may be received by an individual within a specified period with negligible results.

Tomahawk—*(DOD)* An air-, land-, ship-, or submarine-launched cruise missile with three variants: land attack with conventional or nuclear capability, and tactical anti-ship with conventional warhead.

Tomcat—*(DOD)* A twin turbofan, dual-crew, supersonic, all-weather, long-range interceptor designed to operate from aircraft carriers. It carries a wide assortment of air-to-air and air-to-ground missiles and conventional ordnance. Primary mission is long-range fleet air defense with secondary close air support capability. Designated as **F-14.**

tone—*(NATO)* Each distinguishable shade variation from black to white on imagery.

tone down—*(DOD, NATO)* In camouflage and concealment, the process of making an object or surface less conspicuous by reducing its contrast to the surroundings and/or background.

topographic base—See **chart base.**

topographic map—*(DOD, IADB)* A map which presents the vertical position of features in measurable form as well as their horizontal positions. See also **map.**

top secret—See **defense classification.**

torpedo defense net—*(DOD, NATO, IADB)* A net employed to close an inner harbor to torpedoes fired from seaward or to protect an individual ship at anchor or underway.

toss bombing—*(DOD, IADB)* A method of bombing where an aircraft flies on a line towards the target, pulls up in a vertical plane, releasing the bomb at an angle that will compensate for the effect of gravity drop on the bomb. Similar to loft bombing; unrestricted as to altitude. See also **loft bombing; over-the-shoulder bombing.**

total active aircraft authorization—*(DOD)* The sum of the primary and backup aircraft authorizations.

total active aircraft inventory—*(DOD)* The sum of the primary and backup aircraft assigned to meet the total active aircraft authorization.

total dosage attack—*(DOD, NATO)* A chemical attack/fire mission used to build up the required dosage over an extended period of time. Normally employed against troops who have no protection available. See also **surprise dosage attack.**

369

total materiel assets—*(DOD)* The total quantity of an item available in the military system world-wide and all funded procurement of the item with adjustments to provide for transfers out of or into the inventory through the appropriation and procurement lead-time periods. It includes peacetime force materiel assets and war reserve stock.

total materiel requirement—*(DOD, IADB)* The sum of the peacetime force material requirement and the war reserve material requirement.

total mobilization—See **mobilization.**

total nuclear war—*(DOD)* Not to be used. See **general war.**

total overall aircraft inventory—*(DOD)* The sum of the total active aircraft inventory and the inactive aircraft inventory.

total pressure—*(DOD, NATO)* The sum of dynamic and static pressures.

total war—*(DOD)* Not to be used. See **general war.**

touch-down—*(DOD, NATO)* The contact, or moment of contact, of an aircraft or spacecraft with the landing surface.

touch down zone—*(DOD, NATO)* 1. For fixed wing aircraft—The first 3,000 feet or 1,000 meters of runway beginning at the threshold. 2. For rotary wings and vectored thrust aircraft—That portion of the helicopter landing area or runway used for landing.

TOW (missile)—*(DOD)* A component of a tube-launched, optically tracked, wire-command link guided missile weapon system which is crew-portable.

toxic chemical, biological, or radiological attack—*(DOD, IADB)* An attack directed at man, animals, or crops, using injurious agents of radiological, biological, or chemical origin.

toxin agent—*(DOD)* A poison formed as a specific secretion product in the metabolism of a vegetable or animal organism as distinguished from inorganic poisons. Such poisons can also be manufactured by synthetic processes.

Tracer—*(DOD)* A twin-reciprocating engine, airborne radar platform designed to operate from aircraft carriers. Its mission is the detection and interception control of airborne targets. Designated as **E-1B.**

track—*(DOD, IADB)* 1. A series of related contacts displayed on a plotting board. 2. To display or record the successive positions of a moving object. 3. To lock onto a point of radiation and obtain guidance therefrom. 4. To keep a gun properly aimed, or to point continuously a target-locating instrument at a moving target. 5. The actual path of an aircraft above, or a ship on, the surface of the earth. The course is the path that is planned; the track is the path that is actually taken. 6. One of the two endless belts on which a full-track or half-track vehicle runs. 7. A metal part forming a path for a moving object, e.g., the track around the inside of a vehicle for moving a mounted machine gun.

track—*(NATO)* 1. To display or record the successive positions of a moving object; also to lock on to a point of radiation and obtain guidance therefrom. 2. To keep a gun properly aimed, or to point continuously a target-locating instrument at a moving target. 3. The projection on the surface of the earth of the path of a space vehicle, aircraft or ship, the direction of which path at any point is usually expressed in degrees from North (true, magnetic, or grid). 4. One of two endless belts on which a full-track or half-track vehicle runs. 5. A metal part forming a path for a moving object. 6. A mark left on the ground by the passage or presence of a person or object.

track correlation—*(DOD)* Correlating track information for identification purposes using all available data.

track crossing angle—*(DOD)* In air intercept, the angular difference between interceptor track and target track at the time of intercept.

Tracker—*(DOD, IADB)* A twin-reciprocating-engine, antisubmarine aircraft capable of operating from carriers, and designed primarily for the detection, location, and destruction of submarines. Designated as S-2.

track handover—*(NATO)* In air defense, the process of transferring the responsibility for production of a track from one track production area to another.

tracking—*(DOD, NATO)* 1. Precise and continuous position-finding of targets by radar, optical, or other means. *(DOD)* 2. In air intercept, a code meaning, "By my evaluation, target is steering true course indicated."

track mode—*(DOD, NATO)* In a flight control system, a control mode in which the ground track of an aircraft is maintained automatically.

track production—*(NATO)* A function of a surveillance organization in which the active and passive radar inputs are correlated into coherent position reports, together with historical positions, identity, height, strength and direction.

track production area—*(DOD, NATO)* An area in which tracks are produced by one radar station.

track symbology—*(DOD, NATO)* Symbols used to display tracks on a data display console or other display device.

track telling—*(DOD)* The process of communicating air surveillance and tactical data information between command and control systems or between facilities within the systems. Telling may be classified into the following types: back tell; cross tell; forward tell; lateral tell; overlap tell and relateral tell.

track telling—*(NATO)* The process of communicating air surveillance and tactical data information between command and control systems or between facilities within systems. Telling may be classified into the following types:
1. **Back tell**—The transfer of information from a higher to a lower echelon of command.
2. **Cross tell**—the transfer of information between facilities at the same operational level. Also called **lateral tell**.
3. **Forward tell**—The transfer of information to a higher level of command.
4. **Lateral tell**—See **cross tell**.
5. **Overlap tell**—The transfer of information to an adjacent facility concerning tracks detected in the adjacent facility's area of responsibility.
6. **Relateral tell**—The relay of information between facilities through the use of a third facility. This type of telling is appropriate between automated facilities in a degraded communications environment.

tractor group—*(DOD, IADB)* A group of landing ships in an amphibious operation which carries the amphibious vehicles of the landing force.

trafficability—*(DOD, NATO, IADB)* Capability of terrain to bear traffic. It refers to the extent to which the terrain will permit continued movement of any and/or all types of traffic.

traffic circulation map—*(DOD, IADB)* A map showing traffic routes and the measures for traffic regulation. It indicates the roads for use of certain classes of traffic, the location of traffic control stations, and the directions in which traffic may move. Also called a circulation map. See also **map**.

traffic control police (road transport)—*(NATO)* Any persons ordered by a military commander and/or by national authorities to facilitate the movement of traffic and to prevent and/or report any breach of road traffic regulations.

371

traffic density—*(DOD, NATO, IADB)* The average number of vehicles that occupy one mile or one kilometer of road space, expressed in vehicles per mile or per kilometer.

traffic flow—*(DOD, NATO, IADB)* The total number of vehicles passing a given point in a given time. Traffic flow is expressed as vehicles per hour.

traffic flow security—*(DOD, IADB)* The protection resulting from features, inherent in some cryptoequipment, which conceal the presence of valid messages on a communications circuit, normally achieved by causing the circuit to appear busy at all times.

traffic information (radar)—*(DOD, IADB)* Information issued to alert an aircraft to any radar targets observed on the radar display which may be in such proximity to its position or intended route of flight to warrant its attention.

traffic management—*(DOD)* The direction, control, and supervision of all functions incident to the procurement and use of freight and passenger transportation services.

traffic pattern—*(DOD, IADB)* The traffic flow that is prescribed for aircraft landing at, taxiing on, and taking off from an airport. The usual components of a traffic pattern are upwind leg, crosswind leg, downwind leg, base leg, and final approach.

trail—*(DOD, NATO)* 1. A term applied to the manner in which a bomb trails behind the aircraft from which it has been released, assuming the aircraft does not change its velocity after the release of the bomb. *(DOD)* 2. Track (or shadow). (The words "landward" or "seaward" may be used to indicate from which side of enemy unit to shadow.)

trailer aircraft—*(DOD, NATO, IADB)* Aircraft which are following and keeping under surveillance a designated airborne contact.

trail formation—*(NATO)* A formation in which all aircraft are in single file, each directly behind the other. See also **column formation**.

train—*(DOD, IADB)* 1. A service force or group of service elements which provides logistic support, e.g., an organization of naval auxiliary ships or merchant ships or merchant ships attached to a fleet for this purpose; similarly, the vehicles and operating personnel which furnish supply, evacuation, and maintenance services to a land unit. 2. Bombs dropped in short intervals or sequence.

train headway—*(DOD)* The interval of time between two trains boarded by the same unit at the same point.

training aids—*(DOD, IADB)* Any item which is developed and/or procured with the primary intent that it shall assist in training and the process of learning.

training-pay category—*(DOD)* A designation identifying the number of days of training and pay required for members of the Reserve Components.

train path—*(DOD, NATO)* In railway terminology, the timing of a possible movement of a train along a given route. All the train paths on a given route constitute a timetable.

trajectory—See **ballistic trajectory**.

transattack period—*(DOD)* 1. In nuclear warfare, the period from the initiation of the attack to its termination. 2. As applied to the Single Integrated Operational Plan, the period which extends from execution (or enemy attack, whichever is sooner) to termination of the Single Integrated Operational Plan. See also **postattack period**.

transfer area—*(DOD, IADB)* In an amphibious operation, the water area in which the transfer of troops and supplies from landing craft to amphibious vehicles is effected.

transfer loader—*(DOD, NATO, IADB)* A wheeled or tracked vehicle with a platform capable of vertical and horizontal adjustment used in the loading and unloading of aircraft, ships, or other vehicles.

transient—*(DOD)* 1. Personnel, ships, or craft stopping temporarily at a post, station or port to which they are not assigned or attached, and having destination elsewhere. *(DOD, NATO)* 2. An individual awaiting orders, transport, etc., at a post or station to which he is not attached or assigned. *(DOD)* 3. An independent merchant ship calling at a port and sailing within 12 hours, and for which routing instructions to a further port have been promulgated.

transient forces—*(DOD, IADB)* Forces which pass or stage through, or base temporarily within, the area of responsibility of another command but are not under its operational control.

transit area—See **staging area.**

transit bearing—*(DOD, NATO)* A bearing determined by noting the time at which two features on the earth's surface have the same relative bearing.

transition altitude—*(DOD, IADB)* The altitude at or below which the vertical position of an aircraft is controlled by reference to true altitude.

transition altitude—*(NATO)* The altitude at or below which the vertical position of an aircraft is controlled by reference to altitude. See also **altitude; transition level.**

transition layer—*(DOD, NATO)* The airspace between the transition altitude and the transition level.

transition level—*(DOD, NATO, IADB)* The lowest flight level available for use above the transition altitude. See also **altitude; transition altitude.**

transit route—*(DOD, NATO)* A sea route which crosses open waters normally joining two coastal routes.

transmission factor (nuclear)—*(DOD, IADB)* The ratio of the dose inside the shielding material to the outside (ambient) dose. Transmission factor is used to calculate the dose received through the shielding material. See also **half thickness; shielding.**

transmission security—See **communications security.**

transonic—*(DOD, NATO, IADB)* Of or pertaining to the speed of a body in a surrounding fluid when the relative speed of the fluid is subsonic in some places and supersonic in others. This is encountered when passing from subsonic to supersonic speeds and vice versa. See also **speed of sound.**

transparency—*(DOD, NATO)* An image fixed on a clear base by means of a photographic, printing, chemical or other process, especially adaptable for viewing by transmitted light. See also **diapositive.**

transponder—*(DOD, NATO)* A receiver-transmitter which will generate a reply signal upon proper interrogation. See also **responsor.**

transponder india—*(DOD)* International Civil Aviation Organization/secondary surveillance radar.

transponder sierra—*(DOD)* Identification Friend or Foe mark X (selective identification feature).

transponder tango—*(DOD)* Identification Friend or Foe mark X (basic).

transportability—*(DOD)* The capability of material to be moved by towing, self-propulsion, or carrier via any means, such as railways, highways, waterways, pipelines, oceans, and airways.

transport aircraft—*(DOD, NATO)* Aircraft designed primarily for the carriage of personnel and/or cargo. Transport aircraft may be classed according to range, as follows:
   a. **Short-range**—Not to exceed 1200 nautical miles at normal cruising conditions (2222 Km).
   b. **Medium-range**—Between 1200 and 3500 nautical miles at normal cruising conditions (2222 and 6482 Km).
   c. **Long-range**—Exceeds 3500 nautical miles at normal cruising conditions (6482 Km). See also **strategic transport aircraft; tactical transport aircraft.**

transport area—*(DOD)* In amphibious operations, an area assigned to a transport organization for the purpose of debarking troops and equipment. See also **inner transport area; outer transport area.**

transportation emergency—*(DOD, IADB)* A situation created by a shortage of normal transportation capability and of a magnitude sufficient to frustrate military movement requirements, and which requires extraordinary action by the President or other designated authority to insure continued movement of essential Department of Defense Traffic.

transportation operating agencies—*(DOD)* 1. **military**—These agencies are the Military Traffic Management Command, under the Department of the Army, the Military Sealift Command, under the Department of the Navy, and the Military Airlift Command, under the Department of the Air Force. 2. **civil**—Those Federal agencies having responsibilities under national emergency conditions for the operational direction of one or more forms of transportation; they are also referred to as Federal Modal Agencies or Federal Transport Agencies.

transportation priorities—*(DOD, IADB)* Indicators assigned to eligible traffic which establish its movement precedence. Appropriate priority systems apply to the movement of traffic by sea and air. *(DOD)* In times of emergency, priorities may be applicable to continental United States movements by land, water, or air.

transport capacity—*(NATO)* The number of persons, weight or volume of the load which can be carried by means of transport under given conditions. See also **payload.**

transport capacity—*(IADB)* The capacity of a vehicle is defined by the number of persons, the tonnage (or volume) of equipment which can be carried by this vehicle under given conditions.

transport control center (air transport)—*(DOD, IADB)* The operations center through which the air transport force commander exercises control over the air transport system.

transport group (amphibious)—*(DOD, IADB)* A subdivision of an amphibious task force, composed primarily of transports.

transport network—*(IADB)* The complete system of the routes pertaining to all means of transport available in a particular area. It is made up of the network particular to each means of transport.

transport stream—*(DOD, NATO, IADB)* Transport vehicles proceeding in trail formation.

transport vehicle—*(DOD, IADB)* A motor vehicle designed and used without modification to the chassis, to provide general transport service in the movement of personnel and cargo. See also **vehicle.**

trans-shipment point—*(DOD, NATO)* A location where material is transferred between vehicles.

traverse—*(DOD, NATO, IADB)* 1. To turn a weapon to the right or left on its mount. 2. A method of surveying in which lengths and directions of lines between points on the earth are obtained by or from field measurements, and used in determining positions of the points.

traverse level—*(DOD, NATO)* That vertical displacement above low-level air defense systems, expressed both as a height and altitude, at which aircraft can cross the area.

treason—*(DOD, IADB)* Violation of the allegiance owed to one's sovereign or state; betrayal of one's country.

trench burial—*(DOD, IADB)* A method of burial resorted to when casualties are heavy whereby a trench is prepared and the individual remains are laid in it side by side, thus obviating the necessity of digging and filling in individual graves. See also **burial**.

trend—*(DOD)* The straying of the fall of shot, such as might be caused by incorrect speed settings of the fire support ship.

triage—*(NATO)* The evaluation and classification of casualties for purposes of treatment and evacuation. It consists of the immediate sorting of patients according to type and seriousness of injury, and likelihood of survival, and the establishment of priority for treatment and evacuation to assure medical care of the greatest benefit to the largest number.

triangulation station—*(DOD, NATO)* A point on the earth, the position of which is determined by triangulation. Also called **trig point**.

tri-camera photography—*(DOD, NATO)* Photography obtained by simultaneous exposure of three cameras systematically disposed in the air vehicle at fixed overlapping angles relative to each other in order to cover a wide field. See also **fan camera photography**.

Trident—*(DOD)* A general descriptive term for the sea-based strategic weapon system consisting of the highly survivable nuclear-powered Trident submarine, long-range Trident ballistic missiles and the integrated refit facilities required to support the submarine and missile subsystems as well as associated personnel.

Trident I—*(DOD)* A three-stage, solid propellant ballistic missile capable of being launched from a Trident submarine either surfaced or submerged. It is sized to permit backfit into Poseidon submarines and is equipped with advanced guidance, nuclear warheads and a maneuverable bus which can deploy these warheads to separate targets. It is capable of carrying a full payload to 4000 nautical miles with greater ranges achievable in reduced payload configurations. Designated as **UGM-96A**.

Trident II—*(DOD)* A solid propellant ballistic missile capable of being launched from a Trident submarine. It is larger than the Trident I missile and will replace these missiles in Trident submarines in the mid-1980s. It will provide the option to deploy a higher throw weight, more accurate, submarine-launched ballistic missile.

trig list—*(DOD)* A list published by certain Army units which includes essential information of accurately located survey points.

trimetrogon photography—See **fan camera photography**.

trim for take-off feature—*(DOD, NATO)* A flight control system feature in which the control surfaces of an aircraft are automatically trimmed to a predetermined take-off position.

trim size—*(DOD, NATO)* The size of a map or chart sheet when the excess paper outside the margin has been trimmed off after printing.

triple point—*(DOD)* The intersection of the incident, reflected, and fused (or Mach) shock fronts accompanying an air burst. The height of the triple point above the surface, i.e., the height of the Mach stem, increases with increasing distance from a given explosion.

troop basis—*(DOD, IADB)* An approved list of those military units and individuals (including civilians) required for the performance of a particular mission by numbers, organization and equipment, and, in the case of larger commands, by deployment.

troops—*(DOD, IADB)* A collective term for uniformed military personnel (usually not applicable to naval personnel afloat). See also **airborne troops; combat service support elements; combat support troops; combat troops; service troops; tactical troops.**

troop safety (nuclear)—*(DOD, IADB)* An element which defines a distance from the proposed burst location beyond which personnel meeting the criteria described under degree of risk will be safe to the degree prescribed.

troop space cargo—*(DOD, IADB)* Cargo such as sea or barracks bags, bedding rolls or hammocks, locker trunks, and office equipment, which is normally stowed in an accessible place. This cargo will also include normal hand-carried combat equipment and weapons to be carried ashore by the assault troops. See also **cargo.**

troop test—*(DOD, IADB)* A test conducted in the field for the purpose of evaluating operational or organizational concepts, doctrine, tactics, and techniques, or to gain further information on material. See also **service test.**

tropical storm—*(DOD, IADB)* A tropical cyclone in which the surface wind speed is at least 34, but not more than 63 knots.

tropopause—*(DOD, NATO, IADB)* The transition zone between the stratosphere and the troposphere. The tropopause normally occurs at an altitude of about 25,000 to 45,000 feet (8 to 15 kilometers) in polar and temperate zones, and a 55,000 feet (20 kilometers) in the tropics. See also **atmosphere.**

troposphere—*(DOD, NATO, IADB)* The lower layers of atmosphere, in which the change of temperature with height is relatively large. It is the region where clouds form, convection is active, and mixing is continuous and more or less complete. See also **atmosphere.**

tropospheric scatter—*(DOD, NATO)* The propagation of electromagnetic waves by scattering as a result of irregularities or discontinuities in the physical properties of the troposphere.

true airspeed indicator—*(DOD, NATO)* An instrument which displays the speed of the aircraft relative to the ambient air.

true altitude—*(DOD, IADB)* The height of an aircraft as measured from mean sea level.

true bearing—*(DOD, NATO)* The direction to an object from a point, expressed as a horizontal angle measured clockwise from true north.

true convergence—*(DOD)* The angle at which one meridian is inclined to another on the surface of the earth. See also **convergence.**

true convergence—*(NATO)* A change in the azimuth of a great circle from one meridian to another. See also **convergence.**

true horizon—*(DOD, NATO)* 1. The boundary of a horizontal plane passing through a point of vision. 2. In photogrammetry, the boundary of a horizontal plane passing through the perspective center of a lens system.

true north—*(DOD, NATO, IADB)* The direction from an observer's position to the geographic North Pole. The north direction of any geographic meridian.

trunk air route—*(NATO)* An established air route along which strategic moves of military forces can take place.

turbojet—*(DOD, IADB)* A jet engine whose air is supplied by a turbine-driven compressor, the turbine being activated by exhaust gases.

turn and slip indicator—*(DOD, NATO)* An instrument which combines the functions of a turn and a slip indicator.

turnaround—*(DOD, NATO, IADB)* The length of time between arriving at a point and being ready to depart from that point. It is used in this sense for the loading, unloading, re-fueling and re-arming, where appropriate, of vehicles, aircraft and ships. See also **turnaround cycle.**

turnaround cycle—*(DOD, NATO)* A term used in conjunction with vehicles, ships and aircraft, and comprising the following: loading time at departure point; time to and from destination; unloading and loading time at destination; unloading time at returning point; planned maintenance time, and where applicable, time awaiting facilities. See also **turnaround.**

turn indicator—*(DOD, NATO)* An instrument which displays the aircraft's rate and direction of turn.

turning movement—*(DOD, NATO)* A variation of the envelopment in which the attacking force passes around or over the enemy's principal defensive positions to secure objectives deep in the enemy's rear to force the enemy to abandon his position or divert major forces to meet the threat.

turning point—*(DOD, NATO)* In land mine warfare, a point of the centerline of a mine strip or row where strips or rows change direction.

turn-in point—*(DOD, NATO, IADB)* The point at which an aircraft starts to turn from the approach direction to the line of attack. See also **contact point; pull-up point.**

turn-off guidance—*(DOD, NATO)* Information which enables the pilot of a landing aircraft to select and follow the correct taxiway from the time the aircraft leaves the runway until it may safely be brought to a halt clear of the active runway.

twilight—*(NATO)* The periods of incomplete darkness following sunset and preceding sunrise. Twilight is designated as civil, nautical or astronomical, as the darker limit occurs when the center of the sun is 6°, 12° or 18°, respectively, below the celestial horizon.

two-man rule—*(DOD)* A system designed to prohibit access by an individual to nuclear weapons and certain designated components by requiring the presence at all times of at least two authorized persons each capable of detecting incorrect or unauthorized procedures with respect to the task to be performed. Also referred to as the two-man concept or two-man policy.

two-up—*(NATO, IADB)* A formation with two elements disposed abreast; the remaining element(s) in rear.

type command—*(DOD, IADB)* An administrative subdivision of a fleet or force into ships or units of the same type, as differentiated from a tactical subdivision. Any type command may have a flagship, tender, and aircraft assigned to it.

type load—See **standard load.**

types of burst—See **airburst; fallout safe height of burst; height of burst; high airburst; high altitude burst; low airburst; nuclear airburst; nuclear exoatmospheric burst; nuclear surface burst; nuclear underground burst; nuclear underwater burst; optimum height of burst; safe burst height.**

type unit—*(DOD)* A type of organizational entity established within the Armed Forces and uniquely identified by a five-character, alphanumeric code called a unit type code.

type unit data file—*(DOD)* A file that provides standard planning data and movement characteristics for personnel, cargo, and accompanying supplies associated with type units.

U

UGM-27—See **Polaris.**

UGM-73A—See **Poseidon.**

UGM-84A—See **Harpoon.**

UGM-96A—See **Trident I.**

UH-1—See **Iroquois.**

ultraviolet imagery—*(DOD)* That imagery produced as a result of sensing ultraviolet radiations reflected from a given target surface.

uncharged demolition target—*(DOD, NATO, IADB)* A demolition target which has been prepared to receive the demolition agent, the necessary quantities of which have been calculated, packaged, and stored in a safe place. Installation instructions have been prepared. See also **demolition.**

unclassified matter—*(DOD, NATO, IADB)* Official matter which does not require the application of security safeguards, but the disclosure of which may be subject to control for other reasons. See also **classified matter.**

uncontrolled mosaic—*(DOD, NATO)* A mosaic composed of uncorrected photographs, the details of which have been matched from print to print, without ground control or other orientation. Accurate measurement and direction cannot be accomplished. See also **controlled mosaic.**

unconventional warfare—*(DOD)* A broad spectrum of military and paramilitary operations conducted in enemy-held, enemy-controlled or politically sensitive territory. Unconventional warfare includes, but is not limited to, the interrelated fields of guerrilla warfare, evasion and escape, subversion, sabotage, and other operations of a low visibility, covert or clandestine nature. These interrelated aspects of unconventional warfare may be prosecuted singly or collectively by predominantly indigenous personnel, usually supported and directed in varying degrees by (an) external source(s) during all conditions of war or peace.

unconventional warfare—*(NATO)* General term used to describe operations conducted for military, political or economic purposes within an area occupied by the enemy and making use of the local inhabitants and resources.

unconventional warfare forces—*(DOD)* United States forces having an existing unconventional warfare capability consisting of Army Special Forces and such Navy, Air Force, and Marine units as are assigned for these operations.

understowed cargo—See **flatted cargo.**

underwater demolition—*(DOD, NATO, IADB)* The destruction or neutralization of underwater obstacles; this is normally accomplished by underwater demolition teams.

underwater demolition team—*(DOD, IADB)* A group of officers and men specially trained and equipped for making hydrographic reconnaissance of approaches to prospective landing beaches; for effecting demolition of obstacles, clearing mines in certain areas; locating, improving, and marking of useable channels; channel and harbor clearance; acquisition of pertinent data during pre-assault operations, including military information; and visual observation of the hinterland to gain information useful to the landing force; and for performing miscellaneous underwater and surface tasks within their capabilities.

underway replenishment—See **replenishment at sea.**

underway replenishment force—*(DOD, NATO, IADB)* A task force of fleet auxiliaries (consisting of oilers, ammunition ships, stores issue ships, etc.) adequately protected by escorts furnished by the responsible operational commander. The function of this force is to provide underway logistic support for naval forces. See also **force(s)**.

underway replenishment group—*(DOD, IADB)* A task group configured to provide logistic replenishment of ships underway by transfer-at-sea methods.

unexploded explosive ordnance—*(DOD, NATO)* Explosive ordnance which has been primed, fused, armed or otherwise prepared for action, and which has been fired, dropped, launched, projected or placed in such a manner as to constitute a hazard to operations, installations, personnel or material and remains unexploded either by malfunction or design or for any other cause.

Unified Action Armed Forces—*(DOD)* A publication setting forth the principles, doctrines, and functions governing the activities and performance of the Armed Forces of the United States when two or more Services or elements thereof are acting together.

unified command—*(DOD)* A command with a broad continuing mission under a single commander and composed of significant assigned components of two or more Services, and which is established and so designated by the President, through the Secretary of Defense with the advice and assistance of the Joint Chiefs of Staff, or, when so authorized by the Joint Chiefs of Staff, by a commander of an existing unified command established by the President.

uniformed services—*(DOD)* The Army, Navy, Air Force, Marine Corps, Coast Guard, National Oceanic and Atmospheric Administration, and Public Health Service. See also **Military Department; Military Service**.

unilateral arms control measure—*(DOD, IADB)* An arms control course of action taken by a nation without any compensating concession being required of other nations.

unintentional radiation exploitation—*(DOD)* Exploitation for operational purposes of non-information-bearing elements of electromagnetic energy unintentionally emanated by targets of interest.

uni-Service command—*(DOD)* A command comprised of forces of a single Service.

unit—*(DOD, NATO, IADB)* 1. Any military element whose structure is prescribed by competent authority, such as a table of organization and equipment; specifically, part of an organization. 2. An organization title of a subdivision of a group in a task force. 3. A standard or basic quantity into which an item of supply is divided, issued, or used. In this meaning, also called "unit of issue."

unit aircraft—*(DOD, IADB)* Those aircraft provided an aircraft unit for the performance of a flying mission. See also **aircraft**.

unit combat readiness—See **combat readiness**.

unit commitment status—*(DOD, NATO)* The degree of commitment of any unit designated and categorized as a force allocated to NATO.

United States Armed Forces—*(DOD)* Used to denote collectively only the regular components of the Army, Navy, Air Force, Marine Corps, and Coast Guard. See also **Armed Forces of the United States**.

United States Army Special Forces—*(DOD)* Military personnel with cross training in basic and specialized military skills, organized into small, multiple-purpose detachments with the mission to train, organize, supply, direct, and control indigenous forces in guerrilla warfare and counter-insurgency operations, and to conduct unconventional warfare operations.

United States Civil Authorities—*(DOD)* Those elected and appointed public officials and employees who constitute the governments of the 50 States, District of Columbia, Commonwealth of Puerto Rico, United States possessions and territories, and political subdivisions thereof.

United States Civilian Internee Information Center—*(DOD)* The national center of information in the United States for enemy and United States civilian internees.

United States controlled shipping—*(DOD)* That shipping under United States flag plus those selected ships under foreign flag which are considered to be under "effective United States control," i.e., which can reasonably be expected to be made available to the United States in time of national emergency.

United States country team—*(DOD)* The senior, in-country, United States coordinating and supervising body, headed by the Chief of the United States diplomatic mission, usually an ambassador, and composed of the senior member of each represented United States department or agency.

United States Military Service Funded Foreign Training—*(DOD)* Training which is provided to foreign nationals in United States military Service schools and installations under authority other than the Foreign Assistance Act of 1961.

United States Prisoner of War Information Center—*(DOD)* The national center of information in the United States for enemy and United States prisoners of war.

United States Strategic Army Forces—*(DOD)* That part of the Army, normally located in the continental United States, which is trained, equipped, and maintained for employment at national level in accordance with current plans.

unit emplaning officer—*(NATO)* In air transport, a representative of the transported unit responsible for organizing the movement of that unit.

unit equipment—*(NATO)* The equipment prescribed by the table of organization and equipment, or national equivalents pertaining to that unit. See also **establishment.**

unit identification code—*(DOD)* A six-character, alphanumeric code that uniquely identifies each Active, Reserve, and National Guard unit of the Armed Forces. Also called UIC.

unitized load—*(DOD)* A single item, or a number of items packaged, packed or arranged in a specified manner and capable of being handled as a unit. Unitization may be accomplished by placing the item or items in a container or by banding them securely together. See also **palletized unit load.**

unit loading—*(DOD, NATO, IADB)* The loading of troop units with their equipment and supplies in the same vessels, aircraft, or land vehicles. See also **loading.**

unit of issue—*(DOD, IADB)* In its special storage meaning, refers to the quantity of an item; as each number, dozen, gallon, pair, pound, ream, set, yard. Usually termed unit of issue to distinguish from "unit price." See also **unit.**

unit of issue—*(NATO)* See **unit** Part 3.

unit personnel and tonnage table—*(DOD, IADB)* A table included in the loading plan of a combat-loaded ship as a recapitulation of totals of personnel and cargo by type, listing cubic measurements and weight.

unit price—*(DOD)* The cost or price of an item of supply based on the unit of issue.

unit reserves—*(DOD, IADB)* Prescribed quantities of supplies carried by a unit as a reserve to cover emergencies. See also **reserve supplies.**

unit strength—*(NATO)* As applied to a friendly or enemy unit, relates to the number of personnel, amount of supplies, armament equipment and vehicles and the total logistic capabilities. See also **strength.**

unit training assembly—*(DOD)* An authorized and scheduled period of unit inactive duty training of a prescribed length of time.

unit type code—*(DOD)* A five-character, alphanumeric code that uniquely identifies each type unit of the Armed Forces. Also called **UTC**.

universal polar stereographic grid—*(DOD)* A military grid prescribed for joint use in operations in limited areas and used for operations requiring precise position reporting. It covers areas between the 80 degree parallels and the poles.

universal transverse mercator grid—*(DOD, NATO)* A grid coordinate system based on the transverse mercator projection, applied to maps of the earth's surface extending to 84°N and 80°S latitudes. Also called **UTM Grid**.

unknown—*(DOD)* 1. A code meaning information not available. 2. An unidentified target.

unlimited war—*(DOD)* Not to be used. See **general war**.

unobserved fire—*(DOD, NATO, IADB)* Fire for which the points of impact or burst are not observed. See also **fire**.

unpremeditated expansion of a war—*(DOD)* Not to be used. See **escalation**.

unpremeditated war—*(DOD)* Not to be used. See **accidental attack**.

unscheduled convoy phase—*(DOD, NATO)* The period in the early days of war when convoys are instituted on an ad hoc basis before the introduction of convoy schedules in the regular convoy phase.

unsurveyed area—*(NATO)* An area on a map or chart where both relief and planimetric data are unavailable. Such an area is usually labelled "unsurveyed." Or an area on a map or chart which shows little or no charted data because accurate information is limited or not available.

unwanted cargo—See **cargo**.

unwarned exposed—*(DOD, NATO, IADB)* The vulnerability of friendly forces to nuclear weapon effects. In this condition, personnel are assumed to be standing in the open at burst time, but have dropped to a prone position by the time the blast wave arrives. They are expected to have areas of bare skin exposed to direct thermal radiation, and some personnel may suffer dazzle. See also **warned exposed; warned protected**.

up—*(DOD, NATO)* In artillery and naval gunfire support: 1. A term used in a call for fire to indicate that the target is higher in altitude than the point which has been used as a reference point for the target location. 2. A correction used by an observer or a spotter in time fire to indicate that an increase in height of burst is desired.

urgent mining—*(DOD, NATO)* In naval mine warfare, the laying of mines with correct spacing but not in the ordered or planned positions. The mines may be laid either inside or outside the allowed area in such positions that they will hamper the movements of the enemy more than those of our own forces.

urgent priority—*(DOD, IADB)* A category of immediate mission request which is lower than emergency priority but takes precedence over ordinary priority, e.g., enemy artillery or mortar fire which is falling on friendly troops and causing casualties or enemy troops or mechanized units moving up in such force as to threaten a break-through. See also **immediate mission request; priority of immediate mission request**.

US Roland—*(DOD)* A short range, low-altitude, all-weather, Army air defense artillery surface-to-air missile system under development which is based upon the Franco-German Roland III missile system.

utility helicopter—*(DOD, NATO)* Multi-purpose helicopter capable of lifting troops but may be used in a command and control, logistics, casualty evacuation or armed helicopter role.

UTM-grid—See also **universal transverse mercator grid.**

UUM-44A—See **submarine rocket.**

V

valuable cargo—See **cargo.**

value engineering—*(DOD, IADB)* An organized effort directed at analyzing the function of Department of Defense systems, equipment, facilities, procedures and supplies for the purpose of achieving the required function at the lowest total cost of effective ownership, consistent with requirements for performance, reliability, quality, and maintainability.

variability—*(DOD, NATO, IADB)* The manner in which the probability of damage to a specific target decreases with the distance from ground zero; or, in damage assessment, a mathematical factor introduced to average the effects of orientation, minor shielding and uncertainty of target response to the effects considered.

variable safety level—See **safety level of supply.**

variant—*(DOD, IADB)* 1. One of two or more cipher or code symbols which have the same plain text equivalent. 2. One of several plain text meanings that are represented by a single code group; also called **alternative.**

vector—*(DOD)* In air intercept, close air support and air interdiction usage, a code meaning, "Alter heading to magnetic heading indicated." Heading ordered must be in three digits; e.g., "vector" zero six zero (for homing, use "steer").

vector—*(IADB)* A heading issued to an aircraft to provide navigational guidance by radar.

vectored attack—*(DOD, NATO, IADB)* Attack in which a weapon carrier (air, surface, or subsurface) not holding contact on the target, is vectored to the weapon delivery point by a unit (air, surface or subsurface) which holds contact on the target.

vector sights—See **bomb sighting systems.**

vehicle—*(DOD, NATO, IADB)* A self-propelled, boosted, or towed conveyance for transporting a burden on land, sea or through air or space. See also **amphibious vehicle; combat vehicle; commercial vehicle; special-equipment vehicle; special-purpose vehicle; substitute transport-type vehicle; transport vehicle.**

vehicle cargo—*(DOD, IADB)* Wheeled or tracked equipment, including weapons, which require certain deck space, head room, and other definite clearance. See also **cargo.**

vehicle distance—*(DOD, NATO)* The clearance between vehicles in a column which is measured from the rear of one vehicle to the front of the following vehicle.

vehicle summary and priority table—*(DOD, IADB)* A table listing all vehicles by priority of debarkation from a combat-loaded ship. It includes the nomenclature, dimensions, square feet, cubic feet, weight, and stowage location of each vehicle, the cargo loaded in each vehicle, and the name of the unit to which the vehicle belongs.

verification—*(DOD, IADB)* In arms control, any action, including inspection, detection, and identification, taken to ascertain compliance with agreed measures.

verify—*(DOD, NATO, IADB)* 1. To ensure that the meaning and phraseology of the transmitted message conveys the exact intention of the originator. *(DOD)* 2. A request from an observer, a spotter, or a fire-control agency to reexamine firing data and report the results of the reexamination.

vertex height—See **maximum ordinate.**

vertical air photograph—*(DOD, NATO)* An air photograph taken with the optical axis of the camera perpendicular to the surface of the earth.

vertical and/or short takeoff and landing—(DOD, IADB) Vertical and/or short takeoff and landing capability for aircraft.

vertical envelopment—(DOD, IADB) A tactical maneuver in which troops, either air-dropped or air-landed, attack the rear and flanks of a force, in effect cutting off or encircling the force.

vertical interval—(DOD, IADB) Difference in altitude between two specified points or locations, e.g., the battery or firing ship and the target; observer location and the target; location of previously fired target and new target; observer and a height of burst; battery or firing ship and a height of burst, etc.

vertical interval—(NATO) Difference in altitude or height between two specified points or locations.

vertical loading—(DOD, NATO, IADB) A type of loading whereby items of like character are vertically tiered throughout the holds of a ship, so that selected items are available at any stage of the unloading. See also loading.

vertical probable error—(DOD, IADB) The product of the range probable error and the slope of fall.

vertical replenishment—(DOD, NATO) The use of a helicopter for the transfer of materiel to or from a ship.

vertical scale instrument systems—(NATO) A system of vertical scale indicators which display flight and engine information.

vertical separation—(DOD, NATO) Separation between aircraft expressed in units of vertical distance.

vertical separation—(IADB) A specified vertical distance measured in terms of space between aircraft in flight at different altitude or flight levels.

vertical situation display—(DOD, NATO) An electronically generated display on which information on aircraft attitude and heading, flight director commands, weapon aiming and terrain following can be presented, choice of presentation being under the control of the pilot.

vertical speed indicator—(NATO) An instrument which displays rate of climb or descent.
  a. Barometric. An instrument which displays the apparent vertical speed of the aircraft as derived from the rate of change of static pressure.
  b. Instantaneous. An instrument which displays the vertical speed of the aircraft as derived from a combination of accelerometric and barometric sources.

vertical strip—(DOD) A single flightline of overlapping photos. Photography of this type is normally taken of long, narrow targets such as beaches or roads.

vertical take-off and landing—(DOD, NATO, IADB) The capability of an aircraft to take off and land vertically and to transfer to or from forward motion at heights required to clear surrounding obstacles.

very deep draught ship—(NATO) A ship with a laden draught of 13.75 meters (45 feet) or more.

very high—(DOD, IADB) A height above fifty thousand feet.

very low—(DOD, IADB) A height below five hundred feet.

very seriously ill—(DOD, NATO, IADB) A patient is very seriously ill when his illness is of such severity that life is imminently endangered. See also seriously ill.

vesicant agent—See blister agent.

Vigilante—(DOD, IADB) A twin turbojet engine, dual-crew, supersonic all-weather reconnaissance aircraft designed to operate

386

from aircraft carriers. It carries a wide assortment of photographic and electronic surveillance systems. Designated as **RA-5**.

vignetting—*(DOD, NATO)* A method of producing a band of color or tone on a map or chart, the density of which is reduced uniformly from edge to edge.

Viking—*(DOD)* A twin turbofan engine, multicrew antisubmarine aircraft capable of operating off aircraft carriers. It is designed to detect, locate, and destroy submarines utilizing an integrated, computer-controlled attack system and a variety of conventional and/or nuclear ordnance. Designated as **S-3**.

visibility—*(DOD)* In air intercept usage, "Visibility (in miles) is ____."

visibility range—*(DOD, IADB)* The horizontal distance (in kilometers or miles) at which a large dark object can just be seen against the horizon sky in daylight.

visual call sign—*(DOD, NATO, IADB)* A call sign provided primarily for visual signaling. See also **call sign**.

visual identification—*(DOD, NATO)* In a flight control system, a control mode in which the aircraft follows a radar target and is automatically positioned to allow visual identification.

visual interceptor—*(DOD, NATO)* An interceptor which has no special equipment to enable it to intercept its target in dark or daylight conditions by other than visual means.

visual mine firing indicator—*(DOD, NATO)* A device used with exercise mines to indicate that the mine would have detonated had it been poised.

visual report—*(DOD)* Not to be used. See **inflight report**.

vital area—*(DOD, NATO, IADB)* A designated area or installation to be defended by air defense units. See also **area**.

vital ground—See **key terrain**.

voice call sign—*(DOD, NATO, IADB)* A call sign provided primarily for voice communication. See also **call sign**.

voluntary training—*(DOD)* Training in a nonpay status for Individual Ready Reservists and active status Standby Reservists. Participation in voluntary training is for retirement points only and may be achieved by training with Selected Reserve or Voluntary Training units; by active duty for training; by completion of authorized military correspondence courses; by attendance at designated courses of instruction; by performing equivalent duty; by participation in special military and professional events designated by the Military Departments; or by participation in authorized Civil Defense activities.

voluntary training unit—*(DOD)* A reserve unit formed by volunteers to provide inactive duty training in a nonpay status for individual Ready Reservists and active status Standby Reservists who are attached under competent orders and participate in such units for retirement points.

Voodoo—*(DOD, IADB)* A supersonic, twin-engine turbojet, air interceptor. This twin cockpit aircraft carries a variety of air-to-air missiles, both nuclear and nonnuclear. Designated as **F-101**.

VOR—*(DOD, NATO)* An air navigational radio aid which uses phase comparison of a ground transmitted signal to determine bearing. This term is derived from the words "very high frequency omnidirectional radio range."

Vulcan—*(DOD)* An Army air defense artillery gun which provides low-altitude air defense and has a direct fire capability against surface targets. The gun is a 6-barreled, air-cooled, 20-mm rotary-fired weapon.

vulnerability—(DOD, IADB) 1. The susceptibility of a nation or military force to any action by any means through which its war potential or combat effectiveness may be reduced or its will to fight diminished. 2. The characteristics of a system which cause it to suffer a definite degradation (incapability to perform the designated mission) as a result of having been subjected to a certain level of effects in an unnatural (manmade) hostile environment.

vulnerability program—(DOD, IADB) A program to determine the degree of, and to remedy insofar as possible, any existing susceptibility of nuclear weapon systems to enemy countermeasures, accidental fire, and accidental shock.

vulnerability study—(DOD, IADB) An analysis of the capabilities and limitations of a force in a specific situation to determine vulnerabilities capable of exploitation by an opposing force.

vulnerable area—See vital area.

vulnerable point—See vital area.

W

wading crossing—See **deep fording; deep fording capability; shallow fording; shallow fording capability.**

waiting position—*(NATO)* Any suitable position in which naval units can be kept ready for operations at immediate notice. See also **laying-up position.**

walking patient—*(DOD, NATO, IADB)* A patient not requiring a litter while in transit.

Walleye—*(DOD)* A guided air-to-surface glide bomb for the stand-off destruction of large semi-hard targets. It incorporates a contrast-tracking television system for guidance.

wanted cargo—See **cargo.**

war air service program—*(DOD)* The program designed to provide for the maintenance of essential civil air routes and services, and to provide for the distribution and re-distribution of air-carrier aircraft among civil air transportation carriers after withdrawal of aircraft allocated to the Civil Reserve Air Fleet.

warble—*(DOD, NATO)* In naval mine warfare, the process of varying the frequency of sound produced by a narrow band noisemaker to ensure that the frequency to which the mine will respond is covered.

warehouse chart—See **planograph.**

war game—*(DOD, NATO, IADB)* A simulation, by whatever means, of a military operation involving two or more opposing forces, using rules, data, and procedures designed to depict an actual or assumed real life situation.

warhead—*(DOD, NATO, IADB)* That part of a missile, projectile, torpedo, rocket, or other munition which contains either the nuclear or thermonuclear system, high explosive system, chemical or biological agents or inert materials intended to inflict damage.

warhead mating—*(DOD)* The act of attaching a warhead section to a rocket or missile body, torpedo, airframe, motor or guidance section.

warhead section—*(DOD, NATO, IADB)* A completely assembled warhead including appropriate skin sections and related components.

WARM—See **wartime reserve mode.**

WARMAPS—See **wartime manpower planning system.**

war materiel procurement capability—*(DOD)* The quantity of an item which can be acquired by orders placed on or after the day an operation commences (D-day) from industry or from any other available source during the period prescribed for war materiel procurement planning purposes.

war materiel requirement—*(DOD)* The quantity of an item required to equip and support the approved forces specified in the current Secretary of Defense guidance through the period prescribed for war materiel planning purposes.

warned exposed—*(DOD, NATO, IADB)* The vulnerability of friendly forces to nuclear weapon effects. In this condition, personnel are assumed to be prone with all skin covered and with thermal protection at least that provided by a two-layer summer uniform. See also **unwarned exposed; warned protected.**

warned protected—*(DOD, NATO, IADB)* The vulnerability of friendly forces to nuclear weapon effects. In this condition, personnel are assumed to have some protection against heat, blast, and radiation such as that afforded in closed armored vehicles or crouched in fox holes with improvised overhead shielding. See also **unwarned exposed; warned exposed.**

warning area—See **danger area.**

warning net—*(DOD, IADB)* A communication system established for the purpose of disseminating warning information of enemy movement or action to all interested commands.

warning order—*(DOD, NATO)* A preliminary notice of an order or action which is to follow.

warning red—See **air defense warning conditions.**

warning white—See **air defense warning conditions.**

warning yellow—See **air defense warning conditions.**

war reserve materiel requirement—*(DOD)* That portion of the war materiel requirement required to be on hand on D-day. This level consists of the war materiel requirement less the sum of the peacetime assets assumed to be available on D-day and the war materiel procurement capability.

war reserve materiel requirement, balance—*(DOD)* That portion of the war reserve materiel requirement which has not been acquired or funded. This level consists of the war reserve materiel requirement less the war reserve materiel requirement, protectable.

war reserve materiel requirement, protectable—*(DOD)* That portion of the war reserve materiel requirement that is either on hand and/or previously funded which shall be protected; if issued for peacetime use, it shall be promptly reconstituted. This level consists of the pre-positioned war reserve materiel requirement, protectable, and the other war reserve materiel requirement, protectable.

war reserve (nuclear)—*(DOD)* Nuclear weapons materiel stockpiled in the custody of the Department of Energy or transferred to the custody of the Department of Defense and intended for employment in the event of war.

war reserves—*(DOD, NATO, IADB)* War reserves are stocks of materiel amassed in peacetime to meet the increase in military requirements consequent upon an outbreak of war. War reserves are intended to provide the interim support essential to sustain operations until resupply can be effected. See also **materiel inventory objective; M-day force materiel requirement; net inventory assets; other acquisition war reserve requirements; other acquisition war reserve stock; peacetime force materiel assets; peacetime force materiel requirement; peacetime materiel usage; pre-positioned war reserve requirement; pre-positioned war reserve stock; reserve supplies; total materiel assets; total materiel requirement; war materiel procurement capability; war materiel requirement; war reserve materiel requirement; war reserve stock(s).**

war reserve stock(s)—*(DOD)* That portion of total materiel assets which is designated to satisfy the war reserve materiel requirement.

war reserve stocks for allies—*(DOD)* A Department of Defense program to have the Services procure or retain in their inventories those minimum stockpiles of materiel such as munitions, equipment, and combat essential consumables to ensure support for selected allied forces in time of war, until future in-country production and external resupply can meet the estimated combat consumption.

wartime load—*(DOD, NATO)* The maximum quantity of supplies of all kinds which a ship can carry. The composition of the load is prescribed by proper authority. See also **combat load.**

wartime manpower planning system—*(DOD)* A standardized DOD-wide procedure, structure, and data base for computing, compiling, projecting, and portraying the time-phased wartime manpower requirements, demand, and supply of the DOD components. Also called **WARMAPS.** See also **S-day.** *(NATO:* See also **designation of days and hours.**)

wartime reserve mode—*(DOD)* An intentional change in observable electromagnetic emitter parameters or operational procedures intended to reduce the effectiveness of electronic warfare equipment or other detection, classification, and support activities of opposing forces. These modes are deliberately held in reserve for wartime or emergency use and are seldom if ever intercepted or observed prior to such use. Also called **WARM**.

watching mine—*(DOD, NATO)* In naval mine warfare, a mine secured to its mooring but showing on the surface, possibly only in certain tidal conditions. See also **floating mine; mine.**

water suit—*(DOD, IADB)* A G-suit in which water is used in the interlining thereby automatically approximating the required hydrostatic pressure-graident under G forces. See also **pressure suit.**

water terminal—See **alternate water terminal; major water terminal; secondary water terminal; port.**

wave—*(DOD, NATO, IADB)* A formation of forces, landing ships, craft, amphibious vehicles or aircraft, required to beach or land about the same time. Can be classified as to type, function or order as shown: **a.** Assault wave; **b.** Boat wave; **c.** Helicopter wave; **d.** Numbered wave; **e.** On-call wave; **f.** Scheduled wave.

wave-off—See **overshoot.**

way point—*(DOD)* In air operations, a point or a series of points in space to which an aircraft may be vectored.

weapon and payload identification—*(DOD)* 1. The determination of the type of weapon being used in an attack. 2. The discrimination of a re-entry vehicle from penetration aids being utilized with the re-entry vehicle. See also **attack assessment.**

weapon debris (nuclear)—*(DOD, NATO, IADB)* The residue of a nuclear weapon after it has exploded; that is, materials used for the casing and other components of the weapon, plus unexpended plutonium or uranium, together with fission products.

weapon engagement zone—*(DOD, NATO)* In air defense, airspace of defined dimensions within which the responsibility for engagement normally rests with a particular weapon system. Also called **fighter engagement zone; missile engagement zone; short range air defense engagement zone.**

weapons assignment—*(DOD, NATO, IADB)* In air defense, the process by which weapons are assigned to individual air weapons controllers for use in accomplishing an assigned mission.

weapons free—*(DOD, NATO)* In air defense, a weapon control status used to indicate that weapons systems may be fired at any target not positively identified as friendly. See also **weapons hold; weapons tight.**

weapons hold—*(DOD, NATO)* In air defense, a weapon control status used to indicate that weapons systems may be fired only in self-defense or in response to a formal order. See also **weapons free; weapons tight.**

weapons of mass destruction—*(DOD, IADB)* In arms control usage, weapons that are capable of a high order of destruction and/or of being used in such a manner as to destroy large numbers of people. Can be nuclear, chemical, biological, and radiological weapons, but excludes the means of transporting or propelling the weapon where such means is a separable and divisible part of the weapon.

weapons readiness state—*(DOD, IADB)* The degree of readiness of air defense weapons which can become airborne or be launched to carry out an assigned task. Weapons readiness states are expressed in numbers of weapons and numbers of minutes. Weapon readiness states are defined as follows:

391

a. **2 minutes**—Weapons can be launched within two minutes.

b. **5 minutes**—Weapons can be launched within five minutes.

c. **15 minutes**—Weapons can be launched within fifteen minutes.

d. **30 minutes**—Weapons can be launched within thirty minutes.

e. **1 hour**—Weapons can be launched within one hour.

f. **3 hours**—Weapons can be launched within three hours.

g. **released**—Weapons are released from defense commitment for a specified period of time.

weapons recommendation sheet—*(DOD, NATO, IADB)* A sheet or chart which defines the intention of the attack, and recommends the nature of weapons, and resulting damage expected, tonnage, fuzing, spacing, desired mean points of impact, and intervals of reattack.

weapons state of readiness—See **weapons readiness state.**

weapons system—*(IADB)* A weapon and those components required for its operation. (The term is not precise unless specific parameters are established.)

weapons tight—*(DOD, NATO)* In air defense, a weapon control status used to indicate that weapons systems may be fired only at targets identified as hostile. See also **weapons free; weapons hold.**

weapon system—*(DOD, NATO)* A delivery vehicle and weapon combination including all related equipment, materials, services and personnel required so that the system becomes self-sufficient in its intended operational environment.

weapon system employment concept—*(DOD, NATO)* A description in broad terms, based on established outline characteristics, of the application of a particular equipment or weapon system within the framework of tactical concept and future doctrines.

weapon system manager—See **system manager.**

weapon-target line—*(DOD, IADB)* An imaginary straight line from a weapon to a target.

weather central—*(DOD, IADB)* An organization which collects, collates, evaluates, and disseminates meteorological information in such manner that it becomes a principal source of such information for a given area.

weather forecast—*(DOD, IADB)* A prediction of weather conditions at a point, along a route, or within an area, for a specified period of time.

weather map—*(DOD, IADB)* A map showing the weather conditions prevailing, or predicted to prevail, over a considerable area. Usually, the map is based upon weather observations taken at the same time at a number of stations. See also **map.**

weather minimum—*(DOD, IADB)* The worst weather conditions under which aviation operations may be conducted under either visual or instrument flight rules. Usually prescribed by directives and standing operating procedures in terms of minimum ceiling, visibility, or specific hazards to flight.

weather (VAT B)—*(DOD, IADB)* Short form weather report, giving:

a. **V**—*Visibility* in miles.

b. **A**—*Amount* of clouds, in eights.

c. **T**—Height of cloud *top*, in thousands of feet.

d. **B**—Height of cloud *base*, in thousands of feet.

(The reply is a series of four numbers preceded by the word "weather." An unknown item is reported as "unknown.")

weight and balance sheet—*(DOD, NATO, IADB)* A sheet which records the distribution of weight in an aircraft and shows the center of gravity of an aircraft at takeoff and landing.

well—*(DOD)* As used in air intercept, a code meaning, "Equipment indicated is operating efficiently."

what luck—*(DOD)* As used in air intercept, a code meaning, "What are/were the results of assigned mission?"

what state—*(DOD)* As used in air intercept, a code meaning, "Report amount of fuel, ammunition, and oxygen remaining."

what's up—*(DOD)* As used in air intercept, a code meaning, "Is anything the matter?"

wheelbase—*(DOD, NATO, IADB)* The distance between the centers of two consecutive wheels. In the case of vehicles with more than two axles or equivalent systems, the successive wheelbases are all given in the order front to rear of the vehicle.

wheel load capacity—*(DOD, IADB)* The capacity of airfield runways, taxiways, parking areas, or roadways to bear the pressures exerted by aircraft or vehicles in a gross weight static configuration.

which transponder—*(DOD)* A code meaning report type of transponder fitted—Identification Friend or Foe, Air Traffic Control Radar Beacon System, or Secondary Surveillance Radar.

white forces—*(DOD, NATO)* A term used in reporting of intelligence on Warsaw Pact exercises, to denote those units representing opposing forces during such exercises. See also force(s).

whiteout—*(DOD, NATO, IADB)* Loss of orientation with respect to the horizon caused by sun reflecting on snow and overcast sky.

white propaganda—*(DOD, I, IADB)* Propaganda disseminated and acknowledged by the sponsor or by an accredited agency thereof. See also propaganda.

width of sheaf—*(DOD, IADB)* Lateral interval between center of flank bursts or impacts. The comparable naval gunfire term is deflection pattern.

wild weasel—*(DOD, NATO)* An aircraft specially modified to identify, locate, and physically suppress or destroy ground based enemy air defense systems that employ sensors radiating electromagnetic energy.

will not fire—*(DOD)* A term sent to the spotter or other requesting agency to indicate that the target will not be engaged by the fire support ship.

Wilson cloud—See condensation cloud.

window—See chaff.

wind shear—*(DOD)* A change of wind direction and magnitude.

wind velocity—*(DOD, NATO)* The horizontal direction and speed of air motion.

wing—*(DOD)* 1. An Air Force unit composed normally of one primary mission group and the necessary supporting organizations, i.e., organizations designed to render supply, maintenance, hospitalization, and other services required by the primary mission groups. Primary mission groups may be functional, such as combat, training, transport, or service. 2. A fleet air wing is the basic organizational and administrative unit for naval-, land-, and tender-based aviation. Such wings are mobile units to which are assigned aircraft squadrons and tenders for administrative control. 3. A balanced Marine Corps task orgnization of aircraft groups/squadrons together with appropriate command, air control, administrative, service, and maintenance units. A standard Marine Corps aircraft wing contains the aviation elements normally required for the air support of a Marine division. 4. A flank unit; that part of a military force to the right or left of the main body.

wingman—(DOD) An aviator subordinate to and in support of the designated section leader; also, the aircraft flown in this role.

wingman—(NATO) A pilot flying subordinate to and in support of his designated leader; also, the aircraft flown in this role.

withdrawal operation—(DOD, NATO, IADB) A planned operation in which a force in contact disengages from an enemy force.

withhold (nuclear)—(DOD, IADB) The limiting of authority to employ nuclear weapons by denying their use within specified geographical areas or certain countries.

wooden bomb—(DOD) A concept which pictures a weapon as being completely reliable and having an infinite shelf life while at the same time requiring no special handling, storage or surveillance.

working anchorage—(DOD, NATO, IADB) An anchorage where ships lie to discharge cargoes overside to coasters or lighters. See also **emergency anchorage.**

working capital fund—(DOD) A revolving fund established to finance inventories of supplies and other stores, or to provide working capital for industrial-type activities.

work order—(DOD) A specific or blanket authorization to perform certain work—usually broader in scope than a job order. It is sometimes used synonymously with job order.

world geographic reference system—See georef.

wounded—See seriously wounded; slightly wounded. See also battle casualty.

wounded in action—(DOD, NATO, IADB) A battle casualty other than "killed in action" who has incurred an injury due to an external agent or cause. The term encompasses all kinds of wounds and other injuries incurred in action, whether there is a piercing of the body, as in a penetrating or perforated wound, or none, as in the contused wound; all fractures, burns, blast concussions, all effects of biological and chemical warfare agents, the effects of exposure to ionizing radiation or any other destructive weapon or agent.

wreckage locator chart—(DOD) A chart indicating the geographic location of all known aircraft wreckage sites, and all known vessel wrecks which show above low water or which can be seen from the air. It consists of a visual plot of each wreckage, numbered in chronological order, and cross referenced with a wreckage locator file containing all pertinent data concerning the wreckage.

wrong—(DOD) A proword meaning, "Your last transmission was incorrect, the correct version is _____."

X

x-axis—*(DOD, IADB)* A horizontal axis in a system of rectangular coordinates; that line on which distances to the right or left (east or west) of the reference line are marked, especially on a map, chart, or graph.

X-scale—*(DOD, NATO)* On an oblique photograph, the scale along a line parallel to the true horizon.

Y

yaw—*(DOD, NATO)* 1. The rotation of an aircraft, ship or missile about its vertical axis so as to cause the longitudinal axis of the aircraft, ship or missile to deviate from the flight line or heading in its horizontal plane. 2. The rotation of a camera or a photograph coordinate system about either the photograph z-axis or the exterior z-axis. 3. Angle between the longitudinal axis of a projectile at any moment and the tangent to the trajectory in the corresponding point of flight of the projectile.

y-axis—*(DOD, IADB)* A vertical axis in a system of rectangular coordinates; that line on which distances above or below (north or south) the reference line are marked, especially on a map, chart or graph.

yield—See **nuclear yields.**

Y-scale—*(DOD, NATO)* On an oblique photograph, the scale along the line of the principal vertical, or any other line inherent or plotted, which, on the ground, is parallel to the principal vertical.

Z

zero-length launching—*(DOD, NATO, IADB)* A technique in which the first motion of the missile or aircraft removes it from the launcher.

zero point—*(DOD, IADB)* The location of the center of a burst of a nuclear weapon at the instant of detonation. The zero point may be in the air, or on or beneath the surface of land or water, dependent upon the type of burst, and it is thus to be distinguished from ground zero.

zippers—*(DOD)* Target dawn and dusk combat air patrol.

Z marker beacon—*(DOD, NATO)* A type of radio beacon, the emissions of which radiate in a vertical cone shaped pattern.

zone—See **air defense identification zone; air surface zone; combat zone; communications zone; control zone; dead zone; demilitarized zone; drop zone; landing zone; rupture zone; safety zone.** See also **area.**

Z marker beacon—*(IADB)* Equipment identical with the fan marker except that it is installed as part of a four-course radio range at the intersection of the four range legs, and radiates vertically to indicate to aircraft when they pass directly over the range station. It is usually not keyed for identification. Also known as cone of silence marker. See also **beacon.**

zone fire—*(DOD)* Artillery or mortar fires that are delivered in a constant direction at several quadrant elevations. See also **fire.**

zone of action—*(DOD, NATO, IADB)* A tactical subdivision of a larger area, the responsibility for which is assigned to a tactical unit; generally applied to offensive action. See also **sector.**

zone of fire—*(DOD, IADB)* An area within which a designated ground unit or fire support ship delivers, or is prepared to deliver, fire support. Fire may or may not be observed. See also **contingent zone of fire.**

zone I (nuclear)—*(DOD, IADB)* A circular area, determined by using minimum safe distance I as the radius and the desired ground zero as the center, from which all armed forces are evacuated. If evacuation is not possible or if a commander elects a higher degree of risk, maximum protective measures will be required.

zone II (nuclear)—*(DOD, IADB)* A circular area (less zone I), determined by using minimum safe distance II as the radius and the desired ground zero as the center, in which all personnel require maximum protection. Maximum protection denotes that armed forces personnel are in "buttoned up" tanks or crouched in foxholes with improvised overhead shielding.

zone III (nuclear)—*(DOD, IADB)* A circular area (less zones I and II), determined by using minimum safe distance III as the radius and the desired ground zero as the center, in which all personnel require minimum protection. Minimum protection denotes that armed forces personnel are prone on open ground with all skin areas covered and with an overall thermal protection at least equal to that provided by a two-layer uniform.

Z-scale—*(DOD, NATO, IADB)* On an oblique photograph, the scale used in calculating the height of an object. Also the name given to this method of height determination.

zulu time—*(DOD, NATO)* Greenwich Mean Time.

APPENDIX A: DIRECTORY OF DEPARTMENTS, AGENCIES, AND FACILITIES OF THE U.S. DEPARTMENT OF DEFENSE AND U.S. COAST GUARD

DEPARTMENT OF DEFENSE

The Pentagon, Washington, DC 20301–1155
Phone, 202–545–6700

The Department of Defense is responsible for providing the military forces needed to deter war and protect the security of our country.

The major elements of these forces are the Army, Navy, Marine Corps, and Air Force, consisting of about 2.2 million men and women on active duty. Of these, some 515,000—including about 70,000 on ships at sea—are serving outside the United States. They are backed, in case of emergency, by the 2.5 million members of the reserve components. In addition, there are about 1.2 million civilian employees in the Defense Department.

Under the President, who is also Commander in Chief, the Secretary of Defense exercises direction, authority, and control over the Department, which includes the separately organized military departments of Army, Navy, and Air Force, the Joint Chiefs of Staff providing military advice, the unified and specified combatant commands, and various defense agencies established for specific purposes.

Every State in the Union has some defense activities. Central headquarters of the Department is at the Pentagon, the "world's largest office building."

The Department of Defense (DOD) is the successor agency to the National Military Establishment created by the National Security Act of 1947 (61 Stat. 495). It was established as an executive department of the Government by the National Security Act Amendments of 1949, with the Secretary of Defense as its head (63 Stat. 578; 5 U.S.C. 101). Since that time, major amendments have been made to the act by Reorganization Plan 6 of 1953, effective June 30, 1953, and the Department of Defense Reorganization Act of 1958 (67 Stat. 638; 72 Stat. 514). The act of October 21, 1977 (91 Stat. 1172), provided for the establishment of the two positions of Under Secretary of Defense for Policy and Under Secretary of Defense for Research and Engineering.

The Inspector General Act of 1978 (92 Stat. 1101), as amended, provided for the establishment of the Inspector General within the Department of Defense, effective May 2, 1983.

The Department of Defense Authorization Act, 1984 (97 Stat. 614), provided for the establishment of the following positions: Director of Operational Test and Evaluation, Assistant Secretary of Defense (Reserve Affairs), Assistant Secretary of Defense (Command, Control, Communications, and Intelligence), Assistant Secretary of Defense (Development and Support), and Assistant Secretary of Defense (Research and Technology).

In February 1985, under authority of 10 U.S.C. 136, the Assistant Secretary of Defense (Development and Support) was disestablished, and the Assistant

Secretary of Defense (Acquisition and Logistics) was established.

Structure

The Department of Defense includes the Office of the Secretary of Defense and the Organization of the Joint Chiefs of Staff, the Armed Forces Policy Council, the military departments and the military services within those departments, the unified and specified commands, and such other agencies as the Secretary of Defense establishes to meet specific requirements.

In providing immediate staff assistance and advice to the Secretary of Defense, the Office of the Secretary of Defense and the Organization of the Joint Chiefs of Staff, though separately identified and organized, function in full coordination and cooperation.

The Office of the Secretary of Defense includes the offices of the Deputy Secretary of Defense, the Executive Secretary of the Department of Defense, the Assistant to the Secretary and the Deputy Secretary of Defense, the Under Secretary of Defense for Policy, the Under Secretary of Defense for Research and Engineering, 11 Assistant Secretaries of Defense, the General Counsel, the Director of Operational Test and Evaluation, the Director for Program Analysis and Evaluation, the Inspector General, and such other staff offices as the Secretary of Defense establishes to assist him in carrying out his duties and responsibilities. The heads of these offices are civilian staff advisers to the Secretary and perform such functions as he assigns to them.

The Joint Chiefs of Staff are the principal military advisers to the Secretary of Defense as well as the President and the National Security Council. Each member of the Joint Chiefs of Staff, other than the Chairman, is the senior military officer of his respective service and is responsible for keeping the Secretary of his military department fully informed on matters considered or acted upon by the Joint Chiefs of Staff.

Each military department (the Department of the Navy includes naval aviation and the United States Marine Corps) is separately organized under its own Secretary and functions under the direction, authority, and control of the Secretary of Defense. The Secretary of a military department is responsible to the Secretary of Defense for the operation of his department as well as its efficiency. Orders to the military departments are issued through the Secretaries of these departments, or their designees, by the Secretary of Defense or under authority specifically delegated in writing by the Secretary of Defense or provided by law.

Commanders of unified and specified commands are responsible to the President and the Secretary of Defense for the accomplishments of the military missions assigned to them. The chain of command runs from the President to the Secretary of Defense and through the Joint Chiefs of Staff to the commanders of unified and specified commands. Orders to such commanders are issued by the President or the Secretary of Defense, or by the Joint Chiefs of Staff by authority and direction of the Secretary of Defense. These commanders have full operational command over all forces assigned to them.

The Armed Forces Policy Council (AFPC) advises the Secretary of Defense on matters of broad policy relating to the Armed Forces and such other matters as the Secretary may direct. Its members report regularly on important matters that are of interest to the Department of Defense. In addition to the members identified below, such other officials of the Department of Defense and other departments and agencies in the

404

executive branch as may be designated by the Secretary of Defense are invited to attend appropriate meetings of the AFPC. Council membership is as follows: Secretary of Defense, Chairman; Deputy Secretary of Defense; Secretaries of the military departments; Chairman, Joint Chiefs of Staff; Under Secretaries of Defense; Chief of Staff, Army; Chief of Naval Operations; Chief of Staff, Air Force; and Commandant, Marine Corps.

Office of the Secretary of Defense

The Department of Defense is administered by the Secretary of Defense, who is the principal assistant to the President in all matters relating to the Department of Defense. Under the direction of the President, and subject to the provisions of the National Security Act of 1947, as amended, the Secretary of Defense exercises control over the Department of Defense. He is appointed from civil life by the President, with the advice and consent of the Senate. He is assisted in the administration of the Department by a Deputy Secretary of Defense who acts for, and exercises the powers of, the Secretary of Defense and is responsible for the supervision and coordination of the activities of the Department of Defense as directed by the Secretary of Defense.

Executive Secretary of the Department of Defense   The Executive Secretary supports the Secretary and Deputy Secretary by performing the following duties: coordinates DOD participation in the interagency process involving national security management, defense policy, programs, and resources for DOD and with the White House, the National Security Council, the State Department, the Central Intelligence Agency, and other agencies, as appropriate; acts as the Secretariat for both the Armed Forces Policy Council (AFPC) and the Secretary's Performance Review Board; performs liaison with the White House Military Office, including Presidential

support activities; serves as the DOD point of contact for intergovernmental affairs; processes requests for DOD support from the White House and Federal departments and agencies; processes special air mission transportation requests for the Office of the Secretary of Defense and non-DOD agencies; manages and controls all correspondence, information, and action documents for the Secretary and Deputy Secretary; and performs any special project directed by either the Secretary or Deputy Secretary.

Assistant to the Secretary and Deputy Secretary of Defense   The Assistant to the Secretary and Deputy Secretary of Defense staffs noncareer positions throughout DOD; approves staffing for DOD boards and committees; recommends candidates for Presidential boards and committees; approves appointments for DOD headquarters-level experts and consultants; acts as the noncareer DOD contact with the Office of the Assistant to the President for Intergovernmental Affairs; and serves as primary DOD liaison with the White House Personnel Office in dealing with such matters.

Acquisition and Logistics   The Assistant Secretary of Defense (Acquisition and Logistics) is the principal staff assistant and adviser to the Secretary of Defense for management of DOD production procurement, development of procurement regulations, career management of the procurement work force, logistics, installations, associated support functions, and other related matters. The Assistant Secretary participates in the total weapon system acquisition process and specifically chairs the Defense Acquisition Review Council (DSARC) Milestone III review. The Assistant Secretary develops policies, conducts analyses, provides advice, makes recommendations, and issues guidance on DOD plans and programs and requirements determination; develops systems and standards for the administration and management of approved DOD plans and programs; develops plans, programs, and actions to ensure adherence to DOD policies and national security objectives; reviews and evaluates DOD component plans and programs to ensure adherence to approved policies and standards; participates in planning, programming, budgeting, and followup activities related to the Assistant Secretary's responsibilities; promotes coordination, cooperation, and mutual understanding of all matters related to assigned activities, both inside and outside of the Department of Defense, including oversight and policy formulation for international logistics and military construction agreements and implementation of coproduction agreements with North Atlantic Treaty Organization (NATO) allies and other friendly nations in coordination with the Under Secretary of Defense for Policy and the Under Secretary of Defense for Research and Engineering; serves as the primary focal point and principal spokesman and serves on boards, committees, and other groups pertaining to assigned functional areas; develops, coordinates, and maintains regulations as necessary and appropriate to implement the procurement regulatory responsibilities of the Secretary of

Defense. The Assistant Secretary also exercises direction, authority, and control over the Defense Logistics Agency and the Armed Forces Pest Management Board.

Command, Control, Communications and Intelligence   The Assistant Secretary of Defense (Command, Control, Communications and Intelligence (C^3I)) is the principal adviser and assistant to the Secretary of Defense for DOD telecommunications, command, control, and intelligence matters, including related warning, electronic combat, special operations, and reconnaissance activities. The Assistant Secretary serves as the principal DOD focus for staff coordination on all matters concerning these areas and is the principal DOD official responsible for preparing and defending the Department's C^3I program before the Congress. The Assistant Secretary exercises direction, authority, and control over the Defense Mapping Agency, the Defense Communications Agency, the Joint Tactical C^3 Agency, and primary staff responsibility over the Defense Intelligence Agency and the National Security Agency/Central Security Service.

Comptroller   This functional area includes advice and assistance to the Secretary of Defense and Defense components in the performance of the Secretary's programming, budgeting, fiscal management, organizational and management planning, and administrative functions and the design and installation of resource management systems throughout the Department of Defense. Resource management information is collected, analyzed, and reported for the Office of Management and Budget, the Congress, the General Accounting Office, and other agencies outside the Department of Defense. Supervision, direction, and review of the preparation and execution of the Defense budget is provided, and services pertaining to automatic data processing and central data services are administered. The Comptroller provides assistance in identifying, diagnosing, and correcting organizational or management problems. The Assistant Secretary of Defense (Comptroller) exercises direction, authority, and control over the Defense Contract Audit Agency and the Washington Headquarters Services (WHS) through the Deputy Assistant Secretary of Defense (Administration), who has collateral responsibility as Director, WHS.

Health Affairs The Assistant Secretary of Defense (Health Affairs) is responsible for Department of Defense health matters, including preventive medicine, medical readiness, health care delivery, drug and alcohol abuse prevention, and procurement, development, and retention of medical personnel. The Assistant Secretary is required to develop policies, provide advice, make recommendations, and issue guidance on DOD plans and programs; develop systems, standards, and procedures for the administration and management of approved plans and programs; initiate programs and actions to ensure that all DOD health programs adhere to Department policies and national health objectives; promote coordination, cooperation, and mutual understanding within DOD and between the Department and other Federal agencies and the civilian community; serve on health-related boards, committees, and other groups; establish requirements for DOD research and development programs in medical fields and keep abreast of technical developments to provide for an orderly transition to operational status; and establish requirements and standards for medical facilities and materiel acquisition programs. The Assistant Secretary also exercises direction, authority, and control

over the Office of the Civilian Health and Medical Program of the Uniformed Services (OCHAMPUS) and is Director of the Defense Medical Support Activity (DMSA), consisting of the Defense Medical Facilities Office (DMFO) and the Defense Medical Systems Support Center (DMSSC), which includes both the Tri-Service Medical Information System (TRIMIS) and the Defense Enrollment Eligibility Reporting System (DEERS).

Legislative Affairs This functional area includes maintenance of direct liaison with the Congress, the Executive Office of the President, and other Government agencies with regard to legislative investigations and other pertinent matters affecting the relations of the Department of Defense with the Congress; advice and assistance to the Secretary of Defense and other officials of the Department of Defense on congressional Control, Communications and Intelligence (C^3I)) is the principal adviser and assistant to the Secretary of Defense for DOD telecommunications, command, control, and intelligence matters, including related warning, electronic combat, special operations, and reconnaissance activities. The Assistant Secretary serves as the principal DOD focus for staff coordination on all matters concerning these areas and is the principal DOD official responsible for preparing and defending the Department's C^3I program before the Congress. The Assistant Secretary exercises direction, authority, and control over the Defense Mapping Agency, the Defense Communications Agency, the Joint Tactical C^3 Agency, and primary staff responsibility over the Defense Intelligence Agency and the National Security Agency/Central Security Service.

Comptroller This functional area includes advice and assistance to the Secretary of Defense and Defense components in the performance of the

Secretary's programming, budgeting, fiscal management, organizational and management planning, and administrative functions and the design and installation of resource management systems throughout the Department of Defense. Resource management information is collected, analyzed, and reported for the Office of Management and Budget, the Congress, the General Accounting Office, and other agencies outside the Department of Defense. Supervision, direction, and review of the preparation and execution of the Defense budget is provided, and services pertaining to automatic data processing and central data services are administered. The Comptroller provides assistance in identifying, diagnosing, and correcting organizational or management problems. The Assistant Secretary of Defense (Comptroller) exercises direction, authority, and control over the Defense Contract Audit Agency and the Washington Headquarters Services (WHS) through the Deputy Assistant Secretary of Defense (Administration), who has collateral responsibility as Director, WHS.

Health Affairs The Assistant Secretary of Defense (Health Affairs) is responsible for Department of Defense health matters, including preventive medicine, medical readiness, health care delivery, drug and alcohol abuse prevention, and procurement, development, and retention of medical personnel. The Assistant Secretary is required to develop policies, provide advice, make recommendations, and issue guidance on DOD plans and programs; develop systems, standards, and procedures for the administration and management of approved plans and programs; initiate programs and actions to ensure that all DOD health programs adhere to Department policies and national health objectives; promote coordination, cooperation, and mutual understanding within DOD and between the Department and other Federal agencies and the civilian community; serve on health-related boards, committees, and other groups; establish requirements for DOD research and development programs in medical fields and keep abreast of technical developments to provide for an orderly transition to operational status; and establish requirements and standards for medical facilities and materiel acquisition programs. The Assistant Secretary also exercises direction, authority, and control over the Office of the Civilian Health and Medical Program of the Uniformed Services (OCHAMPUS) and is Director of the Defense Medical Support Activity (DMSA), consisting of the Defense Medical Facilities Office (DMFO) and the Defense Medical Systems Support Center (DMSSC), which includes both the Tri-Service Medical Information System (TRIMIS) and the Defense Enrollment Eligibility Reporting System (DEERS).

Legislative Affairs This functional area includes maintenance of direct liaison with the Congress, the Executive Office of the President, and other Government agencies with regard to legislative investigations and other pertinent matters affecting the relations of the Department of Defense with the Congress; advice and assistance to the Secretary of Defense and other officials of the Department of Defense on congressional preparedness; counterintelligence; outer space; personnel, information, physical, and industrial security; international information and communications; psychological operations; and investigative program management and resource control. The Deputy Under Secretary also develops organization and procedures for the discharge of Office of the Secretary of Defense functions in national emergencies, and provides support to DOD and other U.S.

Government or State agencies on civil defense and related matters.

The Deputy Under Secretary for Trade Security Policy serves as the focal point within DOD for the planning and management of all international trade and technology matters of Defense interest and their impact upon U.S. national security. The Deputy Under Secretary also has primary responsibility within the policy cluster for analysis of the interaction of international economic and export control factors affecting U.S. national security and the subsequent development, preparation, and coordination of related DOD positions, plans, procedures, and policy recommendations. He plans, directs, and coordinates a program of policy research pertaining to technology security. Specific topics include international trade in defense-related commodities and technologies, the impact of such trade on U.S. security interests, East-West and free world trade, munitions control, technical information control, and the international aspects of mobilization policy. The Deputy Under Secretary also formulates and recommends policy positions on East-West and free world trade and technology transfer cases reviewed by the multilateral Coordinating Committee (COCOM), reviews munitions license applications for the Under Secretary, and represents DOD at interagency meetings and in discussions with representatives of foreign governments.

The Deputy Under Secretary of Defense for Planning and Resources serves as the principal deputy and adviser to the Under Secretary on all resource- and acquisition-related matters that arise within the PPB and systems acquisition processes. The Deputy Under Secretary manages day-to-day operations of the Defense guidance and exercises direction, authority, and control over the Defense guidance staff; serves as principal deputy and adviser to the Under Secretary on all international financial and economic policy matters of Defense interest, with special emphasis on NATO and other European and Soviet affairs and their impact on U.S. national security. He is responsible for directing the development and coordination of DOD policies, positions, plans, and procedures that relate to the impact of OECD, European, and East-West international financial and economic policy matters on U.S. security interests, mobilization capability, and related interests of U.S. allies. The Deputy Under Secretary additionally is designated to take the overall lead within Defense in coordinating the DOD's participation in interagency review of the national security aspects of U.S. international trade, economic, and financial policies.

International Security Affairs   The Assistant Secretary of Defense for International Security Affairs provides advice and recommends policies, formulates programs, develops plans, and issues guidance to DOD components regarding political-military activities related to international affairs, excluding NATO, other European countries, and the USSR. Oversight is provided for DOD activities relating to law of the sea. The Assistant Secretary provides supervision in the areas of security assistance (i.e., foreign military sales and military assistance programs), Military Assistance Advisory Groups and Missions, and the negotiation and monitoring of agreements with foreign governments, excluding NATO, other European countries, and the USSR. In the area of international economic and energy affairs, the Assistant Secretary provides advice and recommends policies, formulates programs, develops plans, and issues guidance to DOD components. The Assistant Secretary formulates plans and policy related to general purpose forces, non-European regional security requirements, and related budget considerations. The Assistant Secretary provides defense policy oversight on matters pertaining to POW/MIA affairs and acts as principal adviser to the Secretary of Defense on such matters.

International Security Policy The Assistant Secretary of Defense for International Security Policy serves as the focal point for policy planning on strategic international security matters concerning European and NATO affairs, strategic and theater nuclear force planning, and all matters concerning nuclear and conventional, bilateral and multilateral negotiations on arms reductions, defense and space, and East-West security negotiations. The Assistant Secretary formulates policy related to strategic offensive and defensive forces, theater nuclear matters and capabilities, European conventional defense, and the relationship between strategic and theater force planning and budgets. Responsibilities also include implementing policy on nuclear nonproliferation matters and other treaties and agreements, as well as oversight of DOD activities related to the North Atlantic Treaty Organization and bilateral issues with European countries. He additionally oversees the formulation of East-West economic policy, including East-West trade, technology transfer and security issues, including strategic trade and export licensing of dual-use items controlled for national security reasons, and munitions items, and covering issues affecting the defense industrial mobilization base.

Net Assessment The Director of Net Assessment is under the direction, authority, and control of the Under Secretary of Defense for Policy, but maintains a direct channel to the

Secretary of Defense while keeping the Under Secretary informed. The Director formulates, plans, conducts, and prepares net assessments for the Secretary of Defense.

Program Analysis and Evaluation With the direction of the Secretary of Defense, this staff formulates the force planning, fiscal, programming, and policy guidance upon which DOD force planning and program projections are to be based. From the Secretary's guidance the staff defines the Defense objectives, policies, and fiscal constraints to be used as the basis for force planning and for developing changes to the Defense program. The staff analyzes and evaluates military forces, weapons systems, and equipment in relation to projected threats, U.S. objectives, resource constraints, and priorities established by the Secretary of Defense. This staff also identifies issues and analyzes and evaluates alternative programs in terms of how well the programs meet objectives; proposes, guides, monitors, and evaluates studies and analyses by other DOD components; and conducts or participates in special studies as directed by the Secretary of Defense.

Public Affairs This functional area includes Defense public and internal information and audiovisual activities and community relations. Liaison is maintained with and assistance is provided to information media and national and civic organizations with respect to matters relating to activities of the Department of Defense. Approvals are required for military participation in public exhibitions, demonstrations, and ceremonies of national or international significance. The Assistant Secretary of Defense (Public Affairs) ensures a free flow of news and information to the media, appropriate forums, and the American people, limited only by national security constraints and statutory considerations. The Assistant Secretary exercises direction, authority, and control over the Defense Information Services Activity and the American Forces Information Service.

Research and Engineering   The Under Secretary of Defense for Research and Engineering is the principal adviser and assistant to the Secretary of Defense for DOD scientific and technical matters; basic and applied research; environmental services; and development of weapons systems. The Under Secretary has responsibility for research, development, and development testing of all DOD weapons systems. The Under Secretary exercises direction, authority, and control over the Assistant Secretary of Defense (Research and Technology), the Assistant to the Secretary of Defense (Atomic Energy), the Defense Advanced Research Projects Agency, the Defense Nuclear Agency, and the Defense Systems Management College.

Reserve Affairs   The Assistant Secretary of Defense (Reserve Affairs) is responsible for exercising overall supervision of Reserve component matters in the Department of Defense: manpower, personnel, and compensation; research, studies, and evaluation; operations, training, and force structure; mobilization, demobilization, and reconstitution; force mix; weapons systems, equipment, and materiel; construction, installations, and facilities; and readiness and sustainability. In addition, the Assistant Secretary exercises direction, authority, and control over the National Committee for Employer Support of the Guard and Reserve and provides administrative staff support to the Reserve Forces Policy Board.

General Counsel   The General Counsel is the chief legal officer of the Department of Defense with responsibility for all legal services performed within or involving the Department of Defense. The General Counsel is responsible for the preparation and processing of legislation, executive orders and proclamations, and reports and comments thereon. In addition, the General Counsel serves as Director of the Defense Legal Services Agency, providing legal advice and service for the Office of the Secretary of Defense and its field activities, and the Defense agencies.

Operational Test and Evaluation   The Director of Operational Test and Evaluation serves as the principal staff assistant and adviser to the Secretary of Defense on operational test and evaluation (OT&E) in the Department of Defense and the principal OT&E official within the senior management of DOD. The Director of OT&E prescribes policies and procedures for the conduct of OT&E within DOD; provides advice and makes recommendations to the Secretary of Defense and issues guidance to and consults with the heads of DOD components with respect to OT&E in the Department in general, and to specific OT&E programs to be conducted in connection with a major defense acquisition program; monitors and reviews all OT&E programs in DOD to ensure adherence to approved policies and standards; and reviews and makes recommendations to the Secretary of Defense on all budgetary and financial matters relating to OT&E, including operational test facilities and equipment. The Director approves the adequacy of service operational test plans for major programs prior to execution and provides to the Secretary of Defense and Congress an assessment of the operational effectiveness and suitability of the system before it proceeds beyond a low rate of production.

Inspector General of the Department of Defense   The Inspector General serves as an independent and objective

411

official in the Department of Defense who is responsible for conducting, supervising, monitoring, and initiating audits, investigations, and inspections relating to programs and operations of the Department of Defense. The Inspector General provides leadership and coordination and recommends policies for activities designed to promote economy, efficiency, and effectiveness in the administration of, and to prevent and detect fraud and abuse in, such programs and operations. The Inspector General is also responsible for keeping the Secretary of Defense and the Congress fully and currently informed about problems and deficiencies relating to the administration of such programs and operations and the necessity for, and progress of, corrective action.

Intelligence Oversight The Assistant to the Secretary of Defense (Intelligence Oversight) conducts oversight inspections of DOD intelligence and counterintelligence activities to ensure legal compliance and standards of propriety; independently inspects as well as reviews results of additional inspections by the Inspectors General of the National Security Agency and Defense Intelligence Agency, and military service intelligence organizations; evaluates inquiries into allegations of questionable activities to ensure that investigations are rigorously and thoroughly accomplished and that appropriate corrective measures are implemented; reports jointly with the DOD General Counsel to the Secretary of Defense and the President's Intelligence Oversight Board (established under Executive Order 12334 of December 4, 1981) at least quarterly on any DOD intelligence activities of questionable legality or propriety and on significant oversight activities undertaken to ensure compliance with Executive Order 12333, "United States Intelligence Activities," and DOD policies.

Small and Disadvantaged Business Utilization (SADBU) Under the direction of the Secretary of Defense, SADBU administers Department responsibilities under the Small Business Act (92 Stat. 1760; 15 U.S.C. 631), as amended. The Director, SADBU, ensures that a fair share of Department procurements are placed with small businesses, small disadvantaged businesses, and women-owned small businesses; conducts surveillance reviews of selected Department contracting activities' small business programs as well as those of major Department prime contractors; establishes and reviews policies, procedures, and initiatives for inclusion in the Defense supplement to the Federal Acquisition Regulation for the improvement of Department small business and small disadvantaged business programs; manages the Department's labor surplus program; develops and reviews legislative initiatives for increased small business participation in Department procurements; and manages the small business research and development program.

Field Activities

American Forces Information Service
The American Forces Information Service (AFIS), established in 1977 under the supervision of the Assistant Secretary of Defense (Public Affairs), is responsible for the DOD internal information program and DOD visual information policy. The Armed Forces Radio and Television Service (AFRTS), the American Forces Press and Publications Service (AFPPS), and the AFRTS Broadcast Center (AFRTS-BC) function under the Director of AFIS. In addition, AFIS provides policy guidance and oversight for DOD

periodicals and pamphlets, *Stars and Stripes* newspapers, military command newspapers, the broadcast elements of the military departments, DOD audiovisual matters, and the Defense Information School (DINFOS).

(American Forces Information Service, Department of Defense, Room 210, 1735 N. Lynn Street, Arlington, VA 22209–2086. Phone, 202–696–5284)

Defense Information Services Activity

The Defense Information Services Activity (DISA) was established in 1985 under the policy guidance and operational direction of the Assistant Secretary of Defense (Public Affairs). DISA implements DOD policies and programs that pertain to the release of information to the American people. DISA functions include reviewing information intended for public release to ensure compliance with security policies; implementation of the Freedom of Information Act and the Federal Privacy Act programs within the Department of Defense; long-range coordination and planning of public schedules of senior Defense officials; providing editorial services to the Secretary of Defense and the Deputy Secretary of Defense; and serving as the DOD focal point for defense information and publications.

(Defense Information Services Activity, Office of the Assistant Secretary of Defense (Public Affairs), Washington, DC 20301-1400. Phone, 202–697–1180)

Department of Defense Dependents Schools

The Department of Defense Dependents Schools (DODDS) was established in 1974. Under the policy guidance of the Assistant Secretary of Defense (Force Management and Personnel), DODDS is charged with providing quality education, from kindergarten through grade twelve, to eligible minor dependents of military and civilian personnel of the Department of Defense stationed overseas. DODDS, in turn, advises the Assistant Secretary of Defense (Force Management and Personnel) on all matters pertaining to Dependents Schools.

(Department of Defense Dependents Schools, Room 152, Hoffman Building, Alexandria, VA 22331. Phone, 202–325–0188)

Office of Civilian Health and Medical Program of the Uniformed Services

The Office of Civilian Health and Medical Program of the Uniformed Services (OCHAMPUS) was established as a field activity in 1974 under the policy guidance and operational direction of the Assistant Secretary of Defense (Health Affairs). The mission of OCHAMPUS is to administer a civilian health and medical care program for retirees and the spouses and dependent children of active duty, retired, and deceased service members. Also included are spouses and dependent children of totally disabled veterans. OCHAMPUS also administers, for the Uniformed Services, a program for payment of emergency medical/dental services provided to active duty service members by civilian medical personnel.

(Office of Civilian Health and Medical Program of the Uniformed Services, Department of Defense, Denver, CO 80045. Phone, 303–361–8606)

Defense Medical Support Activity

The Defense Medical Support Activity is comprised of two principal elements: the Defense Medical Systems Support Center and the Defense Medical Facilities Office.

The Defense Medical Systems Support Center, under the policy guidance and operational direction of the Assistant Secretary of Defense (Health Affairs), provides control for both information management policy and systems policy within the military health systems arena.

The mission of the Defense Medical Systems Support Center is to ensure that information systems and related communications function efficiently, are supportive of DOD functional requirements for both peacetime and contingency operations, and are integrated to support a planned systems architecture. The four principal subdivisions are the Tri-Service Medical Information System (TRIMIS); the Defense Enrollment Eligibility Reporting System (DEERS); the Office of Mobilization Support and Communications; and the Management Information Support Directorate.

(Defense Medical Systems Support Center, Department of Defense, Suite 1511, 3 Skyline Place, 5201 Leesburg Pike, Falls Church, VA 22041–3203. Phone, 703–756–2530)

The Defense Medical Facilities Office develops and maintains an integrated system for planning, programming, and budgeting for medical facility construction projects (which include construction, replacement, modification, modernization, and supporting facilities) throughout the Department of Defense and for managing the allocation of the financial resources approved for such projects.

(Defense Medical Systems Support Center, Department of Defense, Suite 737, 1717 H St. NW., Washington, DC 20419. Phone, 202–653–0080)

Defense Technology Security Administration

The Defense Technology Security Administration (DTSA) was established by the Deputy Secretary of Defense on May 10, 1985, as a field activity of the Department of Defense. DTSA represents a consolidation of technology security operating functions formerly assigned to USD (Policy) and USD (Research and Engineering) and is responsible for reviewing the international transfer of defense-related technology, goods, services, and munitions consistent with U.S. foreign policy and national security objectives.

(Defense Technology Security Administration, Department of Defense, Room 4C767, The Pentagon, Washington, DC 20301. Phone, 202–697–9347)

Office of Economic Adjustment

The Office of Economic Adjustment is responsible for planning and managing DOD economic adjustment programs and for assisting Federal, State, and local officials in cooperative efforts to alleviate any serious social and economic side effects resulting from major DOD realignments or other actions. The Office also supports the Secretary of Defense in his capacity as Chairperson of the Economic Adjustment Committee, an interagency group established by Executive Order 12049 of March 27, 1978, to coordinate Federal economic adjustment activities. In addition, the Director of the Office of Economic Adjustment also serves as the economic adjustment policy adviser on the staff of the Assistant Secretary of Defense (Force Management and Personnel).

(Office of Economic Adjustment, Department of Defense, Room 3D968, The Pentagon, Washington, DC 20301. Phone, 202–697–9155)

Washington Headquarters Services

Washington Headquarters Services (WHS) was established in 1977. The Deputy Assistant Secretary of Defense (Administration) serves in a dual capacity as the Director, WHS. The mission of WHS is to provide administrative and operational support to certain Department of Defense activities in the National Capital region. Such support includes budget and accounting, personnel management, office services, security, correspondence, directives and records management, travel, building administration, computer services, information and data systems, voting assistance program, and other administrative support as required.

(Washington Headquarters Services, Department of Defense, Room 3E843, The Pentagon, Washington, DC 20301. Phone, 202–695–4436)

Joint Tactical Command, Control, and Communications Agency   The Joint Tactical Command, Control, and Communications Agency (JTC³A) was established in July 1984 by combining assets of the Joint Tactical Communications Program (TRI-TAC) and the Joint Interoperability of the Tactical Command and Control Systems Program (JINTACCS). JTC³A is a joint field activity of the Department of Defense under the control of the Assistant Secretary of Defense for Command, Control, Communications and Intelligence. JTC³A also responds directly to the Joint Chiefs of Staff on policies, tactical operations matters, and C³ requirements of a joint and combined nature. The mission of the Agency is to ensure the interoperability of tactical command, control, and communications (C³) systems for joint or combined operations, including nonstrategic nuclear forces, through the development and maintenance of a joint architecture, interface standards, and interface definitions for tactical mobile C³ systems.

The Agency is manned in three geographic locations: Fort Monmouth, NJ; Washington, DC; and Fort Huachuca, AZ.

(Joint Tactical Command, Control, and Communications Agency, Department of Defense, Fort Monmouth, NJ 07703–5513. Phone, 201–532–7701).

Organization of the Joint Chiefs of Staff

Joint Chiefs of Staff

The Joint Chiefs of Staff (JCS) are the principal military advisers to the President, the National Security Council, and the Secretary of Defense. They constitute the immediate military staff of the Secretary of Defense, serving in the chain of command that extends from the President to the Secretary of Defense, through the Joint Chiefs of Staff, to the commanders of unified and specified commands.

Subject to the authority and direction of the President and the Secretary of Defense, the Joint Chiefs of Staff, in addition to such other duties as the President and the Secretary of Defense may direct, have the following responsibilities:

Preparation of strategic plans and provision for the strategic direction of the Armed Forces;

Preparation of integrated plans for military mobilization and integrated logistic plans;

Recommending to the Secretary of Defense the establishment and force structure of unified and specified commands and the assignment to the military departments of responsibility for providing support to such commands;

Review of plans and programs of commanders of unified and specified commands;

Review of major personnel, materiel, and logistic requirements of the Armed Forces in relation to strategic and logistic plans;

Establishment of doctrines for unified operations and training and for coordination of the military education of

415

members of the Armed Forces;

Providing the Secretary of Defense with statements of military requirements and strategic guidance for use in the development of budgets, foreign military aid programs, industrial mobilization plans, and programs of scientific research and development;

Recommending to the Secretary of Defense the assignment of primary responsibility for any function of the Armed Forces requiring such determination and the transfer, reassignment, abolition, or consolidation of such functions; and

Providing the United States representation on the Military Staff Committee of the United Nations, and when authorized, on other military staffs, boards, councils, and missions.

The Joint Chiefs of Staff consist of the Chairman of the Joint Chiefs of Staff; the Chief of Staff, United States Army; the Chief of Naval Operations; the Commandant of the Marine Corps; and the Chief of Staff, United States Air Force. The Joint Chiefs of Staff are assisted in the performance of their responsibilities by the Joint Staff and the other agencies of the Organization of the Joint Chiefs of Staff.

Chairman of the Joint Chiefs of Staff

The Chairman of the Joint Chiefs of Staff while holding such office takes precedence over all officers of the armed services. Besides participating as a member, the Chairman serves as presiding officer of the Joint Chiefs of Staff, provides agenda for the meetings, works to ensure that business is carried out promptly, and determines when issues under consideration by the Joint Chiefs of Staff will be decided. He informs the Secretary of Defense on issues before the Joint Chiefs of Staff,

including those upon which agreement has not been reached. Subject to the authority, direction, and control of the Secretary of Defense, the Chairman serves as the spokesman for the unified and specified commanders on operational requirements. In consultation with the Joint Chiefs of Staff and with the approval of the Secretary of Defense, he selects the Director of the Joint Staff and manages the Joint Staff through its Director. The appointment of officers to and tenure of officers on the Joint Staff are subject to his approval.

Joint Staff

The Joint Staff, headed by the Director of the Joint Staff, is composed of not more than 400 officers selected in approximately equal numbers from the Army, the Navy (including the Marine Corps), and the Air Force. The Joint Staff is organized into Directorates concerned with manpower and personnel, operations, logistics, plans and policy, and communications, command, and control systems.

Other Agencies

The other agencies of the Organization of the Joint Chiefs of Staff are the Joint Analysis Directorate; the Strategic Plans and Resource Analysis Agency; the Joint Special Operations Agency; the Joint Secretariat; the Directorate for Information and Resource Management; the Office of the Inspector General; and the Advisor for Mapping, Charting, and Geodesy Support. The Joint Materiel Priorities and Allocations Board, Joint Transportation Board, and Military Communications-Electronics Board are concerned with equitable distribution of resources. There are four organizations involving various aspects of hemispheric defense. They are vehicles for promoting military-political cooperation with Canada, Mexico, and other American nations. These organizations are the U.S. Delegation, Inter-American Defense Board; U.S. Section, Canada-U.S. Military Cooperation Committee; U.S. Military Representative, Permanent Joint Board on Defense, Canada-U.S.; and the U.S. Section, Joint Mexican-U.S. Defense Commission. The Joint Electronic Warfare Center provides analytical support to the electronic warfare military aspects of military operations. The Joint Strategic Target Planning Staff and the Joint Deployment Agency are tasked with coordinating plans in critical areas. Additionally, the facilities of the National Military Command System are operationally and administratively responsible to the Operations Directorate of the Joint Staff.

Other major organizations reporting to or through the Joint Chiefs of Staff

include the National Defense University; the U.S. Delegation, United Nations Military Staff Committee; and the U.S. Representative to the Military Committee, North Atlantic Treaty Organization.

Defense Agencies

For operational matters and requirements associated with joint planning that are of primary concern to the Chiefs, the Chairman of the Joint Chiefs of Staff may assign tasks and communicate directly with the Defense Communications Agency, the Defense Nuclear Agency, and the Defense Mapping Agency. The Defense Intelligence Agency, in addition to serving as the intelligence adviser to the Secretary of Defense, is responsible for intelligence and intelligence staff support to the JCS and for intelligence support to the unified and specified commands.

Sources of Information

DOD Directives and Instructions
Correspondence and Directives Directorate, Washington Headquarters Services, Room 2A286, The Pentagon, Washington, DC 20301–1155. Phone, 202–697–4111.
Contracts for Small Business Activities
Contact the Director, Small and Disadvantaged Business Utilization, Office of the Secretary of Defense, Room 2A340, The Pentagon, Washington, DC 20301–3061. Phone, 202–697–9383.
Employment Almost all positions are in the competitive service and are filled from civil service registers. College recruiting requirements are limited primarily to management intern positions at the B.S. and M.S. levels.

For additional information, inquiries should be addressed to the Chief, Staffing

and Support Programs, Directorate for Personnel and Security, Washington Headquarters Services, Room 3B347, The Pentagon, Washington, DC 20301–1155. Phone, 202–697–4211.
Speakers Scheduling of speaking engagements for civilian and military representatives of the Department of Defense is a responsibility of the Director for Programs, Defense Information Services Activity, Office of the Assistant Secretary of Defense (Public Affairs). Speakers on a variety of defense subjects are available in response to invitations at no cost to the local sponsor. However, any speaker can accept transportation, meals, and lodging, if offered by the sponsor of the public event in which he is to participate.

Written requests for speakers should

be forwarded to the Director for Programs, Defense Information Services Activity, Office of the Assistant Secretary of Defense (Public Affairs), The Pentagon, Washington, DC 20301–1400, phone, 202–695–6108, or to the Public Affairs Officer of the nearest military installation.

Films The Department of Defense has certain motion pictures and videotapes available for public, nonprofit exhibition. They are made available from productions required to support training and internal information objectives. There is a catalog of those productions available to the public for sale from the National Technical Information Service, 5285 Port Royal Road, Springfield, VA 22161. Each Service has its own catalog for internal use. Interested persons should contact the nearest installation of each Service to obtain the appropriate address of the film/videotape distribution center serving that area. Additionally, the Public Affairs Office of each Service at its Headquarters, Washington, DC, should be contacted. There is no charge for listings of films. No admission or any other fees may be charged for viewing of films and each film must be shown in its entirety, including all titles at beginning and end; no portion of the film may be reproduced, edited, or cut in any manner; and qualified operators must be provided by the borrower. Interested purchasers of Department of Defense films may also contact the Sales Branch, National Audio-Visual Center, 8700 Edgeworth Drive, Capitol Heights, MD 20743–3701. Phone, 301–763–1882.

Telephone Directory The Department of Defense telephone directory is available for sale by the Superintendent of Documents, Government Printing Office, Washington, DC 20402. Phone, 202–783–3238.

Pentagon Tours Guided tours of the Pentagon are available Monday through Friday, excluding Federal holidays. The 1-hour tours start at the Concourse.

For further information or reservations, call 202–695–1776 or write: Pentagon Tour Director, Room 3C1054, Washington, DC 20301–1400.

For further information concerning the Department of Defense, contact the Chief, Public Correspondence Division, Office of the Assistant Secretary of Defense (Public Affairs), Department of Defense, The Pentagon, Washington, DC 20301–1400. Phone, 202–697–5737.

DEPARTMENT OF THE AIR FORCE

The Pentagon, Washington, DC 20330
Phone, 202–545–6700

The Department of the Air Force is responsible for providing an Air Force that is capable, in conjuction with the other armed forces, of preserving the peace and security of the United States.

The Department of the Air Force was established as part of the National Military Establishment by the National Security Act of 1947 (61 Stat. 495) and came into being on September 18, 1947. The National Security Act Amendments of 1949 redesignated the National Military Establishment as the Department of Defense, established it as an executive department, and made the Department of the Air Force a military department within the Department of Defense (63 Stat. 578).

The Department of the Air Force is separately organized under the Secretary of the Air Force. It operates under the authority, direction, and control of the Secretary of Defense (10 U.S.C. 8010). The Department consists of the Office of the Secretary of the Air Force, the Air Staff, and the field organization.

Office of the Secretary

The Office of the Secretary includes the Under Secretary, three Assistant Secretaries, the Administrative Assistant, the General Counsel, and the Directors of Legislative Liaison, Public Affairs, Space Systems, International Affairs, Small and Disadvantaged Business Utilization, and Auditor General. The heads of these offices are staff advisers to the Secretary for functions he assigns to them.

The Department of the Air Force is administered by the Secretary of the Air Force who is responsible for and has the authority to conduct all affairs of the Department. The principal assistant is the Under Secretary, who acts with full authority of the Secretary on all affairs of the Department. Additionally, the Under Secretary provides overall direction, guidance, and supervision for Air Force space programs and activities. The Special Assistant (International Affairs) is the principal assistant to the Secretary concerning international Air Force activities, politico-military affairs, and international security policy and affairs.

Assistant Secretaries The Assistant Secretary (Manpower, Reserve Affairs and Installations) is responsible for the formulation, review, and execution of Air Force manpower, reserve affairs, and installations plans, policies, and programs. In addition, this person serves as a member of the Reserve Forces Policy Board, the Per Diem, Travel and Transportation Allowance Committee, the Air Force Policy Council, and the Air Force Systems Acquisition Review Council.

The Assistant Secretary (Financial Management) is responsible for the policies and procedures in Air Force planning, programming, and budgeting; cost analysis; accounting; internal audit; management systems, banking, and information systems management. Other responsibilities include reporting for weapons systems, major programs, and management of products and services from the computer industry.

The Assistant Secretary (Research, Development and Logistics) is responsible for the formulation and execution of Air Force research, development, and logistics policies and programs. As the Air Force acquisition executive, this person is responsible to the Secretary for all decisions relating to the acquisition of weapons systems and the command and control systems that support them.

Supporting Offices The Administrative Assistant serves as principal adviser to the Secretary of the Air Force and other statutory appointees on all phases of internal administration and management policies and assures administrative continuity in the Office of the Secretary during changes of top officials.

The General Counsel is the final legal authority on all matters arising within or referred to the Department of the Air Force, except those relating to the administration of military justice and such other matters as may be assigned to the Judge Advocate General.

The Director of Legislative Liaison advises and assists the Secretary and all other principal civilian and military officials of the Department concerning Air Force legislative affairs and congressional relations.

The Director of Public Affairs assists the Secretary and all military personnel and civilians in the Department concerning communication with the Air Force team, community relations, and media relations.

The Director of Space Systems is primarily responsible for assisting the Secretary in discharging his responsibility for the direction, supervision, policy, security, and control of space systems.

The Air Force Audit Agency provides independent internal audit and appraisal of financial, operational, management, and support activities as a service to all levels of management.

The Director of Small and Disadvantaged Business Utilization is responsible for the implementation and execution of the Air Force's program to aid, counsel, and assist small and disadvantaged firms in obtaining a fair proportion of Air Force prime contracts and subcontracts. The Director is also responsible for the Air Force's Labor Surplus Area Contracting Program and for assisting women-owned business firms in obtaining contracts.

Air Staff

Mission The mission of the Air Staff is to furnish professional assistance to the Secretary, the Under Secretary, the Assistant Secretaries of the Air Force, and the Chief of Staff.

Structure The Air Staff is a

management headquarters functional organization under the Chief of Staff, United States Air Force. Titles throughout all organizational levels reflect the functions involved. In addition, there is a board structure, a Chief Master Sergeant of the Air Force, a foreign liaison office, and an administrative management function.

Functions and Activities   Air Staff functions are specialized into well-defined areas to effect the management principles of functionality, integration, flexibility, simplicity, and decentralization. The Air Staff retains those management functions that legally cannot be delegated or decentralized, are needed by the Secretary and Chief of Staff, are essential to respond promptly to the Secretary of Defense, or are required to determine the design and structure of the Air Force in the future.

Chief of Staff   The Chief of Staff is directly responsible to the Secretary of the Air Force for the efficiency and operational readiness of the Air Force. He is a member of the Joint Chiefs of Staff (JCS) of the Department of Defense. He is assisted in all responsibilities, except for JCS, by the Vice Chief of Staff. The Assistant Vice Chief of Staff assists the Chief and Vice Chief in the discharge of their duties.

Special Staff   The Special Staff is an adjunct to the Chief of Staff, independent of the basic staff structure, and provides advisory and support services to both the Chief of Staff and the Air Staff. The Special Staff consists of: Chief, Office of Air Force History; USAF Scientific Advisory Board; Surgeon General; Chief of Chaplains; Judge Advocate General; Chief of Air Force Reserve; Chief, National Guard Bureau; Director, Air National Guard; the Inspector General; Assistant Chief of Staff, Intelligence; Assistant Chief of Staff, Information Systems; Assistant Chief of Staff, Studies and Analyses; and the Director of Administration.

Deputy Chiefs of Staff   The Deputy Chiefs of Staff (DCS's) function primarily as a coordinating level on policy matters and represent the corporate structure. Substantive functions are organized under the DCS's in homogeneous groups that are called Directorates. Under the directorates, functions are further broken down into descriptive groups, divisions, and branches.

Comptroller of the Air Force   The Comptroller of the Air Force functions in the same manner as the DCS's except that he or she is directly responsible to the Assistant Secretary of the Air Force for Financial Management with concurrent responsibility to the Chief of Staff.

Board Structure   The board structure in the Air Staff consists of the Air Force Council and below it the Air Staff Board. The Air Force Council presents the recommendations of the DCS's on an agenda item to the Chief of Staff. The Air Staff Board presents the recommendations of the directors on an agenda item to the staff responsible or sponsors the recommendation before the Air Force Council. Membership on the Council is at DCS, Comptroller, Special Staff level while membership on the Board is at Directorate level.

Field Organization

The major commands, separate operating agencies, and direct reporting units together represent the field organization of the United States Air Force. These commands are organized primarily on a functional basis in the United States and on an area basis overseas. Commands are given the responsibility for accomplishing certain phases of the worldwide activities of the USAF. They are responsible for organizing, administering, equipping, and training their subordinate elements for the accomplishment of assigned missions.

Air Force Logistics Command The Air Force Logistics Command provides worldwide logistical support to the Air Force. This includes procurement, storage, and distribution of supplies and the performance of or arrangement for the performance of depot level maintenance on materiel.

Air Force Systems Command The responsibility of the Air Force Systems Command is to advance aerospace technology, adapt it into operational aerospace systems, and acquire qualitatively superior aerospace systems and material needed to accomplish the United States Air Force mission.

Air Training Command The Air Training Command is responsible for Air Force recruiting and individual training for Air Force officers and airmen. Training includes basic training and indoctrination for recruits; Air Force ROTC flying training; and technical, field, and special training.

Air University The Air University is a major command and is responsible for the higher education of Air Force officers. Education activities include the Air War College, Air Command and Staff College, Air Force Institute of Technology, Civil Air Patrol, Extension Course Institute, and the Air University Center for Professional Development.

Military Airlift Command The Military Airlift Command is a major command of the United States Air Force and a Joint Chiefs of Staff specified command. Its

primary mission is to provide air transportation for personnel and cargo for all the military services on a worldwide basis. In addition, it furnishes weather, rescue, special operations, and audiovisual services for the Air Force.

Strategic Air Command The Strategic Air Command is a major command of the United States Air Force and a Joint Chiefs of Staff specified command. Its primary mission is to organize, train, equip, administer, and prepare strategic air forces for combat, including bombardment, missile, special mission, and strategic reconnaissance units, and to conduct strategic air operations.

Tactical Air Command The Tactical Air Command's mission is to organize, train, and equip forces to participate in tactical air operations. This includes tactical fighter, tactical air reconnaissance, air defense, close combat air support, and joint amphibious and airborne operations. It is the Air Force component of the U.S. Readiness Command, the U.S. Atlantic Command, and provides the Air Force component of the U.S. Central Command. It participates with other services in developing doctrine, procedures, tactics, techniques, training, and equipment for joint operations. It provides combat ready air elements to the Readiness and Central Commands.

Electronic Security Command The Electronic Security Command monitors Air Force communications in all parts of the world to ensure compliance with established communication security practices and procedures. In addition, Electronic Security Command units occasionally conduct research in communication phenomena in support of various elements of the U.S. Government.

Air Force Communications Command The Air Force Communications Command provides base and point-to-point communications, flight facilities, air traffic control, and automated data processing (ADP) services, primarily to the Air Force, but also to other agencies, governmental and civil, national and foreign.

United States Air Forces in Europe
The United States Air Forces in Europe is a major command of the United States Air Force and is the Air Force component of the U.S. European Command. Its primary mission is to organize, train, equip, administer, and prepare assigned forces for combat, including tactical fighter, tactical air reconnaissance, tactical air control, close air support, and defense suppression units to conduct defensive and offensive air operations. It provides combat ready air elements to the U.S. European Command and participates in joint and combined air operations.

Pacific Air Forces   The Pacific Air Forces is a major command of the United States Air Force and is the Air Force component of the U.S. Pacific Command. Its primary mission is to organize, train, equip, administer, and prepare assigned forces for combat, including tactical fighter, tactical air reconnaissance, tactical air control, close air support, and defense suppression units to conduct defensive and offensive air operations. It provides combat ready air elements to the U.S. Pacific Command and participates in joint and combined air operations.

Alaskan Air Command   The Alaskan Air Command is a major command of the United States Air Force. Its primary mission is to conduct aerospace defense operations according to tasks assigned by the Commander in Chief, North American Aerospace Defense Command (CINCNORAD). The Command plans, conducts, controls, and coordinates offensive and defensive air operations, and is the coordinating authority for all

joint military administrative and logistical matters in Alaska, and is the military point of contact for the State of Alaska.

Air Force Space Command   The Air Force Space Command provides resource management and operation of assigned assets for space control, space force application, force enhancement, space support, and strategic aerospace defense. The Command provides a close link between its space activities and, through the Commander in Chief, Aerospace Defense Command and Unified Space Command, the unified and specified command structure.

Separate Operating Agencies   The Air Force Accounting and Finance Center provides technical supervision, advice, and guidance to Air Force accounting and finance field activities and finance operation.

The Air Force Audit Agency provides independent internal audit and appraisal of financial, operational, management, and support activities as a service to all levels of management.

The Air Force Inspection and Safety Center directs the Air Force inspection and safety programs, evaluating operational readiness, accident prevention, and management systems.

The Air Force Office of Special Investigations provides criminal, counterintelligence, personnel security, and special investigative services to Air Force activities; collects, analyzes, and reports significant information about these matters.

The Air Force Military Personnel Center executes personnel plans and programs and supervises procedures applicable to the worldwide management and administration of Air Force military personnel.

The Air Force Intelligence Service provides specialized intelligence service in support of USAF operations through the conduct of comprehensive research,

423

direction of collection activities, processing and dissemination of intelligence information and intelligence, and the exercise of management and control of intelligence systems and special security systems.

The Air Force Operational Test and Evaluation Center manages the Air Force Operational Test and Evaluation (OT&E) program; assesses the operational utility of all major and selected nonmajor Air Force systems using, implementing, and supporting commands as required; and is responsible for recommending policy and for planning, directing, evaluating, and reporting on the Air Force OT&E program.

The Air Force Engineering and Services Center provides specialized engineering and services, technical assistance, and operating support to Air Force bases and organizations. This includes food, laundry, dry cleaning, and linen exchange services; regional civil engineering; and the highly specialized, interdisciplinary civil engineering functions.

The Air Force Commissary Service provides subsistence support to appropriated and nonappropriated fund food activities and to authorized individual patrons. It also operates a resale store system to provide service and facilities for the sale of Department of Defense authorized merchandise at the lowest practical price to authorized patrons.

The Air Force Legal Services Center provides Air Force-wide legal services in the functional areas of military justice, patents, claims and tort litigation, general litigation, labor law, preventive law, and legal aid. It also administers the Federal Legal Information Through Electronics (FLITE) Program for the Air Force as Executive Agent for the Department of Defense.

The Air Force Service Information and News Center plans and executes the USAF internal information program for all military and civilian personnel. It develops, produces, and distributes materials in support of information, orientation, motivation, and unit morale goals and provides information about Air Force people and missions to hometown news media and national commercial magazines.

The Air Force Office of Medical Support assists and supports the Air Force Surgeon General in developing and implementing practices for health care in peacetime and wartime environments. It also performs studies and research on how Air Force medical policies and programs are executed and recommends appropriate modifications to the Air Force Surgeon General.

The Air Force Office of Security Police develops operational policies and practices in peacetime and wartime environments to carry out programs for the security of Air Force resources and information and the delivery of law enforcement services. The Office implements plans, policies, and programs for base defense, management of security police personnel, training, systems and equipment programs, and the physical security of Air Force resources; the information, personnel and industrial security programs and the wartime information security program; maintenance of law and order; prisoner rehabilitation and corrections programs; vehicle traffic management; and the military working dog program.

The Air Force Reserve performs the USAF Chief of Staff field responsibilities of command of the Air Force Reserve and is responsible for participation in the formulation of plans for the management, administration, and execution of programs affecting Air Force Reserve

(AFRes) units and mobilization of these reserves when needed.

The Air Reserve Personnel Center develops personnel management policies, plans, and programs pertaining to Air Force Reserve personnel when they are not on extended active duty and provides personnel management for reserve forces of the Air Force and personnel support for mobilization of these forces.

The Air Force Management Engineering Agency develops and maintains Air Force manpower standards for the purpose of improving manpower utilization; implements the Air Force Management Engineering Program; and exercises direct supervision over assigned Management Engineering teams engaged in developing specialized and functional manpower standards and related data.

Direct Reporting Units   The Air Force Combat Operations Staff provides readiness-oriented, combat-related support to the Chief of Staff, U.S. Air Force. The Staff serves as a permanent nucleus of a centralized, highly responsive, and integrated combat support structure. It includes the combat-related activities of functions such as operations, operations plans, intelligence, logistics, and personnel.

The Air Force Civilian Personnel Management Center directs, develops, manages, and evaluates the wide range of Federal and internal policies and programs affecting Air Force civilians, including foreign nationals, worldwide.

The Air Force Review Boards Office supervises the activities of the Air Force Board for Correction of Military Records (AFBCMR), the Air Force Civilian Appellate Review Agency (AFCARA), and the Air Force Personnel Council. AFBCMR and AFCARA ensure compliance with appropriate legal and policy guidelines in the correction of

military records and in resolving civilian employee complaints. The Personnel Council advises the Air Force Secretariat on matters relating to various personnel policies and the effective management of active and reserve components of the Air Force.

The Air Force Technical Applications Center operates and maintains the United States Atomic Energy Detection System (AEDS) to monitor compliance of signatories to nuclear test ban treaties. AEDS consists of a worldwide network of sensors and collection equipment, analysis laboratories, a depot to support AEDS, and a headquarters staff to perform operational management functions.

The Air National Guard Support Center is responsible for the maintenance, operational, and technical functions essential for the combat readiness of the Air National Guard forces.

The USAF Historical Research Center provides historical and reference services for the Air Force. It serves as a repository for Air Force historical documents and prepares books, monographs, research reports, studies, unit histories, and other historical works relating to the U.S. Air Force and military aviation. The Center carries out various special programs to acquire historical documents and data and answers requests for historical information from both official sources and the public.

The United States Air Force Academy provides a 4-year educational curriculum for cadets that includes a baccalaureate level education in airmanship, related sciences, and the humanities. Besides a classical education, each cadet is trained to appreciate the role of airpower, its capabilities and limitations, high ideals of individual integrity, patriotism, loyalty, honor, physical fitness, sense of responsibility, and a dedication of selfless and honorable service.

The Air Force District of Washington (AFDW) provides logistical and administrative support to Air Force activities in the Washington, DC, area that do not have their own internal support, including Headquarters USAF and the Air Force Secretariat. In addition, AFDW represents the Air Force in matters pertaining to the National Capital Region.

The Air Force Center for Studies and analyses performs studies to assist and support the decision-making process of the Air Force. The Center performs independent studies and evaluations of Air Force requirements, proposals, plans, and programs, while providing comparisons and trade-off analysis. The Center also evaluates critical technical and operational issues and monitors applicable tests and evaluations that address such issues.

The Air Force Center for International Programs provides direction and guidance for the Air Force portion of the military Security Assistance Program for foreign nations and international activities. The Center also coordinates Air Force politico-military policies as they affect Security Assistance matters pertinent to DOD, State Department, and other agencies of the Federal Government.

Sources of Information

Speakers The Air Force will make speakers available for private organizations or community groups. Requests for speakers should be addressed to the Air Force Speakers Branch, Hq USAF (SAF/PACD), Washington, DC 20330. Phone, 202–697–6205 or 2769.

Writers The Air Force will provide assistance to magazine and book authors and researchers who desire to write about the Air Force. Requests should be addressed to the Air Force Office of Public Affairs, Magazines and Books Division (AFOPA–MB), 1221 South Fern St., RMD–159, Arlington, VA 22202. Phone, 202–695–5331 or 5328.

DEPARTMENT OF THE ARMY

The Pentagon, Washington, DC 20310
Phone, 202–545–6700; Information during nonoffice hours,202–695–0441

The American Continental Army, now called the United States Army, was established by the Continental Congress on June 14, 1775, more than a year before the Declaration of Independence.

The mission of the Department of the Army is to organize, train, and equip active duty and reserve forces for the preservation of peace, security, and the defense of our nation. It serves as part of our national military team, whose members include the Navy, Air Force, Marines, and Coast Guard. The Army's mission focuses on land operations; its soldiers must be trained with modern arms and equipment and be ready to respond quickly.

The Army also administers programs aimed at protecting the environment, improving waterway navigation, flood and beach erosion control, and water resource development. It supports the National Civil Defense Program, provides military assistance to Federal, State, and local government agencies, including natural disaster relief assistance, and provides emergency medical air transportation services.

The Department of War was established as an executive department at the seat of government by an act approved August 7, 1789. The Secretary of War was established as its head and his powers were those entrusted to him by the President (1 Stat. 49; 5 U.S.C. 181).

The National Security Act of 1947 created the National Military Establishment, and the Department of War was designated the Department of the Army. The title of its Secretary became Secretary of the Army (61 Stat. 499; 5 U.S.C. 171).

The National Security Act Amendments of 1949 established the Department of Defense as an executive department of the Government and provided that the Department of the

Army be a military department within the Department of Defense (63 Stat. 578; 5 U.S.C. 171).

The Army Organization Act provided the statutory basis for the internal organization of the Army and the Department of the Army. The act consolidated and revised the numerous earlier laws, incorporated various adjustments made necessary by the National Security Act of 1947 and other postwar enactments, and provided for the organization of the Department of the Army in a single comprehensive statute, with certain minor exceptions. In general, the act followed the policy of vesting broad organizational powers in the Secretary of the Army, subject to delegation by him, rather than specifying duties of subordinate officers (10 U.S.C. 3012, 3062).

The Command of the Army is exercised by the President through the Secretary of Defense and the Secretary of the Army, who directly represent him; and, under the law and decisions of the Supreme Court, their acts are the President's acts, and their directions and orders are the President's directions and orders.

Office of the Secretary of the Army

Secretary The Secretary of the Army is the head of the Department of the Army. Subject to the direction, authority, and control of the President as Commander in Chief and of the Secretary of Defense, the Secretary of the Army is responsible for and has the authority to conduct all affairs of the Department of the Army, including its organization, administration, operation, efficiency, and such other activities as may be prescribed by the President or the Secretary of Defense as authorized by law.

The Secretary is also responsible for certain civil functions, such as oversight of the Panama Canal Commission and execution of the Panama Canal Treaty; the civil works program of the Corps of Engineers; Arlington and Soldiers' Home National Cemeteries; and such other activities of a civil nature as may be prescribed by higher authority or authorized by law.

Principal Assistants Subject to the direction and control of the Secretary of the Army, the Under Secretary of the Army, Assistant Secretary of the Army (Civil Works), Assistant Secretary of the Army (Financial Management), Assistant Secretary of the Army (Installations and Logistics), Assistant Secretary of the Army (Manpower and Reserve Affairs), Assistant Secretary of the Army (Research, Development and Acquisition), General Counsel, the Administrative Assistant, Deputy Under Secretary of the Army, Deputy Under Secretary of the Army (Operations Research), Chief of Legislative Liaison, Chief of Public Affairs, and Director, Office of Small and Disadvantaged Business Utilization are authorized and directed to act for the Secretary of the Army within their respective fields of responsibility and as further directed by the Secretary.

This authority extends not only to actions within the Department of the Army but also to relationships and transactions with the Congress and other governmental and nongovernmental organizations and individuals. These officials are responsible for the exercise of direction and supervision over matters pertaining to the formulation, execution, and review of policies, plans and programs within their respective functional areas, including the establishment of objectives and appraisal of performance. Officers of the Army report to the Under Secretary of the Army, Assistant Secretaries of the Army, General Counsel, the Administrative Assistant, Deputy Under Secretary of the Army, Deputy Under Secretary of the Army (Operations Research), Chief of Legislative Liaison, Chief of Public Affairs and the Director, Office of Small and Disadvantaged Business Utilization regarding matters within their respective fields of responsibility.

Army Policy Council   The Army Policy Council is the senior policy advisory council of the Department of the Army. It provides the Secretary of the Army and his principal civilian and military assistants with a forum for the discussion of Army subjects of significant policy interest and an opportunity for members to consult with other members on matters arising within their specific areas of responsibility.

For further information, call 202–695–7922.

Armed Forces Policy Council   The Secretary of the Army serves as a member of the Armed Forces Policy Council, which advises the Secretary of Defense on broad policy matters relating to the Armed Forces.

For further information, call 202–695–0028.

Army Staff

The Army Staff, presided over by the Chief of Staff, is the military staff of the Secretary of the Army. It includes a General Staff, a Special Staff, and a Personal Staff. The Army Staff renders professional advice and assistance to the Secretary of the Army, the Under Secretary of the Army, the Assistant Secretaries of the Army, and other officials of the Army Secretariat.

It is the duty of the Army Staff to: prepare for employment of the Army and for such recruiting, organizing, supplying, equipping, training, mobilizing, and demobilizing of the Army as will assist the execution of any power, duty, or function of the Secretary or the Chief of Staff; investigate and report upon the efficiency of the Army and its preparation for military operations; act as the agent of the Secretary of the Army and the Chief of Staff in coordinating the action of all organizations of the Department of the Army; and perform such other duties not otherwise assigned by law as may be prescribed by the Secretary of the Army.

Chief of Staff   The Chief of Staff is the principal military adviser to the Secretary of the Army and is charged by him with the planning, development, execution, review, and analysis of the Army programs. The Chief of Staff, under the direction of the Secretary of the Army, supervises the members and organization of the Army and performs the duties prescribed for him by the National Security Act of 1947 and other laws. He is directly responsible to the Secretary of the Army for the efficiency of the Army, its state of preparation for military operations and plans therefor.

The Chief of Staff serves as the Army member of the Joint Chiefs of Staff and as a member of the Army Policy Council and the Armed Forces Policy Council. As a member of the Joint Chiefs of Staff, he is one of the principal advisers to the President, the National Security Council, and the Secretary of Defense.

Army General Staff   Under the direction of the Chief of Staff, the Army General Staff renders professional advice and assistance to the Secretary, the Under Secretary, the Assistant Secretaries of the Army, and other Secretariat officials in providing broad basic policies and plans for the guidance of the Department of the Army. The Army General Staff specifically assists the Secretary in the preparation and issuance of directives to implement plans and policies and in the supervision of the execution and implementation of these directives.

Special Staff The Special Staff provides advice and assistance to the Secretary of the Army, the Chief of Staff, other members of the Army Secretariat and Army Staff, and elements of the Department of the Army on specialized matters specifically within their respective fields of responsibility.

The heads of certain Special Staff agencies exercise dual functions of staff and command. These two functions, although vested in a single individual, are separate and distinct in that each involves different responsibilities and duties.

Personal Staff The Personal Staff to the Chief of Staff includes his aides, the Inspector General and his Staff agency, the Chief of Chaplains, the Judge Advocate General, the Auditor General, and any other Army Staff member whose activities he desires to coordinate and administer directly.

Program Areas

Military Operations and Plans
Determination of requirements and priorities for, and the employment of, Army forces strategy formation; strategy application, mid- and long-range and regional; arms control, negotiation and disarmament; national security affairs; joint service matters; net assessment; politico-military affairs; force mobilization and demobilization; force planning, programming structuring, development, analysis and management; operational readiness; overall roles and missions; collective security; individual and unit training; psychological operations; unconventional warfare; counter terrorism; operations security; signal security; military aspects of space and sea; special plans; table of equipment

development and approval; electronic warfare; nuclear and chemical matters; civil affairs; military support of civil defense; civil disturbance; domestic actions; audiovisual activities; command and control; and automation and communications (A/C) programs and activities.

Personnel Management of military and civilian personnel for overall integrated support of the Army, including policies and programs for manpower utilization standards, allocation, and documentation, career development, equal opportunity, leadership, alcohol and drug abuse control, welfare and morale, promotion, retention, and separation; management of the program for law enforcement, correction and crime prevention for military members of the Army; physical security; military compensation, transportation and travel entitlements, the personnel aspects of military construction and housing management; research and development related to training personnel, manpower systems, human factors; management of civilian personnel training; manpower surveys; and safety.

Reserve Components Management of individual and unit readiness and mobilization for Reserve Components, comprised of the Army National Guard and the U.S. Army Reserve.

Intelligence Management of Army intelligence and counterintelligence activities, personnel, equipment, systems, and organizations; Army cryptology, topography, and meteorology; coordination of Army requirements for mapping, charting, and geodesy; and Army industrial security.

Management-Comptrollership Review and analysis of Army programs and major Army commands; management information systems in the financial area, progress and statistical reporting, and

430

reports control; financial management, budgeting, finance and accounting, cost analysis, economic analysis, military pay and allowances, resource management, productivity and value improvement; regulatory policies and programs pertaining to the overall management of the Army; and legislative policies and programs pertaining to appropriation acts affecting the Army.

Research, Development, and Materiel Acquisition   Management of Army research, development, development test and evaluation; planning, programming, and budgeting for the acquisition of materiel obtained by the procurement appropriations for the Army; materiel life cycle management from concept phase through acquisition; and research, development, and military standardization aspects of international military cooperative programs.

Information Management   Automation, communications, audiovisual, records management, publications, and information management.

Logistics   Managment of Department of the Army logistical activities for the movement and maintenance of forces; logistical planning and support of Army and joint service operations; materiel and supply management and maintenance; security assistance; transportation; and Army interservice supply operations.

Engineering   Management of Army engineering, construction, installations, family housing, real estate, facilities requirements and stationing, and real property maintenance activities; environmental preservation and improvement activities; applicable research and development activities for engineer missions to include environmental sciences; Army topographic and military geographic information activities; and engineer aspects of Army strategic and operational plans.

Civil Functions   Civil functions of the Department of the Army include the Civil Works Program, the administration of Arlington and Soldiers' Home National Cemeteries, and other related matters. The Army's Civil Works Program, a responsibility of the Corps of Engineers under the direction and supervision of the Secretary of the Army, dates back to 1824 and is the Nation's major Federal water resources development activity and involves engineering works such as major dams, reservoirs, levees, harbors, waterways, locks, and many other types of structures. These works provide flood protection for cities and major river valleys, reduce the cost of transportation, supply water for municipal and industrial use, generate hydroelectric power, provide recreational opportunities for vast numbers of people, regulate the rivers for many purposes including the improvement of water quality, protect the shores of oceans and lakes, and provide other types of benefits. Planning assistance is also provided to States and other non-Federal entities for the comprehensive management of water resources, including pollution abatement works. In addition, through the Civil Works Program the Federal Government protects the navigable waters of the United States under legislation empowering the Secretary of the Army to prohibit activities that would reduce the value of such waters to the Nation.

Medical   Management of health services for the Army and, as directed for other services, agencies, and organizations; health standards for Army personnel; health professional education and training; career management authority over commissioned and warrant officer personnel of the Army Medical Department; medical research, materiel development, testing and evaluation; policies concerning health aspects of Army environmental programs and prevention of disease; and planning, programming, and budgeting for Army-wide health services.

Inspection Management of inquiries, inspections, and reports on matters affecting the performance of mission and the state of discipline, efficiency, economy, and morale of the Department of the Army.

Religious Management of religious, moral and moral leadership, and chaplain support activities Army-wide; religious ministrations, religious education, pastoral care, and counseling for Army military personnel; liaison with the ecclesiastical agencies; chapel construction requirements and design approval; and career management of clergymen serving in the Chaplains Branch.

Legal Legal advisory services provided for all military personnel and agencies of the Army; review and take final action as designee of the Secretary of the Army on complaints of wrongs by service personnel submitted under the Uniform Code of Military Justice; administration of

military justice and civil law matters pertaining to the Army; administration of Army claims and legal assistance services; operation of the legal system of appellate reviews of court-martial records as provided by the Uniform Code of Military Justice; general court-martial and real property records custodianship; records administration of proceedings of courts of inquiry and military commissions; liaison service with the Department of Justice and other Federal and State agencies on matters connected with litigation and legal proceedings concerning the Army; and career management of Judge Advocate General's Corps officers.

Information Public information, command information, and community relations services and preparation of information plans and programs in support of Army basic plans and programs.

History Advisory and coordination service provided on historical matters, including historical properties; formulation and execution of the Army Historical Program; and preparation and publication of histories required by the Army.

Major Army Commands

United States Army Forces Command
The Commanding General, United States Army Forces Command, commands all assigned active Army forces in the continental United States, the Continental United States Armies, and the United States Army Reserve within the United States and serves as Commander in Chief, United States Army Forces, Readiness Command. He serves, for planning purposes, as Commander in Chief, United States Army Forces, Atlantic. He also commands those

subordinate commands, installations, and activities assigned by Headquarters, Department of the Army and, as directed, provides administrative and logistical support through his subordinate installation commanders to other Department of the Army, Department of Defense, or other Government agencies. In addition, he supervises the training of Army National Guard units within the United States, the Commonwealth of Puerto Rico, and the U.S. Virgin Islands.

The Commanding General of each of

the Continental United States Armies has the primary mission, under the Commanding General, United States Army Forces Command, to command the United States Army Reserve, plan for mobilization, coordinate domestic emergencies, and exercise training supervision over the Army National Guard. The five Army areas are as follows:

First United States Army (Headquarters, Fort George G. Meade, MD)—Connecticut, Delaware, the Distict of Columbia, Maine, Maryland, Massachusetts, New Hampshire, New Jersey, New York, Pennsylvania, Rhode Island, Vermont, Virginia, and West Virginia.

Second United States Army (Headquarters, Fort Gillem, GA)—Alabama, Florida, Georgia, Kentucky, Missisippi, North Carolina, Puerto Rico, South Carolina, and Tennessee.

Third United States Army (Headquarters, Fort McPherson, GA)

Fourth United States Army (Headquarters, Fort Sheridan, IL)—Illinois, Indiana, Iowa, Michigan, Minnesota, Ohio, and Wisconsin.

Fifth United States Army (Headquarters, Fort Sam Houston, TX)—Arkansas, Kansas, Louisiana, Missouri, Nebraska, New Mexico, Oklahoma, and Texas.

Sixth United States Army (Headquarters, Presidio of San Francisco, CA)—Arizona, California, Colorado, Idaho, Montana, Nevada, North Dakota, Oregon, South Dakota, Utah, Washington, and Wyoming.

For further information, call 404–752–2994.

United States Army Training and Doctrine Command

The Commanding General, United States Army Training and Doctrine Command, develops, manages, and supervises the training of individuals of the Active Army and Reserve Components. He also formulates and documents concepts, doctrine, materiel requirements, organizations, and appropriate training systems for the Army in all environments, tactical and nontactical.

He commands installations and activities as may be assigned by Headquarters, Department of the Army, and, as directed, provides administrative and logistical support through his assigned installation commanders to elements and agencies of the Department of the Army, Department of Defense, or other Government agencies that are tenants or satellites of the installation.

For further information, call 804–727–3514.

United States Army Materiel Command

The Commanding General, United States Army Materiel Command, develops and provides materiel and related services to the Army, to Army elements of unified commands and specified commands, and to other United States and foreign agencies as directed. His principal functions include research; development; product, production, and maintenance engineering; testing and evaluation of materiel; production and procurement of materiel; inventory management; and storage and distribution, maintenance, transportation, and disposal of materiel.

For further information, call 703–274–9625.

United States Army Information Systems Command

Functions yet to be determined.

For further information, call 602–538–6161.

United States Army Intelligence and Security Command

The Commanding General, United States Army Intelligence and Security Command, is responsible for supporting the Army at echelons above Corps through counterintelligence, intelligence collection, production, and security operations performed by a worldwide command structure.

For further information, call 202–692–6603.

United States Army Health Services Command

The Commanding General, United States Army Health Services Command, performs health services for

433

the Army within the United States and, as directed, for other governmental agencies and activities. He commands the Army hospital system within the United States and other organizations, units, and facilities as may be directed. He is responsible for the conduct of medical professional education for Army personnel. He is further responsible, under the guidance of the Commanding General, United States Training and Doctrine Command, for the development of medical doctrine, concepts, organizations, materiel requirements, and systems in support of the Army.

For further information, call 512–221–6313.

United States Army Criminal Investigation Command The Commanding General, United States Army Criminal Investigation Command, is responsible for exercising centralized command, authority, direction, and control of Army criminal investigative activities worldwide and for providing investigative support to all United States Army elements. He is charged with, and is responsible directly to the Secretary of the Army and the Chief of Staff for, conducting, controlling, and monitoring Army criminal investigations; developing investigative standards, procedures, and doctrinal policies; operating a criminal intelligence element; operating the United States Army Crime Records Repository; maintaining centralized records of criminal investigative agents; reviewing all investigative reports; operating investigative crime laboratories; planning and conducting protective service operations; and conducting the accreditation/certification program of investigative agents.

For further information, call 202–756–2263.

Military Traffic Management Command The Commanding General, Military Traffic Management Command

(MTMC), is the Executive Director for military traffic management, land transportation, and common-user ocean terminal service within the United States, excluding Alaska and Hawaii, and for worldwide traffic management of the Department of Defense household goods moving and storage program. He administers Department of Defense activities pertaining to Highways for National Defense.

For further information, call 202–756–1724.

United States Army Military District of Washington The Commanding General, United States Army Military District of Washington (USAMDW), commands units, activities, and installations in the National Capital area as may be assigned by Headquarters Department of the Army (HQDA); provides base operation and other support to the Department of the Army, Department of Defense, or other Government activities that are tenants of or are located on USAMDW installations for such support; plans for and executes those missions peculiar to the needs of the seat of government as assigned by HQDA; and provides an organized and responsive defense of designated Department of Defense facilities.

For further information, call 202–475–0520.

United States Army Corps of Engineers The Commanding General, United States Army Corps of Engineers (CGUSACE), serves as the Army's Real Property Manager, performing the full cycle of real property activities (requirements, programming, acquisition, operation, maintenance, and disposal); manages and executes engineering, construction, and real estate programs for the Army and the United States Air Force; and performs research and development in support of these programs. CGUSACE manages and executes Civil Works Programs. These

434

programs include research and development, planning, design, construction, operation and maintenance, and real estate activities related to rivers, harbors, and waterways; administration of laws for protection and preservation of navigable waters and related resources such as wetlands. CGUSACE assists in recovery from natural disasters.

For further information, call 202–272–0001.

Army Components of Unified Commands The missions of the commanding generals of the Army components of unified commands are set forth in directives of the Department of Defense. The Army components of unified commands are major commands of the Department of the Army and consist of such subordinate commands, units, activities, and installations as may be assigned to them by Headquarters,

Department of the Army. In certain unified command areas—such as United States Southern Command and United States Atlantic Command—where the Army does not have a separate, single, and distinct component headquarters or commander, a designated Army commander in the area will be responsible for certain Army "component" functions that must be performed at his location.

Commands:

United States Army, Europe. Phone, 011–49–6221–57–8831.

United States Army, Japan. Phone, 011–81–0462–51–1520.

Eighth United States Army. Phone, 202–694–3475 (Pentagon Korean Liaison Office).

United States Army, Western Command. Phone, 808–471–7471.

Sources of Information

Public Affairs and Community Relations For official Army information and community relations, contact the Office of the Chief of Public Affairs, Department of the Army, Washington, DC 20310–1508. Phone, 202–694–0741.

Environment Contact the Public Affairs Office, Office of the Chief of Engineers, Washington, DC 20314–1000, phone, 202–272–0010; or the nearest Corps of Engineers Division or District Office located in most major cities throughout the United States.

Research Industry may obtain information on long-range research and development plans concerning future materiel requirements and objectives from Commander, U.S. Army Materiel Command, ATTN: AMCPA, 5001

Eisenhower Ave., Alexandria, VA 22333–0001. Phone, 703–274–8010.

Small Business Activities Aids to assist small businesses in obtaining defense procurement contracts are available through the Office of Small and Disadvantaged Business Utilization, Office of the Secretary of the Army, Room 2A712, The Pentagon, Washington, DC 20310–0106. Phone, 202–695–9800.

Contracts Contract procurement policies and procedures are the responsibility of the Deputy for Procurement, Office of the Assistant Secretary of the Army (Research, Development and Acquisition), Room 2E661, The Pentagon, Washington, DC 20310–0103. Phone, 202–695–2488.

Reading Rooms The Pentagon Library,

Room 1A518, The Pentagon, Washington, DC 20310-6000 (phone, 202-697-4301); Discharge Review/Correction Boards, Room 2E165, The Pentagon, Washington, DC 20310-1803 (phone, 202-695-3973).

Publications Requests should be addressed to The Adjutant General HQDA (DAIM-APD), Alexandria, VA 22331-0302. Phone, 202-325-6297.

Films DOD 5040.2-C1 thru 4 lists all Army films available. DA Pamphlet No. 108-4 lists all Army films available to the public. Requests for the loan of Army motion pictures should be addressed to the Commanding General of the appropriate Army Area, ATTN: Audio-Visual Support Center.

Army Historical Program For information concerning the Army Historical Program, write to the U.S. Army Center of Military History, HQDA (DAMH), Pulaski Building, Washington, DC 20314-0200. Phone, 202-272-0291.

Civilian Employment Employment inquiries and applications should be directed to the following: (1) For employment in the Washington, DC, metropolitan area—Personnel and Employment Service—Washington, Room 3D727, The Pentagon, Washington, DC 20310-6800 (phone, 202-695-3383); (2) For employment outside the Washington, DC, metropolitan area—address or apply directly to the Army installation where employment is desired, ATTN: Civilian Personnel Office; (3) For employment overseas—U.S. Army Civilian Personnel Center, ATTN: PECC-CSS, Hoffman II Building, 200 Stovall St., Alexandria, VA 22332-0300 (phone, 202-325-8712).

Military Career Opportunities Information on all phases of Army enlistments and specialized training are available by writing the United States Army Recruiting Command, Fort

Sheridan, IL 60037. Phone, 312-926-3322.

United States Military Academy For information write to Director of Admissions, United States Military Academy, West Point, NY 10996. Phone, 914-938-4041.

Army ROTC The Army Reserve Officers' Training Corps is an educational program designed to develop college educated officers for the Active Army, the Army National Guard, and the Army Reserve. For information, write or contact the Professor of Military Science at the nearest college or university offering the program, or the Army ROTC Regional Headquarters in your area.

Officer Candidate Schools Members of the Active Army may attend the 14-week course at Fort Benning, GA. Members of the Reserve Components may attend a short course at Fort Benning, GA.

Commissioning Opportunities for Women All commissioning sources available to men are available to women.

Army National Guard For information concerning individual training opportunities in the National Guard, contact the Army National Guard, ARO-OAC-ME, Edgewood, MD 21010-5420. Phone, 301-671-4789.

Army Health Professions For information concerning career opportunities in Army Health Professions, write to HQDA (DASG-HC), Washington, DC 20310. Phone, 202-695-1850.

Judge Advocate General's Corps For information concerning career opportunities as a lawyer, military and civilian, write to the Personnel, Plans, and Training Office, Office of the Judge Advocate General, Department of the Army, HQDA (DAJA-PT), Washington, DC 20310-2206. Phone, 202-695-1353.

Chaplains Corps For information

concerning career opportunities as a chaplain, write to the Chief of Chaplains, HQDA (DACH–ZA), Washington, DC 20310. Phone, 202–695–1133.

Arlington and Soldiers' Home National Cemeteries For information write to the Superintendent, Arlington National Cemetery, Arlington, VA 22211–5003. Phone, 202–695–3175.

Speakers Civilian organizations desiring an Army speaker may contact a nearby Army installation or write or call the Community Relations Division, Office of the Chief of Public Affairs, Department of the Army, Washington, DC 20310–1508. Phone, 202–697–5720. Requests for Army Reserve speakers may be addressed to HQDA (DAAR–PA), Washington, DC 20310–2423, or the local Army Reserve Center. Organizations in the Washington, DC, area desiring chaplain speakers may contact the Chief of Chaplains, Department of the Army, Washington,

DC 20310–2700. Phone, 202–695–1137. Information on speakers may be obtained by contacting the Public Affairs Office, Office of the Chief of Engineers, Washington, DC 20314, or the nearest Corps of Engineer Division or District Office.

Freedom of Information and Privacy Acts Inquiries concerning Department of the Army policies pertaining to Freedom of Information Act and Privacy Act matters should be addressed to HQDA (DAIM–FAR–A), Hoffman Building, 2461 Eisenhower Ave., Alexandria, VA 22331–0301, or by calling for Freedom of Information Act matters, or Privacy Act matters, 202–325–6163. In addition, assistance or information concerning requests for records of a specific Army field command, installation, or organization, may be obtained by contacting the local Army installation or organization Information Officer.

For further information concerning the Department of the Army, contact the Office of the Chief of Public Affairs, Headquarters, Department of the Army, Washington, DC 20310–1508. Phone, 202–694–0741.

United States Military Academy

West Point, NY 10996

The United States Military Academy is located at West Point, NY. The course is of 4 years' duration, during which the cadets receive, besides a general education, theoretical and practical training as junior officers. Cadets who complete the course satisfactorily receive the degree of Bachelor of Science and a commission as second lieutenant in the Army.

For further general information concerning the United States Military Academy, contact the Public Affairs Office, United States Military Academy, West Point NY 10996. Phone, 914–938–4261.

For information about Military Academy admission criteria and policies, contact the Office of the Registrar, United States Military Academy, West Point, NY 10996.

DEPARTMENT OF THE NAVY

The Pentagon, Washington, DC 20350
Phone, 202-545-6700

The primary mission of the Department of the Navy is to protect the United States, as directed by the President or the Secretary of Defense, by the effective prosecution of war at sea including, with its Marine Corps component, the seizure or defense of advanced naval bases; to support, as required, the forces of all military departments of the United States; and maintain freedom of the seas.

The United States Navy was founded on October 13, 1775, when Congress enacted the first legislation creating the Continental Navy of the American Revolution. The Department of the Navy and the Office of Secretary of the Navy were established by act of Congress approved April 30, 1798 (1 Stat. 553; 10 U.S.C. 5011, 5031). For 9 years prior to that date, by an act of Congress approved August 7, 1789 (1 Stat. 49), the conduct of naval affairs was under the Secretary of War.

The National Security Act Amendments of 1949 established the Department of Defense as an executive department of the Federal Government, and provided that the Department of the Navy be a military department within the Department of Defense (63 Stat. 578).

The Secretary of the Navy is appointed by the President as the head of the Department of the Navy and is responsible to the Secretary of Defense for the operation and efficiency of the Navy (10 U.S.C. 5031).

The organization of the Department of the Navy is reflected in the organization chart and personnel listing. The Department of the Navy includes the U.S. Coast Guard when it is operating as a Service in the Navy.

Office of the Secretary of the Navy

Secretary of the Navy

The Secretary of the Navy is the head of the Department of the Navy. Under the direction, authority, and control of the Secretary of Defense, the Secretary of the Navy is responsible for the policies and control of the Department of the Navy, including its organization, administration, operation, and efficiency. The members of the Secretary's executive administration assist in the discharge of the responsibilities of the Secretary of the Navy.

During the temporary absence of the Secretary of the Navy, the Under Secretary of the Navy is next in succession to act as the Secretary of the Navy. The Under Secretary functions as deputy and principal assistant to the Secretary, and acts with full authority of the Secretary in the general management of the Department.

Civilian Executive Assistants

The Civilian Executive Assistants to the Secretary are the principal advisers and assistants to the Secretary of the Navy on the administration of the affairs of the Department of the Navy as a whole and are assigned Department-wide responsibilities for areas essential to the efficient administration of the Department of the Navy.

The Civilian Executive Assistants to the Secretary of the Navy are the Under Secretary of the Navy, the Assistant Secretaries of the Navy, and the General Counsel of the Navy. It is the policy of the Secretary to assign Department-wide responsibilities essential to the efficient administration of the Department of the Navy to the Civilian Executive Assistants.

Each Civilian Executive Assistant, within an assigned area of responsibility, is the principal adviser and assistant to the Secretary on the administration of the affairs of the Department of the Navy. The Civilian Executive Assistants carry out the duties in harmony with the statutory position of the Chief of Naval Operations as the principal naval adviser and naval executive to the Secretary on the conduct of activities of the Department of the Navy and the responsibilities of the Chief of Naval Operations and the Commandant of the Marine Corps. Each is authorized and directed to act for the Secretary within his assigned area of responsibility.

The Under Secretary of the Navy is designated as the deputy and principal assistant to the Secretary of the Navy to act with full authority of the Secretary in

the general management of the Department and to supervise the offices and organizations as assigned by the Secretary.

The Assistant Secretary of the Navy (Financial Management) is the Comptroller of the Navy and is responsible for all matters related to the financial management of the Department, including budgeting, accounting, disbursing, financing, internal review, progress and statistical reporting, automatic data processing systems and equipment (ADPE), except ADPE integral to a weapon system, and supervision of offices and organizations as assigned by the Secretary. Under the Comptroller, the Deputy Comptroller of the Navy shall, in addition to other duties, serve as an adviser and assistant to the Chief of Naval Operations and the Commandant of the Marine Corps with respect to financial and budgetary matters.

The Assistant Secretary of the Navy (Manpower and Reserve Affairs) is responsible for the overall supervision of manpower and reserve component affairs of the Department, including policy and administration of affairs related to military (active and inactive) and civilian personnel, and supervision of offices and organizations as assigned by the Secretary, specifically the Naval Council of Personnel Boards and the Board for Correction of Naval Records.

The Assistant Secretary of the Navy (Shipbuilding and Logistics) is responsible for all stages of the acquisition of naval ships funded by the appropriation "Shipbuilding and Conversion, Navy;" all Department of the Navy acquisition programs following full-scale production decision (Milestone III); the business, contractual, manpower, and logistic support aspects of the Department's acquisition programs, including policy and administration of affairs related thereto; the maintenance, alteration, supply, distribution, and disposal of material; all transportation matters; the acquisition, construction, utilization, improvement, alteration, maintenance, and disposal of real estate and facilities, including capital equipment, utilities, housing, and public quarters; industrial preparedness planning; labor relations with respect to contractors with the Department of the Navy; industrial security; the Mutual Defense Assistance Program as related to the supplying of material, including foreign military sales; and supervision of offices and organizations as assigned by the Secretary.

The Assistant Secretary of the Navy (Research, Engineering and Systems) is responsible for all matters related to research, development, engineering, test, and evaluation efforts within the Department, including management of the appropriation, "Research, Development, Test, and Evaluation, Navy;" oceanography, ocean engineering, and closely related matters; the technical aspects of production management and maintenance or alteration of material; Navy acquisition programs through the full-scale production decision (Milestone III), including policy and administration of affairs related thereto, with the exception of the acquisition of naval ships funded by the appropriation "Shipbuilding and Conversion, Navy;" and supervision of offices and organizations as assigned by the Secretary.

The General Counsel provides legal advice, counsel, and guidance to the Secretary of the Navy and the other Civilian Executive Assistants and their staffs on any issue or matter involving the Department of the Navy. The General Counsel provides legal services relating to: general legal issues, litigation, business and commercial law, real and personal property, civilian personnel law, patent law, and procurement of services, including the fiscal, budgetary, and accounting aspects for the Navy and the Marine Corps.

The Staff Assistants

The Staff Assistants to the Secretary of the Navy are the Auditor General of the Navy, the Chief of Information, the Chief of Legislative Affairs, the Director, Office of Program Appraisal, and the heads of such other offices and boards as may be established by law or by the Secretary for the purpose of assisting the Secretary or one or more of the Civilian Executive Assistants in the administration of the Department of the Navy. Each supervises all functions and activities internal to that office and assigned shore activities, if any. Each is responsible to the Secretary or to one of the Civilian Executive Assistants for the utilization of resources by, and the operating efficiency of, all activities under their supervision. The duties of the individual Staff Assistants and their respective offices are provided by law or assigned by the Secretary.

Naval Research   The Office of Naval Research, established by the act of August 1, 1946 (60 Stat. 779; 10 U.S.C. 5150–5153), is headed by a Chief of Naval Research who is appointed by the President by and with the advice and consent of the Senate, and is authorized to act for the Secretary of the Navy on all assigned matters. The Chief of Naval Research is responsible to the Secretary, through the Assistant Secretary of the Navy (Research, Engineering and Systems), for the performance of assigned functions, duties, and responsibilities. The Chief of Naval Research is responsible for the encouragement, promotion, planning, initiation, and coordination of naval research; the conduct of naval research

440

in augmentation of and in conjunction with the research and development conducted by the bureaus, system commands, and other agencies and offices of the Department; the supervision, administration, and control of activities within or on behalf of the Department relating to patents, inventions, trademarks, copyrights, and royalty payments, and matters connected therewith.

Office of Naval Research Detachments are located in Bay St. Louis, Boston, Chicago, and Pasadena. A branch office is located in London, England. Other field activities are: the Naval Research Laboratory, Washington, DC; the Naval Biosciences Laboratory, Oakland, CA; the Naval Ocean Research and Development Activity, Bay St. Louis, MS; and the Office of Naval Research Liaison Office, Far East. In addition, the Office of Naval Research has various resident representatives in geographical areas of extensive research activity.

(Office of Naval Research, Department of the Navy, Ballston Tower No. 1, 800 N. Quincy Street, Arlington, VA 22217. Phone, 202–696–4258.)

Judge Advocate General The Judge Advocate General is the senior officer of the Judge Advocate General's Corps of the Navy and is the Commander of the Naval Legal Service Command. The Judge Advocate General supervises the administration of military justice throughout the Navy, performs the functions required or authorized by the Uniform Code of Military Justice, provides technical supervision for the Naval Justice School at Newport, RI, and has responsibility for such legal duties and services throughout the Department of the Navy as are not provided by the General Counsel of the Navy. The Judge Advocate General maintains a close

working relationship with the General Counsel on all matters of common interest and has responsibility for liaison with other departments and agencies of the Government in appropriate cases.

Officers of the Judge Advocate General's Corps and Judge Advocates of the Marine Corps provide legal services in such matters as legal assistance and tax advice to naval personnel and their dependents, investigations, claims, admiralty, international relations, courts-martial, nonjudicial punishment, civilian personnel law at field activities (under the overall coordination and policy guidance of the Office of Civilian Personnel Law), military personnel law, labor relations, conservation, and environmental protection.

For further information concerning activities of the Judge Advocate General's Corps, contact the Office of the Judge Advocate General, Code 004, Department of the Navy, 200 Stovall Street, Alexandria, VA 22332. For telephone inquiries, contact the Public Affairs Officer, phone, 202–325–9820.

Comptroller Pursuant to the provisions of 10 U.S.C. 5061, the Secretary of the Navy established the Office of the Comptroller of the Navy on June 1, 1950.

The Comptroller is responsible for financial management of the Navy, including budgeting, accounting, progress and statistical reporting, administrative organization, and related managerial procedures.

Auditor General of the Navy The Auditor General of the Navy is responsible for developing and implementing Navy internal audit policies, programs, and procedures within the framework of Government auditing standards and serving as Director of the Naval Audit Service.

The function of internal audit is to objectively evaluate and make recommendations concerning the integrity and reliability of financial and other data used to make management decisions; the adequacy of policies and procedures affecting the expenditure of funds, the safeguarding and efficient use of resources, and the accomplishment of management objectives and program results; and the extent of compliance with applicable policies, procedures, laws, and regulations.

Audits are accomplished through four Naval Audit Service regional offices with support from Naval Audit Service Headquarters. Each regional office has audit responsibility within an assigned geographic area, including responsibility for permanent audit sites and mobile audit teams.

(Auditor General of the Navy, Department of the Navy, Post Office Box 1206, Falls Church, VA 22041–0206. Phone, 703–756–2117.)

Chief of Information The Chief of Information is the direct representative of the Secretary of the Navy and of the Chief of Naval Operations in all public affairs and internal relations matters and is authorized to implement Navy public affairs and internal relations policies and to coordinate those Navy and Marine Corps activities that are of mutual interest.

The Chief of Information is responsible for keeping Navy commands informed of Department of Defense policies and requirements and is the only principal component within the Office of the Chief of Naval Operations authorized to deal directly with the Office of the Assistant Secretary of Defense (Public Affairs).

Principal functions of the Office of Information include making available accurate and timely information about the Navy so that the general public, the press, and Congress may understand and assess the Navy's programs, operations,

and needs; coordination of Navy participation in community events; supervision of the Navy's internal information programs as well as Freedom of Information and Privacy Act coordination.

Field activities of the Chief of Information include six Navy Information Offices (NAVINFO's), two Navy Public Affairs Centers (NAVPACEN's), and one Fleet Home Town News Center (FHTNC).

(Office of Information, Department of the Navy, Washington, DC 20350. Phone, 202–697–5342.)

Naval Council of Personnel Boards
The Naval Council of Personnel Boards, comprised of the Naval Discharge Review Board, Naval Complaints Review Board, Naval Clemency and Parole Board, Employee Appeals Review Board, the Disability Evaluation System, and Naval Physical Disability Review Board, administers, under the Assistant Secretary of the Navy (Manpower and Reserve Affairs), personnel services and support as indicated by each component board's title.

Naval Discharge Review Board: The board reviews, pursuant to 10 U.S.C. 1553, upon its own motion or upon request by or on behalf of former Navy and Marine Corps members, the type and reason for discharge or dismissal received by that former member, except a discharge or dismissal by reason of the sentence of general court-martial. It determines whether, under reasonable standards of naval law and discipline, a discharge or dismissal should be changed and, if so, what change should be made.

Naval Complaints Review Board: The Board reviews, upon request, decisional documents and/or index entries created by the Naval Discharge Review Board after April 1, 1977. The Naval Complaints Review Board determines whether decisional documents conform to those applicable regulations of the Department of Defense and the Department of the Navy.

Naval Clemency and Parole Board: The Board reviews, pursuant to 10 U.S.C. 953–954, Navy and Marine Corps court-martial cases referred to it and grants or denies clemency; and, pursuant to 10 U.S.C. 952, reviews and directs that parole be granted or denied in cases referred to it for review.

Employee Appeals Review Board: The Board renders final decisions, and directs implementation of them, on civilian employee complaints alleging discrimination based on race, color, religion, sex, age, physical or mental handicap or national origin and other civilian employee grievances and appeals properly referred to it.

Disability Evaluation System: The System organizes and administers disability evaluations within the Department of the Navy pursuant to 10 U.S.C., chapter 61, and other applicable provisions of law and regulation. It is comprised of the Central Physical Evaluation Board, regional Physical Evaluation Boards at Bethesda, MD, Great Lakes, IL, and San Diego, CA, the Physical Review Council, and disability evaluation system counselors located at major medical centers. The system considers evidence concerning disabilities of personnel and determines the appropriate disposition in each case.

Physical Disability Review Board: The Board reviews appropriate appeals from the Physical Review Council and renders advisory opinions to the Board for Correction of Naval Records, ensuring conformity with accepted medical principles, pertinent law and regulation, and established personnel policies in each case.

(Naval Council of Personnel Boards, Department of the Navy, Room 905, 801 N. Randolph Street, Arlington, VA 22203. Phone, 202–696–4356.)

Board for Correction of Naval Records

The Board for Correction of Naval Records is a statutory civilian board, established pursuant to the provisions of 10 U.S.C. 1552, to relieve the Congress of the burden and necessity of considering private relief legislation for the correction of errors and injustices suffered by members and former members of the Navy and Marine Corps. The Secretary of the Navy, acting through this board of civilians of the executive part of the Department, is authorized to take action consistent with law and regulation to correct naval or military records of the Department of the Navy where such action is necessary or appropriate to correct an error or to remove an injustice. The Board represents the highest echelon of review of administrative errors and injustices. The Board reviews, on application, actions taken by various boards and officials in the Department.

(Board for Correction of Naval Records, Department of the Navy, Room 2432, Navy Annex, Washington, DC 20370. Phone, 202–694–1765.)

United States Navy

Chief of Naval Operations

The Chief of Naval Operations (CNO) is the senior military officer of the Department of the Navy and takes precedence above all other officers of the naval service, except an officer of the naval service who is serving as Chairman of the Joint Chiefs of Staff. He is the principal naval adviser to the President and the Secretary of the Navy on the conduct of war, and the principal naval adviser and naval executive to the Secretary on the conduct of the activities of the Department of the Navy. He is the Navy member of the Joint Chiefs of Staff.

The Chief of Naval Operations, under the Secretary of the Navy, exercises command over certain central executive organizations, assigned shore activities, and the Operating Forces of the Navy.

The Chief of Naval Operations plans for and provides the manpower, material, weapons, facilities, and services to support the needs of the Navy, with the exception of the Fleet Marine Forces; maintains water transportation services, including sea transportation services for the Department of Defense; directs the Naval Reserve; and exercises authority for matters of naval administration, including matters related to customs and traditions of the naval service, security, intelligence, discipline, naval communications, and naval operations.

The Chief of Naval Operations exercises area coordination authority over all shore activities of the Department of the Navy to ensure that total efforts afford adequate support to the combatant forces and are coordinated among themselves to assure economy and efficiency of operation.

Operating Forces of the Navy

The Operating Forces of the Navy are responsible for naval operations necessary to carry out the Department of the Navy's role in upholding and advancing the national policies and interests of the United States. The Operating Forces of the Navy include the several fleets, seagoing forces, Fleet Marine Forces and other assigned Marine Corps forces, the Military Sealift Command, and other forces and activities as may be assigned by the President or the Secretary of the Navy. The Chief of Naval Operations is responsible for the command and administration of the Operating Forces of the Navy.

The Pacific Fleet is composed of ships, submarines, and aircraft operating throughout the Pacific and Indian Oceans.

The Atlantic Fleet is composed of ships, submarines, and aircraft that operate throughout the Atlantic Ocean and Mediterranean Sea.

The Naval Forces, Europe, includes forces assigned by the Chief of Naval Operations or made available from either the Pacific or Atlantic Fleet to operate in the European theater.

The Military Sealift Command provides ocean transportation (by Government-owned or commercial vessels) for personnel and cargo of all components of the Department of Defense and as authorized for other Federal agencies; operates and maintains underway replenishment ships and other vessels providing mobile logistic support to elements of the combatant fleets; and operates ships in support of scientific projects and other programs for Federal agencies.

Other major commands of the Operating Forces of the Navy are the Commander, U.S. Naval Forces Central Command; Commander, U.S. Naval Forces Southern Command; Commander, Operational Test and Evaluation Force; Commander, Mine Warfare Command; and Commander, Naval Reserve Force.

Navy Command Structure

The Chief of Naval Operations manages and supports the Operating Forces of the Navy through the following executive and functional organization structure.

Office of the Chief of Naval Operations   The Office of the Chief of Naval Operations (OPNAV) is the headquarters of the Navy which advises and assists the CNO in the discharge of his responsibilities. The Office of the Chief of Naval Operations was established basically in its present structure by Executive Order 9635 of September 29, 1945, and later by act of March 5, 1948 (38 Stat. 929, 62 Stat. 66; 10 U.S.C. 141, 171, 5036(b), 5081–5088).

Naval Sea Systems   The Commander, Naval Sea Systems Command, provides material support to the Navy and Marine Corps for ships, submarines, and other sea platforms, shipboard combat systems and components, other surface and undersea warfare and weapons systems, and ordnance expendables not specifically assigned to other system commands.

(Commander, Naval Sea Systems Command, Washington, DC 20362–5101. Phone, 202–692–3328.)

Naval Air Systems   The Commander, Naval Air Systems Command, provides for the material support to the Navy and Marine Corps for aircraft, airborne weapon systems, avionics, related photographic and support equipment, ranges, and targets.

(Commander, Naval Air Systems Command, Washington, DC 20361–0001. Phone, 202–692–2260.)

Space and Naval Warfare Systems   The Commander, Space and Naval Warfare Systems Command, provides material and technical support to the Navy and Marine Corps for space systems, command, control, communications, and intelligence, electronic warfare, and undersea surveillance; provides force warfighting architecture and requirements integration among total naval battle forces; and has responsibility for management of the Navy research and development centers and university laboratories.

(Commander, Space and Naval Warfare Systems Command, Washington, DC 20363–5100. Phone, 202–692–8768.)

Naval Supply Systems   The Commander, Naval Supply Systems Command, provides for the material support to the Navy and Marine Corps for materials, supplies, and supporting services by providing supply management policies and methods and administering related support service systems, and administers the security assistance program.

(Commander, Naval Supply Systems Command, Washington, DC 20376–5000. Phone, 202–695–4009.)

Naval Facilities   The Commander, Naval Facilities Engineering Command, provides for material and technical support to the Navy and Marine Corps for shore facilities, real property, and utilities, fixed ocean systems and structures, transportation and construction equipment, energy, environmental, and natural resources management, and support of the Naval Construction Forces.

(Commander, Naval Facilities Engineering Command, 200 Stovall Street, Alexandria, VA 22332–2300. Phone, 202–325–8543.)

Strategic Systems   The Director, Strategic Systems Program provides for the development, production, and material support to the Navy for fleet ballistic missile and strategic weapon systems, including the missiles, platforms, and associated equipment; security, training of personnel, and the installation and direction of necessary supporting facilities.

(Director, Strategic Systems Program Office,

445

Department of the Navy, Washington, DC 20376–5002. Phone, 202–695–2158.)

Bureau of Naval Personnel The Chief of Naval Personnel directs the procurement, distribution, administration, and career motivation of the military personnel of the regular and reserve components of the United States Navy to meet the quantitive and qualitative manpower requirements determined by the Chief of Naval Operations. He also directs the management and administration of the Navy Civilian Personnel/EEO Programs and develops servicewide programs for improved human resources management.

(Bureau of Naval Personnel, Department of the Navy, Federal Office Building No. 2, Washington, DC 20370–5000. Phone, 202–694–1271.)

Naval Medical Command The Commander, Naval Medical Command, directs the provision of medical and dental services for Navy and Marine Corps personnel and other persons authorized by law; ensures that health care program policies are optimally executed through the acquisition and effective utilization of financial and manpower resources; maintains all assigned activities in a proper state of material and personnel readiness to fulfill assigned peacetime and contingency mission taskings; administers the execution and implementation of contingency support plans and programs that provide for an effective medical and dental readiness capability; acquires, trains, and maintains a force of professional and technical personnel; provides professional and technical medical and dental service to the Fleet, Fleet Marine Force, and shore activities of the Navy; ensures that assigned activities are able to achieve successful accreditation and recognition by appropriate governmental and civilian

agencies and commissions; and ensures cooperation with civil authorities in matters pertaining to public health disasters and other emergencies, in conjunction with maintaining and safeguarding the health of Navy and Marine Corps personnel.

(Naval Medical Command, Department of the Navy, 23d and E Streets NW., Washington, DC 20372–5120. Phone, 202–653–1327.)

Oceanography The Commander, Naval Oceanography Command, and the Superintendent, U.S. Naval Observatory, are responsible for the science, technology, engineering, operations, and those personnel and facilities associated with each, which are essential to explore the ocean and the atmosphere and to provide astronomical data and time for naval and related national objectives. Oceanography examines how naval operations are influenced by the physical environment and applies its findings to the development of technology and methods for improving naval operations.

The Naval Oceanographic Program embraces five major disciplines of physical science to investigate the nature and behavior of the ocean environment in which the Navy operates. They are:

Hydrography—to collect data for the charting of the oceans and to establish geodetic references for navigation;

Oceanography—to define the characteristics of the water volume for use in ocean reporting and prediction, and studies of underwater acoustics, water dynamics, corrosion, and other factors influencing the performance of naval systems;

Meteorology—to define the characteristics of the atmosphere for use in weather reporting and prediction, and studies of upper atmosphere winds and currents, refractive indices for radar performance, and similar factors;

446

Astrometry—to determine the position and motions of celestial bodies required for accurate navigation, operational support, and use in calculating precise geodetic positions and azimuth references on Earth; and

Precise Time—to determine, provide, and manage the distribution of precise time and time interval (frequency), both atomic and astronomical, for use in electronic navigation and command, control, and communications.

(Oceanographer of the Navy, U.S. Naval Observatory, Washington, DC 20390–5100. Phone, 202–653–1295. Commander, Naval Oceanography Command, NSTL Station, Bay St. Louis, MS 39529. Phone, 601–688–4726. Superintendent, Naval Observatory, Washington, DC 20390–5000. Phone, 202–653–1538.)

Naval Space Command The Commander, Naval Space Command, provides operational space systems support to naval forces worldwide and helps prepare the naval service for extended future involvement in space. The Command has operational responsibility for all Navy space-related systems, plus coordination responsibility with other operational activities so that space capabilities are integrated into the Navy's operational plans. The Command identifies fleet operational requirements for space systems, which will be translated into specific program planning and budgeting. The Command has operational responsibility for the Navy Navigation Satellite System, the Naval Space Surveillance System, and elements supporting the Fleet Satellite Communications System of the Naval Telecommunications Systems.

The Command has responsibility for the Relocatable Over-the-Horizon Radar System, a broad area surveillance high-frequency radar that will have the capability to be relocated to prepared global sites to support naval forces; and

the Navy Remote Ocean Sensing System, which is being developed to support fleet users with important oceanographic data supplied from space.

(Naval Space Command, Department of the Navy, Dahlgren, VA 22448. Phone, 703–663–7841.)

Naval Legal Service Command The Commander, Naval Legal Service Command, under the command of the Chief of Naval Operations, is responsible for administering the legal services program within the Department of the Navy and providing command direction for all Naval Legal Service Command activities and resources.

(Commander, Naval Legal Service Command, Hoffman Building No. 2, 200 Stovall Street, Alexandria, VA 22332. Phone, 202–325–9850.)

Naval Telecommunications The Commander, Naval Telecommunications Command, exercises configuration control of the Naval Telecommunications System; commands, operates, and maintains the Naval Telecommunications Command; serves as the operations and maintenance manager of assigned elements of the Defense Communications System; and serves as technical adviser for Navy telecommunications training.

(Commander, Naval Telecommunications Command, 4401 Massachusetts Avenue NW., Washington, DC 20390–5290. Phone, 202–282–0357.)

Cryptology The Commander, Naval Security Group Command, performs cryptologic functions; provides, operates, and maintains an adequate Naval Security Group; approves requirements for the use of existing Naval Security Group capabilities and resources; and coordinates the execution of approved cryptologic programs.

Naval Intelligence The Commander, Naval Intelligence Command, ensures the fulfillment of the intelligence requirements and responsibilities of the Department of the Navy.

(Naval Intelligence Command, Department of the Navy, 4600 Silver Hill Road, Washington, DC 20389. Phone, 202–763–3552; hotline, 202–763–3556.)

Naval Security and Investigative Command The Commander, Naval Security and Investigative Command, commands a worldwide organization, with representation in more than 160 geographic locations, to provide criminal investigative, counterintelligence, law enforcement and physical security, and information and personnel security support to the Navy and Marine Corps, both ashore and afloat. The Naval Security and Investigative Command is comprised of law enforcement professionals who are investigators, crime laboratory technicians, technical investigative specialists, counterintelligence analysts, physical security specialists, and administrative support personnel.

(Naval Security and Investigative Command, Department of the Navy, Washington, DC 20388. For general information, call 301–763–3783, or contact the Operations Control Center/ Headquarters Duty Officer, 301–763–3780.)

Naval Education and Training The mission of the Chief of Naval Education and Training is to provide assigned shore-based education and training for Navy, certain Marine Corps, and other personnel in support of the Fleet, Naval Shore Establishment, Naval Reserve, Interservice Training Program, and

Security Assistance Program; develop specifically designated education and training afloat programs for the Fleet; execute the Navy's responsibility for voluntary education and dependents education; participate with research and development activities in the development and implementation of the most effective teaching and training systems and devices for optimal education and training; and perform such other functions as directed.

(Chief of Naval Education and Training, Naval Air Station, Department of the Navy, Pensacola, FL 32508. Phone, 904–452–3613.)

Naval Information Systems The Director, Naval Data Automation Command, administers and coordinates the Navy Information Systems and administrative management programs. The Director collaborates with all Navy claimants on information systems matters; develops management plans, policy, and procedures; develops information systems, technical standards, and guidelines; plans and develops Navy information systems and architecture; sponsors information systems and technology; sponsors career development and training of information systems and administrative management personnel; and approves system development, acquisitions, and utilization of automated information systems support facilities.

(Director, Naval Data Automation Command, Washington Navy Yard, Washington, DC 20374–2181. Phone, 202–433–4748.)

United States Marine Corps

Commandant of the Marine Corps,
Department of the Navy, Washington, DC 20380–0001
Phone, 202–694–2500

The United States Marine Corps was initially established on November 10, 1775, by resolution of the Continental Congress. The present composition, missions, and functions of the Marine Corps are set forth in the National Security Act of 1947, as amended in 1952.

The primary mission assigned to the Marine Corps is to provide Fleet Marine Forces of combined arms, together with supporting air components, for service with the Fleet in the seizure or defense of advanced naval bases and for the conduct of such land operations as may be essential to the prosecution of a naval campaign. Collateral functions of the Marine Corps are to provide detachments and organizations for service on armed vessels of the Navy and security detachments aboard naval stations/bases and other governmental installations. The Marine Corps is also responsible for developing, in coordination with the other military services, the tactics, doctrine, techniques, and equipment employed by landing forces in amphibious operations. An additional function is to prepare for wartime expansion, in accordance with joint mobilization plans, which may require activation of reserve forces when necessary. Included as a Marine Corps mission is the all-encompassing statement of "performing such other duties as the President may direct."

Structure The National Security Act, as amended in 1978, reaffirms the Marine Corps as a separate service within the Department of the Navy and seats the Commandant of the Marine Corps as a full member of the Joint Chiefs of Staff.

The Marine Corps is composed of Operating Forces and a Supporting Establishment. The actual Operating Forces include three active divisions, one reserve division, three active aircraft wings, one reserve aircraft wing, three force service support groups, and one reserve force service group. The largest of the Operating Forces is the Fleet Marine Force, Pacific (FMFPAC), with major subordinate commands located on the west coast, Hawaii, and in Japan. Included under FMFPAC are two Marine divisions, two Marine aircraft wings, and two Force Service Support Groups. In addition, the headquarters of two Marine Amphibious Forces, four Marine Amphibious Brigades, and two Marine Amphibious Units are being permanently formed. The Fleet Marine Force, Atlantic (FMFLANT), commands the Operating Forces located on the east coast. These forces consist of a Marine division, a Marine aircraft wing, and a supporting Force Service Support Group, and the permanent headquarters of one Marine Amphibious Force, two Marine Amphibious Brigades, and two Marine Amphibious Units.

Marine Corps organization emphasizes the close integration of air-ground operations. Normally, a separate headquarters is task organized for command and control of air-ground units for combat operations, for deployments afloat in amphibious shipping and during training exercises. Marine air-ground task forces, of varying size and capabilities, are organized from the Fleet Marine Forces.

The Marine Corps Supporting

Its traditional peacetime role is to serve as a force-in-readiness. The Marine Corps has a global outlook, and Marines stand ready to be deployed to any part of the world to carry out their assigned missions. The Marines emphasize physical fitness and intensive training. The Marine Corps maintains three rapid response air-ground task forces, elements of which are continuously forward deployed in the Mediterranean Sea, the Western Pacific Ocean, and, intermittently, in the Indian Ocean. These ready forces are responsive to a variety of contingencies worldwide, as directed.

Marine Corps Districts

District	Address
1	605 Stewart Ave., Garden City, NY 11530-4761. Phone, 516-228-5652
4	Bldg. 75, Naval Base, Philadelphia, PA 19112-5000. Phone, 215-897-6301
6	75 Piedmont Ave. NE., Atlanta, GA 30303-2201. Phone, 404-331-6309
8	Bldg. 10, Naval Support Activity, New Orleans, LA 70146-5200. Phone, 504-361-2361
9	10000 W. 75th St., Shawnee Mission, KS 66204-2265. Phone, 913-236-3302
12	Bldg. 7, Naval Station, Treasure Island, San Francisco, CA 94130-5059. Phone, 415-765-5901.

Sources of Information

Consumer Activities Research programs of the Office of Naval Research cover a broad spectrum of scientific fields, primarily for the needs of the Navy, but much information is of interest to the public. Inquiries on specific programs should be directed to the Assistant Chief for Research, Department of the Navy, 800 N. Quincy Street, Arlington, VA 22217-5000. Phone, 202-692-4261.

Environment The Assistant Secretary of the Navy (Shipbuilding and Logistics) is responsible for the conduct of the environmental protection program of the Navy and Marine Corps, and serves as the focal point for the Department in establishing policy in environmental affairs. This is the contact for liaison at the highest level with other Federal and State agencies in addition to private agencies organized on a national level. All environmental impact statements that originate within the Navy and Marine Corps for submission to the Environmental Protection Agency, in compliance with the National Environmental Policy Act, are processed by the Assistant Secretary of the Navy (Shipbuilding and Logistics). This Office maintains close liaison with the Council on Environmental Quality, the Environmental Protection Agency, and the Assistant Secretary of Defense (Health and Environment) in the implementation of the environmental protection program. Other responsible offices within the Department of the Navy are the Environmental Protection, Occupational Safety and Health Division in the Office of the Chief of Naval Operations, and the Office of the Deputy Chief of Staff for Installations and Logistics, Headquarters, U.S. Marine Corps.

Astronomy The United States Naval Observatory provides the astronomical data and precise time required by the Navy and other components of the Department of Defense for navigation, precise positioning, and command, control, and communications. These data also are made available to other Government agencies and to the general public. To broaden the understanding of the mission, functions, and programs of the Naval Observatory, regular night tours and special group day tours are

450

conducted. The night tours are open to the general public and are given every Monday night, except on Federal holidays. Daytime group tours are available if scheduled in advance. Information concerning activities of the observatory and public tours may be obtained by writing to the Superintendent, Naval Observatory, Washington, DC 20390–5100. Phone, 202–653–1543.

Contract Information and Small Business Activities Information in these areas can be obtained from the Assistant Secretary of the Navy (Shipbuilding and Logistics), Department of the Navy, Washington, DC 20350 (phone, 202–692–2202); or from the Assistant Secretary of the Navy (Research, Engineering, and Systems), Department of the Navy, The Pentagon, Washington, DC 20350 (phone, 202–695–6315). Information pertaining specifically to the Marine Corps in the areas of small businesses, minority-owned businesses, and labor surplus activities can be obtained from the Marine Corps Small Business Specialist (LBS), Installations and Logistics Department, Headquarters, U.S. Marine Corps, Washington, DC 20380. Phone, 202–694–1939.

Employment Information Information about civilian employment opportunities within the Department of the Navy in the Washington, DC, metropolitan area can be obtained from the Naval Civilian Personnel Command, Capital Region, 801 N. Randolph Street, Arlington, VA 22203. Phone, 202–696–4567; or the Commandant of the Marine Corps Code (MPC–30), Headquarters, U.S. Marine Corps, Washington, DC 20380. Phone, 202–694–1046.

Speakers and Films Information on how to obtain speakers, films, and exhibits concerning the Navy can be obtained by writing the Office of Information, Department of the Navy, Washington, DC 20350 (phone, 202–697–8711); information on how to obtain Marine Corps speakers can be obtained by writing to the Director of Public Affairs, Headquarters, U.S. Marine Corps, Washington, DC 20380–0001 (phone, 202–694–4080); or by contacting the Director of any Marine Corps District.

General Information Navy and Marine Corps recruiting offices, installation commanders, and Directors of Marine Corps Districts (see above) can answer general inquiries concerning the Navy and Marine Corps and their community and public information programs.

Military Career Opportunities

Navy. Information concerning the numerous career fields available within the Navy, as well as the various enlisted and officer training programs, can be obtained by writing the Commander, Navy Recruiting Command (Code 30), 4015 Wilson Boulevard, Arlington, VA 22203–1991, or by calling toll free, the Navy Information Center, 800–327–NAVY.

Naval Reserve. Information concerning Naval Reserve opportunities can be obtained from the Commander, Naval Reserve Force, New Orleans, LA 70146–5000 (Code 004). Phone, 504–948–1240.

Marine Corps. The Marine Corps conducts enlisted and officer training programs requiring various lengths of service and provides the assurance of specialized skill training and other benefits.

The Marine Corps provides opportunities for training in a variety of technical skills that are necessary in support of ground and aviation combat operations. Radar operation and repair,

451

meteorology, engineer equipment and automotive mechanics, artillery and armor repair, data processing, communications-electronics, jet aircraft repair, avionics, and air control are but a few specialized fields available.

The Marine Corps participates in the Naval Reserve Officers Training Corps Program for commissioning officers in the Marine Corps.

Platoon Leaders Class (PLC) is a Marine Corps program for commissioning officers in the Marine Corps Reserve. Freshmen, sophomores, or juniors in an accredited college may apply for the PLC. The PLC Program provides for financial assistance to undergraduates.

The Officer Candidate Class (OCC) is another program for commissioning officers in the Marine Corps Reserve. Applicants for OCC must be college graduates or must be in their senior year.

Information on the above programs is available at most civilian educational institutions and Navy and Marine Corps recruiting stations. Local telephone directories list the address and telephone number of the Recruiting Station and Officer Selection Officer under U.S. Government. Interested persons also may write directly to the Commandant of the Marine Corps (MR), Washington, DC 20380-0001. Phone, 202-694-2914.

Information concerning Marine Corps Reserve opportunities can be obtained from local Marine Corps recruiting stations or Marine Corps Reserve Drill Centers. Interested persons may also write directly to the Commandant of the Marine Corps (RES), Washington, DC 20380-0001.

United States Naval Academy

Annapolis, MD 21402
Phone, 301-267-4361 (Office of the Dean of Admissions—Candidate Guidance)

The United States Naval Academy offers a 4-year program of academic, military, and professional instruction for the education and training of young men and women for the naval service. Completion of the program normally leads to a commission in the United States Navy or the United States Marine Corps, and to one of seven designated Bachelor of Science degrees in engineering fields, or an undesignated Bachelor of Science degree with major options in 11 fields. Information concerning the United States Naval Academy may be obtained by writing the Superintendent, United States Naval Academy, Annapolis, MD 21402-5000.

For further information concerning the Navy and Marine Corps, contact the Office of Information, Department of the Navy, Washington, DC 20350 (phone, 202-697-7391); or the Director, Division of Public Affairs, Headquarters, U.S. Marine Corps, Washington, DC 20380 (phone 202-694-1492).

DEPARTMENT OF DEFENSE AGENCIES AND JOINT SERVICE SCHOOLS

Defense Advanced Research Projects Agency

1400 Wilson Boulevard, Arlington, VA 22209–2308
Phone, 202–694–3007

The Advanced Research Projects Agency, established in 1958 as an operating agency under the Director of Defense Research and Engineering, was redesignated as the Defense Advanced Research Projects Agency (DARPA) on March 23, 1972. It is a separate agency of the Department of Defense under the control of the Under Secretary of Defense for Research and Engineering.

DARPA has the responsibility to manage high-risk, high-payoff basic research and applied technology programs in projects as may be designated by the Secretary of Defense. The Agency's objective is to select and pursue revolutionary technology developments that minimize the possibility of technological surprise and/or offer potential for major increases in national defense capability. Research and development on projects is taken to the demonstration stage where feasibility and practicality can be assessed, and then the projects are transferred to the appropriate military services. In the performance of its work, the Agency utilizes the services of the military departments, other Government agencies, private industrial and public entities, individuals, and educational or research institutions.

For further information, contact the Defense Advanced Research Projects Agency, 1400 Wilson Boulevard, Arlington, VA 22209–2308. Phone, 202–694–5469.

Defense Communications Agency

Eighth Street and South Courthouse Road, Arlington, VA 22204
Phone, 202–692–0018

The Defense Communications Agency (DCA) was established by direction of the Secretary of Defense on May 12, 1960. It is a separate agency of the Department of Defense under the direction, authority, and control of the

Assistant Secretary of Defense (Command, Control, Communications and Intelligence). DCA also responds directly to the Chairman, Joint Chiefs of Staff, on operational matters and communication requirements associated with joint planning that are of primary concern to the Chiefs.

DCA is organized into a Headquarters and field activities acting for the Director in assigned areas of responsibility. The field organizations also include the White House Communications Agency and Defense Commercial Communications Office.

The mission of DCA is to:

Perform system engineering for the Defense Communications System (DCS) and ensure that DCS is planned, improved, operated, maintained, and managed effectively, efficiently, and economically to meet the long haul, point-to-point, and switched network telecommunications requirements of the National Command Authorities (NCA), the Department of Defense, and, as authorized and directed, other governmental agencies;

Provide system engineering and technical support to the National Military Command System (NMCS) and the Minimum Essential Emergency Communications Network (MEECN);

Provide other engineering and technical support to the Worldwide Military Command and Control System (WWMCCS), as assigned;

Perform system architect functions for current and future Military Satellite Communications (MILSATCOM) Systems;

Provide analytical and automated data processing (ADP) support to the Joint Chiefs of Staff, the Secretary of Defense, and other DOD components as directed and authorized; and

Procure leased communications circuits, services, facilities, and equipment for the DOD where authorized, and for other Government agencies as directed by the Secretary of Defense. Initiate or process actions relating to regulatory and tariff matters, including rates for communications facilities leased by the Department of Defense.

For further information, contact the Director, Defense Communications Agency, Eighth Street and South Courthouse Road, Arlington, VA 22204. Phone, 202–692–0018.

Defense Contract Audit Agency

Building 4, Cameron Station, Alexandria, VA 22304–6178
Phone, 202–274–6785

The Defense Contract Audit Agency (DCAA) was established in 1965 and operates under Department of Defense Directive 5105.36. It is a separate agency under the direction, authority, and control of the Assistant Secretary of Defense (Comptroller).

DCAA performs all necessary contract audit functions for the Department of Defense and provides accounting and financial advisory services to all Defense components responsible for procurement and contract administration. These services are provided in connection with the negotiation, administration, and settlement of contracts and subcontracts.

They include evaluating the acceptability of costs claimed or proposed by contractors and reviewing the efficiency and economy of contractor operations. Other Government agencies may request DCAA's services under appropriate arrangements.

DCAA manages its operations through six regional offices responsible for approximately 430 field audit offices throughout the United States and overseas. Each region is responsible for the contract auditing function in its assigned area.

Regional Offices—Defense Contract Audit Agency

Regional Office	Regional Director	Address
ATLANTA:		
Alabama, Arkansas, Florida, Georgia, Louisiana, Mississippi, North Carolina, South Carolina, Tennessee, Texas (except El Paso and Hudspeth Counties), Virginia (counties west of and including Bath, Rockbridge, Amherst, Campbell, and Pittsylvania), Mexico, Central America, South America, Bermuda, and Puerto Rico and nearby islands	Harvey Della Bernarda	Suite 103, 805 Walker St., Marietta, GA 30060-2731
BOSTON:		
Connecticut, Maine, Massachusetts, New Hampshire, eastern New York (including Long Island), Rhode Island, Vermont, Africa, Europe, Greenland, Iceland, and the Near and Middle East	(Vacancy)	424 Trapelo Rd., Waltham, MA 02154-6397
CHICAGO:		
Illinois, Indiana, Kansas (northeastern portion), Kentucky, Michigan, Missouri (except southwestern portion), western New York, Ohio, western Pennsylvania, Wisconsin, and West Virginia	Robert Hubbard	Suite 652, 527 S. LaSalle St., Chicago, IL 60605-1096
LOS ANGELES:		
Southern California	Patrick Mirch	Suite 1270, 2500 Wilshire Blvd., Los Angeles, CA 90057-4366
PHILADELPHIA:		
Delaware, District of Columbia, Maryland, southeastern New York, New Jersey, eastern Pennsylvania, northern and eastern Virginia	John Stanton	Room 4400, 4th Floor, 600 Arch St., Philadelphia, PA 19106-1604
SAN FRANCISCO:		
Alaska, Arizona, northern California, Colorado, Hawaii, Idaho, Iowa, Kansas (except northeastern portion), Minnesota, Missouri (southwestern portion), Montana, Nebraska, Nevada, New Mexico, North Dakota, Oklahoma, Oregon, South Dakota, Texas, (El Paso and Hudspeth counties), Utah, Washington, Wyoming, Asia (except Middle East), Australia, and Pacific area	Bernard Topf	Box 36116, 450 Golden Gate Ave., San Francisco, CA 94102-3563

For further information, contact the Executive Officer, Defense Contract Audit Agency, Cameron Station, Alexandria, VA 22304–6178. Phone, 202–274–7319. Information regarding employment may be obtained from the regional offices.

Defense Intelligence Agency

The Pentagon, Washington, DC 20301–6111
Phone, 202–697–8844

The Defense Intelligence Agency (DIA) was established as an agency of the Department of Defense by DOD Directive 5105.21, effective October 1, 1961. DIA, under provisions of the National Security Act of 1947, as amended, operates under the control of the Secretary of Defense. Staff supervision of DIA is exercised for the Secretary of Defense by the Assistant Secretary of Defense (Command, Control, Communications and Intelligence). Additionally, the Director of DIA reports to the Chairman of the Joint Chiefs of Staff for the specific purposes of providing the military intelligence support required to perform their statutory and assigned responsibilities and of ensuring that the necessary intelligence support is available to the Unified and Specified Commands.

Under its Director, the Defense Intelligence Agency is responsible for producing and disseminating military intelligence to satisfy the intelligence requirements of the Secretary of Defense, the Joint Chiefs of Staff, major components of DOD, and other authorized requirements. It accomplishes this either by use of internal resources; through the management, control, and coordination of the intelligence functions of other DOD activities; or through cooperation with other intelligence agencies.

DIA provides military intelligence for national foreign intelligence and counterintelligence products and staff support to the Joint Chiefs of Staff.

DIA reviews and coordinates those DOD intelligence functions retained by or assigned to the military departments. It also develops guidance for the conduct and management of such functions for review, approval, and promulgation by the Secretary of Defense.

DIA also has the responsibility of supervising the execution of all approved plans, programs, policies, and procedures for those DOD general intelligence functions and activities for which DIA has management responsibility. It assists in obtaining the maximum economy and efficiency in the use and management of DOD intelligence resources.

For further information, contact the Secretariat, Defense Intelligence Agency, The Pentagon, Washington, DC 20301–6111. Phone, 202–694–4780.

Defense Investigative Service

Buzzard Point, 1900 Half Street SW., Washington, DC 20324–1700
Phone, 202–475–0966

The Defense Investigative Service (DIS) was established by the Secretary of Defense, effective January 1, 1972. DIS is chartered by DOD Directive 5105.42, dated June 14, 1985, and operates under the direction, authority, and control of the Under Secretary of Defense for Policy.

DIS consists of a Headquarters, 2 Operations Centers, the Defense Security Institute, 9 regional offices and their subordinate field offices and resident agencies located in the 50 States and Puerto Rico, the Office of Industrial Security, International-Europe, in Brussels, Belgium; a field office in

Mannheim, Federal Republic of Germany; and the Office of Industrial Security, International-Far East, in Yokohama, Japan.

DIS conducts all Personnel Security Investigations (PSI's) for DOD components and when authorized also conducts PSI's for other U.S. Government activities. These PSI's include investigation of allegations of subversive affiliations, adverse suitability information, or any other situation that requires resolution to complete the PSI.

DIS is responsible for the three major programs involving industrial security: the Defense Industrial Security Program for Safeguarding Classified Information; the Industrial Facilities Protection Program; and the Defense Sensitive Conventional Arms, Ammunition and Explosives Security Program.

DIS also manages the Defense Central Index of Investigations (DCII), a centralized list of all Defense components investigative files, and security clearance information pertaining to Army and Air Force personnel.

Regional Offices—Defense Investigative Service

Regional Offices	Regional Directors
Boston, MA 02210-2192	James B. Witkowski, Jr.
Cherry Hill, NJ 08034-1908	John N. Held
Washington, DC 22331-1000	Charles A. Baldwin
Virginia Beach, VA 23462-2956	Norman H. Hempel
Chicago, IL 60607-4577	W. Graham Bell, Jr.
New Orleans, LA 70160-0155	Frederick E. Robey, Jr.
St. Louis, MO 63188-1900	Thomas L. Eastwood
San Francisco, CA 94129-7700	Alfred W. Hazen
Long Beach, CA 90807-4013	David L. McDonald

For further information, contact the Chief, Office of Information and Public Affairs, Defense Investigative Service, 1900 Half Street SW., Washington, DC 20324–1700. Phone, 202–475–1062.

Defense Legal Services Agency

The Pentagon, Washington, DC 20301–1600
Phone, 202–695–3341

The Defense Legal Services Agency (DLSA) was established by Department of Defense Directive 5145.4, dated August 12, 1981. DLSA is under the direction, authority, and control of the General Counsel of the Department of Defense. It provides legal advice and services for the Office of the Secretary of Defense and its field activities, and the Defense agencies; provides technical support and assistance for development of the DOD Legislative Program; coordinates DOD positions on legislation and Presidential Executive orders; and provides a centralized legislative and congressional document reference and distribution point for the Department, and maintains the Department's historical legislative files. The General Counsel of the Department of Defense serves as the Director of DLSA.

For further information, contact the Administrative Officer, Defense Legal Services Agency, The Pentagon, Washington, DC 20301–1600. Phone, 202–697–8343.

Defense Logistics Agency

Cameron Station, Alexandria, VA 22304–6100
Phone, 202–274–6000 or 6001

Established pursuant to authority vested in the Secretary of Defense, the Defense Logistics Agency (DLA) is an agency of the Department of Defense (DOD) under the direction, authority, and control of the Assistant Secretary of Defense (Acquisition and Logistics) and subject to DOD policies, directives, and instructions.

DLA consists of a Director, a Deputy Director, a Deputy Director for Acquisition Management, a Headquarters establishment, and 25 primary level field activities and their subordinate activities. Some of the subordinate activities of the Defense Fuel Supply Center, the Defense Reutilization and Marketing Service, and the Defense Personnel Support Center operate in overseas areas. There also are a number of Headquarters management support offices that are controlled by Headquarters staff elements.

The mission of DLA is to provide effective and economical support to the military services, other DOD components, Federal civil agencies, foreign governments, and others as authorized, for assigned materiel commodities and items of supply, including weapons systems, logistics services directly associated with the supply management function, contract administration services, and other support services as directed by the Secretary of Defense. Furthermore, DLA administers the operation of DOD programs as assigned.

Under the direction and operational control of its Director, DLA is responsible for the performance of the following major functions:

Materiel management encompassing item management classification, requirements and supply control, procurement, quality and reliability assurance, industrial mobilization planning, storage, inventory and distribution, transportation, maintenance and manufacture, provisioning, technical logistics data and information, value engineering and standardization;

Contract administration services provided in support of the military departments and other DOD components, the National Aeronautics and Space Administration, other designated Federal and State agencies, and foreign governments;

Providing scientific and technical information support services to the Defense Research, Development, Testing and Evaluation community through operation of the centralized management information and technical report data banks at the Defense Technical Information Center and administrative management of nine contractor-operated DOD Information Analysis Centers in selected fields of science and technology;

Administering assigned DOD programs including the DOD Coordinated Procurement Program, Federal Catalog System, DOD Excess, Surplus, and Foreign Excess Personal Property Disposal Program, DOD Retail Interservice Support Program (DRIS), Defense Materiel Utilization Program, DOD Industrial Plant Equipment Program, Foreign Military Sales, operating Military Parts Control Advisory Groups (MPCAG) for standardization of parts at the system equipment design stage, DOD-wide program for redistribution/reutilization of excess Government-owned and rented automation equipment, Defense Automatic Addressing System, Defense Precious Metals Recovery Program, Executive Agent for Materiel Redistribution via the Defense European and Pacific Redistribution Activity (DEPRA), assigned logistics operations contingent to the Federal Emergency Management Program, assigned aspects of the DOD Food Service Management Program, DOD-wide Interchangeable/ Substitutable Program, Military Standard Logistics Systems, Logistics Data Element Standardization and Management Program, Defense Procurement Management Review, providing manpower data support to DOD and other Government agencies assigned, the DOD Hazardous Materiel Data System, and the Program Manager for the Defense Energy Information System;

Monitoring DOD supply relationships with the General Services Administration;

Serving as the operating agency for the DOD Automated Placement Programs, and providing administrative support to the Centralized Referral Activity whose functions are under Assistant Secretary of Defense (Acquisition and Logistics) supervision. These programs are the Centralized Referral System that provides for the placement of displaced DOD employees and returning overseas career employees, the Overseas Employment Referral Program, and the Automated Career Management System (ACMS) for placement of employees registered in the DOD-wide career program for Acquisition/Contracting and Quality Assurance personnel; and

Systems analysis and design, procedural development, and maintenance for supply and service systems as assigned by the Secretary of Defense.

Primary Level Field Activities

Supply Centers The six supply centers are responsible for materiel management of assigned commodities and items of supply relating to food, clothing, textiles, medical, chemical, petroleum, industrial, construction, electronics, and general items of supply. The Defense Fuel Supply Center is also responsible for contracting for commercial petroleum services and coal, as well as all crude oil and petroleum products for the Strategic Petroleum Reserve. Two of the supply centers also perform depot operations functions for assigned commodities.

For further information, call 202–274–6000 or 6001.

Service Centers The six service centers furnish varied support services as follows:

The *Defense Logistics Services Center* is responsible for maintenance of the Federal Cataloging System records including the development and dissemination of cataloging and item intelligence data to the military services and other authorized customers;

The *Defense Industrial Plant Equipment Center* (DIPEC) is responsible for the DOD General Reserve of industrial plant equipment. DIPEC maintains visibility records of all DOD equipment in use by government facilities and contractors and provides specified supply support of industrial plant equipment to the military departments;

The *Defense Technical Information Center* is responsible for the development, maintenance, and operation of the management information system in the field of scientific and technical information; acquisition, storage, announcement, retrieval, and provision of secondary distribution of scientific and technical reports; and primary distribution of foreign technical reports;

The *DLA Administrative Support*

459

Center provides administrative support and common service functions to DLA activities within the Washington, DC, metropolitan area;

The *Defense Reutilization and Marketing Service* is responsible for the integrated management of worldwide personal property disposal operations, including reutilization of serviceable assets, in support of the military services and other authorized customers; and

The *DLA Systems Automation Center* is responsible for the operational execution of the DLA ADP Program and the DLA Telecommunications Program.

For further information, call 202–274–6000 or 6001.

Depots These activities are responsible for depot operations functions for assigned commodities.

Contract Administration Services Regions (DCASR's) The nine DCASR's provide contract administration services including the performance of contract administration, production, quality assurance, and data and financial management activities, and small business/labor surplus programs, within the United States and such external areas as specifically authorized.

For further information, call 202–274–6000 or 6001.

Primary Level Field Activities—Defense Logistics Agency

Activity	Commander (C)/Administrator (A)
Defense Supply Centers:	
Defense Construction Supply Center	Maj. Gen. L.D. Garrison, USAF (C)
Defense Electronics Supply Center	Brig. Gen. H.C. Kammer, USA (C)
Defense Fuel Supply Center	Maj. Gen. J.E. Griffith, USAF (C)
Defense General Supply Center	Brig. Gen. G.C. Ogden, Jr., USA (C)
Defense Industrial Supply Center	Brig. Gen. W.T. McLean, USA (C)
Defense Personnel Support Center	Rear Adm. J.H. Ruehlin, SC, USN (C)
Defense Service Centers:	
Defense Technical Information Center	K.N. Molholm (A)
Defense Industrial Plant Equipment Center	Capt. R.A. Dropp, SC, USN (C)
Defense Logistics Services Center	Col. B. Flynn, USA (C)
Defense Reutilization and Marketing Service	Brig. Gen. T.B. Arwood, USA (C)
DLA Administrative Support Center	Col. J.J. Singsank, USA (C)
DLA Systems Automation Center	Capt W.D. Groves, SC, USN (C)
Defense Depots:	
Defense Depot Mechanicsburg	Col. B.G. Belcher, USA (C)
Defense Depot Memphis	Col. L.M. Jones, USA (C)
Defense Depot Ogden	Capt. R.R. Sareeram, SC, USN (C)
Defense Depot Tracy	Col. D.L. Stoner, USMC (C)
Defense Contract Administration Services Regions (DCASR's):	
DCASR, Atlanta	Capt. S.J. Ligon, SC, USN (C)
DCASR, Boston	Col. M.E. Turcotte, USAF (C)
DCASR, Chicago	Col. J.L. George, USA (C)
DCASR, Cleveland	Col. G.J. Telenko, USA (C)
DCASR, Dallas	Col. J.B. Bryan, USAF (C)
DCASR, Los Angeles	Brig. Gen. J. Serur, USAF (C)
DCASR, New York	Brig. Gen. C.E. St. Arnaud, USA (C)
DCASR, Philadelphia	Capt. C.L. Rech, SC, USN (C)
DCASR, St. Louis	Capt. J.E. Weekes, SC, USN (C)

Sources of Information

Consumer Activities Any questions concerning this program or placement on DOD bidders list should be addressed to DOD Surplus Sales, P.O. Box 1370, Battle Creek, MI 49016. Phone, 616–962–6511, extension 6736 or 6737.

Environment For information concerning DLA's program, contact Defense Logistics Agency, Attn: DLA–WS, Room 4D489, Cameron Station, Alexandria, VA 22304–6100. Phone, 202–274–6357.

Reading Room DLA Library, Room 4D131, Cameron Station, Alexandria, VA 22304–6100. Phone, 202–274–6055.

Procurement Information and Small Business Activities For information, contact Staff Director, Small and Disadvantaged Business Utilization (DLA–U), Room 4B110, Cameron Station, Alexandria, VA 22304–6100. Phone, 202–274–6471.

Publications *How to do Business with the Defense Logistics Agency* and *An Identification of Commodities Purchased by the Defense Logistics Agency* are available free of charge from the Staff Director, Small and Disadvantaged Business Utilization (DLA–U), above address.

An Introduction to the Defense Logistics Agency, as well as other DLA publications, is available from the Superintendent of Documents, Government Printing Office, Washington, DC 20402.

Employment For the Washington, DC, metropolitan area, inquiries and applications should be addressed to Defense Logistics Agency, DLA Administrative Support Center, Attn: DASC–ZE, Room 3A696, Cameron Station, Alexandria, VA 22304–6100. Phone, 202–274–6041. For other areas, contact the local DLA field activity.

DLA has a college recruitment program. Schools interested in participating should direct inquiries to Defense Logistics Agency, Attn: DLA–KS, Room 3D118, Cameron Station, Alexandria, VA 22304–6100. Phone, 202–274–6040.

Films For information on films available for public showing, contact Headquarters, Defense Logistics Agency, Attn: DASC–T, Room 3C547, Cameron Station, Alexandria, VA 22304–6100. Phone, 202–274–6185.

For further information, contact the Executive Officer, Defense Logistics Agency, Room 3A150, Cameron Station, Alexandria, VA 22304–6100. Phone, 202–274–6115.

Defense Mapping Agency

U.S. Naval Observatory, Building 56, Washington, DC 20305–3000
Phone, 202–653–1478

The Defense Mapping Agency (DMA) has some 9,000 employees in more than 50 locations around the world. The mission of the Agency is to:

Enhance national security and support the Nation's strategy of deterrence by producing and distributing to the Joint Chiefs of Staff, Unified and Specified Commands, Military Departments and other Department of Defense users, complete, credible, and effective mapping, charting, and geodetic

461

products, services, and training at the right place and in the right quantity and the right time;

Ensure that U.S. war-fighting forces have available to them effective mapping, charting, and geodetic support should the strategy of deterrence fail;

Provide nautical charts and marine navigational data to the worldwide merchant marine and private vessel operators; and

Maintain liaison with civil agencies and other national and international scientific and operational organizations engaged in mapping, charting, and geodetic activities.

The Defense Mapping Agency was established in 1972, when mapping, charting, and geodesy functions of the Defense Community were combined into this joint DOD agency. DMA is under the direction and control of the Assistant Secretary of Defense (Command, Control, Communications and Intelligence). The director of DMA, a flag officer, is responsible to the Joint Chiefs of Staff for operational matters.

DMA Components

The mapping, charting, and geodesy functions of DMA are principally conducted by its two major production Centers. Aerospace products and support to aerospace manned and unmanned weapons systems are provided to Department of Defense users primarily by the DMA Aerospace Center (DMAAC), which is located in St. Louis, MO. The DMA Hydrographic/Topographic Center (DMAHTC), located in Brookmont, MD, primarily provides nautical products, topographic products, land combat support, and support to ground weapons and naval weapons systems.

The DMA Office of Distribution

Services (DMAODS) is primarily responsible for the distribution of DMA products to the military services and other users. Its headquarters is also located in Brookmont, MD.

The Defense Mapping School (DMS), located at Fort Belvoir, VA, is responsible for providing personnel of the Army, Navy, Air Force, Marine Corps, and other Government agencies with training in all aspects of mapping, charting, and geodesy.

The DMA Inter-American Geodetic Survey (DMAIAGS), headquartered at Fort Sam Houston, TX, conducts a cooperative program to promote and encourage cartographic studies in the Latin American countries. Its goal is to assist Latin American nations in becoming self-sufficient in cartography.

The DMA Special Program Office for Exploitation Modernization (DMASPOEM), located in McLean, VA, is responsible for developing the capability of producing DMA products using softcopy or computerized production techniques.

The DMA Office of Telecommunications Services (DMAOTS), located in Reston, VA, provides overall operational direction and management supervision of DMA Telecommunications Systems and operates and maintains the long-haul systems linking major production centers and field activities.

Components—Defense Mapping Agency

Activity	Director
DMA Aerospace Center (St. Louis Air Force Station, MO 63118-3399)	Col. Robert J. Lemon, USAF
DMA Hydrographic/Topographic Center (Washington, DC 20315-0030)	Col. Hugh P. Johnson, USA
DMA Office of Distribution Services (Washington, DC 20315-0010)	Col. Larry E. Lowe, USA

462

Components—Defense Mapping Agency—Continued

Activity	Director
Defense Mapping School (Fort Belvoir, VA 22060-5828)	Col. David F. Maune, USA
DMA Inter American Geodetic Survey (Fort Sam Houston, TX 78234-5000)	Col. Thomas B. Russell, USA
DMA Special Program Office for Exploitation Modernization (McLean, VA 22102-3692)	Penman Gilliam
DMA Office of Telecommunications Services (Reston, VA 22090)	Annette Krygiel

Sources of Information

Contract Information and Small Business Activities For information, contact the DMA Small and Disadvantaged Business Utilization Specialist, Facilities Engineering and Logistics Office, Defense Mapping Agency, Building 56, U.S. Naval Observatory, Washington, DC 20305-3000. Phone, 202-653-1723.

Employment General employment applications and inquiries should be addressed to the following Personnel Offices:

DMA Aerospace Center: Director, Attn: PO, St. Louis Air Force Station, MO 63118-3399. Phone, 314-263-4965.

DMA Hydrographic/Topographic Center: Director, Attn: PO, 6500 Brookes Lane NW., Washington, DC 20315-0030. Phone, 202-227-2116.

DMA Inter-American Geodetic Survey: Director, Attn: PO, Building 605, Fort Sam Houston, TX 78234-5000. Phone, 512-221-4246.

Executive/Managerial applications should be addressed to the Chief, Civilian Personnel Division, Headquarters, Defense Mapping Agency, Building 56, U.S. Naval Observatory, Washington, DC 20305-3000. Phone, 202-653-1581.

Public Sale of Maps and Charts

Aeronautical Charts Aeronautical charts, published by the DMA Aerospace Center covering foreign areas, are available for sale by the National Ocean Service (NOS) and may be purchased from the following offices:

Distribution Branch (N/CG33), National Ocean Service, Riverdale, MD 20737-1199. Phone, 301-436-6990.

National Ocean Service, Chart Sales and Control Data Office, 632 Sixth Avenue, Room 405, Anchorage, AK 99501. Phone, 907-271-4470.

Domestic aeronautical charts are produced by NOS and may be purchased from NOS Sales Agents established at the principal civil airports or from the offices listed above.

Topographic Maps The DMA Hydrographic/Topographic Center publishes topographic maps of foreign areas. A listing of topographic maps available to the public is contained in the *Defense Mapping Agency Public Sale Catalog,* which is available free of charge from the DMA Office of Distribution Services, Attn: DOCS, Washington, DC 20010. Phone, 202-227-2816.

Topographic maps of the continental United States and Hawaii are not available from DMA, but may be purchased as indicated below:

—For maps east of the Mississippi: U.S. Geological Survey, Eastern Distribution Branch, 1200 South Eads Street, Arlington, VA 22202. Phone, 703-557-2781.

—For maps west of the Mississippi: U.S. Geological Survey, Western Distribution Branch, Federal Center, P.O. Box 25286, Denver, CO 80225. Phone, 303-234-3832.

Nautical Charts A complete list of charts available for sale by the DMA Office of Distribution Services, as well as its authorized sales agents, is tabulated in the DMA *Catalog of Maps, Charts, and Related Products, Part 2—Hydrographic Products* (Volumes I–X). Detailed ordering instructions, as well as the sales agents list, are found in Volume X, *Miscellaneous and Special Purpose Navigational Charts, Sheets and Tables.*

These volumes are available for $2.25 each from the DMA Office of Distribution Services, Attn: DDCP, Washington, DC 20315-0010. Phone, 202-227-2495.

Nautical charts of coastal waterways of the continental United States, Hawaii, Alaska, and U.S. territories may be purchased from NOS, whose address is shown above in the section on aeronautical charts.

For further information, contact the Public Affairs Officer, Defense Mapping Agency, U.S. Naval Observatory, Building 56, Washington, DC 20305-3000. Phone, 202-653-1131.

Defense Nuclear Agency

Washington, DC 20305
Phone, 202-325-7095

The Defense Nuclear Agency (DNA) is the oldest of the Defense agencies. Its history began in 1942 with the creation of the "Manhattan Project," which developed the first atomic bomb. The "Manhattan Project" was dissolved by the Atomic Energy Act of 1946, which also established the Armed Forces Special Weapons Project. The Project was redesignated as the Defense Atomic Support Agency in 1959 and renamed again in 1971 as the Defense Nuclear Agency. The Director, DNA, is under the direction, authority, and control of the Under Secretary of Defense for Research and Engineering. The authority for DNA activities is included in DOD Directive 5105.31.

The majority of DNA activity is associated with nuclear weapons effects research and testing. DNA plans, coordinates, and supervises DOD efforts in this area, including tests assessment, construction and management of simulation facilities, and field experiments. DNA is the central DOD agency for coordination of nuclear weapons development and testing with the Department of Energy. DNA manages the DOD nuclear weapons stockpile and its associated report system and conducts technical investigations and field tests to enhance the safety and security of theater nuclear forces. DNA provides advice and assistance to the Joint Chiefs of Staff and the Services on all nuclear matters, including such related areas as site security, tactics, vulnerability, radiation effects, and biomedical effects.

To accomplish its mission, DNA is organized with its headquarters in Washington, DC, the Field Command in Albuquerque, NM, and the Armed Forces Radiobiology Research Institute (AFRRI) in Bethesda, MD. DNA retains management of Johnston Atoll in the Pacific to ensure its availability as a test site. In addition, DNA managed the restoration of Enewetak Atoll from a nuclear test site to a life-supporting condition that has permitted the return of natives to their home island.

For further information, contact the Administration and Military Personnel Office, Defense Nuclear Agency, Washington, DC 20305. Phone, 202–325–7677.

Defense Security Assistance Agency

The Pentagon, Washington, DC 20301–2800
Phone, 202–695–3291

The purpose of the Defense Security Assistance Agency (DSAA) is to direct, administer, and supervise the execution of approved security assistance plans and programs, such as military assistance and foreign military sales.

The Defense Security Assistance Agency was established on September 1, 1971, by the Department of Defense Directive 5105.38, dated August 11, 1971, as an agency of the Department of Defense. It operates under the direction, authority, and control of the Under Secretary of Defense for Policy. The Director also serves as the Deputy Assistant Secretary of Defense for Security Assistance to the Assistant Secretaries of International Security Affairs and International Security Policy on matters pertaining to security assistance policy.

The Defense Security Assistance Agency works closely with the U.S. Security Assistance Offices worldwide.

For further information, contact the Defense Security Assistance Agency, The Pentagon, Washington, DC 20301–2800. Phone, 202–697–0098.

National Security Agency/Central Security Service

Fort George G. Meade, MD 20755
Phone, 301–688–6311

The National Security Agency/Central Security Service is responsible for centralized coordination, direction, and performance of highly specialized technical functions in support of U.S. Government activities to protect U.S. communications and produce foreign intelligence information. The National Security Agency was established by Presidential directive in 1952 as a separately organized agency within the Department of Defense. In this directive, the President designated the Secretary of Defense Executive Agent for the signals intelligence and communications security activities of the Government. The Agency was charged with an additional mission, computer security, in a 1984 Presidential directive.

In 1972 the Central Security Service

465

was established, in accordance with a Presidential memorandum, to provide a more unified cryptologic organization within the Department of Defense and appointed the Director, National Security Agency, as Chief of the Central Security Service.

The National Security Agency/Central Security Service has three primary missions: a communications security mission, a computer security mission, and a foreign intelligence information mission. To accomplish these missions, the Director has been assigned the following responsibilities:

Prescribing certain security principles, doctrines, and procedures for the U.S. Government;

Organizing, operating, and managing certain activities and facilities for the production of foreign intelligence information;

Organizing and coordinating the research and engineering activities of the U.S. Government that are in support of the Agency's assigned functions;

Regulating certain communications in support of Agency missions; and

Operating the DOD Computer Security Center in support of his role as national manager for telecommunications security and automated information systems security.

Executive Order 12333 of December 4, 1981, describes in more detail the responsibilities of the National Security Agency.

Strategic Defense Initiative Organization

Washington, DC 20301–7100
Phone, 202–695–7060

The Strategic Defense Initiative Organization (SDIO) was established as a separate agency of the Department of Defense under the direction, authority, and control of the Secretary of Defense.

The mission of SDIO is to manage and direct the conduct of research through advanced technology programs that will provide the technological basis for an informed decision regarding feasibility of eliminating the threat posed by nuclear ballistic missiles and increasing the contribution of defensive systems to U.S. and allied security. In the performance of its research, the agency utilizes the services of the military departments, the Department of Energy, private industries, and educational and research institutions.

For further information, contact the Strategic Defense Initiative Organization, External Affairs, Washington, DC 20301–7100. Phone, 202–695–8731.

National Defense University

Fort Lesley J. McNair, Fourth and P Streets SW., Washington, DC 20319–6000
Phone, 202–475–0811

The National Defense University (NDU) was established by the Department of Defense on January 16, 1976, thereby merging the Industrial College of the Armed Forces and the National War College to form a university. Because the two senior service colleges are located at Fort Lesley J. McNair, Washington, DC, their close affiliation reduces administrative costs, provides for the sharing of faculty expertise and educational resources, and promotes a constructive dialog, which benefits both colleges. On August 16, 1981, the Armed Forces Staff College in Norfolk, VA, an institution educating mid-career officers, was incorporated into the National Defense University. This action united the Department of Defense's three joint colleges under one university and allowed NDU to coordinate the curricula and professional development of its students and share resources. At the direction of the Secretary of Defense, the Department of Defense Computer Institute (DODCI) became an element of NDU on September 26, 1982. DODCI, located in the Washington Navy Yard, is responsible for teaching information resources management to senior military and civilian executives within the Department of Defense. Also in 1982, an Institute for Higher Defense Studies was established to provide specialized education in joint matters to both general and flag officers, and Allied officers from selected foreign nations.

The mission of NDU is to ensure excellence in professional military education in the essential elements of national security and their interrelationships in order to enhance the preparation of selected personnel of the Departments of Defense and State, and other governmental agencies for the exercise of senior policy, command and staff functions, the planning of national strategy, and the management of resources for national security.

NDU is pursuing numerous initiatives designed to ensure that its curriculum focuses on critical issues associated with the Nation's current security posture. At the same time, increased emphasis has been placed on achieving a closer relationship between research and education. This is reflected in the studies programs of the two senior colleges. Basic improvements in the scope and thrust of the curricula of both colleges are designed to enrich the educational process while emphasizing the important role played by research in the University's mission.

That role has been enhanced by the establishment of an Institute for National Strategic Studies composed of a publication arm, the NDU Press, and three research-oriented centers: The *Strategic Concepts Development Center (SCDC)* emphasizes studies in theater-level war fighting, employment planning, and the use of joint and combined forces in warfare. The *Mobilization Concepts Development Center (MCDC)* stresses studies on industrial preparedness, mobilization planning, and management and deployment planning. The *War Gaming and Simulation Center (WGSC)* provides simulation and gaming activities to support the educational and research objectives of the University.

In addition to the resident courses taught at the National War College and the Industrial College of the Armed Forces, the University conducts, through its Academic Affairs Directorate, three other programs based on the resident courses, as well as regional and topical symposia. The Reserve Components National Security Seminar is a 2-week course presented to selected reserve component officers at various military installations. Both seminar programs are developed to reflect the NDU resident programs and are conducted by faculty members of NDU, the National War College, and the Industrial College of the Armed Forces. A correspondence course on national security management is offered to regular and reserve officers and civilians who hold key positions in Government or who may be expected to fill such positions in time of emergency mobilization.

For further information, contact the Public Affairs Officer, National Defense University, Fort Lesley J. McNair, Fourth and P Streets SW., Washington, DC 20319–6000. Phone, 202–475–0811.

The National War College

Fort Lesley J. McNair, Fourth and P Streets SW., Washington, DC 20319–6000
Phone, 202–475–1776

The National War College (NWC) provides education in politico-military affairs to selected military officers and career civil service employees of Federal departments and agencies concerned with national security. It is the only senior service college with the primary mission of offering a course of study that emphasizes national security policy formulation and the planning and implementation of national strategy. The 10-month academic program is an issue-centered study in U.S. national security. It consists of a prescribed curriculum and an elective study program. The prescribed portion of the curriculum combines interwoven themes: international politics and the process and substance of security policy formulation. Emphasis is placed on the role of force in national security policy and strategy through the study of major issues likely to affect the national security of the United States. The elective program is designed to permit each student to tailor his academic experience to meet individual professional development needs. Electives include tutorial research, writing, and reading, in addition to individual courses offered at NWC and the Industrial College of the Armed Forces (ICAF).

For further information, contact the Dean of Students and Administration, The National War College, Fort Lesley J. McNair, Fourth and P Streets SW., Washington, DC 20319–6000. Phone, 202–475–1776.

Industrial College of the Armed Forces

Fort Lesley J. McNair, Fourth and P Streets SW., Washington, DC 20319–6000
Phone, 202–475–1832

The Industrial College of the Armed Forces (ICAF) provides senior-level education in management of resources and mobilization in support of national security to selected military officers and career civil service employees of Federal departments and agencies. It is the only senior service college with the primary mission of offering a course of study in resource management for national security. The 10-month academic program focuses on the role of the executive in the national security structure, with emphasis on the allocation and management of resources in dealing with national security problems. The prescribed portion of the curriculum addresses management skills and practices related to human and materiel resources, analytical techniques, global resources issues, and the national economy. The Department of Defense, particularly its management philosophy, systems, and practices, receives major attention. Opportunity is provided the student to choose from a variety of electives offered within the National Defense University. A cooperative M.B.A. program is available with the George Washington University.

For further information, contact the Director of Administrative Services, Industrial College of the Armed Forces, Fort Lesley J. McNair, Fourth and P Streets SW., Washington, DC 20319–6000. Phone, 202–475–1832.

Armed Forces Staff College

Norfolk, VA 23511

The Armed Forces Staff College, established on August 13, 1946, is a joint educational institution operating under the direction of the Joint Chiefs of Staff.

The College conducts two 5 ½-month courses each year. The course concentrates on management of resources, national strategy, and communicative arts, coupled with the makeup, capabilities, and missions of each of the military services, and detailed step-by-step development of a joint and combined plan. Given military scenarios, the students are taught how to combine the various units of the Army, Navy, Air Force, and Marine Corps for a successful joint operation, to include both the transportation and supply requirements to sustain the mission.

Two primary methods of instruction are used. First, the students are assigned to seminars of 20 officers each (with mixed specialties and backgrounds), and this group becomes, in effect, a miniature joint staff. In this environment, the officers learn from each other while assimilating the school's curriculum. The second method of instruction is a guest-lecture program in which major military and civilian leaders, including members of the Joint Chiefs of Staff, address each class and then participate in wide-ranging question-and-answer periods.

For further information, contact the Public Affairs Officer, Armed Forces Staff College, Norfolk, VA 23511. Phone, 804–444–5231.

Department of Defense Computer Institute

Washington Navy Yard, Building 175, Washington, DC 20374
Phone, 202–433–3000

The Department of Defense Computer Institute (DODCI), established by DOD Directive 5160.49 of February 27, 1964, is an element of the National Defense University and a leading educational institute responsible for teaching information resources management (IRM) to senior military and civilian executives within the Department of Defense. In addition, as an element of the National Defense University, the Institute supports the information resources management educational requirements of the University and its constituent colleges.

The mission of the Institute is fivefold: It promotes excellence in information resources management education for DOD senior and intermediate-level executives who oversee the planning, development, and operation of automated information systems (AIS) or who use AIS resources in support of their overall management responsibilities; provides appropriate courses in various aspects of information resources management in response to Department of Defense needs, technological advances, new legislation, and IRM policy initiatives; provides information resources management advisory services to Department of Defense AIS developers and users; provides appropriate courses in various aspects of information resources management in support of the educational mission of the National Defense University and its constituent colleges; and provides technical IRM assistance in support of the National Defense University mission and functions.

For further information, contact the Director of Administration, Department of Defense Computer Institute, Washington Navy Yard, Building 175, Washington, DC 20374. Phone, 202–433–4308.

Uniformed Services University of the Health Sciences

4301 Jones Bridge Road, Bethesda, MD 20814–4799
Phone, 301–295–3030

Authorized by act of Congress, approved September 21, 1972 (86 Stat. 713; 10 U.S.C. 2112), the Uniformed Services University of the Health Sciences was established to educate career-oriented medical officers for the military services. It is a separate agency of the Department of Defense, directly responsible to the Secretary of Defense (Department of Defense Directive 5105.45).

The University currently incorporates the F. Edward Hébert School of Medicine and graduate and continuing education programs. It is located on the Naval Medical Command reservation in Bethesda, MD.

Students are selected by procedures recommended by the Board of Regents and prescribed by the Secretary of Defense. The actual selection is carried out by a faculty committee on admissions and is based upon motivation and dedication to a career in the uniformed services and an overall appraisal of the personal and intellectual characteristics of the candidates without regard to sex, race, religion, or national origin. Applicants must be U.S. citizens. Matriculants will be commissioned officers in one of the uniformed services. They must meet the physical and personal qualifications for such a commission and must give evidence of a strong commitment to serving as a uniformed medical officer. The graduating medical student is required to serve a period of obligation of not less than 7 years.

Currently, there are approximately 625 officers training for their M.D. degrees in the University's F. Edward Hébert School of Medicine and approximately 100 individuals enrolled in one of the University's graduate programs in the basic sciences.

The University's graduate program is fully accredited and is available to both civilian and military applicants. Graduates may receive the PH.D. degree in one of the biomedical sciences, the master of public health degree, or the master of tropical medicine and hygiene degree. In addition, the University serves as the focus for a vigorous continuing medical education program that supports the military services by providing unique training opportunities both at the University's Bethesda campus and at military bases around the world, where such training would not otherwise be available.

For further information, contact the President, Uniformed Services University of the Health Sciences, 4301 Jones Bridge Road, Bethesda, MD 20814–4799. Phone, 301–295–3030.

Defense Systems Management College

Fort Belvoir, VA 22060–5426
Phone, 703–664–6323

The Defense Systems Management College, established July 1, 1971, is a joint service educational institution operating under the direction of the Defense Systems Management College Policy Guidance Council chaired by the Under Secretary of Defense for Research and Engineering. It is the mission of the College to conduct advanced courses of study that will prepare selected military officers and civilian personnel for assignments in program management and to conduct, research, and disseminate information concerning new methods and practices in program management.

The College conducts a 138-day resident course to educate selected intermediate level military officers and civilian personnel in a broad spectrum of program management activities through formal studies, simulation exercises, and case studies. The College also conducts an executive refresher course in program management for senior-level managers and an orientation in systems acquisition for selected generals of the Army and Air Force, flag officers of the Navy, and supergrade civilians in each of the services and the Department of Defense. In addition, special courses are routinely scheduled to disseminate new concepts and methods in program management and respond to the needs of the military departments and Defense agencies. Most of the courses are available to selected persons from other Federal agencies and the defense industry on a space-available basis.

For further information, contact the Office of the Registrar, Defense Systems Management College, Fort Belvoir, VA 22060. Phone, 703–664–3120.

Defense Institute of Security Assistance Management

Wright-Patterson Air Force Base, OH 45433–5000
Phone, 513–255–5850

The Defense Institute of Security Assistance Management (DISAM), established on January 1, 1977, is a joint service educational institute operating under the direction of the Defense Institute of Security Assistance Management Policy Guidance Council, chaired by the Assistant Secretary of Defense for International Security Affairs.

The mission of DISAM is to provide educational, research, and consultation services to managers at all operational levels within the U.S. security assistance community and worldwide. Security assistance is a worldwide program whereby the United States furnishes military and related economic assistance through sales, grants, or loans to more than 100 allied and friendly foreign nations.

DISAM conducts a series of resident and nonresident study courses for U.S. Government and foreign military and civilian personnel, and representatives of defense-related industries assigned to security assistance management positions. These courses are tailored to meet the specific educational requirements of these management personnel and to enlarge their capacity for effective management decisions. Instruction covers security assistance management topics, ranging from the study of governing legislative and policy provisions through the examination of the requisites of program planning and the implementation of financial, logistics, and training management functions.

A basic 15-day course is provided for mid-level managers who are assigned to functional security assistance positions within the United States. Foreign personnel attend a comparable course, and an expanded 20-day course is provided to U.S. personnel assigned to management positions at overseas locations. A variety of 5-day courses are also offered, including a comprehensive executive course for senior-level American managers and officials and a similar course for foreign executive personnel; advanced specialized courses in financial management and program/case management; an industry-oriented course for representatives of U.S. defense-related firms; and a course for U.S. Government personnel assigned as administrative managers of foreign students engaged in technical training and professional education programs at

472

U.S. military installations. Nonresident instruction includes comprehensive, short courses conducted on-site, as required, for U.S. military agencies and mobile training teams, which travel abroad to conduct courses for foreign personnel.

The Institute also engages in a broad research and consultation program directed toward curriculum enhancement and applied research. Unique textbooks and handbooks covering security assistance management topics have been developed and published by DISAM. The Institute also publishes the quarterly DISAM Journal of International Security Assistance Management, which serves as an informational channel for members of the global security assistance community. Consultation services are available to all U.S. and foreign agencies engaged in security assistance management. The Institute's library houses a comprehensive repository of worldwide security assistance-related materials.

For further information, contact the Office of the Registrar, Defense Institute of Security Assistance Management, Wright-Patterson Air Force Base, OH 45433–5000. Phone, 513–255–4144.

Armed Services Board of Contract Appeals

Hoffman Building II, 200 Stovall Street, Alexandria, VA 22332–0700
Phone, Chairman: 202–325–8000; Recorder: 202–325–9070

The Armed Services Board of Contract Appeals was established jointly by the Secretaries of Defense, Army, Navy, and Air Force by charter dated March 20, 1962, as amended on May 1, 1969, September 1, 1973, and July 1, 1979.

Board members, designated as administrative judges, are qualified attorneys at law with at least 5 years of public contract law experience at the time of appointment. The Chairman and two Vice Chairmen are appointed from among Board members jointly by the Under Secretary of Defense for Research and Engineering and the Assistant Secretaries of the military departments responsible for procurement. Decisions are routinely made by majority vote within Board divisions comprised of a division head, two other members, the Board Chairman, and a Vice Chairman. Appeals of unusual difficulty, dispute, or precedential significance are, on reference by the Chairman, decided by majority vote of the Board's Senior Deciding Group comprised of all division heads, the Vice Chairman, and the Chairman.

Pursuant to the Contract Disputes Act of 1978 (41 U.S.C. 601 et seq.) and provisions of the Board's charter, the Board determines with administrative finality (subject only to judicial review) appeals from final decisions of contracting officers on disputes relating to contracts made by elements of the Department of Defense and several civilian agencies under separate delegations of authority. Proceedings are quasi-judicial. Decisions are made strictly on the evidentiary record (testimony and documents) and applicable regulations, statutes, and general law.

In accordance with the Contract Disputes Act and Board rules, the contractor may elect an optional

473

accelerated procedure where the controversial sum does not exceed $50,000 or may elect a small claims (expedited) procedure where the controversial sum does not exceed $10,000.

For further information, contact the Chairman, Armed Services Board of Contract Appeals, Hoffman Building II, 200 Stovall Street, Alexandria, VA 22332–0700. Phone, Chairman: 202–325–8000 or Recorder: 202–325–9070.

UNITED STATES COAST GUARD

2100 Second Street SW., Washington, DC 20593
Phone, 202–426–2158

The Coast Guard, established by the act of January 28, 1915 (14 U.S.C. 1), became a component of the Department of Transportation on April 1, 1967, pursuant to the Department of Transportation Act of October 15, 1966 (80 Stat. 931). The Coast Guard is a branch of the Armed Forces of the United States at all times and is a service within the Department of Transportation except when operating as part of the Navy in time of war or when the President directs.

The predecessor of the Coast Guard, "The Revenue Marine," was established in 1790 as a Federal maritime law enforcement agency. Many other major responsibilities have since been added.

Functions and Activities

Search and Rescue The Coast Guard maintains a system of rescue vessels, aircraft and communications facilities to carry out its function of saving life and property in and over the high seas and the navigable waters of the United States. This function includes flood relief and removing hazards to navigation.

Maritime Law Enforcement The Coast Guard is the primary maritime law enforcement agency for the United States. It enforces or assists in the enforcement of applicable Federal laws and treaties and other international agreements to which the United States is party, on and under the high seas and waters subject to the jurisdiction of the United States, and may conduct investigations into suspected violations of such laws and international agreements. The Coast Guard works with other Federal agencies in the enforcement of such laws as they pertain to the protection of living and nonliving resources and in the suppression of smuggling and illicit drug trafficking.

Commercial Vessel Safety The Coast Guard is charged with formulating, administering, and enforcing various safety standards for the design, construction, equipment, and maintenance of commercial vessels of the United States and offshore structures on the Outer Continental Shelf. The program includes enforcement of safety standards on foreign vessels subject to U.S. jurisdiction and administration and enforcement of vessel personnel manning and crew qualification standards.

Investigations are conducted of reported marine accidents, casualties, violations of law and regulations, misconduct, negligence, and incompetence occurring on commercial vessels subject to U.S. jurisdiction. Surveillance operations and boardings are conducted to detect violations of law and regulations. The program also functions to facilitate marine

475

transportation by admeasuring vessels, supervising the employment and records of employment of merchant marine personnel, and administering the vessel documentation laws.

Great Lakes Pilotage   The Coast Guard administers the Great Lakes Pilotage Act of 1960 that regulates pilotage services on the Great Lakes.

Marine Environmental Response   The Coast Guard is responsible for enforcing the Federal Water Pollution Control Act on navigable waters of the United States and tributaries. Program objectives are to ensure that public health and welfare and the environment are protected when spills occur.

Functions conducted include providing a National Response Center to receive reports of oil and hazardous substance spills, investigating spills, initiating subsequent civil penalty actions when warranted, encouraging and monitoring responsible party cleanups, and when necessary, coordinating federally funded spill response operations. The program also provides a National Strike Force to assist Federal On-Scene Coordinators responding to pollution incidents.

Port and Environmental Safety   This program is administered by the Coast Guard Captains of the Port (COTP's). The Coast Guard is authorized to enforce rules and regulations governing the safety and security of ports and the anchorage and movement of vessels in U.S. waters. Port safety and security functions include supervising cargo transfer operations, both storage and stowage, conducting harbor patrols and waterfront facility inspections, establishing security zones as required, and the control of vessel movement.

Waterways Management   The Coast Guard has a significant role in the safe and orderly passage of cargo, people, and vessels on our nation's waterways. It has established Vessel Traffic Services in six major ports to provide for the safe movement of vessels at all times, but particularly during hazardous conditions, restricted visibility, or bad weather. The Program's goal is to ensure the safe, efficient flow of commerce. The Coast Guard also regulates the installation of equipment necessary for vessel safety.

For further information, call 202–426–2262.

Aids to Navigation   The Coast Guard establishes and maintains the U.S. aids to navigation system that includes lights, buoys, daybeacons, fog signals, marine radiobeacons, racons, and long-range radionavigation aids. Long-range radionavigation aids include loran-C and OMEGA. Aids are established in or adjacent to waters subject to the jurisdiction of the United States, although OMEGA provides global coverage, and loran-C coverage has been established in parts of the Western Pacific, Europe, and the Mediterranean to meet Department of Defense requirements. These aids are intended to assist a navigator to determine a position or plot a safe course or to warn the navigator of dangers or obstructions to navigation. Other aids to navigation-related functions include broadcasting marine information and publishing Local Notice to Mariners and Light Lists.

Bridge Administration   The Coast Guard administers the several statutes regulating the construction, maintenance, and operation of bridges across the navigable waters of the United States to provide for safe navigation through and under bridges.

Ice Operations   The Coast Guard operates the Nation's icebreaking vessels (icebreakers and ice-capable cutters), supported by aircraft, for ice reconnaissance, to facilitate maritime transportation and aid in prevention of flooding in domestic waters. Additionally, icebreakers support logistics to U.S. polar installations and also support scientific research in Arctic and Antarctic waters.

Deepwater Ports Under the provisions of the Deepwater Port Act of 1974, the Coast Guard administers a licensing and regulatory program governing the construction, ownership (international aspects), and operation of deepwater ports on the high seas to transfer oil from tankers to shore.

Boating Safety The Coast Guard develops and directs a national boating safety program aimed at making the operation of small craft in U.S. waters both pleasurable and safe. This is accomplished by establishing uniform safety standards for recreational boats and associated equipment; encouraging State efforts through a grant-in-aid and liaison program; coordinating public education and information programs; administering the Coast Guard Auxiliary; and enforcing compliance with Federal laws and regulations relative to safe use and safety equipment requirements for small boats.

Coast Guard Auxiliary The Auxiliary is a nonmilitary volunteer organization of private citizens who own small boats, aircraft, or radio stations. Auxiliary members assist the Coast Guard by conducting boating education programs, patrolling marine regattas, participating in search and rescue operations, and conducting courtesy marine examinations.

For further information, call 202–426–1077.

Military Readiness As required by law, the Coast Guard maintains a state of readiness to function as a specialized service in the Navy in time of war.

Reserve Training The Coast Guard Reserve provides qualified individuals and trained units for active duty in time of war or national emergency and at such other times as the national security requires. In addition to its role in national defense, the Reserve augments the active service in the performance of peacetime missions during domestic emergencies and during routine and peak operations.

Marine Safety Council The Marine Safety Council acts as a deliberative body to consider proposed Coast Guard regulations and to provide a forum for the consideration of related problems.

For further information, call 202–426–1477.

District and Field Organizations—United States Coast Guard

Organization	Commander	Address
ATLANTIC AREA	Vice Adm. Donald C. Thompson, USCG	Governors Island, New York, NY 10004, 212-668-7196
1st District: Maine, Massachusetts, New Hampshire, Rhode Island, Vermont	Rear Adm. Robert L. Johanson, USCG	408 Atlantic Ave., Boston, MA 02210, 617-223-8480
2d District: Arkansas, Colorado, Illinois, Indiana, Iowa, Kansas, Kentucky, Minnesota, Missouri, Nebraska, North Dakota, Ohio, Oklahoma, western Pennsylvania, South Dakota, Tennessee, West Virginia, Wisconsin, Wyoming	Rear Adm. R.T. Nelson, USCG	1430 Olive St., St. Louis, MO 63103, 314-425-4601
3d District: Connecticut, Delaware, New Jersey, eastern New York, eastern Pennsylvania	Vice Adm. Donald C. Thompson, USCG	Governors Island, New York, NY 10004, 212-668-7196

District and Field Organizations—United States Coast Guard—Continued

Organization	Commander	Address
5th District: District of Columbia, Maryland, North Carolina, Virginia	Rear Adm. Bobby F. Hollingsworth, USCG	431 Crawford St., Portsmouth, VA 23705, 804–398–6000 (switchboard only)
7th District: Florida, Georgia, Puerto Rico, South Carolina, Virgin Islands	Rear Adm. Howard B. Thorsen, USCG	51 SW., 1st. Ave., Miami, FL 33130, 305–350–5654
8th District: Alabama, Louisiana, Mississippi, New Mexico, Texas	Rear Adm. Peter J. Rots, USCG	500 Camp St., New Orleans, LA 70130, 504–589–6298
9th District: Great Lakes area	Rear Adm. Arnold M. Danielson, USCG	1240 E. 9th St., Cleveland, OH 44199, 216–522–3910
PACIFIC AREA	Vice Adm. John D. Costello, USCG	Government Island, Alameda, CA 94501, 415–437–3196
11th District: Arizona, southern California	Rear Adm. A. Bruce Beran, USCG	400 Oceangate Blvd., Long Beach, CA 90822, 213–590–2311
12th District: northern California, Nevada, Utah	Vice Adm. John D. Costello, USCG	2 Government Island, Alameda, CA 94501, 415–437–3196
13th District: Oregon, Idaho, Montana, Washington	Rear Adm. Theodore J. Wojnar, USCG	915 2d Ave., Seattle, WA 98174, 206–442–5078
14th District: American Samoa, Guam, Hawaii, Pacific Islands	Rear Adm. Alfred P. Manning, Jr., USCG	9th Floor, 300 Ala Moana Blvd., Honolulu, HI 96813, 808–546–7109
17th District: Alaska	Rear Adm. Edward Nelson, Jr., USCG	P.O. Box 3–5000, Juneau, AK 99801, 907–586–2680
U.S. COAST GUARD ACADEMY, SUPERINTENDENT	Rear Adm. R.P. Cueroni, USCG	New London, CT 06320, 203–444–8444

For further information, contact the Information Office, United States Coast Guard, Department of Transportation, 2100 Second Street SW., Washington, DC 20593. Phone, 202–426–2158.